Practical Meditations

for Every Day in the Year

on the Life of Our Lord Jesus Christ

Composed chiefly for the use of religious
by a Father of the Society of Jesus

Nihil Obstat: Joannes Rouse, Censor Deput.

Imprimatur: Henricus Eduardus, Archiep. Westmonasterien

NATAL PUBLISHING LLC

ARS LONGA, VITA BREVIS

Cover art by Mauricio A. from Pixabay

Preparatory Prayer

My Lord and my God, I believe that Thou art here present, and that Thy eyes are fixed on me. I adore Thee, and acknowledge I am unworthy to appear before Thee; but, full of confidence in Thy infinite goodness, I beg Thee to give me grace to pass this time of meditation for Thy glory and my spiritual advancement. Enlighten my understanding, touch my heart, strengthen my will, so that I may know Thee better, love Thee more and serve Thee faithfully. I implore this grace by the intercession of our Lady, my holy patrons and guardian angel, etc.

We must labour as well as pray by putting in practice the recommendations of the masters of the spiritual life. Prepare the points of meditation overnight as seriously as if the next day you were going to give them to others; think of them when you are in bed, before going to sleep; recall them as soon as you are awake. During your visit to the Blessed Sacrament, or morning prayers, beg the grace of meditating well. Before saying the preparatory prayer ask yourself, Before whom am I going, and wherefore? Finish the meditation by a *Pater*, followed by a short examen on the causes of the good or ill success of the meditation.

Other Pious Practices

When, in consequence of sickness of body or of mind, you are incapable of making a regular meditation or contemplation, you can run over in your mind the actions which will occupy the day; see how they can be done *well* before God, *well* before men. Make a resolution of performing them thus, and beg God's blessing on each.

You can also complain lovingly to God, as we complain to our director, of our incapacity for meditation, our spiritual miseries (enumerate them), of our poverty in virtue (detail this), etc. If we thus humiliate and annihilate ourselves, and come forth from meditation fully convinced that we are unworthy of the last place, the lowest employment in the house, and are ready to be reprimanded and mortified, it will be a very good meditation. "By the fruit the tree is known," says Jesus Christ. – *Ex fructu arbor agnoscitus.*

Method of Meditation

Remote Preparation. Banish price, sensuality, dissipation; and exercise the contrary virtues – humility, mortification, and recollection.

Immediate Preparation. Read over the meditation the day before. Upon first awaking think of the meditation to be made. Excite appropriate sentiments. Enter upon it with a tranquil mind.

Commencement

Standing, reflect that God is present. Kneeling, adore, and recite the preparatory prayer.
Preludes. Brief review of the subject. Construction of place. Petition for special grace to understand and resolve.

The Meditation

The Mystery. Recall to mind the matter of the meditation.
The Understanding. 1. What is to be considered? 2. What practical conclusion is to be drawn? 3. What are the motives? Is it becoming, useful, agreeable, easy, necessary. 4. How has this been observed hitherto? 5. What is to be done in future? 6. What obstacle is to be removed? 7. What means to be taken?
The Will. Excites affections throughout the meditation more with the heart than the lips. 2. At the end of each practical consideration forms resolutions: practical – particular – suited to present circumstances – based upon solid motives – humble – with fervent supplication for assistance.

Conclusion

Recapitulation. In which the resolutions made are confirmed.
Ejaculation. Taken from the Holy Scriptures or the Fathers, recalling to mind the matter of the meditation, and the resolutions formed.
Colloquy. Addressed to Jesus Christ, the Blessed Virgin Mary, or to any saint.

Reflection

Examen. Of the matter in which the meditation has been made.
Recapitulation. Of the whole meditation. Of the practical conclusions – motives – affections – resolutions – particular inspirations.

January 1: On the three Events of the Day: The Circumcision, the Holy Name of Jesus, the New Year

1st prelude: Represent to yourself the Child Jesus offering for us to His Heavenly Father the first shedding of His blood.
2nd prelude: Let us beg the grace of beginning this year with a renewal of fervor and generosity.

Point I

Consideration: The Feast of this day was instituted in memory of our Lord's voluntary submission to circumcision. Then He began His office of Mediator, and took on Him the tokens, the sufferings and the debt of sin; He offered Himself as a victim of expiation; and shed His blood for the first time. Besides offering up Himself as an *oblation of infinite price*, He consecrated His whole self, and every instant of His mortal life, to our service. How great was this love of God for men!

Application: Let us give back our love for His love. We enter today on a new year; let us consecrate the beginning of it to that God who has so loved us, and let this consecration be so entire that every day and every minute shall be employed in His service, and to His greater glory. We will offer to Him also our soul and body, and be ready to shed the last drop of our blood in proof of our fidelity and our love.

Affections and Resolutions.

Point II: Gift of the holy name of Jesus

Consideration: The angel had said to Joseph: "Mary shall bring forth a son, and thou shalt call His name Jesus, for He shall save His people." It was the custom among the Israelites to name their male children with the circumcision, the eighth day after their birth. This name generally originated from some event which concerned the child, or from a quality with which it was hoped the child would be endowed. Our Heavenly Father alone knew the gifts which His Word made Flesh possessed, and He called Him Jesus, Saviour of the World. The Divine Child verified this beautiful and glorious name by shedding His blood for us, of which a single drop is sufficient, and more than enough, for the redemption and salvation of the whole world.

Application: In the ancient law the newly-born became by circumcision the children of Abraham, and inheritors of the promise which he received. Far happier than they, we become by holy Baptism, of which circumcision was but the faint shadow, the adopted children of God and inheritors of His kingdom; we become Christians and brothers of Jesus Christ, and co-heirs with Him.

There is a glorious meaning in these titles; but if we do not fulfill their solemn meaning, if we bear them in vain, if we dishonor them by our conduct, they will become a judgment and a severe punishment to us.

Affections and Resolutions.

Point III: The new year

Consideration: The blood that Jesus shed for us in the circumcision is the blood of the *New Covenant*, *sanguis novi Testamenti*; a covenant which ought to renew the face of the earth by causing *reality* to succeed to *figures*, the *liberty* of the divine adoption to *slavery*, the *law of charity* to the *law of fear*, which characterized the *old Covenant*.

Application: Let us profit by the circumstances of the new-beginning year, and of the wonderful renewal wrought in the world by the great mystery of this day, to renew in our hearts an increase of fervor and of generosity in the service of God. May this year be a year of fervor and progress! It will pass rapidly, like that which has just ended. If God gives us the grace to see its end, how glad and happy we shall be to have passed it holily!

Colloquy with our Blessed Lady.

January 2: On the Name of Jesus

1st prelude: I will represent to myself the angel saying to Joseph: "Thou shalt call His name Jesus, for He shall save His people from their sins."

2nd prelude: I will beg for the grace really to understand the *greatness*, the *merit* and the *power* of the name of *Jesus*.

Point I: Greatness of the name of Jesus

Consideration: It is great in its origin, for God Himself gives it by means of an archangel. It is great in its signification. Men have sometimes in gratitude given to other men the name of savior of their country. Never have they dreamt of giving to any one the name of Saviour of the World, a name whose meaning, in the full extent of the word, has been so wonderfully realized by the Son of God made man.

Application: With deep reverence we ought to pronounce this great and holy name, "which is," says the Apostle, "above all names." From the earliest ages of Christianity the custom was introduced and became general of bowing or uncovering the head when pronouncing or hearing others pronounce it. Do you not often fail to pay this due veneration, by pronouncing it without attention or devotion even in your prayers?

Affections and Resolutions.

Point II

Consideration: The noble name borne by a son solely by right of heritage is no great merit to him, because its greatness is due to the glory of another. Not so with the name borne by the Son of God. He acquired it by His own merits, by redeeming the human race from the pains of death, which it had incurred, by the sacrifice of His life, and thus He gave back to it a heavenly inheritance. Was there ever a name or a title better deserved?

Application: The names of *adopted son* of God, of *brother and companion of Jesus*, which you bear, are also titles of great value; but you have not merited them. You owe them to the grace of Baptism, to the special grace of your holy vocation. Nevertheless, it is your duty to prove yourself worthy of them; it is your duty to cooperate with grace, so as worthily to bear the names in which you may justly glory. Up to this moment grace has not failed you; but have you corresponded with it? Has your cooperation been generous and persevering? Has it been in proportion to the glorious names you bear?

Affections and Resolutions.

Point III: Power in the name of Jesus

Consideration: The invocation of this name has absolute power over creation. "At the name of Jesus," says Saint Paul, "every knee should bow, of those that are in heaven, on earth, under the earth." By the invocation of this name the Apostles worked the most astonishing miracles, and the faithful drove out demons from the bodies of the pagans. By the invocation of the name of Jesus the martyrs of all ages have triumphed over their torments, the confessors and the virgins have resisted the seductions of the world, and in it Holy Church desires we should find strength and consolation in our last agony.

Application: With what confidence ought we then to invoke it in our temptations, our troubles, our perplexities, and in all our undertakings; and this the more because Jesus has told us Himself, "If you ask the Father anything in My Name, He will give it to you." Let us, then, become familiar with some ejaculatory prayer in which we shall find the name of Jesus, so that it will come naturally to our lips in critical moments, and above all at the awful moment when we shall be struggling with death. Oh, may then our last words be, "Jesus, Jesus, be unto me a Jesus!"

Colloquy with the Infant Jesus.*

*The author of the Spiritual Exercises attaches so much importance to these colloquies, that he wishes we should fix on them with the preparation of the points. They ought greatly to contribute in shedding unction and charm over the meditations; they can be also in conformity with the affections and the resolutions indicated.

January 3: On the Bestowal of the Name of Jesus

1st prelude: I will represent to myself the angel saying to Joseph: "Thou shalt call His Name Jesus, for He shall save His people from their sins."

2nd prelude: Beg the grace of forming your heart after the model of the Heart of Jesus.

Point I: Name of Jesus, reward of humility

Consideration: "His name was called Jesus, Saviour of the World." When was this glorious name given to Him? Was it on the day of His birth, when He was glorified by the angels, venerated by the shepherds? No; but at the moment of His circumcision, when He humbled Himself so as to be made like unto sinners, by wearing in His flesh the mark of sin. It was given to Him, then, in reward for His ineffable humiliations. This in another place the Apostle formally declares: "The Lord emptied Himself, taking the form of a servant; for which cause God hath given Him a name which is above all names."

Application: If you wish worthily to bear the name of Jesus, which was written on our foreheads in Baptism, in Confirmation, and in religious Profession, be humble in heart and soul; be patient and resigned in humiliations, no matter from whom they come. We cannot hope to be the companions of Jesus in glory except so far as we have been the companions of His humiliations.

Affections and Resolutions.

Point II: Name of Jesus, reward of obedience

Consideration: "They called His name Jesus." When did they call Him by it? At the moment when, submitting of His own will to the law of circumcision, He made the sacrifice of His own will and liberty to His Father by binding Himself to observe all His life the harsh requirements of the Mosaic Law; "for every man circumcising himself," says Saint Paul," is a debtor to do the whole law." See, then, what it cost the Incarnate Word to merit for Himself the name of Jesus: "Becoming obedient unto death," says the same Apostle, "for which cause God also hath exalted Him and hath given Him a name which is above all names."

Application: What a happy resemblance there is between us and Jesus! By the vow of obedience we also have made the sacrifice of our liberty, we have subjected our will until death to the yoke of religious observances. But these observances are infinitely more gentle and more easy to fulfill than those imposed by the Mosaic Law. Let us be invariably faithful to them, whatever it may cost us. It is only at this price that the great names we bear will be our title to glory and eternal reward.

Affections and Resolutions.

Point III: Name of Jesus, reward of mortification

Consideration: "They called His name Jesus." When and at what moment? At the same moment when in circumcision He suffered for us; He shed His blood for us, and bound Himself to lead a life of privations, mortifications, and sacrifices, until He ended it by the sacrifice of Himself. It was then that His Heavenly Father gave Him the glorious name of "Jesus, Saviour of the World."

Application: "Jesus," says Saint Peter, "suffered for us from His entrance into the world, leaving you an example that you should follow His steps," leading a life of abnegation and mortification. And let us not think this is only a counsel; for the words of our Lord prove the contrary: "If any man will come after Me, let him deny himself, and take up his cross. He that taketh not up his cross and followeth Me is not worthy of Me." Consequently

the name of disciples of Jesus which we bear will never be our title to glory and reward if we do not resemble our Divine Master by sufferings and by continual mortification. The Apostle calls this the "circumcision of the heart." Let us examine ourselves on this point; let us see how we stand as regards the spirit of mortification, and whether on this head we have perhaps degenerated from our first fervor.
Colloquy with Jesus.

January 4: On the Value of Time

1st prelude: Represent to yourself the Apostle Paul saying, "Whilst we have time, let us work good."
2nd prelude: Beg the grace really to appreciate the value of time and to make a good use of it during the course of the new year.

Point I

Consideration: "Time is as precious as heaven," says Saint Bernard; and nothing is more true, because not only no one will attain heaven without having passed through the trials of time, but he will only obtain it, according to the divine promises, as the reward of a good use of time. This eternal reward can depend upon a single moment well employed. Witness the good thief: his life had been a bad one; he was certainly on the point of death; but in that awful moment, enlightened by grace, he humbly recognized his sins, he implored mercy from our Divine Redeemer; immediately heaven was promised to him, and Jesus said to him, "This day thou shalt be with Me in Paradise."

Application: What respect ought we not to have, then, for the time which is given to us! We ought to value it as much as, nay more than if it were a diamond which would buy a kingdom. For what is an earthly kingdom compared with the kingdom of heaven? And the good employment of time can win for us the eternal possession of that kingdom. And further, each well-employed moment can win for us a new degree of glory and happiness in heaven, a new heaven, so to speak, in heaven itself.
Affections and Resolutions.

Point II

Consideration: "Time is as precious as the Blood of Jesus Christ," adds Saint Bernard, because one good action done in time cannot merit before God save in virtue of redemption; this redemption has been wrought only at the price of the Blood of Jesus Christ; it is His Blood which has made time fruitful; the Blood of God has become like money which represents the value of time.

Application: "The Precious Blood of Jesus Christ" is a consecrated sentence in all languages. What can be more precious? "A single drop of that Blood would suffice," says Saint Thomas, "to redeem the world." How avaricious ought we, then, to be of time, and how should we fear to lose one moment of it! For even God is avaricious of it. He bestows His gifts and graces on us in torrents, but time He gives us only drop by drop; no one ever received two instants of it at once. And how people do waste this precious time! They spend it on trifles, they study how to get rid of it, they use it to offend God and to bring eternal misery.

Affections and Resolutions.

Point III

Consideration: *Time is worth as much as God Himself*: and behold why and how, continues the holy doctor – by every instant well employed we can win the eternal possession of God. Therefore what a severe account will one day be demanded of us! One moment is sufficient to utter an idle word; and Jesus Christ assures us that this loss of time, insignificant as we think it, will not pass unnoticed: "I say unto you, that every idle word that men shall speak, they shall render an account of it on the Day of Judgment."

Application: I believe all this; but is my conduct in accordance with my faith? Do I, in my examen of conscience, call myself to account for the employment of my time? For its loss? And for the causes of this loss? Do I confess this with repentance, with a sincere purpose of amendment? Let us, then, go into a detailed examination, let us see *when*, *where*, and *how* we have lost time, so as to use it better during the course of the new year. The great means of spending it usefully and happily is to make a rule of life, and to be faithful to it.

Colloquy with Our Lady.

January 5: On Employing Time Well

1st prelude: Represent to yourself the Apostle Paul saying, "Whilst we have time, let us work good."
2nd prelude: Beg as the fruit of this meditation the grace to understand well, and to put in practice the means for utilizing and sanctifying time.

Point I

Consideration: *To sanctify time, and never to waste it, we must live continually in a state of grace*. Faith teaches us that no action, however holy and good it may be in itself, can win eternal merit for him who performs it in a state of mortal sin. This is easy to understand, consequently all the time passed in the state of mortal sin is time lost for eternity. What a loss and what a misery! And is it not the misery of the greater number of Christians? How many are they to whom this year, or the greater part of this year, will be thus for ever lost! How they will one day regret it!

Application: If the religious state had no other advantage for you than that of preserving you from this misery, how happy you ought to consider yourself in being called to it, and what sacrifices ought you not to be ready to make, if necessary, to persevere in it until your last breath!

Affections and Resolutions.

Point II

Consideration: *To sanctify time, and never to waste it, we must be in a state of grace and have a pure intention.* All our actions, whether good or indifferent, must be done from supernatural motives – for God, in God's sight. Men see only the exterior, God judges the intention: what we do not do for Him He will not reward. The Scribes and Pharisees did many good works, but through ostentation, and for love of a vain popularity; Jesus Christ tells us in the Gospel that they will not be rewarded – they will have lost their time and labor.

Application: Have we not reason to fear the loss, in part at least, of the merit of many of our good words, because self-love, vanity, the desire of pleasing men, have been secretly mingled with the motives from which we acted? Let us look into the secret foldings of our hearts, and have the courage to question and to answer ourselves.

Affections* and Resolutions.

*We should not be afraid of giving too much time to these pious affections; for it is by them that we should enkindle and stir up the fire of love, thus making our meditation fruitful, and keep up our fervor during the day. Many affections and resolutions will present themselves to those who meditate. They are best when they come from ourselves, or from divine inspiration.

Point III

Consideration: *To sanctify time, and never to waste it, it is further necessary that our action be done fervently, in manner worthy of God.* You perform many good actions with an habitually pure intention; but you do them languidly, in a lukewarm and imperfect way, and the greater part of the time that you have spent in them will be lost, and without merit. This is why the Holy Spirit presses us so strongly, or rather commands us: "In thy works keep the pre-eminence." *In omnibus operibus tuis praecellens esto.*

Application: Happy is the man, happy is the religious, who with vigilance and generosity keeps this divine precept. What a harvest of merits he will lay up in a short time! He will, as the Wise Man says, "in a short space have fulfilled a long time." It depends upon ourselves only to share this happiness. One means among many others is to form a habit of making the sign of the cross when we speak; and before undertaking any important action to add these words, *I wish to perform this action well*; then to examine ourselves when we have done it.

Colloquy with our Blessed Lord.

January 6: Feast of the Epiphany, or of the Kings

1st prelude: To imagine I see the three Kings or Wise Men walking by the light of the star.

2nd prelude: Grant me, Lord, the grace really to understand what *memories*, what *blessings*, and what *duties* this feast should remind me of.

Point I

Consideration: In all ages the Church has celebrated this feast during eight days with an extraordinary splendor, to perpetuate the memory of a great and happy event: the manifestation of Jesus Christ to the Magi, and in their persons to all the people of the earth, enslaved as they were in the darkness of paganism. The word Epiphany means *manifestation* or *appearing*. The historical details are given to us in the Gospel of this day's Mass; it begins with these words: "When Jesus, therefore, was born in Bethlehem of Juda, in the days of King Herod, behold there came Wise Men from the East to Jerusalem: saying, Where is He that is born King of the Jews? for we have seen His star in the east, and are come to adore Him."

Application: The memory of the great even solemnized on this day recalls other thoughts to our minds, and affords us profitable instruction. It reminds us first of the eagerness of Jesus to make Himself known to all by means at once gentle and efficacious – to the Jews who had faith, by an angel; to the Gentiles, by a miraculous star: and it teaches us to be zealous to make God known and loved by all the world without any distinction. It reminds us also of the wonderful sweetness of the ways of Divine Providence, who always proportions the means of salvation to the various dispositions of men, and it teaches us to have an unshaken confidence in that Providence.

Affections and Resolutions.

Point II: The great blessings that the Epiphany recalls to the memory

Consideration: The posterity of Abraham had been chosen to form a people who, in the midst of idolatrous nations, preserved the faith and worship of the true God. But a day was to come when all the nations of the earth were to be called to the same faith, and to form but one nation in Jesus Christ. The promise of this had been made to Abraham, and on this day it was fulfilled by the calling of the Magi, who represented all the idolatrous nations, and consequently our own ancestors. The Epiphany reminds us, then, of the inestimable blessing of our having been called to the true faith, and of having been born and educated by parents who possessed the spirit of faith.

Application: May the memory of these wonderful blessings be ever in our minds, but especially on this day! We ought to show more gratitude because they were the fruit of an undeserved predilection on the part of God. Let us have a dread of ingratitude; it will check the tide of grace.

Affections and Resolutions.

Point III: The sweet and important duties of which the Epiphany reminds us

Consideration: Faith worked great things in the Magi; it made new men of them – spiritual men, saints, apostles, martyrs. It is an ancient tradition that they were baptized by the Apostle Saint Thomas, that they became themselves apostles and martyrs of the faith. The Church of the East and the West honors them as saints; and people go even in our days to visit the singular relics of their heads, carefully preserved, ever since the twelfth century, in the Cathedral of Cologne.

Application: Jesus has enlightened you with the bright light of faith. Let your life be such that it may produce in you more and more abundant fruits of sanctity. It is our greatest and happiest duty. "Faith worketh by charity," says the Apostle; and "where charity is," adds Pope Gregory, "it does great things." Can this be remarked in you?

Colloquy with the Infant Jesus.

January 7: Fidelity of the Magi in obeying the Inspirations of Grace

1st prelude: I will contemplate the Magi following the star which leads them to the cradle of the Savior.

2nd prelude: Grant to us, O Jesus, fidelity to the inspirations of grace.

Point I: The Kings correspond promptly with grace

Consideration: Fidelity to grace supposes, first of all, promptitude in following its inspirations. That of the Magi was wonderful. A star of extraordinary brightness struck upon their sight; an interior voice made them understand its meaning; and immediately breaking all the ties which held them back, they roused themselves to follow it. They could say truly to King Herod, "We have seen the star of the new-born King in the East, and we are come to adore Him." It is probable that many other wise men, who like them were watching the course of the planets, saw the star, and felt themselves interiorly moved to follow it; but they thought they ought to wait for further enlightenment. Their reasoning and their delays prevented them from enjoying the greatest of all favors – the happiness of seeing with their own eyes the Savior of the world.

Application: Perhaps you have lost many graces and merits by your delays in corresponding with the good inspirations which God has sent you; for, generally speaking, to delay is to neglect them. How many times has it not happened that you have had the good thought of utilizing some spare moments by doing an act of charity, paying a visit to the Blessed Sacrament, or some other good work? But you put it off, and nothing was done. Will not an examination of the past tell you that it has been thus?

Affections and Resolutions.

Point II: The Kings correspond generously with grace

Consideration: Fidelity to grace supposes also generosity. It consists in conquering the difficulties and apparent impossibilities which naturally terrify our self-love and cowardice. This generosity was certainly needed by the Magi. The journey they had to undertake was long, the weather severe, and the roads hardly fit to traverse; besides, they knew not wither the star would lead them, and for what length of time they would be absent from their families and their affairs. They had also to meet criticism and ridicule of their countrymen. Nothing of all this stopped them; they gave themselves up with an entire confidence to Him who had called them by these manifest signs.

Application: Why am I so often unfaithful to grace – unfaithful to the resolutions based upon the highest motives – unfaithful to certain practices of piety and mortification, the importance of which I know so well? Is it not very often because I fail in generosity – because I allow myself to be discouraged by the fear of imaginary difficulties?

Affections and Resolutions.

Point III: The Kings correspond perseveringly with grace

Consideration: Fidelity to grace supposes, in the third place, perseverance. Such was the fidelity of the Magi that nothing could stop them, not even the disappearance of the star as they drew nigh to Jerusalem, and the extraordinary indifference of the inhabitants of that city. God rewarded their constancy. The star reappeared, and led them to the feet of our Divine Savior.

Application: How little do we persevere, and for how short a time! Where at noontide is the execution of the resolutions made in the morning? Has it not even happened to you often to be

unfaithful before the end of your undertakings to the resolutions made when you began them? Is it astonishing, then, that we make so little progress? Let us try to do better from today. Let us beg of God, by the intercession of the holy Kings, the perseverance and generosity in which we have been wanting.
Colloquy with the Infant Jesus.

January 8: Three Circumstances during the Journey of the Magi

1st prelude: To imagine I see the Magi in desolation at the disappearance of the star.
2nd prelude: I will be the grace to understand the various accidents which befell the holy Kings, and to derive spiritual profit from them.

Point I: Disappearance of the star

Consideration: The Magi being near to Jerusalem, the star disappeared.

Deprived of this heavenly light, which had been until now their guide and their consolation, what were they to do? They were not discouraged; they went into the city. On the advice of King Herod, they betook themselves to the authorized teachers – to the doctors of the law – to learn from them where the Messiah should be born. On hearing the reply, that it would be at Bethlehem, they immediately took the road which should lead them thither.

Application: God treats His faithful servants as He did the Magi. Sometimes He gives them light and consolation; sometimes He withdraws these, and leave them alone in a sort of dark night, to try them, and to purify their faith and their love. What ought we, then, to do? Let us imitate the holy Kings; let us lay aside all discouragement; adore the designs of God; relax none of our duties or our pious practices, and, waiting for the light to return to us, have recourse, with humility and docility, to the advice of our directors. Have you done this?
Affections and Resolutions.

Point II: The reappearance of the star

Consideration: God made no delay in rewarding the humble confidence and docility of the Magi. They had scarcely left Jerusalem, following the directions given to them, when the star reappeared, and, says Saint Matthew, "they rejoiced with exceeding great joy; and it went before them until it came and stood over where the Child was."

Application: Such is and such will always be the result of the desolations and divers trials through which God causes us to pass, provided we imitate the fidelity and constancy of the holy Kings. But, alas! How often we are unfaithful and inconstant! Instead of persevering in our resolutions, and of having recourse to our spiritual guides, we become relaxed and dissipated, we run in search of consolation to creatures. Does not this apply to you?

Affections and Resolutions.

Point III: The place where the star stood still

Consideration: What must have been the surprise of the Magi when they saw the spot over which the star was standing! It was above a deserted stable, in which they found a little Infant, wrapped in swaddling clothes, lying on a little straw in a manger, in company with His Mother (who did not differ from other women), an artisan, and some poor shepherds. What a trial of their faith! How can they recognize in this Child the promised King of Israel, the Savior of mankind? Here was enough to disgust them, to wound their pride, and to discourage them; but the Magi were humble, and God manifests Himself and "gives grace to the humble." Suddenly grace enlightens them; they understand the great mystery of the voluntary humiliations of the Savior God; they adore Him, and their souls are flooded with ineffable delight; the stable is changed for them into paradise.

Application: Recall all that you have heard, read, and meditated upon concerning the necessity and excellence of humility, of the extraordinary gifts, the wonderful graces with which God is pleased to enrich souls who are truly humble – who seek Him only, live only for Him.

Colloquy with our Blessed Lady.

January 9: Alarm, Hypocrisy and Disappointment of King Herod

1st prelude: Represent to yourself Jesus Christ saying: "Woe to you, hypocrites!"

2nd prelude: Beg for singleness of heart, and pure intentions.

Point I: Alarm of Herod

Consideration: At the question of the Magi as to where the King of the Jews, whose star they had seen, was born, Herod, says the Evangelist: "was troubled, and all Jerusalem with him." Why does this terrible and sudden alarm come upon King Herod? Is it some serious affair of state? Does he fear that some misfortune will overtake the people committed to his care? No, it is selfishness, ambition, jealousy – in one word, passion. He feared that he or his posterity would be supplanted.

Application: Make a careful examination of yourself. You also are sometimes subject to trouble, to sadness, to discouragement; but what does it arise from? Is it from some reasonable cause? Because God is offended? Because you have offended Him? Because souls are lost? The Church is persecuted? Is it not rather because you have been humbled, reprimanded, or your wishes contradicted? Because you were deprived of something to which you clung, or were afraid that such would be the case? It is passion, then, that is at the bottom of all this; pride, vanity, self-love, jealousy, or ill-regulated attachment to yourself and your own ease. Ought you not to own this? Examine yourself.

Affections and Resolutions.

Point II: Hypocrisy of Herod

Consideration: The following is narrated in the Gospel: "Herod, privately calling the wise men, learned diligently of them the time of the star which appeared to them; and, sending them into Bethlehem, said, God and diligently inquire after the Child; and when you have found Him, bring me word again, that I also may come and adore Him." What was Herod's real design in taking this step, which apparently arose from a feeling of respect and piety? We learn it from what followed. It was to find out the age and the dwelling of the Divine Child, that he might put Him to death; and for fear of any doubt as to His identity, he orders a general massacre of all the children of the same age born in the neighborhood of Bethlehem. Was there ever a more abominable project concealed under blacker hypocrisy?

Application: All hypocrisy, even when it does not serve as a mantle for crime, is odious to God and men. To a certain point, it is, however, more common than we think. To assume the appearance of virtue, without caring about its reality, is hypocrisy.

To obey orders, or conform to rule, only because we are observed, and to pretend that we approve of our superior and of his orders in his presence, whilst we condemn him in his absence; to speak otherwise than we think, so as to obtain what we desire; to speak ill of one's self, so as to attract praise; and the like, are all evidently kinds of hypocrisy.
Affections and Resolutions.

Point III: Disappointment of Herod

Consideration: "The hope of the hypocrite shall perish," says the Holy Ghost. Herod is a proof of this. The angel of the Lord ordered the Magi to return by another way; and later on he told Joseph to fly with the Child into Egypt. By this the wicked plans of King Herod were baffled; and the massacre of the children of Bethlehem only peopled heaven with new saints, and made the tyrant the execration of his fellow men and of posterity.

Application: The impious men who never cease to persecute Jesus Christ in his Church in her members can do nothing against us without God's permission. Let us trust in Him; He knows how to turn all their plots to their confusion and to our advantage.
Colloquy with the Infant Jesus.

January 10: Offering of the Magi

1st prelude: I will represent to myself the Magi at the manger opening their treasures.
2nd prelude: I will beg the grace of imitating them in their deep feelings of faith, generosity and love.

Point I: What is it that they offer?

Consideration: Among the Orientals it is a universal custom, which continues to this day, that no one comes before a king or powerful prince without offering him presents. The Magi had taken care not to omit this custom. After having adored the Infant Jesus by prostrating themselves on the earth, they opened their treasures, and, says the Evangelist, "offered Him gifts – gold, frankincense and myrrh." These presents were most precious productions of their native land, but, by a secret disposition of Providence, they also represent the three eminent characteristics of the Messiah. His eternal and universal royalty is represented by gold; His divinity by frankincense; and His humanity by myrrh.

Application: "Thou shalt not appear before Me empty." Such was the precept given by the Lord to the people of Israel after He had enriched them with the spoils of Egypt. He gives the same to us, whom He has enriched with the spoils, or rather the infinite merits, of His blood and His death. It is therefore, says Saint Chrysostom, a want of devotion if we adore God without offering Him something. Each time, then, that we prostrate ourselves at the foot of the holy tabernacle, let us add to our acts of adoration the offering of some mortification or some generous resolution.
Affections and Resolutions.

Point II: How did they offer it?

Consideration: The feelings which accompanied the presents of the Magi were their chief merit. What were these? Feelings of joy and generosity: they offered their superb gifts with all their hearts. Feelings of humility: they were grieved not to be able to offer Him gifts a thousand times more precious. Feelings of love and of the tenderest filial devotion: they bound themselves for ever to the service of Him whom they recognized as their King and their God.

Application: As religious, we have the happiness of surpassing the Magi. By making the three perpetual vows of poverty, chastity and obedience, we offer and immolate ourselves on the altar of the love of God.

But the perfection of this immolation requires repeated acts of self-abnegation. Let these be united with the feelings with which the Kings made their offerings, and all will be of great price in the eyes of God.
Affections and Resolutions.

Point III: How Jesus received what they offered Him

Consideration: If it be true, as we cannot doubt, that God values our gifts, not according to their actual worth, but according to the feelings which accompany them, with what goodwill must He have received the gifts of the holy Kings, looking on them with eyes full of love! And it is no less true that He *never lets Himself be outdone in generosity*. There is no doubt that He gave them in return gifts infinitely more precious – gifts of grace and of final perseverance.

Application: How consoling and encouraging are these thoughts! They recall to our memory the promise given by Jesus Christ Himself, that our smallest offerings, and our most trifling good actions, even if it be but "a drop of cold water," in His name,

will not lose their reward. Animated by this faith, encouraged by these words, let us often renew our good intentions, so that all our actions may be meritorious and pleasing to God.
Colloquy with the Infant Jesus.

January 11: Happiness of the Magi

1st prelude: Behold the Magi overwhelmed with joy at the foot of the manger.
2nd prelude: Beg the grace to share somewhat of this joy.

Point I: The Magi admitted to the knowledge of Jesus

Consideration: One of the first thoughts that come to the mind when we hear the Gospel story of the calling of the Magi is the thought of the happiness which fell to their lot. What a happiness indeed, to have been miraculously called from the Gentile darkness to the divine light of the Incarnate Word; to have been taught the sublime lessons of the Gospel even before they were preached to the world! To what did they owe this wonderful happiness in preference to so many millions who lived and died in infidelity and sin? To the mercy and predilection only of the Savior God.

Application: You also have been the object of this same predilection of God; He caused you to be born of Catholic parents, who taught you from your tenderest infancy the knowledge and love of Jesus. You might have been born, as so many are, of Paga, Mahometan, or Jewish parents, and how great then would have been your misery in time and eternity! To what do you owe your preservation, your being so richly supplied with means of salvation and of sanctification? Is it not solely to the mercy of your Savior?
Affections and Resolutions.

Point II: The Magi admitted to the society of Jesus

Consideration: We can easily believe that the three Kings stayed more than one day at this happy resting-place after their long and difficult pilgrimage; they had consequently the wonderful happiness of having the society of Jesus, which till then had been given only to Mary, Joseph and a few shepherds. What happy hours they passed in that company! What graces they received from it! And how they congratulated themselves on having obeyed the invitation of the star!

Application: This happiness you share with them. You, whom

the star of vocation has led into a religious family, to which Jesus has really bequeathed His Spirit, and perhaps His name; in the midst of which He is pleased to mark His presence by a wonderful Providence, and to shed His graces and favors with profusion; that privilege especially of being everywhere, like him, the object of hatred to the wicked – what happy days, days rich in merit, are you permitted to pass, while waiting till grace and perseverance shall lead you into the glorious society of Jesus in heaven!
Affections and Resolutions.

Point III: The Magi admitted to the kiss of Jesus

Consideration: We may also believe that the Magi not only contemplated at their leisure the beautiful countenance of the Divine Child, but also, to crown their happiness, that they received Him from the loving hands of Mary into their arms; that they were permitted to cover Him with kisses, and to press Him to their hearts. What blissful moments were these, and what abundance of light, love, and sanctity they received!

Application: You envy their happiness, but do not you share it with them each time that you receive Him in Holy Communion? Then you are permitted, not only to press Jesus in your arms and to your breast, but to receive Him into your heart, to be incorporated with Him, to be identified with Him. How is it, then, that, after so many Holy Communions, you are yet so little advanced in the love and intimacy of Jesus? Seek for the cause of this, and remedy it.
Colloquy with the Infant Jesus.

January 12: On the Grace of Vocation given to the Magi

1st prelude: I will represent to myself Jesus Christ saying those words, "I have chosen you."
2nd prelude: I will beg the grace of a continual increase of reverence and love for my holy vocation.

Point I: The vocation of the Magi was a purely gratuitous grace

Consideration: Certainly God was not obliged to diverge from the ordinary ways of Providence in their favor, by calling them and guiding them by a miraculous star; and , on the other side, it is not unlikely that among so many millions of Gentiles there were many who had as much or more title than they had to be called to the knowledge of the Messiah. To what, then, did they owe so great a favor? Only to the free predilection of their Lord.

Application: And I – to what do I owe my vocation? Is it to the innocence and holiness of my youth? No, my conscience answers me. Is it to the superiority of my moral and physical qualities? No, for I have known many far superior to me in these respects. To what, then, do I owe it? Only to the free choice of the Lord, as a free predilection. "You have not chosen Me, but I have chosen you." These are the words of Jesus.

Affections and Resolutions.

Point II: The vocation of the Magi was a grace of conversion

Consideration: Born, educated, and living in the midst of heathen darkness and vice, it is to be presumed that the Magi were walking with the majority in the broad path that leads to destruction. The grace of conversion drew them away for ever from it, set them in the narrow path of justice, and made them new men in Jesus Christ our Savior.

Application: Where were you before the star of vocation rose to enlighten you? You were in the midst of a corrupted and corrupting world; all that you saw and heard tended to evil. And how did you then live? How far did you allow yourself to be carried by the seducing torrent of vice? Recall your past life. See in what sins and perhaps in what habitual sins, you were living. Where would this life have led you, if not to your eternal ruin? The grace of your vocation drew you away, and brought you into the narrow path of virtue and salvation. Happy vocation! It was for you also a "grace of conversion."

Affections and Resolutions.

Point III: The vocation of the Magi was a grace of sanctification

Consideration: It made them see clearly the nothingness of all that is not God, and filled their hearts with the holy ardor of charity. From henceforth they made rapid progress in the practice of exalted virtue. All the three are honored with the title of saint, and have been invoked for nineteen centuries by the Church.

Application: It is the light and unction of your grace of vocation that has shown you the vanity of the world, that has broken the bonds which bound you to it, and made you resolutely enter on a state of life where you make a profession of perfection, and are obliged to tend towards it. To conquer your human inconstancy, you are bound by perpetual vows. These vows

contain for you at once the obligation of tending towards sanctity, and the most efficacious means of attaining it. Be faithful to them, and one day you will be the companions in glory and happiness of the holy Kings in heaven.
Colloquy with our Blessed Lord.

January 13: Departure of the Magi, and their Return to their own Country

1st prelude: To imagine I see the Magi prostrate at the feet of Jesus before they depart.
2nd prelude: I will beg the grace never to leave the presence of Jesus Christ without the feelings that were then in their hearts.

Point I: Departure of the Magi

Consideration: It will be difficult for you, or rather impossible, to form even a faint idea of the happiness and spiritual delight which the Magi tasted in the company of the Infant Jesus. Oh, how willingly would they have passed their lives there! But they were obliged to separate from Him; and how did they part? With great regret; thanking Him with all their hearts for having so marvelously called them to Him; begging His blessing and His help; consecrating themselves entirely to His interests and glory; desirous to make Him known and loved by all men.

Application: Thus ought we to leave the real Presence of Jesus Christ each time that we visit Him in the Sacrament of His Love, or to receive Him in Holy Communion. Has it been thus? Have we not often left Him with none of this? But rather with strange coldness, strange insensibility? Perhaps because we have approached Him with too little faith, too little earnestness.
Affections and Resolutions.

Point II: Return of the Magi

Consideration: "Having received an answer in sleep, that they should not return to Herod, they went back another way into their country." We might add, with other feelings, far more perfect ones than those which had animated them before; feelings, not simply of a pious curiosity, but of an entire abnegation of themselves, contempt of the possessions of earth; a perfect love for Jesus, and an ardent desire to work and suffer much for Him. These were the wonderful effects of the intimate communications that they had enjoyed with the Author of all good and all sanctity.

Application: Such ought to be the result and fruit of our communications with God in meditation. Mass, visits, and especially our Holy Communions. And wherefore is it not thus? Do not these holy exercises bring us into intimate contact with the same God who wrought such a happy change in the minds and hearts of the Magi? If it be not thus, some obstacle must be in the way. What is this obstacle with you?

Affections and Resolutions.

Point III: Perseverance of the Magi

Consideration: The honors that the Church renders to the Magi, and the veneration with which she preserves their wonderful relics, is a certain proof that they persevered in fervor, and in the pious sentiments they had learnt at the foot of the manger of Bethlehem; and that they persevered in them, not only for a few months, but during the thirty-three years which elapsed before the Gospel was preached, when they were made Christians by Baptism, and soon after sealed their profession of the faith with their blood.

Application: Look into yourself. Remember what was your fervor during the happy years of your novitiate. That fervor, which has been constantly stimulated by your spiritual directors since that time, should have been continually on the increase; has it not been rather the contrary with you? Have you not been wanting in perseverance?

Colloquy with our Blessed Lady.

January 14: Three Thoughts useful to retaining your Fervor on waking each Morning

1st prelude: I will imagine I hear Jesus Christ say these words, "If thou didst know the gift of God in this thy day."

2nd prelude: I will beg the grace of increasing in fervor during the whole course of this year.

Point I

Consideration: May the fruit of the Octave of the Epiphany be an increase of fervor in us! Let us try to animate ourselves every day from our first waking, by one or another of the three thoughts which will be the subject of this meditation.

First thought: *This day is given to me only to glorify God, to heap up merits for heaven.* Yesterday is no longer mine, tomorrow is uncertain, today is in my possession. How happy I shall be this evening, if I have spent the day holily, and have not lost any of it! God will demand from me a severe account of this day, of each hour, of each minute, because there is not one that I ought not to use for His glory, and which I cannot use to gain my eternal happiness.

Application: Is this thought often before my mind when I awake? Do I occupy myself earnestly with it while I dress? It is a most useful one to awaken generous feelings in us, and to keep the warmth of our fervor alive. It produced this effect on the saints, and produces it now daily in many religious, who are in earnest about their spiritual advancement.

Affections and Resolutions.

Point II

Second thought: *God has bestowed on this day graces, perhaps special ones, which ought to contribute powerfully to my advancement, and to my final perseverance.* To what dangers, then, shall I not expose myself by neglecting to correspond with them? What regrets shall I have later on! What a loss will be the result for me in time and eternity!

Application: This second thought will make us throughout the day very attentive and docile to the inspirations of grace; let us, however, acknowledge that, either from dissipation or cowardice, it has not always been thus – that often *we receive the gift of God in vain.* And ought it not to make us fear lest we incur the blame and the punishment reserved for the ungrateful?

Affections and Resolutions.

Point III

Third thought: *This day perhaps will be your last.* It will really be so for a hundred thousand of my fellow creatures. According to statistics, that is the number of deaths daily. Who can assure me I shall not be among the number? If I knew that it was to be so, what should I do today? With what scrupulous attention should I avoid the smallest sin! With what ardor should I devote myself to perform all my actions well, even the smallest, and to omit nothing to render myself most pleasing in God's sight! Nothing further is needed to sanctify me.

Application: We have an infallible means of attaining this

happy result – it is, to follow the counsel that Saint Anthony gave to his disciples. “My dear children,” said he, “try to live each day as if it were to be the last of your life.” Why do we not do this? So many motives invite us to do it. Would it not prevent us from ever being surprised by death? It may be sudden, but it never can be *unexpected.*
Colloquy with our Blessed Lord.

January 15: The Virtues practiced by Mary in her Purification

1st prelude: I will represent to myself our Lady humbly presenting herself at the entrance of the Temple.
2nd prelude: I will beg the grace to imitate her in the virtues of which she gives us the example.

Point I: Obedience of Mary

Consideration: The fortieth day after the birth of Jesus, Mary went to the Temple, as the law of Moses prescribed, to be purified, not from sin, but from the legal stain that she was accounted to have contracted like other mothers. It was not necessary; for Mary became a mother by the operation of the Holy Spirit, and remained a pure virgin. She had not therefore contracted any legal spot, and the law of purification was not binding on her. However, she submitted to it from love of the law, and to avoid giving scandal to her neighbors, who were ignorant of the great mystery worked in her favor.

Application: Do you not remark a great contrast between your obedience and that of our Blessed Lady? She obeyed in difficult matters, although she was really exempt; and you escape under a slight pretext from easy and light observances. Have you not often been guilty of this, and in certain circumstances given great disedification to your brethren?
Affections and Resolutions.

Point II: Humility of Mary

Consideration: In submitting to the law of purification, Mary consented to lose the prestige of one of her great privileges. She lost in the eyes of men the glory of her virginity, of which she was so jealous, by being reckoned among the other women in the outer court of the Temple. She passed for an ordinary woman, who needs purification before she can be admitted to the second court.

But Mary was humble. She delighted in humiliations, and she believed that God knew her virginal purity, and that was sufficient. She was little disturbed at the judgments of men.

Application: Do we reason thus? Do we act in this manner? Alas! Little anxious to be stainless before God, we devote all our efforts to appear spotless before men; and provided that we do not incur reprimand from our superiors, we flatter ourselves that all is well – that we are all right before God. What a fatal delusion! Affections and Resolutions.

Point III: Mary's spirit of poverty

Consideration: The law of purification enjoined on the mother to offer, by the hands of the priest, a lamb of the first year and a dove, or at least two doves or two young pigeons. The former was the offering of the rich, the latter of the poor. We should imagine that Mary could, with the gold the Magi had brought, have made the offering of the rich; but for love of humility she was contented to make that of the poor. Where did she learn that esteem and love of voluntary poverty, of which no daughter of Juda had ever given her the example? It was doubtless from the example of her Divine Son, who chose to be born in a stable, in the midst of complete privation.

Application: Let us have, like her, ever before our eyes Jesus, the King of heaven and earth, becoming for our sakes so poor that "He had not where to lay His Head," as He told us Himself, and we shall also have an esteem for poverty; we shall love it as our mother; we shall not regret sometimes to feel its effects. Colloquy with our Lady.

January 16: Presentation of the Infant Jesus in the Temple

1st prelude: Look at our Lady offering the Infant Jesus to the Eternal Father.
2nd prelude: Beg grace from God to make offerings to Him worthy of Him.

Point I: Mary carries the Infant Jesus to the Temple

Consideration: "They carried Him to Jerusalem to present Him to the Lord, as it is written in the law of the Lord." According to this law, besides submitting to the purification, the parents were obliged to bring their firstborn, and to redeem him by a small sum, in token of gratitude that the destroying angel had spared the firstborn of the Hebrews on the night on which he struck dead those of the Egyptians.

Application: This law plainly teaches us that God loves or rather exacts from us a grateful remembrance of our preservation from harm, and of the favors which He has poured upon us. Recall to your mind the evils of body and soul that God has averted from you, and the innumerable favors both of nature and grace which He has poured upon you, and ask yourself, Has my gratitude always been in proportion to so many benefits? Have I at least preserved a grateful remembrance of them?

Affections and Resolutions.

Point II: Mary offers the Infant Jesus to the Lord

Consideration: The offering that Mary made of her Son was infinitely more perfect than that of other mothers. For them the presentation and the redemption of their firstborn was but an act of obedience to the law – a legal ceremony, followed by a feast or family rejoicing, which occupied the greater part of the day.

Mary in reality offered and sacrificed her well-beloved Child to the Lord as a victim who was one day to be immolated for the redemption of the world, and with a heart full of sublime feelings she spent the day in recollection, prayer and good works, without omitting anything which custom demanded from her.

Application: Let us endeavor, like Mary, to render our offerings pleasing to the Lord, making them in a spirit of faith and love. Let us also celebrate worthily the Lord's Day and the principal feasts of the year. These holy days are nothing more, to many Christians who abstain from profaning them, than days of relaxation, enjoyment and good cheer; and the beautiful ceremonies of the Church are only to them pious amusements. How few there are who sanctify these holy days as they ought to be sanctified? Does not conscience reproach you on one or other of these heads?

Affections and Resolutions.

Point III: Jesus offers Himself by the hands of Mary

Consideration: While Mary presented and offered up to the Lord her dear Child, He, possessing the full and perfect use of His reason, though He did not let it appear, offered Himself by Mary's hands to God His Father as the most worthy victim, of which all the preceding had been only the types.

Application: Jesus willed that His whole mortal life, not excepting His tenderest infancy, should be a continual immolation of Himself – an uninterrupted act of love; and we – we have begun so late to love Him, to devote ourselves to His divine service! Colloquy with our Lady.

January 17: Meeting of the Infant Jesus and Simeon in the Temple

1st prelude: Represent to yourself Simeon holding the Infant Jesus in his arms.
2nd prelude: Beg the grace to share in the favors which were poured on the holy old man.

Point I: The old man Simeon guided by the Holy Ghost

Consideration: "There was in Jerusalem," says Saint Luke, "a man named Simeon; and this man was just and devout, waiting for the consolation of Israel, and the Holy Ghost was in him. And he came by the Spirit into the Temple; and His parents brought in the Child Jesus to do for Him according to the custom of the law." How was it that the holy old man came into the Temple at the precise day, hour and moment when Mary entered with her Divine Child? Because he was led by the Spirit of God, who, by secret inspirations, guided all his steps and all his actions; a favor that he had merited by his piety, his ardent faith, and his habitual docility to the inspirations of grace.

Application: Happy is the man, happy is the religious, who has the Holy Ghost for his guide! He will escape many dangers; he will have daily occasions of practicing virtue and of increasing in merit; while the Christian who is guided by the spirit of the world will fall from error into error, from precipice to precipice. Have you not in your time experienced this?
Affections and Resolutions.

Point II: The old man Simeon enlightened by the Holy Ghost

Consideration: The Divine Child whom Mary bore in her arms had nothing to distinguish Him in the eyes of men from other children. His Divinity was veiled under the feeble tokens of humanity. So He was not remarked either by the priests or their assistants. Simeon only, suddenly enlightened by the Holy Ghost, pierced the veil; recognized in the feeble Infant the "Word made flesh," the Messiah expected for four thousand years, and he cried out, "Now Thou dost dismiss Thy servant, O Lord, according to Thy word, in peace. Because my eyes have seen Thy salvation, a light to the revelation of the Gentiles, and the glory of Thy people Israel."

Application: What a difference between the worldly man, however clever he may be, and the holy man, guided by the light of the Holy Ghost! The one sees only with his bodily eyes; the other sees also with the eyes of faith. The one sees in creatures only the material part, that which is captivating, and to which he gives his heart; the other sees the infinite perfections of God, and continually united himself to God by means of creatures. Which of these two do you resemble?

Affections and Resolutions.

Point III: The favors poured by the Holy Ghost on the holy old man Simeon

Consideration: "The Holy Ghost," adds Saint Luke, "had told Simeon, just and devout, that he should not see death before he had seen the Christ of the Lord." God is faithful to His promises. Generally He gives more than He promises. Here is a proof of it; for it was given to Simeon not only to see the Infant Jesus, but further, to receive Him into his arms. "He also took Him into his arms." With what wonderful delight his soul was then filled! How many graces and favors were then poured on him! What a sweet assurance to him that he should die full of years, of joy and of consolation!

Application: The reason Simeon had such extraordinary graces vouchsafed to him was that his life had been entirely passed in the love and service of God. If your life has not always been thus spent, let it at least be so for the future, and you will have a well-founded hope, or rather an assurance, of dying also in the peace and joy of the Lord.

Colloquy with our Blessed Lord.

January 18: On the words *Nunc dimittis servum tuum in pace*

1st prelude: I will picture to myself Simeon at the moment when he said these words, "Now Thou dost dismiss Thy servant in peace."

2nd **prelude**: I will beg the grace of sharing at my death in the dispositions of the holy old man.

Point I: Two dispositions regarding death

Consideration: "Now Thou dost dismiss Thy servant in peace." Simeon, after having seen the promised Redeemer, begged to die. He looked upon himself only as a prisoner who desired to escape at once. And, in fact, since the sin of Adam, this mortal body, which was a palace for the soul in a state of innocencc, is now only a dark and miserable prison. The Christian and the religious who are unfaithful to their duties leave it with regret, like state prisoners who are only expecting a sentence of death from their judges; the faithful Christian and religious, on the contrary, quit it not only with resignation but with joy, as the prisoners unjustly accused goes forth, to whom judgment will be but a restoration and a triumph.

Application: Which of these will you resemble at your last hour? What will by your dispositions then? The future, you will say, is hidden from us; and that is true. However, as death is generally but the echo of life, ask yourself, "If now I had to appear before my Judge, what would be my dispositions?" And when you have the answer to that question, you will know what remains for you to do, that you may have nothing to fear from death, but everything to hope.

Affections and Resolutions.

Point II: Two lawful reasons for desiring death

Consideration: "Who shall deliver me from the body of this death? I desire to be dissolved and to be with Christ." In these two texts, or rather in this double sigh which bursts from the heart of the Apostle, we find two lawful motives for desiring death; the first is, to be freed from the miseries of life, especially from the necessity of fighting continually against the desires of the flesh and the rebellion of the senses; the second is, to see Jesus, the Spouse of our souls, in His glory, to be more intimately united with Him, and to be able to love Him with a perfect and unchangeable love. Both are lawful, but the second is more perfect than the first.

Application: We are religious, we have renounced the deceitful pleasures of the world; on the other hand, we groan continually under the inseparable sufferings of soul and body, and nevertheless we are still so attached to the world. We fear to leave it, to cross the threshold of death, which ought to lead us to those joys of Paradise that Jesus Christ has promised us. What can this proceed from, if not from our want of faith and confidence? To us also Jesus makes this reproach: "O thou of little faith, why didst thou doubt?"

Affections and Resolutions.

Point III: Two means of assuring a happy death

Consideration: "It cannot be," says Saint Augustine, "that he who has lived well should have a miserable death." The first and surest means, then, of making a good and holy death is to live well – to live as a good Christian and a good religious. Without that we are under a delusion, or presumptuous; for "it is rare," adds the same saint, "that we die well if we have not lived well." The second means is pointed out to us by the author of the *Imitation*: "Happy is the man who has the thought of death ever before his mind." It consists in frequently recalling the thought of death – especially in difficult temptations – to ask ourselves, then, What should I think of this at the hour of death?

Application: See how far you are careful and faithful in practicing these means of obtaining that greatest of all blessings – a holy death. Weigh well the importance of it, and you will be faithful. You will spend each day, beginning from this one, as you will wish to have spent it at the hour of death.

Colloquy with Saint Joseph, patron of a happy death.

January 19: Prophesies of the holy old man Simeon

1st prelude: I will imagine I see Mary listening to the words of the holy old man Simeon.

2nd prelude: I will try to understand the mysteries and the truths of faith.

Point I: Prophesies relating to Jesus

Consideration: When giving back the Infant Jesus to Mary, Simeon, suddenly enlightened as to the future, uttered these memorable words: "This Child is set for the fall or for the resurrection of many, and a sign that shall be contradicted." The eighteen centuries which have passed since this prophecy was uttered have proved its truth and especially the time in which we live – a time in which we see wonderful conversions and spiritual resurrections brought about by the zeal of so many missionaries; and also systematic and impious opposition to the Church of Jesus Christ on the part of those who are reckoned among His disciples.

Application: But can it be possible that Jesus, our loving Savior, can become for a religious – the occasion of spiritual ruin, of a greater reprobation? Yes; and ecclesiastical history can furnish, alas, too many proofs of it. How many religious we see who, losing little by little the spirit of their holy state, have re-learnt the spirit of the world – who have become the living contradictions of the maxims of Jesus Christ, and whose ruin has been more fatal and terrible because they have had so many graces and blessings poured on them!

Affections and Resolutions.

Point II: Prophesies relating to Mary

Consideration: Simeon, addressing himself especially to Mary, said to her these severe words: "And thy own soul a sword shall pierce." This prophecy, strictly speaking, was not fulfilled till on Calvary the soul of Mary underwent inexpressible sufferings, and bore the most cruel martyrdom; when she saw her Divine Son dying on the Cross and was unable to die with Him. But may we not say that this martyrdom, by the anticipated knowledge that was given to her, began from this day, and was then a martyrdom of thirty-three years' duration? A martyrdom without parallel; and so much more meritorious before God, that it was not visible to the eyes of men, and no one could soften its bitterness by compassion.

Application: When you have to endure sufferings, and sometimes severe ones, of soul or body, which are not visible to others, and which no one thinks of pitying, console yourself that you have some resemblance to your Mother; console yourself with her by the thought that God is witness of your martyrdom, and that He is pleased with the offering that you make, to endure it all your life for love of Him. Oh, what merit does an unknown martyrdom possess before God, and what wonderful consolation there is for a religious who loves to have it known only to God! What has been your way of acting in moments of trials and desolation?

Affections and Resolutions.

Point III: Prophesies relating to men

Consideration: "And," added Simeon, "out of many hearts thoughts may be revealed." When the persecution against Jesus and His disciples prevailed, the true dispositions of each heart were revealed. Then it was seen who really loved God, who were ready to lose all, to sacrifice all – possessions, rest, health, parents, reputation, even life itself – rather than displease Him, forsake Him, and be lost for ever by sin.

Application: Alas! Your love for God has not perhaps been able to meet blame or mockery – perhaps not even the fear of incurring the disapprobation of men. Humble yourself before God for your want of firmness, perseverance, and generosity; try to have always before your mind those words of Jesus Christ: "Fear ye not them that kill the body, and are not able to kill the soul; but rather fear Him that can destroy both soul and body into hell." They will arm you with invincible strength and courage.

Colloquy with Jesus and Mary.

January 20: Importance of Salvation

1st prelude: Represent to yourself Jesus Christ saying these words: "Seek ye therefore first the kingdom of God and Him justice."

2nd prelude: Beg for a strong impulse of the will to act in all things according to the sense of these words.

Point I: The business of salvation is doubtless the most important of all others, because it is a business which concerns eternity.

Consideration: To pass from this world to a happy eternity, and thus to escape everlasting punishment, is what we mean by the words "work out your salvation." The business of salvation, then, is the business of eternity – the eternity of our soul and body. All other affairs, however important we may think them, are not and cannot be more than affairs of time. And what is time? What are sixty or eighty years compared to eternity?

Application: What blindness and folly it is, then, to busy ourselves and disquiet ourselves more for the interests of time than those of eternity; to lose, or even expose ourselves to the danger of losing, eternal salvation for the momentary enjoyment of some terrestrial happiness or some sensual pleasure! Nevertheless, such is the blindness and folly of the greater number of men. Look at what is passing around you. Has not this folly been yours? Is it not still yours in some respects?

Affections and Resolutions.

Point II: The business of salvation is doubtless the most important of all, because if we once fail, the loss is irreparable

Consideration: For all other misfortunes there is a remedy: we can do over again a work that is spoilt; we can recover a lost fortune; we can rebuild a house burnt down; but if salvation be once lost, the evil is without remedy – *semel periisse aeternum est periisse*. We shall not return to life; we shall not come forth from hell. "These shall go," said Jesus Christ, "into everlasting punishment."

Application: What conclusion ought we to draw from this consideration? Saint Paul tells us, "with fear and trembling work out your salvation." And think not that this conclusion does not strictly apply to you, because you are in the religious state; for the Apostle, though confirmed in grace, applies it to himself. "I was with you," he writes to the Corinthians, "in weakness, and in fear, and in much trembling;" and again: "I chastise my body and bring it into subjection, lest perhaps when I have preached to others I myself should become a castaway." "Ah," cried Pope Saint Gregory, "we ought never to think we have done enough when it is a question of eternity" – Nulla satis magna securitas, ubi periclitatur aeternitas. And besides, did not the angels fall from heaven, and from heaven into hell?

Affections and Resolutions

Point III: The business of salvation is the most important of all, because it is the only business absolutely necessary

Consideration: Many things are relatively necessary. An office is confided to you; you are obliged in conscience to do what it requires from you. That is necessary, but not absolutely so. God can do it without you; others can do it for you. What alone is absolutely necessary is, that you save yourself, work out your own salvation. It is a personal affair; no one can do it for you – neither your superiors, nor your brethren, nor even God. "He who created you without your help," says Saint Augustine, "cannot save you without it."

Application: Woe, then, to the religious who is not fervent, and does not seek his own sanctification. The vigilance of his superiors can indeed restrain him within the bounds of external regularity, but they cannot save him or sanctify him. He has reason to fear lest

in the midst of so many means of salvation he should be lost. "Therefore," says the author of the *Imitation*, "however it may be with others, neglect not thyself."
Colloquy with Jesus, the Author of our salvation and sanctification.

January 21: How to know the Importance which belongs to the Business of our Salvation

1st prelude: Represent to yourself Jesus Christ saying these words: "Seek ye therefore first the kingdom of God and Him justice."
2nd prelude: Beg the grace of really understanding your own dispositions regarding your salvation.

Point I: He who has at heart an affair above all others – for example, a lawsuit on which his whole fortune depends – thinks of it at all times and in all places.

Consideration: The thought pursues him in spite of himself, day and night; in his social pleasures, his conversations, his walks, his meals, his work. It is his first thought in the morning, his last at night: in one word he is, as we say, entirely preoccupied.

Application: Do you remark a likeness to yourself in this as regards your salvation? Does the thought accompany you everywhere? Is it generally your first thought upon waking, your last thought before closing your eyes? If there is none of this, if generally your mind is occupied with vague, idle, earthly or worldly thoughts, judge for yourself if you really have the business of your salvation more than any other at heart, and what there is for you to hope for or to fear in eternity.
Affections and Resolutions.

Point II: He who has one affair above all others at heart is always afraid of its failure, that some accident should mar its success

Consideration: And the more important this affair is, the greater his uneasiness and his fears. This fact experience teaches us daily.

Application: What affair is more important than that of your salvation? If, then, it causes you neither fear nor uneasiness, while so many others disturb you daily, it is a clear proof that you do not sufficiently appreciate the importance of your salvation, or that you are far from having it at heart beyond all other affairs. In this case ought you not to conclude that you are living in a false security, and that you ought to fear the more because you do not fear enough? For he who is without fear of failure takes no serious means to attain success; and salvation is the reward of energy and striving; for, says Jesus Christ, "The kingdom of heaven suffereth violence, and the violent bear it away."

Affections and Resolutions.

Point III: He who has an affair at heart beyond all others never thinks he has done enough to ensure its success

Consideration: Look at the man implicated in a lawsuit which concerns his fortune – he is continually seeking new means of defending it. After one consultation he has another; after one arrangement he makes another; he never thinks he has done enough. Is this not the case?

Application: It would be the same with us, and with far more reason, if we had the business of our salvation and eternity seriously at heart. Far from imitating the lukewarm religious who confines himself in everything to what is strictly necessary, we should never think we have taken sufficient precautions, or used sufficient means; never think we have done enough to obtain final perseverance. Do you remark this in yourself? What ought you to think about yourself?

Colloquy with our Blessed Lord.

January 22: The Flight into Egypt

1st prelude: See the Holy Family journeying towards Egypt.
2nd prelude: Beg for the faith and resignation of which they give us the example.

Point I: The Holy Family receive the order to fly into Egypt

Consideration: "An angel of the Lord appeared in sleep to Joseph, and said to him, "Arise, and take the Child and His Mother, and fly into Egypt."

Joseph and Mary, though poor, lived happily in the company of Jesus. They were without fear or distrust. However, "Herod, perceiving that he was deluded by the wise men," had taken measures to destroy the Infant Jesus. But God watched over those to whose care He had been confided; He warned them of Herod's designs, and showed them the means of escaping them.

Application: Let us learn by this to understand the Providence of God over His servants. He does not promise to spare them afflictions and persecutions, but He promises to watch over them, to direct them by lawful superiors, and to act in such a manner that everything works together for their good. He knows how also, when it seems good to Him in times of great danger, to defeat the plots of the wicked. We see this in the history of the flight into Egypt, and in a number of facts recorded in the Bible and in the history of the Church.

Affections and Resolutions.

Point II: The order to depart is communicated by Joseph to Mary

Consideration: "An angel of the Lord appeared in sleep to Joseph, and said to him, Fly into Egypt." Why did not the angel give the order to Mary, who was more holy and more dear to God than Joseph? Because he was the legal husband of Mary, and consequently the head of the Holy Family, and it is necessary to the maintenance of order that inferiors should be directed by superiors, event when the former excel the latter in holiness; for it is not to the worth of a man that we ought to trust the direction of our souls, but to God in the person of those who hold His place, and of whom He has said, "He that heareth you heareth Me."

Application: Am I always submissive to this doctrine and to this order established by God? Has it not happened sometimes that I have obeyed unwillingly, or failed in respect to a superior, because he was younger in age or in religion than I was? If it be so, it is a certain proof that I do not understand the economy of the order established by God; that I have a very imperfect idea of the virtue of obedience, and that my acts of submission have been frequently rather acts of deference and policy than acts of supernatural virtue, which are alone worthy of recompense.

Affections and Resolutions.

Point III: Reflections on the order the angel gave to Joseph

Consideration: "Fly into Egypt, and be there until I shall tell thee; for it will come to pass that Herod will seek the Child to destroy Him." Remark here how on one side the angel exacts from Joseph and Mary an act of blind obedience by concealing from them the length of their exile – "be there till I shall tell thee"; and then, on the other side, he explains the motives and the reasons why they are exiled; for "it will come to pass that Herod will seek the Child to destroy Him."

Application: It matters little whether superiors give the motive of their orders or not; often discretion forbids them to give it. Sometimes it is better to say what it is, either to make the urgency or the way of performing the command better understood; or to condescend to the weakness and the imperfections of their inferiors, who, anxious to secure the merit of obedience, should desire a simple command only. We see that this has ever been the wish of perfect religious. Let us follow them, and let us always aspire to the most perfect obedience.

Colloquy with our Lady and Saint Joseph.

January 23: Wonderful Obedience of Joseph and Mary

1st prelude: See the Holy Family journeying towards Egypt.
2nd prelude: Beg for the faith and resignation of which they give us the example.

Point I: Their obedience was blind

Consideration: They obeyed blindly, with an entire and perfect submission of judgment. They did not ask why God did not arrest the arm of Herod rather than send them into exile; or if they must be exiled, why they should not go into the country of the Magi, who knew them so well, rather than to Egypt, whose inhabitants were hostile to the people of Israel; nor why the order to depart was not given to them soon enough to enable them to prepare for their journey. God spoke to them by His delegate; it was enough; they thought of nothing but obeying, persuaded that there is nothing better than to do what God wills, because He wills it, as He wills it.

Application: Let us try to obey, like Mary and Joseph, not only courageously, but also blindly, i.e., without wanting to know the reason of the command; for, in fact, if we execute a command after having asked for the reason of it, and because the thing seems right and useful, is it not true to say we are obeying our own ideas rather than the will of God, and that we no longer, strictly speaking, do what God wills, because He wills it, as He wills it – that therefore our obedience will lose much of its merit?

Affections and Resolutions.

Point II: Their obedience was prompt

Consideration: They obeyed promptly, without the slightest interval between the order and its execution, Joseph, says the Evangelist, rose at once, informed Mary of the command from heaven, and she, submissive and resigned, took the Child in her arms, and both set out that same night, without waiting for the dawn of day: "who arose, and took the Child and His Mother by night, and retired into Egypt."

Application: How far removed are we too often from this prompt obedience! How slowly and with what hesitation do we attend to the different community exercises! How unfaithful we are in obeying the first stroke of the bell, often for a vain excuse, commonly suggested by sensuality or caprice, in spite of a certain disquiet of conscience, or, what is worse, without any disquiet! Nevertheless, it may be the cause of great harm; especially when we have to watch over those who are confided to our car. If Joseph had not promptly obeyed the voice of the angel, to what dangers would he not have exposed the sacred Charge confided to him? Affections and Resolutions.

Point III: Their obedience was generous

Consideration: They obeyed generously, without uttering a word of murmur, without testifying regret or sorrow that duty called them so abruptly from their neighbors and friends, without showing the slightest trouble or disquietude about the future. Ah! It was because Jesus was all to them, and they knew that with Him they would surmount all difficulties, and that nothing would be wanting to them.

Application: Let us always remember that in exchange for the sacrifice we have made of our will and liberty, God binds Himself to conduct us by our superiors to the end of our pilgrimage to our heavenly country. This thought will banish all fear, all hesitation; we shall obey generously, and be always victorious. Assured of the help of the Omnipotent, we shall cry out with the Apostle, when the idea of impossibility presents itself to us: "I can do all things in Him who strengthens me," – Omnia possum in eo qui me comfortat. Let us embrace these dispositions, and preserve them in our hearts.

Colloquy with the angel who gave the Holy Father the order to fly into Egypt, and witnessed their wonderful obedience.

January 24: On three Kinds of Obedience

1st prelude: Represent to yourself the Apostle saying these words: "Be obedient in the simplicity of your heart, as to Christ."
2nd prelude: Be earnestly as the fruit of this meditation the spirit of true obedience.

Point I: Servile obedience

Consideration: Servile obedience, as the word indicates, proceeds from fear – not of God, but of men; fear of punishment, of reproach, of humiliation, or privation of some favor. It is the obedience of hirelings: while they are under their master's eye, they do what they are commanded, they conform to the rules as he has laid down; but as soon as they are alone, they are unfaithful, and only follow their own humor. It is evident that in this there is neither the virtue nor merit of obedience, nothing but constraint and servility.

Application: We are religious, we have made the vow of obedience of our own free choice; it would seem, then, that our obedience can have nothing in common with this servility, this mockery of obedience. Nevertheless, let each from his heart ask himself, "When I am alone, and have no fear of being seen, am I as faithful to all that the rule and obedience have laid down as if I were under the eye of my superior? If the contrary frequently takes place, is it not an indication that servile fear has something, if not much, to do with the motive of my obedience?"

Affections and Resolutions.

Point II: Obedience from policy

Consideration: This second kind of obedience is founded on this maxim: It is always useful to be on good terms with superiors; it is a means of avoiding disagreeable things, and of obtaining little favors. This obedience, then, is an entirely human one; it has nothing more in common than the first with the virtue of obedience, it is simply selfishness. The world thinks it cleverness, but it is duplicity before God.

Application: Have policy and duplicity never been mingled with your obedience? In your submission to your superiors, do you seek to please them for the sake of God, or for your own sake? Do you think of your superiors as you speak of them? Do you speak of them as you do to them? Do you blame them interiorly, or before some of your brethren, for what you have approved and praised before their face? By these signs you can know the value of your obedience.

Affections and Resolutions.

Point III: Supernatural obedience

Consideration: This is the third kind of obedience, or rather it is the only one which deserves the name, the only true and meritorious obedience, the only one pleasing to God and worthy of man. It is founded on faith, on that undeniable principle that God's will is to govern men by other men whom He has appointed to be the guardians and visible representatives of His supreme authority, so that every man may live in the subjection which he owes to Him. He who obeys on this principle does not, strictly speaking, obey men, his equals, but God in the person of men. He can say, "I recognize God only as above me; I submit only to God."

Application: How great and how noble is the Christian and the religious who obeys in this way; and how pleasing to God and meritorious his obedience is even in the smallest things! Renew the resolution to avoid carefully all that is contrary to this obedience, and thank God for having made you understand the greatness, the consolation, the merit of this obedience of faith and love.

Colloquy with our Blessed Lord.

January 25: Return of the Holy Family from Egypt

1st prelude: Look at the Holy Family travelling toward their native country.

2nd prelude: Beg for an entire submission to the will of Divine Providence.

Point I: Perseverance of Joseph

Consideration: Joseph dwelt in Egypt wit the Child Jesus and Mary *until the death of Herod*, which took place some years after the massacre of the Innocents; but it is commonly believed that he did not receive the order to return from Egypt till three years later. This long sojourn in a strange country would, as it seems to us, have been extremely painful to Joseph and Mary, and have made them long eagerly for the moment of departure; but no, the single thought, "We are where God wishes us to be," made the sojourn in Egypt not only endurable but pleasant; on the other hand, the

Gospel never hints that they were in want of any necessary. Providence, then, provided for all their wants.

Application: Let us learn by this to remain quietly on the spot and in the conditions in which we have been or may be placed by obedience, persuaded that it is God who directs us by our superiors. If it seems to us at first sight that we really do not know how to act in a new position, let us promptly resist these first unfavorable impressions. A few days' effort at self-conquest will subdue them. Let us firmly resist also all those ideas of changing our place or employment with are so frequent in our inconstant nature. How many religious, from not having followed these rules, have fallen victims to lamentable delusions, and even lost their vocation!

Affections and Resolutions.

Point II: Tranquility of Joseph

Consideration: An angel of the Lord appeared in sleep to Joseph in Egypt, saying: "Take the Child and His Mother, and go into the land of Israel." We may suppose (and many of the Father assure us of it) that God disposed some hearts in Egypt towards Joseph, so that he could practice his trade, and that he became at length used to his new position, and contented with it. It would then have been likely that he would regret sorely having to quit it, and undertake a long journey without exactly knowing where he could take up his abode; nevertheless, he left all at the first injunction of the angel, without hesitation or reply.

Application: It will probably cause you suffering some day when you have to leave a house, an office, or brethren with whom you have lived a long while. Besides, after middle age all changes of our dwelling, even of our room, of office, or of superior, are trying to nature, and often become the occasion of a most painful sacrifice; if this sacrifice is demanded from you, make it heartily. Your generous obedience will have a great recompense, as had that of Saint Joseph.

Affections and Resolutions.

Point III: Prudence of Joseph

Consideration: "But hearing that Archelaus reigned in Judea in the room of Herod his father, he was afraid to go thither." It seemed to him that the Child Jesus would not be safe in the dominions of a prince who was son and successor of Herod, and like him in cruelty; on the other hand, *the land of Israel*, which the angel named, had various provinces, governed by different princes. But into which of these territories would it be well for him to go? He wanted light; he sought and found it in prayer; "being warned in sleep, he retired into the quarters of Galilee, and coming, he dwelt in a city called Nazareth."

Application: The conduct of Joseph in this circumstance teaches us to act with deliberation in everything; in all our doubts and perplexities, after having reflected well, we should, before acting, have recourse to humble and fervent prayer. What troubles of conscience, and what useless regrets, we should spare ourselves by constantly following these rules of conduct!

Colloquy with Saint Joseph.

January 26: The Holy Family go up to the Temple at Jerusalem

1st prelude: See the Holy Family prostrate in prayer in the Temple.

2nd prelude: Beg for a lively faith and an ardent piety, in presence of Jesus Christ concealed in our tabernacles.

Point I: Joseph goes up to keep the Pasch at Jerusalem

Consideration: "And His parents went every year to Jerusalem at the solemn day of the Pasch," to adore God in His Temple. That the Israelites, so inclined to idolatry, might be always kept in mind of the unity of God and the worship due to Him, they were only permitted to build one Temple – the Temple of Jerusalem. The law obliged all men, and boys come to a certain age, to go there three times a year, at the feasts of the Pasch, Pentecost and Tabernacles. This was not much in itself, but considering the long and difficult journey so many had to make, it was a good deal; and pious men like Joseph felt keenly not being able to go oftener to satisfy their devotion.

Application: Far happier than the Israelites, we have everywhere churches and oratories dedicated to our Lord, where He dwells not only in Spirit as in the Temple, but in Person, though hidden from our eyes. We have only a few steps to take before we can enter them. He invites us tenderly to come to Him, anxious to pour His favours on us. How do we respond to His invitation? How many time a day do we go to visit Him, to lay before Him our homage and our supplication? Occasions of doing it come so often as if of themselves. Do we not neglect them, even when perhaps an interior voice bids us profit by them?

Affections and Resolutions.

Point II: Mary accompanies Joseph

Consideration: "And His parents went every year to Jerusalem at the solemn day of the Pasch." We see by these words of the Evangelist that Mary went also to fulfil the Paschal duty at Jerusalem, although the law did not oblige women to do so. She never asked what was of strict obligation, but what was most likely to promote the glory of God, her own sanctification, and the edification of her neighbor.

Application: This conduct of Mary ought to be the invariable rule of every true religious. It is the constant teaching of all the masters of spiritual life that, to make progress in the ways of perfection, we must add that which is of supererogation to that which is of obligation, not only in matters of piety, but in mortification, charity, zeal, and all other virtues. Have I followed this rule? Have I not, on the contrary, confined myself to what is of strict obligation, and thus deprived myself, by being illiberal towards God, of the gifts of His bounty? The danger of such conduct is that we run the risk of often being unfaithful to what is of obligation.

Affections and Resolutions.

Point III: Jesus, aged twelve years, accompanies Mary and Joseph

Consideration: Let us follow in spirit the Holy Family in their pilgrimage to Jerusalem. What eager love directed their steps! With what religious delight they ascended the steps of the Temple! In what grave and respectful attitudes they placed themselves! Sometimes they were prostrate, sometimes they knelt, or stood with their eyes raised to heaven. Let us penetrate into their souls, and try to gain an idea of the ardent devotion with which they gave glory to God, thanked Him for His blessings, offered themselves as victims of expiation for the sins of the world, and begged for an abundance of divine benedictions on the people of Israel and on all men.

Application: What beautiful models are here before our eyes, both as to our exterior manner, and as to the affections we ought to

nourish in our hearts each time that we appear before God in His Temple, especially during the Holy Sacrifice! How have I copied this model?
Colloquy with the Holy Family.

January 27: Jesus lost, and found again in the Temple

1st prelude: I will represent to myself Mary and Joseph seeking the Child Jesus.
2nd prelude: I will beg the grace of living always in a close union with Jesus.

Point I: Jesus remains at Jerusalem unknown to His parents

Consideration: The Gospel story proposed for our meditation today is full not only of mystery but of great instruction, for it has pleased the Incarnate Word, says Pope Saint Gregory, to reach us by His actions no less than by His words – *Ipsa facta Verbi verba sunt.*

By remaining unknown to His parents in Jerusalem, in spite of the suffering that they would feel and which He felt Himself, He wished to teach men to put the interests of God's glory above natural inclinations, even the most lawful ones; He wished especially to teach religious that they should die entirely to the affections of flesh and blood, by changing the natural attachment to their relatives and friends into a spiritual one.

Application: To change filial affection into a spiritual love is not to destroy but to perfect it; in a certain sense, to make it divine. Have I always understood and practiced this doctrine? In consequence of not understanding it well, or rather, not practicing it well, many religious have become the victims of fatal delusions, and have at last lost their vocation.
Affections and Resolutions.

Point II: His desolate parents seek Him for three days

Consideration: "And having fulfilled the days," says Saint Luke, "when they returned, the Child Jesus remained in Jerusalem, and His parents knew it not. And thinking He was in the company, they came a day's journey," (and when the evening came, the hour when each family reunited in the inns,) "they sought Him among their kinsfolk and acquaintance, and not finding Him, they returned into Jerusalem seeking Him." Mary and Joseph loved Jesus with their whole hearts; He was all in all to them, He was the life of their life. When they lost His sweet Presence, the world became a melancholy desert to them. How great, then, must have been their sorrow and their agony! Who can form an idea of it?

Application: Why is it that when you have lost Jesus by sin you are so little touched and afflicted? Is it not because you love Him so feebly, because He is far from being all to you? Further, in the language of the saints, *to lose Jesus* is not only to be separated from Him by mortal sin, and to be less united to Him by affection to venial sin, but also to be deprived of the sweetness and consolation of His sensible Presence. We can *lose Jesus* in this third manner, without its being our fault. The sighs and tears of God's greatest servants show us this. Nevertheless, says the author of the *Imitation*, it is often our own fault; because we do not seek after compunction of heart, we are unmortified and dissipated.

Affections and Resolutions.

Point III: They find Him again in the Temple

Consideration: After three days' search, they found Him in the Temple, sitting in the midst of the doctors, hearing them and answering them. His Mother, drawing Him aside, said to Him, "Son, why hast Thou done so to us? Behold, Thy father and I have sought Thee sorrowing." He answered her, "How is it that you sought Me? Did you not know that I must be about My Father's business?"

Application: Mary and Joseph teach us never to rest till we have found Jesus again, when we have lost Him by one of the three ways indicated in the preceding point. Have we done this? Jesus teaches us on His side to let all considerations about parents and families give way to the service of God, to whom we ought to devote ourselves entirely and before all things. Have we constantly followed this rule of conduct?

Colloquy with our Blessed Lord.

January 28: Jesus leaves Jerusalem and goes down to Nazareth

1st prelude: See the Child Jesus walking between Mary and Joseph.

2nd prelude: Beg the esteem and love of retreat and retirement.

Point I: Jesus leaves the City of Jerusalem

Consideration: Jesus, aged twelve years, had given in the Temple, even to the doctors of the law, a striking proof of His divine wisdom. "All that heard Him were astonished at His wisdom and His answers." We should imagine that this favourable beginning would have induced Him to commence the course of His preaching; nevertheless, He did nothing, but resigned Himself to His parents' care, as is natural for children of His age. "He went down with them" - *descendit cum eis* – and came far away, to bury Himself at Nazareth in a kind of solitude. He did not leave it until long afterwards, when the moment fixed by the good pleasure of His Heavenly Father arrived; restraining in Himself the zeal that would have made Him hasten to the rescue of souls.

Application: Let us remember the reflection we have made, that the actions of Jesus are instructions. What does He teach us now? 1. That before coming forward and professing to teach others, we should teach ourselves, in silence and retreat, virtue and knowledge, especially the knowledge of sanctity. 2. That we ought not to be eager or even desirous to leave this retreat till we are called from it by our superiors. 3. When we are called to the active life, placed in a house or a fixed employment, we ought not to mingle in the noise and conversations of the world more than is necessary, persuaded that we shall be nowhere so secure or so happy as in our cell alone with God. What have been our feelings and our conduct on this point?

Affections and Resolutions.

Point II: Jesus returning to Galilee

Consideration: We contemplated, the day before yesterday, to our great edification, the Holy Family prostrate in prayer in the Temple. Let us contemplate them now on the journey from Jerusalem to Galilee; we shall find there fresh matter for edification. Let us fix our eyes at first on Mary and Joseph, having the Child Jesus between them. What gravity, what religious modesty in their walk and in their whole appearance! In the movements of the head and eyes we see none of that curiosity and levity which are so natural to us, and often so hurtful. Let us listen to the conversation which sometimes interrupts their silence and prayer. It runs upon the mysteries of the kingdom of heaven, on the great things that Jesus would perform in the world for the glory of God. The answer given by the Child Jesus to His Mother, "Did you not know that I must be about My Father's business?" leads us to suppose this. If it were given to us to look into their souls, we should see them occupied with pious affections and meditations. The Gospel proves this by saying of Our Lady especially, "And His Mother kept all these words in her heart."

Application: To draw fruit from this meditation, let us see what there is in common or in contrast between the Holy Family and us, when alone or in company, when we are out of the house, walking or traveling. This comparison will make us see in what we have failed, and in what we ought to reform.

Affections and Resolutions.

Point III: Jesus dwells at Nazareth

Consideration: The Son of God, who had chosen the vilest place in the opinion of man for that of His birth, a deserted stable, chose for His abode during nearly thirty years in the land of Israel the little town of Nazareth, of which the proverb ran, "Can anything of good come from Nazareth?"

Application: Why did Jesus Christ act thus? Doubtless to confound our vanity, which makes us desire and seek a dwelling in great centers of population, apparently to do a great work, but in reality to be put more forward, more appreciated, praised, and applauded. Look into the depths of your own heart, does it not tell you there is some truth in this? And if it be thus, what matter of confusion for you! Jesus, who is infinite wisdom, flies from admiration, notice and applause, and you seek after them. Are you not injuring yourself, doing yourself immense harm, by losing in great part the merit of your good works?

Colloquy with the Holy Family.

January 29: On the Mystery of the Hidden Life of Jesus

1st prelude: Represent to yourself the little house of Nazareth where the Holy Family lived.

2nd prelude: Beg the grace of understanding well the great mystery of the hidden life of Jesus.

Point I: The mystery of the hidden life of Jesus

Consideration: Jesus came into the world not only to give life to the human race by His death, but also to bring it by His divine teaching to the knowledge of the truth, to the worship and love of the true God. He had to convert the world; and to accomplish this immense work, He had only thirty-three years before Him. It would seem, therefore, that He had no time to lose; we should expect to see Him as soon as possible come before men, as sent by God and the teacher of the human race. But no – and here is the mystery – until thirty years of age He remained unknown to the entire world, living in the obscure workshop of a carpenter!

Application: When in contemplation we place ourselves in spirit before the obscure retreat of the Divine Saviour, we are tempted to say with His disciples, *Manifest ate ipsum mundo* – Manifest Thyself, Lord, undeceive the world; it is lost: while here, Thou dost nothing to save it, and Thou art losing time, which is so precious. And Jesus answers us, Are you also yet without understanding? – *Sine intellectu estis?* You say that I do nothing. I do the will of My Father, and that alone is great and praiseworthy. You say that I lose time; and I teach men – those especially who will hereafter aspire to perfection – to subdue their pride, to live without complaint or murmur, unknown and despised by the world, in an obscure spot, if obedience demands it of them. Who can after this complain that he is not place or employed according to his merit and his talents?

Affections and Resolutions.

Point II: Meaning of this mystery

Consideration: To have a more complete knowledge of the hidden life of Jesus, the end that He had in leading it, and all the gratitude we owe Him, let us recollect that the miseries of the world, which the Savior came to remedy, sprang from pride; that it is still the permanent cause which threatens to bring back the same disorders. He had especially to make men understand and adopt the only remedy for pride – *humility*. This is the tendency of the first lessons He gave to the world: "Learn of Me, because I am meek and humble of heart. Blessed are the poor in spirit. Every one that exalts himself shall be humbled; and many that are last shall be first."

Before all things He preached humility; He proclaimed its absolute necessity. But if He had contented Himself with preaching it, without practicing and teaching it in a striking manner, we should have understood the lesson; but our pride, so deeply rooted in our souls, would have resisted; it would have said,

"Jesus in truth had eloquently preached humility, self-forgetfulness, the contempt of the world and of its disdain; but He has been Himself highly thought of, constantly admired, praised and applauded." The lessons and the exhortations of the Savior would have been useless; pride, and the disorders that spring from it, would have been triumphant.

Application: There is no one who does not feel the truth of this conclusion, however little he may know himself. If he looks into the depth of his heart, he ought to say to himself: "If now, even when I have Jesus before my eyes placed so low, and as it were annihilated in the opinion of men, it costs me so much to conquer my pride, not to be troubled or to complain when others are preferred to me, when I am withdrawn from some office of honor, or employed in some inferior or humiliating one, what would it be if this divine model had not been given to me? How should I ever have subdued my pride, or loved and practiced humility?" Colloquy with Jesus hidden and unknown at Nazareth.

January 30: Nature, Motives, and Practice of a pure Intention

1st prelude: I shall imagine I hear Saint Paul say: "Do all to the glory of God."
2nd prelude: I will beg from God help to acquire the habit of always acting with a pure intention.

Point I: Nature of a pure intention

Consideration: Our state of life very much resembles that of Jesus in the house of Nazareth. The greater part of our days is passed within a cloister. We lead there a life hidden from the world. How can we, how ought we to sanctify it? Especially by a pure intention, which enhances our smallest actions in the eyes of God. Let us try to understand well the *nature*, the *motives*, and the *practice* of this pure intention. Intention is an act of the will, by which man tends towards an end. If this end is good, the intention is so also; but that it may be meritorious before God, it must have a supernatural end; and he who possesses it must be in a state of grace. We may have at one time many supernatural ends, either directly or indirectly regarding God. By one single action, then, we can amass a great variety of merits.

Application: Every reasonable man is supposed to act for some

determined end; but there are a great number who take no account of their intentions. What a loss of merit, which is for ever irreparable! Do you belong to this category of Christians or religious so little mindful of their eternal interests?
Affections and Resolutions.

Point II: Motives of a pure intention

Consideration: Many motives lead us and urge us always to act with a pure intention, and attentively to watch over ourselves that it may be so; the first is its *extreme importance*. On our intentions depends in great measure the value of our actions before God, and consequently the value of time, which must decide our eternity; because time is only a succession of actions which make up our short life in this world. The second motive is the *obligations that we have*; we belong entirely to God, and consequently we ought by a pure intention to devote all to Him, even the most indifferent actions; as says the Apostle, "Whether you eat or drink, or whatsoever else you do, do all to the glory of God." The third motive is its *facility*, i.e., the practice of a pure intention, as we shall show in the following point.

Application: Take these motives into serious consideration, weight the value of each, and doubtless you will feel a desire spring up in your heart of attaining the practical perfection of all that a pure intention denotes, especially as, in the state of grace which religious life makes so easy, you ought not to meet with any serious difficulty in its execution.
Affections and Resolutions.

Point III: Practice of a pure intention

Consideration: All consists of two practices, of which we ought to try to learn the habit: first, to have a settled form containing many intentions, which we will repeat every morning with great intensity of will; then renew it often throughout the day, for fear it should have been spoilt or destroyed by vain-glory or self-love.

Application: Look into yourself; see where you are as regards these two practical points. Have you preserved intact the habit of repeating every morning the form so rich in pure intentions, which you were taught in the novitiate? Have you the habit of renewing it often during the day? How often do you renew it? Do you make use of any means to recall it, if necessary, to your memory?
Colloquy with our Blessed Lord.

January 31: Jesus a Model of Obedience in his Hidden Life

1st prelude: See the Child Jesus obeying Mary and Joseph with perfect grace.
2nd prelude: Beg for the knowledge, esteem and practical love of the obedience of faith.

Point I: Qualities of the obedience of Jesus

Consideration: "He was subject to them" – *erat subditus illis*. In these three words the Holy Ghost has chosen that the history of our Savior's life till His thirtieth year should be contained and transmitted to future ages. He seemed to care only for obedience. Because obedience is the only solid proof of the humility that Jesus, by the mystery of His hidden life, wished, before all things, to teach men; without humility we cannot please God; without obedience we cannot flatter ourselves that we are humble. But what ought our obedience to be? Jesus has chosen to be the living model of it. Let us attentively study this model. He *was subject to them*. *Who*? The God of heaven and earth, who made man. To *whom*? To Mary and to Joseph, two holy creatures, certainly, but nevertheless simple creatures, the work of His hands. *In what*? In all things – there is no mention of any exception. And *how* did He obey? – promptly, entirely, constantly, lovingly and with perfect grace.

Application: Imagine you hear Jesus saying to you: "I have given you an example, that as I have done, so you do also": and, looking back, yourself, see if your obedience is habitually modelled on that of your Divine Master: if it has the same qualities; if it gives joy and happiness to your superiors, as that of Jesus made the joy and happiness of Mary and Joseph.
Affections and Resolutions.

Point II: Principle of the obedience of Jesus

Consideration: The exterior actions of men spring from some interior principle or determined motive. What was the principle of the beautiful and perfect obedience of the Child Jesus? Fear? Certainly not. Interest or hope of reward? Again, no. What had the Ruler of the Universe to fear or hope from men? What, then, was the principle of it? No other than the will of God His Father manifested through His representatives Mary and Joseph. Is not this what is meant by the words so familiar to our Savior? – *Ita, Pater, quoniam sic plactium est coram te* – "Yea, Father, for so it hath seemed good in Thy sight," to give me Mary for a mother and Joseph for my legal father; *fiat voluntas tua* – "Thy will be done." I will be obedient to them in all things, as to Thee, for love of Thee. Properly speaking, then, Jesus did not obey creatures, Mary and Joseph, but God His Father, in the persons of Mary and Joseph.

Application: Here is the idea of supernatural obedience – the obedience of faith, springing from this principle of faith; that the invisible God wills to be represented by a visible representative; that He wills to govern men by other men invested with His authority, and of whom it is written: "He that heareth you, heareth Me; and he that despiseth you, despiseth Me." To obey from this principle is great, noble, and meritorious; it is to see God only in the person of superiors. Can we flatter ourselves we have thus habitually obeyed? Have we not obeyed sometimes, perhaps often, from purely human and natural motives, which are consequently without dignity or great merit before God?

Affections and Resolutions.

Point III: Merit of the obedience of Jesus

Consideration: By this perfect obedience the Child Jesus, from His tenderest years, enhanced the merit of His smallest actions in the eyes of His Father; and as time is only the uninterrupted series of interior and exterior acts, what an immense treasure of merit did not Jesus as man acquire for us during the thirty years of His hidden life!

Application: We have come into religion to enrich ourselves with merits for eternal life. Let us try to excel in the virtue of obedience, and we shall obtain our desire; while leading a common life, hidden from the eyes of the world, we shall heap up immense treasures for heaven, even if we had not besides the occasion of performing notable acts of zeal, penitence, and charity.

Colloquy with Jesus.

February 1: Modesty, Gentleness and Piety of Jesus in His Hidden Life

1st prelude: Represent to yourself Jesus Christ saying: "I have

given you an example, that as I have done to you, so you do also."
2nd prelude: I will beg for ardent desire of reproducing in myself especially the *gentleness*, the *modesty*, and the *piety* of Jesus.

Point I: Gentleness of Jesus

Consideration: Jesus did not content Himself by being a perfect model of obedience in His hidden life; He gave us also the example of many other virtues which the religious should endeavor to acquire in the retirement of the cloister before he enters upon his apostolic career. The Holy Ghost makes special mention of three: gentleness, modesty and piety. "I beseech you," says the Apostle, "by the mildness and modesty of Christ"; and Isaias, speaking of the promised Messiah, said the spirit of godliness, or piety should rest on Him. It is of importance, then, for us to study the character of these virtues, so that we may adopt and excel in them. "Gentleness," says Saint Thomas Aquinas, "is the virtue of a noble soul." Those who possess it rise above all injuries; and even at the moment when they are attacked they remain tranquil – they do not lose their peace of heart.

Application: Do you find the mark of Christian gentleness in yourself? Rather, does it not often happen that you give way to disquiet, impatience, irritation, anger, or studied coldness towards your brethren for frivolous reasons, even for the mere suspicion that they despise you? If this be so, humble yourself, repent and amend.

Affections and Resolutions.

Point II: Modesty of Jesus

Consideration: *Modesty*, which the Apostle mentions in common with gentleness, has a charm and an attraction for the hearts of others, and, besides, it gives great edification, and adds much lustre to all the other virtues. The modesty of Jesus as a child, of Jesus in His youth, was more than angelic, it was divine. How wonderful and charming was His modesty in His looks, His words, His walk, in every movement of His Body, in all His intercourse with others, in the simplicity and uniformity of His exterior life! "He shall not be sad or troublesome," says the Prophet Isaias.

Application: See how far you resemble this living example of modesty; do you words breathe humility, self-forgetfulness, reserve, discretion, a desire to edify your neighbor, to glorify God?

Or do they not rather breathe vanity, boasting, presumption and levity? In your looks, in your walk, in your way of behavior, out of the house or in the house, is the religious modest and dead to himself to be perceived, or a worldly and vain man, seeking himself in all things?
Affections and Resolutions.

Point III: Piety of Jesus

Consideration: Filial piety, that feeling of tenderness and devotion which is natural in the heart of the child for his father, is the third special virtue attributed by the Holy Ghost to Jesus living in His retreat at Nazareth. *The spirit of piety shall rest upon Him.* Jesus had no need, as we have, to unite Himself with God His Father by prayer and contemplation, and yet how diligent He was in prayer! Certainly if in His active life He spent whole nights in it – *erat pernoctans in oration Dei* – we may believe that He devoted to it the greater part of His time in His hidden life.

Application: For us who are not able to see God our Father, if we do not raise ourselves in spirit to Him by prayer, contemplation, and other religious exercises, He can never awaken within us the feelings of devoted filial piety which should animate our hearts. We ought, therefore, to have a great esteem for prayer, and be diligent in it. Is it thus with us?
Colloquy with Our Lord.

February 2: Feast of the Purification, or Candlemas Day

1st prelude: Look at Mary in the Temple offering the Infant Jesus to the Lord, and Jesus offering Himself by the hands of Mary.
2nd prelude: Beg for the spirit of generosity and sacrifice.

Point I: What did Mary do for us on this day?

Consideration: Mary has given us a wonderful example of humility and obedience by submitting, without any obligation, to the law of purification, and thus being willing to pass in public opinion for an ordinary and sinful woman. But what should still more excite our admiration and love is, that she made to-day the most heroic sacrifice imaginable, by offering to God the Father the only object of her love – her Jesus – to be the victim of expiation of our sins, the price of our redemption. She did, in truth, like other mothers, pay the ransom for her Divine Child, and He was given back to her; but it was only that she might nourish Him and watch over Him, as a victim who is prepared for the sacrifice.

Application: What a sight is here before your eyes! The love of God's glory and the salvation of souls triumphing in Mary over maternal love and tenderness! Alas, how far are we from such abnegation, from such fervent love of God and of our neighbor! We who care more for our own interests than those of God's glory and the souls committed to our care – we who avoid the execution of our duties, or some little sacrifices by a thousand excuses; let us try to go out of ourselves, to rise once for all above ourselves, and to become more worthy of our Mother.

Affections and Resolutions.

Point II: What did Jesus do for us on this day?

Consideration: A little child of six weeks old, but possessing the perfect use of reason, He offered Himself, by the hands of Mary, to His Heavenly Father to be the ransom of the human race, which was groaning under the yoke of the devil; to be the victim of expiation for the injury done by sin to the Divine Majesty; to be finally, by the shedding of His Blood, the victim of universal expiation. God the Father accepted this offering, the only one worthy of Him; and from that day Jesus began than long martyrdom of thirty-three years which ended only with His last sigh on the cross.

Application: From the cradle to the tomb, the life of your Divine Savior and model was nothing less than a continual immolation of Himself for the glory of His Heavenly Father and the sanctification of souls; it was a life of sacrifice, and ended by the sacrifice of Himself. Here is the *ideal* of a true religious, who by the three vows of poverty, chastity and obedience, and by the solemn engagement of laboring for the salvation of his neighbor, offers and immolates himself entirely on the altar of the love of God. Are you approaching, or at least are you trying to approach, this ideal of religious perfection?

Affections and Resolutions.

Point III: What ought we to do for Jesus and Mary on this day?

Consideration: We ought to respond as far as we can to the love which Jesus and Mary have shown us. We also ought to go to the Temple and present ourselves to the Lord; and while the candles are blessed and offered, we should offer ourselves without reserve on the altar of sacrifice which was raised by the hands of Jesus and Mary, desiring to be there consumed by the holy fire of divine love.

Application: Every memory belonging to this feast should contribute to reanimate our fervor, to give us fresh earnestness in God's service, and in the execution of our duties and the sacrifices which zeal for souls demands from us. We have now entered on another month, the second month of the year; let us try to improve upon what we have done well in the first month, or at least to make up for what we have neglected.
Colloquy with our Lady.

February 3: On the Words "Jesus advanced in Wisdom and Age and Grace with God and Men"

1st prelude: Look at the three persons of the Holy Family in the little dwelling of Nazareth.
2nd prelude: Beg the grace of feeling an ardent desire of making progress in the practice of perfection.

Point I: Jesus advanced in wisdom before men

Consideration: "Jesus advanced in wisdom"; meaning that, as He grew up, He allowed a greater wisdom, a greater perfection to manifest itself in His whole conduct, so that in the eyes of those who were observing Him, He appeared to progress like other men, whose intellectual development depends on age and experience; while in Jesus were *hid all the treasures of wisdom and knowledge* from the moment of His Incarnation. He advanced, then, by constant progress in perfection and sweetness, edifying and charming all those who saw Him more and more.

Application: How enviable is the lot of those religious who, following the steps of their divine model, ardently desire, and happily obtain, the grace of becoming better as they advance in age? They console their superiors, they edify their brethren, they rejoice the Heart of Jesus, they prove that they are fulfilling their first duty of tending towards perfection. Am I in the number of those who thus follow the steps of Jesus Christ? Do I not rather belong to the category of those who consume themselves in mere desires, who remain stationary, or rather fall back instead of advancing?

Affections and Resolutions.

Point II: Jesus advanced in grace with God

Consideration: "Jesus advanced in grace with God." In what sense did Jesus advance in grace who was grace and sanctity itself? It means that He went on practicing acts of virtue which were greater, more arduous, more generous and more perfect in their nature. The virtues that He practiced in His cradle, He practiced in a higher degree in His hidden life, in a higher degree again in His public life, and to a heroic degree in His last moments. We are told also that Jesus advanced in grace with God, which signifies that the acts of virtue which He performed not only attracted the respect of men, but also, and far more, the approval of His Heavenly Father, because they were in every sense eminent acts of virtue sanctified and exalted by the purest intention and the most ardent love.

Application: I ought here to ask myself two questions: first, Do my acts of virtue become more perfect as I advance in age? Are they more numerous and more generous? Do they attest greater victories gained over myself? Second, Is the intention which accompanies them more pure, more free from all self-love?

Affections and Resolutions.

Point III: Jesus advanced in perfection in an obscure life

Consideration: How did Jesus advance continually in perfection and merit? By leading an unnoticed, a domestic life; by doing what men who live in their families generally do. Contemplate what He did in the humble dwelling of Nazareth – you will see nothing else. In vain will you look for those striking actions which attract the attention of the world.

Application: How instructive and encouraging is every part of the life of our divine model! If He bids us advance after His example in perfection before God and before men, He makes it very easy for us by giving us the proof in His own person that we can do it in all situation by the most ordinary actions of domestic or community life. Why do we not do it, then? How we shall one day regret not having done it, having lost such precious time, not having understood that it concerned our dearest interests!

Colloquy with Jesus.

February 4: Ash Wednesday
Series of Meditations on the Passion of Our Lord Jesus Christ

Remark: As the date of Ash Wednesday varies every year between February 4 and March 10, we can take from the *intermediate or intercalary month* (see pages 251 - 305) as many meditations as are wanted before Ash Wednesday arrives. When we come to that day, we should take the following meditation, "On the requisite Dispositions for the holy Time of Lent," and then those that follow until the Feast of the Sacred Heart of Jesus inclusively. After this Feast we can take the remaining meditations of the *intermediate month, i.e.,* those that were not used before Lent. They will furnish sufficient matter until July 1, with which the last six months of the year begin.

The natural place for this series of meditations is at the end of the life of our Lord Jesus Christ. They are put here to be used in Lent, the most suitable time to meditate on the Passion. This reason sufficiently authorizes the inversion of the *order of time* generally followed by other writers.

On the requisite Dispositions for the holy Time of Lent

1st prelude: Represent to yourself Adam at the moment when, after his condemnation, he hears the humiliating words, "Dust thou art, and unto dust shalt thou return."
2nd prelude: Beg of God that He will deign to penetrate you with the feelings the Church desires us to be inspired with today.

Point I: First disposition requisite: Humility

Consideration: "Remember, O man, that dust thou art, and unto dust shalt thou return." Who uttered these bitter words? God Himself, nearly six thousand years ago. To whom did He address them? To Adam, our first parent, as soon as, in punishment for his sin, the sentence of death had been pronounced on him and his posterity: "Because thou hast eaten of the tree whereof I commanded thee that thou shouldst not eat, cursed is the earth in thy work," said the Lord. "In the sweat of thy face shalt thou eat bread, till thou return to the earth of which thou was taken; for dust thou art, and unto dust shalt thou return." But why did God add these last words, which do not increase in any way the punishment already given? It was doubtless to subdue and annihilate the pride of Adam, and inspire him with such deep humility as would dispose his heart to salutary penance. Thus we see that Adam, who had begun to excuse himself, answered not, but accepted the penance imposed, and persevered in it, humble, penitent, and resigned for the long space of nine hundred years. God was pleased with this penance, and our first parent was saved by it through the merits of the future Redeemer.

Application: We have sinned in Adam, we have sinned ourselves, we are very guilty, we have great need of doing penance, of imploring pardon; God is ready to give it to us. But we have seen that the first feeling He seeks in the heart of a sinner is humility, and a conviction of his own unworthiness. The first disposition then into which we ought to try to enter and in which to persevere during Lent – that time of universal penance – is a profound humility, springing from the knowledge of our nothingness and our sins. It is this which should form the principal merit of our works of penance.

Affections and Resolutions.

Point II: Second disposition requisite: Compunction

Consideration: "Remember, O man, that thou art dust, and unto dust shalt thou return." Who is it that utters again, every year on this day, the same words that God pronounced in the terrestrial paradise? Our holy Mother Church by the mouth of her ministers. And to whom does she address them? To each of us, to all the faithful who assemble in the house of God. And at what moment? At the same moment when she places ashes on our foreheads – the emblem of death and penance. It is as if she said, O man, be thou who thou mayest, remember that thou must die and become like unto this dust, because of sin; remember, that if thou dost not penance for thy sins, thou wilt only rise again from the dust of the tomb to pass in body and soul into a place of eternal torments.

Application: The Church obliges us to listen to those grave and terrific truths only to inspire us, from the first day of Lent, with holy and deep compunction. Compunction of heart is the second essential disposition for whomever desires to attain one of the principal ends of Lent – salutary penance. If our works of mortification and penance are accompanied by sentiments of true contrition and humility, they will be pleasing before God, for, says the royal Prophet, "a contrite and humbled heart, O God, Thou wilt not despise." *Cor humiliatum Deus non despicies*. If we are wanting in these dispositions, ought we not to fear that all the

practices of Lent, even the most painful ones, will be of little use to us?
Colloquy with Our Lord.

Thursday after Ash Wednesday: Entrance of Jesus into the Garden of Olives

1st prelude: Look at Jesus walking resolutely in the midst of His Apostles towards the Garden of Olives, to begin His dolorous Passion.
2nd prelude: Beg the grace of meeting with firmness to difficulties which we encounter in the service of God and the practice of perfection.

Point I: When Jesus had said these things, He went forth with His disciples over the brook Cedron, where there was a garden, into which He entered.

Consideration: Fix, O my soul, thy eyes on thy Saviour, whom thou hast so often chosen for thy model; see how resolutely He goes forth to the combat, and draws after Him by His words and example His faithful disciples. "But that the world may know that I love the Father, and as the Father hath given Me commandment, so do I. Arise, let us go hence."

Go where? To the battle, to death. How full these words are of love, obedience, and courage!

Application: You see in this the generosity, the great heart of Jesus. How different are you, who, far from resolutely meeting occasions of conquest and suffering, fly from them continually, with so much care and ingenuity! How shameful in you, who have made profession of imitating Jesus Christ more perfectly than ordinary men, who have the glory of bearing His name, fighting under His standard, and sharing with Him labours, privations, and sufferings! Examine yourself, with a sincere desire of knowing how far you merit these reproaches.
Affections and Resolutions.

Point II: "Then Jesus came with them into a country place which is called Gethsemani; and He said to His disciples, Sit you here, while I go yonder and pray."

Consideration: Remark how Jesus prepares for prayer. He retires into a solitary place, and separates Himself from the company of men, even of His intimate friends. He only invites them to watch and pray with Him. *Sustinete hic et vigilate mecum.* (Matthew 26)

Application: O Jesus, how well doest Thou teach me how I ought to pray and meditate profitably on Thy holy law! After Thy example, when I enter the place where I am about to pray, I will say to all distracting thoughts, "Stay you here, while I go yonder and pray"; and then afterwards I will vigilantly shut them out from my mind and heart, or at least prevent them from fixing themselves there.

Affections and Resolutions.

Point III: "And He taketh Peter and James and John with Him, and He began to fear."

Consideration: Why did the Saviour give such a glorious preference to these three disciples, and choose them to be near His person at the time of the great mysteries of His strife and His agony? The Gospel does not tell us; but we may believe that as they witnessed His glory and happiness on Mount Thabor, it was His will that they should witness also His humiliation and agony on the Mount of Olives.

Application: How inconsistent we are! We appreciate and envy the privilege of the three beloved disciples, whom Jesus allowed to be with Him in His agony, and we do not understand that it is a favour given to us when He sends us an occasion of suffering with Him. Far from being grateful for it, we complain, we give way to discouragement or distrust. Is this acting reasonably and with faith? Let us acknowledge our inconsistency, and humbly beg our loving Saviour to give us grace so to meditate on His sorrowful Passion that we may draw from it a love of the cross, sorrow for our sins, compassion and resignation.

Colloquy with our Blessed Lord in suffering.

Friday after Ash Wednesday: Affliction of the Soul of Jesus

1st prelude: See Jesus Christ saying to His disciples: "My soul is sorrowful, even unto death."

2nd prelude: Beg for Christian resignation in intense sufferings.

Point I: "He began to grow sorrowful, and to be sad; to fear, and to be heavy."

Consideration: Man had sinned by misusing the faculties of his soul, before he misused his senses and the members of his body. Therefore, by the suffering of His soul, Jesus chose to begin His Passion. These sufferings were immense, above all created strength. He experienced them under every form, and no part of His soul was exempted, because He willed to give His Heavenly Father an entire and superabundant satisfaction, and to us a proof of infinite love.

Application: From the first step in His sorrowful Passion, Jesus unveiled the love for men, for each of us, which fills His Heart; for we were all present before Him, and we can say with the Apostle, "He loved me, and delivered Himself for me." The murderers could not touch His soul, but Jesus did what they had no power to do – He suspended by miracle the ineffable joy with which the beatific vision filled His soul, and left it a prey to the terrible agony which the thought of death, and especially a cruel and violent one, naturally causes.

Affections and Resolutions.

Point II: "Then He saith to them, My soul is sorrowful, even unto death."

Consideration: "My soul is sorrowful unto death" means that He was overwhelmed with the sufferings and agony of one who dies by a violent death, and who is pressed down by terrible trouble of mind. What was the cause of this load of sorrow? First, the repulsive sight of the sins of men which His Father had laid on Him because He had offered Himself as the Victim of universal expiation. *Posuit Dominus in eo iniquitates omnium nostrum* – "The Lord hath laid on Him the iniquity of us all." Secondly, the vivid and detailed representation of all the torments, all the insults, that He had to undergo. Finally, the terrible thought of the uselessness of His death to a vast number of men who would harden themselves in sin. *Quae utilitas in sanguine meo*?

Application: Behold, then, O my soul, the cause of thy Saviour's immense sufferings. Dwell on them one by one, and see how far thou hast contributed to them during thy life, and particularly since thou hast made a profession of loving and serving Him more perfectly.

Affections and Resolutions.

Point III: "Stay you here and watch with Me, while I go yonder and pray."

Consideration: How did Jesus feel in the extreme desolation of His soul? First, He speaks to His three chosen disciples, and asks them to share His sorrow, and watch with Him; then He has recourse to prayer. He acted thus as Man, to serve as our model.

Application: We thus learn what in our interior troubles we *may* do and what we *ought* to do: we *may* seek alleviation in communicating them to a pious and discreet friend; but as men, after all, cannot give us the supernatural strength that we need, we *ought* to have recourse to prayer, and wait upon God. Have you acted thus? Have you imitated those who obstinately shut themselves up when in trouble and temptation, at the risk of falling into dejection and melancholy? Or have you gone to the other extreme of those who communicate their interior suffering to everybody, and forget one thing only – that of resorting to God in prayer, and to those whom He has given as guides in the spiritual life, so that they may receive counsel and consolation?
Colloquy with Jesus suffering.

Saturday After Ash Wednesday: Prayer of Jesus in the Garden of Olives

1st prelude: See Jesus prostrate with His face on the earth.
2nd prelude: Beg constant fidelity to all the rules for praying well.

Point I: "And going a little farther, kneeling down He prayed, and He fell upon His face."

Consideration: Remark the extraordinary signs of respect and humility which Jesus Christ showed in His prayer to His heavenly Father. He knelt down, He fell upon His face on the earth, and He remained thus prostrate as if He was unworthy to raise His eyes to heaven. He was penetrated with the thought of the infinite majesty of Him to whom He spoke as man, and as a sinful man, bearing the weight of our iniquities. Remark also the deep feelings of filial piety expressed by the words, "My Father, if it be possible, let this chalice pass from Me."

Application: Why is our manner so often wanting in respect and propriety when we pray or meditate? Is it not because we think too little of the infinite majesty of God, and of our infinite unworthiness? Happy is the man who before he prays is accustomed to ask himself, "Before whom as I going to appear, and wherefore?" His manner will be always respectful; and as the body has a powerful influence over the soul, so a humble and pious exterior will tend very much to produce respect in the mind, the imagination, and all the powers of the soul. Have we not all often had the experience of this?

Affections and Resolutions.

Point II: "Nevertheless not as I will, but as Thou wilt."

Consideration: Jesus gives us the example of wonderful and heroic resignation. Like unto us in all things in His human nature, He experienced a vivid horror at the sight of death, and at the thought of the horrible sufferings and fearful humiliations which were to precede it. He supplicated and implored His Heavenly Father, with groaning and tears, to spare Him these agonizing sacrifices. And nevertheless, He declared that He was ready to endure them if it were His will; and He did finally submit to them with the most entire and perfect resignation.

Application: Behold, how we ought to pray when we ask God to exempt us or deliver us from something which is repugnant to our taste or natural inclination. We are not forbidden to supplicate earnestly that the bitter cup, the sufferings, the contradictions, which are so distasteful to nature, may depart from us, but we should always declare that, after all, we desire that His holy will may be done in us in everything, and this we ask for every day when we say, "Thy will be done on earth as it is in heaven."

Affections and Resolutions.

Point III: "He prayed the third time, saying the selfsame words."

Consideration: Jesus interrupted His prayer three times to go to the assistance of His disciples, who were wrapped in a false security at the moment of the greatest danger; but immediately afterward He went back to pray, and repeated with great earnestness the same petition: "My Father, if this chalice may not pass away, but I must drink it, Thy will be done."

Application: Two things are taught us by this. First, that we ought not to apply ourselves so long to prayer as to neglect works of charity or zeal; neither ought we to devote ourselves to these works to the neglect of prayer; but that we should sanctify zeal by prayer, and enrich prayer by zealous and charitable labours. Secondly, that we ought not to make prayer consist of a variety of

forms and expressions, nor be weary of repeating the same petition.
Colloquy with God the Father.

First Week of Lent, Sunday: Agony of Jesus in the Garden of Olives

1st prelude: Imagine you see Jesus in His agony bathed in blood.
2nd prelude: Beg for courage and perseverance in the spiritual combat.

Point I: "Being in an agony, His sweat became as drops of blood trickling down upon the ground."

Consideration: The Saviour's death upon the heights of Calvary before the world became a striking proof of His divinity. The Roman centurion, says Saint Mark, "seeing that, crying out in this manner, He had given up the ghost," said, "Indeed this man was the Son of God." And the soldiers who were with him *watching Jesus* said the same thing. His death was not, then, preceded by that agony which is the strongest proof of man's impotence – struggling in vain against his dissolution. But Jesus, choosing to submit to all our humiliations and sorrows, *anticipated the time of His agony*. He suffered it before His other torments. And it was the more terrible and cruel because it was not the effect of physical exhaustion, but of an interior struggle between feeling and the will.

Application: What a great proof of love, and what a profitable lesson, Jesus teaches us by this! To soften the agony of death for us, and to merit for us the grace of supporting it with patience and resignation, He voluntarily endured and offered to His Father for us the most painful of agonies. Have I really understood this love? And what effect has it produced in me?
Affections and Resolutions.

Point II: "As drops of blood trickling down upon the ground."

Consideration: This bloody sweat, of which there are few examples in history, makes us understand what was passing in the soul of Jesus during His agony of nearly two hours; it shows us how great was the terror and suffering He endured, and especially how violent was the battle going on in His soul between nature repulsing with terror the chalice of bitterness, and the will firmly resisting the repugnance of nature.

Application: Most certainly our Lord could have avoided this terrible and humiliating agony, but He chose to submit to it for our instruction and encouragement. Let us learn from it never to fall back from the execution of any duty, however painful it may be; and if we cannot get through it without great repugnance, and in spite of ourselves, as it were, let us be consoled by the thought that this natural dislike does not destroy the merit of what we do or suffer for God. Jesus has assured us of this in His own Person, and how encouraging it is!
Affections and Resolutions.

Point III: "And there appeared to Him an angel from heaven strengthening Him."

Consideration: The humble supplication of Jesus in His agony were not in vain. An angel came to visit Him, who strengthened His body, restored the vigour He had lost in His agony, and also fortified His soul, praising His resignation, and showing Him all that His Passion should do for His Father's glory, and for the happiness of men. What Jesus as man had conditionally asked for, was not in truth given to Him, but His prayer obtained a wonderful and consoling answer.

Application: Behold what will infallibly be the fruit of your recourse to God in your troubles and anguish. Never do we pray in vain. If you do not obtain release from a heavy cross which weighs on you, the angel of divine consolation will shed the unction of grace in your heart. You will feel within you fresh strength and vigour of soul. Your cross will appear light to you. You will bear it with sweet resignation, sometimes with sensible joy, always with a fresh increase of merit. You will have obtained what you asked for.
Colloquy with Jesus in agony.

First Week of Lent, Monday: Necessity and Manner of doing Penance, especially during Lent

1st prelude: Look at Jesus Christ saying these words: "Except you do penance, ye shall all perish."
2nd prelude: Beg the spirit of penance, united to deep feelings of humility and compunction.

Point I: God imposes penance on us as a duty

Consideration: The command that God gives us to do penance

is formal and universal. He does not say, Except you do penance, you shall perish *perhaps* or *probably*, but simple, *you shall all perish*. And why shall we perish? Because we are sinners, and after the loss of baptismal innocence there is no other road to heaven but that of penance. Again, why? Because the flesh rebels against the spirit, and continually inclines us towards sin; consequently, says Saint Paul, "If by the spirit you mortify the deeds of the flesh, you shall live – *Si autem spiritu facta carnis mortificaveritis, vivetis*.

Application: We are, then, obliged to do penance, and a penance proportioned, says the Council of Trent, to the number and gravity of our sins. We are obliged to do it at all times, but especially in the holy time of Lent; and all of us, whatever may be our age or our strength, we can all do penance in one way or another. The Fathers of the desert, men eminent for their penance, made it consist principally in *fasting, vigils* and *austerities*. We shall see, in the three points of this meditation, how we can practice these three kinds of penance. And first as regards fasting. If we cannot observe it in all its rigour, we can observe it in part; we can retrench our ordinary food, and confine ourselves with due discretion to what is absolutely necessary; we can mortify our taste in eating and drinking by depriving ourselves habitually of dainties. Consider before God what you can and will do during these days of penance, and be faithful to what you resolve upon. Affections and Resolutions.

Point II: Our vocation makes penance a duty

Consideration: In virtue of our vows and of the double end of our vocation, we are obliged to tend to perfection by continually contradicting our natural inclinations, and obtaining the salvation of our neighbor at the expense of our comfort, often of our health; and all this evidently requires the spirit of sacrifice and mortification, or of a continual penance.

Application: The penitents of the desert united to their fasts, vigils and hard labor. If, like them, or like many religious at this day, we are not obliged to break our sleep at midnight or watch in the Sanctuary, let us at least rise quickly from sleep always at the first sound of the bell, whatever fatigue or difficulty we may experience; let us at least *watch* in our meditation, and in all our spiritual exercises, *never* giving way to sleep or spiritual torpor. This will be a very painful struggle.

Affections and Resolutions.

Point III: Our own interest make penance a duty

Consideration: It is an article of faith that all that we have not expiated in this world by penance will be expiated rigorously by the fire of purgatory; therefore, said Saint Augustine, *do penance or burn – Aut poenitendum aut urendum*. We must choose. Can we hesitate, if we value our dearest interests? If we do, we shall be very blind, and our own enemies; and the more so, because we have so many fruitful means of doing penance and of paying off our debts.

Application: Besides the means already pointed out, can we not, by the continual mortification of our senses and our bodies, imitate, at least at a distance, the *corporal mortifications* of the Fathers of the desert? To habituate ourselves to kneel or sit without a comfortable support; to pass through the streets or public places without ever satisfying our curiosity; to observe silence and other points of rule most exactly and constantly, is to do penance, and, if continuous, it becomes a severe one. This is to live in the practice of a continual abnegation of ourselves.

Colloquy with Jesus Christ.

First Week of Lent, Tuesday: Jesus reproves His Disciples, and goes to meet the Traitor Judas

1st prelude: Look at Jesus when He says these words: "Sleep ye now, and take your rest: behold, he is at hand that will betray Me."

2nd prelude: Beg grace to draw great fruit from this meditation.

Point I: And He cometh to His disciples, and findeth them asleep; and He saith to Peter, Simon sleepest thou? What, couldst thou not watch one hour with Me?

Consideration: This reproach so confounded the three Apostles that the Evangelist says "they knew not what to answer Him." It must have been especially bitter to Saint Peter, who such a short time previously had been making protestations of fidelity and constancy. This was why our Divine Savior addressed him personally: "Simon, sleepest thou? What, while I, thy Master, have prayed and endured an extreme agony, hast thou not had the courage to watch one hour with Me in prayer, though I expressly commanded thee to do so; and thou are about this moment to be attacked by thy enemies?" Certainly the reproach was well deserved.

Application: Alas, how many times you have deserved the same reproach by your frequent languor and slumbering in your spiritual duties, and especially during the hour of meditation! – that precious time which is given to you that you may foresee and prepare for all that the glory of your Divine Master and your own greatest interests demand from you during the day.

Affections and Resolutions

Point II: "Watch ye and pray, that ye enter not into temptation. The spirit indeed is willing, but the flesh is weak."

Consideration: Spiritual lukewarmness, united to that presumption which makes us imagine we are going to do some great good, is a very dangerous state, and leads those who indulge in it into fatal delusions. Because they intend to do well, and are, like the Apostles, prodigal in grand promise, they think all is right with them, and they keep themselves in a false security; as if there were not a great difference between willing and doing a thing, and as if we had of ourselves strength to work out our salvation. Jesus Christ tells us the contrary, when He says, "The spirit is willing, but the flesh is weak"; and that is why He immediately adds these solemn words: "Watch and pray." Be always on your guard, always distrustful of self, always armed with prayer; for if not, you will certainly fall under temptation, under the deceitful attacks of your enemies.

Application: Examine yourself carefully, and dread any delusion about your state – a delusion so much the more to be feared because faults and negligences, if they become habitual, cease to inspire us with fear.

Affections and Resolutions.

Point III: "And leaving them, He went again and He prayed… Then He cometh to His disciples, and said to them, Sleep ye now, and take your rest; behold, the hour is at hand, and the Son of Man shall be betrayed into the hands of sinners. Rise, let us go; behold, he is at hand that will betray Me."

Consideration: The firmness with which Jesus Christ now goes forward to meet tortures and death, the mere thought of which had thrown Him into an agony, shows plainly the powerful effects of prayer – of that long and fervent prayer that He had made to His

Father. We shall also see, in the shameful flight of the Apostles at the first danger, the loss that the soul sustains which neglects to seek God in fervent prayer.

Application: It is from prayer and communication with God that we draw the strength we need in occasions of difficulty. If in our daily meditation we were careful to foresee these occasions, to animate ourselves to meet them, and humbly beg for grace, we should never lose courage; at the critical moment we should say with Jesus, "The hour is come; let us go and practice the resolutions made this morning under the inspiration of grace." We should then count as many victories as we have struggles.

Colloquy with our Divine Savior. We can also make it with the saint of the day, or any other to whom we have a devotion.

First Week of Lend, Wednesday: Treason of Judas

1st prelude: Behold the traitor Judas giving Jesus a kiss.
2nd prelude: Beg from God a salutary fear, and a great distrust of yourself.

Point I: "As He yet spake, behold Judas, one of the twelve, came and with him a great multitude with swords and clubs."

Consideration: We have today to meditate on a great and awful mystery of perversion. Judas, one of the twelve chosen disciples of Jesus, taught by Him for three years, confirmed in the faith by so many miracles, loaded with favors, is become the tool of those who plot the death of the Lord. He has sold Him to them for thirty pieces of silver. He comes treacherously to deliver Him into their hands. Alas, such is the depth of blindness and perversity into which by degrees avarice has plunged Judas! We may, indeed, cry out with David – taught by his own weakness: "What is man?" *Quid est homo*?

Application: Let the misery of another serve as a warning to you. See if there be not certain passions in you which have never been conquered, or which, after having been repressed, have little by little regained their former empire. There need not be many of these; one alone can suffice to overcome the virtue of him on which we thought we were fully able to rely. The history of the Church and of religious orders has recorded too many fallings-away and apostasies which were cause by a single ill-regulated

passion not found out.
Affections and Resolutions.
Point II: "And forthwith coming to Jesus, he said, Hail, Rabbi; and he kissed Him."

Consideration: What revolting hypocrisy! Under the appearance of the most respectful affection, Judas concealed the blackest perfidy. By a kiss he pointed out and delivered up his Divine Master to the fury of His enemies. Did he, then, believe that he could deceive God, as he had deceived men? Oh, how does passion blind its victims!

Application: There is no one who does not detest the crime of Judas; but are there not Christians in our days who renew it by making a sacrilegious Communion? What are they doing in reality but delivering up Jesus as far as they can, under the cloak of piety, to the demons who are in their hearts? May God preserve us from such a crime! But there are acts of hypocrisy less revolting, but which we ought nevertheless to fear and detest, such as contenting ourselves with exterior virtue and piety; being more careful about regularity before superiors or brethren than when alone; alleging false pretexts to attain our ends; and other things of this kind. Is not this hypocrisy and dissimulation, and have we nothing to reproach ourselves with under this head?
Affections and Resolutions.

Point III: "And Jesus said to him, Friend, whereunto art thou come? ... Judas, dost that betray the Son of Man with a kiss?"

Consideration: Which is the more wonderful – the goodness and ineffable sweetness of Jesus, or the hardness of heart of Judas? "My friend"; by giving that name to Judas, Jesus signified that He was still ready to pardon him. By asking him, "Whereunto art thou come?" He wished to help him to look into himself, to recognize and abhor his crime. But Judas was untouched. Our Divine Lord made another effort to convert him: He showed him that He knew his treachery, and was horrified at it, by these words: "Judas, dost thou betray the Son of Man with a kiss?" But all was in vain; he remained obstinate.

Application: The extraordinary gentleness of Jesus ought to redouble our love for Him; and the inconceivable hardness of the traitor Judas should fill us with salutary fear, and an extreme distrust of ourselves, no matter how many years we have been in religion, or to what degree of virtue we believe we have attained. Let us ask that this may be the fruit of this meditation in the Colloquy with our loving Savior.

First Week of Lent, Thursday: Jesus is taken captive – Flight of the Apostles

1st prelude: Behold the soldiers falling backwards before Jesus, and the Apostles running away.
2nd prelude: Beg the grace of a faithful attachment to Jesus Christ by the bonds of love.
Point I: "Jesus therefore, knowing all things that should come upon Him, went forth, and said to them, Whom seek ye? They answered Him, Jesus of Nazareth. Jesus saith to them, I am He. As soon, therefore, as He said to them, I am He, they went backward, and fell to the ground. If, therefore, you seek Me, let these go their way. Then Simon Peter, having a sword drew it, and struck the servant of the high-priest, and cut off his right ear. And the name of the servant was Malchus. But Jesus, having touched his ear, healed it."

Consideration: Why did Jesus multiply the proofs of His Divinity by wonderful miracles at the moment when He began His sorrowful Passion? In order that He might show that He was taken prisoner, bound and "offered because it was His own will," as Isaias had foretold. *Oblatus est quia ipse voluit.* If it had not been thus, how would the martyrs have replied to the insult of their tyrants? What folly to adore a God who was put to death by men! And how could they have convinced them that this violent death was not the result of powerlessness, but of the love of Jesus for the human race?

Application: Let us learn to recognize and appreciate the indulgent goodness of God to men. If He obliges them to believe, with humility mysteries which they cannot understand, only because He tells them, He helps their belief, not by grace alone, but by the testimony of miracles which appeal to the senses, and which He is ready to renew as often as circumstances require it. Affections and Resolutions.

Point II: "Then they took Jesus, and bound Him."

Consideration: How great was the blindness of the Jews! In

spite of the wonderful miracles of goodness and power which they had witnessed, they persevered in their criminal intention – they dared to lay hands on Jesus. And because He gave Himself up into their hands, they thought that they had conquered. Alas, we often have proof that even miracles are unable to convert the man who indulges his passions. Passion blinds a man, and stifles in him the voice of reason and of conscience. See, on the other hand, the gentleness of Jesus! He lets Himself be taken, bound, loaded with fetters, pushed about, struck and grossly insulted in the way from Gethsemani to the city of Jerusalem.

Application: The bonds of original sin and our own sin held us captive under the yoke of the devil, and exposed us to hell. There was no power in men or angels to break our bonds. Jesus Christ alone could, and His love for us made Him do it. He allowed Himself to be loaded with fetters to give us the liberty of the children of God. Do we think often of this? Do we think of it enough?

Affections and Resolutions.

Point III: "Then the disciples all leaving Him, fled."

Consideration: Behold, then, the end of the promises and eager protestations of the disciples. All had assured their beloved Master that they were determined never to forsake Him, *to go with Him to prison and to death.* But as soon as they saw Him in the hands of the soldiers, they all, without exception, shamefully forsook Him, and sought their safety in flight. Then were the words of Jesus verified: "All you shall be scandalized in Me this night," meaning they should be unfaithful. Because they saw Him bound and led to prison they lost faith in His Divinity, His omnipotence, and forsook Him; "for it is written, I will strike the Shepherd, and the sheep shall be dispersed." Such was the fatal consequence of their presumption, and their neglect of gaining strength by prayer before the struggle, as our Divine Savior had expressly recommended them to do.

Application: We condemn the inconstancy and cowardice of the Apostles; we blame them for having, by their desertion and flight, so cruelly afflicted the heart of our loving Savior. But do we not, therefore, condemn ourselves – we who have been so inconstant, so cowardly in following Jesus – we who are habitually unfaithful to our promises and resolutions, and that from the same

causes to which we attribute the inconstancy and shameful desertion of the Apostles?
Colloquy with our Lord.

First Week of Lent, Friday: Jesus led from the House of Annas to the Tribunal of Caiphas

1st prelude: To imagine I see Jesus in the midst of the soldiers, bound and led like a criminal, in the city of Jerusalem.
2nd prelude: Beg for constancy and a continual increase of generosity in the service of God.

Point I: "And they led Him away to Annas first, for he was father-in-law of Caiphas, who was high priest that year, and Annas sent Him bound to Caiphas, where the scribes and the ancients were assembled."

Consideration: The series of humiliations for our loving Savior has now commenced. All the streets, all the public places, all the tribunals of Jerusalem, have witnessed the helplessness to which His enemies gloried in having reduced Him. He was dragged in succession, in the midst of hooting, from Annas to Caiphas, from Caiphas to the Council, from the Council to Pilate, from thence to the praetorium to be scourged, then to the steps to be shown to the people; finally, He was led down into the public place, from whence He went forth, bearing His cross, to Calvary.

Application: Let us learn from the example of our Divine Master never to resist the orders of superiors, to pass from one house to the other, from one employment to another, as they judge proper. These changes will be sometimes frequent, and often painful to nature. They may cause temptations to impatience or weariness. Let us, then, cast our eyes on Jesus, and the difficulties will disappear.
Affections and Resolutions.

Point II: "The high priest, therefore, asked Jesus of His disciples, and of His doctrine, Jesus answered him, I have spoken openly to the world; ask them who have heard what I have spoken to them."

Consideration: The question of the high priest was twofold – on the disciples of Jesus and His doctrine. Our Divine Savior passed over the first in silence. Alas, what good testimony could He bear of His disciples? At this very moment one was denying Him, and the others were hidden, for fear of sharing their Master's fate. He loved them too much to blame them; He was silent. As to His doctrine, the questions put to Him were dictated by malice, by the secret desire of finding a pretext for blame and condemnation. Jesus contented Himself by appealing to public testimony, showing plainly that He knew their guilty intentions, and that He had nothing to fear from a severe but just examination of all that He had said and taught. Our Divine Master gives us an example of silence when we cannot speak well of our neighbor, unless our rule, or the law of charity, compels us to manifest some faults of our brethren. We may learn from Him, also, to be watchful over our words, to be reserved in conversation, and to make a careful preparation of what we have to say in public; so that if we are afterwards falsely accused, we may be able to appeal to the testimony of those who heard us.

Affections and Resolutions.

Point III: "And when He had said these things, one of the servants standing by gave Jesus a blow, saying, Answerest Thou the high-priest so? And Jesus answered him, If I have spoken evil, give testimony of the evil; but if well, why strikest thou Me?"

Consideration: It is almost impossible for us to understand the intensity of the outrage thus offered to our God and our loving Savior. He received a blow, the greatest insult one man can give another, in the open court, from the hand of a servant; and it was given as a mark of correction from a brutal man, to Him who is Master of the creation and Infinite Wisdom. What revenge did He take for this cruel insolence? He returned a meek and prudent answer, and showed not the slightest resentment.

Application: Compare your conduct with that of your Lord. Are you patient and gentle under slight injuries, or even imaginary ones? And yet, who are *you*?

Colloquy with our Divine Lord.

First Week of Lent, Saturday: Jesus accused and examined at the Tribunal of Caiphas

1st prelude: Imagine you see Jesus standing with His hands bound, before iniquitous judges.

2nd prelude: Ask to obtain solid virtue, and especially the grace of knowing when to be silent and when to speak.

Point I: “And the chief priests and the whole council sought false witness against Jesus, that they might put Him to death, and they found none.”

Consideration: So holy was our Lord’s life that His sworn enemies, even though they brought a great many witnesses – and those false ones – against Him, could find nothing of which to accuse Him, nothing that was even the shadow of sin, or a single imperfection.

Application: The life of a religious ought to be so perfect that the wicked who watch him closely should not be able to find fault with him in word or deed, either in public or private life. Can this be truly said of you? What do others think and say of you, or are they too much afraid of wounding your pride and self-love to speak the truth? And, supposing that men have nothing with which to reproach you, are you innocent in the eyes of Him who sees our hearts, our motives, and intentions?

Affections and Resolutions.

Point II: “And the high priest, rising up, said to Him, Answerest Thou nothing to the things which these witness against Thee? But Jesus held His peace.”

Consideration: Wonderful indeed was this silence of our Lord. His honor, reputation, and life were in peril, and it seemed as if He could so easily justify and defend Himself, and obtain a triumph. But He left His defence in the hands of His Father, and was silent.

Application: What a contrast there is between us and our Master! He is silent under false accusation, and we, who glory in being His disciples, cannot hear a reproof that we know we deserve, or a kind observation, without beginning to defend and excuse ourselves; sometimes even at the expense of truth. Have I not often had self-reproach on this head?

Affections and Resolutions.

Point III: “And the high priest said to Him, I adjure Thee by the living God, that Thou tell us if Thou be Christ, the Son of the living God. Jesus said to him, Thou hast said it.”

Consideration: We learn a valuable lesson from this: as long as our Lord’s own Person was concerned, He kept silence; but when it was a question of His Father’s glory, or the salvation of souls, or a point of faith, He spoke, and confessed the truth; and He confessed it freely and unreservedly, though He knew it would cost Him His life.

Application: It is a matter of great difficulty to know when to speak and when to be silent; it requires thought, calmness of mind, and great firmness of character. We shall find that our indiscreet words have arisen from our deficiency in one or other of these qualities. Have we not sometimes also sacrificed truth by keeping silence, or being guilty of dissimulation, or keeping back the truth without a rightful cause?

Colloquy with our loving Savior.

Second Week of Lent, Sunday: Jesus condemned as a Blasphemer

1st prelude: Behold Jesus, gentle and humble, in the midst of bloodthirsty men, who cry out, "He is guilty of death."

2nd prelude: Beg grace to know and love Jesus Christ ever more and more.

Point I: "Then the high priest rent his garments, saying, He hath blasphemed; what further need have we of witnesses?"

Consideration: How detestable was the hypocrisy of Caiphas and his party! Under an appearance of piety and zeal, they hid the mortal hatred they bore our Lord, and their long-conceived plan of putting Him to death. Not wishing to enrage the people against them, they sought a specious excuse for their conduct; and Caiphas made sure he could find one by adjuring Jesus to say if He were really the Son of God; for if He said no, he should be able to condemn Him as an imposter, because the people had believed him to be God; if He said yes, he would sentence Him as a blasphemer; and then he would use some of the expressive signs customary to the Jews, to make people believe he was overwhelmed with horror at the sin. The wicked are indeed very ingenious.

Application: Have I never dissimulated? Have I never imposed on men, on my brethren, or my superiors? Have I never concealed a wrong intention under a fair exterior, or tried to justify in my own eyes some forbidden pleasure in which I take delight? But it is God who will judge me; therefore what use is there in all this? What will be the end of it?

Affections and Resolutions.

Point II: "Behold now you have heard the blasphemy, what thing you? But they, answering, said, He is guilty of death."

Consideration: The judges who pronounced this sentence upon the All-holy were men inflamed with hatred and blinded by passion. They hated Him because He had confessed the truth, and done righteously.

Application: In this world the innocent are often calumniated and oppressed by the crafty, and it is permitted by God, for wise and merciful reasons. And so, in this instance, Caiphas was the instrument by which God, made man, should complete the sacrifice of His life in reparation to His father for the sins of mankind. That wicked sentence of death opened to us all the gates of eternal life.

Affections and Resolutions.

Point III: "But they, answering, said, He is guilty of death."

Consideration: If we look on Jesus according to the expression of the Apostle, as the *new Adam*, who is to expiate the sin of the *first Adam* and the innumerable sins of his whole posterity in His own Person, then indeed "He is guilty of death." *Reus est mortis*. It was in this sense that the Eternal Father ratified the sentence pronounced against His Son, and He Himself accepted it in loving silence.

Application: O my soul, thou hast sinned in Adam, thou hast sinned thyself, thou didst cause the death of Jesus. The sentence, "He is guilty of death," has been pronounced by divine justice against thee; but the Son of God made man became thy substitute, accepted it in thy stead, and gave back to thee eternal life.

Colloquy with our Blessed Lord.

Second Week of Lent, Monday: Motives for Penance derived from the Thought of the Evil which Sin has wrought

1st prelude: Imagine you see Saint Peter saying to the people of Jerusalem, "Be penitent therefore, and be converted, that your sins may be blotted out."

2nd prelude: Beg for a strong impulse of the will to comply with the Apostle's precept.

Point I: Multitude of our sins

Consideration: Go over the past years of your life in spirit –

before and after your First Communion, before and after your entrance into religion, the places where you have lived, the sins you have committed; run rapidly over the commandments of God and the Church, the obligations attached to your vows, the offices and employments that have been confided to you; and you will be surprised and terrified at the sight of your innumerable sins. What would it be if you saw them as God sees them!

Application: For a single mortal sin, Adam and his posterity were condemned to death and eternal torments; for a single venial sin, those great friends of God, Moses, David and Ezechias, were severely punished – a feeble shadow only, however, of the punishment in the next world for the smallest sin. What ought I, then, to expect, who have committed so many sins? I have nearly forgotten them, but God forgets nothing. He will leave nothing unpunished, not even the slight fault of an *idle word*. Our Lord Himself has told us so. We have many motives, then, to induce us to do real and continual penance; and in this holy time we shall receive special graces, which will make the practice of it easier. "Behold, now is the acceptable time."

Affections and Resolutions.

Point II: The injury that sin is to God

Consideration: Each mortal sin is a threefold injury to God, and its malice is infinite because His Majesty is infinite. We injure Him by *insubordination* and *rebellion*: God commands, and we do not obey. We injure Him by *contempt*: we prefer a transitory and vile enjoyment, sometimes a disgraceful one, to God and His laws. We injure Him by *ingratitude*: we make use of His gifts to offend and insult Him. Each venial sin is also a threefold injury; it is certainly of a slighter kind, but still its malice is so great that if by a single venial sin we could change all the lost souls into saints who should praise God eternally in Heaven, we might not commit it, because the praises of all the human race could not compensate to God for the injury done to Him by one venial sin. And the sins which you have committed against the Lord your God have contained malice such as this; and both faith and reason teach us that this malice increases in proportion to the light and grace we have received. What ought we, then, to think about our venial sins? Who can count them? What an additional motive for penance during these chosen days, of which the Divine Office says, "The

days of penance are come, to reclaim us from our sins"!
Affections and Resolutions.

Point III: The injury done to our Lord by sin

Consideration: Our sins have been an injury to our Lord Jesus Christ. The Prophet Isaias speaks of our Lord as the Man of Sorrows above all other men; and it was our sins that made Him so; the sins of the whole world laid on Him; and God beheld Him as the guilty one, on whom the weight of divine justice was to fall. "He was bruised for our sins," says the Holy Ghost. *Attritus est propter scelera nostra.* They were our sins which scourged Him, which crowned Him with thorns, which struck Him, spat upon Him, nailed Him to the cross, and made Him die upon it.

Application: This thought ought to overwhelm us with shame: there were times in my life when, in union with the cruel Jews, I cried out, "Let Him be crucified," and "Not this man, but Barabbas – not this man, but my passion." There have been times when, in union with the murderers, I ran the nails into my Savior's hands and feet. I have done this, as far as I could, every time I committed a mortal sin. And every time I have committed a venial sin I have added fresh suffering to the open wounds of Jesus. Thoughts like these armed the holy penitents of the desert against themselves. Imitate them during these holy days of universal penance and expiation.

Colloquy with our Divine Savior.

Second Week of Lent, Tuesday: Jesus made the Sport of the Soldiers and the Servants of Caiphas

1st prelude: Behold Jesus in the midst of vile soldiers and insolent servants, who pour on Him insults and outrages.

2nd prelude: Beg the grace of knowing the value of humiliations, and of loving them, after the example of Jesus Christ, your King and your model.

Point I: "And the men who held Him mocked Him."

Consideration: When Caiphas, triumphant at having condemned Jesus, when to take his night's rest, he left his captive in the hands of the guard, or, rather, gave Him up to the insolence of his servants and of the soldiery of the praetorium. They immediately dragged Him into a subterranean prison for criminals.

What a humiliation for our Blessed Lord! There was no rest for Him there. The hatred that they knew their masters had for Jesus stirred them up, and, gathering around Him, they made brutal sport of Him, and tried which could excel the other in showering ridicule, scorn, blasphemy and curses on Him; and this scene of horror lasted throughout the rest of the night. Try to form a vivid idea of the suffering and humiliation of our Lord, made the sport of vile and insolent men during the whole night, without a moment's rest; and then nights of suffering will appear more endurable to you, and the days which perhaps you have to spend among children, or others who are vulgar, ungrateful, and petulant, will seem less wearisome, less unbearable.

Affections and Resolutions.

Point II: "Then did they spit in His face."

Consideration: They spat in His face! If this were not recorded in the Gospel, we could not have believed that the brutality and cruelty of men could go so far, or that God made man could have allowed and borne such an insult, the greatest and the most keenly felt which could be given to the lowest of men. But our Lord allowed it, and bore it again and again, without a movement, without a word, as it had been foretold by the Prophet Isaias. "I have not turned away my face from them that spat upon Me."

Application: And yet men often complain, become indignant, and long to be revenged, if they are injured, or even if they are not sufficiently considered or treated as they think they deserve. Ought they not rather to fall at the feet of Jesus, and cry out with Saint Bernard, "What, shall my Master and my King be insulted and spat upon by His vilest subjects, and shall I be honored, who have deserved for my sins to be cast with the refuse of the human race to the bottom of hell? No, never! Let me rather be forgotten and despised by all men in this world, that I may obtain mercy in eternity."

Affections and Resolutions.

Point III: "And they blindfolded Him, and smote His face. And they asked Him, saying, Prophesy, who is it that struck Thee?"

Consideration: In grief and silence we will contemplate the King of Glory covered with reproach, and drinking to the very dregs that cup of humiliation which He accepted in the Garden of Olives. He is seated on a block of wood, His hands are bound, His eyes blindfolded, He is surrounded by coarse, half-intoxicated men, who, one after the other, strike Him on the face and buffet Him, and cry out, Prophesy, who is it that struck Thee? And then they pour a flood of insults and blasphemies on Him. Who is suffering these insults? Why does He thus humble Himself?

Application: When we meditate on the three degrees of humility, we often resolve that we will rather be despised and thought nothing of by the world, be contemned and looked down upon with our Master, than be esteemed and highly exalted before men. What progress have we made in the practice of these resolutions?

Colloquy with our Blessed Lord.

Second Week of Lent, Wednesday: Saint Peter's threefold Denial

1st prelude: Behold the Apostle in the hall of Caiphas, standing near the fire, in company with the soldiers and servants of the high priest.

2nd prelude: Ask the grace of knowledge, and distrust of self.

Point I: "Now when Peter was in the court below, there cometh one of the maid-servants of the high priest, and when she had seen Peter warming himself, looking on him she said, Thou also wast with Jesus of Nazareth. But he denied before them all, saying, Woman, I know Him not."

Consideration: Peter, having recovered from his terror in the garde3n, followed Jesus afar off to the hall of Caiphas, and there, in answer to a woman's voice, the Prince of the Apostles denied his Lord. A short time before, he, more than all the other Apostles, had been boasting of his unchangeable fidelity. Great indeed was his weakness, grievous indeed was his fall.

Application: The fall of Saint Peter shows us how weak is human nature, and makes us tremble for ourselves. But every effect has a cause, therefore let us look into what caused the Apostle's fall. The Fathers give four reasons for it. He was presumptuous of his own strength, he had neglected prayer and vigil with his Master, he was rash in exposing himself to temptation, and he indulged tepidity and idle curiosity. "Peter followed Him afar off, and sat with the servants to see the end."

When we think over our falls, and the false steps we have taken in life, we may easily trace them to one or other of these causes. Affections and Resolutions.

Point II: "And again he denied with an oath: I know not the man."

Consideration: As the danger increased, Saint Peter's fear grew stronger, and he fell lower still. His first denial had been a cowardly falsehood; but his second was a perjury. His sins followed fast upon each other, and became more and more deadly.

Application: If once we give way to our passions, once yield to human respect, gluttony, curiosity, anger, sensuality, or any other sin, we shall soon be carried farther. Never let us venture to say, I will do what I wish for this once, and then I shall be at rest; or, I will go thus far in what is wrong, but no farther. This is a fatal delusion, and springs from a want of self-knowledge. The passions are like fire, which never says, "It is enough." So said Saint Augustine, speaking from experience. And can we not confirm it? Affections and Resolutions.

Point III: "And after the space as it were of one hour, one of the servants of the high priest saith to him, Did I not see thee in the garden with Him? Surely thou also art one of them? But he began to curse and swear, saying, I know not this man of whom you speak."

Consideration: Rapid and fearful was the Apostle's downward course. In less than two hours he thrice denied his Lord, twice he perjured himself; and finally confirmed his false-swearing by a fearful imprecation on himself. What shame and grief he then gave to the Heart of his Master, who at that very moment was standing only a little way off, enduring cruel insults for love of him!

Application: Why did our Lord permit him, who was to become the head of the Church, to fall so low? And why was it published to the whole world in the Gospel? The Fathers give reason for it. They say, in the first place, it was that Saint Peter and his successors, the chief pastors of the Church, should excel in humility, and have a deep sympathy for the weakness of their people. Secondly, that the world, perceiving on what a weak foundation in itself the Catholic Church is built, should recognize that it is indeed the work of God, not of men, and that its existence is a wonder and a marvel. Thirdly, as a warning to men, that, no matter to what height of sanctity they have attained, they are still very weak, and stand in continual need of divine grace. We will therefore bless and exalt the wisdom of Divine Providence. Colloquy with our Lord.

Second Week of Lent, Thursday: Repentance and Conversion of Saint Peter

1st prelude: Look at the Apostle Saint Peter weeping over his sin.
2nd prelude: Beg for the grace of true contrition.

Point I: "And the Lord, turning, looked on Peter."

Consideration: How inexpressibly great was the goodness of our Blessed Lord! He was in the midst of His sufferings; horrible insults and blasphemies were being poured upon Him; but He forgot Himself, and thought only of His faithless disciple. That grievous fall of Saint Peter's had wounded Him more than all His other injuries. "The Lord turned," says the Gospel, "and looked upon Peter." It was a glance of mingled reproach and mercy, which instantly wrought his conversion.

Application: And day by day this same goodness of our Lord is manifested towards numbers of poor sinners. He prevents them by His grace. He looks mercifully on them, dealing with them as He did with the penitent King David when he cried out, "Look Thou upon me, and have mercy on me." Terror had so completely taken possession of Saint Peter in the hall of Caiphas that it had blinded him to the extent of his sin. Our Lord came to his assistance, and opened his eyes; and from that day forward his gratitude to his loving Savior was fervent and continual. If we think over our past sins, we shall recollect how often grace has prevented us, and roused us from the sleep of death. Deep, then, ought to be our gratitude.

Affections and Resolutions.

Point II: "Peter remembered the word that Jesus had said to him: Before the cock crow twice, thou shalt thrice deny Me."

Consideration: Sudden and wonderful was the change which one look from Jesus wrought in the heart of the faithless disciple. In an instant the darkness which encompassed his soul disappeared; he saw clearly the greatness of his sin; he remembered all his Master's forewarnings at the Last Supper and in the Garden of Olives. And his heart was filled, not with despair, but with the deepest contrition. He was transformed into the model of a true penitent.

Application: Wonderful, indeed, is the work of grace! Silently it penetrates into the soul, enlightening and strengthening it, showing it the instability of creatures, the guilt and horror of sin, filling it with a deep and salutary contrition. It makes the sinner shed tears of mingled grief, love and joy; it purifies the soul from all unruly affections; disengages it from the world, and draws it upwards to God.

Affections and Resolutions.

Point III: "And going forth, he wept bitterly."

Consideration: The fall of Saint Peter had been a grievous and a public one, and his repentance was generous and fervent. Without a moment's delay, he fled from the place and the company which had occasioned his fall; and when alone he began to shed those bitter tears which may be said never to have ceased till his death. He mourned over the humiliation of his fall, the thought of his ingratitude, the grief and pain he had given to his Divine master at the very moment when He was manifesting His love for him. Not only did our Blessed Lord pardon His penitent disciple, but He gave him back all the privileges which had been granted to him before his fall.

Application: If we, like the Apostle, have been unfaithful, let us also imitate him in his repentance. The remembrance of our past ingratitude, and of God's goodness to us, should inspire us with deeper humility, more steadfast trust, and an unbounded generosity in works of charity; and thus, with the help of God's grace, we shall be enabled to bring good out of evil.

Colloquy with our good Lord.

Second Week of Lent, Friday: Jesus delivered by His People to Pontius Pilate, the Roman Governor

1st prelude: Look at our Divine Lord passing along with His hands bound, amidst the hooting multitude, towards the palace of the Roman governor.

2nd prelude: Beg for a more fervent love of your Blessed Savior.

Point I: "And when morning was come, all the chief priests and ancients of the people took counsel against Jesus, that they might put Him to death."

Consideration: Hastily and eagerly, before the day broke, the unjust judges roused themselves from sleep, and assembled together. Their only motive was to satisfy their hatred against their innocent Victim, and to carry out their plan for putting Him to death. How diligent they were to accomplish their terrible crime!

Application: We ought to blush with same when we see how much more earnest these wicked men were in doing evil than we often are in doing good. They were much more ready to rise early that they might take counsel how to put Jesus to death than we are that we may give Him glory by our prayer and by our visits to the Sacrament of His love.

Affections and Resolutions.

Point II: "And they bought Him bound, and delivered Him to Pontius Pilate, the governor."

Consideration: It was His own people who rejected our Lord, and delivered Him to the Gentiles; those very people on whom He had poured so many blessings and who had cried out in wonder at His gracious miracles, "He hath done all things well: He hath made both the deaf to hear, and the dumb to speak." Great indeed was their treachery and ingratitude; and what and additional humiliation and grief this must have been to our Divine Lord!

Application: There is not a heart which does not swell with indignation at the remembrance of the treacherous ingratitude of the Jews; but are not many Christians equally as wicked when, by sacrilegious Communions, they deliver Jesus to the company of the evil one, who reigns over their hearts; and when, by their sins, they daily return evil for good to the loving Savior from whom they have received a thousand times more graces and favors than did the Jews?

Affections and Resolutions.

Point III: "They went not into the hall, that they might not be defiled."

Consideration: How astonishing were the false consciences and blindness of these men! They were well instructed in their religion, yet they demurred about contracting a legal stain by entering the house of a heathen, and were not afraid to indulge their envy and hatred by conspiring against the life of an innocent man.

Application: Are there not many people, and those even in

religious life, who scrupulously observe indifferent matters, and who either neglect, or seldom attend to, essential ones; who are faithful to certain self-chosen pious practices, but who do not mind omitting their obligations? Are there not others also who pique themselves on their regularity in exteriors, whilst they neglect interior matters? Are not all these people misled by a false conscience? Have we nothing to reproach ourselves with on these heads? Let us make a detailed and careful examination of conscience.
Colloquy with Jesus.

Second Week of Lent, Saturday: The Despair and Death of Judas

1st prelude: Look at Judas throwing down the thirty shekels of silver before the chief priests.
2nd prelude: Beg the grace of never giving way to temptations of despair or despondency.

Point I: "Then Judas, who had betrayed Him, seeing that He was condemned, repenting himself, brought back the thirty pieces of silver to the chief priests and ancients."

Consideration: When Judas agreed to betray his Divine Master for thirty pieces of silver, he expected that, being God as well as man, He would deliver Himself from the hands of His enemies, as He had often done before; but finding that his avaricious plan was defeated, and that Jesus gave Himself up and was about to suffer death, he was overwhelmed with horror at the thought of his crime, and of the eternal shame that would rest on him. The much-coveted money pressed on his conscience with a crushing weight; and cursing it from his heart, he took it back to the chief priests who had given it to him.

Application: Such is the ordinary result of sin. Before we commit it, we only see the pleasant side, and we are blind to its consequences; but as soon as the harm is done, there come remorse and shame; then we are horrified at our folly, and instead of enjoyment, we find it has brought us nothing but misery and regret. And this is equally true of lesser sins. What does our past experience teach us on this point?
Affections and Resolutions.

Point II: "Saying, I have sinned in betraying innocent blood. But they said, What is that to us? Look thou to that."

Consideration: When Judas went to confess his sin to the chief priests, a sin to which they themselves had tempted him, he hoped they would be able to comfort him, or at least interest themselves in the matter; but he received no other reply than the scornful words, "What is that to us? Look thou to that"; and when he heard it, the measure of his despair was filled up.

Application: Never let us reckon on assistance or sympathy, or even esteem, from those whom we have served against our own conscience and the law of God. Outwardly, perhaps, they will praise or flatter us, but in their secret hearts they will condemn us for our weak and cowardly consent to what we know to be wrong.

Affections and Resolutions.

Point III: "And casting down the pieces of silver in the Temple, he departed, and went and hanged himself."

Consideration: The terrible despair of Judas was the greatest of all his sins. His conviction that his crime was unpardonable was a virtual disbelief in God, who is infinite in all His attributes. The laws of men, which must be *finite*, cannot exceed the *infinite* goodness of God. If he, like Saint Peter, had thrown himself, humbled and contrite, at the feet of Jesus, he would also have been pardoned.

Application: We are all human, all liable to fall, and to fall very low. But if we unhappily commit sin, let us at once drive away all thoughts of despair, and imitate the humble repentance of Saint Peter, trusting, as he did, in the omnipotent mercy of God. Then we shall share the glories of heaven with the penitents who have become saints; and, to strengthen our resolution, let us often say, with holy King David: "In Thee, O Lord, have I hoped; let me never be confounded." And in times of temptation, let us remember those beautiful words of Saint Augustine: "If you feel afraid of God, throw yourself into His bosom."

Colloquy with our Father in heaven.

Third Week of Lent, Sunday: Jesus accused by His People before Pilate

1st prelude: Behold the crowd of people assembled before Pilate's

palace, vociferating against Jesus.
2nd prelude: Ask for grace to enable you to support false imputations in a Christian spirit.

Point I: "Pilate therefore went out to them, and said, What accusation bring you against this man? They answered and said to him, If He were not a malefactor, we would not have delivered Him up to you."

Consideration: We cannot but feel great indignation when we see the rulers of the Jews instigating the crowd to accuse Jesus, their Messiah, of a crime, and to hate Him; He who had never harmed anyone, but who had shed blessings around Him at every step. They were indeed filling up the measure of their ingratitude and unbelief.

Application: This frightful picture is daily reproduced before our eyes. Our Lord and His holy faith are still hated, still calumniated, and often by hose upon whom His best gifts have been poured; those whose rank and talents have raised them above their fellow creatures, but who only use their superiority to mislead their inferiors, and stir them up against our Lord, and against His Church. We should not, however, have bitter feelings towards them, but rather pity them; for the longer their punishment is delayed, the greater it will be.
Affections and Resolutions.

Point II: "Pilate therefore said to them, Take you Him, and judge Him according to your law. The Jews therefore said to him, It is not lawful for us to put any man to death."

Consideration: The Scribes and Pharisees were the accusers of our Lord, but they would not pass sentence on Him, even when Pilate authorized them. They wanted to make Him appear more guilty in the eyes of the people by receiving His condemnation from the chief magistrate; they wanted to avert the odium of His death from themselves, and they wanted Him to be crucified, the most shameful and most cruel mode of death, and commonly used by the Romans, but seldom by the Jews, not being decreed by any of their laws, and so, under a pretence of justice, they hypocritically hid their wickedness. Without knowing or intending it, they were fulfilling prophecy, and bringing the designs of our merciful Lord to pass. He had foretold the manner of His death, and for love of us was willing to drink the cup of suffering and humiliation to the very dregs. Thus by their crimes the intentions of God were carried out.

Application: Such are and always will be the dealings of Divine Providence. Let us never give way to distrust or waver in our faith when we see the wicked obtain a momentary triumph, and succeed in their evil designs. God, who in His infinite wisdom order the whole course of circumstances, will turn all things to His own glory and the good of His Church.

Affections and Resolutions.

Point III: "And they began to accuse Him, saying, We have found this man perverting our nation, and forbidding to give tribute to Caesar, and saying that He is Christ the King."

Consideration: Three especial accusation were brought against Jesus; they accused Him of perverting the people, of refusing to pay tribute, and of assuming the name of Christ the King. The first two were notoriously false, for He had preached and practiced the exact contrary; the third was false also in the sense in which they meant it – in the sense of an earthly kingdom, in opposition to that of Caesar. It was the height of shameless insolence to utter such calumnies against the innocent in the presence of the chief judge, and before the whole nation.

Application: If our Lord was willing to become the victim of wicked calumny without defending Himself, or even being disturbed by it, should we not make little account of men's judgment, when our own conscience tells us we have acted rightly? Have we profited by the lessons of our Divine Master? In what particular should we correct ourselves?

Colloquy with our Blessed Lady.

Third Week of Lent, Monday: Motives for Penance derived from the Thought of the Loss which the Sinner incurs

1st prelude: Imagine you see Saint John the Evangelist writing to the Church of Laodicea: "Be zealous therefore, and do penance."

2nd prelude: Beg grace to enable you to make reparation for the past by abundant penance.

Point I: Loss of God's friendship

Consideration: By mortal sin we lose God's friendship, sanctifying grace, the inheritance of the beatific vision, and all the privileges given to us in holy Baptism. In a state of mortal sin we are God's enemies, children and slaves of the devil; and we are under a curse. Perhaps we have spent days in this miserable state; perhaps even a great part of our lives. The thought of this is a bitter one, and caused such deep grief to Saint Augustine, that his only consolation was to immolate himself daily, by constant penance, on the altar of the love of God.

Application: During these days of universal penance, let us imitate the saint; and if God's mercy has preserved us from frequent mortal sin, let us think of those countless venial sins which give us sufficient cause for penance; for if venial sin does not deprive us of God's friendship, it certainly diminishes it. Every venial sin deprives us of a measure of God's love, and of a corresponding degree of glory in heaven. If we try to number our venial sins, we shall see how large a measure of grace we have lost, and what a loss it has been. Let us hasten, as far as lies in our power, to make reparation for it by fervent penance.

Affections and Resolutions.

Point II: Loss of supernatural life

Consideration: Mortal sin, in the second place, deprives our soul of supernatural life. That life consists in our union with God by the bonds of love. Mortal sin breaks this tie, interrupts this union; and, while separated from God, the soul is like a dead body – incapable of a meritorious action. Our best works are dead; every day, every month, passed in this state, is lost for all eternity.

Application: Would that our eyes were enlightened by the bright beams of faith, so that we could really understand and calculate the amount we have already lost! For we should then most earnestly try by penance to regain at least a portion of it. Venial sin does not *destroy* this supernatural life, but it weakens it; the soul is less fruitful in good works; and these works are less pleasing to God, less meritorious. Moreover, our human imperfection is so great that our best works are always marred by it, and lose somewhat of their merit. The saints tried to compensate for all this by great penance, and by constant mortification. Ought we not to imitate them, we who have sinned so much, and repented so little?

Affections and Resolutions.

Point III: Loss of sanctity

Consideration: Mortal sin, in the third place, robs the soul of its beauty, and renders it odious in the eyes of God and His holy angels; as says the Scriptures, "They are become abominable." One mortal sin changed and angel into a demon, and cast him down from heaven to hell. How, then, must a soul, defiled by numerous mortal sins, appear in the eyes of God? What will be its destiny in eternity, when the punishment will be in proportion to the sins committed?

Application: Perhaps you have incurred this penalty; and if so, you have a strong motive to induce you to embrace hardship and penance, and persevere therein unto the end. For, after all, although it may be certain that you have sinned grievously, yet it is not at all equally certain that your penance has been sufficient. The Church also tells us that the slightest venial fault leaves a stain upon the soul; and that "nothing defiled can enter heaven" are the words of the Holy Ghost. We have daily stained our souls, and made few efforts to cleanse them; therefore our purgatory and our exclusion from heaven will last much longer. Ponder deeply upon this; if we could but understand what it is to endure the pain of purgatory for one moment, what it is for one moment to be deprived of the beatific vision, the utmost rigor of penance would seem light to us.

Colloquy with our Blessed Lady.

Third Week of Lent, Tuesday: Interrogation of Jesus at Pilate's Judgment-seat

1st prelude: Behold Jesus Christ, firm yet submissive, before the Roman governor, Pontius Pilate.

2nd prelude: Beg for grace to make this meditation well.

Point I: "Pilate therefore went into the hall again, and called Jesus, and said to Him, Art Thou the King of the Jews? Jesus answered, My kingdom is not of this world. If My kingdom were of this world, My servants would certainly strive that I should not be delivered to the Jews; but now My kingdom is not from hence."

Consideration: Jesus Christ was not King of the Jews, nor of this world, in the ordinary sense of the word; this was not His will. His kingdom is the Church, the assembly of all those who willingly follow His teaching and observe His laws. The Church is in the world, but not of it. She came down from heaven, and earth is but the place of her pilgrimage and of her trials. She will return to heaven, and there the glorious and everlasting kingdom of Jesus and His disciples shall last for ever. This was the kingdom He meant when He said to Pilate, "My kingdom is not of this world"; and again, when He says to His disciples, "Seek ye first the kingdom of God."

Application: How great is our happiness in being made, by holy Baptism, children of the Church and subjects of Jesus Christ, and, by professing the Christian faith, to be among the number of the elect! If we choose, the kingdom of heaven is ours. What assurance of this do we need? That we should be full of the spirit of our Holy Mother the Church; that though *in* the world, we be not *of* the world; that our life should be more celestial than terrestrial; that we should live in spirit in heaven, as the Apostle says, "Our conversation is in heaven."

Affections and Resolutions.

Point II: "Pilate therefore said to Him, Art Thou a king, then? Jesus answered, Thou sayest that I am a king. For this was I born, and for this came I into the world; that I should give testimony to the truth. Every one that is of the truth heareth my voice."

Consideration: Pilate's conduct gives us a striking example of human instability. He was really desirous to know the truth concerning the wonderful Being whom the world thought of in such different ways, and who was now before him; and this desire increased after he had heard Him say, "For this came I into the world; that I should give testimony to the truth." Naturally he asked, "What is truth?" and apparently he eagerly awaited the reply. Yet, when it was given, it had no effect on him; he took no further heed, and went out quickly from the judgment-hall.

Application: We fully condemn the weakness and vacillation of Pilate; but let us examine if there be not some similarity with him in our conduct. Before beginning some of our actions, or deciding in difficult circumstances, we are accustomed to invoke the Holy Ghost: "Come, Holy Ghost," thus entreating to know His will; but do we not often decide hastily without recollecting ourselves sufficiently to hear His reply? And do we not often hear the voice of God in our souls, and pay no attention to it? Do we not thus

imitate the vacillation of the Roman judge?
Affections and Resolutions.

Point III: "He went out again to the Jews, and saith to them, I find no cause in Him."

Consideration: Pilate, a wise and experienced man, at the first sight of the case felt sure the crimes alleged could not be proved. However, in his position as judge, he questioned the accused upon the nature of the kingdom that He claimed. The answers of Jesus showed him clearly that His kingdom was not in opposition to the rules of this world; and he therefore pronounced Him to be innocent, saying, "I find no cause in Him."

Application: Pilate, though vacillating, was just, and a lover of truth. If he had been as firm as he was just, he would never have condemned Jesus to death. But he feared to get into trouble, and he grew weak and timid. The Jews craftily worked upon his fears, and extorted the unjust sentence from him. This is the devil's way with us: he studies our weak points, and takes advantage of them; and if we are off our guard, he entraps us with subtle snares.
Colloquy with Jesus our Master.

Third Week of Lent, Wednesday: The wonderful Silence of Jesus before Pilate's Judgment-seat

1st prelude: Behold Jesus standing calm and silent in the midst of the clamour and accusations of the people who were stirred up against Him.
2nd prelude: Beg for grace faithfully to imitate the great example our Lord then gave us.

Point I: "And when He was accused by the chief priests and ancients, He answered nothing."

Consideration: The first accusations which the Jews brought were so vague and untruthful that Pilate rejected them, and declared our Lord's innocence. It was beneath our Lord's dignity to reply to some of the points; and besides, the sanctity of His life answered for Him, confounding His calumniators, but proving His divinity. He did indeed try to hide it under His humanity, but it was revealed by His answers to the judge.

Application: Happy is the man whose conduct is an unanswerable defense against the false accusations of the wicked and envious! Happier still if his conscience bears witness to his constant endeavor to be spotless before God. Are we among this happy number?

Affections and Resolutions.

Point II: "And Pilate again asked Him, saying, Answerest Thou nothing? Behold in how many things they accuse Thee. But He answered him never a word; so that the governor wondered exceedingly."

Consideration: The astonishment of Pilate was not surprising. What would seem more natural for an accused man standing before a tribunal from which there was no appeal, and whose death was eagerly sought after, than to defend himself, and exert every effort to declare his innocence, especially when called upon to do so by a judge favorable to his cause? But Jesus was silent. He who often by a single word had confounded His enemies and turned the anger of the people against them, now would not utter one. Pilate could not understand the calm dignity of our Lord's silence, seeing clearly that it did not proceed from pride or resentment.

Application: We are better off than Pilate, for we know why our Blessed Lord kept that heroic silence. He was determined to die for us; and having manifested the truth, He would not say a single word to save His own life. And also, He chose by this painful silence to expiate our sins of the tongue, and to teach us to control our desire of answering our superiors haughtily when they reprove us, or our wish to give a sharp and angry retort to those who wound our feelings, or injure us in any ways.

Affections and Resolutions.

Point III: "But they were the more earnest, saying, He stirreth up the people, teaching throughout all Judea, beginning from Galilee to this place."

Consideration: When Pilate had seen and acknowledged that the accused was innocent, his duty was to silence the accusers, and dismiss them with the contempt they deserved. But this he dared not do. The Jews, perceiving his weakness, tried to take advantage of it. They began to clamor and importune him to grant the request which was against his conscience; and they succeeded only too well.

Application: Our great enemy the devil acts in the same way towards us; as soon as he sees us hesitating between God and

creatures, or conscience and our passions, he takes advantage of our weakness, and grows bolder than ever. He pours his arguments into our ears, terrifies us with the sight of imaginary difficulties, and lets us have no peace till we consent to sin. Let us, then, taught by Pilate's example, be on our guard against our own weakness, and without indulging any unreasonable fear of the tempter, never give in an inch to him; let us firmly resist his first suggestion, arming ourselves, as the Apostle says, with the shield of faith and prayer.
Colloquy with Jesus Christ.

Third Week of Lent, Thursday: Jesus insulted at the Court of Herod

1st prelude: Let us picture to ourselves Jesus reviled and insulted, and treated as a fool at Herod's court.
2nd prelude: Beg for grace to understand the indignities which Jesus bore for love of us.

Point I: "And when he understood that He was of Herod's jurisdiction, he sent Him away to Herod, who was also himself at Jerusalem; and Herod, seeing Jesus, was very glad for he hoped to see some miracle wrought by Him."

Consideration: Herod was a vain and degraded man; he had put Saint John Baptist to death; and he wanted the Savior of the world, of whom he had heard so much, to work a miracle before him, not that he might be touched and converted, but simply to gratify his vanity and curiosity. But God does not grant extraordinary graces to such men as these. He reserves them for the humble, who deem themselves unworthy of them. He delights to pour them on those who are emptied of self, dead to self-love, seeking only His greater glory. These souls ask for extraordinary graces or miracles only that they may serve Him better, or gain others to His service.

Application: The reason why we receive so few extraordinary graces is, that we either lack these dispositions altogether, or have made little progress in them; and after having perhaps passed many years in our holy vocation, we are very unlike those who, powerful in word and work, had the same vocation, and of whom wonderful things are recorded.
Affections and Resolutions.

Point II: "And he questioned Him in many words; but He answered him nothing. And the chief priests and scribes stood by, earnestly accusing Him."

Consideration: Wonderful indeed was the silence and passiveness of our Divine Lord before the tribunal of Herod, to which His cause was referred. He was accused of greater crimes still, but His accusers so outwitted themselves, that He could in a few words have confounded them, and turned the tide in His favor. Yet He held His peace. He went there to receive a sentence for life or death, and if He had chosen to work a miracle at Herod's desire, He would have found protection; but He would work none. It is in reality a greater miracle to triumph thus completely over every human feeling than to raise the dead; but the world cannot understand this. The calm silence of our Lord was looked upon by Herod and his court as helplessness and stupidity, and they treated it as such.

Application: Our Lord kept silence to punish Herod's pride and to teach us to mortify ours. Our pride is our greatest trial; in spite of ourselves it makes us desire esteem, notice, praise and applause from men, especially from the great ones of the earth. Have we fought steadfastly and victoriously against this unruly passion of pride?

Affections and Resolutions

Point III: "And Herod with his army set Him at naught, and mocked Him, putting on Him a white garment, and sent Him back to Pilate."

Consideration: Let us contemplate Jesus, the King of glory, the eternal Wisdom, standing before Herod, insulted by the coarse and stupid mob; let us follow Him in spirit, wearing the fool's robe, through the streets of Jerusalem, amidst the jeerings of the populace and the immense crowd of strangers which the Pascal feast had brought into the city, and we shall see that the prophecy of Jeremiah was fulfilled to the very letter: "I am made a derision to all My people."

Application: This meditation ought to produce great fruit in us. When we contemplate Jesus Christ as the true way, which leads us unto life, as the living model of perfection, it should kindle in our hearts and ardent desire to become like unto Him, to serve Him willingly, to be ready, in imitation of Him and for His love, to be despised, insulted, reviled, and even looked upon as a fool, although we have done nothing to deserve this treatment: this is the *foolishness of the Cross*. Many of God's servants have travelled by this road; why should not we follow in their footsteps? Colloquy with our Blessed Lady.

Third Week of Lent, Friday: Barabbas compared with and preferred to Jesus

1st prelude: Behold our Divine Lord before all the people compared with an infamous robber.
2nd prelude: Beg for grace never to hesitate between the Creator and the creature.

Point I: "They therefore begin gathered together, Pilate said, You have a custom that I should release one unto you at the Pasch. Whom will you that I release unto you: Barabbas, or Jesus, that is called Christ?"

Consideration: Pilate knew and acknowledged the innocence of our Lord; it was against his conscience to condemn Him; but his self-interest bade him gratify the Jews, or he would lose favor in the eyes of Caesar. Conscience being on the one hand, and interest on the other, he tried to get out of the difficulty. He sent Him to Herod, not being able to find out what He was guilty of; then he offered the people their choice between an odious criminal and the Savior, whom till lately they had reverenced so much. But his plans proved futile, and after some further attempts which were all useless, always shrinking back from doing his duty, he completed his evil work by condemning the innocent, and thus lost his own soul.

Application: How true are those words of our Lord's, "No man can serve two masters"! It is impossible to steer a middle course between God and the world; we cannot hover between virtue and vice, though the transgression may be a slight one. A friendship which is inordinate, though it may be based on motives of zeal, may cause us perplexity and trouble of conscience. Our own good sense and our confessor tell us to decide at once to give it up entirely. But we answer, No, you expect too much; but I will be more careful for the future. My case is an especial one. This is a delusion of self-love which leads to nothing. What does our experience tell us on this head?

Affections and Resolutions.

Point II: "But the chief priests and ancients persuaded the people that they should ask Barabbas, and take Jesus away. The whole multitude cried out together, Away with this man! And release unto us Barabbas."

Consideration: Let us try to understand as far as we can the extent to which the insults of Jesus were carried. He is placed on a level, or, as we say, weighed in the balance with Barabbas, the greatest criminal which the prisons then held, by the chief magistrate, before all the people; and to the astonishment even of Pilate, Barabbas was preferred to Jesus by unanimous consent. All, says holy writ, with one voice cried, "Not this man, but Barabbas."

Application: Who among us, then, can dare to complain that he is not treated as he deserves; that others are preferred before him; that he is put last of all? If we remember how often in past life we have imitated the Jews by allowing sin to reign in our hearts, rather than God our Savior, we shall count ourselves unworthy of a place in God's house, and still more unworthy of the meanest office therein.

Affections and Resolutions.

Point III: "And as he was sitting in the place of judgment, his wife sent to him, saying: Have thou nothing to do with that just man; for I have suffered many things this day in a dream because of Him."

Consideration: Most interpreters believe that the uneasiness of Pilate's wife was caused by an inspiration of grace, and that it obtained her salvation. The Greeks even honor her as a saint, under the name of Claudia Procula. Be this as it may, the warning thus sent to Pilate was an extraordinary grace vouchsafed to him at the critical moment, when he was hesitating between doing a great act of justice, which would have won his salvation, and an atrocious crime, which brought fearful misery on him both in this world and the next; for we know that he fell into disgrace and was banished, and finally destroyed himself.

Application: How many times and in how many ways have our guardian angels and our directors warned us and tried to strengthen us, when our passions had obtained such a mastery over us that our judgment was darkened, and we were hesitating between good and evil! All these warnings were extraordinary graces. How have we corresponded with them? How have we profited by them? Colloquy with our Blessed Lord.

Third Week of Lent, Saturday: Pilate tries to save Jesus from the Fury of the Jews

1st prelude: Imagine you see Pilate pleading with the crowd on behalf of Jesus.
2nd prelude: Beg the grace to persevere till the end in our holy vocation.
Point I: "Pilate saith to them, What shall I do, then, with Jesus, that is called Christ? They say all, Let Him be crucified."

Consideration: The efforts that Pilate made to rescue Jesus from His enemies only incensed them the more against Him, because they thought He would escape from them. Of the three classes who were concerned in bringing about His death, Pilate, the people, and the priests, the priests had the greater guilt. Yielding to a base jealousy, they invented and sustained the accusations, they excited and seduced the people, they overpowered the judge by the cries of rage and fury which they put into the mouth of the crowd: their sin was very terrible; for the sanctity of their office, and the greater light and grace they had received, ought to have made them models to their people instead of a scandal.

Application: Here is another melancholy proof of the truth of the old saying, *Optimi pessima corruption* – The best when corrupted become the worst; and this we unhappily see too often in our own days, when priests or religious become infidels or apostates; they seem as if they wanted to deaden their own consciences, or entirely to efface the seal of their sacerdotal consecration or religious profession.
Affections and Resolutions.

Point II: "The governor said to them, Why, what evil hath He done?"

Consideration: This question ought to have opened the eyes of the Jewish people. It reminded them of the public life of Jesus, every step of which had brought down blessings on them. Even among this very multitude there might have been found many whom He had miraculously cured – to whom He had given sight, hearing, or the use of their limbs – and a still greater number whom He had delivered from the possession or temptations of the devil.

Application: During the whole of our lives, and especially since we entered religion, we can remember nothing but wonderful graces and blessings; they constantly flash across our minds, and the memory of them ought to increase our love and devotion to Jesus, our Divine Lord. How is it, then, that we correspond so little with these grace, that we are so lukewarm in His service? Let us search into the causes of this, fight against it, and overcome it if possible.

Affections and Resolutions.

Point III: "And he said to them the third time, I find no cause of death in Him. I will chastise Him, therefore, and let Him go."

Consideration: Pilate was guilty of the grossest injustice. Three times had he declared that the prisoner brought before him was innocent, and yet he condemned Him to a cruel and shameful punishment. His aim was to save Him at least from death, by exciting compassion for His sufferings, under the punishment to which He was sentenced. He did not see that he was actually clearing the way for the death by crucifixion, which the Jews were aiming at, for it was often the custom to precede crucifixion by scourging.

Application: How often have our passions made us act like fools! Have we not, from pride or sensuality, tried to escape the humiliations and mortifications which we ought to seek after, especially in religious life? Or have we not sought for pleasures and distinctions which we knew well would do us harm? Are we, then, on our guard against our passions, and do we fight manfully against them?

Colloquy with our Divine Master.

Fourth Week of Lent, Sunday: The Scourging of Jesus Christ

1st prelude: Behold our Lord Jesus Christ bound to the pillar.

2nd prelude: Let us beg for grace of making our meditations on our Lord's sufferings as fruitful as those of so many holy souls.

Point I: The preparation for the scourging

Consideration: "Pilate took Jesus, and scourged Him." Our innocent Lord heard Himself sentenced to the humiliation and suffering of scourging. He was dragged to the place of punishment. He saw the preparations for it; and He felt all its horror by anticipation. How terrible must this fear and horror have been to His sensitive nature! But He never wavered in His purpose of bearing all for us, and He went resolutely forward.

Application: How differently do we act! How often do we not only waver, but actually shrink back from carrying out our resolutions! And only because we are terrified by the anticipation (which generally exaggerates matters) of the trouble or suffering they would cost us; for instance, rising at the proper time in all seasons, doing such or such an act of penance or mortification, keeping to a certain position in prayer, or faithfully fulfilling a particular duty. Is no this true?

Affections and Resolutions.

Point II: The suffering of the scourging

Consideration: The horror of this punishment is beyond the power of words to describe; but in order to realize it as far as possible, imagine yourself undergoing it: imagine your clothes torn off, yourself covered with blood and bound to the pillar, while strong men, armed some with whips, some with straps, some with cords and iron spikes, scourge you till their arms drop with fatigue, until your body is but one sore, your flesh torn, and the ground covered with your blood. Then, perhaps, you may form some idea of the suffering of that scourging which your Divine Savior endured for you.

Application: In all your troubles, whether of mind or body, fix your eyes on Jesus your King bound to the pillar; the sight of Him will make all your sufferings seem light, and you will bear them with courage and with love.

Affections and Resolutions.

Point III: The motives for the scourging

Consideration: It was a cruel and cowardly expedient on Pilate's part to appease the people and to save Jesus from death. Our Lord bore it from His heroic love for us. He gave up His Body into the hands of the executioners, that He might expiate, in His innocent flesh, the shameful and countless sins with which men of all ages and conditions have degraded and do daily degrade their bodies; sins by which they dishonor and trample under their feet the image of God, in whose likeness they were created.

Application: Had I but once grievously offended against holy purity, I ought to say to myself, Here is my work! It is I who, by the hands of the executioners, have torn the Body of Jesus, who have covered it with blood and wounds; and besides this, the memory of my frequent acts of self-indulgence ought to be sufficient to produce in me a deep compunction, a contempt of myself, and an ardent desire to labor and suffer much for the love of Him to whom I caused such bitter sufferings.

Colloquy with Jesus bound to the pillar.

Fourth Week of Lent, Monday: Motives for Penance inspired by the Thought of Death

1st prelude: Imagine you see a religious on his deathbed.

2nd prelude: Ask for grace to live the life of a penitent, that so you may die the death of a saint.

Point I: Penance will strengthen the dying religious

Consideration: Our truest consolation at the hour of death will be our having passed a life of penance. If we were to say to a dying religious, "Your last moment, my brother, is drawing near; all is ending for you in this world; but take comfort – you have borne an important part; you have held, one after another, the highest posts in your order; you have won a great name amongst learned men and among orators; your works and your writings will keep your name alive": - do you think it would give him much comfort? No, indeed; he would answer you, "What will all this avail me in eternity?" "I have been," said a celebrated religious when dying – "I have been superior in the largest houses of my order; I have been a popular and applauded preacher; and all of it is *nothing* to me now. I have faithfully kept my rule, and *that is something*; it is the only thing that consoles me in this awful moment."

Application: The greatest comfort, then, we shall have on our deathbeds is the knowledge that we have been true religious; that we have been crucified with Jesus to the world and to ourselves by continual mortification. "Yes," says the author of the *Imitation*, "he shall be full of comfort and hope in his death, who in his life lived under the yoke of religious discipline and self-abnegation." If I were to die now, should I find comfort in looking back on the past?

Affections and Resolutions.

Point II: Penance will encourage the dying religious

Consideration: When a good man is dying, he is not in fear and sorrow at the thought of leaving the fair things of this world, but only on account of his past sins, and of those words of the Holy Ghost: "Be not without fear about sin forgiven"; and again, "Man knoweth not whether he be worthy of love or hatred." But what reassurance and what peace we can find in those other words of the Holy Spirit: "Thou overlookest the sins of men for the sake of repentance"! The memory of having expiated by mortification the insult which sin is to God, of having paid off many debts owing to divine justice by means of penance, will also comfort us. Saint Hilarion was thus preserved from the fear of death. "What, my soul," said he, "thou hast carried the cross for seventy years, and now dost thou fear to leave the world to appear before God?"

Application: If we desire, when death is drawing near, to share the calm trust felt by the saints, even those whose lives had not always been spotless, we should imitate their penance, and especially during this precious time of Lent, of which more than half has already passed. Let us be in earnest about it, and defer it not to the hour of sickness or the time of old age. "While you are in health," says Saint Thomas a Kempis, "you can perform many works of satisfaction; but you know not what you will be able to do when sickness overtakes you."

Affections and Resolutions.

Point III: Penance will be the joy of the dying religious

Consideration: When the labourer joyfully gathers in a rich harvest, all his past labour seems as nothing; the joy and satisfaction of the result far outweighs his former trouble and privation.

Application: This is an emblem of the joy and happiness which the penitent and mortified religious will feel when he is about to reap the fruits of all the austerities of the religious life, when he is on the point of receiving the reward promised by our Lord to those who renounce all worldly pleasures to bear the cross after Him. And what will be his bliss when he shall have entered into the joy

of his reward? What memory of the past will then be a joy to him? Saint Peter of Alcantara gave us some idea of it when he appeared in glory to Saint Teresa, and said, "O blissful penance, which has purchased for me so great a reward!" In thoughts like these we shall find courage and strength to live and persevere unto the end in the practice of holy penance.
Colloquy with our Blessed Lord.

Fourth Week of Lent, Tuesday: The Insults which preceded the Crowning with Thorns

1st prelude: Behold our Blessed Lord sitting on a block of wood, holding a reed in His hand, His head crowned with thorns and insulted by the guards of the Roman governor.
2nd prelude: Beg for feelings of deep grief and compunction.

Point I: The insults offered to Jesus

Consideration: After the outrage of scourging, fearful insults were heaped upon our Divine Lord. Pilate's soldiers, who had led him to the court of Herod, were anxious that these insults should excel those offered to Him there. He had there been treated as a fool; they would now crown him as a fool, as the king of fools; as says Holy Writ, "taking Jesus into the hall, gathered together unto Him the whole band, and stripping Him, they put a scarlet cloak about Him, and platting a crown of thorns, they put it upon His head, and a reed in His right hand. And bowing the knee before Him, they mocked Him, saying, Hail, King of the Jews! And spitting on Him, they took the reed and struck His head, and they gave Him blows."

Application: If we carefully think over all the details, and even every word of this narrative, written under the inspiration of the Holy Spirit, we shall see how truly the prophet Jeremias had foretold of the Messiah, "He shall be filled with reproaches." If we then ask ourselves, Who is it that is thus treated? For what reason? Our hearts will surely burn with love.
Affections and Resolutions.

Point II: The terrible pain of the crowning with thorns

Consideration: "And platting a crown of thorns, they put it on His head." They not only placed it on His head, but pressed it in, by striking it on the top with a reed, as the Evangelist tells us.

Conceive, if possible the sufferings our Lord then endured. Why did He not sink beneath this additional torment, following so rapidly upon His scourging? Did He work a miracle to blunt the edge of His sufferings? No; but He exerted His miraculous power that He might not sink under sufferings which would have caused His death; so that no one else might ever suffer as He had done. And all this was for love of me!

Application: It was the will of our Divine Lord that His head, which had escaped the scourging, should also bear its distinct punishment, that He might expiate our sins of thought – the many thoughts and desires of pride, ambition, rebellion, hatred, vengeance, impurity, and injustice with which the heads of men are filled, so that they lose all thought of the presence and justice of God.

Affections and Resolutions.

Point III: The wonderful patience of Jesus

Consideration: With what wonderful patience did our Blessed Lord bear these extraordinary insults and sufferings! His eyes were not bandaged now, as they were when in Herod's court. They mocked Him as a prophet. He looked upon the insulting homage which one soldier after another offered him in ridicule. He saw the spittle which they dared to throw in His face. He saw the arms of the insolent soldiers raised to strike Him; and yet He never moved His head to escape their blows. When they snatched the reed from His hand, He let them have it; when they gave it Him back again, He took it, fulfilling to the very letter the prophesy of Isaias, "I have not turned away My face from them that spit upon Me."

Application: While we gaze upon this wonderful patience, we should remember our own impatience at the least contradiction. What ought we to think of our secret but eager desires for the praise and adulation of the world; of the resentment which enters and dwells in our hearts against those who have offended or looked down upon us? "If," says the author of the *Imitation*, "Jesus, covered with ignominy, was always before your minds, you would desire rather to be beneath the feet of all men, than to exercise superiority over any one." We should, then, ardently long to be despised and to suffer for the love of Jesus. How far have we advanced in thus following the true disciples of our Lord?

Colloquy with our patient Lord.

Fourth Week of Lent, Wednesday: Pilate shows Jesus to the People, saying, "Behold the Man"

1st prelude: Behold our Lord Jesus covered with blood and wounds, crowned with thorns, wearing a purple mantle, and with a reed in His hand, exposed to the gaze of the multitude.
2nd prelude: Ask for grace to give more love and glory to Jesus, because He was thus mocked and reviled.

Point I: "Jesus, therefore, came forth bearing the crown of thorns and the purple garment; and he said to them, Behold the Man."

Consideration: Even the heart of the Roman governor was touched when he beheld our Lord covered with blood and wounds, and insulted as a mock king. He thought that the Jews would equally be moved at the sight, and would demand the liberation of Him whose death they had been clamouring for. With this intention he brought Him forth to the front of the judgment-hall, and presenting Him to the people, said, "Behold the Man."

Application: Holy Church addresses these words to every faithful soul, that they may have a tender compassion for the sufferings and humiliations of our Divine Lord. And God the Father also addresses them to us, that our hearts may be inflamed by love for His Divine Son, so shamefully treated for love of us; and ought we not to be moved even to tears when we know it was our sins which brought all this upon Him?

Affections and Resolutions.

Point II: "When the chief priests and the servants had seen Him, they cried out, saying, Crucify Him, crucify Him!"

Consideration: When Pilate exposed Jesus to the gaze of the multitude, he thought it would be unnecessary to plead for Him in many words. He only said, "Behold the Man"; and he imagined there would be a universal cry for pardon and mercy. And doubtless this would have been the case, if he had not been dealing with a people excited by the implacable hatred of the priests and doctors. The pride and self-love of these men had been wounded, and they had sworn to have the life of Jesus, not afraid, by shedding innocent blood and the blood of a God, to draw down on themselves and their people fearful punishment. Pilate, to his astonishment, had no other answer than an outcry of rage, "Crucify

Him, crucify Him!"

Application: Here is an example to what lengths our passions, and especially wounded pride, will go. It blinded these clear-headed men to their own interests; it stifled all sense of justice and the fear of God in their breasts. And in the same way the religious who is determined not to submit to his superiors is indifferent to the loss of his vocation, the violation of his vows, and the detriment to his reputation. If he is told that those who have respected him as a religious will despise him when he is a worldling, he is unmoved. Remind him of the most touching or the most terrifying truths of religion, show him Jesus Christ humble and obedient unto death, even the death of the cross, it is all in vain. Passion never stops to reason; its victims are obstinately blind, and fall over the precipice. God grant that there may not be any examples in our own days to verify the truth of what we have been considering!

Affections and Resolutions.

Point III: "Pilate saith to them, Take Him you, and crucify Him. The Jews answered him, We have a law, and according to our law he ought to die, because He made Himself the Son of God."

Consideration: The real crime of Jesus in the eyes of the priests and doctors was the He had seen through their hypocrisy, and thrown them into the shade by the superiority of His teaching, the sanctity of His life, and the renown of His miracles. But they took good care not to bring this motive forward, for they were not willing to expose the base passion of envy which possessed them.

Application: Such are the workings of our passions. We do not see the true motives of our actions, and we fasten upon the imaginary faults of others. A religious or a priest rebelling against obedience will tell you that the fault is all on the side of his superiors – that they are prejudiced, ignorant, and unjust; and that for his own honor's sake, and even in his zeal for the glory of God and the salvation of souls, he is obliged to act as he does. In reality, wounded self-love is the foundation of it all. May God preserve us from becoming the victims of this passion!

Colloquy with our Blessed Lord.

Fourth Week of Lent, Thursday: The last Interrogation of Jesus, and the Weakness and Timidity of Pilate

1st prelude: Look at the meek but resolute countenance of Jesus, as He stands before the faint-hearted and cowardly judge and the infuriated people.
2nd prelude: Beg for grace never to give way to any fear but the fear of God.

Point I: "He ought to die, because He made Himself the Son of God. When Pilate therefore had heard this saying, he feared the more."

Consideration: This last accusation of the Jews, "He made Himself the Son of God," far from creating a belief in His guilt in the mind of the judge, only made him believe the mysterious truth, and filled him with fear. The words and demeanor of our Lord had already made him suspect His divinity, not with that certainty which faith gives to us, but with such a conviction as a pagan could feel. But it was sufficient to have made him fear the vengeance of God.

Application: Pilate was astonished and terrified at the thought that he might perhaps be standing in the presence of God, and about to commit a grievous crime against Him. He dared no take a single step further in the matter without inquiring into the truth of the assertion. And what have we done, who know and firmly believe that we are always in the presence of God, who searches the inmost recesses of our hearts? We have not been afraid to insult Him, to commit iniquity in His sight, to defy His terrors, even with the awful examples before us of His punishments.
Affections and Resolutions.

Point II: "And he entered into the hall again, and he said to Jesus, Whence art Thou? But Jesus gave him no answer. Pilate therefore saith to Him, Speakest Thou not to me? Knowest Thou not that I have power to crucify Thee, and I have power to release Thee? Jesus answered, Thou shouldst not have any power against Me, unless it were given thee from above; therefore he that hath delivered Me to thee hath the greater sin."

Consideration: Pilate's question was not about the birthplace of our Lord, for that he already knew, but concerning His descent and genealogy. But he was not worthy to be taught the wonderful mystery of our Lord's eternal being and His Incarnation; such truths are revealed only to the pure and humble. Our Lord therefore only rebuked him that he had not power save from God, and warned him with wonderful gentleness against the crime he was about to commit.

Application: Why does not God speak to you? Why does He give you so little of His divine light? It is because you are not prepared to listen to Him – because by constant infidelity to grace, you lose the power God has given you of discerning between good and evil.

Affections and Resolutions.

Point III: "And from henceforth Pilate sought to release Him. But the Jews cried out, saying, If thou release this man, thou art not Caesar's friend; for whosoever maketh himself a king speaketh against Caesar."

Consideration: This last threat of the Jews put an end to the struggle that had been going on in the breast of the cowardly governor. The fear of offending a mortal prince prevailed over his reason, over justice, the warnings of conscience, and even the fear of drawing down divine vengeance. His head was confused, his heart fainted within him, and he hastened to deliver up Jesus to death.

Application: There is no one who does not detest the criminal cowardice of Pilate; and yet in these days there are a great many Christians who give up their sacred obligations from human respect. Let us give thanks to God for having drawn us out of the world, where human respect and self-interest reign supreme, and many fall victims before them.

Colloquy with the Mother of Jesus.

Fourth Week of Lent, Friday: Jesus unjustly condemned – His Resignation

1st prelude: Consider Jesus, who "delivered Himself to him that judged Him unjustly."

2nd prelude: Ask for victory over your passions.

Point I: "And he [Pilate] saith to the Jews, Behold your King! … Shall I crucify your King? The chief priests answered, we have no king but Caesar. Then, therefore, he delivered Him to them to be crucified."

Consideration: Never did judge pronounce a more unjust sentence, for He that was condemned as the worst of malefactors had been four times publicly proclaimed innocent. How did it happen that Pilate, naturally right-minded and well-intentioned, descended to such cowardly wickedness? We know the reason; from the beginning he wanted energy and resolution to oppose the popular fury, for he was aware that "for envy they had delivered Him."

Application: Nothing is more to be dreaded than the first giving way to passion; generally, the first false step paves the way for others, and brings us only too often to a point from which we should formerly have shrunk with horror. Thus we learn how men once distinguished for their qualities of heart and mind, even religious who were long the edification of their brethren, have fallen into heresy, apostasy, and even infidelity. They merely yielded in the beginning to some slight temptation of wounded self-love or sensuality, but in the end they were blinded by passion and became its victims.

Affections and Resolutions.

Point II: "And Pilate, taking water, washed his hands before the people, saying, I am innocent of the blood of this just man. Look you to it."

Consideration: When those charged with the maintenance of law and order fail in their duty, the consequences are usually as fatal to their subordinates as to themselves. We have a proof of this here; if Pilate, when convinced of our Lord's innocence, had censured his enemies as they deserved, and given Him back justified to the affection of the people, he would have had no part in the guilt of the chief priests, nor in that terrible imprecation which was unconsciously pronounced against himself, and which has hung over him these nineteen hundred years: "His blood be on us and on our children."

Application: Far be from us any feeling of bitterness against our superiors when they wisely and firmly maintain religious disciplines, reprove our failings and, when required, vigorously oppose the first symptoms of our disorderly inclinations. If we do otherwise, do we not follow the example of the Jews, or of the sick who are angry with the doctors who prescribe them bitter but

necessary medicine?
Affections and Resolutions.
Point III: "And they took Jesus and led Him forth, and, bearing His own cross, He went forth to that place which is called Calvary."

Consideration: Saint Peter speaks of the perfect submission with which Jesus accepted His unjust sentence, "He delivered Himself to him that judged Him unjustly"; that is, He looked on it as coming from God the Father, who makes use of the malice or the mistakes of men to accomplish His designs, and in expiation of the sins of the world. The design of God here was to make reparation to Him and to redeem mankind by the death of His Divine Son. And it was this that our Lord had ardently desired from the first moment of His Incarnation; judge, therefore, of the joy and eagerness with which He laid the heavy cross upon His shoulders.

Application: Our Lord here teaches us how to meet the persecution and ill-treatment of wicked men, and how we should receive the humiliations, or even the punishments, that our superiors may inflict upon us by mistake. How has it been with you in such instances? If you have Jesus always before your eyes, nothing will seem difficult; all your glory and happiness will be in bearing the cross after Him.
Colloquy with Jesus, the model and King of martyrs.

Fourth Week of Lent, Saturday: Jesus falls beneath the Cross; Simon carries the Cross after Him

1st prelude: Behold Jesus falling three times under the weight of His cross.
2nd prelude: Ask for grace to follow Him in the way of suffering and humiliation.

Point I: "And the soldiers led Him into the court of the palace;... and after they had mocked Him, they took off the purple from Him, and put His own garments on Him; and they led Him out to crucify Him,... into the place called Golgotha, which being interpreted, is the place of Calvary; and with Him they crucify two thieves."

Consideration: Let us observe how our Lord, amidst every circumstance of His Passion, is insatiable not merely of sufferings, but of shame and humiliation. He submits to the ignominy of crucifixion in the place where the vilest criminals suffer, in company with two of them, not in borrowed garments, in which He might not have been recognized, but in those which He wore on the day of His triumphant entry into Jerusalem.

Application: What does our Lord teach us here, we who call ourselves specially His disciples? Not to be ashamed of, but rather to glory in, His livery – that is to say, in contempt, raillery, rcbuffs, injuries, and persecutions endured in His service; to rejoice in thus closely resembling our model and Master. How does this agree with your feelings, desires or fears?

Affections and Resolutions.

Point II: "And, as they led Him away, they laid hold of one Simon of Cyrene, coming from the country, and they laid the cross on him to carry after Jesus."

Consideration: Jesus fatigued and exhausted by fasting, by being hurried from place to place, and by the loss of blood, falls beneath the weight of the cross. Tradition tells us that He fell thrice; twice, gathering up His little remaining strength, He rose and continued His journey, but the third time, the Jews, fearing that He would die upon the way, and that they would thus be deprived of their expected pleasure, forced Simon to bear the cross to the summit of Calvary.

Application: Does it not seem astonishing that no one out of all that crowd, many of whom had been miraculously healed by Him, and who besides still secretly believed in Him, came forward to offer to carry our Lord's cross? Must this not have wounded so tender a heart as that of Jesus; and do not we also wound Him when we refuse to follow Him in the path of suffering and humiliation, out of unfounded fear or human respect?

Affections and Resolutions.

Point III: "They forced one Simon a Cyrenian, the father of Alexander and of Rufus, to take up His cross."

Consideration: It seems from these words that Simon at first showed great reluctance to carry our Lord's cross; but from the fact of the evangelist's making special mention of his name and that of his two sons, we may believe that, enlightened by divine grace, he bore it as became a true disciple, and was, as well as his children, richly rewarded; and, according to a generally admitted tradition, all three became celebrated in the Church as either bishops or martyrs.

Application: Let us renew our love and esteem for the cross, the source of our glory and happiness. In the cross is salvation; in the cross is life; in the cross is protection from enemies, says the *Imitation*. In the cross is infusion of heavenly sweetness; in the cross is strength of mind; in the cross is joy of spirit; in the cross is height of virtue; in the cross is perfection of sanctity. There is no health of soul, nor hope of eternal life, but in the cross. Take up, therefore, thy cross and follow Jesus, and thou shalt go into life everlasting.

Colloquy with Jesus suffering.

Fifth Week of Lent, Sunday: Holy Women weep over Jesus; Jesus meets His Mother on His sorrowful Journey

1st prelude: Behold those women amongst the multitude who bewailed and lamented Jesus, and specially His holy Mother.
2nd prelude: Ask for the grace of tender compassion.

Point I: "And there followed Him a great multitude of people, and of women who bewailed and lamented Him."

Consideration: We do not learn that all the multitude were filled with the same compassionate tenderness as these holy women; many, perhaps the greatest number, apart from the enemies of Jesus, were attracted by mere curiosity, and were quite indifferent to the fate of their Lord about to die for them.

Application: Thus in our own times a great multitude follow in spirit the various phases of our Lord's Passion during this holy season of Lent, and you amongst the number can do so with more leisure than ordinary Christians, and at least give an hour a day to this exercise. But what are your impressions during this hour? Are you, like these holy women, touched with love, compassion, and contrition at the thought that it is for your sins, and for your sake, that Jesus suffers and is about to die?

Affections and Resolutions.

Point II: "And their followed Him… women who bewailed and lamented Him."

Consideration: Although Saint Luke, speaking of these holy women, makes no special mention of our Blessed Lady, we may piously believe, in accordance with universal tradition, that the Son and the Mother met upon the road, particularly as Saint John says explicitly that Mary stood by the cross when Jesus reached the end of His journey. Who can express the feelings of the heart of this the most loving of mothers, when, making her way through the crowd, she stood face to face with her Divine Son, disfigured, bruised, crowned with thorns, covered with wounds and blood, surrounded by soldiers and executioners, who loaded Him with imprecations, and dragged Him to death?

Application: God willed that our Blessed Lady should be thus afflicted; and she above all the saints might have the largest share in the Passion of her Son and in the work of our redemption, and thus accumulate more merit and richer treasures of sanctity than all who have yet lived or shall live. Do not be astonished, therefore, do not murmur, above all, do not be discouraged, if God sends you much suffering and tribulation, but believe that He does so to increase your love and your merit.

Affections and Resolutions.

Point III: "But Jesus, turning to them, said, Daughters of Jerusalem, weep not for Me, but weep for yourselves and your children."

Consideration: Here let us admire the greatness of our Lord's tenderness to others. He forgets His own sufferings in His care for them. He warns them of evil days to come, and warns them to prepare for them by tears and penance.

Application: How different is our Lord's conduct from ours! When we are suffering in body or mind, do we not often forget what we owe to others, fancying that every one ought to be interested in us and pity our condition; and if they do not do so, do we not indulge in ill-humor and discontent? If we look at our Lord, we shall be more generous, less occupied with ourselves, more attentive to the wants of those around us, making it a rule never to let others suffer through us.

Colloquy with our Blessed Lady meeting her Divine Son.

Fifth Week of Lent, Monday: Motives for Penance drawn from the Thought of Judgment

1st prelude: I will imagine myself before the judgment-seat of

Jesus Christ, with two unshaken witnesses beside me, my guardian angel and Satan.
2nd prelude: I will ask for grace to know myself, that I may be able to judge myself here.
Three things are to be feared in the particular judgment: 1. The judge; 2. The account to be rendered; 3. The sentence.

Point I: The Judge

Consideration: By penance we may make the judge favourable to us. The judge is our Lord Himself, whom we have neglected, offended and injured, with all the malice of sin, and so often, so deliberately, even when He loaded us with benefits. Now He is a God of mercy, ready to pardon at the first sign of repentance; as His mercy was infinite, so will be His justice; not the smallest fault, not an idle word, He has said, will pass unperceived, but will be severely punished in purgatory. These thoughts filled holy Job with fear. Who shall reprove His way to His face? And who shall repay Him what He hath done?

Application: What have you not to expect, or rather to fear, from your judge, you who have perhaps long lived in a state of tepidity, which blinds man as to the number and gravity of his faults, or maintains him in false security? What, then, should you do? Our Lord tells you: "Be at agreement with thy adversary betimes, whilst thou art in the way with him"; that is, according to Saint Augustine, with God who is your judge, and whose enemy sin has made you; and you can do so, if "ye be humbled, therefore, under the mighty hand of God," to use Saint Peter's words, "and be penitent therefore, and be converted, that your sin may be blotted out."
Affections and Resolutions.

Point II: The account to be rendered

Consideration: By penance we may lighten the account we shall have to give. What an account! All will be passed in review by One from whom nothing can be hidden: the time lost in useless things; the good left undone, the good ill-done; all our thoughts, intentions, words and actions; and, what is worse for the religious, all the means of salvation and sanctification lavishly bestowed upon him daily and hourly. The judgment will be severe in proportion to the grace received, says Saint Cyprian, following the words of our Lord, "Unto whomsoever much is given, of him much shall be required."

Application: These truths filled even the penitents of the desert with fear; they never thought they had sufficiently atoned for their past lives. The only means of consolation under this dread were tears and constant mortification, a life of continual penance until death. Imitate them; try to lighten by such a life of penance and mortification your heavy account of sin, imperfection and negligence; and do it with special generosity during this holy season, two-thirds of which are already gone.

Affections and Resolutions.

Point III: The sentence

Consideration: By penance we may insure a favorable sentence. The sentence of the judge will be irrevocable – life eternal or death eternal; the first securing the soul of the just endless glory and the delights of heaven, although it may for a while be detained in a place of expiation; the second condemning the soul of the sinner to Satan and the eternal pains of hell.

Application: You earnestly desire to be amongst the number of the elect, to enter into the immediate possession of heave. It is possible: with the grace of God, endeavor to live as a holy religious, expiating by constant penance and mortifications all that yet tarnishes the purity of your soul. This is the infallible but indispensable means of insuring what you so much desire. Oh, how joyfully, after such a life, will you meet death! And why should you not do so?

Colloquy with Jesus doing penance for us.

Fifth Week of Lent, Tuesday: Jesus on Calvary – The Soldiers give Jesus Gall to drink, and strip Him of His Garments

1st prelude: Imagine you see Jesus surrounded by His executioners, who strip Him of His garments.

2nd prelude: Ask for grace to grow in the knowledge and love of Jesus.

Point I: "And they came to the place that is called Golgotha, which is the place of Calvary."

Consideration: There are numerous mysteries connected with the place which our Lord chose for consummating His sacrifice: it was the spot where God commanded Abraham to offer up Isaac;

where the Jews were accustomed to execute great criminals; and where, according to tradition, Noah buried Adam's head, which he had taken in the Ark with him, the Hebrew word Golgotha signifying "chief" or "head." The special mention of the place by the four Evangelists, of the Hebrew name Golgotha, instead of the latinized Greek "cranium," the place of Calvary, appears to give authority to the tradition always maintained by the Jews, according to the testimony of Tertullian, Origen, Saint Athanasius, and the greater number of the Fathers.

Application: Let us meditate on these mysteries, for they are full of instruction. The sacrifice of Jesus recalling to mind that of Abraham, should inspire us with love and gratitude to Him and His eternal Father, who thus fulfilled the typical sacrifice of the great patriarch; next, our Lord's choice of the place used for the execution of criminals should remind us that He suffered for us criminals, for each one of us; and lastly, His dying on the spot where lie the ashes of our father Adam should show us how His death destroys the empire of death, and gives us a right to life eternal.

Affections and Resolutions.

Point II: "And they gave Him wine to drink, mingled with gall, and when He had tasted He would not drink."

Consideration: It was the custom to give those condemned to death wine mixed with myrrh, either to strengthen them or to partly destroy their sense of feeling; but by a refinement of cruelty, gall was mixed with the wine given to our Lord. He took it; He tasted it; but, as the Gospel says, He would not drink.

Application: Why did our Lord thus taste this bitter draught, and then refuse to drink it? He tasted it – 1st, to suffer in the sense of taste, which His executioners had not been able to touch; 2ndly, to expiate our intemperance and sensuality in the use of food; 3rdly, to encourage us, after His example, to mortify our taste, or at least to resist our appetites, and never to exceed the bounds of religious temperance. On the other hand, He would not drink, because He would not in any degree assuage the sufferings which it was His will to endure to their utmost extent.

Affections and Resolutions.

Point III: Jesus stripped of His garments

Consideration: The Roman law ordered that those condemned

to be crucified should be stripped of their garments, thus adding shame to their other torments. Therefore Jesus, having tasted the bitter draught His executioners gave Him, was despoiled of His garments, which, by the weight of the cross, and His frequent falls, adhered so closely to His bleeding form that they could not be removed without opening His wounds, and causing Him fresh agony.

Application: Why did our Lord will to suffer this fresh martyrdom of confusion and pain? To teach us, and to encourage us by His example, never to withdraw from any sort of shame, suffering or privation in His service should we even become a laughing-stock to the world, and be deprived of everything, like the dead man carried out to burial. This renunciation must be absolute fact, or at least in affection. Jesus Christ requires it. He says, "If any man will follow Me, let him deny himself, and take up his cross and follow Me." What should we think of the religious who dreads the ridicule with which the world treats his habit or his poverty, or of the religious who tries to please the world by studying his appearance, as far as the little he possesses allows him?

Colloquy with our Blessed Lady.

Fifth Week of Lent, Wednesday: Jesus crucified between two Thieves

1st prelude: Behold Jesus lying on the cross, and the executioners who nail Him to it by the strokes of their hammers.

2nd prelude: Ask for lively sentiments of compunction and compassion.

Point I: "And it was the third hour, and they crucified Him."

Consideration: Jesus is come to Calvary, to the appointed place and at the hour appointed from all eternity for the consummation of His sacrifice. Let us go there in spirit: what do we see? – the Roman soldiers dispersing the crowd, Jesus standing by the huge wooden cross, the executioners each holding a nail and hammer. Our Lord is commanded to place Himself upon His cruel couch. He obeys without a reply; He lies down upon the cross; He stretches Himself upon it. An executioner asks for His right hand; He gives it; it is seized, and fastened to the cross by an enormous nail, with redoubled blows which re-echo around. But Jesus utters neither a cry of sorrow nor a murmur of complaint.

Application: He was crucified for us; for me, for my sins, and for the love of me, Jesus endured these fearful torments, the very thought of which makes nature shudder. The evangelist contents himself with the simple words, "They crucified Him." Can I contemplate Him nailed to this cross without emotion, without being touched to the heart, and affected to tears of love and compassion?

Affections and Resolutions.

Point II: Jesus is raised up on the cross

Consideration: What a terrible punishment to be stretched upon the cross, with hands and feet nailed and in this manner to wait for death! But this punishment did not suffice the love of Jesus; He suffered tenfold, a hundredfold more. The cross upon which He was nailed was raised, and firmly fixed in the rock. He remained hanging to it by the whole weight of His body, supported only by the nails, dying by inches. We can scarcely bear to think of such suffering, in which a minute must seem a day, but which Jesus bore for three mortal hours; and this for me and for love of me!

Application: O Christian, O religious, whoever you are, here pause and ask yourself – 1st, What are and what can my sufferings ever be, compared to the sufferings of my King and my Savior? 2ndly, What have I done till now for this Savior, who has loved me to such an excess, and what can I do now for the love of Him?

Affections and Resolutions.

Point III: "And with Him they crucify two thieves, the one on His right hand, and the other on His left; and the Scripture was fulfilled, which saith, And with the wicked He was reputed."

Consideration: Jesus, as the King of Martyrs, not only willed His sufferings to be incomparably great, but also His humiliations: so it was that He to whom is due all glory in heaven and earth made Himself like the worst of criminals, and even by the good was accounted an impostor; thus was the height of infamy joined to the height of suffering.

Application: Let us kneel in spirit before Jesus suspended in ignominy on the cross, reconciling heaven and earth, between which He hangs; blotting out by His blood, as the Apostle expresses it, the handwriting of the decree that was against us. Let us repeat, in the words that the Church employs at each Station in the Way of the Cross, "We adore Thee and we bless Thee, O Christ, because by Thy holy cross Thou hast redeemed the world." Colloquy with Jesus on the cross, or with His Mother standing beneath it.

Fifth Week of Lent, Thursday: First Word of Jesus on the Cross

1st prelude: Imagine you see Jesus raised on the cross, and hear Him say, "Father, forgive them; for they know not what they do."
2nd prelude: Ask for a spirit of gentleness and charity.

Point I: "Father, forgive them; for they know not what they do."

Consideration: The blood of Abel cried to heaven for vengeance, and the vengeance of heaven fell without delay upon Cain and his descendants. The crime of the Jews who nailed their Messiah, the Holy of holies, on the cross was infinitely greater. Yet at His last hour, instead of asking His Heavenly Father to manifest His justice by confounding His enemies and establishing His innocence, the first words of Jesus were, "Father, forgive them; for they know not what they do." What an example of gentleness and charity!

Application: Jesus is your model, whom you have promised so often to follow, specially in His gentleness and charity. But examine how you have done so. Jesus, innocence itself, so horribly treated, prays for His murderers, and even excuses their guilt, whilst *you*, perhaps, nourish feelings of bitterness and revenge against those who have wronged you but very slightly, over-estimating their offence, or attributing to them intentions which they may never have entertained.

Affections and Resolutions.

Point II: "And Pilate wrote a title also, and he put in upon the cross; and the writing was, Jesus of Nazareth, the King of the Jews, in letters of Greek, Latin and Hebrew."

Consideration: Pilate's motive in placing this apparently honourable inscription above the cross, in the three then best-known languages, was to mortify the Jews, who had compelled him to condemn our Lord unjustly; but at the same time he unconsciously fulfilled the words of Jesus, "He that humbleth himself shall be exalted," as well as the prophecy that the Gospel should be made known to Hebrews, Greeks and Romans, and from them should spread into every country, and be proclaimed in every tongue.

Application: Remark here the admirable providence of God, and how He obtains His ends in spite, and even by means, of the perversity of man; this we see every day, and therefore why shouldst thou, O devout soul, be so fearful and mistrustful in His service? Let us repose upon His providence, and no one can harm us; in the words of the Apostle, we know that "to them that love God all things work together unto good."

Affections and Resolutions.

Point III: "Then the chief priests of the Jews said to Pilate, Write not, The King of the Jews; but that He said, I am the King of the Jews. Pilate answered, What I have written, I have written."

Consideration: The inscription Pilate ordered to be placed above the cross wounded the pride of the chief priests, who came in a body to the governor requesting him to change it; but Pilate, so weak and timid before, was firm now, and only replied to their imperious demand, "What I have written, I have written."

Application: Here Pilate, although a heathen, gives us a lesson; he teaches us not to change our resolutions lightly, particularly those we have formed in retreats, but to adhere to them at whatever cost. So that under any pretext whatever – and pretexts are rarely ever wanting to those tempted to abandon their resolutions – let us stand firm and say, "What I have written under the inspiration of grace, when God spoke to my heart, is to remain unaltered, and I will not depart from it."

Colloquy with the Almighty Father beholding His crucified Son.

Fifth Week of Lent, Friday: Feast of the Dolours of Our Blessed Lady

1st prelude: Imagine you see our Blessed Lady standing at the foot of the cross.

2nd prelude: Ask the grace of tender compassion towards our dearest Mother in her bitter sorrow, and to understand how much, in what manner, and wherefore she suffered.

Point I: How much she suffers

Consideration: Let us enter into the spirit of the Church this day, and fix, as she does, our thoughts exclusively upon Our Lady's sufferings; she suffers on our account and for us. To understand in some measure how much she suffers, we must conceive the idea of a mother, the tenderest of mothers, who loves nothing so much as her son, her only son; this Son, the greatest of the children of men, she is force to see die in the prime of His days, by no natural death, but by the hand of the executioner, surrounded by an angry mob, nailed living on a cross, after having been covered with wounds from head to foot, crowned with thorns; to behold Him struggling with death for three long hours, without being able in the least to assuage His agony! Did ever mother suffer such a martyrdom? But what passes our comprehension is, that we may truly say that she endured this martyrdom for thirty-three years, knowing, to the smallest particular, all that awaited her from the hour of Simeon's prophecy. Well does the Church style her Queen of Martyrs, and apply to her the words of the Psalmist, "My life is wasted with grief, and my years in sighs."

Application: Let us think of this when thus gazing on the picture of our Lady at the foot of the cross, and we shall find our hearts filled with love, compassion, and childlike devotion; we shall account our sufferings but trifles, and gain courage to bear or surmount them.

Affections and Resolutions.

Point II: In what manner she suffers

Consideration: How did our Lady endure so many and so great sufferings? 1st, with perfect resignation and without a word of complaint; 2ndly, with admirable conformity to all the designs of Almighty God in the cruel and ignominious death of her Son; 3rdly, with generosity apparently impossible in a mother; 4thly, with constancy beyond heroism, standing beneath the cross till Jesus breathed His last sigh; lastly, with invincible sweetness and charity, joining her Divine Son in praying for His murderers.

Application: Mary is here the Queen and pattern of martyrs; see how far you are conformed to her example in the slight sufferings you endure.

Affections and Resolutions.

Point III: Wherefore she suffers

Consideration: Wherefore did God will that our Lady's whole

life should be passed in suffering, who had nothing to expiate like the rest of mankind? The Fathers of the Church reply that, to merit the title of Queen of Saints, she was obliged to surpass them all in her resemblance to her Son, so pre-eminently the Man of Sorrows; in love to God, which is proved by suffering for Him; in merit, which is gained also by suffering; and in sacrifice, for the greater glory of God and the salvation of souls.

Application: If God, wishing to bestow a mark of His peculiar love upon our Lady, could not find anything more precious than the cross, ought we to consider ourselves miserable when He gives us a share in it also, even should He decree that we carry it to the end? If so, He only treats us as He did her whom He loved best; let that thought console us, and let us carry our cross willingly after our dearest Mother.

Colloquy with our Blessed Lady.

Fifth Week of Lent, Saturday: The penitent Thief – the Second Word on the Cross

1st prelude: Behold Jesus crucified between two thieves.
2nd prelude: Ask for great docility in following the inspirations of grace.

Point I: "And one of those robbers who were hanged blasphemed Him saying, If Thou be Christ, save Thyself and us. But the other, answering, rebuked him, saying, Neither dost thou fear God, seeing thou are under the same condemnation?"

Consideration: The striking contrast between the two thieves offers at once a mystery and a lesson. The mystery is this, that both these thieves witness the superhuman charity and patience of our Lord, who hangs between them praying and suffering for both of them alike; but nevertheless, the one remains an impious blasphemer to the end, and dies impenitent; whilst the other, docile to the first movements of grace, opens his eyes and heart to the truth, and dies the death of the predestinate, baptized, as Saint Cyprian says, in his own blood. The Church calls upon the faithful to venerate him, under the name of Dismas, on the 25th of March.

Application: The practical lesson to be derived from the above mystery is, that God gives each man grace sufficient for his salvation, although He gives more largely to some than to others.

But He also requires His creatures' co-operation; thus, however great the graces bestowed on the good thief, he would not have been either converted or saved without his correspondence with these graces. And it follows that we religious, who have received extraordinary graces, must not look upon our salvation as therefore secure. What alone can give us a moral assurance of salvation is a faithful correspondence to each successively given grace.

Affections and Resolutions.

Point II: "And we indeed [suffer] justly, for we receive the due reward of our evil deeds; but this man hath done no evil. And he said to Jesus, Lord, remember me when Thou shalt come into Thy kingdom."

Consideration: We go straight to God, and ensure not only His forgiveness, but draw down upon us still greater favours, when, like the penitent thief, we acknowledge our misdeeds and accept our punishment with contrition and resignation, joining humble and confident prayer to our submissive confession. The good confession of the divinity of our Lord, which was then, as it were, annihilated, made by the penitent thief, shows us that, besides his justification, he received the gift of faith in an eminent degree.

Application: We are all weak; you have often considerable faults of which your conscience accuses you. Do you imitate the penitent thief? Do you not try to deceive yourself respecting them, or to hide or deny them before others? And with what sort of grace do you receive the correction they require?

Affections and Resolutions.

Point III: "And Jesus said to him, Amen, I say to thee, This day thou shalt be with Me in paradise."

Consideration: What consoling and encouraging words for the penitent thief in his last hour, surrounded by everything that renders death terrible and induces despair – agonizing pain, the remembrance of the past, the dread of the future! How great the power of one single fervent prayer! Here it changes a hardened sinner into a saint. He only asked our Lord to remember him; and our Lord gave him, with the remission of all his sins, the promise of a happy death, to be followed by bliss eternal.

Application: How wrong, therefore, to distrust the love of God, or the efficacy of prayer! However guilty or miserable we may be, or have been, prayer contains a virtue in itself, apart from the holiness of the man who offers it; and the more wretched in our case, the more we should have confidence in its being answered. "That is very encouraging; but sometimes," you say, "I feel as if I could not pray in the least"; then make use only of the prayer of the penitent thief, "Lord, remember me," so poor, so miserable; never shall we do so in vain.

Colloquy with our merciful Lord.

Sixth Week of Lent, Palm Sunday: Jesus on the Cross, abandoned, stripped and blasphemed

In this meditation we have tried to unite two subjects without interrupting our consideration of the Passion – Jesus dying on the cross, and His triumphal entry into Jerusalem six days before.

1st prelude: Behold Jesus, so short a time since triumphantly received, abandoned and blasphemed.

2nd prelude: Ask for the grace to detach yourself from the world, that you may attach yourself to God alone.

Point I: "And all His acquaintance… stood afar off, beholding these things."

Consideration: All the ceremonies of Palm Sunday, the blessing of the palms, the procession, the chanted hosannas, are instituted by the Church to recall the triumphal entry of Christ into Jerusalem on that day. What a contrast, at only six days' interval, between the honors then rendered to our Lord and the affronts and blasphemies that greet Him now! Then, a great multitude that was come to the festival, when they heard that Jesus was coming to Jerusalem took branches of palm-trees and went forth to meet Him; and now He is condemned to death, He is left alone, abandoned by His friends, who stand afar off beholding him!

Application: Let us learn from this not to count upon the help or consolation of our friends, particularly in times of misfortune or persecution; and to bear the want of sympathy even from our brethren and superiors, content to have God alone for the witness of our sorrows and sufferings. Happy is the religious who has early learnt this lesson; he is never heard to complain of neglect or want of consideration on the part of others. Jesus abandoned on the cross is sufficient for him.

Affections and Resolutions.

Point II: "The soldiers, therefore, when they had crucified Him, took His garments, and they made four parts, to every soldier a part; and also His coat."

Consideration: Six days before, the inhabitants of Jerusalem, not satisfied with welcoming our Lord in triumphal procession, spread their garment in His way, and strewed them before Him. And how do they treat Him now? Thy strip Him of His garments and divide them before His eyes into four parts!

Application: Jesus, thus deprived of all things, even of those considered absolutely necessary to existence, which worldly men seek so eagerly, often to their soul's cost. Jesus suffers Himself to be thus despoiled with perfect calmness; for He is detached from everything below. Let us thank Him for having called us to the profession of holy poverty, the source of our peace, security, and happiness.

Affections and Resolutions.

Point III: "And they that passed by blasphemed Him, wagging their heads, and saying... If thou be the Son of God, come down from the cross. In like manner also the chief priests, with the scribes and ancients."

Consideration: Another contrast, not less striking than the preceding ones. Six days ago the multitude that formed the procession from Bethphage to Jerusalem were crying with one voice, "Hosanna to the Son of David! Blessed is He who cometh in the name of the Lord, hosanna in the highest!" And now this same multitude, after having denied the Messiah they so lately had received in triumph, mock and blaspheme Him even in the very agonies of death!

Application: Today they cry Hosanna, they reverence and applaud Him; tomorrow it is, Crucify Him! And He is forgotten, disdained, and despised. Such is the history of earthly greatness; what folly, therefore, if in the exercise of your sacred ministry, or in any other work, you seek for notice, fame or applause! In doing so, not only will you lose all merit in the sight of God, but you will lose likewise the esteem of men, who detest vanity, particularly in a religious.

Colloquy with our Blessed Lady.

Sixth Week of Lent, Monday: Motives for Penance drawn from the Thought of Hell

1st prelude: Imagine a lost soul asking for an hour in which to do penance.
2nd prelude: Ask for the grace to do penance, moved by the consideration of eternal reprobation.

Point I: We have deserved hell

Consideration: I have merited hell – first motive. Adam, by his disobedience, drew down upon himself the sentence of everlasting condemnation. God, it is true, gave him certain hope of escaping it when He foretold the advent of a Redeemer; but on the condition that he should do penance all the days of his life. "In the sweat of thy face shalt thou eat bread", was the command. With what gratitude did Adam receive this gracious commutation of his punishment, long and severe as it was! So in modern days, criminals condemned to death have sometimes their penalty altered to servitude for life.

Application: If you have committed one mortal sin, you ought to say to yourself, "I have merited hell, as did also our first father Adam; and if I am to escape, it is also on the condition of leading a life of penance." Thus the Council of Trent, speaking in general terms, says: "All the life of a Christian should be a life of penance." How much more true is this, if you have sinned yourself, even though it be but once! Besides, if you go down to hell in spirit, and behold the punishments which the lost endure, and which last to all eternity, suffering in this life will seem light, and you will say, with Saint Augustine, "Here below, O Lord, burn, cut, and spare me not, so long as Thou sparest me in eternity!"

Affections and Resolutions.

Point I: The fear of hell

Consideration: Hell threatens me – second motive. The words of our Lord are explicit: "Except you do penance, you shall all likewise perish." How is this? Because pride and concupiscence, which since the Fall have infected our mind and heart, rule our actions, and will infallibly lead us into every species of sin and disorder, without the practice of constant penance and mortifications. The history of religious orders proves this.

Humiliation is the penance of the intellect; and how many, in rejecting it, have become apostates before God, if not before man! Mortification is the penance of the heart; and how many, unwilling to endure it, who have begun in the spirit, afterwards indulge the desires of the flesh, as the Apostle Saint Paul tells us! Think of those amongst them whom you have known. Think of the dangers that you yourself have run.

Application: The Church does well to exhort us tenderly to penance from the first Sunday in Lent. Let us embrace it willingly. This is Holy Week. We should strive, therefore, to do more than we have yet done.

Affections and Resolutions.

Point III: Others are lost

Consideration: Beings more perfect than myself are eternally lost – third motive. The angels have fallen in heaven, and from heaven they were cast into hell. Faith assures us so. They had no time for penance; immediate punishment followed their offence – another and no less terrible truth. The renegade Judas had been called and formed by our Lord Himself to the practice of religious perfection and the apostolic functions. He spent three years with Jesus, and there secretly fostering an evil inclination, he at length became capable of conceiving and executing the most detestable of crimes, which led him to despair, suicide and hell.

Application: "Wherefore, he that thinketh himself to stand, let him take heed, lest he fall"; repressing every evil inclination by continual mortification. Such is the practical conclusion of the Apostle Saint Paul: "But I chastise my body and bring it into subjection, lest perhaps when I have preached to others, I myself should become a castaway." Let us reason as did Saint Paul; let us act as he did, and we shall be saved with him.

Colloquy with our merciful Lord.

Sixth Week of Lent, Tuesday: Third Word on the Cross: "Behold thy Mother!"

1st prelude: Look at our Lady and Saint John at the foot of the cross.

2nd prelude: Ask for an increase of love for Jesus and Mary.

Point I: "Now there stood by the cross of Jesus His Mother."

Consideration: His Mother stood by the cross. Here we must pause and consider two admirable and apparently incompatible things: *our Lady's extraordinary grief,* and *her heroic courage*. It is difficult to conceive how she, the most loving of mothers, could behold her Son nailed alive to the cross, and suffering a three hours' agony, and remain standing beneath it. Many painters, it is true, have depicted her fainting and overwhelmed at its foot, but without any scriptural warrant. Saint John says explicitly *she stood*; and the Fathers agree that, standing thus, though, according to the prophecy of Simeon, her whole soul was pierced through as by a sword, she united herself to the sacrifice of her Divine Son.

Application: This supernatural strength was certainly the effect of a miracle of grace; but was no less also the fruit of her fidelity under all the trials which her faith and constancy had before suffered. God gives His graces in proportion to our correspondence with them. Let us also be generous and steadfast under our more ordinary trials, and we shall be strengthened under greater ones. Look back on your past life, and you will be convinced of this truth.

Affections and Resolutions.

Point II: "When Jesus therefore had seen His Mother and the disciple standing whom He loved, He saith to His Mother, Woman, behold thy son."

Consideration: Admire the calmness of Jesus, who forgets Himself in the midst of His agony, to recommend her to the care of His virgin disciple, who was henceforth to sustain and console her to the end of her life. "Woman, behold your son!" and at that moment He filled the heart of the beloved Saint John full to overflowing with the tenderest and most generous love that ever son felt for this admirable Mothers.

Application: Here our Lord teaches us to rise above our own sorrows, or rather to put them aside and forget ourselves for others. In giving His Mother merely the name of Woman, He would have us understand the less we act by the impulse of merely *natural* affection, the more we may rely upon His power to supply our needs and upon the protection of the Mother He has given us.

Affections and Resolutions.

Point III: "After that, He saith to the disciple, Son, behold thy Mother."

Consideration: Our Lord, having cared for His afflicted Mother, bethought Him of His beloved disciple, and wishing to give him a last mark of His love, places our Lady from henceforth under his protection. "Behold thy Mother" are the words with which He turns His dying eyes on Saint John; words full of consolation for us all, for the Fathers unanimously concur in believing that our Lord here used Saint John as the representative of all the faithful, and that from this moment He filled the heart of Mary with an overflowing love for mankind, so that her Maternity became, in a certain degree, as unlimited as the Divine Paternity itself.
Application and Colloquy of love, devotion and confidence in our Blessed Mother.

Sixth Week of Lent, Wednesday: Fourth and Fifth Words on the Cross

1st prelude: Imagine you see Jesus on the cross in the midst of the darkness that overspread the earth at noon-day.
2nd prelude: Ask for the grace of love and compunction.

Point I: "Now from the sixth hour there was darkness over the whole earth until the ninth hour."

Consideration: This miraculous darkness, mentioned even by contemporary pagan writers, lasted nearly three hours, all nature seeming to mourn its Maker. But the Jews remained unconvinced by this prodigy, as well as by the other extraordinary circumstances attendant on or subsequent to the death of the Messiah, although they had been distinctly foretold by their prophets.

Application: Saint Gregory the Great makes striking reflections upon this excessive blindness. "All the elements," he says, "gave their testimony to their Creator's advent: His birth was announced by a star; the sea became firm beneath his footsteps; the sun grew dark, the earth trembled, and the rocks were rent at His death, whilst those that were in Limbo returned once more to earth; yet still the Jews, harder than the very rocks, remained obstinate in their unbelief." Alas that there should be Christians whose eyes are blinded and their hearts hardened by sin no less deplorably than these Jews!
Affections and Resolutions.

Point II: "And about the ninth hour, Jesus cried with a loud voice, saying, Eli, Eli, lama sabacthani? That is, My God, My God, why hast Thou forsaken Me?"

Consideration: These are the words of King David, who in the 21st Psalm, nine centuries before, speaks of the Passion rather as an historian than a prophet. Our Lord used them at this solemn moment to afford the Jews another proof that He was the Messiah predicted by the prophets, and as a proof to us of succeeding generations that His divinity in no degree alleviated the bitterness of His agony.

Application: "My God, My God, why hast Thou forsaken Me?" This plaintive cry of a Son abandoned, it is true, but perfectly resigned to His Father's will, teaches us that His faithful followers must know how to support the withdrawal of sensible consolation, even when we are most earnestly promoting His glory; and also that in these moments of darkness we are not forbidden to cry aloud to our hidden Father, provided our will is entirely in conformity with His good pleasure.

Affections and Resolutions.

Point III: "Afterwards Jesus, knowing that all things were now accomplished, that the Scripture might be fulfilled, said, I thirst."

Consideration: Our Lord had told the Jews that all that had been uttered by the prophets respecting the Messiah should be exactly accomplished in Him. Thus King David had said in the 28th verse of the 68th Psalm, "In my thirst they gave me vinegar to drink." Our Lord accordingly said, "I thirst," knowing that the soldiers would offer him this bitter beverage. Immediately one of them took a sponge and filled it with vinegar, and put it on a reed and gave it to Him to drink.

Application: After having considered the perfect exactness and heroic fidelity with which our Lord carried out to His last sigh the smallest details regarding Himself of which the prophets had spoken, what ought you to think of your want of care in your daily duties, your infractions of the rule, on the pretext that they are matters of little moment?

Colloquy with our Lord on the cross.

Sixth Week of Lent, Holy Thursday: Sixth Word on the Cross

1st prelude: Imagine you behold your crucified Lord uttering the words, "It is consummated."
2nd prelude: Ask that you may be able to say the same words at the hour of your own death.

Point I: "When Jesus therefore had taken the vinegar, He said, It is consummated."

Consideration: Consider how truly our Lord at the end of His earthly life could say, "It is consummated; all that I owed to God My Father in reparation of His glory; all My labours, sufferings, and humiliations": to use His own words, "I have glorified Thee on the earth, I have finished the work which Thou gavest Me to do."

Application: How happy the religious who on his deathbed can say that he has faithfully accomplished all that God, his neighbor, and his holy vocation required of him; who since his entrance into religion has made God, the salvation of souls, and his own perfection his only aims; who has observed his rule, satisfied his superiors, and edified his community in spite of difficulties, sacrifices and humiliations! Truly can he also say, "It is consummated; I am happy, I die content and full of hope." Can you speak thus? Look back on the past; death is the echo of life. Affections and Resolutions.

Point II: "It is consummated."

Consideration: The send of these words is best completed by those which Jesus had uttered some hours before: "And now I am not in the world, and these (His disciples) are in the world, and I come to Thee." As if He would say, "All is consummated; nothing now keeps Me in the world; I leave it willingly." Those who have no attachment to the world do not regret leaving it. The Heart of Jesus had no attachment except for men: He had come into the world to save them, He loved them ardently, and now death is about to separate Him from them! How, then, could He leave them without regret? By a prodigy of ineffable love He instituted at the Last Supper the Sacrament of the Holy Eucharist, and after dying for us, deigns, by means of this same Sacrament, to remain perpetually with us.

Application: It was on Holy Thursday that the institution of this wonderful Sacrament took place; the Church solemnly celebrates it not only in her office, in the gospel and prayers of the Mass, but in her ceremonial, which is peculiar to this day. In cathedrals the bishop, in communities the abbot or superior, alone offers up the Holy Sacrifice; the other priests receiving communion from his hand, after the example of the Apostles communicated by Jesus Christ.

Affections and Resolutions.

Point III: "It is consummated."

Consideration: There is no doubt that our Lord, in giving utterance to these words, had in His mind the great act of the night before, when He celebrated the Pasch with His Apostles. He had substituted, in place of the sacrifices of the old law and of the Paschal law, the sacrifice of Himself, which will last to the end of time. He had said, "With desire have I desired to eat this Pasch with you."

Application: This, then, is the festival of the Christian Pasch; let us rejoice at commemorating it at the same time as the Apostles, and prepare ourselves with suitable dispositions, renewing our acts of faith, hope, confidence and desire. Colloquy with our loving Savior.

Sixth Week of Lent, Good Friday: Last Word on the Cross

1st prelude: Imagine you behold our Lord, and hear Him say: "Father, into Thy hands I commend My spirit."

2nd prelude: Ask for a holy and happy death.

Point I: "And Jesus, crying with a loud voice, said, Father, into Thy hands I commend My spirit."

Consideration: Let us carefully meditate, one by one, on these last words of our Lord, the same that the priest will use by our deathbed. "My Father"; what sweetness dwells in that word! how well fitted it is to soften the bitterness of death, and to give confidence in the last struggle! "Into Thy hands I commend my spirit." (Commend signifies rather, according to the Greek text, deposit, or place.) I commend or place my spirit into Thy hands, into the hands which created it, which gave it to me, for a time united to a mortal body, to glorify Thee on earth; now death separates it from its lifelong companion, till the moment of the resurrection, and till then I commend it into Thy fatherly hands.

Application: Try often to make use of this last word of our Lord, particularly before sleep, the likeness of death; that at the hour of death it may be in your heart, and so spring naturally to your lips. As you utter it, unite your thoughts and affections to those of Jesus Christ, who in commending His soul to His Father, as Saint Athanasius says, commended to God also the souls of all mankind.

Affections and Resolutions.

Point II: "And saying this, He gave up the ghost."

Consideration: Thus dies Jesus, our loving Savior, at the precise moment He willed to die, without suffering the agony He had previously endured in the Garden of Gethsemani. He dies abandoned and calumniated, but His death is followed by an immediate testimony to both His innocence and His divinity by the centurion at the foot of the cross exclaiming at the sight, "Indeed this was a just man; indeed this man was the Son of God!" Jesus is dead! But He has overcome death, and opened to us the gates of everlasting life. He is dead; but from His Heart, pierced by the lance, flows the life-giving Sacraments of His spouse the Church, which is to bring forth till the end of time an innumerable multitude of children throughout the world. He is dead, His body remains nailed to the cross; but His Soul enjoys the Beatific Vision, and has received the adoration of the inhabitants of limbo.

Application: O Body and Soul of Jesus, that have suffered so much for me, what can I do in return? I adore and bless you, and, recalling the words of the Apostle, that Christ died for all, that they also who live may not live to themselves, but unto Him who died for them, I will endeavor, O my Jesus, to die more and more to myself, to the world, and to all that displeases Thee.

Affections and Resolutions.

Point III: "And bowing His head, He gave up the ghost."

Consideration: Contemplate the inanimate Body of our loving Redeemer. Those eyes, that have shed so many tears of tenderness and compassion over sinners; that mouth, which never opened but to glorify God or to comfort man; those pierced hands, ever ready to aid and bless; those wounded feet, moving only by obedience, never weary of seeking His lost sheep. Oh, what glory in heaven will surround all those bodily powers used here below for the glory of God and the salvation of souls!

Colloquy with Jesus crucified.

Sixth Week of Lent, Holy Saturday: The Burial of Our Lord

1st prelude: Be present in spirit at the descent from the cross and the burial of Jesus.
2nd prelude: Ask for grace to pass this the last day of Lent holily.

Point I: "And after these things [an hour after the death of our Lord], Joseph of Arimathea (because he was a disciple of Jesus, but secretly, for fear of the Jews) besought Pilate that he might take away the Body of Jesus. And Pilate gave leave. He came therefore, and took away the Body of Jesus. And Nicodemus also came, he who at first came to Jesus by night, bringing a mixture of myrrh and aloes, about a hundred pounds weight. They took therefore the Body of Jesus, and bound it in linen cloths, with the spices, as the manner of the Jews is to bury. Now there way, in the place where He was crucified, a garden, and in the garden a sepulcher, wherein no man had been laid. There, therefore, because of the parasceve of the Jews, they laid Jesus, because the sepulcher was nigh at hand."

Consideration: Behold the mournful scene at the foot of the cross: the crowd and the soldiers are already gone, the three Marys and the Apostle Saint John are left alone; at length God sends two men to their help, two who before their conversion were weak and fearful, but whom grace has made bold and resolute; they mount the ladders, they remove the nails that pierce that sacred Body. Their hands unfasten Jesus and place Him in the arms of His Blessed Mother; it is they, too, who aid this most sorrowful Mother to bind His sacred Body in linen cloths, with spices, and who place it at last in the glorious sepulcher of which Isaias has spoken in prophecy.

Application: Consider, here, how God acted towards His well-beloved Son; He who was formerly humiliated and abandoned is now honored and cared for after death. So will God act towards us if we humbly and lovingly resign ourselves to His will in adversity.

Affections and Resolutions.

Point II: "And the next day, which followed the day of preparation, the chief priests and the Pharisees came together to Pilate, saying, Sir, we have remembered that that seducer said while He was yet alive, After three days I will rise again. Command, therefore, the sepulcher to be guarded until the third day, lest perhaps His disciples come and steal Him away, and say to the people, He is risen from the dead. So the last error shall be worse than the first. And Pilate said to them, You have a guard; go, guard it as you know. And they, departing, made the sepulcher sure, sealing the stone, and setting guards."

Consideration: Admire the providence of God in all these circumstances – in the new sepulcher, near where our Lord was crucified, hewn out of a rock, as well as the sealing of the stone and placing a guard; the precautions taken by His enemies making it impossible even to approach Him in His grave. Our Lord permitted it, to place the truth of His resurrection beyond dispute – a truth which is the basis of His Gospel.

Application: We believe in an ever-working Providence; far be it from us to look on events here below as chances or accidents; far from us that despondency which occasionally overpowers the most devoted servants of Our Lord at beholding the temporary triumphs of impiety. It was when the disciples of Jesus thought all was lost that their Master overcame the grave and confounded His enemies for ever. Far from us also that melancholy which the sight of death or a funeral sometimes produces; let us conquer it by the consoling thought of the resurrection, from which we shall pass, as did our Lord, from death unto life eternal.

Colloquy with Jesus in the sepulchre.

Easter Sunday: The Resurrection of our Lord

"This is the day which the Lord hath made; let us be glad and rejoice therein." (From the Gradual of the Mass for Easter Sunday.)

1st prelude: Behold Jesus coming out of the grave.

2nd prelude: Ask that the fruit of your meditation may be a heart filled with holy gladness. There are three great motives for this gladness.

Point I: Motives for rejoicing first with our Lord.

Consideration: "He is risen; He is not here!" Such was the greeting of the angel to the holy women who had come very early in the morning to visit the place where Jesus was laid. What joy must have overwhelmed their hearts at the words! What joy even now fills the hearts of the faithful when they hear them repeated in the Mass of this great day! He is risen! He, Jesus, our Father and our King, over whose sorrowful Passion we have been so lately mourning, "dieth no more, death hath no more dominion over Him." Conqueror over death and all His enemies, He rejoices in His glorified humanity, and all power is given unto Him in heaven and in earth, even in hell itself; therefore let us rejoice with Him and with His Church, who has this day thrown off her mourning garb, and changed her accents of lamentation for strains of gladness, mingled with the oft-repeated Alleluia. "He is not here, for He is risen, as He said, Alleluia, Alleluia!"

Application: Here let us renew the holy gladness which was to be the fruit of our meditation, and which is one of the elements of happiness and progress in the spiritual life. All seems easy to us when in such dispositions; labours and crosses become delightful; we may be said to run rather than to walk in the way of perfection; and, best of all, our actions become more agreeable to God and more meritorious for ourselves, for God loveth a cheerful giver. Look back on your past experiences of joy and sorrow, and you will see the truth of this.

Affections and Resolutions.

Point II: Motives for rejoicing secondly with our Blessed Lady

Consideration: No one doubts that our Lord first appeared to His Blessed Mother; but how can we form an idea of the joy that filled her heart at sight of this beloved Son, now as radiant and beautiful as He had been before disfigured by His agony and crucifixion?

Application: The sorrows and joys of a mother are the sorrows and joys of her children. Mary is our Mother; so let our joy this day be as deep as our previous sorrow, and in proportion to the childlike love we bear her. Let our joy go beyond this day, and produce in us all its holy and blissful effects.

Affections and Resolutions.

Point III: Motives for rejoicing for ourselves

Consideration: What ineffable joy springs from this thought alone – that the resurrection of our Lord is the type and the pledge of the resurrection of each one of us! This is no pious belief; it is an express article of faith; "knowing," as Saint Paul says, "that He who raised up Jesus will raise us up also with Jesus, and those who have slept through Jesus will God bring with Him." It is this that makes us cry out with the same Apostle, "O death, where is thy victory? O death, where is thy sting?"

Application: Let us deeply impress this thought on our minds, and we shall never suffer long from sadness; in all our tribulations of soul or body let us say, I believe in the resurrection of the body, and the life everlasting. If we suffer, we shall also reign with Him. Colloquy with Jesus risen.

Easter Monday: The wonderful Perfections of our Lord's glorified Body

1st prelude: The same as in the preceding meditation.
2nd prelude: Ask for grace to comprehend the perfections of our Lord's glorified Body, and to have our share in them with Him on the great day of the resurrection.

Point I: The immortality and impassibility of our Lord's Body

Consideration: As soon as our Lord's Soul was reunited to His Body, the latter received the property of impassibility. This Body, formerly subject to all human infirmities – cold, hunger, weariness, the pains and sorrows of death – became absolutely impassible and immortal: "Death shall have no more dominion over Him."

Application: How had Jesus, as man, merited such glorious gifts? By His death and sufferings, endured for His Father's glory and man's salvation. We shall receive the same gifts on the like conditions; therefore, why should we so greatly fear death? Let us sanctify our sufferings by accepting them, as well as death itself, with entire resignation to the will of our Heavenly Father, offering them up in expiation of our sins, and those of others, after the example of our Divine Lord. The more we suffer with Him, the larger our share in the wonderful perfections of His glorified Body. Happy the Christian, happy the religious, who bears this in mind! How great will be his courage, how perfect his submission under every affliction!

Affections and Resolutions.

Point II: The spirituality and agility of our Lord's glorified Body

Consideration: A *spiritual* body is one that has *spiritual* properties, such as the power of penetrating matter, of passing at a single act of will from one place to another, at whatever distance;

how, or in what way, we cannot comprehend, much less explain. Nevertheless, such were the properties of our Lord's glorified Body. He proved that He possessed them by appearing several times in the midst of the disciples, when the doors of the rooms in which they were gathered together were shut, and disappeared again without their being able to follow Him.

Application: Such, again, will be the perfection of the glorified bodies of the just after the resurrection; I shall one day partake of them. In the words of Saint Paul, "It is sown a natural body, it shall rise a spiritual body," provided that I endeavor to live a spiritual life. "If by the spirit you mortify the deeds of the flesh, you shall live," as the Apostle Saint Paul expresses it. Does my conscience testify that I have done this?

Affections and Resolutions.

Point III: The lucidity of our Lord's glorified Body

Consideration: Those that walk in the dark provide themselves with a light. For Jesus risen there is no more darkness. His glorified Body is its own light. The splendours of His divinity, flowing from His Soul to His Body, have made Him more radiant than the sun at noon-day. The Apostles had once before seen something of this glory, on the day of His transfiguration.

Application: If I share the resurrection of the just, such will also be the radiance of my body; the more brilliant in proportion to the mortifications to which it has been subjected, and the labours it has endured for the glory of God and the salvation of souls.

Colloquy with God the Father in thanksgiving for these perfections of our Lord's glorified Body.

Easter Tuesday: The Marks of the five Wounds in the glorified Body of our Lord

1st prelude: Bring before your mind these bright and radiant wounds of our Lord's glorified Body.

2nd prelude: Ask for grace to understand the mystery of His retaining them after His resurrection.

Point I: The wounds of Jesus titles of glory

Consideration: A prince returning in triumph to his kingdom is proud of the wounds he has received in battle; therefore we must not be surprised that our Lord chose to bear in His now glorified

Body the marks of the wound He received in His terrific combat against sin and death. There were, besides, other reasons for His choice. He wished to show us the esteem He has for suffering and infamy endured in the cause of God, and to encourage us to endure them likewise; for it is suffering and humiliation that bring us at length to glory and never-ending happiness.

Application: It was from contemplating the wounds and the humiliations of their Lord that the saints drew their generosity and contempt for the world; it enabled them to regard fame, honour, and pleasures as naught, to rejoice in bearing the livery of their Divine Master, in suffering as He did hardships, labor, and ignominy, stimulated rather by the desire of resembling Him than of acquiring merit by so doing. How do you imitate these faithful servants of Christ?

Affections and Resolutions.

Point II: The wounds of Jesus the refuge of the unfortunate

Consideration: Our Lord has retained these wounds also to remind us of what He has done for love of us, and to assure us of His never-failing protection. These wounds are even open to receive and shelter us; they are so many eloquent voices pleading for us before the heavenly throne. How can He who sits thereon refuse His beloved Son whatever He asks?

Application: We often complain of dryness in prayer, even in our visits to the Blessed Sacrament; of the little love, almost the indifference, we feel for the Person of our Lord; and of our powerlessness against our innumerable difficulties and temptations. And what is our remedy? Let us seek it in the wounds of Jesus; let us contemplate them; let us enter therein in spirit, and all our subjects of complaint will disappear. Saint Augustine says, "In every misery I have found no more efficacious remedy than the wounds of Jesus. Within them I rest in peace and safety."

Affections and Resolutions.

Point III: The wounds of Jesus a justification of Providence

Consideration: Our Lord has, besides, retained these wounds to confound the wicked at the last judgment, who have not profited by His Passion, as well as to rejoice the elect, who have corresponded with the designs of His wonderful and merciful Providence respecting them.

Application: We wish and we trust to be found among the

number of the elect. Our desire and our confidence will be well founded, if based upon an earnest endeavor to form within ourselves the likeness of our crucified God. Then with what joy shall we press our dying lips upon the five wounds of the crucifix! How shall we rejoice throughout all eternity!
Colloquy with Jesus showing His wounds.

Wednesday in Easter Week: Fruits of the Resurrection

1st prelude: Imagine you hear our Lord saying, "Have confidence; I have overcome the world."
2nd prelude: Ask for grace to share in the abundant fruits of the Resurrection.

Point I: The Resurrection the foundation-stone of Faith

Consideration: Our Lord made constant use of the miracle of His approaching resurrection during His ministry on earth to support the doctrines which He taught; and it was directed by Him also that all the precautions taken by the Jews only served to prove the stupendous fact more clearly. The Apostles, besides, perpetually brought forward the Resurrection as the basis of the faith they preached. "If Christ be not risen again," Saint Paul writes, "your faith is vain, for you are yet in your sins."

Application: How happy am I to possess a faith so clearly divine, and all the gifts and graces belonging to the religious state! Do I show my gratitude by my works as well as my words?
Affections and Resolutions.

Point II: The Resurrection of our Lord the pledge and assurance of our own

Consideration: My own resurrection to life eternal, to a life, if I only take care to secure it, of bliss eternal, is as certain as the resurrection of my Lord. In the words of infallible truth, "As in Adam all die, so also in Christ all shall be made alive." "Those who have slept with Jesus shall God bring with Him."

Application: What consolation there is in the thought that this body, which I watch over with such care, will one day be given back to me endowed with new and wonderful powers! It will be immortal, with an immensely increased capacity for enjoyment, drawn from the contemplation of the Infinite. Death viewed in such a light is no loss, but rather a gain to the Christian and fervent

religious, a source of the sweetest hope, and inexpressible comfort.
Affections and Resolutions.

Point III: The Resurrection our encouragement under labors and infirmities

Consideration: A man contemplates the falling to pieces of the house he lives in with the utmost sorrow; but if he learns that it is to be rebuilt more beautifully than before, his sorrow is changed into joy. Our body is the dwelling-place of the soul. It is not a very stable one, however; in spite of all our care, sooner or later it falls to pieces. It is a saddening thought, but we know that God has promised to raise it up again infinitely more beautiful, and that it can never again be destroyed. "If our earthly house of this habitation be dissolved," says Saint Paul, "we have a building of God, a house not made with hands, eternal in heaven" (2 Cor. v.1). "Our Lord Jesus Christ will reform the body of our lowness," made like to the body of His glory; "for this corruptible must put on incorruption, and this mortal must put on immortality."

Application: If we never lose sight of such thoughts, we shall not spare health, strength or any bodily faculty whatsoever, in the service of the sick, in the work of instruction, or in the severer labors of the priesthood; and should we fall under their weight, and die, still in the prime of life, we may say with Saint Paul, "to die is gain."
Colloquy with our Lord.

Thursday in Easter Week: The Resurrection – Type of the Spiritual Resurrection

1st prelude: Imagine you hear the Apostle Saint Paul saying "that as Christ is risen from the dead by the glory of the Father, so we also may walk in newness of life."
2nd prelude: Ask earnestly for the grace of a *true* and *outward spiritual* resurrection.

Point I: "The Lord is risen."

Consideration: The Lord is risen; He has left the grave; He has entered upon a new life more perfect than the first, and subject to none of its infirmities. So ought we at this holy season to rise from the grave of sin, imperfection, and tepidity, to a more perfect and fervent life, exempt, as far as possible, from our past defects.

Application: Examine yourself upon your sins, your habitual faults, the means you use to avoid them, and also those that you had best employ to begin resolutely upon a new life in conformity with the plan you laid down for yourself on entering religion.
Affections and Resolutions.

Point II: "The Lord is risen indeed."

Consideration: The Lord is risen *indeed*; not only in appearance, as Saul was raised up by Samuel; nor for a time only, as Lazarus was raised by our Lord; but in deed, and no more to die. "Christ rising from the dead, dieth now no more; death shall no more have dominion over Him."

Application: Such should also be our spiritual resurrection, a resurrection *indeed*; a real passage from a life more or less tepid to one of fervor, befitting our holy profession – to a life based upon the resolution to persevere in the grace of God, and to fall no more into our former state of faithlessness and langur, which, little by little, would lead us back into the sleep of death.
Affections and Resolutions.

Point III: "The Lord is risen indeed, and hath appeared to Simon."

Consideration: Our Lord put the fact of His resurrection beyond dispute not *once* only, but several times, during the forty days He remained on earth. He allowed them to touch Him, and ate with them.

Application: The third mark of our spiritual resurrection must be *exterior*. It must not be known only to God, but appear before men, our superiors, our community, our inferiors – before all with whom we come in contact. They must perceive the change in us, and rejoice at it: perhaps our former negligences and defects have annoyed or grieved them, perhaps even they have scandalized our neighbors; we must endeavor to edify them in proportion.
Colloquy with our risen Lord.

Friday in Easter Week: The Sepulchre of Jesus Christ become glorious

1st prelude: Bring before your mind the glories of the holy Sepulchre.
2nd prelude: Ask for grace to despise all that perishes in the grave.

Point I: Worldly glory ends with the tomb, where heavenly glory begins – the inheritance of our Lord and of His faithful followers.

Consideration: What is the portion of those men, seculars or religious, who made worldly glory the mainspring of all their actions? Nothing but the oblivion of the grave; and if their names be held in remembrance, "what do they gain," as Saint Augustine expresses it, "by being praised where they are not, whilst they are tormented where they are now?" How different was our Lord from these men! He sought the glory of His Father only throughout His whole life. He died the victim of love, blasphemed and despised, but the greater His humiliation, the greater His glory. His glory began in the tomb. "His sepulcher shall be glorious," said the prophet Isaias. He left it to be crowned with the eternal glory of heaven; and it has been ever since the object of honor and veneration of pilgrims from every part of the world.

Application: Thus also the faithful servants of our Lord will be glorified, who have, like their Master, trodden under foot the glories of the world, and sought in all the greater glory of God. Unknown and despised of men, their sepulcher will also be glorious in the great day of the resurrection; and they too will leave it to receive a crown of everlasting glory. We believe this, and yet do we not often cherish, more or less openly, a desire for worldly praise and esteem, even in the most sacred functions?

Affections and Resolutions.

Point II: The wealth and power of this world end with the grave, where the riches of heaven begin

Consideration: A great prince, feeling death drawing near, exclaimed: "Today I have treasures, palaces, and an army at my disposal; tomorrow what will be mine? Perhaps nought but the horrors of the tomb." Such are the thoughts that overwhelm the dying who have placed all their happiness in wealth and power; whilst our Lord, who passed His whole life in poverty and voluntary obedience, received in the tomb the fullness of life, the power of judging all men as their sovereign arbiter, and the empire of the universe.

Application: Thus also His faithful servants, who, after His example and for His love, have chosen poverty and self-renunciation, will be glorified. He assures us Himself that every one that hath left home, or brethren, or sisters, or fathers, or mothers, wife, or children, or lands, "for His name's sake," shall receive a hundred-fold, and shall possess life everlasting. Let us rejoice that we have listened to the divine voice and followed the evangelical counsels; but let us beware lest, after having generously abandoned all that was ours, perhaps great possessions, we do not attach ourselves to trifles.

Affections and Resolutions.

Point III: The joys and delights of the world end with the grave, where those of heaven begin

Consideration: How unhappy is the fate of the man of pleasure at the moment of death. He has ever before his eyes the awful thought that terrified and finally converted Saint Augustine: "A few moments of pleasure, and an eternity of torment." How different is the death-bed of the faithful disciple! He can say with his Lord, "It is consummated; the sacrifice that I made of worldly pleasures, and all that it has cost me, Thou hast turned, as the Psalmist expresses it, into joy, and hast compassed me with gladness"; and he can conclude with the Apostle, "I have fought a good fight; I have finished my course; I have kept the faith. As to the rest, there is laid up for me a crown of justice, which the Lord, the just judge, will render to me on that day."

Application: As long as we do not forget these truths, we shall count as nothing the sacrifice of every earthly enjoyment, secure of eternal enjoyment, *even in our bodies*, in proportion to our sacrifices.

Colloquy with Jesus glorified.

Saturday in Easter Week: Our Lady before and after the Resurrection

1st prelude: Bring before your mind the joy of our Lady at our Lord's first appearing to her.

2nd prelude: Ask for grace to bear sorrow, so as to merit a share in the joys of your blessed Mother.

Point I: Affliction of our Lady

Consideration: What greater grief can afflict a mother than to be violently parted from an only son? What must, then, have been the depth and extent of our Lady's grief during the desolate interval between the burial and the resurrection of our Lord! How long must the time have appeared to this most loving Mother, sighing for the Son so cruelly snatched away from her, and ardently longing once more to behold Him!

Application: Is it thus that I, an exile from the sensible presence of my Lord, sigh for the moment when I shall behold his glorified humanity, and be eternally united to Him in heaven? Alas, no; and why? Because I know and love Him so little; because I am so attached to earth and to creatures.

Affections and Resolutions.

Point II: Consolation of our Lady

Consideration: Imagine the joy of a mother who unexpectedly beholds the son she has believed dead, and for whom she has long wept, and you will have some faint idea of our Lady's joy when our Lord appeared to her after His glorious resurrection. Her joy was in proportion to her grief, and to the glory she was to share with her Son in heaven; and to her applies the prophecy of King David, "According to the multitude of my sorrows in my heart, Thy comforts have given joy to my soul."

Application: Here we find powerful motives for rejoicing in slights and crosses suffered for our Lord, for self-sacrifice and continual mortification. These things, it is true, are hard and bitter to nature; but the joys of the resurrection will enable us to bear them, and will make them sweet and easy. Let us remember the words of the Apostle, verified in our blessed Mother, "As you are partakers of the sufferings, so shall you be also of the consolation."

Affections and Resolutions.

Point III: Alternations of consolation and desolation experienced by our Lady

Consideration: We cannot doubt that our Lord who appeared so often to His Apostles, appeared still oftener to His Mother, always filling her heart with fresh joy by His presence. But these appearances were of short duration, leaving a desolate void in that loving heart. Thus, during the forty days between the Resurrection and the Ascension, our Lady experienced continual alterations of joy and sorrow, of consolation and desolation.

Application: After the same manner does our Lord treat His servants. Sometimes He overwhelms them with His consolation and the sensible sweetness of His presence; then He abandons them to themselves, leaving mind and heart alike dry. We, too, frequently experience these alternations of soul. Let us learn to

profit by them, to grow strong, and to advance in the service and love of God, according to the advice of all masters of the spiritual life. How far has our conduct been in conformity to such teaching? Have we anything to reform in this matter?
Colloquy with our Blessed Lady.

Low Sunday: The Holy Women at the Sepulchre

1st prelude: Imagine you see the holy women going to the Sepulchre, bringing the spices they had prepared.
2nd prelude: Ask for grace to grow in love, confidence and generosity.

Point I: Their departure for the sepulchre

Consideration: The burial and embalming had been hurried over on account of the Jewish Sabbath, which began on Friday at sunset: the holy women known as the three Marys – viz., Mary Magdalen, Mary the mother of James and Joseph, and Mary the Mother of James and Salome – hastened to the sepulcher with the earliest dawn on the first day of the week, that they might again embalm the Body of their beloved Master.

Application: Who can refrain from admiring the fervor and courage of these holy women, who left the town alone, whilst all was still darkness, climbing the hill of Calvary, and making their way straight to the sepulcher, regardless of the soldiers guarding it? What made them so fervent and courageous? It was their love. Oh, if you loved as they did, how much you would undertake and execute for the glory of God and the salvation of souls! How perseveringly and perfectly you would perform your spiritual duties! And what progress you would make! For love makes all things easy, and never thinks it has done enough.
Affections and Resolutions.

Point II: Their embarrassment on the way

Consideration: The stone which the chief priests and the Pharisees had placed at the door of the sepulcher, and sealed with their seal, must surely have presented itself as an insurmountable obstacle to the pious designs of the holy women. On their way they asked each other, "Who shall roll us back the stone from the door of the sepulcher?" but nevertheless they continued their journey, occupied only with the single idea of paying the last duties to their beloved Master.

Application: It may happen to you to meet with apparently insurmountable difficulties in the execution of commands, in pious undertakings, or in the practice of good resolutions; but do not yield to discouragement; imitate these holy women, and go on with a blind confidence, doing what you can, persuaded that God will supply the rest, if it is necessary for His glory or the good of His creatures. Do you act thus?

Affections and Resolutions.

Point III: Their arrival at the sepulcher

Consideration: "And looking, they saw the stone rolled back, for it was very great." God worked a miracle for these women who showed such persevering, ardent love. As they approached the sepulcher, an earthquake rolled back the stone that barred their entrance, and the soldiers on watch, struck with terror, "became as dead men."

Application: Thus does God often come to the help of those that trust in Him, contrary to all the laws of human wisdom, as Saint Paul says of Abraham, who against hope believed in hope. Certainly ordinary means ought not to be neglected; but confidence in the goodness and the power of God should rise above and often silence human wisdom. See how far you are imbued with such trust.

Colloquy with our risen Lord.

First Week after Easter, Monday: The Resurrection announced to the Holy Women by an Angel

1st prelude: Imagine the empty sepulcher, and the astonishment and joy of the holy women.

2nd prelude: Ask to share their holy joy and their love of Jesus.

Point I: The angel reassures the holy women

Consideration: The holy women, terrified by the earthquake, knew not what to do; but were reassured by the angel seated on the stone which he had rolled back from the door of the sepulcher. "Fear not you," said he to them; "for I know that you seek Jesus who was crucified." Remark, that the same angel who thus addresses the holy women had so alarmed the soldiers on guard that they had taken flight. Wherefore this difference in his conduct? Because the soldiers' and the holy women's presence at the sepulcher was due to very opposite reasons: perversity and unbelief had drawn thither the former, love and faith the latter. Remark, too, why the holy women are told not to fear. Because they sought Jesus crucified.

Application: Whenever you are attacked by fear or disturbed by trouble, go likewise to Jesus crucified; kneel for a few seconds before your crucifix, and you will speedily recover strength and peace of mind.

Affections and Resolutions.

Point II: The angel announces the Resurrection

Consideration: The angel not only reassures the holy women, but announces the mystery of the Resurrection. "Why seek you the living with the dead? He is not here, for His is risen, as He said. Come and see the place where the Lord was laid." Convincing proof! He is not here, He has left the grave. Saint Luke adds, "And going in, they found not the Body of the Lord Jesus."

Application: What would be your happiness, how great the joy of your superiors and your brethren, if, risen spiritually with Christ, you were indeed changed – if your words and your conduct proved that you had left behind, buried as it were in the tomb, your evil habits, your many imperfections! It depends upon yourself: you must join your efforts *constantly*, *perseveringly*, to the divine grace offered to you at this holy season with greater profusion than at any other.

Affections and Resolutions.

Point III: The angel commands the holy women to publish the Resurrection abroad

Consideration: "And going quickly, tell ye His disciples that He is risen." These were the words of the angel to his overjoyed hearers. See in them the loving kindness of our Lord. All His disciples had fled from Him in His Passion. After His death they had seemed to discredit the prediction of His resurrection by giving way to excessive grief, as if they thought His cause and their own were hopeless. But nevertheless our Lord hastens to console, to reassure, and to encourage them by the voice of His angel and the holy women, although they appeared to deserve neglect and punishment than such gracious favors. But Jesus only follows the loving-kindness of His Sacred Heart.

Application: Acknowledge that it is to the loving-kindness of the same Sacred Heart that you owe so many natural and supernatural graces, whilst you have, during perhaps many years, grieved this Divine Heart by your sins, and even since your conversion have loved it with so feeble and lukewarm a love. Colloquy with our Lord.

First Week after Easter, Tuesday: Jesus appears to Saint Mary Magdalen

1st prelude: Imagine Saint Mary Magdalen in contemplation before the sepulcher, and then our Lord's appearing suddenly to her.
2nd prelude: Ask for a share in her faith, her love, and her joy.

Point I: Saint Mary Magdalen stands alone at the sepulchre

Consideration: Whilst the two other Marys return home to spread abroad the joyful tidings of the Resurrection, Saint Mary Magdalene stands "at the sepulchre without, weeping." Love kept her there, rapt her beyond herself, and caused those tears; love for her Divine Master, the Beloved of her soul.

Application: Saint Mary Magdalene here offers us an example of a perfect contemplative. If we look into ourselves, shall we not find that we are very far from imitating it, despite all the advantages we possess in living free form the distractions and turmoil of the world? How comes this? The *Imitation* gives our answer: "Because there are few that know how to sequester themselves entirely from perishable creatures."
Affections and Resolutions.

Point II: Two angels appear to Saint Mary Magdalene

Consideration: Whilst Saint Mary Magdalene, lost in contemplation, remained with her eyes fixed upon the sepulchre, she saw "two angels in white sitting, one at the head, and one at the feet, where the Body of Jesus had been laid. They say to her, Woman, why weepest thou? She saith to them, Because they have taken away by Lord, and I know not where they have laid Him."

Application: The only cause of Saint Mary Magdalene's deep affliction was the loss of the sensible presence of Jesus. How happy should I be if this were the only, or at least the principal, cause of my sorrows – the loss of that sensible presence which once made me rejoice in my vocation, and find such peace and consolation in the practice of virtue amidst privations and difficulties!

Affections and Resolutions.

Point III: Jesus appears to Saint Mary Magdalene

Consideration: Jesus had been present invisibly whilst His faithful servant had been thus giving such touching proofs of her love and sorrow. He was pleased by them, and desired to reward her. "Whilst she had thus said, she turned herself back and saw Jesus standing, and she knew not that it was Jesus… She said to Him, Sir, if thou hast taken Him hence, tell me where thou hast laid Him, and I will take Him away. Jesus saith to her, Mary!" At that single word she recognized her Lord, and threw herself at His feet.

Application: What consoling lessons we may find in this apparition of our Lord! To whom did He appear? To a penitent sinner. How came she to merit so great a favor? 1st, by the generosity of her love; 2nd, by her share in the Passion; 3rd, by her ardent desire of seeing Jesus, and her perseverance in seeking Him. Let us also desire to see Jesus glorified in heaven, let us often tell Him that we love Him, and prove our love by our generosity in His service; and thus, whatever may have been our past faithlessness, we may be certain of a large share in His abundant favours.

Colloquy with our risen Lord.

First Week after Easter, Wednesday: Jesus appears to the two other Marys

1st prelude: The astonishment and joy of the two Marys.

2nd prelude: Ask for a share in our Lord's favors.

Point I: Mary the Mother of James, and Mary of Salome return to the city

Consideration: The angel had commanded the holy women to declare the Resurrection to the disciples, but they were not all three obliged to return together to the city. Mary Magdalene remained, as we have seen, by the sepulchre, and the two other Marys hastened towards Jerusalem, where the disciples were hiding themselves. "And they went out quickly from the sepulchre with fear and great joy, running to tell His disciples." They, too, were rewarded, for they were favored by our Lord's meeting them, as we shall see.

Application: From the difference between the conduct of Saint Mary Magdalene and the other Marys, we may learn that it is not from any action taken by itself that we acquire merit and reward, but from the motive and intention which accompany it. Suppose that, having some spare time at your disposal, you make a visit to the Blessed Sacrament; one of your companions performs instead an act of charity, or employs himself usefully: your merit and reward will be the same, if the same love of God was the motive of your different actions.

Affections and Resolutions.

Point II: Jesus appears to the holy women

Consideration: The prompt obedience of the two Marys was extraordinarily rewarded. As they hastened on their way, "behold, Jesus met them, saying, All hail! But they came up and took hold of His feet, and adored Him. Then Jesus said to them, Fear not. Go, tell My brethren that they go into Galilee; there they shall see Me."

Application: Admire our Lord's goodness to His loving and obedient servants, the tender sweetness of His words, "All hail," "Fear not," and again, "Tell My brethren." He calls them His brethren, though they had abandoned and even denied Him; thus showing His forgiveness and forgetfulness of their past guilt towards Him.

Affections and Resolutions.

Point III: The disciples do not believe the holy women

Consideration: The disciples, when they heard the tidings brought by the holy women, treated them, in the words of Saint Luke, "as idle tales; they believed them not." Yet our Lord had clearly predicted His death and His resurrection on the third day. Were the disciples, then, obstinate unbelievers? No; but their faith was, as it were, in bonds. They doubted practically rather than systematically.

Application: Have we not often been like them? We believe that God beholds us always, and in all places, yet how many things we do that displease Him greatly! We know the words of our Lord, "As long as you did it to one of these My least brethren, you did it to Me"; and we judge, grieve, and despise our brethren. We are

practical, not systematic unbelievers, as the disciples were. Whither will such a course lead us? What should we think of it? Let us reflect and resolve.
Colloquy with Jesus.

First Week after Easter, Thursday: The Apostles Saint Peter and Saint John go to the Sepulchre

1st prelude: Imagine the Apostles on their way thither.
2nd prelude: Ask to profit by their example.

Point I: The Apostles set out

Consideration: The Apostles did not all receive the tidings of the holy women with the same incredulity. Saint Peter and Saint John half believed and half doubted, and resolved to assure themselves of the fact by personal observation. "Peter therefore went out and that other disciple, and they came to the sepulchre"; thus following the impulse of reason and conscience, without troubling themselves as to the words and actions of the rest.

Application: How happy should I be if my conduct had been always like theirs, making God, my conscience and the obligations of my holy state the rule of my life! Alas, have I not perhaps often adopted a course of speech and action at least irregular and imperfect, either from cowardice or human respect, and finding excuses in my tepidity? Examine yourself in these respects.
Affections and Resolutions.

Point II: As they approach the sepulchre their speed increases

Consideration: The Gospel says "they both ran together," so eager were they to reach the sepulchre, and to discover what had become of their beloved Master. It was their love that thus gave wings to their feet, and made them not walk but run on their way thither.

Application: Do you fulfill the duties that God and obedience enjoin upon you with the like promptness and energy? If your conscience bears witness in your favor, it is a proof of fervor, and rejoice; but if not, have you not reason to fear – particularly if age or infirmities warn you that you are approaching the term of your days – and endeavor to avoid deathbed regrets?
Affections and Resolutions.

Point III: Saint John allows Saint Peter to enter into the sepulchre before him

Consideration: Although Saint John, the younger and swifter of the two, came first to the sepulchre, he tells us himself that "he went not in," out of respect for Saint Peter, to whom our Lord had given primacy and jurisdiction. To their great surprise, all they found therein were "the linen cloth and the napkin that had been about His head."

Application: Saint Peter, it is true, had sinned grievously by his threefold denial of his Lord; yet Saint John did not fail to show him the honor and respect which were his due as his superior. This should teach us not to look at the errors and imperfections of superiors, but to consider them as the representatives of God, bearing in mind our Lord's words, "He that heareth you, heareth Me; and he that despiseth you, despiseth Me." Have my thoughts, words and actions been in conformity to this doctrine? This is a most important question.

Colloquy with our risen Lord.

First Week after Easter, Friday: Our Lord appears to Saint Peter

1st prelude: Imagine the Apostle when he first beholds his Divine Master.

2nd prelude: Ask for a share in the love and devotion with which he was filled.

Point I: Reflection of Saint Peter

Consideration: While Saint John returned to the city as swiftly as he had come, to tell all he had seen, Saint Peter followed him slowly, "reasoning" with himself "of all these things that had happened"; fear and hope, joy and sorrow, love and contrition, contending for mastery within his breast.

Application: What an example for you! Often you are alone, either working, or travelling from one place to another in town or country. Oh then, like Saint Peter, occupy yourself with some mystery of faith, or go over your morning meditation, thereby preparing your heart and mind, in a favorable manner, for the reception of divine grace. What a powerful motive to animate you! What efforts have you already made to familiarize yourself with this practice, and with what success? Affections and Resolutions.

Point II: Our Lord shows Himself to Saint Peter

Consideration: "And He was seen of Cephas." Saint Paul here leaves no doubt that Saint Peter – to whom Our Lord gave the name of Cephas, which, by interpretation, is Peter – was the first of the Apostles favored by the apparition of their Divine Master. Saint John, the beloved disciple, had stood beneath the cross and received the last sigh of His Redeemer; but it was not to him that our Lord first showed Himself, but to Peter, who had publicly denied Him. We may well believe that this appearance was accompanied by the most tender and reassuring words, designed to convince the penitent Apostle of his Lord's full forgiveness for the past.

Application: What conclusion should we draw from our Lord's behavior to Saint Peter? That God pardons as God – that is to say, *entirely*, without *reserve or remembrance of the past*. He loves and even caresses the sinner, as if he had never offended Him. "For the gifts of God are without repentance," as Saint Paul says.

Affections and Resolutions.

Point III: Peter confirms his brethren in the faith

Consideration: No doubt our Lord's motive in thus first appearing to Saint Peter, who had denied Him, was, amongst others, to restore him in the opinion of the rest, and to preserve his authority amongst them as the chief of the Apostles. We see that Saint Peter's testimony was at once received by his brethren, when they affirmed, "The Lord is risen indeed and hath appeared to Simon"; and thus he fulfilled the mission confided to him by his Divine Master, "And thou, being once converted, strengthen thy brethren."

Application: Remark the goodness of the Lord to all of us and in everything. Let us praise and bless Him, and conform ourselves to His example. Thus, when it is our duty to find fault with anyone to whom respect is owing, let us be careful to bear his position in mind. Unless it is necessary to repair a public scandal, never reproach such an one before others. Do not point out his errors either in his absence, or even mention them in confidential discourse.

Colloquy with our Lord.

First Week after Easter, Saturday: Our Lord appears to the Disciples on their Way to Emmaus

1st prelude: Imagine you see our Lord walking with two disciples, unrecognized by them.

2nd prelude: Ask that you may ever walk in the presence of God.

Point I: The two disciples on their way to Emmaus

Consideration: Saint Luke tells us that, evening on the day of the Resurrection, two of the disciples were on their way to Emmaus, a little town at the distance of sixty furlongs from Jerusalem, where one of them had some property. No doubt they required some distraction after the sorrowful scenes through which they had so lately passed; but the Passion and death of their Master was still the only theme of their discourse on the journey thither.

Application: We are not forbidden to take relaxation at proper times, or to seek sympathy and assistance when wearied or sorrowful: these things are not even incompatible with a desire for perfection. But where do we seek our distractions and our consolations? Very often, perhaps, in long and frivolous conversation; in dissipation of spirit; in light reading; or, in what is more dangerous, the pleasures of sense. This is a grievous and lamentable error. True consolation is not to be found in creatures, apart from God. Have you not found it so more than once?

Affections and Resolutions.

Point II: Our Lord joins them without making Himself known

Consideration: "And it came to pass, that while they talked and reasoned with themselves, Jesus Himself also drawing near, went with them; but their eyes were held that they should not know Him." Why did our Lord deign to join them? To correct their errors, to give them instruction and consolation, and to strengthen them in the right way.

Application: Such should be likewise the aim of our conversation, even at recreation, with those with whom we live, as also with those whom we occasionally meet, at home or abroad. Charity and duty oblige us to try that they should be the better for our intercourse; or that, at least, they should bear away from it something good. Have we no negligence to reproach ourselves with on this point – habitual negligence, perhaps?

Affections and Resolutions.

Point III: Our Lord questions the disciples

Consideration: "And He said to them, What are these discourses that you hold with one another as you walk, and are sad?" Why did our Lord, who knew the innermost thoughts of men, thus question His disciples? His design, in thus drawing from their own lips the false and worldly ideas they entertained respecting the promised Messiah, was to make them see their errors more clearly, in order to ensure their correction.

Application: Let us learn from this how we can best correct the faults of others. We, too, should question them, drawing the avowal from their own mouths, and showing them the gravity and fatal consequences of the errors into which they have fallen. They will then be properly disposed to receive correction; it will be truly useful to them; and we shall have conferred a lasting and solid benefit upon them. Is this wise line of conduct yours, or have you not rather exasperated those whom it was your duty to reprove? Colloquy with Jesus risen.

Second Sunday after Easter: On the Gospel for the Day

1st prelude: Imagine our Lord saying, "I am the good Shepherd."
2nd prelude: Endeavor to learn the sentiments of His Sacred Heart, that you may conform your own thereto.

Point I: Jesus tells the Pharisees that He is the good Shepherd

Consideration: Our Lord uses this tender and touching figure to express the love His Sacred Heart bears us, and to draw to it the hearts of men. Imagine you behold a good shepherd surrounded by his sheep. What is his greatest anxiety? Is it not for the safety of his flock? He thinks of them night and day, and is ever on the watch lest any mischance should befall them. His love for them knows no bounds. If, despite his vigilance, a single sheep wanders from the fold, he gives himself no rest till he has found it and carried it home; should there be any sickness amongst the flock, he tends them unceasingly; he devotes himself altogether to them. In short, his delight is to be with them, and to lavish every sort of care upon them.

Application: Apply these considerations to Jesus, the Shepherd of our souls, and you will find that the ardent love and unceasing vigilance there described fill His Heart towards mankind, but in a

much more elevated and perfect degree. Has He not completely forgotten Himself for us? Did He not become poor to make us rich? Did He not deliver Himself up to death to give us life?
Affections and Resolutions.

Point II: "I know My sheep, and Mine know Me."

Consideration: What does our Lord wish us to understand by these words? He means to say that He reads the heart; that there are Christians, and even religious, who are good sheep in appearance only, and in the eyes of men; that there are others who are in reality good sheep, and known as such in the All-seeing Eye that cannot be deceived.

Application: Ponder these words, examine yourself upon them, ask yourself if you are one of the faithful flock known to our Lord. The good sheep seeks his master's company. Do you love to be with Jesus, and to visit Him often in the Blessed Sacrament? The sheep knows and follows his master's voice. Do you know and follow it likewise when He speaks through holy inspirations, or through your superiors and your rule? The good sheep is known by gentleness, simplicity, and openness. Are not you prone to envy, bitterness, and dissimulation? Answer these questions truly, and you will see what you ought to do.
Affections and Resolutions.

Point III: "And I lay down My life for My sheep."

Consideration: Our Lord tells us "that the hireling, whose own the sheep are not, seeth the wolf coming, and leaveth the sheep and flieth." That is, he is faithful only as long as neither trouble nor sacrifice is demanded of him; whilst the good Shepherd, on the contrary, "giveth His life for the sheep."

Application: What a contrast between the conduct of the hireling and that of the good Shepherd! The hireling thinks of nothing but of his own interest and of himself; whilst the other acts from motives of supernatural love and charity. Our Lord uses the hireling as a type of the Pharisees, who noised their good actions abroad, "that they may be honored of men." He speaks of Himself under the figure of the good Shepherd, seeking only and in everything the glory of His Heavenly Father. Examine yourself, your intentions, the motives of your speech and actions, and make some generous resolutions for the future. Humbly ask that you may be faithful to them.

Colloquy with the good Shepherd of your soul.

Second Week after Easter, Monday: Jesus reproves and instructs the two Disciples

1st prelude: Imagine our Lord saying: "I am the good Shepherd."
2nd prelude: Ask that you may profit by the lessons our Lord gives His disciples.

Point I: Our Lord reproaches the disciples with their incredulity

Consideration: Our Lord, having drawn the avowal of their prejudices and their incredulity from the lips of the two disciples themselves, severely reproves them thus: "O foolish and slow of heart to believe in all things which the prophets have spoken." This was severe, but it was neither bitter nor in anger; the disciples received it with humility and without remark, for they felt that it was dictated by charity.

Application: Nothing is more fatal than the acquisition of bad habits; they little by little so become part of ourselves that we are unable, though we may wish, to shake them off. "Habit becomes second nature," said Saint Augustine. The religious need not fear this danger; vigilant and charitable superiors warn him of his omissions in time, and, if necessary, rebuke him energetically, so that he may see the evil of his way before it is too late, and correct himself. This is a great advantage; let us appreciate it as it deserves, and not imitate the sick man who gets angry with the surgeon, who, to cure him, is often obliged to cause him pain. Receive correction according to your rule, and, as the two disciples did, without reply, humbly or rather gratefully, with the sincere desire of amendment. Have we acted thus?

Affections and Resolutions.

Point II: Our Lord undeceives and instructs the disciples

Consideration: For correction to be of real service, it is necessary that the person blamed should feel that he is in the wrong, and for this he requires instruction. This was our Lord's mode of proceeding with the two disciples, showing them that the prophecies concerning the Messiah entirely contradict their prejudices, and establish His reign upon self-abnegation and humility. "Ought not Christ," He says, "to have suffered these things, and so to enter into His glory?"

Application: Thus we clearly see the only road which leads to eternal salvation pointed out by the Infallible Word Himself – the way of the cross. Should I think myself wiser, that I deserve to fare better than my Master; that I can gain an immortal crown without struggle or suffering, by leading a soft and idle life? Would not this be the height of absurdity?
Affections and Resolutions.

Point III: Jesus explains the meaning of the Scriptures to the two disciples

Consideration: "And beginning at Moses and the prophets, He expounded to them in all the Scriptures the things that were concerning Him." Wherefore did our Lord, who might have enlightened the minds of the two disciples by a single ray of His grace, enter into this long exposition of the prophetic writers? To teach us that we are to obtain and preserve the comprehension of divine things by diligently reading the Holy Scriptures and spiritual books.

Application: Is not your neglect of or carelessness in spiritual reading the cause of your want of faith and light, even in Holy Communion? Examine yourself; and if you feel the accusation just, resolve to correct yourself in so important a point of spiritual life.
Colloquy with the good and loving Shepherd of our souls.

Second Week after Easter, Tuesday: The Disciples constrain our Lord to remain with them, and share their Hospitality

1st prelude: Imagine the three travelers at the entrance of Emmaus.
2nd prelude: Ask our Lord to enter into our hearts as a guest, and to prepare them to receive Him fittingly.

Point I: Jesus made as though He would go farther

Consideration: "When they drew nigh to the town whither they were going, He made as though He would go farther." Nevertheless, our Lord fully intended to confer on these disciples the wonderful privilege of becoming their guest, and of making Himself known to them that very day; but He desired that this favor should be granted only at their pressing invitation.

Application: God willingly comes and enters into your soul,

takes up His dwelling there, and manifests His presence by heavenly graces and favors – "My delights are to be with the children of men" – but He will be sought for and invited with fervor and perseverance. Therefore, if it seems to you that He is far from you, and that your soul is void of those movements of grace His presence creates, ask yourself if you and your tepidity and reserve toward Him are not the cause.

Affections and Resolutions.

Point II: The disciples constrain our Lord to remain with them

Consideration: The disciples – whose hearts had burned within them in the way, during the discourse of the unknown pilgrim who had joined them – entreated Him not to leave them on their arrival at their destination. From entreaty they proceeded to argument: "Stay with us," they said, "because it is toward evening, and the day is now far spent," adding action to word, "they constrained Him," as the Gospel expresses it. "And He went in with them."

Application: The practical conclusion we may draw is this: that, if we wish to own our spiritual insensibility, and to draw our Lord and His sensible graces into our souls, we must use a sort of holy violence towards Him; redoubling, at certain seasons, our devout practices and mortifications, till, like the disciples, we constrain Him to yield to our desires. Like them, we may urge "that it is now towards evening," and "that the day (of our life) is now far spent" and tending, perhaps without our suspecting it, towards its decline.

Affections and Resolutions.

Point III: Jesus yields to their entreaties

Consideration: The entreaties of the disciples, and the gentle violence they used towards Him, pleased their Divine Lord. He yielded, and went in with them. They were full of joy, and did their best to show Him hospitality; yet still they knew not the dignity of their guest. What would they have done had they known?

Application: But I know the guest whom I receive into my heart at Holy Communion. How ought I to receive Him? How prepare for His reception? How have I done it hitherto? What ought I to do in future?

Colloquy with the disciples at Emmaus.

Second Week after Easter, Wednesday: Our Lord makes Himself known to the Disciples

1st prelude: Imagine our Lord seated at table with the two disciples, at the moment He makes Himself known.
2nd prelude: Beg for grace to share the happiness they enjoyed at that moment.

Point I: They knew their Lord in the breaking of bread

Consideration: "And it came to pass, whilst He was at the table with them, He took bread, and blessed and brake, and gave to them." The generality of commentators maintain that our Lord gave them His divine Self, under the appearance of bread, in the same manner as at the Last Supper. As soon as they had received, the Gospel adds, "their eyes were opened, and they knew Him." This was, as it ever is, the effect of the Holy Eucharist, to enlighten the understanding, and fill it with the knowledge of God and divine things.

Application: But if so, how comes it that I, having so often received this same Eucharist, am still so unenlightened, and have made so little progress in the knowledge of divine things and the ways of God? Doubtless because my dispositions have not been what they should be, and that my preparation or thanksgiving has been negligent.

Affections and Resolutions.

Point II: Our Lord vanishes out of their sight

Consideration: No sooner had the disciples known their Lord in the breaking of bread than He vanished out of their sight. Thus, to their sorrow, they lost His sensible presence, though they still felt its effects.

Application: It may be asked why our Lord vanished so speedily out of His disciples' sight without waiting for any act adoration or of gratitude from them. Ascetic writers reply, "Perhaps to teach us that, after having performed a good action, we ought to avoid rather than seek thanks and praise for it. Perhaps, again, to show us that we ought not to count upon the sweetness of the sensible presence of Jesus, which is only a transitory consolation granted us in this valley of tears." Are you not habitually too sensitive to slights from your fellows, and too little sensitive to the deprivation of divine favors?

Affections and Resolutions.

Point III: The disciples return in haste to Jerusalem

Consideration: After having received this wonderful favor, the two disciples, in the words of the Gospel, "rising up the same hour, went back to Jerusalem; and they found the eleven gathered together, and those that were with them." Why did they go with such speed, when it was growing late, and they were already fatigued by their journey? To glorify their Divine Master, to make known His resurrection to their brethren without delay, and repair the scandal they had given by refusing to believe the testimony of the holy women.

Application: Let us learn first to forget ourselves, and to spare no pains when the glory of God is concerned, and never to hesitate in promptly and generously repairing any scandal that we may have unfortunately given.

Colloquy with Jesus.

Second Week after Easter, Thursday: Jesus appears to the Apostles and Disciples gathered together

1st prelude: Picture the surprise and joy of the Apostles at the sight of Jesus.

2nd prelude: Ask for an increase of veneration, love and devotion for our Lord's Person.

Point I: Jesus appears in the midst of them when the doors were shut

Consideration: "Now it was late that same day, the first of the week, and the doors were shut where the disciples were gathered together, for fear of the Jews. Now whilst they were speaking of these things [the apparition at Emmaus], Jesus stood in the midst of them, and saith to them, Peace be to you; it is I; fear not." Remark the moment that the Lord appeared to the Apostles and disciples. It was when they were assembled together in recollection and retirement, strongly united by the ties of brotherly love, speaking together of Him, desiring to see Him, and on the guard against their enemies.

Application: If you wish God to communicate Himself to you, 1st, preserve peace and union with your brethren, do not withdraw yourself from the community; 2nd, be habitually recollected, only

occupied with the thought of God; 3rd, familiarize yourself with ejaculatory prayer, by which you ask Him to come to you; 4th, love to speak of the things of God; 5th, cherish a wholesome fear within yourself, and watch over your senses. Do you act thus?
Affections and Resolutions.

Point II: The disciples suppose they see a spirit

Consideration: Our Lord, seeing that the disciples supposed they saw a spirit, said to them, "Why are you troubled, and why do thoughts arise in your hearts? See My hands and feet, that it is I Myself; handle and see; for a spirit hath not flesh and bones as you see Me to have. And when He had said this, He showed them His hands and feet. The disciples, therefore, were glad when they saw the Lord," their fears and perplexities all vanishing at the sight of their Lord, giving place to feelings of complete joy and confidence.

Application: The effects of the presence of God within the soul and the certain marks of the good Spirit, are peace, calmness, and holy joy, which fill the heart, detach it from creatures, and make us properly appreciate the happiness of giving one's self to God by the three vows of religion. How blessed the religious whom his Lord thus deigns to visit!
Affections and Resolutions.

Point III: Our Lord eats before the disciples

Consideration: "But while they yet believed not, and wondered for joy, He said, Have you anything to eat? And they offered Him a piece of broiled fish and a honeycomb; and when He had eaten before them, taking the remains, He gave to them." Remark here the goodness of our Lord. He condescends to an action which seems unbefitting His glorified Body, that He may fully convince His followers of the truth of His resurrection – that glorious truth upon which that Gospel rests which they were called to preach to the whole world.

Application: Let us learn, from the example of our Lord, not to be disgusted with anything, however humiliating and repugnant to nature, that is demanded of us in the service of our neighbor, and above all in that of our brethren. Let us try, too, to inspire in them, as well as in ourselves, a lively faith in the Resurrection and in the ineffable joys of heaven, to sustain and encourage us under all the trials of this mortal life. Colloquy with our risen Lord.

Second Week after Easter, Friday: The Peace which our Lord gives His Disciples

1st prelude: Imagine our Lord standing in the midst of His Apostles and disciples.
2nd prelude: Ask for the preservation and increase of peace with God, your neighbor and yourself.

Point I: Our Lord says to His Apostles: "Peace be to you."

Consideration: These words, "Peace be to you," are the first addressed by our Lord to His Apostles when He showed Himself on the evening of His resurrection. Peace of the soul and of the heart; the only true happiness in this life. And He repeats them three times in two successive visits. Why three times? To make us understand that there are three sorts of peace He desires for us – peace with God, our neighbor, and ourselves.

Application: What value do we set upon that highest of heavenly gifts, peace with God? The answer is easy; this peace, we know, consists in the full and entire conformity of our will with that of God. His will is manifested to us through the commandments and counsels, the orders of our superiors, and our rule; all we need do, then, is to ask ourselves, How have I conformed my words, thoughts and actions to these standards? With what eagerness, exactness, love and generosity? Affections and Resolutions.

Point II: Our Lord again wishes His disciples peace

Consideration: "And after eight days, again His disciples were within, and Thomas with them. Jesus cometh, the doors being shut, and stood in the midst, and said, Peace be to you." Peace with God should always go hand-in-hand with peace with our neighbors, particularly with our brethren and fellow labourers. It is the fullness of this peace, based upon charity and fraternal union, that our Lord desired for His disciples. It was specially necessary to them, for the least division between them might have produced the failure of their mission, that mission which was to reunite all the nations of the earth by the ties of mutual faith, hope and charity.

Application: How happy those religious communities where peace, that fruit of brotherly love, reigns supreme! How unhappy those where it is not to be found! The two great conditions for preserving this peace are – 1st, to bear with the defects of others;

2nd, to give others nothing to bear from us. How do you observe these rules? Are peace and union ever disturbed by your fault, by disputes, rudeness, offended susceptibility?
Affections and Resolutions.

Point III: Jesus wishes peace to His disciples for the third time

Consideration: "He said, therefore, to them again, Peace be to you." If we would possess in its entire plenitude the peace our Lord desire for His disciples, we must acquire *peace with ourselves*. This interior peace consists in the witness of a good conscience, in the submission of the sense and passions to reason, and of reason to faith.

Application: This peace can never be perfectly acquired in this world, where the flesh and self-love will ever rebel against the spirit and the will of God. The peace of our souls during this life must be sought in a perpetual and resolute combat against all our unruly inclinations. "It is by resisting the passions, and not by serving them, that true peace of heart is to be found," truly says the *Imitation*.
Colloquy with Jesus, the Author of peace.

Second Week after Easter, Saturday: The Mission of the Apostles – Our Lord gives them the Holy Ghost and the Power of forgiving Sins

1st prelude: Imagine our Lord in the midst of the Apostles.
2nd prelude: Ask that you may have a proper appreciation of the gifts He bestows upon them.

Point I: The mission of the Apostles

Consideration: Our Lord, having again given His peace to the Apostles, said to them, "As the Father hath sent Me, I also send you"; that is to say, "For the same ends – to glorify God and to save man; and by the same means – prayer and preaching, in the midst of persecution, and every sort of obstacle; and with the assurance of the same reward: "and I dispose to you, as My Father has disposed to Me, a kingdom; that you may eat and drink at My table in My kingdom, and may sit upon thrones judging the twelve tribes of Israel." What a sublime mission – to be thus the ambassadors of Jesus Christ, and to co-operate with him in the salvation of the world.

Application: This mission is ours likewise, the end of our vocation being nothing else but the glory of God and the salvation of souls. Wherever we are sent, our Lord says to us, through our superiors, "As the Father hath sent Me, I also send you." Do we comprehend the dignity of our vocation?

Affections and Resolutions.

Point II: Our Lord bestows the Holy Ghost upon His Apostles

Consideration: The mission of the Apostles was as infinitely above their strength as ours is above our own. Therefore, as the Gospel says, "He breathed on them, and said the them, Receive ye the Holy Ghost"; thus communicating to them mysteriously that Holy Spirit which is in Him, and proceeds from Him and from the Father, that they might live henceforth as dead to the world, and by It alone – a spirit entirely opposed to the spirit of the world, to self-love, pride, cupidity, and ambition; a spirit of self-sacrifice, humility, mortification, poverty, and charity.

Application: Examine yourself carefully and see if you follow and are ruled by the spirit of the world or that of Jesus Christ, and in what degree.

Affections and Resolutions.

Point III: Our Lord gives His Apostles power to forgive sins

Consideration: Our Lord immediately continued, "Whose sins you shall forgive, they are forgiven them; and whose sins you shall retain, they are retained." By these words, our Lord bestowed upon the Apostles and their lawfully ordained successors the wonderful power of forgiving sins, without any restriction as to their number or heinousness. What goodness and liberality!

Application: Let us try to understand all the value of this power. What hope of salvation would remain to us without this second plank after shipwreck – as the Council of Trent styles the Sacrament of Penance – we who are so weak and so subject to temptation? How often have you thanked the Lord for instituting this Sacrament? Perhaps you have considered it a painful yoke, or even abused it sacrilegiously. What fruit have you drawn from it? What have been your dispositions and preparation for it?

Colloquy with our Divine Lord.

Third Sunday After Easter: On the Patronage of Saint Joseph (March 19)

1st prelude: Imagine you hear Jesus saying, "Go to Joseph."
2nd prelude: Ask for great confidence in Saint Joseph.

Point I: Saint Joseph patron and protector of Christian families

Consideration: Saint Joseph, as the legal husband of the Blessed Virgin, was the head of the Holy Family. He supported them by the labor of his hands; he governed and guided them in obedience to direction from on high, manifested to him by the ministry of angels; and the Evangelist gives us reason to suppose that Jesus and Mary obeyed him strictly. It is no wonder, then, that he is looked upon and invoked as the protector or those Christian families who desire to follow the laws and conform to the will of God.

Application: Every religious community is a family, and all the members of it look on the same superior as their father in God. They live under the same roof, follow the same rule, and call each other by the name of brethren. The feast of Saint Joseph's Patronage is, then, a special feast for our community. It reminds us of the gratitude and reverent devotion we owe to our holy and powerful protector. Let us recall to mind the trials, the difficulties, and the dangers of every kind that the order to which we belong has passed through for so many years – perhaps even for centuries – and we shall have no doubt that it is owing to the protection of Saint Joseph that it still subsists, full of life and vigor, while so many ruins are on every side of it.

Affections and Resolutions.

Point II: Saint Joseph the special protector and patron of Christian youth

Consideration: The Gospel tells us that the Child Jesus submitted to the direction of Saint Joseph, and obeyed him in everything as well as Mary. "And He was subject to them." We may say that he had charge of the education of Jesus as a child, youth and young man. He enjoyed the greatest happiness a father can have – seeing Him increase in age and in wisdom before God and before men. We cannot, therefore, doubt that Saint Joseph takes a particular interest in, and extends a special *protection* over, children and over those whose office it is to educate the young.

Application: Perhaps your employment is to labor in the education of children and young people in schools and colleges. It is a glorious work, but also a most difficult one. You want to succeed in it. *Ite ad Joseph*, go to Joseph, and you will obtain what you desire.
Colloquy with our holy and glorious patron.

Third Week after Easter, Monday: On the Gospel of the preceding Sunday

1st prelude: Imagine you hear Jesus saying these words: "Amen, amen, I say to you, that you shall lament and weep, but the world shall rejoice."
2nd prelude: Ask for a sovereign contempt for anything which does not lead to God.

Point I: Joy of the children of this world

Consideration: When our Lord was about the leave this world, He said to His disciples, "A little while, and you shall not see Me, because I go to the Father. You shall lament and weep, but the world shall rejoice." We see, then, how our Lord has portioned our the possessions of this life. To the good He gives crosses and tears; to the worldly, whom the Bible calls the "children of the world," He gives riches and material enjoyments. This is because, in His goodness and sovereign justice, He desires that the former should be purified by momentary sufferings from the smallest stains of sin; and that the others should have a passing reward for their naturally good actions, which have no merit in eternity, He gives to them the joys of this world. What a melancholy lot! They are apparently happy, but in reality very unfortunate; always tormented by the thirst for gaining something, and the fear of losing it; bending under the yoke of violent, disgraceful and insatiable passions; tormented by remorse of conscience, terrified at the thought of death and eternity.

Application: Have you always taken this view of worldly happiness? Have you not rather sometimes envied it, and said to yourself, "Why have I embraced such an austere kind of life? I could as easily have saved my soul while living in the world, enjoying my liberty, taking part in innocent pleasures." If this be the case, it is to be feared that your faith has been growing weak, that lukewarmness has darkened your understanding, and allowed ill-regulated affections to spring up in your heart. A religious who is in this case runs a great risk of losing the grace of his vocation, of falling into delusions, and of losing his soul

Affections and Resolutions.

Point II: Sorrow of the children of God

Consideration: The world shall rejoice, and you shall be made sorrowful. The privations, persecutions, and sufferings of every kind which Jesus Christ foretold to His Apostles as their portion in this world, make worldly men look on them as unfortunate beings, leading a most sorrowful life. They pity their fate because they do not know the hidden manna of the cross, because they have never tasted the consolations and unspeakable joys which God gives to those who suffer for love of Him. The Apostle experienced them when he exclaimed, "I exceedingly abound with joy in all our tribulation." And Saint Augustine knew them when he said to those who pitied him for his severe penances, "The tears that you see me shed are sweeter than all the pleasures that I ever tasted in the world."

Application: The words *tears* and *sorrow* were not meant by our Lord in the sense we commonly attach to them. They mean the exact opposite of the senseless laughter and sinful joys of the world. "There is," says Saint Paul, "a sorrow of the world, and a sorrow that is according to God." The latter affects the exterior alone – it is an apparent sorrow only; and in the depths of the soul there is joy, an unspeakable joy, a foretaste of the joys of heaven, of which the worldly cannot form an idea. "As sorrowful, yet always rejoicing."

Affections and Resolutions.

Point III: The eternity reserved for each of these classes

Consideration: "I will see you again, and your heart shall rejoice; and your joy no man shall take from you." These are the closing words of Sunday's Gospel; and they assure us that the privations, the tears, and the passing sorrow of the *children of God* will be succeeded by an eternity of joy and delight in heaven. Our Lord has told us this also in these words of encouragement: "Blessed are they that mourn, for they shall be comforted." But the *children of this world* will have a different lot; their passing joy will be changed into tears and eternal torments. "Woe to you that

now laugh," says Jesus Christ, "for you shall mourn and weep." What a contrast! A moment of joy, and eternal suffering; a moment of suffering, and an eternity of joy and bliss.
Colloquy with our Divine Lord.

Third Week after Easter, Tuesday: Unbelief of the Apostle Thomas

1st prelude: Imagine you see Thomas in his presumptuous isolation from his brethren.
2nd prelude: Beg the grace of a wise mistrust of self.

Point I: Isolation of the Apostle Thomas

Consideration: The appearance of Jesus to His Apostles the very day of His resurrection filled them with joy, consolation and courage. They became perfectly happy. One of them only – Thomas – had no part in this happiness, because he was separated from his brethren, and was absent from the place where they assembled together for prayer. "Now Thomas, one of the twelve, was not with them when Jesus came."

Application: The religious who isolates himself from his brethren, or without reason is absent from the community exercises, runs a risk of losing many graces and special favors, and even of falling into sin. Have you not had experience of this? Whether you have or not, it is a certain fact that when a religious without lawful reason does not rise at the same hour as the rest, does not join in meditation, examen, vocal prayer, and even in recreation with the community, he loses the special graces that God has bestowed on these exercises made in common. He is not where God wishes him to be.
Affections and Resolutions.

Point II: Obstinate unbelief of Thomas

Consideration: Besides the fault of separating himself from his companions, Thomas was guilty of the most obstinate unbelief. Though the Apostles, the disciples, the holy women and probably our Blessed Lady, assured him that their Divine Master was risen again – that they had seen Him, heard Him, touched Him with their hands – he would not receive their testimony. He obstinately refused to believe in the resurrection of Jesus Christ.

Application: A fault very rarely happens by itself, but is

generally followed by a second worse than the first; and the second by a third, worse again than the preceding. Question your past life; perhaps it will tell you this is unhappily too true. Take care not to have this sad experience over again.

Affections and Resolutions.

Point III: Pride and presumption of Thomas

Consideration: Avarice had led Judas to his ruin and pride was about to cause that of Thomas. It led him to imagine himself more enlightened than all his brethren, to treat them as weak-minded men, and obstinately remain the only one who did not believe. And with the intolerable pride he had great presumption. "Except I shall see in His hands the print of the nails, and put my finger into the place of the nails, I will not believe." He laid down the law to his Master; he dictated to Him the conditions of an act of faith in the truth of His resurrection, and exposed himself to His just anger.

Application: We are justly shocked at the conduct of Thomas, but let us take care; we are not more infallible than he was; and if this Apostle, who had spent three years in the school of our Divine Lord, could thus err from over-great confidence in himself, we ought to act and speak with great circumspection. And how often we are wanting in it! Let us thank our Lord for having preserved us from the evil consequences which might have resulted from our want of discretion, and pride. Let us renew the resolution of being modest and circumspect in maintaining our opinions, especially when they are in opposition to the general one.

Colloquy with our Divine Lord.

Third Week after Easter, Wednesday: Jesus shows Himself to Thomas in the Presence of all the Apostles, and of many of the Disciples

1st prelude: Let us imagine this holy and solemn meeting.

2nd prelude: Beg the grace of knowing your faults, and of making a prompt reparation for them.

Point I: Jesus enables Thomas to discover his error

Consideration: The first Sunday after Easter, Jesus appeared again, as He had done eight days before, to the Apostles gathered together in the upper chamber. But this time Thomas was with them. "After eight days again, His disciples were within, and

Thomas was with them." It was because Thomas we there, as the Gospel expressly mentions, that our Lord especially came; and why? That he might convert this unbelieving Apostle, and bring back a lost sheep into the path of life. How good was our Divine Lord! He took the first step towards the sinner; for if Thomas had been left to himself, what would have become of him? He had already persisted for eight days in his unbelief, and we may reasonably imagine that he would have continued in it, and been lost for all eternity.

Application: Have you not also, and perhaps more than once, passed a considerable time in habitual sin? And have you not been brought out of it, instead of being overtaken by death, through the mercy of God, who prevented you by His grace? "The mercies of the Lord that we are not consumed," says Jeremias. Can you not also say the same with profound wonder and gratitude?

Affections and Resolutions.

Point II: He enabled him also to repair the scandal he had given

Consideration: It is a remarkable circumstance in this history, that our Lord would only appear to Thomas in the presence of the other disciples. His reason was, to give Thomas an occasion of repairing before them all the scandal and the sorrow he had caused them. "The words of God are perfect," says the prophet. He bestowed on the Apostle the grace of a sincere conversion, and gave him also by His providence the means of making it entire and exemplary.

Application: If you have scandalized or wounded by word or deed those with whom you live, or with whom you have some relation, seize the first occasion which Providence gives you of repairing the harm you have done; and if the reparation ought to be public because the fault has been public, make it with a good heart, humbly and sincerely. You will not lose the good opinion of others. "To acknowledge we were in error yesterday shows that we are wiser today," says the proverb.

Affections and Resolutions.

Point III

Consideration: He enables him to do this without injury to his reputation. "Jesus cometh, the doors being shut, and stood in the midst." The circumstance mentioned in the Gospel – "the doors being shut" – contains not only a mystery, but a valuable lesson.

Our Lord teaches us never to tell our neighbors' faults except to those who have the right to hear them, nor to reprove anyone publicly except before those who witnessed his fault. For our Lord showed Himself to Thomas only before those whom he had scandalized and grieved by his unbelief.

Application: Have we always followed these rules of justice and charity? Have we not, to give a mark of confidence, manifested the faults of others – not to those whose duty it was to correct them, but to those who had nothing to do with them? Ask yourself if you have not reproaches, and very grave ones, perhaps to make to yourself on this point.

Colloquy with our Divine Lord.

Third Week after Easter, Thursday: The Apostle Thomas is converted, and confesses the Faith

1st prelude: Imagine you see the Apostle humble and repentant at the feet of Jesus.

2nd prelude: Ask the grace to share the same feelings, especially at the moment of receiving absolution.

Point I: Jesus invites Thomas to touch His wounds

Consideration: What must have been the fear and astonishment of Thomas when he beheld before him that Divine Master whom he had treated so badly! He had denied His veracity in refusing to believe in the resurrection which He had so often foretold and desired His Apostles to believe; he had been dictating conditions simply from his own judgement and whim, by saying, "Except I shall see in His hands the print of the nails, and put my finger into His side, I will not believe." After such pride and presumption he might well fear a most just indignation. And nevertheless, what did Jesus say and do? He graciously condescended to what Thomas had demanded, with nothing more than a gentle reproach. "He saith to Thomas, Put in thy finger hither, and see My hands; and bring hither thy hand, and put in into My side; and be not faithless, but believing."

Application: And in the same way, that He may gain a soul, the good Shepherd actually condescends to yield, as we may say, to our inclinations, our weaknesses, our whims. How infinite is His goodness and gentleness! Have you not experienced it? Look attentively over the past, especially over the circumstances of your vocation and your entrance into religion, and you will find proofs of the same goodness and gentleness which made allowance for your character, your temperament, and your wishes, even capricious ones.

Affections and Resolutions.

Point II: Jesus accepts repentance and profession of faith from Thomas

Consideration: The brightness and glory of the Divinity shining in the glorified Body of Jesus, the sweet words that fell from His lips, and above all His wonderful gentleness, in one instant converted and gained the heart of the Apostle. Forgetting all else, he could only utter these words: "My Lord and my God! My Lord and my God!" The words were few, but they expressed a great deal; they contained the strongest profession of faith in the *humanity and divinity* of Jesus; they were a powerful expression of the feelings of veneration, repentance, submission, hope, love and devotion which were burning in the heart of Saint Thomas. They were very pleasing to our Lord, and the sin of the penitent Apostle was forgiven and forgotten.

Application: This may teach us that the worth of our prayers does not consist in the number and choice of the words we use, but in the disposition of heart from which they spring. We learn also how ready our Lord is to hear and to pardon us; to give us back His grace, even after we have grievously offended Him. It is our want of faith and confidence that hinders us from being purified from the stains of our sins, and causes us to remain so poor in grace and merit.

Affections and Resolutions.

Point III: Jesus declares the great merit of faith

Consideration: Let us remark how our Divine Lord answered the Apostle's declaration of faith: "Because thou hast seen Me, Thomas, thou hast believed; blessed are they that have not seen, and have believed." What is the meaning of these words? Clearly that the merit of faith and its reward in heaven will depend no on miraculous evidence, but in blindly submitting our understanding to the revealed word of God.

Application: This lively faith which our Lord commended is an especial grace and gift from God. We must therefore beg for it

from the Author of all grace; and we must beg for its continual increase, after the example of the Apostles, when they said, "Lord, increase our faith." Why is our faith so weak, so unfruitful in deeds of zeal and sanctity? Because we do not ask earnestly enough to have it strengthened and increased within us.
Colloquy with Jesus.

Third Week after Easter, Friday: Appearance of Jesus on the Shore of the Sea of Tiberias

1st prelude: Imagine you see the bark from which Peter and his six companions are throwing their nets in vain for the whole night.
2nd prelude: Beg for grace never to labor without gathering fruit for eternity.

Point I: Peter and the other disciples pass the night in fishing

Consideration: This memorable appearance is thus recorded by Saint John: "There were together Simon Peter, and Thomas who is called Didymus, and Nathanael, who was of Cana in Galilee, and the sons of Zebedee, and two others of His disciples. Simon Peter saith to them, I go a-fishing. They say to him, We also come with thee. And they went forth, and entered into the ship." How united the Apostles were in feelings and wishes! Peter said he was going to fish, and all the others were ready to join him.

Application: There is nothing more beautiful and more likely to preserve charity in community life than to know how to give up our own ideas and inclinations to follow those of others, when they are not contrary to the law of God or the rule. Have I done this? Is there not rather in me an inclination to contradict others? Am I not too attached to my own opinion? And have I not in consequence differed with others, and even had useless and dangerous disputes in words?
Affections and Resolutions.

Point II: They labor all the night and take nothing

Consideration: And that night they caught nothing. This long and fruitless labor was arranged by Providence. It was the will of God that when our Lord was away from them, they should catch nothing during the whole night; and when He was with them, they should take a quantity of fish with one throw of their net; and this was to teach us that our labors will have no result for eternal life if our Lord is not present in our souls by sanctifying grace, and we are not closely united to Him by purity of intention and by a spirit of prayer.

Application: There are no men and no religious more to be pitied than those who labor much and gain nothing, or very little, for eternity. Who are these unfortunate beings? First, those who are knowingly in the state of mortal sin, deprived of sanctifying grace; and this number is a very large one. Secondly, those who, being in a state of grace, lose altogether or in part the merit of their good works, because they have a bad intention in doing them, or because *they have no good intention at all.*

Affections and Resolutions.

Point III: They perceive Jesus on the shore and do not recognize Him

Consideration: "And when the morning was come Jesus stood on the shore; yet the disciples knew not that it was Jesus. Jesus therefore said to them, Children, have you any meat? They answered Him, No." Our Divine Lord knew very well that they had taken nothing, that they were pressed by hunger, and exhausted by fatigue. He had determined to supply their wants by a miracle, but He chose to question them, to make them tell out their trouble with their own lips, and kindle in their hearts and earnest desire for assistance.

Application: Our knowledge of the misery of our soul, the humble confession of it, and our ardent desire for help, prepare us to receive the gifts of God. Is it not because you have been wanting in these dispositions that you have had such a small share in the favors of our Lord? Examine yourself, and be assured that the more your weakness makes you despair of yourself, the more right you have to pray with confidence, and the more assurance you have of help.

Colloquy with Jesus.

Third Week after Easter, Saturday: Miraculous Draught of Fishes – Jesus recognized by His Disciples

1st prelude: Imagine you see the Apostles in the ship, and Jesus near them on the shore.

2nd prelude: Beg for the spirit of obedience and fervor.

Point I: Reward of the blind obedience of the Apostles

Consideration: By the knowledge and humble confession of their helplessness, Jesus had prepared His disciples to receive an extraordinary favor. He then said to them, with that tone of authority which was habitual to Him – as Saint Matthew tells us, "He was teaching them as one having power" – "Cast the net on the right side of the ship, and you will find. They cast therefore, and now they were not able to draw it for the multitude of fishes." This unexpected success against all probabilities was the reward of the prompt and blind obedience of the Apostles to the voice of Him who seemed to speak to them in the name of God, for "their eyes were held," so that they did not recognize their Divine Master.

Application: If we wish to see all our undertakings crowned with perfect success, let us be the children of obedience, submissive in faith and in love to those who direct or command us in the name and with the authority of God. Let us imitate the Apostles, and, like them, abstain from all replies and objections. Let us obey promptly and blindly, trusting to the word of Him whose hand is omnipotent, and who has told us "an obedient man shall speak of victories." Do we habitually obey in this manner, doing what the rule, the duties of our office, and our superiors require from us?

Affections and Resolutions.

Point II: Reward of the virginity of Saint John

Consideration: The miraculous draught would, we should have thought, at once have revealed to the disciples to whom they owed it. Nevertheless, John, the beloved disciple, was the only one who pierced the veil which surrounded Jesus, and he said to Peter, "It is the Lord." Why had Saint John this supernatural light in preference to the other disciples? Saint Jerome tells us it was the prerogative of his virginity; "it was the virgin disciple only who recognized the King of virgins." The purity of his heart had won for him a special place of preference in the Heart of Jesus; and in this we see the literal fulfilment of our Savior's words, "Blessed are the pure in heart, for they shall see God."

Application: We often complain of being habitually in a state of spiritual darkness and dryness, of having so little of that light which at once enlightens the soul, fills it with a sweet unction, and

wonderfully confirms it in the love of God. Where shall we look for the cause of this? May it not be, perhaps, because we have taken little care to preserve and increase our purity of heart? Are you not among those whose want of mortification and recollection leads them into many faults? Even if these faults are light ones, they leave stains in our soul and keep light back from it.
Affections and Resolutions.

Point III: Saint Peter's burst of fervor

Consideration: "Simon Peter, when he heard it was the Lord, cast himself into the sea." Saint Peter's transport of love for his Divine Master was so great that he could not wait for the progress of the ship. He was impatient to be with Him whom he loved, and love does not wait to reason. He never thought of the dangers he might run by throwing himself into the sea. To go to Jesus, to be with Him as soon as possible, was his sole thought, and he saw no difficulties in the way.

Application: In this conduct of the Apostle we find all the marks of real fervor and of divine love so well described by the author of the *Imitation*: "Love oftentimes knoweth no measure, but is fervent beyond all measure, attempts what is above its strength, pleads no excuse of impossibility; it is, therefore, able to undertake all things, while he who does not love would faint and lie down." Do you sometimes experience the effects of love like this?
Colloquy with Jesus.

Fourth Sunday after Easter: On the Gospel of the Day

1st prelude: Imagine you see Jesus Christ speaking to the Apostles of the mission of the Holy Ghost.
2nd prelude: Beg for a spirit of disinterested love.

Point I: Disinterested love of Jesus Christ in sending the Holy Ghost

Consideration: "And now I go to Him that sent Me, and none of you asketh Me, Whither goest Thou? But because I have spoken these things to you, sorrow hath filled your heart. But I tell you the truth; it is expedient to you that I go." Such was the disinterested love of Jesus Christ for us. It was not the rest, the bliss, and the glory promised to His sacred humanity that He thought of in His Ascension, but our interest, our advantage. To the very last moment of His sensible presence on earth He forgot Himself, and thought only of us. It was thus during the whole course of His life, from the stable where He wept – not from sorrow, but from compassion – until Calvary, when He said to the women who pitied Him, "Daughters of Jerusalem, weep not for Me, but weep for yourselves and your children."

Application: Compare you love for God with that disinterested love that He has shown you, and see what you ought to think of it. You will probably find that your love is not worthy of the name, so much is self-love mixed up in it. And in the generous efforts that you sometimes make to avoid sin or to practice virtue, is it not principally, if not entirely, the fear of punishment, or the hope of reward, which influences you?

Affections and Resolutions.

Point II: Promise of the Holy Spirit

Consideration: "If I go not, the Paraclete will not come to you; but if I go, I will send Him to you." Why could not the Apostles receive the Holy Ghost before the Ascension of Jesus Christ? One reason which the interpreters of Scripture give, and which Saint Augustine especially insists upon, is, that the attachment of the Apostles to the corporal presence of their Master was too human and sensible, and the love they bore Him was too natural, to imperfect. It was necessary that the sensible object of their love, the *humanity* of the Word, should be taken from them, for if not, they could not receive the plenitude of the Holy Spirit, nor become really spiritual men.

Application: If, in one sense, the presence even of Jesus Christ was an obstacle to the reception by the Apostles of the fullness of the Holy Ghost, what should you think of the affection that you have for many objects, the deprivation of which touches you so keenly, and affects you so deeply, and especially of those over-great attachments, or particular friendships, that you indulge in? These affections and friendships are always foolish, and often very hurtful, because they generally rest only on sympathy or sensible attraction; they degenerate frequently into familiarity or misplaced confidence; they are a loss of time, and they disturb that sweet and entire peace of conscience which those only enjoy whose thoughts and affections are given to God alone. Besides, knowing what a leaning we always have towards evil, it is to be feared that these

natural affections may become sensual or even sinful. What does experience tell you about this? What ought you to do?
Affections and Resolutions.

Point III: Operations of the Holy Spirit

Consideration: "And when He is come He will convince the world of sin, and of justice, and of judgment; He will teach you all truth." When the Spirit of God really possesses a soul, it always produces two effects: 1st, a spirit of sanctity, reproaching us with the slightest sin, correcting and rectifying our defective judgments, and showing us the great insufficiency of our imaginary goodness; 2nd, a spirit of light, instructing us about our duties, helping us to understand and relish eternal truths, ever showing us new means and new practices of advancing in perfection.

Application: Do you perceive and feel these wonderful operations of the Holy Spirit? Are you docile to them? Are you attentive to the movements they produce in your heart? If you cannot answer yes, ought you not to conclude that you are not an interior man, or that you are very insensible, if not indocile, to the attractions of grace? And ought you not further to fear lest you deserve the reproof Saint Stephen gave to the Jews, "stiff-necked, in the heart you always resist the Holy Ghost"?
Colloquy with the Holy Ghost.

Fourth Week after Easter, Monday: Jesus works another Miracle in Favor of the seven Disciples

1st prelude: Imagine you see the seven disciples receiving the miraculous bread from the hands of Jesus.
2nd prelude: Beg for grace worthily to receive the Eucharistic Food.

Point I: Jesus provides the repast of the disciples by miracle

Consideration: "As soon, then, as they came to land, they saw hot coals lying, and a fish laid thereon, and bread." They were exhausted by fatigue, faint with hunger: but they had neither fire nor food, and it would have taken a long time to have procured either. Jesus provided for them by another miracle, so that in an instant they had all they needed. But that they should have the pleasure of adding the fish they had caught, and of tasting something of their own, He said, "Bring hither of the fishes which you have now caught." And He invited them to the repast, saying, "Come and dine." What a refinement of love and goodness did our Lord thus show to His poor servants!

Application: And thus does He daily act towards us: it is by a continual miracle of His power and goodness that the earth brings forth food for our nourishment; we owe it all to Him; yet, by requiring us to do our part, He lets us have the satisfaction of thinking we are tasting the fruit of our own labors. Again, it is He, and He only, who by the help of His grace gives supernatural merit to our good works; and yet He grants us a reward in proportion to our efforts, as if all the merit were our own, and as if He would let us have the satisfaction of thinking we have made our own fortune, while in reality, "it is His own gifts that He crowns in His elect," as Saint Augustine so beautifully says: *Sua in nobis Deus dona coronat*. Do you think often enough of this indulgent goodness of God towards you? Do you not often fail in giving Him the gratitude which is due to Him, and attribute to yourself too great a share in your good deeds?

Affections and Resolutions.

Point II: Jesus makes Himself gradually known to the disciples

Consideration: One remarkable circumstance of this appearance to the seven disciples was, as the Gospel tell us, that "none of them who were at meat durst ask Him, Who art Thou? Knowing that it was the Lord." We must, therefore, conclude that our Lord appeared to them under some form which veiled Him from their sight; they could not *see* that it was He, and yet they *knew* it, as the Evangelist says – meaning that they *believed* it without doubting. What gave them this faith? The exterior testimony of a miracle and the interior voice of grace.

Application: Is not this our case when we are in adoration before the Blessed Sacrament, or approach the holy altar? We do not then *see* Jesus Christ; He is veiled from our eyes under the appearance of bread; but we *know* that it is He; we believe it without doubting, being assured of it by the testimony of faith, and by the unction of grace from that Divine Lord, who speaks and acts within us. We ought, then, to try to equal the respect and love which the disciples gave to His adorable Person. Do you do this habitually?

Affections and Resolutions.

Point III: Jesus sits down to table with His disciples and serves them

Consideration: Our Lord, not yet weary of showing His love and care to His dear disciples, "cometh," continues the Evangelist, "and taketh bread, and giveth them, and fish in like manner."

Application: Here is at once the image and the pledge of what our loving Lord will one day do in our heavenly home for His faithful servants; to those especially who, after the example of the Apostles, have abandoned all for Him. He deigns to tell us this Himself. "I am in the midst of you as he that serveth you – all they which have continued with Me in My temptations; and I dispose to you as My Father hath disposed to Me, a kingdom, that you may eat and drink at My table in My kingdom, and may sit upon thrones judging the twelve tribes of Israel." Let us expand our hearts at the thought of these encouraging and glorious promises. Colloquy with our loving Savior.

Fourth Week after Easter, Tuesday: Jesus searches the Heart of Saint Peter, and appoints him Head of the Church

1st prelude: Imagine you see our Lord saying to Peter: "Simon, son of John, lovest thou Me more than these?"
2nd prelude: Beg for the grace of ardent love.

Point I: Vocation of Saint Peter to be Sovereign Pontiff

Consideration: The miraculous draught should have reminded the disciples of Our Lord's promise, "I will make you to be fishers of men." Simon Peter had a larger share in it than the others, by the ordering of Providence, because he was to take greatest part in fishing for souls; he was to be placed at the head of the Apostles in the position of Sovereign Pontiff. To hold this great dignity worthily, he required great sanctity, or love, which is the perfection of sanctity. This was the reason that "when therefore they had dined, Jesus saith to Simon Peter, Simon, son of John, lovest thou Me more than these? He saith to Him, Yea, Lord, Thou knowest that I love Thee. He saith to him, Feed My lambs."

Application: We also, by the grace of a religious vocation, are raised above seculars, and called to take a greater part in the search for souls. But this vocation obliges us, both before God and men, to tend to a higher degree of charity or sanctity. To us also, to each of us, our Lord puts this question, "Lovest thou Me more than these?" What answer can we give Him from the depths of our hearts?

Affections and Resolutions.

Point II: Threefold protestation of love from Saint Peter

Consideration: "He saith to him again, Simon, son of John, lovest thou Me? He saith to Him, Yea, Lord, Thou knowest that I love Thee. He saith to him, Feed My lambs. He saith to him the third time, Simon, son of John, lovest thou Me? And he said to Him, Lord, Thou knowest all things; Thou knowest that I love Thee. He said to him, Feed My sheep." By these last words, "Feed My sheep," not only the lambs, but their mothers, Jesus Christ placed both the faithful and their pastors under the charge of Saint Peter and his lawful successors. He made him the only visible head of His Church, that He might thus ensure its perfect unity until the end of time.

Application: With what great modesty Saint Peter speaks! No longer, as on the night of the Last Supper, does he say he is certain about his love; but now he appeals to his Master, who knows the depths of the heart. His past faults and weaknesses have made him humble and diffident of himself, but not distrustful of the goodness of his Lord. Imitate him in this, and you, like him, will draw good out of evil. Remark also with what eagerness and what happiness Saint Peter seized the occasion thus offered to him of repairing the scandal of his threefold denial by a threefold and fervent declaration of love. If you have compromised the respect due to your holy state by any public fault, seize upon the first occasion of making reparation for it.

Affections and Resolutions.

Point III: Grief of the Apostle Saint Peter

Consideration: "Peter was grieved because He had said to him the third time, Lovest thou Me?" The poor fisherman of Galilee was about to be promoted to the highest dignity, and crowned with honors by the Son of God Himself. Such a distinction should naturally have filled him with joy and happiness. But however, the Evangelist tells us, he was sad and grieved. Why was he in such trouble? Because he was afraid of not *really* having the love for his Divine Master which he *believed* he had, or of failing a second time in the manifestation of it. Our Lord's three questions awoke this fear in his heart, and he could think of nothing else.

Application: Happy is the religious in whom the love of God and the desire of increasing in it reigns supreme, and who has no other cause for fear or trouble than that of decreasing in fervor or generosity in the service of the Lord his God!
Colloquy with our Lord.

Fourth Week after Easter, Wednesday: Jesus foretells the Martyrdom of the Cross to Saint Peter and reproves his Curiosity

1st prelude: Imagine you see Jesus Christ saying to Saint Peter: "Follow Me."
2nd prelude: Beg for grace to follow Jesus faithfully in little things, so that you may also following Him in great things.

Point I: Jesus foretells the martyrdom of the cross to Saint Peter

Consideration: Peter, while he declared aloud his love for Jesus, was not without fear. Was he, he asked himself, sure of his perseverance if he met with some great temptation like that before which he had fallen? The doubt was agony to him; and Jesus graciously comforted him by the assurance that he would be generous and faithful. "Amen, amen I say to thee, when thou shalt be old, thou shalt stretch forth thy hands, and another shall lead thee whither thou wouldst not"; and "this He said," remarks the Evangelist, "signifying by what death he should glorify God"; by the death of the cross – death endured for justice' sake – martyrdom. This was the reward given to the Apostle's love, and by this he was to glorify the great rank and dignity to which he had been raised.

Application: We should fear rather, then, such offices of superiority in religion – for they ought to be to those who are placed in them only a laborious and painful burden. We should look on them only as a long and severe martyrdom, which a true religious should submit to, but never seek after. We should see also in the crosses that God sends us only the proofs of His love, and the means of making Him some return for it. Have we looked upon them in this light?
Affections and Resolutions.

Point II: Jesus bids Peter follow in His steps

Consideration: Jesus, after having assured Saint Peter that He should be faithful unto death, walked forward, and said to him, "Follow Me." What did our Lord mean by giving the Apostle, who was ready for martyrdom, a command so easy to obey? To show him that to be faithful in great things, we must be habitually faithful in little ones; and that to be able to make painful and heroic sacrifices when required, we must have a habit of making slight and easy ones. This was, in fact, what He had taught before His Passion, when He said, "He that is faithful in that which is least, is faithful also in that which is greater."

Application: Everyday experience confirms the truth of this doctrine; we never see those who are habitually faithful to their rule fall into great errors; we always remark, on the contrary, that in times of great trial they remain faithful even to martyrdom. And this grace of martyrdom, which no one can merit, was the reward of their fidelity in little things, and of the constant mortification which it implies. Before they were martyrs for the faith, they were martyrs to their rule, even to its smallest details. Is not this the meaning of that beautiful Antiphon of the Office for Martyrs: "Behold the saints, how great torments they have all suffered, that they might securely attain the palm of martyrdom"?

Affections and Resolutions.

Point III: Jesus reproves Peter for his curiosity

Consideration: "Peter, turning about, saw that disciples whom Jesus loved following, and he said, Lord, and what shall this man do? Jesus saith to him, So I will have him to remain till I come, what is it to thee? Follow thou Me."

Application: It is an ordinary temptation in community life to busy ourselves or mix ourselves up in the affairs of others – to judge or interpret in a wrong sense the words and actions of others. If this temptation comes to you, say to yourself what our Lord said to Saint Peter, What is it to thee? Thou art not the superior charged to watch over the others; thou wilt not be asked to give account for others, but only for thyself. This is the best means of conquering this temptation. Have you made use of it? How often? And with what success?

Colloquy with our Lord.

Fourth Week after Easter, Thursday: Appearance of our Lord to the five hundred Disciples

1st prelude: Represent to yourself Jesus standing in the midst of the five hundred disciples, who are transported with joy at the sight of their Master.
2nd prelude: Ask of Him to give you often the joy and refreshment of His sensible presence.

Point I: Eagerness of the disciples to see Jesus

Consideration: "A few days before the Ascension," writes Saint Matthew, "the eleven disciples went into Galilee, unto the mountain where Jesus had appointed them"; where "He was seen," adds Saint Paul, "by more than five hundred brethren at once." This appearance is the only one of which the time and place were known beforehand. Not only Jesus Himself, but the angel had announced it long before; which accounts for the number of witnesses being so much greater than on any preceding occasion – "more than five hundred." Imagine with what intense eagerness the greater part of these, who had not seen the Lord since His resurrection, would hasten to the appointed place, urged on by the natural desire to see a dead man raised to life; and still more by the more perfect motive of longing to show their reverence, love, and gratitude to their risen Lord; and also, we may well believe, inspired with the hope of receiving, not only His blessing, but special graces and favors.

Application: If it were now to be revealed that Jesus would appear visibly in some appointed place, how eagerly men would repair thither, even at the cost of a long and troublesome journey! The mere thought of coming into the presence of their God and Savior, the Giver of all good gifts, with the expectation of receiving some special favor, would make the most toilsome journey seem light and easy; and yet – O marvelous thought! – this very God and Savior is in the midst of these same men, in a multitude of temples; and what do we see? Instead of hastening to Him, they will not go near Him. This is, indeed, a most mysterious inconsistency. You are shocked, grieved, but are you in no degree guilty yourself? How often do you visit Jesus in the Blessed Sacrament? What are your thoughts when you kneel before Him? Affections and Resolutions.

Point II: Weak faith of some of the disciples

Consideration: "And seeing Him they adored," says Saint Matthew; "but," he adds, "some doubted" the reality of His resurrection. *Quidam autem dubitaverunt*; and because their faith was weak, their love was cold. Their distrust and uncertainty contrasted sadly with the lively faith and eager joy of the rest; they were dull and cold amidst the holy zeal and fervor of their brethren. This must have been a source of great grief to the other disciples, and doubtless also to the Sacred Heart of Jesus.

Application: Is not this a picture of what we see at the present day in even the most exemplary communities? Do we not too often see, amongst a number of religious who are full of faith and fervor, because they have been faithful to the grace of their holy vocation, others who *seem to doubt*, or to have lost consciousness of the solemn obligations imposed upon them by their vows, who, constantly hovering between good and evil, have fallen into a state of relaxation and tepidity, and have become, through their irregularities, a source of grief to their brethren, and of painful anxiety to their superiors?

Affections and Resolutions.

Point III: The reproach of Jesus to the disciples

Consideration: Jesus said to His disciples, "O foolish and slow of heart to believe in all the things which the prophets have spoken!" This reproach did not proceed from impatience or ill-humor, but from the love of Jesus for His disciples, even while they remained in error and unbelief. They attributed their Master's death to weakness, and could no longer believe in His omnipotence. For this reason Jesus added to His reproof the explanation necessary to convince them of their error. He said, "Ought not Christ to have suffered these things, and so to enter into His glory? And beginning at Moses and all the prophets, He expounded to them in all the Scriptures the things that were concerning Him."

Application: Learn first, from this example, never to reproach anyone out of resentment or spite, but only from duty and charity; an further, always endeavor to instruct those whom you are obliged to reprove, in order that they may acknowledge and amend their errors. Have you followed this rule of conduct?

Colloquy with our risen Lord.

Fourth Week after Easter, Friday: Jesus sends His Apostles to preach and baptize throughout the whole World

1st prelude: Represent to yourself Jesus Christ saying to His disciples: "All power is given to Me in heaven and in earth. Going therefore, teach ye all nations."
2nd prelude: Ask the grace of perfect fidelity to your vocation.

Point I: All power is given to Jesus

Consideration: Jesus said to His disciples, "All power is given to Me in heaven and in earth." What an exalted idea do these few words give us of our Blessed Lord in His human nature! "All power is given to Me in heaven." He reigns there over all the countless legions of angels in heaven; He bestows offices and kingdoms there on whomsoever He will: "I dispose to you," He said to His Apostles, "as My Father hath disposed to Me, a kingdom." He causes the gifts of the Holy Spirit, the treasures of sanctifying grace, to descend from thence upon His friends, which are able to raise us in one moment to the greatest heights of perfection. "And all power is given to Me in earth." He is therefore the arbiter of life and death. Nothing can resist Him; neither the world nor the devil, nor all the powers of hell combined, can hurt a hair of the head of those whom He protects.

Application: Let us praise Jesus for the power and the glory which He has won by His sufferings and humiliations; and let us rejoice that we have obeyed His invitation, and have renounced the world and left all things to consecrate ourselves entirely, irrevocably, to the service of so powerful and generous a King, who has promised us (they are His own words), "Every one that hath left house, or brethren, or sisters, or father, or mother, or wife, or children, or lands, for My Name's sake, shall receive an hundredfold, and shall possess life everlasting."

Affections and Resolutions.

Point II: The Apostles are commissioned to evangelize the world

Consideration: The words on which we have just been meditating, viz., "All power is given to Me," had prepared the Apostles to receive the mission which Jesus was about to confide to them – the mission to preach the Gospel in all the world, to bring all men into the one Fold of the Church, and to lay the foundation of that kingdom of which He had so often spoken, both before and after His resurrection: He gave it therefore in these words: "Go ye into the whole world, and preach the Gospel to every creature."

Application: Observe that Jesus did not execute the great work of the conversion of the world Himself, but entrusted it to His Apostles – men who were in themselves wholly unfit for such an undertaking. Learn from this, if you are elected to any office or superiority, not to depend wholly upon yourself, as though no one else were capable of discharging its duties; and also, never to refuse any office that obedience may impose upon you under the excuse that you are unfit for it. Trust in the help of Almighty God, who takes pleasure in doing great things through weak instruments.

Affections and Resolutions.

Point III: The command to baptize in the name of the Blessed Trinity is joined to the mission of preaching

Consideration: After saying, "Teach ye all nations," Jesus immediately added, "baptizing them in the name of the Father, and of the Son, and of the Holy Ghost." The conditions, therefore, of admission into His Church are a profession of faith in the Holy Trinity, and baptism in the name of the Three Divine Persons. It is also our chief defense against the assaults of the devil, and our best safeguard against all dangers, to invoke the Most Holy Trinity, making at the same time the sign of the cross, the instrument of our redemption, whereby also we make a public profession of our faith, and an acknowledgement of the benefits we have received from the Father, the Son, and the Holy Ghost.

Application: Always make the sign of the cross with great attention and devotion, in order to reap all possible benefit from it. Colloquy with the Three Persons of the Adorable Trinity.

Fourth Week after Easter, Saturday: Continuation of the Preceding Subject: Organization of the Church

1st prelude: Represent to yourself the Apostles surrounding Jesus, and listening to Him.

2nd prelude: Ask for a truly apostolic spirit of faith and zeal.

Point I: The deposit of the Faith is confided to the Apostles

Consideration: It was through the bond of faith, by a belief in the same doctrines, the same Sacraments, the same precepts of morality, that the faithful throughout the world were to be united in one body, forming the Church of Jesus Christ, the heritage of God. Our Blessed Lord, therefore, before His ascension, provided for the unity and indefectibility of the faith which He had preached to mankind and left to His Apostles. And this He did, first, by commanding them to teach men to believe and practice all that He had taught, without either adding to it or taking from it. *Docentes eos servare omnia quoecumque mandavi vobis* – "Teaching them to observe all things whatsoever I have commanded you." Secondly, by sending the Holy Ghost upon them, the Spirit of Truth: "And I send the promise of My Father upon you, the Spirit of Truth." Thirdly, by assuring them that the successors of Saint Peter should always retain the gift of infallibility in faith and morals; saying to that great Apostle, "I have prayed for thee, that thy faith fail not."

Application: More than nineteen hundred years have elapsed since Jesus Christ founded His Church, and yet we see it remaining unchanged to the present day. The Church alone has stood firm, unaltered, unshaken, amidst all the changes and revolutions of the world. The deposit of Faith confided to the Apostles has been preserved intact. Examination of the traditions of the Church will convince us that we believe now all the same doctrines which were first announced by Jesus Christ and his Apostles, and that consequently we are in the true Church *militant* on earth, from whence we may hope to pass into the Church *triumphant* in heaven.

Affections and Resolutions.

Point II: Salvation is promised to true believers

Consideration: "He that believeth and is baptized shall be saved; but he that believeth not shall be condemned." If we attentively consider these words of our Divine Lord, we shall find in them a powerful motive both of joy and fear; of *joy*, because they point out a secure and easy way to eternal salvation; of *fear*, because they declare the condemnation, not only of obstinate heretics, but also, in different degrees, of two kinds of Catholics, only too numerous, alas, at the present time. They contain an *explicit* condemnation of those who venture to speak lightly of certain doctrines, and thus seem to approve of the detestable principle that *it matters little what a man believes, provided he leads a good life*; and an *implicit* condemnation of those who, while they profess to adhere strictly to every article of faith, lead lives little in accordance with their belief. Now Saint James declares that "faith without works is dead," and our Blessed Lord says that God will "render to every man according to his works."

Application: Are we not ourselves, to a certain extent, among the number of these last? Examine seriously what is your belief concerning the malice and the pernicious effects of venial sin; concerning the obligations of your vows, the duties of your office, the reverence due to God, especially in time of prayer, the importance of beginning each day well, etc. Then examine what is your conduct in all these respects: in other words, what is your *practical* faith.

Affections and Resolutions.

Point III: The gift of miracles is promised to the early Christians

Consideration: Jesus promised the gift of miracles to the Apostles, and their immediate followers, in confirmation of their preaching, and to strengthen the faith of their converts. "These signs," He said, "shall follow them that believe: in My name they shall cast out devils, they shall speak with new tongues, they shall take up serpents; and if they shall drink any deadly thing, it shall not hurt them; they shall lay their hands upon the sick, and they shall recover." And we learn from history that all these promises were literally fulfilled.

Application: Let us here admire the wisdom and goodness of God, who always proportions the means to the end; He works miracles to persuade the Gentiles to receive the true Faith, but when it has once been accepted and established, He withdraws the gift, that He may leave us the full benefit of making acts of faith.

Colloquy with Jesus.

Fifth Sunday after Easter: On the Gospel of the Day: Motives of Confidence in Prayer

1st prelude: Behold Jesus saying to His disciples: "Amen, amen I say to you, if you ask the Father anything in My name, He will give it you."

2nd prelude: Ask for a continual increase of faith, and confidence in prayer.

Point I: Motives of confidence on the part of God

Consideration: Want of confidence is one of the chief causes of the inefficacy of our prayers. And yet what powerful motives we have for confidence! Motives drawn from the thought of God, from the thought of ourselves, and from the thought of our neighbor, when we use intercessory prayer. On the part of God, let us remember that He is almighty, and consequently can grant all that we ask; He is omnipresent, and therefore can hear us everywhere, and knows even our most secret desires; He is our tender Father, and loves us more than we love ourselves. If we still have doubts, they must surely be dispelled by those gracious words of our Divine Lord: “If you ask the Father anything in My name, He will give it you.”

Application: How is it that, whilst we acknowledge these truths, we pray ordinarily with so little confidence? We seem to cherish a kind of foreboding that our prayers will not be granted, or else to imagine some immense distance between God and ourselves, in which they will be lost before they reach Him. Or is it that we look on God only as a severe Judge alienated from us by our past sins and present infidelities? Let us examine ourselves carefully on these points, for often these motives of distrust are so hidden that they influence us without our being able to perceive it. Affections and Resolutions.

Point II: Motives drawn from ourselves

Consideration: Our own helplessness and spiritual misery ought to inspire us with the greatest confidence, for God requires of us that we should aim at perfection, and we ourselves desire it; but we find ourselves powerless to attain it without His help and the constant succor of grace. Our Lord Himself teaches us this when He says, “Without Me you can do nothing.” But He also says, “Ask, and it shall be given you.” If it were not so, God would require an impossibility of us, which it would be absurd to oppose.

Application: We may draw a most consoling and encouraging conclusion from these considerations – namely, that the weaker we find ourselves, the more unable to rise from our sins and conquer our bad habits, the more right we have to trust in the efficacy of our prayers. This is self-evident, and yet have we not often acted as though the contrary were true? Have we not fallen into despair or discouragement after our falls? And when tepidity or disgust for spiritual things has taken possession of us, have we not left off praying, or lost all confidence in our prayers, as though God would not hear them? Let us acknowledge our errors, and be careful to avoid a repetition of them.

Affections and Resolutions.

Point III: Motives drawn from our neighbor

Consideration: We have three power motives for confidence when we prayer for others, especially for sinners, or for any who have been recommended to our prayers: 1st, that we are performing an act most pleasing to Almighty God; 2nd, that we are fulfilling a duty; 3rd, that it is a disinterested act of charity. We can pray with more boldness for another than for ourselves, and with more confidence in proportion to his need.

Application: When we look at the impiety and immorality which surround us, or on the apparent uselessness of our efforts to convert others, or save the souls confided to our care, are we not tempted to look upon them as incurable? Do we not feel inclined to leave off praying for them – to leave them to their fate? Far be such a thought from us; it is contrary to charity, and an insult to God.

Colloquy with our Blessed Lord.

Fifth Week after Easter, Monday: The Rogation Days

1st prelude: Place yourself in spirit in the procession among the faithful.

2nd prelude: Beg the grace to enter into the spirit of the Church.

Point I: Origin of the Rogation Days

Consideration: The origin of the Rogation Days or the three days of prayer and abstinence immediately preceding the Feast of the Ascension, may be traced to Saint Mamertus, Bishop of Vienne in Dauphine, in the fifth century. From the time that the Burgundians invaded this country, it had been visited every year with grievous calamities, which were looked upon as chastisements from God. The year 470 was a terribly fatal one to the city of Vienne; and the holy Bishop then made a vow to establish *rogations*, or public prayers and processions, in his diocese every year. The people gladly co-operated with him, and he then appointed the ceremonies for the three days before the Ascension, prescribed the fast to be observed, and chose three churches outside the walls of the town as the places to which the processions should be made. The prayers were answered, the scourge was removed, and the other French bishops adopted the same plan in their respective dioceses. Towards the end of the eighth century, Pope Leo III imposed the observance of the Rogation Days as an obligation on the whole Latin Church; but, in consideration of the Paschal season, he changed the fast into an abstinence.

Application: See with what wisdom Divine Providence makes use of what would seem adverse circumstances, to introduce new practices of devotion, and thus nourish the faith and fervor of the faithful.

Affections and Resolutions.

Point II: The object of this devotion

Consideration: In order to conform ourselves to the spirit of the Church during these three days, we ought to keep steadfastly before our minds the ends she had in view in appointing them. These ends are not only deliverance from some passing danger, but our preservation from all the numberless evils, both of soul and body, which threaten us; the attainment of all that is necessary for our spiritual and temporal welfare, and especially the blessing of God on the fruits of the earth at this particular season of the year when they begin to bud forth.

Application: We, above all men, are bound to make generous efforts to obtain the ends proposed by the Church. As religious, we ought to be distinguished above all others by our zeal and by the exercise of a more ardent charity. We ought to place ourselves as intercessors between an offended God and His guilty creatures, and turn away the judgements their sins provoke, by our prayers, penance, and acts of mortification. Do we fully realize this truth? Do our acts bear witness to our faith in this respect?

Affections and Resolutions.

Point III: Means to obtain these ends

Consideration: The chief end proposed by the Church in appointing the Rogation Days being the public welfare, she appoints means adapted to its attainment. She imposes on all who are not legitimately dispensed a strict abstinence; she appoints solemn public prayers and processions, to which she invites all the faithful, and during which litanies are chanted. In these public prayers, all the different necessities, both of the state and private individuals, are enumerated. What blessings might not be thus obtained if only the people were faithful to what is demanded of them!

Application: If we cannot join in the public processions, let us at least say the litanies for ourselves in the churches, in the presence of the people. Let us say them with all possible devotion, trying to enter into the spirit of the Church, and uniting ourselves in spirit with those who are singing them so solemnly in procession.

Colloquy: it will consist of some few invocations of the litanies.

Fifth Week after Easter, Tuesday: Last Appearance of Jesus before His Ascension

1st prelude: Behold Jesus seated at table with the eleven Apostles.
2nd prelude: Beg to be permitted to share the feelings of the Apostles.

Point I: Love of Jesus for His Apostles

Consideration: "He appeared to the eleven as they were at table." These words clearly demonstrate that His appearance was for the *Apostles alone*, whose number was reduced to eleven by the apostasy of Judas. To them Jesus desired to give the last moments of His glorious life on earth, as to them He had given the last moments before His death. And by sitting at table with the, which is a proof of the greatest intimacy amongst friends, He gave them on both those occasions a proof of His singular love for them. Why did He thus love them? First, because His Father had given them to Him to aid Him in the work of our salvation: "To Me Thou gavest them" (Saint John xvii. 6); secondly, because they had forsaken all things to follow Him: "Behold, we have left all things, and followed Thee" (Saint Matthew xix. 27); and thirdly, because they were destined to labor and suffer more for Him than the other disciples.

Application: We also have been chosen by Jesus Christ out of the world to co-operate with Him in the salvation of souls; we also have left all things to follow Him. Have we not, then, some claims

upon His love?
Affections and Resolutions.

Point II: Assurance of His protection

Consideration: The hour was fast drawing near when the Apostles and disciples were about to be forever deprived of the sensible presence of their Divine Master in this world. This thought naturally filled them with trouble and sorrow. To reassure and console them, Jesus declared that He would be separated from them only in appearance, but that in reality He would be always near to help and protect them. He declared this most explicitly, saying, "Behold, I am with you all days, even to the consummation of the world" (Saint Matthew xxviii. 20).

Application: Jesus Christ is, indeed, with us to the present day, not only as God, but as Man – by His corporal presence in the Blessed Sacrament, and even more intimately present than before His Ascension; for then He was only in one place at a time, whereas now He is in many places at once; everywhere, indeed, where there is a church and a tabernacle. Then He could only communicate with men by entering their houses and sitting down with them at table; now He communicates Himself to us by entering our hearts, becoming our food, and incorporating Himself with us.

Affections and Resolutions.

Point III: Promise of the Holy Ghost

Consideration: The Apostles were fully aware of their ignorance and weakness. They were terrified at the prospect of the difficulties that lay before them, discouraged, disheartened. To revive their fainting hearts, therefore, Jesus gave them the promise of a speedy outpouring of His Holy Spirit: "Stay you in the city," He said, "till you be endued with power from on high," and changed into other men.

Application: It is good and profitable to be deeply conscious of our weakness and insufficiency, but we must never let ourselves be cast down by this thought; if we are tempted to discouragement we must instantly turn to Jesus, and invoke with great confidence the aid of the Holy Spirit. He will hasten to enlighten and strengthen us. Have not our discouragements and fretfulness often been caused by our failure in these respects? Let us for the future be more circumspect. Colloquy with our Blessed Lord.

Fifth Week after Easter, Wednesday: General Reflections on all the Appearances of our Blessed Lord

1st prelude: Think of the joy which filled the hearts of the disciples each time that Jesus appeared to them.
2nd prelude: Ask Him to manifest Himself often to your soul, to prepare it for a perfect union with Him in heaven.

Point I: Number and motives of the different appearances

Consideration: The holy Evangelists have recorded only the nine appearances which form the subjects of the foregoing meditations; but it is clear, from the very context of their words, that the number was really much greater, especially from the following words of Saint Luke: "To whom also He showed Himself alive, after His Passion, by many proofs, for forty days appearing to them, and speaking of the kingdom of God" (Acts i. 3). These frequent manifestations were to confirm the faith of His Apostles and disciples in His resurrection, to accustom them gradually to His approaching separation from them, and also to prove, by so many sudden appearances, that He was always invisibly present with them.

Application: Jesus deals in this manner even now with holy souls; besides always invisibly present with them, He sometimes gives them sensible tokens of His presence, either by some special illumination, or by causing them to feel a vivid transport of joy and love. This happens frequently in Holy Communion, when He causes them to realize clearly that the bread which they eat is "the living Bread which came down from heaven." Have we never experienced these signs of the sensible presence of Jesus? Affections and Resolutions.

Point II: Time and place of the apparitions

Consideration: It is impossible to define the exact time or place of the numerous apparitions of our Blessed Lord. They did not take place at regular intervals, but more or less frequently, according to the dispositions of those who were the objects of them; neither were they at any fixed time or place, but sometimes in the night, sometimes in the day, sometimes in the house, and sometimes in the open air.

Application: We may learn from these considerations that no position, or employment, or occupation, however distracting, need be any obstacle to the secret communications between our soul and God; and that we need never imagine that we have altogether lost them because we have been for a long time deprived of them. Our chief concern should be to dispose ourselves always to receive them by great purity of heart and fervor.

Affections and Resolutions.

Point III: Manner and duration of the apparitions

Consideration: They all had these points of resemblance, that they were vouchsafed to only the Apostles and disciples, and that they were *sudden*, *unexpected*, and of *short duration.* Jesus appeared to them when they were least expecting Him, and almost always disappeared from their eyes just when they were most enjoying His presence and conversation.

Application: Jesus acted thus, 1st, to show us that He reserves these favors for those who are most truly devoted to Him; 2nd, to make us desire His presence and consolations, yet without too great an attachments to them, since they can be neither lasting nor perfect, except in heaven; and finally, that we may keep a constant watch over ourselves, and be at all times prepared to receive His visits.

Colloquy with our Lord.

Fifth Week after Easter, Thursday: Feast of the Ascension

1st prelude: Look at Jesus ascending in a cloud from the midst of His disciples.

2nd prelude: Beg Him to give you the grace to experience in yourself something of the same feelings which animated the Apostles.

Point I: Mysteries of the Feast of the Ascension

Consideration: Saint Luke relates the circumstances of this great feast in the following words: "And He led them out as far as Bethania; and lifting up His hands He blessed them: and it came to pass whilst He blessed them, He departed from them and was carried up into heaven." Saint Mark says He was "taken up into heaven, and sitteth on the right hand of God"; and Saint Luke again, in the first chapter of the Acts of the Apostles, "While they looked on, he was raised up, and a cloud received Him out of their sight; and while they were beholding Him going up to heaven, behold two men stood by them in white garments, who also said, Ye men of Galilee, why stand you looking up to heaven? This Jesus, who is taken up from you into heaven, shall so come, as you have seen Him going into heaven. Then they returned to Jerusalem from the mount which is called Olivet."

Application: Let us try, on this great festival, to gaze with the eyes of our mind upon Jesus rising slowly from the earth, passing through the clouds, making His triumphal entry into heaven, advancing to the foot of His Father's throne attended by celestial spirits, and receiving a glorious crown, and full power over His enemies. "Sit Thou at My right hand, until I make Thy enemies Thy footstool" (Psalm cix. 1,2). Let us ask Him to draw our hearts to Himself, and to raise our thoughts and affections to heaven, that we may dwell there in spirit, as we pray in the Collect of the Mass. Affections and Resolutions.

Point II: The joyfulness of the Feast of the Ascension

Consideration: It is said that the disciples returned to Jerusalem "with great joy"; and yet they had just suffered the pain of a most bitter parting. Whence, then, came this joy? Because their Divine Master has returned to His kingdom as a Conqueror. Because, on His entrance into heaven, He opened its gates, which the sin of our first parents had closed, to all believers. Because, by thus exalting His human nature, He ennobled ours, and made it capable of contemplating the divine nature. Because He had promised to prepare a place for them also in heaven, and to intercede for them with His Father: "I go to prepare a place for you… I will ask the Father" (Saint John xiv).

Application: Let these be also the motives of our joy. Let us meditate devoutly on them, and engrave them deeply on our hearts, that nothing may ever efface them, and, as our Lord promised His disciples, "your joy no man shall take from you." In the midst of whatever tribulations, we will exclaim with the Apostle, "I exceedingly abound with joy in all our tribulations"; and again: "Knowing that as you are partakers of His sufferings, so shall you be also of His consolations."

Affections and Resolutions.

Point III: The fruits of the Ascension

Consideration: The remembrance of this great mystery, and of the promises connected with it, filled the Apostles with a courage and constancy which were proof against all temptations. They all went to meet death joyfully, "rejoicing that they were accounted worthy to suffer reproach for the name of Jesus"; and declaring that "the sufferings of this time are not worthy to be compared with the glory to come, that shall be revealed in us."

Application: We too shall reap similar fruits from this meditation, if we keep faithfully in our hearts the thoughts with which it has inspired us. Let us ask our Divine Lord to impress it indelibly upon our hearts.

Colloquy with our Lord.

Novena to the Holy Ghost (Friday): Motives for making this Novena

1st prelude: Let us behold in spirit the Apostles assembled in the upper chamber at Jerusalem with our Lady.

2nd prelude: Let us ask grace to make this Novena with great fervor.

Point I: Excellence of the Novena: First motive

Consideration: Immediately after the Ascension the Apostles returned to Jerusalem, and, according to the command of their Divine Master, remained in the upper room with Mary, the Mother of Jesus, and the other disciples, in number a hundred and twenty. They continued in prayer, expecting the coming of the Holy Ghost, during *nine days*. From this was derived the practice of preparing for certain great feasts by a Novena of prayers and good works. The Novena of Pentecost was first made by the Apostles, so that it is not only apostolical, but may even be called of divine institution, since the Apostles made it in obedience to a formal command of Jesus Christ. What, then, must be its excellence, and with what devotion ought we to observe it.

Application: If on this account the Novena should be dear to all Christians, it ought to be especially so to us who are religious, and have more in common with the Apostles. Like them, we are enrolled in the army of Jesus Christ; like them, we have left all to follow Him; like them, we have no fixed place of abode, but are always ready to go whithersoever obedience, the glory of God, and the salvation of souls may call us.

Affections and Resolutions.

Point II: End and advantages of the Novena: Second motive

Consideration: Why did our Blessed Lord command His Apostles to make this novena? That they might dispose and prepare themselves to receive the gifts of the Holy Ghost, without which they would have remained forever what they then were – nothing in themselves, and of no use to others; absolutely incapable of attaining the end of their sublime vocation – but with which all would become possible and even easy to them.

Application: Why ought we to make this Novena with extraordinary fervor? For the same reasons. For certainly we are not greater than the Apostles; we are not better able than they were to dispense with the assistance of the Holy Spirit, and to fulfill the duties of our vocation; to arrive at that degree of perfection which it requires of us, and to save the souls of others both by word and work.

Affections and Resolutions.

Point III: Necessity of this Novena: Third motive

Consideration: When our Blessed Lord promised the Holy Ghost to His Apostles, He brought forward a third motive to urge them to a more careful preparation for receiving Him: the wickedness of the world, the miseries of the time in which they lived, the snares that surrounded them, the persecutions that would fall upon them: "In the world you shall have distress"; "you shall be brought before governors and kings for My sake"; "they shall deliver you up to councils, and in the synagogues you shall be beaten"; "they will lay their hands on you and persecute you."

Application: We too live in days of tribulation, and the rage of the wicked against the religion of Jesus Christ and those who profess it is not diminished. Religious especially are exposed to dangers and persecutions, and need supernatural courage and prudence in dealing with their enemies. Where shall we seek this but from the Spirit of counsel, fortitude and piety?

Colloquy with our Lady.

Second Day of the Novena (Saturday): Method of making the Novena

1st prelude: I will attentively consider the Apostles and disciples, assembled with Mary, and preparing themselves to receive the

Holy Ghost.
2nd prelude: I will ask the grace to understand and imitate their preparation.

Point I: Retreat and recollection of the Apostles

Consideration: God, says Saint Augustine, desires to bestow the gifts of the Holy Spirit abundantly upon us; but He wills that we should rightly dispose ourselves to receive them. How then shall we do this? The example of the Apostles will teach us better than any sermons. They retired into an upper chamber, where they passed their time in recollection and silence, broken only by pious conversations; keeping watch over themselves, and meditating on all that Jesus had taught them, especially on the attributes and operations of the Holy Ghost, whom He had promised to them.

Application: If, then, I desire to receive an abundant outpouring of the gifts of the Holy Ghost, I must above all things during this Novena, keep myself recollected, and be more than ordinarily careful to keep my rule, to observe silence, to guard my senses, and to watch over every irregular affection, so as to avoid the least sin, which would be the chief obstacle to interior peace and a reception of the gifts of God.

Affections and Resolutions.

Point II: Prayer and unity of the Apostles

Consideration: To their recollection the Apostles joined continual and earnest prayer, mindful of their Divine Master's words, "How much more will your Father from heaven give the good Spirit to them that ask Him?" And their prayer was the more efficacious and pleasing to God, because they made it in common, all uniting together in using the same words and asking the same favor. This, too, Jesus had taught them, when He said, "If two of you shall consent upon earth concerning anything whatsoever they shall ask, it shall be done to them by My Father who is in heaven."

Application: We too, during this Novena, must be men of prayer, adding to our ordinary devotions some especially addressed to the Holy Ghost. We cannot doubt that God will hear and answer these prayers, since we make them in common, and for the same object, after the example of the Apostles. The words of Saint Luke may be applied to our own community: "All these were persevering with one mind in prayer."

Affections and Resolutions.

Point III: The Apostles have recourse to Mary

Consideration: Convinced of the power of Mary over the Heart of Jesus, the Apostles not only strive to increase their fervor by her example, but entreat her to supply for their imperfections, and to present their humble petitions to her Divine Son; they persevered in prayer "with Mary the Mother of Jesus." It is also the opinion of many of the Fathers that the coming of the Holy Ghost was hastened on account of the powerful intercession of Mary.

Application: Let us also seek her intercession; let us beg of her to aid our efforts, to be in the midst of us, and to present our desires to her Divine Son. Let us ask her to obtain for each of us the grace not to forfeit any of the special graces which God may intend to bestow upon him on the Feast of Pentecost.
Colloquy with our Lady.

Third Day of the Novena (Sunday): On the Gospel of the Day – The Testimony borne by the Holy Ghost and the Apostles to Jesus

1st prelude: Consider Jesus saying to His Apostles: "When the Paraclete cometh, He shall give testimony of Me, and you shall give testimony."
2nd prelude: Ask for unbounded confidence in the mysterious operations of the Holy Ghost.

Point I: How the Holy Ghost bore witness to Jesus

Consideration: The Holy Ghost bore witness to Jesus in the most striking manner. He proved to the world that Jesus is the Son of God, the Savior of men, the Judge of the living and the dead He led men to worship a crucified God, and to crucify their own flesh with all its concupiscences. He made the cause of Jesus to triumph over all the malice of those who opposed the preaching of His Gospel; He gave courage to women and children, making them despise a cruel death and suffer the most fearful torture for the love of Jesus.

Application: Jesus had foretold these marvelous effects of the operation of the Holy Ghost, who was the guide the Church after His Ascension. He had solemnly promised to send Him to the Apostles, telling them that without His help they could do nothing, while with it they would work miracles of conversion and sanctification. He desired, nevertheless, that they should ask for Him, and dispose themselves to receive Him by constant and fervent prayer; and it is only under the same conditions that we can hope to produce any fruit in our labor for souls. Experience must have taught us that, without the cooperation of the Holy Spirit, all our efforts are vain and fruitless. Hence comes the practice introduced from time immemorial in the Church and in religious communities, of invoking the Holy Ghost before every important undertaking, and even before all the ordinary actions of the day. Do we make this invocation with real piety and devotion?

Affections and Resolutions.

Point II: How the Apostles gave testimony to Jesus

Consideration: After saying, "He shall give testimony of Me," Jesus immediately added, "and you shall give testimony in Jerusalem, and in all Judea, and Samaria, and even to the uttermost part of the earth." We know how faithfully the Apostles fulfilled this great and glorious mission. They made known their Master's name in all the world, and caused Him to be adored in spite of all the opposition of men and devils. They destroyed the idols, and overthrew the temples of the false gods of the heathen. They changed the whole world from Pagan to Christian, and founded the Church of Jesus Christ, which nineteen centuries have neither changed nor shaken.

Application: Observe that they who worked all these miracles were twelve poor fishermen, weak and ignorant persons. Why did the Son of God choose such instruments to lay the foundations of His Church? First, to prove, by convincing evidence, that it is not a human, but a divine institution, claiming therefore our obedience and submission; secondly that the thought of our own weakness and unworthiness should not deter us from undertaking great things for the glory of God and the salvation of souls.

Affections and Resolutions.

Point III: How we may bear testimony to Jesus

Consideration: To bear testimony to Jesus is to work for His glory, to make Him known, loved and served, by all the means in our power. Whoever does this, cooperates with the Holy Ghost and the Apostles in the greatest and holiest cause for which it is possible to labor.

Application: We who are enrolled in the army of Jesus are

under a special obligation to labor for the triumph of this cause. We may do it without being priests or missionaries, by our words, our actions, our prayers and our example. Do we thus act? Let us see wherein we have hitherto failed, and repair it by redoubled zeal for the future.

Colloquy with the Holy Ghost.

Fourth Day of the Novena (Monday): The Apostles and Disciples as Models of the Spirit of Prayer

1st prelude: Represent to yourself the Apostles and disciples in prayer in the upper chamber.

2nd prelude: Ask for grace to pray well, after their example.

Point I: The Apostles pray with faith and reverence

Consideration: According to Saint Luke, prayer was the chief occupation of the Apostles and disciples during the nine days that followed the Ascension. But how did they pray? With great faith, a keen sense of the presence of God, and consequently with great exterior and interior recollection. Since His Ascension, Jesus had no longer been visibly present with them. As man He was parted from them, but as God they knew that He was still in the midst of them, seeing and hearing all that they did. They therefore observed the greatest reverence and modesty both in words and actions.

Application: Behold here the first conditions of acceptable prayer. It must be accompanied by a lively faith, and a firm conviction that God sees and hears us, that His eye pierces into the inmost recesses of our hearts, and reads our most secret thoughts. Have we this faith? If so, we shall always be modest and reverent in our exterior, and attentive to our words. This follow as a matter of course. If, therefore, we pray without this reverence and attention, we have but little faith, and our prayers can avail but little.

Affections and Resolutions.

Point II: They pray with humility and confidence

Consideration: The prayer of the Apostles and disciples was accompanied by a deep humility and great confidence. Their humility proceeded from the remembrance of their past infidelities, and their consciousness of their own weakness and inability to accomplish the work entrusted to them. On the other hand, this very weakness led them to place great confidence in the efficacy of prayer, which their Divine Lord had told them would obtain all their desires and supply all their needs.

Application: "The prayer of him that humbleth himself shall pierce the clouds," says the Wise Man. Have not our prayers often failed for want of humility? And yet how many motives have we for humility! Our past sins, our frequent infidelities, and the uncertainty of our final perseverance. If we keep these things constantly in mind, we shall always pray with a humble and contrite heart, and this will increase both our confidence and our fervor.

Affections and Resolutions.

Point III: They pray with resignation and perseverance

Consideration: The Apostles prayed with perfect resignation as regarded the time when it might please God to send His Holy Spirit. They knew that He would be granted to their prayers; but being ignorant of the day and hour when He would come, they resolved to persevere for as long as it should please their Divine Lord to keep them in suspense. Their perseverance was rewarded on the tenth day, when they received the fullness of the gifts of the Holy Ghost.

Application: Have we not sometimes, at least by implication, attached certain conditions to our prayers with regard to time? Because our prayer was not granted at once, we have abandoned it, and so failed in resignation and perseverance. This is the cause of our prayer remaining unanswered: it is our own fault.

Colloquy with our Lady.

Fifth Day of the Novena (Tuesday): The Apostles adopt Measures to fill up the Place of the Traitor Judas

1st prelude: Consider Saint Peter speaking to the other Apostles and disciples.

2nd prelude: Beg the grace of constant fidelity to your vocation.

Point I: Saint Peter proposes to choose a successor to Judas.

Consideration: In the midst of their prayers, the Apostles did not neglect their duties. These need never interfere with one another. The apostasy of Judas had apparently disturbed the intentions of Jesus, who had chosen *twelve* Apostles to be the witnesses throughout all the world of His resurrection and His teaching. But the malice of men cannot hinder the designs of God. Peter, the head of the Apostolic College, felt himself inspired from on high. Saint Luke records that he rose up in the midst of his brethren, and said, "Men, brethren, … the Scriptures must needs be fulfilled; … for it is written in the book of Psalms, … And his bishopric let another take … Wherefore of these men who have companied with us all the time that the Lord Jesus came in and went out among us, … one of these must be made a witness with us of His Resurrection." The whole assembly agreed to the proposition of Saint Peter, and at once took steps to ascertain on whom the choice of God would fall.

Application: When a religious is tempted to renounce his vocation, let him not be guilty of the folly or vanity of supposing that either the cause of God, or that of his order, will suffer from his defection. On the contrary, we learn by this example that God will provide a worthier substitute for him. He alone will be the loser, and another will wear his crown. I may, perhaps, owe my vocation to the infidelity and apostasy of another.

Affections and Resolutions.

Point II: The assembly proposes Barsabas and Matthias

Consideration: The votes of the assembly being equally divided between "Joseph, called Barsabas, who was surnamed Justus, and Matthias," there seemed to be some difficulty and risk of contention in making a decision. To put an end to the doubt, they had recourse to prayer, and cast lots to discover the will of God in the matter. All with one voice said, "Thou, Lord, who knowest the hearts of all men, show whether of these two Thou has chosen,… and they gave them lots."

Application: We, too, sometimes have doubts and perplexities. Shall we ask such a favor, such a dispensation? Shall we apply to some superior for a change of abode, or of employment? We are at a loss how to decide. Let us follow the example of the Apostles – pray that God would make known His will to us. Have we always acted thus? Have we not mistaken our own desires, or substituted our own will for the will of God?

Affections and Resolutions.

Point III: God Himself decides in favor of Matthias

Consideration: "The lot fell upon Matthias, and he was

numbered with the eleven Apostles." The will of God being manifested, every one submitted to it with perfect unanimity, and all discord instantly ceased. All were at once ready to acknowledge the elect of God as one of the twelve Apostles of Jesus Christ; and neither did Matthias show any symptom of pride, nor Barsabas of jealousy.

Application: Call to mind, and be ready to practice the golden rule of Augustine – *In dubiis libertas*: *in certis unitas*. In things doubtful and not decided by authority, let every one be free to think or choose as he will; but in what is authoritatively laid down, let there be perfect unanimity both in thoughts and words. This rule is an excellent means for preserving peace and charity amongst brethren. Let us be faithful to it, and be willing to yield to others in things indifferent.

Colloquy with our Lord.

Sixth Day of the Novena, Wednesday: Our extreme Need of the Gifts of the Holy Ghost

1st prelude: Consider the Apostles, weak and ignorant men, hiding themselves for fear of the Jews.

2nd prelude: Let us ask the gifts of wisdom, understanding, and counsel.

Point I: What the Apostles were, and what we are, without the gift of wisdom

Consideration: The first gift of the Holy Ghost is *wisdom*, which consists in understanding how to appreciate things at their real value. *Sapientia a sapere*. Before receiving this gift, did the Apostles esteem and value the things of God and their own eternal salvation more than all the fleeting pleasures of this world? No, they were men of earthly minds, occupied entirely with the care of their bodies, and the desire to rise in the world and in their Master's favor. "There was a strife among them, which of them should seem to be greater," and they cared but little, in comparison, to watch or pray with Jesus.

Application: Behold what the Apostles were, and what we all are, without the gift of wisdom; cold and indifferent in spiritual things, in exercises of piety, humility, mortification, penance; finding a thousand excuses for shortening or omitting them; whilst we are full of activity about worldly matters and all that concerns our temporal welfare. Let us examine ourselves honestly on this point.

Affections and Resolutions.

Point II: What the Apostles were, and what we are, without the gift of understanding

Consideration: We see clearly in the holy gospels what the Apostles were before they received the gift of understanding – that is to say, before they were supernaturally enlightened so as to comprehend the divine mysteries. They understood nothing of those "mysteries of the kingdom of heaven" which our Divine Lord explained to them. They always interpreted His words in a material and carnal sense, so as to merit from Him the severe rebuke, "Are ye also yet without understanding?"

Application: This was their condition, and is also ours, without the gift of understanding – a condition incapable of comprehending the things of God, or of contemplating His divine perfections. The very world in which we live exhibits them to us – puts them as it were under our very hand – and yet we do not see them! We are like blind persons before a picture. The most touching spiritual books are read or explained to us, and we understand nothing of them; we are as indifferent as if we had literally no power of comprehension. Is not this but too true?

Affections and Resolutions.

Point III: What the Apostles were, and what we are, without the gift of counsel

Consideration: What were the Apostles without the gift of counsel? Inconstant and vacillating in their thoughts, their affections, their conduct; drifting with the stream; feeble and inconsistent. Desiring to follow Jesus in the way of the evangelical counsels, and yet cherishing earthly hopes in their hearts. One day full of zeal and courage, the next cast down and sad.

Application: Such also are we without the gift of counsel. Full of hesitation, darkness of mind, and false judgements, which make us the sport of our imagination, of the illusions of the devil, and of circumstances. Beginning and breaking off, willing and not willing, changeable as the wind, inconstant in everything, unable to make any solid progress. Is not this often a subject of complaint with us before God? Colloquy with the Holy Ghost.

Seventh Day of the Novena (Thursday): Continuation of the same Subject: Our extreme Need of the Gifts of the Holy Ghost

1st prelude: Consider the Apostles, weak and ignorant men, hiding themselves for fear of the Jews.
2nd prelude: Beg earnestly for the gifts of fortitude, knowledge, piety and the fear of the Lord.

Point I: What the Apostles were, and what we are, without the gift of fortitude

Consideration: Before being endued with "power from on high," the Apostles were indeed men of good will, but weak, timid and cowardly in the extreme. At the Last Supper they all made strong protestations of fidelity to their Divine Master, and declared themselves ready to follow Him to prison and death; and yet the moment they saw Him taken by the soldiers of the high priest, they all forsook Him and fled.

Application: Is not this a faithful picture of our own state when we are left to ourselves? Strong in promises, protests, and good resolutions, but weak and cowardly when it comes to putting them into practice. Breaking our firmest resolutions almost as soon as we have made them; yielding to the very smallest temptation; always finding some excuse for neglecting some point of our rule, or some duty of our office; often unable to make the slightest effort in even a trivial matter, such as awaking at our appointed time.
Affections and Resolutions.

Point II: What the Apostles were, and what we are, without the gift of knowledge

Consideration: Our Divine Lord wished to convince the world that His religion was not the work of men. He therefore made choice, for its propagation, of twelve Galilean fishermen – poor, ignorant, uneducated, unintellectual, caring only for the trade by which they gained their livelihood. Such were the Apostles, and such they would always have remained, without the gift of knowledge, which they received at Pentecost.

Application: If we happen to be better educated, and to have more opportunities of progress in secular learning, let us at least admit that we are but very little advanced in the science of the saints, and that we have cared less to perfect ourselves therein than to study other matters which are comparatively vain and unprofitable, though we are bound as religious to aim at a high degree of sanctity, and to bring others to it by our example and teaching.

Affections and Resolutions.

Point III: What the Apostles were, and what we are, without the gift of piety and the fear of God

Consideration: How imperfect was the love of the Apostles for their Divine Master! It was far less a pure sentiment of childlike affection than the spirit of self-interest and egotism. They loved Him more for their own sakes than for His. Hence came the cowardice and treachery of their conduct towards Him especially at the time of His Passion and death.

Application: Have we not similar conduct to reproach ourselves with? Do we really love God for Himself, and not for our own advantage? When we abstain from offending Him, is it not chiefly to avoid the punishment of sin, the torments of hell, the sufferings of purgatory? And when we make voluntary acts of any virtue, is it not chiefly for the sake of the reward promised to them? These dispositions are certainly not sinful or even blameworthy, but they are far removed from that *piety, filial fear*, and *perfect charity* infused into the hearts of the Apostles by the Holy Ghost on the Day of Pentecost.

Colloquy with the Holy Ghost.

Eighth Day of the Novena (Friday): On the principal Ends of the Coming of the Holy Ghost

1st prelude: Represent to yourself Jesus saying to His Apostles: "If I go not, the Paraclete will not come to you."

2nd prelude: Ask the grace to attain the ends proposed by God in the descent of the Holy Ghost.

Point I: The Holy Ghost came to console the Apostles

Consideration: In order to keep up our fervor till the end of the Novena, let us meditate on the great ends for which our blessed Lord promised to send the Holy Ghost upon His Apostles and disciples. First it was that He might be with them after His own Ascension, to take His place in comforting and encouraging them in all the trials of life, and especially in the hard labors of their apostolate. "A little while, and now you shall not see Me," He had said to them, "because I go to the Father… I will not leave you orphans… I will ask the Father, and He shall give you another Paraclete, that He may abide with you forever." His promise was fulfilled. When they first began to preach, the Apostles were beaten and cast into prison; but, far from being disheartened or afflicted, "they went from the presence of the council rejoicing." The Holy Ghost worked the same miracle for the early Christians, though subjected to the most dreadful persecutions; for Saint Luke writes that "the Church… was filled with the consolation of the Holy Ghost."

Application: We also must expect to meet with many trials, difficulties, and contradictions on fulfilling the duties of our state; but if the Holy Ghost be with us, we shall endure them not only with resignation, but with joy, and crosses and humiliations will become our greatest delight. How diligently, then, ought we to seek and to entertain this blessed Spirit!

Affections and Resolutions.

Point II: He was to be their Guide

Consideration: The second end which God had in view in sending down the Holy Ghost upon the Apostles was to shed upon their souls the clear light of faith, and to give them a more perfect understanding of the truths which Jesus had only partially revealed, and also to show them things to come. We know this from the words which our Blessed Lord addressed to them on the eve of His death: "I have yet many things to say to you; but you cannot bear them now. But when He, the Spirit of Truth, is come, He will teach you all truth, - and the things that are to come He shall show you."

Application: What the Holy Ghost did for the Apostles and early Christians He will also for all who strive to attract Him into their hearts and retain Him there. It is for this reason that on all important occasions the Church begins by imploring the light and assistance of the Holy Ghost, and that the practice has obtained in religious communities of reciting frequently during the day either the *Veni Creator* or the *Veni Sancte Spiritus*. How do we make these invocations? With our lips only, or with our hearts also? Let us examine ourselves on this point.

Affections and Resolutions.

Point III: He was to impart a divine unction to their words

Consideration: The Apostles were to glorify Jesus Christ not only in themselves, but in others, by making them know, love and practice His divine teaching, by inspiring them with a horror of vice and love of virtue; in a word, by making them saints. The third end of the descent of the Holy Ghost was to enable them to accomplish this task, so far beyond their natural strength. "For," said our Blessed Lord, "I will give you a mouth and wisdom, which all your adversaries shall not be able to resist and gainsay. For it is not you that speak, but the Spirit of your Father that speaketh in you."
Colloquy with the Holy Ghost.

Ninth Day of the Novena (Saturday): Eve of Pentecost: The Dispositions suitable for the Coming of the Holy Ghost

1st prelude: Let us represent to ourselves the assembly in the upper chamber.
2nd prelude: Let us ask grace to prepare ourselves for the great feast of tomorrow, by recollection, prayer and union with Mary.

Point I: Recollection

Consideration: We are approaching the end of our Novena; let us, then, renew our fervor, that we may not lose its fruits. Let us call to mind, and put in practice with redoubled ardor, all the means that may conduce to that end. The first of these is recollection, which produces peace in the soul and union with God. The Apostles taught in retirement from the world, in silence and solitude.

Application: If we cannot spend this day in retirement from the distractions of the world, in silence and retreat; if the preparations for tomorrow's feast even add to our ordinary interruptions and occupations – let us try to make a solitude in our hearts, a kind of secret chamber into which we may retire; let us avoid all the causes of dissipation, such as over-eagerness in our work, unnecessary conversations, useless goings to and fro; let us keep guard carefully over our senses and observe strictly the rules of modesty and silence, that we may be "interior men, closely united to God, lending, but not giving, ourselves to exterior things" (*Imitation*).
Affections and Resolutions.

Point II: Prayer

Consideration: Prayer is the second means which was pointed out from the first day of the Novena as indispensable for obtaining a large outpouring of the gifts of the Holy Ghost. The Apostles might have seemed to be excused from it, since they had receive from Jesus Christ Himself the *assurance* that the Holy Ghost would come down to them will all His gifts; but yet they never ceased to pray earnestly for Him, until they had received Him. They knew well that the gifts of God, though bestowed liberally and by His free grace, must yet be also the fruits of persevering prayer.

Application: Let us call to mind the days of the Novena that have already passed, and examine if there has been any relaxation in our prayers. Our inconstancy makes it but too probable; and if we find it to have been the case, let us try today to compensate for it by redoubled fervor. Do not say that your numerous occupations today will hinder you from praying much, for Holy Scripture says, "Let nothing hinder thee from praying always." We do not pray with our hands, but with our hearts. Let your external occupations be accompanied by frequent raisings of your heart towards God, and they will be changed into prayers. We may thus pray all day long without interruption.

Point III: Invocation of our Lady

Consideration: There is a third means which adds greatly to the efficacy of the two preceding. We have not neglected to mention it before; but we must take special notice of it today, the last day of the Novena. This means is the intercession of our Lady, of whom the world's Redeemer was born, and "through whose intercession," says Saint Bernard, "God grants all our petitions."

Application: Let us, then, today fix our eyes upon our glorious and powerful Mother. Let us ask her with great confidence to unite her prayers to ours, as she united them on this day to those of the Apostles and disciples, and to obtain for us, as she did for them, a copious outpouring of the gifts of the Holy Ghost. We should do well to insert her name in all our ejaculatory prayers, and we shall do this the more readily as Saturday is always consecrated to her honor.

Colloquy with our Lady.

Feast of Pentecost: On the Mysteries of the Day

1st prelude: Behold with the eye of faith the upper chamber at the moment of the descent of the Holy Ghost.
2nd prelude: Ask for grace to understand rightly the threefold object of this great feast – the descent of the Holy Ghost, the promulgation of the Gospel, and the establishment of the Church.

Point I: The descent of the Holy Ghost on the Apostles and disciples

Consideration: Ten days after His Ascension, and on the fiftieth day after Easter (Pentecostes), Jesus fulfilled the promise He had so often made to His Apostles of sending them His Holy Spirit. We read in the second chapter of the Acts that "when the days of the Pentecost were accomplished, they were altogether in one place: and suddenly there came a sound from heaven, as of a mighty wind coming, and it filled the whole house where they were sitting. And there appeared to them parted tongues as it were of fire, and it sat upon every one of them: and they were all filled with the Holy Ghost, and they began to speak with divers tongues, according as the Holy Ghost gave them to speak." It is in these few and simple words that Saint Luke records the great and mysterious event which substituted the Christian feast of Pentecost for the Jewish one; an event which changed the Apostles in one moment from carnal and ignorant into spiritual and eloquent men, eminent both in wisdom and holiness, gifted with an invincible zeal and courage, and thenceforward fully capable of executing their great commission of evangelizing mankind and changing the whole face of the earth.

Application: We celebrate today the anniversary of this great event, and that not only by commemorating it as we commemorate our Lord's resurrection at Easter, but by seeking to renew it within ourselves. In this respect the feast of Pentecost differs from all others; for others are feasts of gratitude for past mercies, whereas in this we celebrate a mystery which is continually renewed in the Church, and which will be renewed in the souls of the faithful, even to the end of the world. At this very day we may venture, according to the promise of Jesus Christ, to ask, and to expect with the same confidence as the Apostles, the descent of the Holy Ghost upon ourselves, and the communication of His gifts. Among all the

religious who have been making this Novena, many will receive this great favor, though not outwardly, that being now no longer necessary. May we be among this number!
Affections and Resolutions.

Point II: The promulgation of the Gospel

Consideration: The second event of which we celebrate the anniversary today is the promulgation of the Gospel. Beginning in Jerusalem on the feast of Pentecost, and blessed with extraordinary success by the conversion and baptism of three thousand Jews, it extended rapidly over all the known world through the inspired preaching of the Apostles. Even during their lifetime, Jesus was adored in every nation under the sun. The prophecy was fulfilled: *Et renovabis faciem terrae* – "Thou shalt renew the face of the earth"; and "I will pour out My Spirit upon all flesh."

Application: Through the uninterrupted succession of Sovereign Pontiffs, Bishops and priests, successors of Saint Peter, of the Apostles, and of the seventy-two disciples, the Gospel, with all its spiritual and temporal advantages, has reached us. On this day we commemorate this great blessing, and render thanks for it to Almighty God. All are bound to do this; but for us who are religious it is not enough. We have been called to an apostolic life and work, and we must today renew our zeal, and examine whether by our words, our example, our prayers, our works of penance, in short, by all the means within our power, we contribute as much as in us lies to extend the kingdom of God among souls. Let us see wherein we have failed, and how we can do better for the future.
Affections and Resolutions.

Point III: Establishment of the Church

Consideration: The nations who were converted by the preaching of the Apostles, although so different in disposition and character, yet formed but one family, having the same faith, the same laws, the same Sacraments, the same Head. This great family, spread over all the world, is the Church of Jesus Christ – one, holy, catholic. For more than nineteen hundred years the "gates of hell" have fought against it; but they have not prevailed, and never shall prevail. We celebrate today the memory of its establishment. This is the third object of the great solemnity of Pentecost.
Colloquy with the Holy Ghost.

Whit-Monday: Mysterious Circumstances of the Feast of Pentecost

1st prelude: Behold with the eye of faith the upper chamber at the moment of the descent of the Holy Ghost.
2nd prelude: Ask for the most loving and childlike devotion to Jesus Christ and His holy Church.

Point I: The time of this Feast

Consideration: The Christian Pentecost occurred on a Sunday, the fiftieth day after the Sunday of the Resurrection. That day was the one following the Great Sabbath, or Jewish Pasch; from whence it follows that the descent of the Holy Ghost did not take place on the Jewish Pentecost, but on the day following (Cornelius a Lapide, *in Act. Apost.*). This circumstance, divinely ordained, inaugurated a great and solemn mystery, namely, *the succession of the New Law to the Old.* The Old Law, suited to the hard-heartedness of the Jews, was a law of *fear* and *bondage*, given in the midst of thunders, engraved on *stone*; the New Law, on the contrary, is a law of *love* and *liberty*, written by the Holy Ghost Himself on the hearts of the faithful, when He fills them with the interior spirit of love and filial piety.

Application: Let us thank God for having been born and baptized under the law of grace, and seek to perfect in ourselves the interior law of love. This must be done in three ways: 1st, we must treat God with the greatest confidence, like a tender Father, and not a hard master or severe tyrant; 2nd, we must be actuated always by the spirit of love, and not by that of fear; 3rd, we must serve God our Lord for Himself, and not for the sake of any reward. What is our state in this respect? Have we a true spirit of love? What progress have we made therein?
Affections and Resolutions.

Point II: The place

Consideration: On the Day of Pentecost the twelve Apostles, presided over by Saint Peter, and all the other faithful disciples were assembled, with Mary in the midst of them, in the upper room already consecrated by the mysteries of the Last Supper. This was the place chosen by the Holy Ghost to communicate Himself to men, and which He filled throughout with His divine truth, but without extending Himself outside of it. This house, we are told, represents the Church, or "the assembly of the faithful who profess the true doctrine of Jesus Christ, under obedience to the successor of Saint Peter" (*Mechlin Catechism*). There alone is the Holy Spirit given; from thence alone flow the holy Sacraments, the only true means of eternal salvation. "There is no salvation out of the Church."

Application: What a blessed privilege to have the Church for our Mother! Through her we inherit eternal life. She showers down fresh graces upon us every day. What return can we make to her? We can love her, honor her by the purity of our lives, pray earnestly that God would render her victorious over her enemies, and give her the whole world for her inheritance, according to the promise of our Blessed Lord; and offer to God for these ends our health, our talents, our learning and even our lives. Can we do more? Yes; we can use all our influence with others to induce them to love and honor the holy Church, and to undertake her defence against her enemies. We can recommend and endeavor to spread that excellent institution, the Propagation of the Faith. Let us examine what we have done, what we have not done, and what we intend to do.

Colloquy with our Lord.

Whit-Tuesday: The outward Signs employed by the Holy Ghost in the Mystery of Pentecost

1st prelude: To see the tongues of fire which rested on the heads of the Apostles and disciples.

2nd prelude: To ask for grace to comprehend the mystery hidden under the symbols of wind and tongues of fire.

Point I: The symbol of a mighty wind

Consideration: "And suddenly there came a sound from heaven, as of a mighty wind coming." By the rushing sound of a whirlwind approaching the house and being arrested there, the Holy Ghost desired to warn the Apostles of His coming, and also to attract a large concourse of people, so as to give an opportunity for the preaching of the Gospel; and that they might, by baptizing a great number of Jews, lay on that very day the foundation of the Church, substituting it for the synagogue. This symbol was, moreover, a singularly appropriate one, for it represented the vehemence of the zeal with which the Apostles would preach the Gospel throughout the world, and in spite of all obstacles.

Application: Let us ask the Holy Spirit to breathe into our souls His divine inspiration, detaching them from all earthly objects, and raising them up to heaven. Let us ask Him to fill all the powers of our soul, as He "filled all the house" where the Apostles were sitting. We have every reason to hope for such a favor, but we must not be discouraged if we do not immediately obtain it, remembering that "the Spirit breatheth where He will." He will come, as it has been foretold of Him, *suddenly*, and when we least expect Him.

Affections and Resolutions.

Point II: The symbol of tongues

Consideration: No sooner were the Apostles warned of the coming of the Holy Ghost than "there appeared to them parted tongues, as it were of fire, and it sat upon every one of them." Why did Almighty God choose this outward sign of the presence of His Holy Spirit? Because it was the Holy Spirit alone who could so inspire the tongues of the Apostles as to enable them to preach the Gospel in all the world. For this purpose the *gift of tongues* was bestowed upon them, as we read in the Acts of the Apostles: "They were all filled with the Holy Ghost, and they began to speak with divers tongues."

Application: Our tongues are, perhaps, not intended to be employed like those of the Apostles or apostolic missionaries; but we are certainly bound to use them for the glory of God and the benefit of our neighbor; especially we who are consecrated to God by religious vows. Let us remember that the *gift of speech*, of which the *gift of tongues* is only an extension, is one of the most precious gifts of God to man. He will demand a strict account of our use or abuse thereof, and how rare it is to find anyone who never abuses it! Saint James says: "If any one offend not in word, the same is a perfect man." We have, indeed, here sufficient matter for self-examination.

Affections and Resolutions.

Point III: The symbol of fire

Consideration: It is said that these tongues were "as it were of fire." It is the nature of fire to enlighten, warm, dilate, purify and consume; it therefore rightly represents the operations of the Holy

Ghost in the hearts of the Apostles. He illuminated them with the light of faith; He enkindled in them the love of God and their neighbor; He enlarged their hearts, so that thenceforward God alone could fill them; He purified them from every stain, and transformed them in such a manner that they became one with Himself.

Application: The Holy Ghost still performs the same miracles in the hearts of those who receive Him, especially during the feast of Pentecost. Why should He not work them in our regard? The Novena we have just completed, and His own desire to impart His gifts to us, ought to give us the fullest confidence. Let us ask, and we shall receive.

Colloquy with our Lady.

Wednesday in the Octave of Pentecost: Miraculous Operations of the Holy Ghost in the Hearts of the Apostles

1st prelude: Let us behold the eyes of the Apostles glistening with the fire which fills them.

2nd prelude: Let us ask to be partakers of the miraculous effects of the operations of the Holy Ghost in the Apostles.

Point I: Wonderful transformation of the Apostles

Consideration: Simultaneously with the appearance of the tongues, the Apostles were all "filled with the Holy Ghost," and transformed into quite different men: from being timid, proud, vacillating, and slaves of their passions, they became suddenly marvels of knowledge, strength, humility, constancy, and holiness – purified from all stain of sin, and confirmed in sanctifying grace. What their Divine Master had not chosen to do Himself in the course of three years was accomplished by the Holy Ghost in one moment, and without any effort on the part of the Apostles.

Application: The Holy Ghost still performs the same miracles, through less sensibly, in the hearts of those who are docile to His inspirations, and especially when they receive the holy Sacraments worthily. We receive them frequently, and yet we complain of being so little illuminated in divine things – so weak, so ready to fall under temptation, so constantly relapsing into the same faults and imperfections; almost always in a state of tepidity. Let us examine if the fault is not entirely in ourselves – in our negligence,

or want of fervor in receiving the Sacraments.
Affections and Resolutions.

Point II: Admirable zeal of the Apostles

Consideration: The first use which the Apostles made of the gifts of understanding and of tongues was to publish the glory and greatness of God; and by their burning zeal and eloquent words to make Jesus, His Divine Son, known, loved, glorified and obeyed. This was the language of the Holy Ghost, in opposition to the language of the world, which generally is employed to speak of ourselves, and praise our own works, seeking thereby to obtain esteem and admiration for ourselves.

Application: Are we influenced by the Spirit of God, or by the spirit of the world and of vainglory? If we take pleasure in speaking of God; if we seek to bring the lost sheep into the true Church, and to make known the religion of Jesus Christ, we speak the language of the Holy Ghost; but if, on the contrary, we speak only of ourselves, we may conclude that He does not really dwell in our hearts, since it is out of the abundance of the heart that the mouth speaketh.

Affections and Resolutions.

Point III: Admirable constancy of the Apostles

Consideration: The zeal of the Apostles quickly raised them up enemies: the wicked turned them into ridicule, the Scribes calumniated them, the princes of the people had them cast into prison and beaten with rods, and even threatened them with death, if they dared to preach any more in the name of Jesus. But, far from being alarmed or discouraged, the Apostles only continued with redoubled zeal to preach Jesus and the Resurrection, answering any who sought to hinder them in the memorable words, "If it be just in the sight of God to obey you rather than God, judge ye." "For we cannot but speak the things which we have seen and heard… We ought to obey God rather than men."

Application: If we act in like manner, we shall meet with the like treatment: we shall be unjustly accused, calumniated, persecuted. But let us not therefore be discouraged. We must not regulate our conduct according to the world's praise or blame, but according to the law of God, the rules of our order, and the commands of our superior and spiritual guides. If we act thus, we shall be secure from error, and our zeal will be discreet, faithful and blessed with success both for ourselves and our neighbors. Colloquy with our Lady.

Thursday in the Octave of Pentecost: First Sermon of Saint Peter

1st prelude: Imagine that you behold the Apostles standing in the midst of a crowd of Jews eager to hear them speak.
2nd prelude: Ask grace to proclaim the Word of God, or to hear it proclaimed, so as to obtain great fruit.

Point I: The audience of Saint Peter

Consideration: The strange report of the “mighty wind” had attracted a great crowd to the house inhabited by the Apostles. There were then, as Saint Luke tells us, “dwelling at Jerusalem, Jews, devout men out of every nation under heaven” – Jews who faithfully observed the obligation of visiting the Temple once every year. Saint Peter’s audience therefore consisted of persons from all parts of the world, speaking all manner of different languages; so that they may justly say he spoke to the whole world, since they would be sure, on their return to their homes, to publish abroad the words of the Apostles, and the striking miracle which accompanied them; namely, “that every man heard them speak in his own tongue.” Thus the seed of the Gospel was sown throughout the world, even before the dispersion of the Apostles, who had afterwards only to water and make it fruitful, causing it to bring forth numerous Christian communities.

Application: Let us here observe how admirably Divine Providence adapts the means to the ends which are to be accomplished, or to the work appointed to men. The mission of the Apostles was to publish the Gospel throughout the whole world, and to found the Catholic or Universal Church. But how could they do this? The wonderful circumstances we have just recorded will supply the answer. Let us then trust God implicitly, and rest assured of His assistance in all the labors required of us by obedience, in all the difficulties and sacrifices which the obligation of aiming at perfection imposes upon us. He will supply all our needs, even, if it should be necessary, by miraculous intervention. Affections and Resolutions.

Point II: Saint Peter’s discourse

Consideration: Let us consider its matter and its form. Its matter was simply a collection of texts from Holy Scripture, announcing the coming of the Holy Ghost, and its marvelous effects; together with the life, death and resurrection of Jesus of Nazareth, the promised Messiah, that Just One whom, as Saint Peter told his hearers, they themselves had crucified and slain. In its form we see a wonderful freedom and energy of expression, united with rare prudence and wisdom. Instead of beginning with harsh rebukes, which would only have exasperated his hearers, the Apostle calls their attention to the various prophecies, and shows them, with masterly eloquence, how they had been deceived by their rulers into demanding the death of their Redeemer, the Author of life! This was the surest way to lead them to repent and condemn themselves; as, in fact, actually happened.

Application: If we have to correct or punish others, let us imitate the conduct of the Apostle, which was inspired by the Holy Ghost. Let us first endeavor by all means to convince the guilty of their error, and to lead them to acknowledge it. But let us avoid all harsh and bitter expressions, and suppose that their conduct has arisen from ignorance, or the persuasion of others. In this manner we shall gain their hearts, and obtain all that we desire from them. If we have to receive correction, let us behold in him who administers it a tender father performing a painful duty only for our good.

Affections and Resolutions.

Point III: Success of Saint Peter

Consideration: This was most marvelous: three thousand persons were converted to the true Faith, placed themselves under the direction of the Apostles, were baptized and received the gift of the Holy Ghost. Five thousand more soon followed their example. The Church was founded and organized, and even during the lifetime of the Apostles was spread through every portion of the habitable globe.

Application: We must never despair of the success of any work undertaken with a good intention; though we must look for it not to our efforts, but to the assistance of the Holy Ghost. Have we not sometimes forgotten this?

Colloquy with the Holy Ghost.

Friday in the Octave of Pentecost: Miraculous Operations of the Holy Ghost in the early Christians

1st prelude: Behold the first Christians assembled with the Apostles to sing the praises of God.
2nd prelude: Ask the Holy Ghost to renew in our souls what He effected in theirs.

Point I: Miraculous detachment

Consideration: The gifts of wisdom and of understanding so plentifully bestowed upon the early Christians, had a marvelous effect in entirely weaning their affections from earthly possessions and honors. These things became henceforward only obstacles and hindrances to them in the acquisition of heavenly treasures. Therefore, "their possessions and goods they sold, and divided them to all, according as every one had need;… and all things were common unto them." Thus, being free from all worldly cares, they thought only of heavenly things. They enjoyed great peace and joy, serving God without distraction or hindrance.

Application: We too have been taught by the Holy Ghost that Christian perfection consist in entire detachment from earthly goods; and have also received the grace to renounce them at once and for ever by the vow of holy poverty in a religious order approved by the Church. Happy poverty! Happy community life! It gives us all the advantages enjoyed by the early Christians, and also puts us in possession of eternal life, according to our Blessed Lord's promise: "Every one that hath left house or brethren… for My name's sake, shall receive an hundredfold, and shall possess life everlasting."

Affections and Resolutions.

Point II: Miraculous charity

Consideration: Not less wonderful in the eyes of the world than the spirit of poverty was the spirit of love and union which reigned among the early Christians. Although differing in nation, in manners, in habits, all were so united in heart and mind that, as Saint Luke says, "they had but one heart and one soul"; they spoke the same language, they prayed together, they ate together, they shared the same joys, and were ready to share the same sorrows and to make the same sacrifices. Men were constrained to believe in the divine origin of a religion which produced such fruits, and the number of converts increased daily.

Application: The works of God are the same in every age; the love and paternal union which the Holy Ghost inspired in the early Christians, to the astonishment of a self-seeking world, still flourish in religious communities, as we can joyfully testify. Let us show our gratitude by carefully avoiding all that could injure the perfection of community life, such as singularity, contention, particular friendships, or special privileges; desiring nothing more than to be in all things like our brethren; loving them with a supernatural charity, in all sincerity and simplicity, and always ready to do them service, even at the cost of our ease and comfort.
Affections and Resolutions.

Point III: Miraculous piety

Consideration: "And they were persevering in the doctrine of the Apostles, and in the communication of the breaking of bread, and in prayers." Before their conversion these very disciples had been worldly-minded men, whose whole religion consisted in certain external observances, without interior devotion; as our Blessed Lord had once complained: "This people honoreth Me with their lips, but their heart is far from Me." But now these same men have become interior, spiritual, contemplative – full of the most tender piety. This was the third miraculous operation of the Holy Ghost in their hearts. How did they preserve and increase this gift? By persevering in the doctrine of the Apostles, in prayer and communion.
Colloquy with the Holy Ghost.

Saturday in the Octave of Pentecost: Miraculous Transformation in human Society effected by the Holy Ghost

1st prelude: Consider the words of David: "Thou shalt send Thy Spirit, and they shall be created; and Thou shalt renew the face of the earth."
2nd prelude: Ask for a large outpouring of the gifts of the Holy Ghost.

Point I: Benevolent institutions

Consideration: What was the state of society before the coming of the Holy Ghost? Idolatry and superstition, tyranny and oppression, reigned everywhere; the most revolting vices were even worshipped! The breath of the Holy Spirit swept away these abominations, and substituted for them the reign of truth, justice and virtue. What was the condition of the poor and the unfortunate? They were treated with neglect and contempt, as the objects of the malediction of the gods. Even among the most civilized pagans there was no attempt at any asylum or refuge for the destitute and suffering. They had not the spirit of charity. This could only come from God. It was shed abroad with the greatest profusion by the Holy Ghost, as Saint Paul says, in his Epistle to the Romans: "The charity of God is poured forth in our hearts by the Holy Ghost, who is given to us." This divine charity began without delay to "renew the face of the earth," covering it with hospitals and charitable institutions of all kinds for the sick, the destitute, for old age, for children, raising up benevolent societies and religious communities of men and women devoted to the service of others, even at the cost of their lives. The martyrs of charity everywhere accompanied the martyrs of the faith.

Application: How blessed are those who, following in the footsteps of the Apostles, carry the Gospel into heathen lands! And not less blessed they who, for love of God, and by the duties of their institute, devote themselves to the service of the poor and ignorant. Are they not almost canonized already by the sentence of Jesus Christ: "Come, ye blessed of My Father; for I was hungry, and you gave Me to eat… Amen I say to you, as long as you did it to one of these My least brethren, you did it to Me"? We who have left all to devote themselves to the service of the sick and needy are among this happy number if we are faithful to our obligations. Affections and Resolutions.

Point II: Abolition of slavery

Consideration: Before the coming of the Holy Ghost and the preaching of the Gospel, more than half the human race was oppressed under the yoke of the most cruel slavery. In pagan Rome, the centre of civilization, a single individual often possessed many thousands of slaves. And in the eyes of their masters these slaves were looked upon as no better than mere beasts of burden; they were put to death for a mere whim or caprice, compelled to destroy each other in the amphitheaters for the amusement of the people, sacrificed on the altars of their false gods, or rather, of devils. Reason had in vain lifted up her voice against these horrors by the mouth of philosophers. It was reserved for the Holy Ghost to abolish them by the mouth of the Apostles, and to proclaim to the world that "there is no respect of persons with God," and that with Him there is neither "bond nor free, but Christ is all and in all." These fundamental principles, constantly insisted upon by the holy Pontiffs, successors of the Apostles, at length prevailed, and succeeded in civilizing the world.

Application: How great is the blindness and ignorance of those who attribute the blessings of civilization not to the Divine Author of all good, but to merely natural causes! They do not, or will not, see that these natural causes, this progress of the mere human spirit, have produced no such results in lands where the Gospel is still unknown. Let us pray for those who are still in the darkness and misery of error, and oppressed by cruel tyranny, and earnestly endeavor to break off from ourselves the yoke of human respect and unruly passions.

Colloquy with the Holy Ghost.

Feast of the Most Holy Trinity: The Blessings we owe to the Three Persons

1st prelude: Listen to Jesus Christ saying: "Teach ye all nations, baptizing them in the name of the Father, and of the Son, and of the Holy Ghost."

2nd prelude: Ask the grace to know and to feel interiorly all the love and gratitude you owe to each one of the Three Persons of the Blessed Trinity.

Point I: Love and benefits of God the Father

Consideration: The mystery of the Holy Trinity is the greatest of all mysteries. The feast which the Church has appointed to be celebrated on this day in its honor is, as it were, the compliment and gathering up into one of all the feasts of the ecclesiastical year. It is a mystery quite beyond our comprehension, the finite being incapable of understanding the infinite; but we must adore it with the deepest humility, the most tender love, the most lively gratitude, for it is the source of all good to us. In order to excite these sentiments, let us call to mind all that we owe to the love of the Three Persons of the Most Holy Trinity. "I believe in God the

Father Almighty, Creator of heaven and earth." Omnipotence, and the work of creation, which implies omnipotence, is the special attribute of the Father, because He is the first principal from which the two other Persons proceed. To Him, then, I owe my existence, my preservation, and all that had conduced to my preservation; without Him I should be nothing, and should always have remained nothing.

Application: God saw from all eternity, in the nothingness out of which you were created, millions of possible beings, who would have served Him better than you have done, and glorified Him more; why, then, has He created you rather than them? Out of a gratuitous love of predilection: "I have loved thee with an everlasting love." To this love you owe it that you have been preserved from so many dangers in which others have perished, and that you enjoy so many peculiar favors both of nature and grace. Love demands love in return. What return have you made to so loving and generous a God and Father? Perhaps you have loved Him but little, and served Him grudgingly.

Affections and Resolutions.

Point II: Love and benefits of God the Son

Consideration: The love of God the Son for us has been manifested in a still more striking manner than by the benefit of creation, namely, by that of *redemption*, which has not only ransomed us from slavery and death, but reinstated us in all our primitive rights. What would be thought in the world if the son of a king should take the place of a criminal, and offer his life for him?

Application: This is what the Son of God has done for each one of us. "He debased Himself," says the Apostle, "taking the form of a servant, becoming obedient unto death, even the death of the cross." From which the Apostle concludes that we ought henceforth to live only for Him who died for us: "That they also who live may not now live to themselves, but unto Him who died for them." Have we given this proof of our love and gratitude to Him?

Affections and Resolutions.

Point III: Love and benefits of the Holy Ghost

Consideration: The love of the Holy Ghost manifests itself especially in our sanctification and adoption. He sanctified us in our Baptism, purifying our soul from all stain, filling it with divine charity, and all those prerogatives of sanctifying grace which raise us to the dignity of adopted sons and heirs of God, and co-heirs of Jesus Christ. In the words of Saint Paul, "The charity of God is poured forth in our hearts by the Holy Ghost, who is given to us." For the "Spirit Himself giveth testimony to our spirit that we are the sons of God; and if sons, heirs also, heirs indeed of God and joint-heirs with Christ." He has also sanctified us in our Confirmation, and in partaking of the other Sacraments; and still further by the attractions of His grace leading us to the perfection of our state, or to the religious life.

Application: How many benefits have I received without any merit on my part, and even in spite of my great unworthiness! "What shall I render to the Lord," to the Three Persons of the Blessed Trinity, "for all the things that He has rendered to me?" Colloquy with the Three Adorable Persons of the Holy Trinity.

Monday after Trinity Sunday: Relations of the Christian with the Holy Trinity

1st prelude: Listen to Jesus Christ saying: "Teach ye all nations, baptizing them in the name of the Father, and of the Son, and of the Holy Ghost."

2nd prelude: Ask grace to understand rightly our relations with the Three Persons of the Most Holy Trinity.

Point I: Our relations with God the Father

Consideration: What is a Christian? A man who has a special relationship to God the Father, whose child he became in holy Baptism. What Jesus Christ is by *nature*, the Christian is by *adoption*. He receives by spiritual regeneration, according to his capacity, what the Word received in His eternal generation. "You have received," says Saint Paul, "the spirit of adoption of sons, whereby we cry Abba, Father." What an honor would be conferred on the son of a poor man if he were adopted by some powerful monarch, and invested with all the privileges of a legitimate son! Yet this is but a faint image of our adoption by God in holy Baptism.

Application: What are our obligations towards so generous and loving a Father? Surely to love Him with all our hearts, and to prove our love: 1st, by avoiding all that could displease Him, even the most trivial faults or transgressions of our rule; 2nd, by trying to please Him more and more by the practice of virtue; 3rd, by striving diligently after the perfection of our state, according to the words of Jesus Christ: "Be ye therefore perfect, as also your heavenly Father is perfect."

Affections and Resolutions.

Point II: Our relations with God the Son

Consideration: What is a Christian? A man who has a special relationship, or rather many special relationships, with God the Incarnate Son. He is His brother by his very nature; and by baptism he is a member of His mystical body. "Now you are the body of Christ," says Saint Paul, "and member of member." But this is not all. In Holy Communion we become incorporated with Him, according to His own words: "He that eateth My flesh, and drinketh My blood, abideth in Me, and I in him." Living with His life, identified as it were with Him, "we are," says Saint Peter, "made partakers of the divine nature." What can be more blessed and glorious!

Application: What ought to be our return for these great privileges? Saint John will tell us, in a few but memorable words: "He that saith he abideth in Him, ought himself also to walk even as He walked." In this manner we shall put in practice that beautiful expression of Saint Cyprian, "*Christianus alter Christus*." – The Christian is another Christ.

Affections and Resolutions.

Point III: Our relations with God the Holy Ghost

Consideration: What is a Christian? A man who enters through baptism into special relations with the Holy Spirit, whose *living temple* he becomes; a truth which the great Apostle constantly refers to: "Know you not," he writes to the Corinthians, "that your members are the temple of the Holy Ghost, who is in you?" And it is worthy of remark that the ceremonies used in baptism are the same as those for the consecration of churches.

Application: The Apostle himself draws the practical conclusion from this great truth; for after saying, "Your members are the temple of the Holy Ghost," he immediately adds, "Glorify and bear God in your body." Make your body, that is, an instrument for the glory of God; keep it free from all stain, adorn it with virtue and good works, as an altar is dressed and tended.

Colloquy with the Three Persons of the Holy Trinity.

Tuesday after Trinity Sunday: The Sign of the Cross reminds us of the Holy Trinity

1st prelude: Listen to Jesus Christ saying: "Teach ye all nations, baptizing them in the name of the Father, and of the Son, and of the Holy Ghost."
2nd prelude: Ask grace to honor the Holy Trinity as much as possible in making the sign of the cross.

Point I: In the name of the Father

Consideration: When you say these words, in making the sign of the cross, add, at least mentally, *who created me in His image, and for heaven*. These words are a meditation in themselves: *who created me*, out of nothing, by His almighty power, and still more by His electing love, instead of so many others who would have served Him better. *In His image*: how beautiful and precious, then, must my soul be in the sight of the angels? It is the living portrait of God, and like another God upon earth – "I have said, You are gods." *And for heaven*: to be happy there forever, body and soul, full of glory and joy unspeakable.

Application: Such are a few of the thoughts which may occupy your mind when, in making the sign of the cross, you add the words, *Who created me in His image for heaven*. And these thoughts will excite suitable affections.

Affections and Resolutions.

Point II: And of the Son

Consideration: Add to these words in like manner, *who has redeemed me by His Blood, with so much love.* Redeemed from the slavery of the devil, from the eternal damnation to which sin had subjected me, and from which none but the Son of God could deliver me. *Who has redeemed me*, not with silver or gold, but with *His Blood*, with *every drop of His Blood. And with so much love*: the purest and most disinterested love possible, since He had nothing to gain by loving me, being Himself the Infinite God.

Application: You will have no difficulty in drawing practical conclusions from these thoughts. Being redeemed by the Son of God, you belong no longer to yourselves, but to Him. You must therefore live for Him, and glorify Him by the holiness of your

life, and also by the ardor of your zeal for other souls redeemed by Him; and you must have an unbounded confidence that, having given Himself for you, He will refuse you nothing.
Affections and Resolutions.

Point III: And of the Holy Ghost

Consideration: Add again to these words, *who has sanctified me, and adopted me as the child of God. Sanctified* by His mysterious operations in the holy Sacraments, particularly in Baptism and Confirmation. *Sanctified* by His divine inspirations and graces, especially by the grace of my holy vocation. *And adopted as the child of God*: adopted in the fullest sense of the word, and with all the privileges of a true adoption.

Application: These thoughts will remind us of the solemn obligations of our Baptism, our Confirmation, our vocation; they will make us docile, and obedient to the inspirations of the Holy Ghost, and true children of God. We may thus derive great benefit from this method of making the sign of the cross: In the name of the Father, who has created me in His image, and for heaven; and of the Son, who has redeemed me with His Blood, and with so much love; and of the Holy Ghost, who has sanctified me, and adopted me as the child of God, I desire to begin and end this day, this action, &c.
Colloquy with the Blessed Trinity.

Novena to the Sacred Heart of Jesus: First Day (Wednesday)

1st prelude: Consider Jesus Christ showing His Heart, and saying: "Behold this Heart, ,which has loved men so much."
2nd prelude: Ask for grace to begin this Novena well.

Point I: Object of this devotion

Consideration: The *material* or *sensible* object of this devotion is the Heart of the Incarnate Word, inseparably united to His humanity and His divinity, and as much an object of worship as Jesus Christ Himself, with whom it is identified. The *spiritual* or *abstract* object is the love of Jesus Christ, of which His Heart is the symbol. In whatever way, therefore, we consider it, the *object* of this devotion is all that we can imagine most worthy of our adoration. It is the Heart of a God who loves us tenderly; it is Jesus Christ Himself, represented by the most noble organ of His humanity, and the most beautiful attribute of His divinity – His love.

Application: We think ourselves happy if we possess, or even if we only press with our lips, a relic of the true cross, one of the nails, one of the thorns, which pierced the hands and head of Jesus. But what are these, deserving as they are of our veneration, compared with the Heart of Jesus? Oh, may our devotion during this Novena be worthy of its great and most sacred object. May it increase a thousandfold our love and devotion to the Sacred Heart! Affections and Resolutions.

Point II: Motives of devotion to the Sacred Heart

Consideration: *Motives on the side of Jesus Christ*. No devotion can be more acceptable to Him, because none can more powerfully remind us of all that He has done and suffered for us. His Heart has the same feelings as our own. We are pleased when those to whom we have rendered some service are grateful to us. He shares this feeling, as His own words plainly show. On the eve of His death, when He gave power to His Apostles to consecrate bread and wine, He said twice to them, "Do this for a commemoration of Me"; adding, "For as often as you shall eat this bread, and drink the chalice, you shall how the death of the Lord until He come." You shall show forth or recall to men that death which I endured for love of them, and to save them from eternal damnation.

Motives drawn from the consideration of Jesus Christ present on our altars. By this devotion we may make reparation for the insults and blasphemies of heretics, and the coldness and indifference of Catholics, which wound His Sacred Heart.

Motives on our own side. We shall find this devotion a most efficacious means, 1st, to nourish the interior life; 2nd, to pay the debt of gratitude which we owe to our Divine Redeemer; 3rd, to preserve and increase our fervor; and 4th, to obtain for ourselves and for others an abundant share of the graces which flow unceasingly from this Sacred Heart.

Application: What numerous and excellent motives for cultivating this devotion, and promoting it amongst others! And have we not been slack and remiss in doing it? To renew our fervor, let us call to mind the words which our Blessed Lord Himself addressed to Saint Margaret Mary Alacoque: "Behold this Heart, which has loved men so much, and which is loved by them

so little!" And those other words: "I promise that My Heart shall expand, and shed its love abundantly on all who shall honor it, or cause it to be honored" (*Life of Saint Margaret Mary*).
Affections and Resolutions.

Point III: Novena, or practical devotion to the Sacred Heart

Consideration: The better we prepare ourselves for great feasts, the more graces we may expect to receive; for God demands our cooperation. Moreover, this preparation strengthens our faith and confidence, which are the first conditions required by our Lord for the working of any miracle. This is the origin of Novenas, and especially of the Novena to the Sacred Heart.

Application: To insure its success, determine now what you will do each day; what prayers you will use, what visits to the Blessed Sacrament, what mortifications.
Colloquy with the loving Heart of Jesus.

Second Day of the Novena (Thursday): Corpus Christi: The Love of the Heart of Jesus manifested in the Institution of the Holy Eucharist

1st prelude: Listen to Saint John the Evangelist saying: "Jesus having loved His own who were in the world, He loved them unto the end."
2nd prelude: Ask for grace to understand the miracles of love which the Heart of Jesus works in the holy Sacrament of the Eucharist.

Point I: Jesus in the Holy Eucharist as the Companion of our exile

Consideration: The love of the Heart of Jesus has found means to perform a prodigy impossible to human love – *to die for the beloved object, yet without being separated from it*. This He did by the institution of the Holy Eucharist. By means of this ineffable Sacrament, Jesus Christ dwells really in our hearts, and in the midst of us, though veiled from our eyes. Making Himself thus the *companion of our exile*, He multiplies His presence over all the world, that no one may be deprived of it; and from the interior of the tabernacle He calls to us, as from an abyss of mercy, "Come to Me, all you that labor and are burdened, and I will refresh you."

Application: Let us take advantage of the great festival today, the solemnity of Corpus Christi, to offer to the Heart of Jesus our tribute of love, gratitude, and veneration; to make reparation for having so frequently disregarded His loving invitations, so seldom visited Him in the Sacrament of His love, so often grieved His Sacred Heart by our coldness and infidelity, though we actually live under the same roof with Him.

Affections and Resolutions.

Point II: Jesus in the Holy Eucharist as a Victim perpetually offered for us

Consideration: This is the second miracle which the love of our Divine Savior works for us. By means of the Holy Eucharist He renews continually in the Holy Sacrifice of the Mass the offering which He made on Calvary on Good Friday. He is here also both priest and victim, offering Himself by the hands of His minister. The only difference between the Sacrifice of the Cross and that on our altars is that the first was a bloody sacrifice, while the other is unbloody; Jesus being therein slain, according to the language of theology, *only by the sword of the words of consecration*, by virtue of which words His Body is separated from His Blood. From this we conclude, with Saint John Chrysostom, *that the Sacrifice of the Mass is of equal value with that of the Cross*.

Application: What a blessing and happiness to be able duly to participate in this holy sacrifice; if not as a priest, yet as a server or assistant! But how do we assist thereat? With faith, reverence, devotion, or with coldness, and out of mere custom, neglecting the acts of devotion we were once in the habit of making?

Affections and Resolutions.

Point III: Jesus the food of our souls in the Holy Eucharist

Consideration: The love of Jesus in the Holy Eucharist is shown most of all by His vouchsafing to become therein the food of our souls, and so identifying Himself with us that "we live in Him and He in us." Listen to His own words: "Take ye, and eat; this is My Body." "He that eateth My Flesh, and drinketh My Blood, abideth in Me, and I in him."

Application: How is it after so many Communions we are still so imperfect, so *unspiritual, so unlike Jesus Christ*? It must be for want of the right dispositions; for want of fervor in our preparation, or thanksgiving, or even in the very reception of the Blessed Sacrament.

Colloquy with the Sacred Heart.

Third Day of the Novena (Friday): Purity of the Heart of Jesus

1st prelude: Behold Jesus saying these words: "Blessed are the clean of heart."
2nd prelude: Ask the grace to keep your heart pure from the corruption of the world.

Point I: The Heart of Jesus is pure from all stain of sin

Consideration: The Heart of Jesus, formed out of the blood of an Immaculate Virgin, was itself immaculate, and always free from the smallest taint of sin. Our Blessed Lord even condescended to offer a proof of this to His calumniators, when, after having said that "from the heart come forth" all manner of sins, He demanded of them: "Which of you shall convince Me of sin?" They did, indeed, attempt to do so on the day of His Passion, but with so little success that Pilate was compelled to proclaim publicly: "I find no cause in Him." He was also incapable of sin by virtue of the hypostatic union of the humanity with the divinity. It was impossible that the breath of sin should ever for a moment sully the perfect purity of that most adorable Heart.

Application: How different, also, are our hearts from that of Jesus! His is pure and immaculate; ours stained from the very beginning with the guilt of original sin, and still more deeply stained afterwards by that of so many actual sins; sins of youth, sins of each succeeding day, which, though they may seem little in our eyes, are, in the just judgment of God, stains only to be effaced by voluntary penance in the flames of purgatory.

Affections and Resolutions.

Point II: The Heart of Jesus is exempt from all temptation to sin

Consideration: The Apostle Saint Paul, though confirmed in grace, declared that day and night his soul was troubled by temptations and continual excitements to sin. He groans bitterly over this misery. But our Blessed Lord experienced nothing of this kind. He did, indeed, permit the devil to tempt Him, but those temptations were purely exterior; they could never reach His Heart, or trouble its perfect peace and serenity, which are among its greatest perfections.

Application: Whatever care we may take to repress the irregular motion of sin, we can never be wholly free from them in this world. The evil inclinations implanted by the sin of our first parents will always be a source of trial and temptation to us. It is only by a constant struggle that we can keep them in subjection. We are thus constrained to live always at war with ourselves, or, as the Apostle expresses it, with "our old man." But let us take courage; the fiercer the struggle, the more glorious will be the victory, and the brighter our crown in heaven. Moreover, the Heart of Jesus is always open to us as a sure refuge and resting-place. Affections and Resolutions.

Point III: The Heart of Jesus is exempt from even the thought of sin

Consideration: If we may say of the Mother of Jesus that never, by virtue of her Immaculate Conception, did so much as an evil thought disturb the peace of her heart, much more may we say this of her Divine Son. Jesus Christ was, moreover, absolute master over all the movements of His Heart. He could open or close it at will to the emotions of joy, grief, etc.

Application: It is very different, alas! with us. We are troubled with bad thoughts, even in spite of ourselves. They follow and persecute us everywhere, and at all times, even in our prayers, even before the altar. We have still the seeds of original sin in our hearts. "The imagination and thought of man's heart are prone to evil from his youth." We are often tempted to complain of this, but do we not often increase the evil by allowing too much liberty to our sense, especially to our eyes, with the Holy Ghost calls the windows of the soul? "Death is come up through our windows." Colloquy with the Heart of Jesus.

Fourth Day of the Novena (Saturday): Humility of the Heart of Jesus

1st prelude: Behold Jesus showing you His Heart, and saying: "Learn of Me, for I am humble of heart."
2nd prelude: Ask for grace to grow in the esteem and practice of humility.

Point I: Humility of the Heart of Jesus

Consideration: *Humility of heart or of will*, as distinct from *humility of mind or of intellect*, is a virtue, or habitual disposition and state of the will, by which a man forgets himself, and seeks only the glory of God in all things. Dead to himself, the humble man lives only for God; God alone is the object of his thoughts, of his intentions; the only motive and end of all that he does, desires, fears, or hopes, because to God alone all glory and honor are due. Such was our Blessed Lord during the whole of His mortal life, as His own words testify: "I seek not My own glory." Witness also the whole course of His life, which Saint Paul sums up briefly in the words: "He humbled Himself" – *Semetipsum exinanivit.*

Application: Do we find a like humility in ourselves? Do we seek always the glory of God alone, or have we not in the secret depth of our hearts some self-love, or desire for the esteem of men, even in our holiest actions? If so, we have not yet learnt to copy the humility of our Divine Master.

Affections and Resolutions.

Point II: Humility of the Heart of Jesus shown by His words

Consideration: True humility, though deeply hidden in the heart, will manifest itself in words, for "out of the abundance of the heart the mouth speaketh," says our Blessed Lord. And thus it showed itself with Him in His intercourse with men. Did He ever seek to exalt Himself? No; "My glory is nothing," He said. He spoke always of His Father's glory; and this in terms of such magnificence, and under such attractive figures, that the Apostles, filled with wonder, said to Him, at the Last Supper: "Lord, show us the Father, and it is enough for us."

Application: Let us here examine ourselves, and consider whether those with whom we are intimate have reason to think that our hearts are full of the thought of God, and that we desire above all things to promote His glory. Do we not rather speak often of ourselves, and that even in our own praise, vaunting our good works past or present, our qualities or talents? Do we not often blame others, defend our own opinions obstinately, answer with bitterness those who may contradict us? If so, can we flatter ourselves that we are really *humble of heart*? Let others answer this question for us: they will say, "Even thy speech doth discover thee," for it is full of thyself.

Affections and Resolutions.

Point III: Humility of the Heart of Jesus manifested in His acts

Consideration: The whole life of our Blessed Lord upon earth was only a series of humiliations. He endured them voluntarily to make reparation for the insulted Majesty of His Father, to pay the debt of our pride, and to set us an example of humility. He was born in a stable; He lived for thirty years unknown to the world; and during the three years of His public ministry He allowed envy and calumny to accuse Him of being a seducer, an impostor, and possessed by the devil. He died as a malefactor between two thieves. Could He have done more to abase and annihilate Himself?

Application: We, too, should act thus, if we were truly *humble of heart*. Instead of seeking after praise, honors and marks of esteem, we should seek to be hidden from men, that we may please God alone; to shut ourselves out from the world, that our hearts may be free for God only; and at least we should not be troubled or disturbed if we are spoken against, reproved, or humbled. Colloquy with Jesus Christ.

Fifth Day of the Novena (Sunday): Obedience of the Heart of Jesus

1st prelude: Behold Jesus Christ showing you His Heart, and saying: "I have given you an example [of obedience], that as I have done to you, so you do also."
2nd prelude: Ask for grace to copy faithfully your divine model.

Point I: Submission of the Heart of Jesus to His Father

Consideration: Obedience is the first-fruit of humility. Jesus is *humble of heart*; therefore He is docile and obedient of heart. He tells us that He makes the will of His Heavenly Father His own. "Father, … not My will, but Thine be done"; and that He submits and conforms Himself to it in everything: "I do always the things that please Him." And this even in things most repugnant to nature; witness His agony in the Garden of Gethsemane. His obedience was perfect, because the foundation on which it rested was perfect; He did the will of His Father, because it was the will of His Father: "Yea, Father, for so hath it seemed good in Thy sight."

Application: What an excellent example is here proposed for our imitation! Have we followed it by trying to make the will of God our own? By accepting all the various circumstances of our life, whether agreeable to us or not, with *an entire submission of heart* to the will of God, without whose permission nothing can befall us in this world? Have we obeyed Him always in a spirit of faith and love?

Affections and Resolutions.

Point II: Submission of the Heart of Jesus to Mary and Joseph

Consideration: "And He was subject to them." *Erat subditus illis*. These three words contain the whole life of Jesus Christ during the thirty years that He spent in retreat with Mary His Mother, and Joseph His foster-father. But what is this? A God subject to two creatures? Is there not something in this inconsistent with the sovereign dominion of the Divinity over all creation? No; because the obedience of Jesus is really given to God His Father, who is represented to Him by Mary and Joseph.

Application: This is the true model of obedience, the obedience of faith; submission to God in the persons of those who represent Him to us, and of whom He has said: "He that heareth you heareth Me." This is the obedience of the perfect religious, which, far from degrading, exalts and ennobles him. To obey thus is to have the same will with God. Is it in this spirit that we obey our lawful superiors, without having regard to their personal qualifications? If so, our obedience will be perfect, like that of our Divine Master, as far as is possible for us; it will be prompt, generous, unlimited, and full of merit before God.

Affections and Resolutions.

Point III: Admirable submission of the Heart of Jesus to all kinds of persons

Consideration: On the same principle which we have been consideration, Jesus obeyed and submitted to even the most wicked men, and those whose hypocrisy He had proclaimed to the people. Caiphas, in his office of high priest, adjured Him to say if He were the Son of God or not, and immediately Jesus breaks the silence He had hitherto observed, and answers him fully. He submitted even to the heathen: Pontius Pilate, as the governor of Judea, condemned Him to death, and He accepted the sentence without a word of reply. He even obeyed His executioners: when they ordered Him to stretch out His arms on the cross, He immediately did it, with perfect submission of heart and will. Thus He became, as the Apostle says, "obedient unto death, even the death of the cross." It was for love of us, and also for our instruction and encouragement, that Jesus gave us these examples

of obedience. Bear them in mind, and you will never complain of having harsh superiors, or commands too difficult to obey. With Jesus on the cross before our eyes, no act of obedience will seem too hard for us.
Colloquy with the Sacred Heart of Jesus.

Sixth Day of the Novena (Monday): Meekness of the Heart of Jesus

1st prelude: Behold Jesus Christ showing us His Heart, and saying: "Learn of Me, because I am meek."
2nd prelude: Ask for grace to understand, esteem and love meekness.

Point I: Meekness of the Heart of Jesus manifested in His whole Person

Consideration: Of all qualities, meekness is the most universally loved and appreciated. A gentle, kind-hearted man is not sooner known than loved. Everyone feels drawn to him, and desires his friendship. What a marvelous attraction, then, must the sweet Heart of Jesus have for men! We read in the holy Gospels that as many as four thousand followed Him once for three days without having any food, so great was the charm which His gentleness and meekness shed around Him.

Application: Do we desire to know if our meekness at all resembles that of our Divine Master? Let us judge it by its fruits. Have we the sympathy and confidence of our brethren? Do they seek our company gladly, especially in times of trouble? Or do they keep aloof from us, for fear of being annoyed and contradicted?
Affections and Resolutions.

Point II: The meekness of His words

Consideration: Every page of the holy Gospels bears witness to this. What could be more sweet than these words? "I am the good Shepherd. The good Shepherd giveth His life for His sheep." Or again: "Jerusalem! Jerusalem!... how often would I have gathered thy children as the bird doth her brood under her wings; and thou wouldst not." And again, the words He addressed to the traitor Judas in the very act of consummating his crime: "Friend, whereto art thou come? Judas, dost thou betray the Son of Man with a kiss?" What meekness, above all, in the prayer which He made on the cross for His executioners; "Father, forgive them, for they know not what they do."

Application: If it be true that from the abundance of the heart the mouth speaks, must we not conclude that our hearts are still far from being like that of our Divine Savior? We are so harsh in our judgments of others; so ready to exaggerate their faults, to reprove them, to publish them. Jesus answers with such meekness when unjustly accused, and we break out into sharp words when told of our real faults. Jesus finds an excuse for His executioners, and we are angry if we only imagine that someone desires to do us an injury.

Affections and Resolutions.

Point III: The meekness of His actions

Consideration: How severely was the meekness of Jesus tried! During the whole course of His life He was exposed to the hatred, calumnies and insults of the doctors and rulers of the Jews. They even told Him to His face, before all the people, that He was possessed with a devil, and worked miracles by the power of Beelzebub, the prince of the devils. And yet His meekness never failed; it remained unchanged to the very last. He may indeed justly say to us, "Learn of Me, for I am meek and humble of heart."

Application: It is easy enough to be gentle and patient when all goes well with us and everyone is kind and considerate to us; there is no merit in it under such circumstances. But to be really "meek and humble of heart" is to be able to bear wrongs patiently, and to render good for evil, after the example of Jesus Christ. Let us strive earnestly to do this, that so the words of our Blessed Lord may be applied to us: "Blessed are the meek, for they shall possess the land."

Colloquy with the Sacred Heart.

Seventh Day of the Novena (Tuesday): Generosity of the Heart of Jesus

1st prelude: Behold Jesus showing you His Heart, and saying: "Behold this Heart, which has loved men so much."

2nd prelude: Ask for a heart wholly devoted to the interests of

Jesus Christ.

Point I: The generosity of the Heart of Jesus is shown by the sacrifice which He made of His reputation

Consideration: We commonly measure the generosity of a man by the greatness of the sacrifices which he makes for his fellow creatures. We may do the same with the generosity of the Heart of Jesus. What has He not sacrificed for us? May we not say that He only shared our goods in order that He might be able to sacrifice them for us? Of all that we possess, that which we guard most jealously, and with good reason, is our honor, our reputation; and this Jesus was content to sacrifice as a reparation for the dishonor which sin had done to His Heavenly Father, and to reconcile us to Him. He not only submitted silently to the most atrocious calumnies, but He died stripped of all reputation. As He hung on the cross, His enemies dared Him to come down if He were the Son of God: "Let Christ come down now from the cross, that we may see and believe." But He descended not, leaving them to conclude that He had not the power, that He was an impostor, the basest of men. And thus He died.

Application: God will probably not require of us so entire a sacrifice of our reputation as He has demanded of certain great saints; amongst others, of Saint John of the Cross, who was imprisoned, and died the victim of a calumny, without uttering one word of complaint. But what our Lord does and will ask of us, is to sacrifice all feeling of resentment when, either through malice or inadvertence, someone may have injured our reputation; to receive in silence, as our rule commands, any reprimand or penance given for a fault which we have not committed. Though these little sacrifices are not heroic, they will be pleasing to God, and merit a reward.

Affections and Resolutions.

Point II: It is shown by the sacrifice which He made of all the enjoyments of life

Consideration: Jesus was innocence itself; He had no sins to expiate; He therefore had a full right to enjoy all the pleasures of this life. But, nevertheless, He made a generous sacrifice of them, passing His whole life subject to the most severe privations, and sufferings both of body and soul, such as no one had ever endured. And this because He had taken upon Himself to make satisfaction to the divine justice for all our criminal indulgences; and also that He might encourage us by His example to lead a life of penance.

Application: We are guilty creatures; we have much to expiate. If we have not strength or courage for severe penances, let us at least practice some little ones in a spirit of sacrifice; let us mortify ourselves in something during the day, and suffer without complaining. This is surely little enough, and yet how seldom we do even this!

Affections and Resolutions.

Point III: His meekness manifested in the sacrifice of His life

Consideration: The most generous sacrifice that one man can make for another is, according to our Blessed Lord's own words, the sacrifice of his life – to die to save another from death. This, then, is what Jesus has done for us, for each one of us. We can all say with the Apostle, "He loved me, and delivered Himself for me."

Application: Is this great proof of the love of Jesus always present in our minds? Does it excite us to gratitude? And does this gratitude show itself in works, in a readiness to make sacrifices? Do we not, on the contrary, suffer many opportunities of making them to be lost? Our hearts are indeed most unlike the adorable Heart of Jesus.

Colloquy with the Sacred Heart.

Eighth Day of the Novena (Wednesday): Zeal of the Heart of Jesus

1st prelude: To hear Jesus Christ saying to us: "Pray ye therefore the Lord of the harvest that He send laborers into His harvest."

2nd prelude: To ask for a zeal conformable to the zeal of the Heart of Jesus.

Point I: Ardent zeal of the Sacred Heart

Consideration: Zeal for the glory of God and the salvation of souls is nothing else but the love of God running over from our own hearts upon others, desiring to win them to God and to see them united with us in heaven. The measure of our love is, therefore, the measure of our zeal. What, therefore, must have been the zeal of that adorable Heart, which loved both God and man with an ineffable love! These few words may give us some faint idea of it: "I am come to cast fire on the earth, and what will I but that it be kindled in all hearts?" "I have a baptism wherewith I am to be baptized, and how am I straitened until it be accomplished!" – that is to say, "until I have consummated the sacrifice I so ardently desire to make of my life."

Application: To procure the glory of God and the salvation of souls was always the most ardent desire of the saints, because they were full of the love of God. We find proof of this in almost every psalm of the holy King David. "For the zeal of Thy house hath eaten me up," he says; "and the reproaches of them that reproached Thee are fallen upon me." "Mine eyes have sent forth springs of water, because they have not kept Thy law." "Let all peoples give praise to Thee." If we cherish the like sentiments in our hearts, we too shall find a thousand means of exercising our zeal for the glory of God and the salvation of souls.

Affections and Resolutions.

Point II: Extent of the zeal of the Sacred Heart

Consideration: Great as was the zeal of our Divine Lord, He restricted its exercise to the inhabitants of Palestine, because such was His Father's will, to which He was in all things perfectly conformed. But His Heart embraced the whole world; He prayed perpetually for its conversion during His hidden life, and during the three years of His public ministry He prepared His Apostles for this great work, promising to by Himself with them "even to the consummation of the world."

Application: After the example of our Divine Master, let us learn – 1st, to let our zeal be governed by obedience, even should this compel us to retrain it within the narrow bounds of a life apparently common and obscure; 2nd, not to envy those who may be called to a more brilliant career in the exercise of their zeal, but rather to do all we can to help them; 3rd, to let our zeal embrace the whole world, taking part in the good work everywhere, as much as lies in our power, by prayers and alms.

Affections and Resolutions.

Point III: Triumph of the zeal of the Sacred Heart

Consideration: "And I, if I be lifted up from the earth, will draw all things to Myself." This is the prophecy of the triumph of our Blessed Lord's zeal. And what a triumph! Idolatry vanquished and made despicable; the name of God known and adored everywhere;

the way of salvation opened freely to all men; more than eleven million, in every condition of life, bearing witness for the faith by a cruel martyrdom! And is it not even now a triumph that so many persons, even of the weaker sex, draw from the Heart of Jesus a zeal which gives them courage to forsake all things and follow the evangelical counsels, or go into distant and barbarous lands as missionaries.

Application: We have the happiness of being consecrated entirely to works of zeal by our holy vocation; but how little fruit do we reap from our labors, because our faith is so weak, our charity so cold! Let us seek both in the Heart of Jesus.
Colloquy with the Sacred Heart.

Ninth Day of the Novena (Thursday): Kindness and Tenderness of the Heart of Jesus

1st prelude: Think that you see Jesus showing you His Heart, full of goodness and tenderness for men.
2nd prelude: Ask for grace to conform your heart to the Heart of Jesus.

Point I: Tenderness of the Heart of Jesus shown by His tears

Consideration: Kindness or goodness of heart is a disposition which inclines a man to do good to his fellow men, and to compassionate their misfortune. "Goodness," says Saint Leo the Great, "is the nature of God." How great, then, must be the goodness of the Heart of Jesus! In how many ways His tenderness showed itself! First, by *tears*. Even on the occasion of His triumphal entry into Jerusalem, He was moved to tears by the thought of the miseries which would so soon burst upon the devoted city. "Seeing the city, He wept over it." And again, Saint John tells us that He was deeply touched and moved to tears by the death of Lazarus and the grief of Martha and Mary: "And Jesus wept."

Application: How little do we know of this tenderness of heart! Even the sight of a crucifix, which reminds us of the Passion and death of Jesus, draws no tears from our eyes. The sight of so many sinners, who crucify Him afresh every day, has no power to move us. And the thought of so many souls who go down daily into hell costs us not a single sigh. We do not even weep over our own sins.

Affections and Resolutions.

Point II: Kindness of the Heart of Jesus shown by His words

Consideration: What a depth of tenderness breathes in these words, which came not only from the lips but from the Heart of Jesus! "Come to Me, all you that labor and are burdened, and I will refresh you." "It is I, fear ye not." "Be of good heart, son; thy sins are forgiven thee." "Daughters of Jerusalem, weep not over Me, but weep for yourselves and for your children." "I am the good Shepherd. The good Shepherd giveth His life for His sheep." "Be merciful." "I will have mercy, and not sacrifice."

Application: Do our words thus show forth the goodness and tenderness of our hearts? Do we never judge rashly and speak harshly of our neighbor's conduct, finding fault with it when perhaps we do not understand his motives? If so, unlike are our hearts to the Sacred Heart of Jesus!

Affections and Resolutions.

Point III: Kindness of the Heart of Jesus shown by His actions

Consideration: The whole life of our blessed Lord was spent in *doing good*. He never saw suffering, either bodily or mental, without healing or consoling it. Let us take two instances out of a thousand others. Near the city of Naim, He met a widowed mother, inconsolable for the loss of her only son. And He was "moved with mercy" for her, and raised her son to life. On another occasion, when four thousand men had followed Him for three days in the desert, He said to the Apostles: "I have compassion on the multitude… lest they faint in the way." The expressions, "moved with mercy," or "have compassion," occur no less than eight times in the holy Gospels.

Application: We therefore do a great injury to the Heart of Jesus when we doubt His mercy, or the pardon of our sins in the Sacrament of Penance; when we look upon His yoke as heavy and difficult to bear; when we exchange confidence for fear, and fear for discouragement, or even despair. Let us be most careful never to offer Him such an insult as this.

Colloquy with the Sacred Heart.

Feast of the Sacred Heart: Our duties towards the Heart of Jesus dwelling in our Tabernacles

1st prelude: Behold Jesus showing you from the tabernacle His Heart inflamed with love, and saying: "My son, give Me thy heart."
2nd prelude: Ask Him with great fervor to kindle the fire of His love in your heart.

Point I: What does the Heart of Jesus do for men in the Blessed Sacrament?

Consideration: It performs there the office of a *mediator*, continually interceding for us. If God does not utterly exterminate the human race on account of sins which cry for vengeance to heaven, we know that it is because the Heart of Jesus is perpetually pleading with Him, "Father, forgive them, for they know not what they do." It performs the office of a *priest*, sacrificing Itself every day for us on a thousand altars. It performs the office of a *father*, feeding us with its own flesh and blood. It performs the office of a *master* and *teacher*, instructing us, by its very condition in the Blessed Sacrament, in the virtues most necessary for us – silence, recollection, humility, contempt of the world, patience, resignation, devotion.

Application: These are but a few of the claims which the Heart of Jesus has upon our love. We know them; we understand and feel what it requires of us in return; and yet we are so cold, so dead, even before the Blessed Sacrament, even in our Communion! Whence does this proceed? Is it not from too strong an attachment to the world and to ourselves? Or perhaps from certain affections which, if not sinful, are at least sensual, taking too strong root in our hearts.

Affections and Resolutions.

Point II: What do men do for the Heart of Jesus?

Consideration: Not to speak of Jews and heretics, what return does Jesus receive from those who believe in His True Presence in the Blessed Sacrament? From some, it is true, He receives the homage of adoration day and night, and that gratitude and filial devotion which are His due; but only from a few. And what does He receive from others? Neglect, disdain, contempt, profanation, sacrilege.

Application: Have we nothing to reproach ourselves with on this head in the past or in the present? What shall we say even now of our negligence in visiting the Sacred Heart in the Blessed Sacrament – where it is always burning with love for us – of our many distractions, our little care to make devout preparation and thanksgiving for Holy Communion? Have we not good reason to fear that our dispositions are not such as the Sacred Heart desires to see in us?

Affections and Resolutions.

Point III: What does the Heart of Jesus expect of us, especially at the present time?

Consideration: It expects that we should make reparation to it, by extraordinary devotion and fervor for all the contempt, injuries, and profanations of which so many Catholics are guilty; that to this end we should visit it frequently on this great feast; that we should receive Holy Communion and hear Mass with great devotion, and, if possible, also go to Benediction, and there, in union with the priest, make an act of reparation to the Sacred Heart; or, if we are not able to do this, that we should make it privately.

Application: What powerful motives are there at the present day to urge us to do this with all our hearts! Which of us does not owe many blessings and graces to the Heart of Jesus? Who has not numerous sins and infidelities to make reparation for, many graces and benefits to pray for? Add to these private motives other more public ones, especially those which affect the Catholic Church, now so bitterly persecuted, and we shall never tire of finding a thousand different ways of honoring the Sacred Heart.

Colloquy with the Sacred Heart.

Intercalary Month

Meditation I: Motives, Signs and Means of Spiritual Progress

1st prelude: Behold Jesus Christ saying to you: "Be you therefore perfect, as also your Heavenly Father is perfect."

2nd prelude: Ask for grace to make constant progress in virtue.

Point I: Motives of spiritual progress

Consideration: 1st, Its *obligation.* As religious we are obliged to aim at and tend towards Christian perfection. Our Blessed Lord's words, "Be you therefore perfect," are for us a positive command. Not a command to attain absolute perfection, which is impossible for any mere creature, but to aspire to it, to seek always after greater perfection by generous and constant efforts – in other words, to make progress in virtue. 2nd, Its *utility*. To make progress in virtue is to increase our merit, and thereby to increase our glory and happiness in heaven. 3rd, Its *facility*. Our circumstances are so favorable; instead of obstacles and hindrances we have abundance of every kind of help.

Application: Whence comes it, then, that we are still so imperfect, that we make so little progress? From the weakness and inconstancy of our will. We *wish*, but we do not *will* efficaciously. We begin, and leave off again. Progress supposes effort, and we make no effort. We draw back at the smallest difficulty.

Affections and Resolutions.

Point II: Signs of spiritual progress

Consideration: These are a few of the signs by which you may know if you are making progress in perfection: 1st, if you feel more deeply the happiness of your holy vocation, and value it more and more; 2nd, if you fall less frequently into certain venial sins to which you were accustomed; 3rd, if you conquer temptations more easily; 4th, if your acts of mortification are more frequent; 5th, if from time to time you have certain attractions which give you more devotion in Holy Communion, in visits to the Blessed Sacrament, etc.; 6th, if you feel more contempt for the world and for all that is not God, and less difficulty in ridding yourself of self-love; 7th, if you bear crosses and humiliations with more courage, patience and resignation.

Application: Try to derive great profit from these considerations; they will greatly enlighten you, and either fill you with joy, or cover you with confusion and shame.

Affections and Resolutions.

Point III: Means for spiritual progress

Consideration: There are three principal ones; the first is to gird on your spiritual armor every morning on first waking, resolving to make the day fruitful in victories and good works. The second is to maintain, as far as possible, a spirit of interior joy and confidence. This is a great help in the service of God, as holy David declares: "I have run the way of Thy commandments, when Thou didst enlarge my heart." The third means, which includes all others, is to preserve your original fervor, or to renew it if it has grown slack. Why do novices generally make such rapid progress? Because they are fervent.

Application: Use these means. Use especially those which are most suited to your circumstances or needs, and they will bring you joy for all eternity.

Colloquy with our Blessed Lord.

Meditation II: Baptism of Jesus Christ: His public Life

1st prelude: Behold Jesus taking leave of His Blessed Mother, and going to be baptized before commencing His public life.

2nd prelude: Ask for perfect detachment from all worldly and domestic ties.

Point I: Public life of Jesus

Consideration: The public and active life of Jesus succeeded His hidden and contemplative life. The moment appointed by the eternal decrees had arrived. The peaceful life which He had led for more than twenty years in the holy home of Nazareth was to come to an end. He must exchange it for a public life, for the laborious and painful work of the ministry. He must give up the society of His Holy Mother and of all His friends, to live on alms among coarse and rude men. All this must have been *naturally* as repugnant to the sweet and tender Heart of Jesus as it would be to ours. But He stifled the voice of nature, and listened only to that of obedience and zeal for souls.

Application: Let us do the like, feeling convinced that nothing can be better or safer for us than to go, or to remain, wherever obedience, or rather the voice of God Himself, calls us through our superiors. We have left all things for God; do not let us take back any part of the sacrifice by attaching ourselves too strongly to any person or place, or even to certain spiritual consolations, which perhaps one office affords us more opportunities of than another.

Affections and Resolutions.

Point II: Baptism of Jesus

Consideration: Jesus desired to commence His public life by an act of great humility, by receiving the Baptism of penance at the hands of His precursor. "Jesus," says Saint Matthew, "came from

Galilee to Jordan, unto John, to be baptized by him. But John stayed Him, saying: I ought to be baptized by Thee, and comest Thou to me? And Jesus, answer, said to him: Suffer it to be so now, for so it becometh us to fulfill justice." That is to say, We shall give God the glory which is justly due to Him – I by an act of profound humiliation, you by one of blind obedience; and we shall thus repair the injustice done to God by the pride and rebellion of man.

Application: Our Blessed Lord taught us two great lessons by this act: 1st, that as Baptism is the first and most necessary of all the Sacraments, so humility is the first and most necessary of all virtues; 2nd, that it is by humility, and the obedience which springs from it, that we can best please God, and draw down His blessings on our labors. If these have hitherto been unfruitful, it is perhaps because we have not acted on these principles.

Affections and Resolutions

Point III: Glorification of Jesus

Consideration: "He that shall humble himself shall be exalted." This was accomplished at the baptism of Jesus; for we read: "Jesus being baptized, forthwith came out of the water, and lo! The heavens were opened to Him, and He saw the Spirit of God descending as a dove, and coming upon Him. And behold a voice from heaven, saying: This is my beloved Son, in whom I am well pleased."

Application: The same favor which Jesus Christ, as man, merited by the deep humility of His baptism – in which He mixed with penitents as one of themselves – has been granted gratuitously to us in our baptism. As soon as the holy water was poured upon our head, the heavens, which before had been closed to us by original sin, were opened, and the Holy Ghost descended upon us, and a voice from heaven said: This is now My beloved child.

Colloquy with Jesus.

Meditation III: Jesus is led by the Spirit into the Desert

1st prelude: Imagine Jesus alone in a frightful desert.

2nd prelude: Ask for a ready obedience to the impulses of grace.

Point I: Jesus, obedient to the impulse of the Spirit, goes into the desert

Consideration: "Jesus, being full of the Holy Ghost, returned from the Jordan, and was led by the Spirit into the desert, for the space of forty days." Though Jesus Christ possessed, as man, the fullness of wisdom and grace, and was perfectly secure against all error, surprise or illusion, He would not act except according to the leading of the Holy Ghost, to which He submitted with the utmost docility, as is clear from the sacred text.

Application: It is the same Spirit who, by the victorious impulse of grace, has led and drawn us from the midst of a deceitful world into the happy desert of religion; who keeps us there by the attractions of His grace, and who never ceases to guide and urge us onward in the way of perfect. What progress should we not have made if we had always been faithful and docile to His inspirations! But what we have not done in the past, let us do now with constancy and generosity; and since the voice of God is not heard in the midst of noise and tumult, let us diligently keep ourselves in a state of recollection and interior peace. Let us fly from the world, and love solitude; for it is written: "I will allure her, and will lead her into the wilderness, and I will speak to her heart." Affections and Resolutions.

Point II: Jesus prays and fasts in the desert

Consideration: The obedience of Jesus to the Holy Spirit was generous and heroic. It led Him to separate Himself from the world, and retire into a frightful desert, there to remain during forty days, with no companionship but that of wild beasts. "He was with beasts." He had no roof to shelter Him from the inclemency of the weather, and He fasted rigorously during the whole time, taking no food whatever. "He ate nothing in those days. He also spent the whole time in contemplation, interrupted only by the tears He shed over our miseries, and the prayers He addressed to His heavenly Father on our behalf. Thus from the baptism of penance He passed on to works of penance, and thus prepared Himself for His public life and ministry.

Application: Let us learn these two lessons from our Divine Master: 1st, that holy baptism, which to the early Christians was a call to martyrdom, is to every one a call to penance, and obliges us to live in the constant exercise of penance: "The life of a Christian ought to be a perpetual penance" (Council of Trent); 2nd, that we ought to prepare ourselves for active work by retreat, prayer and

mortification, if we wish our labors to be crowned with success. Let us examine how far we have thus acted.
Affections and Resolutions.

Point III: Jesus is tempted in the desert

Consideration: "Jesus was led by the Spirit into the desert, to be tempted by the devil." In Himself He had no inclination to evil, and therefore He permitted the devil to tempt Him. But why should He suffer this terrible and humiliating trial? For our instruction and encouragement. He desired to teach us that temptations are not sins, but that, on the contrary, they serve to keep us humble, watchful, fervent, and thereby more pleasing to God; that they are independent of our will; that neither holiness nor solitude exempts us from them, and that therefore they ought never to trouble or discourage us.

Application: Let us then take courage, and lay to heart the words of the Apostle: "God is faithful; who will not suffer you to be tempted above that which you are able, but will make also with temptation issue; that you may be able to bear it."
Colloquy with our Blessed Lord.

Meditation IV: On the three Temptations of Jesus as recorded in the Gospels

1st prelude: Represent to yourself the devil in a human form approaching Jesus to tempt Him.
2nd prelude: Ask for grace to understand and avoid the snares of the devil.

Point I: Temptation of gluttony

Consideration: The devil, like a skillful tempter, studies our natural dispositions of body and mind, in order to draw us the more easily into sin. Seeing, therefore, that Jesus, "when He had fasted forty days and forty nights, afterwards was hungry," he pretended to take compassion on Him, and approaching Him in human form, said: "If Thou be the Son of God, command that these stones be made bread." It was a temptation of gluttony, in the suggestion that He should satisfy the demands of nature by a miracle, instead of waiting till His Heavenly Father supplied them by the ministry of angels. Jesus rebuked him in the words of Deuteronomy: "Not in bread alone doth man live, but in every word that proceedeth from the mouth of God."

Application: If we are tempted to gluttony – as, for instance, to forestall the appointed hour for meals, to exceed the bounds of religious moderation, to seek too eagerly for what gratifies our palate, or to eat and drink simply for enjoyment, etc. – let us say to ourselves these same words: "Not in bread alone doth man live," but in the spiritual food of the soul. Let us feed the body for necessity, but the soul in abundance. What folly would it be to entertain our body at the expense of our soul – of our eternal salvation! Affections and Resolutions.

Point II: Temptation of vainglory

Consideration: Though defeated, the devil returns to the charge. He tries another more subtle form of temptation, addressed to the intellect, which is naturally influenced by the renown of brilliant actions. Having been permitted to exercise power over the body of Jesus, "he took Him up into the holy city, and set Him upon a pinnacle of the temple, and said to Him: If Thou be the Son of God, cast Thyself down; for it is written, that He hath given His angels charge over Thee, and in their hands shall they bear Thee up, lest perchance Thou dash Thy foot against a stone." Such a miracle would have established the authority of Jesus, and prepared the way for the success of His preaching. We must admit that the devil made use of a most specious pretext to tempt Him to vain-glory. But Jesus only replied: "It is written again, Thou shalt not tempt the Lord thy God."

Application: Let us take warning to be always on our guard against the deceits and snares of the devil. He never retires from the assault. Even our victories furnish him with fresh matter for temptation. If you have resisted gluttony by abstaining from certain delicacies at table, he will inspire you with thoughts of vain-glory, or of contempt for those who have not done like yourself. At other times, he will transform himself into an angel of light, and suggest some evil to you in the disguise of virtue. For instance, anger, strife, vengeance, under the disguise of zeal; intemperance or idleness, under the pretense of care for your health. He will persuade you to run into danger, and in other ways tempt God, under the pretense of being a valiant soldier and meriting the palm of victory in heaven.

Affections and Resolutions.

Point III: Temptation of ambition

Consideration: The devil, insolently taking advantage of the permission to tempt Jesus in every way, took Him to the top of a high mountain, and causing Him to see from thence all the kingdoms of the world, said to Him: "To thee will I give all this power, and the glory of them; for to me they are delivered, and to whom I will I give them. If Thou, therefore, wilt adore me, all shall be Thine. Then Jesus saith to him, Begone Satan; for it is written, The Lord thy God shalt thou adore, and Him only shalt thou serve. Then the devil left Him; and behold angels came and ministered to Him."

Application: Behold how the devil seduces men by lying and false promises, flattering our pride and our evil inclinations. Will you let him deceive you? Behold, on the other hand, how faithful and generous God is in consoling those who resist temptation steadfastly, even sending His angels to strengthen them.
Colloquy with our Blessed Lord.

Meditation V: On Temptations in general

1st prelude: Consider holy Job in the midst of his cruel temptations, saying: "The life of man upon earth is a warfare."
2nd prelude: Ask for grace to be faithful and victorious in this warfare with temptations.

Point I: Sources of our temptations

Consideration: We are necessarily exposed to temptations on account of original sin, which has implanted its seeds in us, as the earth contains the seeds of all noxious plants. They come to us primarily from the disorder which sin has introduced into our heart, from pride and concupiscence; they come, secondly, from the devil, who, in his despair at having lost heaven, has sworn to spare no pains to hinder us from gaining it; they come, in the third place, from the world – from all the evil that we see and hear around us.

Application: We have no right, therefore, to be surprised at the frequency or violence of our temptations, or to expect that age or circumstances will be any security against them. Neither have we any right to attribute all our temptations to the devil, since we often cause them by our own curiosity, intemperance, or idleness, by allowing too much liberty to our senses, or by indulging in certain dangerous intimacies and friendships, against the warning of our conscience. In such cases we cannot fairly accuse the devil of our temptations, nor will such an excuse avail us before the judgment-seat of God.

Affections and Resolutions.

Point II: Remedy for our temptations

Consideration: "Watch ye, and pray, that ye enter not into temptation." Watching, united to prayer, is then the remedy proposed to us by Jesus Christ against all temptations. And wherein ought our watching to consist? 1st, In observing carefully what things are occasions of sin to us, and avoiding them as far as may be in our power; 2ndly, in studying the sources whence our temptations most commonly arise, that we may the more easily apply a remedy; 3rdly, in guarding and mortifying our senses, especially our eyes, for the Holy Spirit says: "Death is come through our windows"; 4thly, in noticing carefully the first impressions of evil, the first suggestions of the evil one, that we may meet them with prompt and energetic resistance; 5thly, in a constant spirit of recollection, without which this prompt attention and resistance is impossible. "Watch and pray." Pray from the first moment of your waking; adding to the resolution of fighting valiantly against your temptations a demand for the graces necessary to obtain a victory, without which your resolutions will be useless; if we are left to our own strength, we are certain to fail. Pray with humility, but also with the greatest confidence, pray especially at the time of temptation, calling upon the holy names of Jesus and Mary, and you will never be overcome.

Application: With what care, with what perseverance, and with what success, have you used these remedies?

Affections and Resolutions.

Point III: The use of our temptations

Consideration: Our temptations serve to keep us humble. They detach us from the world, and draw our thoughts and desires to heaven; they also lead us to pray with more devotion; they supply us with a means of making reparation for our sins, and gaining merit; they strengthen us in the practice of virtue, and revive our decaying fervor.

Application: It is therefore a great mistake to complain, to be

discouraged, or to think that God is angry with us because we are violently tempted. "Because thou wast acceptable to God," and the angel to Tobias, "it was necessary that temptation should prove thee." These words ought to fill our hearts with a holy joy and consolation.
Colloquy with our Blessed Lord.

Meditation VI: Jesus manifested and acknowledged by Saint John the Baptist, his Precursor

1st prelude: Behold Saint John the Baptist pointing out Jesus to the people.
2nd prelude: Ask for grace to forget yourself, and seek only the glory of God.

Point I: Saint John the Baptist pointing out Jesus to the people

Consideration: On leaving the desert, Jesus when to visit and console His precursor, who was suffering under grievous persecution. John, when he saw his Divine Master approaching, pointed Him out to the assembled multitude, saying, "Behold the Lamb of God. … The same is He that shall come after me, who is preferred before me, the latchet of whose shoes I am not worthy to loose … He it is that baptizeth with the Holy Ghost… This is the Son of God… He must increase; and I must decrease."

Application: We here see a man of undoubted sanctity, and held in the highest reputation, voluntarily lowering himself in the eyes of the people, and seeking to be forgotten by them, in order to fix their attention exclusively on the Savior of the World. This is how the saints humble themselves, that God may be exalted. They keep silence about their own merits, and love to praise others. These are the men to whom God loves to communicate Himself, and to enrich with His consolations and graces. You complain, perhaps, that you are deprived of them; may it not be because God sees that you seek only your own advantage and the esteem of men, even perhaps at the expense of others?
Affections and Resolutions.

Point II: He calls Jesus the Lamb of God

Consideration: John, seeing Jesus approaching, said, "Behold the Lamb of God. Behold Him who taketh away the sin of the world." He is called the Lamb of God – 1st, because He is the true and only victim worthy of being offered to God, or capable of expiating the sins of the world; 2ndly, because His meekness and long-suffering, in spite of our provocations, are like the gentleness of a *lamb*; 3rdly, because as a lamb suffers itself to be put to death without uttering a cry, so He spoke only words of pardon for His executioners. It was under this form that Isaias represented the promised Messiah, and His precursor hoped, by reminding them of this, to make the Jews recognize Him.

Application: Let us show ourselves worth of being disciples of the Lamb of God by these three signs: by uniting the sacrifice of ourselves to that of Jesus by the constant practice of mortification; by a gentle, charitable and patient behavior to everyone, even to those who are unfriendly to us; and by offering ourselves to Jesus as victims of love, desiring to suffer much for His glory and the salvation of souls, even should it cost us our life.

Affections and Resolutions.

Point III: He procures disciples for Him

Consideration: Saint John had assembled together a great number of disciples by his preaching, and by the report of his holiness. This might have tempted an ordinary man to vanity and ambition; but the saints care not for their own glory, they seek only the honor of God and the good of souls. Far from seeking to increase the number of his disciples, Saint John made every effort to detach them from himself and transfer them to Jesus, taking every opportunity of praising and exalting Him before them.

Application: True zeal is not afraid of the success of others; it rejoices in whatever good is done by them. False zeal, on the contrary, is secretly jealous of the good done by others, especially when it sees itself surpassed in success or in reputation; and this jealousy often shows itself in indirect blame or unkind criticism. We shrink from this description; but are we sure that we are ourselves quite free from such feelings?

Colloquy with our Blessed Lord.

Meditation VII: Jesus calls Disciples to Him

1st prelude: Behold Jesus in the midst of his four first disciples.
2nd prelude: Ask for grace to be always among the number of His most fervent disciples.

Point I: Choice of the four first disciples

Consideration: After having preached alone for some months, like the early prophets, Jesus sought to assemble disciples round Him. The first of these came from His holy precursor. The fact is thus recorded in Saint John's Gospel: Two disciples of Saint John the Baptist, having heard him say, "Behold the Lamb of God, … followed Jesus." And they said to Him, "Rabbi (which is to say, being interpreted, Master), where dwellest Thou? He saith to them, Come and see. They came and saw where He abode, and they stayed with Him that day. And Andrew, the brother of Simon Peter, was one of the two… He findeth first his brother Simon, and saith to him, We have found the Messias… And he brought him to Jesus. And Jesus, looking upon him, saith, Thou art Simon, the son of Jona; thou shalt be called Cephas, which is interpreted Peter. On the following day He would go forth into Galilee, and He findeth Philip. And Jesus saith to him, Follow Me."

Application: Andrew, John, Simon or Peter, and Philip were, then, the four priviledged mortals who were called by the Savior of the World to be His first disciples. Their vocation may seem to have been a mere accident, but it was decreed by God from all eternity. Examine the beginning of you vocation; it will seem to have been the result only of favorable circumstances; but with the eye of faith you will perceive the result of an eternal choice on the part of God.

Affections and Resolutions.

Point II: Condition of these first disciples

Consideration: They were honest, hardworking, and pious men, but of low birth, Galilean fishermen, and as such, despised by the Jews; ignorant and obscure men, held in contempt by the world. Why were such men chosen by our Divine Lord? First, to undeceive the world, which can see nothing great or estimable except in riches and honors; secondly, to exalt poverty and simplicity when found united with virtue and honesty; thirdly, to preserve the disciples themselves from all danger of pride in the high office to which they were predestined; but fourthly, and chiefly, to convince the world that the establishment and the triumph of the Church were not the work of man.

Application: If you consider this attentively, you will not be inclined, like some religious, to be ashamed of low birth, or to pass

yourself off for something different from what you really were in the world, by any affectations of language or manner; neither will you be vain of the rank you may have held, or the fortune you may have possessed there. Either of these things will be injurious to you, both before God and man, as you very well know.
Affections and Resolutions.

Point III: The manner of their vocation

Consideration: All were not called in the same direct manner, but none were admitted into the company of Jesus except provisionally at first, and on probation. The free disposal of their goods and their person was still left to them; it was only after a certain time of trial that they were allowed to make profession of the perfect poverty and apostolic life of Jesus.

Application: Call to mind the beginning, progress, and fulfillment of your vocation, and you will see that it much resembles that of these first disciples. You will also notice, with admiration and joy, that after the lapse of nineteen centuries, the superiors of religious orders still follow the rules traced out by their Divine Master, in the reception of candidates. These thoughts will increase your esteem and love for your holy vocation, and your desire to correspond faithfully with its grace.
Colloquy with Jesus, the Author of your holy vocation.

Meditation VIII: Interview of Jesus with Nathanael

1st prelude: Behold Jesus talking with Nathanael.
2nd prelude: Ask for the simplicity and guileless spirit which Jesus praised in Nathanael.

Point I: Prejudices of Nathanael

Consideration: No sooner did Philip know Jesus than he hastened to make Him known also to his friend Nathanael, who is thought to be the same as Saint Bartholomew. "We have found," he said, "Him of whom Moses in the law and the prophets did write, Jesus the son of Joseph of Nazareth." Thus was Nathanael called to the great privilege of the knowledge and friendship of Jesus. But he was on the point of losing this great grace through a fatal prejudice. He answered contemptuously, "Can anything of good come from Nazareth?" And it was only with great difficulty that his friend persuaded him to "come and see."

Application: How many at the present day are kept from Jesus, from His Church, from His Sacraments, by some prejudice! They are indeed worthy of our compassion; but are religious wholly free from this misfortune? You are recommended some book for your spiritual reading, but you have a prejudice against the author, and you refuse. Your director advises the practice of certain devotions, which would greatly benefit your soul, but you have been prejudiced against him, he is too particular, etc. You will perhaps find many such instances if you examine yourself carefully.

Affections and Resolutions.

Point II: Straightforwardness of Nathanael

Consideration: The contempt which Nathanael entertained for Nazarenes fell upon Jesus personally. But our Blessed Lord was not offended at this, because He saw him to be free from malice, and honestly seeking the truth. Far from reproaching him, He praised him: "Behold," He said, on seeing him approach, "an Israelite indeed, in whom there is not guile." Blessed indeed is the man who merits such praise from the lips of Jesus. Happy the religious who can flatter himself that in all things he goes straight to God in the simplicity of his heart, having no other intention or desire but to please Him. Very different is the case of one who thinks only of appearing virtuous and exact before men, without being really so in the sight of God.

Application: To which of these two description do we belong? The question is a most important one, and deserves our most serious consideration; especially as we are very apt to deceive ourselves on this subject, our pride being always ready to flatter us, and lead us to seek the esteem of men.

Affections and Resolutions.

Point III: Nathanael's profession of faith

Consideration: Nathanael, astonished at the portrait drawn of him by one who had never seen him, exclaimed, on the impulse of the moment, "Whence knowest Thou me? Jesus answered and said to him, Before that Philip called thee, when thou wast under the fig-tree, I saw thee." In one moment the eyes of the chosen disciple were opened; he felt convinced that no mere man could thus see things secret and hidden, and he exclaimed, with the most lively faith, "Rabbi, Thou art the Son of God, Thou art the King of Israel! Jesus answered and said to him, Because I said to thee, I saw thee under the fig-tree, thou believest: greater things than these shalt thou see… You shall see the heavens opened, and the angels of God ascending and descending upon the Son of Man."

Application: Let us seek God, like Nathanael, with simplicity of heart, and He will reveal Himself to us; He will send lights and graces to us out of heaven, and we shall experience the truth of the inspired words, "He that is a little one, let him turn to Me."
Colloquy with our Blessed Lord.

Meditation IX: Manifestation of Jesus in His first Miracle at the Marriage in Cana of Galilee

1st prelude: Behold Jesus and Mary among the guests at the marriage-feast.
2nd prelude: Ask of God miracles of grace for yourself.

Point I: Presence of Jesus and Mary at the wedding feast

Consideration: "And the third day," after the interview with Nathanael, "there was a marriage in Cana of Galilee, and the Mother of Jesus was there. And Jesus also was invited, and His disciples." One is here tempted to ask why our Divine Lord should have honored this humble marriage with His presence, rather than the nuptials of some person of high rank. First, then, it was to fulfill a duty of friendship and regard towards His Mother's family, for we find that the bridegroom at this feast was Simon the Canaanite, son of Cleophas, the brother of Saint Joseph, who afterwards became one of the twelve Apostles; secondly, to show His esteem for virtue in a humble rank of life; thirdly, to promote honour and respect for the marriage contract, ordained by God from the beginning of the world, and soon to be raised to the dignity of a Sacrament.

Application: Our Blessed Lord here teaches us that our renunciation of the world need not hinder us from conforming to the customs of society and friendship in our relations with our friends, provided we do not thereby transgress any duty to God, to our neighbor, or our rule. He also teaches us to hold every condition of life in honor, and to show more respect to virtue than rank.
Affections and Resolutions.

Point II: Care of Mary for her guests

Consideration: “And the wine failing, the Mother of Jesus said to Him, They have no wine.” Let us here consider two points – the hospitable care of our Lady, and the confidence with which she addresses herself to her Divine Son. Perceiving that the small quantity of wine (the ordinary beverage of the country) set apart for the use of her guests was exhausted, and that they would be put to inconvenience, without waiting to be asked, she briefly remarked to her Son, “They have no wine.” She did not even make any request, so perfect was her confidence that the mere statement of her need would be sufficient; and though He seemed to repulse her by his reply, “Woman, what is it to Me and to thee? My hour is not yet come,” she nevertheless “saith to the waiters, Whatsoever He shall say to you, do ye.”

Application: We see here how compassionately our Lady interests herself in even the most trifling things which concern us, and also what power she has with God, who is willing to grant all things through her intercession. Our confidence in her should be unlimited, since she can dispose of the infinite power of her Divine Son. Do we wish to obtain miraculous favors? She teaches us what method to adopt – *to do all that Jesus shall say to us* by the mouth of our superiors; in other words, *blind obedience.*

Affections and Resolutions.

Point III: Miracle worked by Jesus for the sake of Mary

Consideration: Mary’s expectation was not disappointed. Jesus, anticipating the appointed time for her sake, worked His first miracle in public, changing into wine the water with which He had caused six water-pots of stone, each containing two or three measures, to be filled. Thus did He, as the Evangelist says, “manifest His glory,” or divinity, “and His disciples believed in Him.”

Application: The miracle which Jesus performed in Cana for the wedding guests He repeats daily for us in a still more wonderful and excellent manner, when, by the ministry of His priests, He changes wine into His Blood, and gives it us to drink, with the promise that they who drink it shall never die. Let us show our gratitude for so much love by increased care and reverence in preparing ourselves to receive His Most Precious Blood. Colloquy with Our Lord Jesus Christ.

Meditation X: Jesus leaves His Holy Mother: He invites His Disciples to leave all, after His Example

1st prelude: Consider Jesus saying to you: "Follow Me."
2nd prelude: Ask for grace to make constant progress in the imitation of Jesus Christ.

Point I: Jesus leaves His Mother: His perfect detachment

Consideration: After leaving Cana, Jesus "went down to Capharnaum, He and His Mother and His brethren and His disciples, and they remained there not many days." These last words, "they remained there not many days," are very remarkable. They refer to the last days which He spent under the same roof with His Mother and other relations. Form that time we may truly say that He had neither Mother nor home any more on earth. He was thenceforth only "the Son of Man"; one sent from God, and entirely given up to His divine mission, going about from place to place wherever the glory of God and the salvation of souls called Him.

Application: It behoves apostolic men, and those religious who have embraced an active life, to change their place of abode frequently. Their rule obliges them to go wherever obedience calls them, to work for the greater glory of God and the good of souls. These frequent changes are often very trying to nature; have we submitted to them promptly, and in a spirit of indifference? Affections and Resolutions.

Point II: Jesus invites Andrew and Peter to make the act of renunciation of which He has set them the example

Consideration: Jesus, having given an example of the perfect renunciation of all natural affections, in order to devote Himself exclusively to His divine mission, invited those of His disciples who were to share that mission and to perpetuate it, to make the same act of self-sacrifice. "Jesus, walking by the sea of Galilee," says Saint Matthew, "saw two brethren, Simon, who is called Peter, and Andrew his brother, casting a net into the sea (for they were fishers); and He saith to them, Come you after Me, and I will make you fishers of men. And they, immediately leaving their nets, followed Him," bursting asunder all domestic ties, renouncing all property and all liberty to dispose of themselves, and resolving to imitate the voluntary poverty, the perfect chastity, and the laborious work of their divine Master.

Application: We see here the first example of the *practice* of the evangelical counsels, which are so contrary to the maxims of the world and the inclinations of nature. Who would ever have embraced them, if God made Man had not first set the example? We must certainly attribute it as much to the force of example as to the workings of divine grace that the first disciples embraced them so promptly. If you wish to draw others to the practice of virtue, you must preach by example as well as precept.

Affections and Resolutions.

Point III: Jesus invites James and John to make the same sacrifice

Consideration: "And going on from thence, He saw other two brethren, James, the son of Zebedee their father, mending their nets, and He called them. And they forthwith left their nets and father, and followed Him."

Application: What admirable generosity and correspondence with grace do we here see, both in the father and his sons! There is neither hesitation on one side, nor complaint or opposition on the other. Oh, what a happiness for us, if we have corresponded generously with the first grace of our vocation! Oh, why have we not corresponded with the same fidelity to every other!

Colloquy with Our Blessed Lord.

Meditation XI: Zeal of Jesus for His Father's House

The first Easter, from which is commonly reckoned the commencement of the three years' public ministry of our Lord Jesus Christ.

1st prelude: Behold Jesus driving the buyers and sellers out of the Temple with a scourge.

2nd prelude: Ask for great zeal for the glory and the house of God.

Point I: Ardent zeal of Jesus

Consideration: "And the Pasch of the Jews was at hand, and Jesus went up from Jerusalem." But this year He went not as a simple worshipper, but as a Master and Reformer, and He proclaimed Himself such by a striking act of authority: "He found in the Temple them that sold oxen and sheep and doves, and the changers of money sitting. And when He had made, as it were, a scourge of little cords, He drove them all out of the Temple, the sheep also and the oxen, and the money of the changers He poured out, and the tables He overthrew." He was resolved to put an end to a scandalous, sacrilegious, and inveterate abuse which a sordid love of gain had established. For this reason Jesus outwardly manifested indignation and anger, without, however, permitting the interior peace of His soul to be disturbed.

Application: To show *just* anger is not only no sin, but often an act of virtue and a necessity. "Be angry and sin not." It is sometimes necessary with our inferiors or subjects to make them feel the seriousness of their faults, and sometimes with ourselves. Perhaps you have long been addicted to some habit of sin which causes scandal or secret remorse; you must get rid of it. Use a holy indignation and the rod of divine justice against yourself, and lay it not aside till you have conquered yourself.

Affections and Resolutions.

Point II: Discretion of the zeal of Jesus

Consideration: "And to them that sold doves, He said, Take these things hence." Why this greater consideration for these persons? Because they were poor, more ignorant, and less guilty than the others. Moreover, if He had dealt with them as with the first mentioned, He would have deprived them of their only means of subsistence, which would have been most repugnant to His infinite goodness. He therefore only frightened without hurting them.

Application: Learn to temper your zeal with discretion, and to moderate it by charity. Do we not often fail in this, and is it not the cause of many failures? Indiscreet zeal does more harm than good.

Affections and Resolutions.

Point III: Justification of the zeal of Jesus

Consideration: Jesus was pleased to justify His severity to the Jews in these words: "Make not the house of My Father a house of traffic." What ought to be the thoughts of a Christian in considering these words? If Jesus judged it to be a profanation deserving of the most severe punishment to buy and sell in the Temple what was necessary for the sacrifices therein offered, how must He regard the public and secret sins by which our churches, so much holier than the Temple at Jerusalem, are profaned? With what severity will He not one day punish them!

Application: Let us apply these words to ourselves. Do we seek to make reparation for the insults offered to God in the holy place by exterior reverence and devotion? Have we not, on the contrary, much negligence and many irreverent looks and gestures to reproach ourselves with?
Colloquy with Our Lord on the altar.

Meditation XII: On Zeal for the Glory of God

1st prelude: Consider the words of Saint Paul: "Do all for to the glory of God."
2nd prelude: Ask for a great zeal for the glory of God.

Point I: Nature of zeal for the glory of God

Consideration: *The extrinsic glory of God*, as He has manifested Himself in the work of creation, consists in receiving from man, a being gifted with intelligence, and alone capable of knowing the Author of his being and of all the wonders of the universe, the acknowledgement that all honor and glory belong to God alone, together with the most profound reverence and adoration, and an entire offering of himself. *Zeal for the glory of God* consists in an ardent desire to inspire others with these feelings, and, if possible, to fill all hearts with them.

Application: What can be more just and equitable than this *zeal for the glory of God*? Every good son has naturally his father's glory and interests at heart. God is the Father of all. We owe Him our life and all that we possess. Ought not, then, zeal for His glory to be our most natural feeling? Ought not all men to be constantly blessing and praising Him? But, alas, it is not so. The truth is, most men still deserve the reproach addressed by Moses to the children of Israel: "He forsook God who made him, and departed from God his Savior." Though we are religious, do we not sometimes deserve this reproach? Do we not sometimes think more of ourselves than of God, and resent an injury done to ourselves more than an insult offered to Him?
Affections and Resolutions.

Point II: Excellence of zeal for the glory of God

Consideration: Nothing can possibly be greater or more excellent than the end which God Himself had in view in all His works. And this end was Himself and His own glory. "The Lord has made all things for Himself." This also was His end in creating man in His own image. "I have created him for My glory." Hence the conclusion, or rather the precept, of the Apostle: "Whether you eat or drink, or whatsoever you do, do all to the glory of God." What a privilege for man to work for the same end as God! Could he desire a higher destiny?

Application: To us especially, as religious, it belongs to promote not only the glory, but the *greater glory*, of God. First in ourselves, offering Him a perpetual homage; striving to know and do His holy will in all things, and never to oppose it by the very least contradiction; and then to promote it in others, by laboring to make them love and serve God, and by cooperating in all good works, if not actively, at least by offering our prayers and Communions, or the holy sacrifice of the Mass, for them.
Affections and Resolutions.

Point III: Great merit of zeal for the glory of God

Consideration: Since nothing can be more excellent than works undertaken *for the glory of God*, it follows that nothing can be of greater merit in His sight, or procure greater glory for us in eternity, according to His own words: "Whosoever shall glorify Me, him will I glorify."

Application: These considerations should make us anxious to seize every opportunity of exercising zeal for the glory of God. We shall find such opportunities everywhere, even without going out of the house, in leading others to perfection by our good example, and thus making them instrumental to the glory of God.
Colloquy with Our Blessed Lady.

Meditation XIII: Nicodemus comes to Jesus by Night

1st prelude: Behold Nicodemus, a man greatly respected both for his age and authority, humbly questioning and listening to Jesus.
2nd prelude: Ask Jesus to make the energy of your will always correspond with the light of your understanding.

Point I: Courage and cowardice of Nicodemus

Consideration: The more than human authority which Jesus had shown in driving the buyers and sellers from the Temple had caused a great commotion in Jerusalem. "Many believed," says Saint John, "seeing His signs which He did." "And there was a man of the Pharisees, named Nicodemus, a ruler of the Jews." He was an upright man, in search of truth. He believed that Jesus was a true prophet, and thought it his duty to seek instruction from Him. But to do this it was necessary to set human respect at defiance, and to brave the anger of the rulers, who had openly declared themselves against Jesus, calling Him a Nazarene impostor, and a deceiver of the people. Nicodemus had courage enough to trample these difficulties under foot, but with a sad mixture of cowardice; that no one might notice him, he "came to Jesus by night."

Application: Is not this mixture of courage and cowardice that we see in Nicodemus a faithful portrait of ourselves? We have had courage to forsake all things for the love of God, and to embrace a manner of life painful to our nature; we have courage to persevere in our choice, and yet what unfaithfulness to our rule, to our resolutions, to our duties, do we not constantly fall into, out of cowardice, human respect, or lukewarmness? Let us make a firm determinations that by the grace of God it shall be so no longer. Affections and Resolutions.

Point II: Light and darkness of Nicodemus

Consideration: Nicodemus, on approaching Jesus, said to Him: "Rabbi, we know that Thou art come a Teacher from God; for no man can do these signs which Thou dost, unless God be with him." This profession of faith shows Nicodemus to have been much more enlightened than the other members of the council, and yet he was still groping in thick darkness. He did not recognize Jesus as the Messiah; or at all events he so far misapprehended His doctrines as to deserve the reproach, "Art thou a master in Israel, and knowest not these things?"

Application: We are not wanting in the intelligence which concerns the excellency of Christian perfection; we perhaps have enough proficiency in it to be "masters in Israel," and to teach others. But when it becomes a question of acting according to our knowledge, we are suddenly involved in darkness; the motives for keeping certain resolutions, such as to rise at the first sound of the bell, to take a reproof silently, to observe an abstinence, etc., no longer appear to us sufficiently conclusive, and we give up our resolutions. We reconsider them. Have we not often noticed in ourselves this contrast of light and darkness, generosity and

weakness? What a subject for humiliation before God, and distrust in ourselves!
Affections and Resolutions.

Point III: Goodwill and procrastination of Nicodemus

Consideration: Nicodemus went out from his interview with Jesus an altered man. His mind was illuminated with the light of faith, and his heart enkindled with the love of his Lord. He had become His faithful and fervent disciple. Nevertheless, he does not seem eager to express his faith by acts. He never even mingles among the disciples who follow Jesus. It was not till two years later, and the death of Jesus, that he signalized himself by an heroic act of piety and devotion, boldly going to Pilate to demand the body of his Divine Master, and providing it with a magnificent burial.

Application: Perhaps we too, notwithstanding a certain amount of goodwill, have been slow in the actual service of God. Perhaps we have as yet done nothing great or heroic for Him. But let us not be discouraged. Nicodemus redeemed his tardiness heroically, and he merited to be counted among the saints (Martyrology, August 3). Let us follow his example.
Colloquy with our Blessed Lord.

Meditation XIV: Jealousy of Saint John the Baptist's Disciples

1st prelude: Behold Saint John teaching his disciples, who are animated with a mistaken zeal for his glory.
2nd prelude: Ask for forgetfulness of self, and a true zeal for God's glory.

Point I: Jealousy of Saint John the Baptist's disciples

Consideration: After the conversions and miracles which had taken place in Jerusalem, "Jesus and His disciples came into the land of Judea, and baptized… Jesus Himself did not baptize, but His disciples." This excited the jealousy of Saint John the Baptist's disciples, and they went to him and complained: "Rabbi, He that was with thee beyond the Jordan, to whom thou gavest testimony, behold He baptizeth, and all men come to Him."

Application: We have here a proof that even good people are liable to envy, and that this passion sometimes puts on the appearance of zeal; for the zeal of the disciples of Saint John for his glory caused them to view the success of Jesus and His disciples with displeasure. Instead of rejoicing, they were grieved at it. Do we find nothing of the kind in ourselves? When good is done by some other order, or even when we find ourselves eclipsed and surpassed by one of our brethren, do we rejoice, or do we feel the sting of jealousy? Does not our readiness to blame and criticize answer for us?

Affections and Resolutions.

Point II: Disinterestedness of Saint John the Baptist

Consideration: Saint John's disciples expected to find him share their feelings; but they were greatly mistaken. There is no envy in the hearts of the saints; wholly detached from themselves and their own interests, they seek only the glory of God. This disinterestedness was most remarkable in the precursor of Jesus Christ: his only reply to the complaints of his disciples was to exalt Jesus and depreciate himself. "He that cometh from above is above all. I am sent before Him." "My joy therefore is fulfilled."

Application: How rare, even amongst Christians, is this perfect detachment and forgetfulness of self! It charms while it astonishes us in a secular person, but it is expected, and with good reason, from a religious. In what degree do we possess it? If we are thoroughly rooted in this virtue, we shall gladly hear and repeat the praises of those who are more highly gifted and more esteemed than ourselves. If we cannot do this, we must conclude that we are not yet detached from the world and from ourselves.

Affections and Resolutions.

Point III: Abnegation of Saint John the Baptist

Consideration: "He must increase, but I must decrease." Saint John the Baptist carried his disinterestedness to the extent of a total abnegation of self. He not only loses sight of his own works, and rejoices in the still greater ones of Jesus, but he even desires that these last should wholly eclipse his own in the sight and esteem of the world.

Application: If we desire to escape the attacks of vainglory and envy, we must, after this example, so completely subdue our pride as to aim at an entire abnegation of ourselves, and a desire to be forgotten and despised by others. We need not despair of reaching this perfection: all things are possible to grace.

Colloquy with our Blessed Lord.

Meditation XV: On Pride and its fatal Effects

1st prelude: Behold Lucifer falling from heaven down to hell.
2nd prelude: Ask for a salutary fear of the spirit of pride.

Point I: Nature of pride

Consideration: In order to be secure against the attacks of envy and other unruly passions we must trace them to their source, which is pride, the result and the punishment of original sin, as the Holy Ghost teaches in these memorable words: "Never suffer pride to reign in thy mind or in thy words, for from it all perdition took its beginning."

Application: To be convinced of this truth, we have only to consider the nature of this terrible and mortal sin. *Pride is the inordinate love of our own glory.* Hence proceed vainglory and ambition, which in their turn produce intrigues, hypocrisy, human respect; hence proceed lying, prevarication, contumacy, obstinacy, contentions, divisions; hence, again, proceed selfishness and jealousy, which lead to endless sins against charity. We feel annoyed at the success of others; we rejoice at their faults or misfortunes; we injure them, by suspicions and rash judgements, in our own esteem, and often also in that of others, by detraction, calumny, malicious insinuations, and the like.
Affections and Resolutions.

Point II: The sin of pride

Consideration: The desire for our own glory is called unruly, because it is directly opposed to the supreme rule of justice. To every one his due. Now God alone is the author of all that is good and excellent in His creatures; to Him alone therefore is due all the honor and glory thereof: *Soli Deo honor et Gloria.* But the proud man exalts *himself* on account of his gifts, either of nature or of grace. He makes use of them to gain the praise and esteem of others, and thus puts himself, as it were, in the place of God. Is it surprising, then, that God should abominate him? "Every proud man is an abomination to the Lord." "God resisteth the proud, but to the humble he giveth grace."

Application: In order to understand more clearly what is the sinfulness of pride in God's sight, and to conceive a lively horror of it, call to mind the terrible chastisements inflicted on the pride of the angels, of our first parents, of Pharaoh, of Nabuchodonosor, of Antiochus, and so many others recorded in Holy Scripture; consider also how severely God punished pride in the holy kings David and Ezechias, who had only been guilty of vanity – one in numbering his subjects, and the other in showing the treasures of his palace. Remember also how God has threatened to abandon the proud to their own evil passions, even to the most shameful excesses. How many religious have fallen through pride into apostasy or profligacy!

Affections and Resolutions.

Point III: Misery of pride

Consideration: How sad is the case of a proud religious! His is wretched because his labors, his watchings, his struggles, will have no reward in heaven. "They have" already "received their reward," as our Lord told the proud Pharisees. Wretched because instead of the esteem of men, which he seeks, he will receive only their contempt. "Pride is hateful before God and man." Wretched because he is perpetually tormented by the desire to increase his reputation, and the fear of losing it; always agitated by dark suspicions or vain apprehensions.

Application: If experience has taught you the truth of all this, hasten to profit by it; redouble your vigilance and energy in resisting this most powerful enemy of your salvation and progress in perfections.

Colloquy with our Blessed Lady.

Meditation XVI: On the Nature and Necessity of Humility

1st prelude: Behold Jesus Christ saying to you: "Many that are first shall be last, and the last first."

2nd prelude: Ask for grace to increase continually in the knowledge, love and practice of humility.

Point I: Nature of humility

Consideration: Humility is the root of all virtues, as pride is the root of all sins. Saint Bernard thus defines it: "An acquired virtue or habit, by means of which man despises himself and desires to be despised by others." In other words, it is a disposition or habit of mind and heart by which man, seeing nothing in himself but sin, and the inclination to sin, despises himself, and esteems God alone, the source of all good, being content, and even desirous, to be forgotten and despised by men, that God alone may be praised and glorified.

Application: To ascertain if we possess this virtue, let us apply to ourselves the rule of Jesus Christ: "By the fruit the tree is known." Let us examine our thoughts, words and actions. *Our thoughts*. If we care less what God thinks of us than what men think, and are more anxious to please men than God; if our thoughts tend to exalt ourselves, to the desire for superiority, or for a position of mark in the world, we have not humility. *Our words*. If we think ourselves humble because we sometimes speak ill of ourselves, because we often accuse ourselves of our faults before the community, while at the same time we fret and complain if others speak ill of us, reprove, humble or injure us, we may rest well assured that we are not really humble, and still less if we have recourse to lies or excuses to palliate our faults. *Our actions*. However good and praiseworthy they may seem before men, if we have sought our own glory in them, we may be sure that before God we are devoid of humility; and if so, how can we ever become good religious?

Affections and Resolutions.

Point II: Necessity of humility

Consideration: The same is true of humility as of faith, that without it, it is impossible to please God; because without humility we worship ourselves, and thus become hateful and abominable in the sight of God. Without humility no virtue is possible, because it is the root of all virtues. Without humility there is no grace, for God "giveth grace to the humble"; without grace we cannot merit; and without either virtue or merit we cannot enter heaven; consequently without humility there is no salvation. Our Lord expressly tells us this. "Unless you be converted, and become as little children, you shall not enter into the kingdom of heaven." He said this on the occasion of a dispute having arisen amongst His Apostles as to which of them should be the greatest; He therefore especially referred to the *humility and simplicity* of children. Still more evidently, without humility there can be no progress in perfection; and we are bound by our vows to aim at perfection; and we are bound by our vows to aim at perfection. Without humility we are useless, to almost useless, to others, and yet we are bound to labor for their salvation. How can God bless labor in which we seek our own glory? Without humility, therefore, we can never attain the double end of our vocation; we can have not hope of persevering in it, nor can we ever find in it the peace and happiness which we sought. Is not this a true interpretation of our Savior's words: "Learn of Me, because I am meek and humble of heart"?

Application: Are we well persuaded of the necessity of humility? What means do we adopt to acquire it? And with what success? Let us answer these questions in all sincerity, *before God.* Colloquy with Jesus Christ.

Meditation XVII: On the Advantages and Properties of the Virtue of Humility

1st prelude: Consider Saint Peter saying: "To the humble He giveth grace."
2nd prelude: Ask for grace to reach a high degree of humility.

Point I: Advantages of humility

Consideration: We may apply to humility what has been said of wisdom: "All good things came to me together with her." Happy, then, the religious who possesses her! His progress in virtue will be rapid and constant, his joy continual. In fact, the humble religious, being fully convinced of his own unworthiness, and of the infinite majesty of God, has necessarily: 1st, a good intention, which makes all his actions meritorious; 2ndly, the love of God, and consequently the love of crosses and sufferings, because love is proved by things painful to nature; 3rdly, zeal for the glory of God, which he desires to promote in himself and others; he would gladly bring all men to the feet of Jesus Christ; 4thly, distrust of himself, and consequently prudence, and modesty, and discretion in his words; 5thly, obedience, docility, and that perfect openness with superiors to which they lead; 6thly, patience, and resignation under all trials, which appear to him far less than he deserves from the justice of God; 7thly, indifference to all places or offices, for he thinks himself unworthy of all, and yet capable of anything by the help of God; 8thly, charity and kindness – he is severe with himself, but indulgent to others; 9thly, and finally, peace of heart – he is never unhappy. Neglect, contempt, injuries, which disturb the proud man, are his delight. As a great saint once said, "He carries heaven about with him" (Bellarmine, *de V. Sol.*)

Application: These considerations will make us love and esteem humility as the "pearl of great price" spoken of by our Blessed Lord, and like the merchant man in the parable, we shall gladly sell all that we have to buy it.

Affections and Resolutions.

Point II: Properties of humility

Consideration: Let us examine well the nature and properties of humility, that we may avoid certain very common mistakes. Many imagine that humility is something forced and unnatural, while in reality it is most conformable to truth and justice; but for the disorder consequent upon original sin, we should all be naturally humble. Others think that humility forbids us to conceal our faults, to sustain our just rights and privileges, to let our talents be known to others, or even to ourselves, to allow ourselves to be respected or esteemed by our subordinates for our wise and careful management of affairs. All this is a mistake. None of these things are contrary to humility, when they are necessary for the glory of God, or the good of souls, and when we have no other end in view, no desire for our own interests or aggrandizement.

Application: Behold Mary, the most humble of virgins; she acknowledges and publishes to all the world the great privileges and graces she has received: "He that is mighty hath done great things to me" but she ascribed all the glory to God: "My soul doth magnify the Lord." Again, consider Saint Paul. He vigorously maintained his rights as a Roman citizen before the heathen; and before the Asiatic Christians he put forward his labors and revelations as a claim upon their love, respect and obedience; but he did it only for the furtherance of the Gospel. When it concerned only himself personally, he suffered persecutions and injuries in silence, and regarded himself as the last of the Apostles. Others, again, think that humility is the same as cowardice, that a humble man must not undertake great or enterprising works. On the contrary, when a proud man would recoil before difficulties and the fear of failure or ridicule, the humble man, putting all such thoughts aside, goes steadily forward. Nothing seems impossible to him, for he says with the Apostle: "I can do all things through Him who strengtheneth me."

Colloquy with Our Lady.

Meditation XVIII: On the principal Means to acquire and strengthen Humility

1st prelude: Consider the words of the Apostle: "He humbled Himself, for which cause God also hath exalted Him."
2nd prelude: Ask for courage to practice all means of acquiring and increasing humility.

Point I: To avoid all that wounds humility

Consideration: If we desire the friendship of any one, we avoid all that could wound him. If, then, we desire to obtain humility as the companion of our life, we must be careful above all that nothing in our thoughts, words or actions should savour of pride, or nourish vanity. We must not swell with complacency on any good actions in our past lives, but rather remember our sins as a contrast to them; we must meet temptations to pride by interior acts of humility; we must avoid speaking of ourselves, either ill or well, without sufficient cause; we must be silent when we are reproved; we must not seek to domineer in conversation, or to impose our own opinion upon others. In our bearing and manner we must avoid all affectation, immodesty, singularity, pretense, and, in a word, all that wounds humility.

Application: Have we been careful in these things, which even common sense points out to us as necessary to obtain humility? It is true they are only negative means, but if we neglect them, all others will be useless.

Affections and Resolutions.

Point II: To take advantage of every opportunity to practice humility

Consideration: Moral virtues are never infused, like theological ones. We must acquire them for ourselves, and practice them diligently. Thus, it is a common saying, "There is no humility without humiliations." What hinders us is a want of courage to deny ourselves in good earnest; and often our superiors dare not mortify us, lest they should only exasperate us. God, however, takes pity on us, and sends us humiliations, which are all the more salutary that they are not our own choice. Sometimes these take the form of mental sufferings, doubts, scruples, painful and humiliating temptations, which oblige us to seek help or consolation like simple novices; sometimes of sickness, weakness, disease, which incapacitates us from fulfilling our duties, and makes us useless to the community, when we had thought ourselves indispensable to it; sometimes it is a painful misunderstanding – the failure of our most anxious efforts – an undeserved reproof, when we have mistaken the meaning of some order of our superior's or when he has mistaken our motives; or again, it may be some cruel calumny which strikes at our reputation.

Application: When God permits these things, it is only for our good, and to procure for us opportunities of aspiring to a high degree of humility. Let us profit by them. Far from complaining, or being cast down by them, let us pray, with holy King David, "It is good for me that Thou hast humbled me."

Affections and Resolutions.

Point III: To make frequent acts of humility

Consideration: The religious who really desires to advance in humility does not rest satisfied with the humiliations which God sends him, but makes many exterior and interior acts of humility during the day.

Application: Let us do likewise. First let us be exact in all acts of humility practiced in the community, and be careful to make them in a spirit of humility; then let us make ourselves familiar with interior acts, and the exterior ones will become easy to us, and sources of great consolation.

Colloquy with Jesus Christ.

Meditation XIX: Interview of Jesus with the Woman of Samaria – her Conversion and Zeal

1st prelude: Behold Jesus sitting down to rest by Jacob's Well.
2nd prelude: Ask for grace to sanctify both your fatigues and your recreations.

Point I: Weariness of Jesus

Consideration: We read in the Gospel that, early in the first year of our Lord's public ministry, His holy precursor was cast into prison, where he afterwards ended his life by martyrdom. The mission of Jesus was thenceforward more openly manifested. But, being persecuted in Judea, He determined to return to Galilee, passing through Samaria. It was a long and painful journey, and when He arrived at Sichar, a city of Samaria, "Jesus, being wearied with His journey, sat thus at the well. It was about the sixth hour."

Application: We too are often fatigued, exhausted, overcome and so long for rest. What a consolation to think that our weariness resembles that of our Lord in being the result of works of charity for the glory of God and the salvation of souls! Such fatigues will merit for us a great increase of joy in heaven, while the weariness of worldly men is sterile and unprofitable. Let us sustain and encourage ourselves with these thoughts, and say with Saint Augustine, "The labor is short, the reward is eternal."

Affections and Resolutions.

Point II: Repose of Jesus

Consideration: Jesus Christ, being in all things like to us, was really fatigued, and really desired to rest when He sat down at Jacob's Well. But He made a good use of His repose by entering into conversation with a poor sinful woman of Sichar who had come to draw water, which conversation proved her conversion, and that of many of her fellow citizens.

Application: We have here, in the person of our Divine Lord, the perfect model of a true religious, who ought to be always on the look-out, even in his hours of rest and recreation, for some means of furthering the glory of God and the good of souls, which are the true ends of his vocation. Have we not sometimes heard one of our brethren, after this example, relate some anecdote at recreation, or out walking, which tends to edify as well as to amuse, and thus often benefits not only the community, but any strangers who may happen to be present?

Affections and Resolutions.

Point III: Indefatigable zeal of Jesus

Consideration: Observe with how much patience and dexterity our Blessed Lord leads the Samaritan woman to self-knowledge and repentance. First He takes occasion, from the water which she draws, to suggest a desire for the living waters of grace; then He desires her *to fetch her husband*, in order to make her acknowledge the licentiousness of her life; then, by reminding her of all she had done in her past life, He opens her eyes, and causes her to exclaim: "Sir, I perceive that Thou art a prophet." Then in answer to her questions, He reveals Himself to her as the promised Messiah. She recognizes her Savior; from a sinner she becomes and apostle. She hastens to the town, and brings the inhabitants in crows to the feet of Jesus.

Application: Has not God dealt thus with ourselves? Has He not led us by gentle steps to the knowledge of ourselves, of the vanities of the world, and then on further to the love and practice of the evangelical counsels? Let us thank Him for this, and deal in a like manner with those entrusted to our charge. Often we fail from indiscreet zeal and overhaste, instead of waiting for a favorable opportunity.

Colloquy with our Blessed Lord.

Meditation XX: Faith of the Inhabitants of Sichar – Mission of Galilee

1st prelude: Behold Jesus saying, "My food is to do the will of Him that sent Me."

2nd prelude: Ask for grace to know and do in all things the holy will of God.

Point I: Mysterious food of Jesus

Consideration: The Samaritan woman returned to the city, and said to the people: "Come and see a man who has told me all things whatsoever I have done." The disciples meanwhile, having returned from their expedition to buy food, "prayed Him, saying, Rabbi, eat." But He said to them: "I have meat to eat which you know not. My meat is to do the will of Him that sent Me, that I may perfect His work." (Perfect, that is, the work of creation, by the redemption and sanctification of mankind.)

Application: Let us consider these words attentively; they will enable us to understand how eagerly Jesus desires our sanctification, more eagerly than a famished man desires food. A brief reflection on what Jesus has done for ourselves in particular will still more convince us of this truth. We shall also learn that, in order to conform ourselves to the desires of Jesus Christ, we must try to ascertain what are the designs of God in our regard, and correspond faithfully therewith. We shall further learn that we can never show sufficient zeal for the glory of God and the salvation of souls, and that hunger, thirst, weariness, or any other inconveniences, are not for a moment to be compared with it. Have we anything approaching this zeal?

Affections and Resolutions.

Point II: Sojourn of Jesus in Sichar

Consideration: No sooner had the people of Sichar, yielding to the woman's entreaty, seen and heard Jesus than He so charmed them that "they desired Him that He would tarry there." Our Blessed Lord granted their desire: "And He abode there two days. And many more believed in Him because of His own word; and they said to the woman, We now believe, not for thy saying; for we ourselves have heard him, and know that this is indeed the Savior of the world."

Application: What an honor for these Samaritans to have been the first to recognize Jesus as the *Savior of the world*! What a blessed privilege to have believed in Him, and found the treasures of faith and sanctifying grace – the pledge of eternal happiness! And all this was the fruit of a short visit and a few instructions. To know Jesus is enough; and if we only knew Him, we could never offend Him.

Affections and Resolutions.

Point III: Mission of Jesus in Galilee

Consideration: Jesus went straight from Sichar to Galilee, to open a mission which, through the fame of its miracles, was to stir up the people, verify His teaching, extend His reputation, and serve as a model for all future missions. "He departed and went into Galilee." And He "began to preach, and to say, Do penance, for the kingdom of heaven is at hand. Repent, and believe the Gospel… And the fame of Him was spread forthwith into all the country of Galilee."

Application: If we are commissioned to teach others, let us seek to establish our reputation and win confidence, not by working miracles, which God does not require of us, but by the testimony of a blameless life, and let us, like our Divine Master, make the fundamental truths of religion our ordinary subjects of instruction.

Colloquy with Jesus.

Meditation XXI: Cure of the Ruler's Son at Capharnaum

1st prelude: Behold an afflicted father kneeling at Jesus' feet.
2nd prelude: Ask for unbounded confidence in the mercy and goodness of God.

Point I: An afflicted father appeals to Jesus

Consideration: The first miracle by which our Blessed Lord proved His divine mission, and inspired men with faith in Him, was performed for the consolation of an afflicted father, a man of high rank, and well known in Galilee. Saint John thus records it: "There was a certain ruler, whose son was sick at Capharnaum. He having heard that Jesus was come… into Galilee, went to Him and prayed Him to come down and heal his son, for he was at the point of death."

Application: It was *sorrow* which brought this ruler to the knowledge of Jesus, and was the instrument of his salvation. We must not, therefore, look upon the afflictions sent us by God as evils, and complain of them, as perhaps we have been tempted to do. We may observe that this ruler delayed coming to Jesus till his son was at the last extremity. This was an error, which we must not imitate. We must not wait to ask God's help till we have exhausted all human means, and sought consolation in vain from creatures. It we act thus, is it surprising that God should delay to help us?
Affections and Resolutions.

Point II: Jesus reproves the ruler

Consideration: The ruler's hope of obtaining the cure of his son sprang from a very imperfect faith. He did not believe that Jesus could cure him from a distance. Our Blessed Lord therefore said to him: "Unless you see signs and wonders, you believe not." The afflicted father received this reproof with humility, and at the same time repeated his request with respectful confidence: "Lord, come down, before that my son die." These good dispositions obtained for him a more perfect faith, and also the favor that he requested. "Jesus saith to him, Go thy way; thy son liveth. The man believed the word that Jesus said to him, and went his way."

Application: Jesus treats us as He treated this ruler. If He seems to refuse what we ask, or to delay granting it, it is either to make us value it more, or to give us an opportunity of practicing patience, resignation, faith, and confidence. We must never weary of asking Him for what we want; He will grant it in the end.
Affections and Resolutions.

Point III: Favors granted by Jesus to the ruler

Consideration: However firmly the poor father might believe the word of Jesus, we can easily imagine how eagerly he must have hurried over the fourteen leagues which separate Cana from Capharnaum, that he might see with his own eyes the fulfillment of it. The time must have seemed double its real length to him. But what must have been his joy when "his servants met him, and they brought him word saying that his son lived," that "yesterday at the seventh hour the fever left him. The father therefore knew that it was at the same hour that Jesus said to him, Thy son liveth; and himself believed and his whole house."

Application: Oh how good and liberal is our Divine Lord! He is not satisfied with granting a perfect cure to the child of this afflicted father, but He bestows on himself, on his son, and on all his household *the gift of faith*, and, as we may well believe, also that of final perseverance, and of eternal salvation! What ought not to be our love and gratitude to so generous a benefactor?
Colloquy with Jesus.

Meditation XXII: Sojourn of Jesus at Capharnaum

1st prelude: Behold Jesus preaching in the synagogue at Capharnaum.
2nd prelude: Ask for a docile and obedient spirit.

Point I: Jesus takes up His abode at Capharnaum

Consideration: After preaching for a few days at Cana, Jesus went to Capharnaum, where He fixed His residence, rather than at Nazareth, or any other town in Galilee. This was probably because Capharnaum was the most populous town in Galilee, and also had more facilities of communication with the surrounding country and villages, on account of its position at the point where the river Jordan empties itself into the sea of Galilee or Tiberias. "Leaving the city Nazareth, He came and dwelt in Capharnaum." It was, therefore, a place peculiarly suited for the preaching of the Gospel, and also for the exercise of the infinite charity of Jesus in works of mercy. The inhabitants greatly needed the display of such charity, for they were thoroughly corrupted by the riches and luxury which their extensive commerce had introduced amongst them.

Application: The rule of those religious who by their institute are obliged to go wherever there are miseries to console or souls to save, binds them to an entire *indifference* for all places of abode, with the obligation, if a choice is left to them, of selecting that wherein they can do the most good, without regard to any personal feeling. This rule has been dictated by the example of our Lord Himself, and therefore commands our utmost reverence.

Affections and Resolutions.

Point II: Jesus preaches in the synagogue of Capharnaum

Consideration: As soon as Jesus arrived at Capharnaum, "forthwith," says the Evangelist, "upon the Sabbath days going into the synagogue, He taught them. And they were astonished at His doctrine. For he was teaching them as one having power, and not as the Scribes."

Application: The words of Jesus made very different impressions on the people from the teaching of the Scribes, not only because He spoke as a Master and Lawgiver, but because He practiced what He taught, and that every word and action spoke of forgetfulness of Himself, and zeal for His Father's glory and salvation of souls. The Scribes, on the contrary, openly contradicted their teaching by their lives, and their whole conduct betrayed self-interest. Such a course can never produce any fruit in saving souls.

Affections and Resolutions.

Point III: Jesus delivers one possessed with a devil

Consideration: "And there was in their synagogue a man with an unclean spirit, and he cried out, saying: What have we to do with Thee, Jesus of Nazareth? Art Thou come to destroy us? I know Thee who Thou art, the Holy One of God. And Jesus threatened him, saying: Speak no more, and go out of the man. And the unclean spirit, tearing him, and crying with a loud voice went out of him. And they were all amazed, insomuch that they questioned among themselves, saying: What thing is this? What is this new doctrine? For with power He commandeth even the unclean spirits, and they obey Him. And the fame of Him was spread forthwith into all the country of Galilee.

Application: We here see: 1st, the misery of one who by any sin, especially the sin of impurity, gives the devil possession of his heart; 2ndly, how powerless is the fury of the devils against those who fly to Jesus for help; 3rdly, how God brings good out of evil. All the rage of this unclean spirit turned only to the advantage of the Gospel, by raising the reputation of Jesus, and disposing persons to accept His teaching. Let us not, then, be scandalized at

the evils which God permits the devil to work in the world; He will turn them to His own glory, and the good of His Church: of this we may be well assured.
Colloquy with Jesus.

Meditation XXIII: Jesus in the House of Saint Peter – Cure of his Mother-in-Law

1st prelude: Behold Jesus raising up the mother-in-law of Simon Peter from a bed of sickness.
2nd prelude: Ask for the love of Jesus, the grace to imitate Him in everything; to be of one heart and one mind with Him.

Point I: Jesus dwells in the house of Simon Peter

Consideration: After the striking miracle which Jesus had worked in Capharnaum, and which had won Him universal admiration, He might have reckoned on an honorable reception from any of the richest and noblest families in the town. But He had no thought of this; for we read that, "immediately going out of the synagogue, they came into the house of Simon and Andrew, with James and John"; thus voluntarily making choice of a poor and humble abode. He was also actuated by a motive of charity, for "Simon's wife's mother lay in a fit of a fever."

Application: Do we, like our Divine Master, prefer to be meanly and poorly lodged? Do we choose rather to visit those whom we may benefit by our charity or zeal than those who would flatter our vanity by outward marks of respect, especially if we have just performed some public act of charity or generosity? Do we never visit others for self-indulgence, sensuality, or some still more unworthy motive? Let us ask ourselves these questions honestly.
Affections and Resolutions.

Point II: Jesus cures Simon's mother-in-law

Consideration: As soon as Jesus had entered the house of Simon, where his wife's mother lay ill, "forthwith they tell Him of her. And coming to her, He lifted her up, holding her by the hand; and immediately the fever left her."

Application: We learn from this passage of the holy Gospel, first, that true charity always *takes the initiative*. The disciples did not wait for the sick woman to ask them; of their own accord they entreated their Master to work a miracle in her favor, as soon as He had set foot in the house. We also learn that intercession for the sick and suffering is very pleasing to God, and appeals forcibly to His Heart. The prayer of the disciples was at once granted; the sick woman was instantly cured. Let us, then, strive to anticipate the desires and necessities of our suffering brethren – our charity will not fail to be rewarded.

Affections and Resolutions.

Point III: Jesus receives a just return of gratitude

Consideration: As soon as the sick woman was cured, we read that, "immediately rising, she ministered to them." With what overflowing sentiments of love, joy and gratitude she must have performed this duty of hospitality; *with what care and diligence*!

Application: This poor woman's eagerness to show her gratitude seems only right and natural to us. She owed Him her life, her health, and the use of her limbs; what could be more natural than that she should employ them in the service of her benefactor? It is true; but let us apply the same rule to ourselves. Do not we also owe to God our life, our health, all our bodily and mental powers? Are we not equally bound, in justice and gratitude, to use them for His greater glory, and that with the utmost fervor and diligence?

Colloquy with our Lord.

Meditation XXIV: Jesus interrupts His Labors of Charity for Prayer

1st prelude: Behold Jesus retiring from the town into solitude, to give Himself to prayer.

2nd prelude: Ask for the spirit of prayer, united to that of zeal and charity.

Point I: Jesus takes compassion on all infirmities

Consideration: "And when it was evening, after sunset, they brought to Him all that were ill, and that were possessed with devils. And all the city was gathered together at the door … But He, laying His hands on every one of them, healed them." Observe here the extreme goodness of our Divine Lord, who let all approach Him without difficulty or ceremony, and who never betrayed the smallest annoyance or impatience, either on account of the lateness of the hour, the pressure of the crowd, or His own weariness. He might have got rid of the people more quickly by curing them all at once; but He preferred laying His hands on each one separately, and addressing a few words of consolation to each. *Singulis manus imponens*.

Application: Let us imitate our Divine Master in this conduct. It is most edifying to see a religious, a superior, always kind-hearted and cheerful, easily accessible to everyone, and forgetting his own sufferings to minister to others. But this is a degree of perfection quite beyond nature. Have we striven to acquire it? And with what success?

Affections and Resolutions.

Point II: Jesus retires into solitude to pray

Consideration: "And rising very early," says Saint Mark, "going out, He went into a desert place, and there He prayed." By this example our Blessed Lord teaches us, first, to escape from the sight of men after having performed any good action, to avoid the danger of vainglory; secondly, to recollect ourselves in retreat and solitude, after our works of charity, to avoid distractions; thirdly, to support work with prayer, choosing for the latter the earlier portion of the day, in order to draw down the blessing of God on our labors.

Application: Let us ask ourselves solemnly before God how far we conform ourselves in this respect to the example of our Divine Master, and thus provide against our many temptations to vainglory and distractions of various kinds.

Affections and Resolutions.

Point III: Jesus passes through Galilee

Consideration: No sooner had the people of Capharnaum discovered our Lord's place of retirement than "the multitudes sought Him, and came unto Him; and they detained Him; … to whom He said, To other cities also I must preach the kingdom of God, for therefore I am sent." "And Jesus went about all Galilee, teaching in their synagogues, and preaching the gospel of the kingdom, and healing all manner of sickness, and every infirmity among the people. And His fame went throughout all Syria,… and much people followed Him."

Application: We know not whether to admire most the untiring zeal of Jesus, or the eagerness and docility of the people. We must

not only admire, but imitate. In our works of zeal and charity let us be generous, and know no limit within the bounds of possibility. This is our mission; a high and noble, though arduous one. To succeed in it we must be closely united with Him who has sent us. "For," He says, "without Me you can do nothing."
Colloquy with our Lord.

Meditation XXV: The Detachment which Jesus requires from us

1st prelude: Behold Jesus Christ saying: "Whosoever doth not carry his cross and come after Me, cannot be My disciple."
2nd prelude: Ask for perfect detachment.

Point I: Detachment from the riches and honors of the world

Consideration: "A certain Scribe came and said to Jesus, "Master, I will follow Thee whithersoever Thou shalt go. And Jesus saith to him, The foxes have holes, and the birds of the air nests; but the Son of Man hath not where to lay His head." Most interpreters are of opinion that this reply of Jesus, who sees the thoughts of the heart, implies that the Scribe expected to obtain riches and honor by following one already so high in public reputation. Being, however, undeceived by our Lord's profession of strict poverty, he drew back, having no desire to share it.

Application: We are happier than the Scribe, inasmuch as we have received grace to renounce the world for a life of evangelical poverty and humility. But let us be on our guard; we have heard of religious who, being priests, have left the cloister for the sake of ecclesiastical dignities and honors; and of others who, being lay brothers, have quitted it in the hope of being elevated to the priesthood. History furnishes us with many such instances.
Affections and Resolutions.

Point II: Detachment from parents

Consideration: After the withdrawal of the Scribe, Jesus, looing with an eye of love upon one of His hearers, deigned to call him to the apostleship of which the Scribe was unworthy. He said to him, "Follow Me." He was ready to give up everything for the sake of his vocation: he only asked leave to delay following it for a short time. "Lord," he said, "suffer me first to go and bury my father." He wished to take care of his father during his old age, and not leave him till after his death. Our Lord refused his request, saying to him, "Let the dead bury their dead; but go thou and preach the kingdom of God."

Application: If your affection for your parents, or their opposition to your vocation, has not been a hindrance to you, be eternally grateful for this blessing; but be careful to avoid another snare into which many have fallen. Seeing their father or mother in distress and difficulty, they have been tempted to leave their order for the sake of consoling or supporting them, often only to become a burden to their parents, and a prey to bitter regret, remorse or despair.

Affections and Resolutions.

Point III: Detachment from relations and friends

Consideration: Saint Luke mentions another who also desired to delay obeying our Lord's call. "I will follow Thee, Lord," he said; "but let me first take my leave of them that are at my house. Jesu said to him: No man putting his hand to the plough, and looking back, is fit for the kingdom of God."

Application: In these words our Blessed Lord teaches us that those who, like ourselves, have left all to follow Him in the way of perfection, must not occupy themselves with the temporal interests of their relations or friends, but think only of advancing daily towards the end of their holy vocation.

Colloquy with Our Blessed Lord.

Meditation XXVI: Jesus and His Disciples overtaken by a Tempest

1st prelude: Behold the boat of Peter, tossed by the waves and in danger of sinking, while Jesus sleeps in it.

2nd prelude: Ask for unshaken confidence in Divine Providence.

Point I: Sleep of Jesus: terror of the disciples

Consideration: "And He saith to them that day, when evening was come, Let us pass over to the other side. And when He entered the boat, His disciples followed Him. And when they were sailing, He slept. And behold a great tempest arose in the sea, so that the boat was covered with waves; but He was asleep upon a pillow."

Application: Two things especially strike us in this event, recorded so minutely by three Evangelists: 1st, that the tempest threatened to shipwreck them, in spite of our Lord's presence; and 2ndly, that He slept calmly during the storm. From these facts we may draw two practical conclusions: 1st, that it is a great mistake to suppose ourselves abandoned by God because we are exposed to violent temptations or frightful persecutions; and 2ndly, that it is equally wrong to give way to fear, as though our Divine Lord were not with us, and watching over us to shield us from harm.

Affections and Resolutions.

Point II: The disciples appeal to Jesus

Consideration: The disciples, finding all their efforts to save the boat useless, "came to Him and awaked Him, saying: Lord, save us; we perish." "Master, doth it not concern Thee that we perish?" "And Jesus saith to them: Why are ye fearful, O ye of little faith?" He did not find fault with them for awaking Him from sleep, but for having doubted His care for them and thought Him powerless to help them while He was asleep.

Application: Let us fly to Jesus in every danger, as the disciples did; but let us not, like them, delay till we are at the last extremity; and especially let us beware of any want of faith or confidence, and doubt of His Divine Providence, because, for our greater good, he may seem to sleep, and to be deaf to our prayers, while He is only delaying to grant them.

Affections and Resolutions.

Point III: The disciples reproved; the tempest calmed

Consideration: Jesus, who had only permitted this storm to arise that He might show His divine power, and strengthen the confidence of His disciples, quelled it with a single word: "Rising up, He rebuked the wind, and said to the sea, Peace; be still. And the wind ceased, and there was made a great calm… And they feared exceedingly; and they said to one another, Who is this that both wind and sea obey Him?"

Application: Both the majesty and the almighty power of our Divine Lord are here manifested in the most striking manner. Which of us does not feel proud and happy to belong to Him – to be allowed to fight under His standard? Let us thank Him for having called us to this great privilege, and offer ourselves anew to Him unreservedly and courageously.

Colloquy with our Lord.

Meditation XXVII: Jesus and His Disciples overtaken by a Tempest (continued)

1st prelude: Behold the disciples in the boat, struggling with the tempest.
2nd prelude: Ask for wisdom to read the designs of God for His Church and for souls.

Point I: The barque of Peter a type of the Church

Consideration: The barque of Peter is a type of the Church. As it was exposed during the whole night to the fury of the winds and waves, so the Church is exposed to the fury of the devil and his satellites, and will be so exposed till the end of the world, during the *night* – that is to say, till the dim light of faith is exchanged for the full glory of the Beatific Vision. And as the boat seemed often in danger of being wrecked, so has the Church often appeared to be on the point of destruction. Towards the end of the eighteenth century her fall was predicted with the greatest confidence by unbelievers. But Jesus was asleep in the ship. It could not perish. At the moment appointed by His divine wisdom, He awoke, and rebuked the tempest, and there was a great calm. And so it will ever be; always attacked and threatened with shipwreck, but always victorious, the Church will pursue her way across the stormy sea of this world, till she enters the haven of her eternal rest.

Application: We must therefore not be disturbed or scandalized when we see our holy Mother the Church persecuted, oppressed, and despoiled by impious men. Saint Augustine says that God wills that it should be so: 1st, that all the world may see that the Church is a divine and not a human institution; 2ndly, that she may be like her Divine Founder, who "ought… to suffer these things, and so to enter into His glory"; 3rdly, lest calm and prosperity should cause relaxation and corruption; 4thly, that being constantly harassed by her enemies and purified in the fire of tribulation, she may always retain her primitive strength and beauty.
Affections and Resolutions.

Point II: The barque of Peter a type of the faithful soul

Consideration: The ship containing the disciples, and Jesus with them, is also, according to Saint Augustine, a type of the faithful soul. It too is always exposed in this world to storms and tempests, and is never at rest. There is neither time nor place, says Saint Thomas a Kempis, that can shelter you from the storms of temptation. When you think yourselves most secure, when Jesus is nearest to you – as after a Retreat or a fervent Communion – you will be suddenly overwhelmed with scruples, disgust, impure imaginations, and all manner of horrible temptations, which, like a raging sea, will threaten to engulf you. But Jesus, who has permitted the storm for your spiritual good, has also defined its limits. At His command, peace and serenity will return when you least expect it, making you feel with redoubled confidence that the Lord is sweet. The lives of the saints are full of these alternations of storm and calm, consolation and desolation.

Application: Practical conclusions: 1st, never reckon on perfect peace and serenity; 2ndly, be always prepared for a violent storm; 3rdly, in times of desolation, and even of the fiercest temptation, never for a moment lose confidence in Jesus Christ; 4thly, beware of changing any of your resolutions at such times; 5thly, wake Jesus – appeal to Him for help, as the disciples did; 6thly, when the storm is over, examine your behavior during it – how far you have acted upon these rules and the advice of your spiritual directors, and make resolutions accordingly.
Colloquy with Jesus Christ.

Meditation XXVIII: Jesus among the Gerasenes – Healing of the Demoniacs

1st prelude: Behold the demoniac at the feet of Jesus, and our Lord saying: "Go out of this man, thou unclean spirit."
2nd prelude: Ask for the grace of perfect charity.

Point I: Misery of a Gerasene possessed by an unclean spirit

Consideration: Having shown that all nature and the elements were subject to Him, Jesus wished to show that evil spirits were equally so. An opportunity soon occurred. Scarcely had He landed in the country of the Gerasenes when two men possessed with devils cast themselves at His feet. Of one of these Saint Mark says expressly that he had "an unclean spirit." His case was a most miserable one. It would seem that in describing it the Evangelist desires to set before us the misery of anyone, religious or secular, who is a slave to the vice or devil of impurity. "No man could bind him, not even with chains; for, having often been bound with fetters and chains, he had burst the chains." He was "exceeding fierce, so that none could pass by that way." When asked his name, he replied, "My name is Legion, for we are many." "And he wore no clothes, and was always days and night in the mountains, crying and cutting himself with stones."

Application: Here we see the wretched condition of the impure man. Mad with passion, nothing can control or restrain him; he cares neither for his reputation, his health, or his religious vows; he is insensible to the horror of sacrilege, and to the fear of judgment and hell; he seizes upon others, either for his accomplices or victims, so that it is dangerous to go near him, or hold intercourse with him. Legion is the true name for the vice of impurity, for it always draws an infinity of other vices after it. Finally, the nakedness, the savage wanderings, and the wild howlings of the demoniac bear witness to the description given by the Holy Ghost: "Man, when he was in honor, did not understand; he hath been compared to senseless beasts, and made like to them." He is a misery to himself, without either the will or the power to cure his misery.

Affections and Resolutions.

Point II: Joy of the Gerasene after his deliverance

Consideration: Jesus, being touched with compassion at so fearful a sight, said, in a loud voice: "Go out of the man, thou unclean spirit." The devils, thus driven out, asked leave to enter a herd of swine which was feeding near. "And Jesus immediately gave them leave… And the heard with great violence was carried headlong into the sea, being about two thousand, and were stifled in the sea." At the same moment the demoniac was suddenly changed, and became as quiet and gentle as a lamb. The people, who had assembled in crowds at the report of this miracle, were astonished to see "him that was troubled with the devil, sitting, clothed, and well in his wits." He meanwhile, not knowing how sufficiently to express his gratitude, "began to beseech" Jesus "that he might be with Him" as His disciple. But Jesus, satisfied with his good intention, "admitted him not, but saith to him: Go into thy house to thy friends, and tell them how great things the Lord hath done for thee… And he went his way, and began to publish in Decapolis how great things Jesus had done for him. And all men wondered."

Application: Let us frequently meditate on all that Jesus has done for us, and show our gratitude by proclaiming His mercies. Affections and Resolutions.

Point III: Blindness of the Gerasenes

Consideration: The Gerasenes, when they saw what was done, and that they had lost their herd of swine, came to Jesus, and "besought Him to depart from them, for they were taken with great fear." Jesus punished their selfishness and stupidity by granting their prayer. "He, going up into the ship, returned back again."

Application: Let us thank God that we are saved by the vow of poverty from temptations of avarice, and detach ourselves still more perfectly from all that is not God and does not lead to Him. Colloquy with our Blessed Lord.

Meditations XXIX: Return of Jesus to Capharnaum – Cure of a Paralytic

1st prelude: Behold the paralytic carried in his bed to Jesus.
2nd prelude: Ask for such faith and confidence as he had.

Point I: Active faith of the paralytic

Consideration: The joy of the inhabitants of Capharnaum at the return of Jesus compensated for the insult offered Him by the Gerasenes. As soon as it became known that He was in the house, the crowd increased around it till it was almost impossible for anyone to get near, and especially for those who were carrying the sick. We read that four men brought one who was sick of the palsy: "And when they could not find by what way they might bring him in, because of the multitude, they went up upon the roof, and let him down through the tiles with his bed into the midst before Jesus."

Application: This ingenious expedient strikes us with admiration at its singularity, boldness, and promptitude. It was most pleasing to our Divine Lord, and was immediately crowned with success. But what caused the great eagerness of the paralytic? His desire to be cured of his disease. "Ah! If we only felt he diseases of the soul as we do those of the body," says the holy author of the *Imitation*, "we should find plenty of bold and persevering expedients to remedy them." And our efforts would be

successful. We should get rid of that spiritual paralysis which hinders us, perhaps for years, from making any progress, and which threatens to become incurable.
Affections and Resolutions.

Point II: Spiritual cure of the paralytic

Consideration: "Jesus, seeing their faith, said to the man sick of the palsy: Be of good heart, son; thy sins are forgiven thee." He had sought only the cure of his bodily disease, and he receives also that of his soul. Jesus excites in his heart a true contrition for his sins; and grants him a full remission of them. And this He does before curing the palsy, to show that his chief end in coming into the world was to save souls, and to remind us that we should be infinitely more solicitous about the sanctification of our soul than the health of our body.

Application: In spite of this lesson, most men live as though they had no soul to save. Is it so with us in any degree? Are our *first thoughts*, on waking in the morning, for our soul or our body? How often in the day do we think of the one in comparison with the other? And do we not much more often speak of our bodily ailments, and the remedies that might relieve them, than of our spiritual miseries and the means of curing them? Do we not also sometimes indulge our body to the detriment of our soul?
Affections and Resolutions.

Point III: Bodily cure of the paralytic

Consideration: The spiritual cure of the paralytic was immediately followed by the healing of his bodily disease. By this cure, so evidently miraculous, Jesus desired to prove to the Scribes and Pharisees that He was really God, and really had power to forgive sins, which the Scribes disputed. For this reason He said: "That you may know that the Son of Man hath power on earth to forgive sins (then saith He to the man sick of the palsy), Arise, take up thy bed, and go into thy house. And he arose and went into his house."

Application: "And the multitude seeing it," says the Evangelist, "feared and glorified God, that gave such power to men." Let us unite with them in praising God, who has committed to His priests the power to absolve our sins.
Colloquy with our Lord.

Meditation XXX: The Vocation of Saint Matthew

1st prelude: Behold Jesus saying to Matthew: "Follow Me."
2nd prelude: Ask for grace to correspond faithfully with your holy vocation.

Point I: The wonderful vocation of Saint Matthew

Consideration: When Jesus was leaving Capharnaum, "passing by, He saw Levi, the son of Alpheus, sitting at the receipt of custom, and He saith to him: Follow Me." This was, in every respect, a remarkable vocation. First, the person called was a publican or tax-gatherer; this was an employment odious in the sight of the people, on account of the facilities it afforded for those who followed it to enrich themselves by fraudulent practices. Next, he was called while actually employed in counting his unjust gains. Finally, it was, as we might say, a *passing call*, consisting only of one look, one word – "Follow Me."

Application: We shall, perhaps, find some similar circumstances in our own vocation. For instance, why should God have called us in preference to so many others more worthy of so great a privilege? It may be, too, that His call came when we were actually indulging some evil passion. If so, how grateful ought we to be for so signal a mercy!

Affections and Resolutions.

Point II: Prompt obedience of Saint Matthew

Consideration: The readiness and fidelity of Saint Matthew in corresponding with his vocation are no less admirable than his vocation itself. As soon as he heard the words of Jesus, "he rose up and followed Him." Julian the Apostate declared that this was either a false account, or an act of madness. And, indeed, it cannot be explained, except by the miraculous operations of divine grace, which *in one moment* can change a sensual and avaricious man into a spiritual and mortified one. The world has often witnessed such miracles of grace; but it does not understand them, because it has no faith, and faith is necessary for their comprehension. Blessed are they who not only understand, but have experienced them.

Application: Are not we ourselves among these latter? Have we not received many graces independently or even in spite of ourselves? How often, when we were resisting grace, and thinking

only of the world and ourselves, its powerful attraction compelled us to see the nothingness of all that is not God, that is not eternal, and urged us to follow the evangelical counsel, "Follow Me," in the way of voluntary poverty!
Affections and Resolutions.

Point III: The striking gratitude of Saint Matthew

Consideration: Illuminated by grace, Saint Matthew now understood the real value of his vocation, and was anxious to prove his gratitude for it before both God and man. He invited Jesus to a magnificent banquet "in his own house," which our Lord was pleased to accept. Saint Mark tells us that "many publicans and sinners sat down together with Jesus and His disciples." The new convert had invited them in the hope of bringing them also to the feet of Jesus, perhaps even of persuading some of them to embrace, like himself, a life of voluntary poverty. He thus gave a double proof of his gratitude.

Application: Let us imitate the gratitude of Saint Matthew by seizing every opportunity of bringing men to God, and, if possible, of inspiring them with a love and desire for the religious life.
Colloquy with our Lord.

Meditation XXXI: On the Excellence of our Vocation

1st prelude: Let us imagine Jesus Christ saying to us: "You have not chosen Me, but I have chosen you."
2nd prelude: Let us ask grace to correspond perfectly with our vocation.

Point I: The origin of our vocation

Consideration: Its origin is undoubtedly divine. The thought of leaving parents, fortunes, pleasures, liberty, in a word, all that is dearest to the heart of man, to embrace a life of mortification and self-sacrifice could never come from ourselves; it is too contrary to all our natural inclinations. Neither could it comes from the world, which looks upon it as folly and madness; and still less from the devil, who hates it. It can therefore only have come from God. As our Blessed Lord Himself says: "You have not chosen Me, but I have chosen you." And again: "All men take not this word [of perfect continency], but they to whom it is given."

Application: Our vocation, then, comes straight from heaven, from God. If we keep this in mind, all our thoughts and actions will also be heavenly, great, noble, and generous. We shall never degenerate into a certain type of religious, who are so narrow-minded that they are always occupied with thoughts of their own reputation, their own health, their own comfort; always taken up with themselves, and thus rendered incapable of any heroic sacrifice.

Affections and Resolutions.

Point II: The end of our vocation

Consideration: For what end have we entered religion? To escape the dangers and seductions of the world; to avoid offending God; to secure our eternal salvation; to attain a high degree of glory and happiness in heaven, by a close conformity with Jesus Christ through the practice of the evangelical counsels; to suffer our purgatory in this world; in a word, to become saints.

Application: Do we often recall these thoughts, as Saint Bernard did, who said to himself every morning on first waking, "Bernard, Bernard, wherefore didst thou come hither?" By doing so we shall, like him, constantly renew our fervor, and speedily arrive at a high degree of perfection.

Affections and Resolutions.

Point III: The rewards promised to our vocation

Consideration: We may still better appreciate the excellence of our vocation, if we consider the promises which our Divine Lord has attached to it. They surpass in magnificence those which are attached to any other good words; from whence we may conclude that in His sight the religious life surpasses every other in excellence. "There is no man," He says, "that hath left house, or parents, or brethren, or wife, or children, for the kingdom of God's sake, who shall not receive much more in this present time, and in the world to come life everlasting."

Application: Behold here a powerful motive to love and esteem our holy vocation, and an incitement to perseverance which should make us eager to surmount all difficulties; for should we not be ashamed to let those who labor only for a temporal reward surpass us in courage and generosity?

Colloquy with our Lady.

Meditation XXXII: The Raising of Jarius' Daughter

1st prelude: Behold Jesus taking the daughter of Jarius by the hand, and raising her to life.
2nd prelude: Ask for great faith and confidence in prayer.

Point I: Jarius' prayer

Consideration: The day following the vocation of Saint Matthew, "a certain ruler," named Jarius, "came up and adored" Jesus, "saying, My daughter is at the point of death; come, lay Thy hand upon her, that she may be safe, and live." This prayer was so pleasing to Jesus that it obtained several miracles. Let us therefore consider its qualities for our own profit. 1 st, it was *humble* and *reverent*, as both the words and manner of the suppliant show; 2 nd, it was *earnest* and *pleading*, coming from the heart of an afflicted father; 3 rd, it was *simple* and *childlike*; Jarius makes his request without any superfluous words, and trusts it to the mercy of Jesus, to the tenderness of His Heart.

Application: Do our prayers always breathe this humility, this exterior and interior reverence so due to the majesty of God? And their earnest, coming from hearts which feel their misery, and know that they cannot remedy themselves? Are they not often wanting in confidence and simplicity? Perhaps in answering these questions we shall find out why our prayers seem so often to be unavailing.
Affections and Resolutions.

Point II: Jairus' faith

Consideration: As Jarius returned to his house, followed by Jesus, who had *immediately* granted his prayer, "some came from the ruler of the synagogue's house, saying, Thy daughter is dead; why dost thou trouble the Master any further?" But Jarius, instead of giving way to despair, turned to Jesus, and said, "Lord, my daughter is even now dead; but come, lay Thy hand upon her, and she shall live." And Jesus answered, "Fear not; believe only, and she shall be safe." In this touching history we hardly know whether most to admire the faith of Jarius, or the promptitude of our Blessed Lord in recompensing it.

Application: Let us not only admire but imitate the faith and confidence of this Jewish ruler, or rather the *constancy* of his faith; for this is where we so often fail: the least difficulty discourages us, whereas the confidence of Jarius only increased where ours would be shaken. Let us also imitate the promptitude of Jesus in granting the request of Jarius, and render *at once* any service that is demanded of us. "He who gives quickly, gives doubly," says the proverb. We lose all the merit of our good actions if we perform them grudgingly.

Affections and Resolutions.

Point III: The miracle granted to the faith and prayer of Jarius

Consideration: "When Jesus was come to the house of the ruler,... He went in, and taking her by the hand, cried out, saying, Maid, arise. And her spirit returned, and she rose immediately. And He bid them give her to eat. And her parents were astonished."

Application: "And the fame thereof went abroad into all that country," adds Saint Matthew. And no wonder; for what miracle could cause a greater sensation than the raising of a dead person to life? And yet, says Saint Bernard, the resurrection, or the solid and lasting conversion, of an inveterate sinner is a still greater miracle. If God has worked this miracle for us, what gratitude do we not owe Him? But there is one miracle still greater, adds the same holy doctor – namely, the resurrection or real conversion of a degenerate religious form a state of tepidity to one of fervor. If such a miracle is needed in our case, let us not despair of obtaining it: all things are possible to the prayer of faith.

Colloquy with our good Lord.

Meditation XXXIII: Three Miraculous Cures

1st prelude: Behold Jesus surrounded by the sick and suffering.
2nd prelude: Ask for grace to increase in the knowledge and love of Jesus.

Point I: Miraculous cure of the woman with an issue of blood

Consideration: On the same day that He raised Jairus' daughter to life, Jesus performed three other miraculous cures. The first was that of a woman diseased with an issue of blood for twelve years, who, "when she had heard of Jesus, came in the crowd behind Him, and touched His garments; for she said, If I shall touch but His garment; I shall be whole. And forthwith... she felt in her body that she was healed of the evil." We must allow that the means employed by this poor woman were not such as human wisdom would have suggested. Perhaps she hesitated herself before using them; she did it, however, in obedience to a divine inspiration.

Application: It is a great mistake to give up the execution of any pious intention because certain objections occur to our mind. "It will often happen," says the author of the *Spiritual Exercises*, "that after framing some pious intention, you will be tempted to abandon it; it will seem to you strange, compromising, dictated by vanity, too difficult, or even impossible. These are snares of the devil; despise them, and go steadily forward." It is not by following the dictates of human wisdom that we shall obtain miracles."

Affections and Resolutions.

Point II: Miraculous cure of two blind men

Consideration: "And as Jesus passed from thence, there followed Him two blind men, crying out and saying, Have mercy on us, O Son of David. And when He was come to the house, the blind men came to Him. And Jesus saith to them, Do you believe that I can do this unto you? They say to Him: Yea, Lord. Then He touched their eyes, saying: According to your faith be it done unto you. And their eyes were opened."

Application: After the example of these blind men, let us seize every opportunity of obtaining graces and favor from God. Let us persevere in our supplications, though they may at first seem unavailing; and above all, let us make frequent acts of faith in the power and goodness of our Divine Savior. He would seem to make this faith the condition and the measure of His gifts. "According to your faith be it done unto you."

Affections and Resolutions.

Point III: Miraculous cure of a dumb demoniac

Consideration: No sooner had Jesus cured the two blind men than "they brought Him a dumb man possessed with a devil." He was suffering from a double affliction, and the more to be pitied as he was unable to solicit aid for himself. Happily, other charitable persons did this for him. The Heart of Jesus was touched with compassion; without even waiting to be asked, He commanded the devil to release his prey; and immediately "the dumb man spoke."

Application: How pitiable is the state of those whom the devil

makes dumb in the confessional – dumb in prayer, dumb when duty or charity requires them to speak! Let us take compassion on their misery, and try to help them. Especially let us imitate the readiness of Jesus to come forward to the assistance of those who are hindered by a natural reserve, or any other motive, from asking our help.
Colloquy with our Blessed Lord.

SECOND YEAR OF THE MINISTRY OF JESUS CHRIST

July 1: Cure of the Paralytic at the Pool of Jerusalem

1st prelude: Imagine you hear Jesus saying to the man paralysed for thirty-eight years: "Take up thy bed, and walk."
2nd prelude: Beg for unshaken confidence in the goodness of Christ.

Point I: Our Lord take notice of the paralytic

Consideration: "After these things," says Saint John (*i.e.*, after the cure of the issue of blood, the two blind men, and the deaf and dumb), there was a festival day of the Jews, and Jesus went up from Capharnaum to Jerusalem. He went to celebrate the Pasch publicly for the second time. From this Pasch began the second year of His ministry. He chose to inaugurate it, if we may so speak, by a wonderful miracle, which will form the subject of our meditation. At one of the gates of Jerusalem there is, says the Evangelist, "a pond, which in Hebrew is named Bethsaida, having five porches. In these lay a great multitude of sick, of blind, of lame, of withered, waiting for the moving of the water. And an angel of the Lord descended at certain times into the pond, and the water was moved. And he that went down first into the pond after the motion of the water was made whole of whatsoever infirmity he lay under. And there was a certain man there that had been eight-and-thirty years under his infirmity."

Application: Jesus Christ, being the sovereign lawgiver, was not bound to observe the Jewish Pasch, but yet He did so. This should teach us how faithfully we ought to observe the laws, the rules, and the established customs of our community. In certain cases we might lawfully claim exemption from them; but let us rather keep them from love of regularity, and to give edification.

And this will be very meritorious before God. Is this you habitual practice? Our Lord teaches us another lesson. When He arrived at Jerusalem He chose to remain among those that were afflicted, and singled out the most wretched of them all. Do you follow your Divine Master in this respect? Whom do you prefer among those committed to your care? Is it the most forsaken? Is it those who stand in need of especial care? Or is it not those rather by whose qualities or natural gifts you are attracted? Examine yourself. Be on your guard against yourself.

Affections and Resolutions.

Point II: Jesus cures the paralytic

Consideration: Jesus, touched with compassion when he saw a man who had lost the use of his limbs for so many years, *saith to him*, "Wilt thou be made whole?" The poor man thought the question was one of reproach, and answered, "Sir, I have no man, when the water is troubled, to put me into the pond. For whilst I am coming, another goeth down before me. Jesus saith to him, Arise, take up thy bed, and walk."

Application: It is a great consolation to learn that it was the extremity of the paralytic's misery which drew the attention of our Lord to him in preference to so many others. Far be, then, from us all thoughts of discouragement or distrust at the sight of our miseries and our spiritual infirmities, however great or deeply-seated they may be. Let us go to Jesus, guided and supported by the hand of our spiritual director, that "*faithful friend*" whom the paralytic stood in need of, and we shall obtain the cure of our spiritual diseases. But after we are cured, let us remember what our Lord said to the paralytic. "Thou art made whole; sin no more, lest some worse thing happen to thee."

Colloquy.

July 2: Feast of our Lady's Visitation

1st prelude: Imagine you see our Blessed Lady entering the house of Zacharias to visit Saint Elizabeth.

2nd prelude: Beg for grace to pay all your visits in the same spirit in which our Lady paid hers.

Point I: Motives of the visit

Consideration: Saint Luke, after having related the history of the Incarnation, in which the account of the miraculous conception of Saint John the Baptist occurs, immediately adds these words: "And Mary, rising up in those days, went into the hill-country in haste, into a city of Juda (Hebron), and saluted Elizabeth. And Mary abode with her about three months." Why did our Blessed Lady undertake these painful journey, which occupied four days? The Fathers tell us it was done – 1 st, in obedience to inspiration; 2 nd, from courtesy, that she might rejoice with Elizabeth, her near relative, in the great miracle wrought in her favor, and which the archangel Gabriel had revealed to her; 3 rd, in charity, that she might be a help to Elizabeth in a time of difficulty, and co-operated in the sanctification of her child.

Application: Religious are sometimes obliged to pay visits and make journeys, and to many they have proved occasions of sin and of final ruin; and this because they were too frequent and were undertaken from vanity, from a weariness of retirement, from a desire of pleasure. Be on your guard against these motives; let your visits be always regulated by *obedience*, by *courtesy*, or by *charity*, and they will be always useful to your neighbor and yourself. Have you acted always on these your principles? Have you not sometimes concealed your real motives when you gave your reasons to your superior? Have you presumed permission to make these visits? Have you always tried to spread, as the Apostle says, the good odor of Christ?

Affections and Resolutions.

Point II: The fruit of this visit

Consideration: Mary brought joy and happiness with her into the house of Zacharias. Elizabeth was filled with the Holy Ghost; the mystery of the Incarnation was revealed to her, and she prophesied; the child whom she carried in her womb was cleansed from original sin, confirmed in grace, endowed with the use of reason, and thus rendered capable of gaining merit. Mary was present at his birth, and she obtained for his father a restoration of his speech, and he began to prophesy. There was a universal joy, shared in by all their neighbors. Elizabeth had foretold it when she cried out, "Whence is this to me, that the Mother of my Lord should come to me?"

Application: Blessed is the house and happy is the soul which the Mother of God deigns to visit. The Son delights to honor His

Mother by pouring an abundance of graces on those who have an especial veneration for her, and who strive to propagate her devotion. It is the will of God that we should obtain everything by Mary. If you desire that she should often visit you, honor her, and draw others to honor her as much as you can. Examine whether on this point you can improve, and let your zeal be redoubled.
Affections and Resolutions.

Point III: The virtue and merit of this visit

Consideration: If it be a truth that our virtues increase in proportion to the acts of virtue that we practice, what great merit Elizabeth must have obtained by the visit of Mary to her! For in her all virtues were shining in their splendor. She possessed faith, obedience, mortification, fervor, modesty, generosity, and zeal, and especially humility and charity. She, the Mother of God, had come to congratulate Elizabeth, as if the latter were superior to her in grace and favor; then she waited on her for three months as a humble servant. She had heard herself called "Blessed among women"; but she instantly attributed all that had been accomplished in her to God only. "He that is mighty hath done great things to me." The whole *Magnificat* breathes forth a perfume of wonderful virtue.

Application: Reflect upon these virtues in detail, and try to reproduce them in yourself; this is the best way to please our Lady. You will thus deserve her visits, and gain great merit.
Colloquy with our Blessed Lady.

July 3: On the great Prerogatives of our Blessed Lady

1st prelude: Imagine that you see our Lady at the moment when, having been congratulated by Elizabeth, she says these words: "He that is might hath done great things to me."
2nd prelude: Beg the grace of understanding the privileges which were given to Mary before, during and after the Incarnation of the Word.

Point I: Privileges given to Mary before the Incarnation

Consideration: Mary was destined for the greatest of dignities, and God, who, says Saint Thomas, always proportions the gifts of His grace to the dignity to which we are called, conferred upon her privileges which no one can ever share. Many of the Fathers point out twelve principal ones, represented by the twelve stars surrounding the marvelous woman spoken of in the Apocalypse. Four of them were given before the Incarnation of the Word: 1. Preservation from original sin in her conception; a privilege which the Church has proclaimed as a dogma of faith under the title of the Immaculate Conception. 2. Plentitude of grace, with which she was invested from her entrance into life. 3. The use of reason given to her at the same time, that she might correspond with grace. 4. Knowledge of the great value of virginity, to which Mary at the age of three years bound herself by vow at her presentation in the Temple.

Application: We should often unite in spirit with the angels, the Church and all the servants of our Lady to congratulate her on the wonderful prerogatives with which it has pleased the Almighty to endow her. This will be sure to please her, and dispose her heart more and more towards us! It will be a means of obtaining special graces, more particularly that of persevering in our vow of chastity, and of a continual increase in perfection before God and men, after her example.

Affections and Resolutions.

Point II: Privileges given to Mary at the Incarnation

Consideration: The first of these privileges, and the one dearest to the heart of Mary, was that, in becoming a month, she still remained a virgin; she had the joys of maternity and the glory of virginity at one and the same time. The second was, that for nine whole months she entirely possessed the Son of God incarnate in her virginal womb. He lived by her and with her. The third, that while for nine months the Body of the Word made flesh grew within her, Mary, in the same proportion, received continual increase of grace. The fourth, that she became the channel of the grace which God intends to bestow on man; and this privilege is acknowledged by the Church when she salutes Mary by the title of "Mother of divine grace, pray for us."

Application: While meditating on the wonderful privileges of our dearest Mother, and especially on the last we have mentioned – that she is the channel of grace which falls from heaven upon earth – ask yourself if your devotion and your habit of having recourse to our Lady is all it should be, or if it is not capable of a great increase, and if this be not the reason why you make so little

progress, and have such little success in your works of zeal.
Affections and Resolutions.

Point III: Privileges given to Mary after the Incarnation

Consideration: First privilege: She was exempted from the curse which fell on sinful Eve – "In sorrow shalt thou bring forth children" – in consequence of her Immaculate Conception. Second privilege: She was made worthy to bear the title, which no other can, of co-operatrix in the redemption of the human race. Third privilege: When her life on earth was ended, she had none of the suffering or the regret that other human beings have; her death was a transport of love. Fourth privilege: She was carried to heaven by angels not only in soul, as the saints are, but in body and soul, clothed with all the gifts of immortality.

Application: You can have a large share in these privileges of our Lady. Be zealous in bringing back lost sheep to the fold of Jesus Christ, and you will really co-operate in the work of redemption. Endeavor to live like a true religious, and you will certainly share the joys of heaven in body and soul with Mary.
Colloquy with our Blessed Lady.

July 4: Hypocrisy and Jealousy of the Pharisees

1st prelude: Imagine you hear Jesus replying to the false accusations of the Pharisees.
2nd prelude: Ask for a humble and compassionate heart.

Point I: The Pharisees accuse the disciples of Jesus

Consideration: Jesus, having fulfilled all the paschal duties, left Jerusalem and returned into Galilee. "And it came to pass," says Saint Luke, "on the second first Sabbath as He went through the corn fields His disciples, pressed by hunger, plucked the ears and did eat, rubbing them in their hands." The law expressly allowed this to be done (Deut. xxiii); but the Pharisees, who prided themselves on their exact observance of the Sabbath day, condemned it as a crime, saying, "Why do ye that which is not lawful on the Sabbath days?"

Application: It is easy to see through the cloak of zeal under which the Pharisees tried to hide their jealousy; and everyone condemns and detests their conduct. But as this hideous passion easily finds access into the hearts even of religious, we should see whether we can discover any marks of it in ourselves. The following are some of them: Narrowly to observe the conduct of those we dislike, to spy out their actions, relate their slightest faults with malice and exaggeration, to judge them harshly, to put an evil interpretation on all their actions, even their intentions. Find out from these signs what you ought to think about yourself.

Affections and Resolutions.

Point II: Jesus defends His disciples

Consideration: The accusation made by the Pharisees was likely to bring discredit on the disciples, and to strengthen the people in an erroneous belief. Our Lord therefore enlightened them, defended His disciples, and put their accusers to silence. "And He said to them, have you never read what David did, and they that were with him?" And then He continued: "The Sabbath was made for man, and not man for the Sabbath; therefore the Son of Man is Lord of the Sabbath also."

Application: We should learn from this that we may keep silence when personally attacked, but not when the glory of God, the rights or doctrines of the Church, or the welfare of our neighbors, are in question. To be silent then, when we can answer the accusation, would be a withholding of the truth, and cowardice, and would in some cases cause us to share in the guilt. "There is," says the Wise Man, "a time to keep silence, and a time to speak." Happy is he who has learnt this wise discernment, and rules his life accordingly. How have you acted? Have you not been generally more prompt and eager in defending your wounded self-love than in supporting and defending the cause of God?

Affections and Resolutions.

Point III: Jesus confounds the Pharisees

Consideration: Our Lord, wishing to let the Pharisees see that He could read the secrets of their hearts, and that He well knew they were actuated by jealousy only, said to them: "If you knew what this meaneth, I will have mercy and not sacrifice, you would never have condemned the innocent."

Application: Let us take care never to deserve a similar reproof; never to speak or act from secret malice hidden under the garb of virtue; never to observe the letter rather than the spirit of God's commandments and our rule; never to be harsh and unmerciful in our judgments of our brethren, blaming and condemning them on

slight grounds or by appearances only. Examine yourself on these points, acknowledge and lament over the faults you may have committed; and that you may not fall into them again, beg earnestly of our Lord to increase in you paternal charity and humility.
Colloquy with our Divine Lord.

July 5: The Choice and Vocation of the twelve Apostles

1st prelude: Imagine you see Jesus Christ at the moment when He proclaims the names of the twelve Apostles.
2nd prelude: Beg for grace to correspond faithfully to the grace of vocation.

Point I: Our Lord's choice of His twelve Apostles

Consideration: The Lord began the second year of his ministry by an act of the greatest importance for the future. He founded the Apostolic College, and thus laid the foundation of His Church, which was to perpetuate His mission among men. "He called unto Him His disciples, and He chose twelve of them, whom He would Himself, whom also He named Apostles: Simon, whom He surnamed Peter, and Andrew his brother; James and John, Philip and Bartholomew, Matthew and Thomas, James the son of Alpheus, and Simon who is called Zelotes, and Jude the brother of James, and Judas Iscariot, who was the traitor."

Application: From out of the numerous disciples who followed Jesus, He chose twelve only – a mystical number, typified seventeen centuries before by the twelve princes or chiefs of the twelve tribes of Israel. Glorious and happy was the lot of those whom the Son of God chose out by a grace of predilection. He chose twelve *whom He would Himself.* Let us rejoice with them and for them; and let us rejoice also because our Lord has chosen us in preference to so many others who were more worthy.
Affections and Resolutions.

Point II: Circumstances of His choice

Consideration: Our Blessed Lord made an extraordinary preparation for this choice. "The evening before," says Saint Luke, "He went out into a mountain, and He passed the whole night in the prayer of God." Had He any need of this retreat, of this night-long prayer, that His choice might be a good one? No, answers

Saint Ambrose; but it was His will to give us an example, and to teach us an important lesson.

Application: Our Lord thus teaches us by His example, 1st, never to undertake any important matter without taking counsel of the Father of Lights, without earnest prayer; 2nd, when we pray, to withdraw as much as possible from the world, from the turmoil of life. How have I followed this divine teaching? In what way can I, or ought I, to amend my conduct?

Affections and Resolutions.

Point III: Particulars of this choice

Consideration: Most singular and inexplicable does it appear to us to find among the chosen twelve the traitor Judas. Was our Lord, then, deceived in him, or did He really call him to the apostolate? Interpreters tell us that our Lord chose Judas because He earnestly desired to have him for an Apostle. Judas ruined himself by his treason; but our Lord still chose him, to teach us that a man who has received the most excellent gifts of God has still the power of using or abusing them as he chooses, and that those who are called to the holiest state may still be lost, and ought therefore to work out their salvation with fear and trembling, as Saint Peter tells us; and it teaches us to distinguish between the body and an individual, between the office and the man.

Application: We ought to derive great profit from these lessons for ourselves and for the instruction of others. To those who fear God, says the Apostle, all things work together for good; the treachery of one should make us tremble and mistrustful of self, the perseverance of the others should give us great confidence in the omnipotent grace of God.

Colloquy.

July 6: Sermon on the Mount: "Blessed are the poor in Spirit"

1st prelude: Imagine you see Jesus seated on the mountain, and giving the wonderful lessons of His Gospel to the world.

2nd prelude: Beg for grace both to receive and understand the Gospel teaching, and to induce others to receive it.

Point I: Circumstances of the sermon

Consideration: Our Lord chose the twelve Apostles that He might *send them to preach*, and thus transmit by them and their successors in the apostolate His divine doctrines to all nations and all generations. He immediately began to teach them what they were to say. When He came down to the foot of the mountain, where the people could see and hear Him, He found "a very great multitude of people from all Judea and Jerusalem, and the sea-coast both of Tyre and Sidon. He had drawn them thither by His Providence, to accomplish His will of having many witnesses to the truth that the doctrine preached by the Apostles and their successors was indeed His Gospel, the pure Word of God, without any intermixture of human teaching. "And when He was set down, His disciples came unto Him." He began to speak, and delivered a long discourse called the Sermon on the Mount, which contains the substance of the law of God, and all evangelical perfection.

Application: Let us show our gratitude to God, who allowed us to be born in the bosom of the Catholic Church, the only guardian of the eternal truth taught by the Son of God. Whoever, then, makes it the rule of his life shall be saved. As religious, we have contracted an obligation of observing it more perfectly than the rest of the faithful. Happy indeed are we to be bound by such an obligation. It will win an immense increase of glory for us in heaven. Have you been faithful to this obligation?

Affections and Resolutions.

Point II: Teaching of Jesus Christ on poverty. First Beatitude.

Consideration: Our Lord commenced His discourse by laying down the principles of true happiness. These had been corrupted by pagan vices and Jewish prejudices, as they now are by a proud and sensual world. And there is a great contrast between the beatitudes which the world proclaims, and those of Jesus Christ. The world says, "Blessed are the rich"; our Lord says, "Blessed are the poor"; not exactly the poor by birth, but poor in spirit, detached in heart and mind from the possessions of the earth for the love of God. Why are they blessed? "Because," says our Lord, "theirs is the kingdom of heaven"; because even in this life, having neither fear nor anxiety, they are in peace, which is a foretaste of heaven.

Application: Among the poor whom Jesus Christ calls blessed we can distinguish three classes: 1 st, the actual poor, perfectly resigned to the will of God; 2 nd, the rich who are really poor in spirit; 3 rd, the voluntary poor, who have stripped themselves forever of all things to follow Jesus Christ in poverty. To this last class we have the happiness to belong; and to it especially belong those wonderful promises of our Lord, as we learn from the words, "There is no man who has left house or lands for My sake and the Gospel's, who shall not receive a hundred times as much now in this time, and in the world to come life everlasting." These words ought to fill our hearts with holy joy and courage.

Affections and Resolutions.

Point III: Teaching of Jesus Christ on riches

Consideration: Our Lord's teaching upon poverty showed plainly enough what we ought to think about riches, and those who cling to them as their dearest possession. But lest we should not fully understand this, he added these terrible words, "Woe to you that are rich, for you have your consolation"; meaning that they are so entirely taken up with material enjoyments that they live in complete forgetfulness of their last end, and at length death comes suddenly upon them, they are destitute of merit, loaded with sins, and they fall into eternal misery.

Application: Look around you, and see what is passing in the world. Do you not see this condemnation of our Lord verified? Let it teach you, then, the unspeakable favor that God has done you by withdrawing you from the world; show Him your gratitude, and redouble your zeal to undeceive those whose desire for temporal enjoyments is drawing them away from the path of salvation.

Colloquy.

July 7: On religious Poverty

1st prelude: Imagine you hear Jesus saying, "Blessed are the poor in spirit."

2nd prelude: Ask for grace to love and esteem holy poverty.

Point I: Excellence of religious poverty

Consideration: The strongest proof we can have of the excellence of religious poverty is that our Lord set a great value on it, and chose it Himself for the companion of His whole life, from the cradle to the grave. He highly exalted it, saying, *Beati pauperes spiritu*. He gave it to us as a counsel, and has promised great rewards to those who practice it. It was highly valued by the first Christians following His example, and then as time went on by all the saints, especially the founders of religious orders, who, together with their numberless followers, bound themselves by vow to live in perpetual poverty, knowing from the teaching of the Church that a vow increases the merit of the practice of poverty.

Application: Let us strive to renew our esteem and love of holy poverty; far from being ashamed of it before men, let us glory in it, and try to make the lovers of this world understand the folly and disappointment of the pursuit of riches; and how noble and wise a thing it is to exchange the fleeting and perishable possessions of earth for the eternal treasures of the world to come.

Affections and Resolutions.

Point II: Essence and spirit of religious poverty

Consideration: The essence of religious poverty, or of the vow of poverty, consists in having nothing of our own, that is, independent of our superior; therefore it follows that a religious cannot, without sinning more or less grievously, receive, give, exchange, or lend anything without permission from his superior. He, on the other hand, being but the administrator of the property of the community, cannot dispose of it either to inferiors or strangers, but according to the spirit of the rule and the greater good of the community.

Application: Have we always thus understood and practiced holy poverty? Have we not sometimes infringed the rules under vain pretexts, at least in small matters? Let us be on our guard, for these little transgressions will easily lead to great ones, under some delusion or other. But religious who are alive to their true interests will not be contented with the essence of poverty; they will look to its perfection, the spirit of poverty. The religious who is penetrated with it looks on poverty as his inheritance; far from taking offence at a refusal, or of murmuring when he has to suffer privation, he thinks himself too well treated, because he has the poverty of Jesus Christ always before his eyes. He takes great care of everything given for his use, and he receives with humble gratitude, like the beggar who lives upon alms, the food and clothing which is bestowed on him. He feels himself to be unworthy of them, because he has so often abused the gifts of his Creator.

Affections and Resolutions.

Point III: Advantages of religious poverty

Consideration: 1st, It removes the greatest obstacle to eternal salvation, attachment to the possessions of earth: "A rich man shall hardly enter into the kingdom of heaven," says Jesus Christ. 2 nd, It is a pledge of eternal possessions and a superabundance of joy: "Thou shalt have treasure in heaven," says our Lord again. 3 rd, It places us in the path of perfection, according to the words of our Lord: "If thou wilt be perfect, go sell what thou hast and give to the poor, and come follow Me." The entire detachment from earthly possessions is a powerful help in uniting us to God by charity, in which consists all perfection. *Plenitudo legis caritas* – The fullness of the law is love. And as regards this present life only, what blessings does religious poverty bring upon us? We feel them better than we can express them. We shall feel them better still at the hour of death.

Application: We should have these thoughts always in our minds, and the difficulties that we meet in our vocation and in keeping our vows will appear slight indeed to us.

Colloquy with Jesus Christ, the great model of voluntary poverty.

July 8: Sermon on the Mount: Second, third, fourth and seventh Beatitudes

1st prelude: Imagine you hear Jesus saying, "Blessed are the meek," "Blessed are ye that weep," "Blessed are they that hunger and thirst after justice."

2nd prelude: Beg the grace of being among the number of these blessed ones.

Point I: The second and seventh Beatitudes

Consideration: "Blessed are the meek" – not only those who are so naturally, but also and especially those who, though naturally fiery and passionate, have obtained a mastery over impatience, anger, the desire of revenge, and all other feelings incompatible with peace of heart – "for they shall possess the land." According to Saint Augustine, because they shall hold earthly possessions in peace, being loved and esteemed by all. According the Saint Bernard, because they shall possess the land of their own hearts, be masters of their own actions (for the angry man is not his own master). According to Saint Jerome and the majority of doctors, because they shall possess by right of heritage the land of the living – heaven, according to the words of David: "I believe to see the good things of the Lord in the land of the living."

Application: Great blessings, then, even in this life are promised to meekness. It is worth the trouble it will give us to acquire it in perfection; this consists in being able to control the first burst of impatience, to live peacefully with bad-tempered people, to preserve liberty of spirit and an unbroken peace in the midst of the vicissitudes of life. There is a superior degree of this perfection on which our Lord has bestowed a separate blessing (the seventh), that of being able to preserve or restore peace and union among men, among our brethren. "Blessed are the peacemakers," continued our Lord; for they shall so resemble God their Father that they shall be worthy in an especial manner to be called "the children of God." How do I stand as regards the perfection of meekness, of peace with myself, with others?
Affections and Resolutions.

Point II: Third Beatitude

Consideration: "Blessed are ye that weep;" namely, those who are full of compunction, who delight in weeping and mourning before God over the miseries of their exile, the wounds of their soul, and especially at the thought of the many injuries done to God, of the numerous souls who are falling every instant into hell, and of the number of unhappy beings who are rushing blindly thither. They are blessed, says Jesus, because they "shall be comforted" in this life by the unction of grace, and by the unspeakable sweetness which is found in the tears of compunction. "I have found greater happiness," said Saint Augustine, "in weeping at the foot of my crucifix than I found in frequenting theatres." Because they shall be comforted without end or measure in heaven.

Application: Before your entrance into religion, perhaps you hardly knew even the name of compunction; perhaps you were even among the number of those to whom our Lord addressed those terrible words: "Woe to you that now laugh; for you shall mourn and weep." How everything around you invites you to compunction, and reminds you of the motives for it! Why is it, then, that you feel it so rarely, and that the effects of it are so little visible in your conduct? Is it not because you are too dissipated, too unmortified.
Affections and Resolutions.

Point III: Fourth Beatitude

Consideration: "Blessed are they that hunger and thirst after justice." Jesus Christ, then, declares that fervent religious are blessed who are trying to become better, more pure, more humble, more mortified, more united to God, never thinking they have sufficiently obeyed the precept, "Be you therefore perfect, as also your Heavenly Father is perfect." But does He not at the same time condemn the conduct of the lukewarm religious, who thinks he has done enough by keeping out of grievous faults, and by remaining at the point which he has attained?

Application: Are you among the former of these classes? If so, rejoice greatly, for you shall share their happiness. Like them, you will taste, even in this life, the peace and joy of divine consolations; and after this life you will be satisfied with the abundance of heavenly delights. Fear, then, above all things, to degenerate from your first fervor, and to fall little by little into lukewarmness.

Colloquy.

July 9: Sermon on the Mount: Fifth, sixth and eighth Beatitudes

1st prelude: Imagine you hear Jesus Christ saying, "Blessed are the merciful, blessed are the clean of heart, blessed are they who suffer persecution."

2nd prelude: Beg the grace of being among the number of these privileged souls.

Point I: Fifth Beatitude

Consideration: "Blessed are the merciful," who, compassionating the sufferings of others, try to help them; not simply from human and natural motives, but from a principle of faith. Works of mercy are enjoined on us by our Lord's precept when He said, "Be ye therefore merciful, as your Father also is merciful"; and He has deigned to represent the needy in His own person. At the day of judgment He will say: "Come, ye blessed of My Father; I was hungry, and you gave Me to eat. Amen I say to you, as long as you did it to one of these My least brethren, you did it to Me."

Application: If you belong to an order especially devoted to corporal works of mercy, rejoice in it, and fulfill you duties fervently, with a pure intention before God. If you belong to an educational order, you have no less cause for joy; you can accomplish greater works still – the spiritual works of mercy. To convert sinners and bring them back to God, to instruct the ignorant, to root out sinful prejudices, to inculcate the truths and maxims of the faith which men are so determined to misrepresent, etc.; how have you performed these duties? With patience? With generosity? Do you obtain help in them from God? Our Lady? The angels and saints? By the sanctity of your life, your prayers, and your mortifications?

Affections and Resolutions.

Point II: Sixth Beatitude

Consideration: "Blessed are the clean of heart; for they shall see God." There are many degrees of purity of heart: the first is freedom from mortal sin; the second, freedom from deliberate venial sin and all affection for sin; the third, freedom from the least ill-regulated affection; the fourth, freedom from those imperceptible stains which hinder our entrance into heaven; the fifth consists of that perfect purity of intention by which a man sees, feels and loves nothing but God. Great is the reward promised to this last degree – they shall see God; in this world by the great lights given to them, and in the other by the Beatific Vision, which will be in proportion to these different degrees.

Application: To which of these degrees are you trying to attain? With what fervor and perseverance are you using the means for attaining it? Are you making a good use of confession? The particular examen, silence, solitude, recollection, vigilance over your heart and your senses? Every effort will be richly rewarded; to each degree of purity with be given a further degree of eternal happiness.

Affections and Resolutions.

Point III: Eighth Beatitude

Consideration: "Blessed are they that suffer persecution for justice's sake." This applies to those who faithfully observe the law of God; and if they are religious, all the rules and observances of their institute; who are faithful and intrepid in using every means their zeal can suggest to them for defending the cause of God, for procuring His glory, saving souls, and preserving the rights of the Church. Their reward will be in proportion to their

labors and dangers; "theirs is the kingdom of heaven," says our Lord. Do not complain of those who wish you ill, and malign you because you are religious; rather pity and pray for them. They do you a service by wishing you evil. If you say that you care little for outward persecution, that you do not suffer personally from it, but that it is very painful to you to meet with coldness and a kind of opposition on the part of your brethren toward you, ask yourself if this be not caused by your want of regularity, your haughtiness or eccentricity of character, your obstinacy of disposition, or hastiness of temper? If this be the case, you are not suffering for justice's sake, but for the faults that you can and ought to correct. Do this, and all your cause for complaint will vanish. You will be beloved of God and men.
Colloquy with our Divine Master.

July 10: Sermon on the Mount: Qualities of an apostolic Man

1st prelude: Imagine you see Jesus Christ on the mountain surrounded by His Apostles.
2nd prelude: Beg for the qualities which distinguish apostolic men.

Point I: The salt of the earth

Consideration: All religious bodies, with a few exceptions, are devoted to works of charity and zeal; consequently one can say that all religious, though they may not be priests, ought to be apostles. To them also Jesus Christ was speaking when He said to His Apostles in figurative language that they should become the salt of the earth, or they would be good for nothing. Let us listen to His very words: "You are all the salt of the earth; but if the salt lose its savor, it is good for nothing any more."

Application: If you desire to learn whether you are this "salt of the earth" in the sense in which our Lord spoke, you should consider the proper qualities of salt; it preserves food from corruption, and makes what was insipid pleasant to the taste. This is what you should do for the souls committed to your care, whether they be children in schools or youth in colleges, or the sick whom you have to nurse in their homes or in the hospitals. You should be your diligence and zeal labor to preserve them from the corruption of sin, and induce them to render themselves pleasing to God by the practice of virtue. It is true that this is the work of grace; but grace seldom acts without our cooperation. What have you done, what are you habitually doing, to merit the assistance of grace?

Affections and Resolutions.

Point II: The light of the world

Consideration: Our Lord, after telling His Apostles that they were to be the salt of the earth, went on to say they were to be the light of the world; by which He meant that they were to drive out the darkness of idolatry from the whole world; they were to cause the one true God to be known, adored and faithfully served unto the ends of the earth; they were to convert and sanctify the human race. We know how faithfully they fulfilled their sublime mission. Saint Paul, speaking to the Christians at Miletus, gives us an idea of their zeal when he says, "You know from the first day that I came into Asia in what manner I have been with you and taught you, publicly and from house to house. I ceased not with tears to admonish every one of you night and day."

Application: Here is a picture of a zealous religious; in all places, at all times, and in all circumstances, he is seeking and finding occasions of saying a word which will enlighten the mind and kindle the fire of divine love in the heart; in all places and at all times he is preaching, without appearing to do so. The light and the unction which he has received in prayer naturally flow from his heart and from his lips. People always leave him feeling that they have been enlightened and drawn nearer to God. Do you recognize yourself in this portrait? Are your brethren and others edified by intercourse with you, and especially by your conversation?

Affections and Resolutions.

Point III: The living image of Christian perfection

Consideration: "A city seated on a mountain cannot be hid. So let your light shine before men, that they may see your good works and glorify your Father who is in heaven." We learn from these words what is the third quality by which we should be distinguished. We should constantly give edification before men: we should draw them towards God by the silent language of our conduct, a language which is more persuasive than the most eloquent words.

Application: Is your conduct such as this in the house and out of it? Can your superior say of you to your brethren, Copy him?

Can you say to those whom you have to do with what the Apostle said to the Corinthians, "Be ye followers of me, as I also am of Christ"? Happy indeed would it be for us if we all verified the powerful declaration of Saint Cyprian in answer to pagan objections, *"Nos non pulchra loquimur sed pulchra vivimus* – "We think far less about speaking well than acting well."
Colloquy.

July 11: Feast of Saint Norbert's Triumph, Founder of the Order of the Premonstratensians

(The saints who have founded religious orders should naturally have a particular interest for us. Saint Norbert was born 1080; died June 6, 1134; canonized 1582. His order, according to Pere Helyot, possessed at the close of the eighteenth century 50 provinces, 130 houses of men, and 400 of women.)

1st prelude: Imagine you see the saint in glory.
2nd prelude: Beg of him to take us under his powerful protection.

Point I: Conversion of Saint Norbert

Consideration: Norbert was born at Xanten, in the duchy of Cleves, of parents allied to the royal family. After having passed through college with extraordinary success, he was ordained a subdeacon, obtained a rich canonry, and soon after was named chaplain to the emperor, Henry IV; but his conduct was very unworthy of his holy calling. Until he was thirty he passed his life at court in dissipation and amusement. God in His mercy struck him with a severe blow, to draw him out of his evil ways. One day, as he was riding to Freten in Westphalia, for some worldly entertainment, a clap of thunder threw him on the ground half-dead. When he came to himself, he cried out, like another Saul, "Lord, what wilt Thou have me to do?" An interior voice replied: "Fly from evil, and do good; seek peace in retreat and penance." Immediately Norbert was changed into another man, left the court, gave all his goods to the poor, cast aside his rich clothing, put on a poor cassock, and went to the monastery of Saint Sigebert near Cologne, and there did exemplary penance.

Application: After the example of Saint Norbert, let us be docile to grace, whether it speaks to us by gentle inspirations or by extraordinary lights. If we have imitated him in his faults, let us imitate him also in his penance, and persevere in it, like him, until death. Have you not given up the practice of penance, at least in some degree?

Affections and Resolutions.

Point II: Evangelical life of Saint Norbert

Consideration: After passing two years in retirement, Norbert was inflamed with zeal for the glory of God and the salvation of souls. Scarcely was he ordained priest than he began to preach penance, and wrought numberless conversions. The Bishop of Laon, struck by his sanctity, was determined to keep him in his diocese. Norbert chose for his dwelling-place a deserted valley called Premontre. It was decreed by God that it should be the cradle of the future order which was to bring forth so many saints, and immortalize the name of Norbert. He was soon surrounded by forty disciples, the first thirteen of whom came from Brabant. He gave them rules full of wisdom, founded on the rule of Saint Augustine. His institute was approved in a solemn bull by Pope Honorious II (February 1125). The following year Norbert was forced to accept the archbishopric of Magdeburg. He held this see eight years without diminishing either his austerities or his care for the order he had founded.

Application: If it has not been given to you, like Saint Norbert, to found an order or become a great missionary, try at least to sanctify yourself in the order to which God has called you, and to help on the sanctification of your brethren by your good example. Both of these are obligations: do you seriously reflect on them?

Affections and Resolutions.

Point III: Triumph of Saint Norbert

Consideration: Among the many miracles which the saint wrought, there is one which has made him illustrious; and this was the victory he won over heresy and the sectaries of Tanchelin. This fanatic had revived the horrors and excesses of the ancient Gnostics over a vast extent of the country of which Antwerp was the center. At the entreaty of the bishops and princes Norbert went to Antwerp, and acted in such a manner that before his departure Catholic worship was reestablished, and the use of the Sacraments vigorously resumed. The grateful clergy gave the saint the church of Saint Michael, which became one of the most celebrated abbeys of the order, and the Holy See allowed the children of Saint

Norbert to celebrate every year, on the 11th of July, a feast called "Feast of Saint Norbert's Triumph." Pope Gregory XVI, wishing to revive the memory of this great event, extended the permission to celebrate this feast to all the clergy of the Catholic diocese of Malines, in which Antwerp is situated.
Colloquy.

July 12: Sermon on the Mount: Exact Observance of the Law

1st prelude: Behold Jesus seated on the mountain.
2nd prelude: Beg for a great esteem and ardent love of religious discipline.

Point I: Fidelity to every point of discipline.

Consideration: "Do not think that I am come to destroy the law. I say unto you, until heaven and earth pass, one jot or one tittle shall not pass of the law till all be fulfilled." These words teach us that an exact observance of the rule and religious discipline is pleasing to our Lord. In fact, what distinguishes us from seculars is, that we give up for the love of God our liberty even in the smallest details of our life; we bear the yoke of the rule, and of community life; and hence it is that the Church gives us the name of *regulars*. We falsify, then, both our name and the engagements we have contracted before God and before the Church, if we make little account of certain points of religious discipline or of rule.

Application: Examine yourself upon your disposition in respect to the observances of community life. To form a correct judgment, it is well to go into details. Are you exact in rising promptly and with devotedness? In going to the different exercises at the first sound of the bell – to the visit to the Blessed Sacrament, mediation, prayers said in common? Are you faithful in observing silence, modesty, and religious gravity?
Affections and Resolutions.

Point II: Dangers of the least infraction of religious discipline

Consideration: Meditate earnestly on these words of our Lord, which follow those just quoted: "He therefore that shall break one of these least commandments, and shall so teach men, shall be called the least in the kingdom of heaven; for I tell you that unless you justice abound more than that of the Scribes and Pharisees, you shall not enter into the kingdom of heaven." Then consider what the author of the *Imitation* says: "A religious man that lives not in discipline [that is, who excuses himself from what is irksome to him] lies open to dreadful ruin. He who does not shun small defects, by little and little falls into greater." Then you will understand the presumption and peril of an *habitual* neglect of certain points of rule – peril for yourself, and peril for others from your bad example.

Application: If you feel yourself guilty, try to discover the source of the evil, that you m ay remedy it. Generally it is dissipation which destroys the interior life: then our spiritual duties are performed negligently; there is a void in the heart, which we try to fill by seeking for intercourse with seculars, under some idle excuse of zeal or propriety; then it naturally follows that we excuse the great evils that prevail in the world, to excuse our own infidelity to the rule, looking on them as trifles.

Affections and Resolutions.

Point III: Advantages of a strict observance of discipline

Consideration: Meditate further on the following words of our Divine Master: "He that shall do and teach them [i.e., the smallest precepts] shall be called great in the kingdom of heaven"; *great*, because he will have shown great generosity in the service of God; great, because by his example, still more than by his words, he will have done much to secure the perseverance and spiritual progress of his neighbor, especially his brethren in religion.

Application: This thought is a most encouraging one, and we shall be always faithful to the smallest observances is we can but always keep them in mind. Let us beg of God that it may be thus, and that the words of the author of the *Imitation* may be applicable to our community: ""Oh, how sweet and comfortable it is to see brethren fervent and devout, regular and well-disciplined!"

Colloquy with Saint Joseph.

July 13: On Fervor in serving God

1st prelude: Imagine you hear Saint Paul saying, "In spirit fervent, serving the Lord."

2nd prelude: Beg for grace to set a just value on fervor.

Point I: Nature of fervor

Consideration: That exactitude in observing all the points of religious discipline which we have meditated on supposes fervor of spirit; for in reality fervor is nothing more than promptitude in devoting our whole self with all our heart to the service of God. If this be the habitual disposition of the soul, it is worthy to be called a virtue (for all virtue is habitual); though, strictly speaking, fervor is only a *quality* of the virtue of religion, according to Saint Thomas; according to others, of the virtue of charity. Therefore it is plain that a fervent religious will be faithful to the smallest observances of his rule, in which he sees the expression of the will of God.

Application: Weigh well these words of the *Imitation*: "Our fervor and progress ought to be every day greater; but now it is esteemed a great matter if a man can retain some part of his first fervor." It is very humiliating to find an author so versed in the knowledge of men making such an assertion. At first we are tempted to dispute it; but do we not find it fulfilled in ourselves? Compare the first year of your religious profession with the last: in which of the two were you most exact and fervent? What remains of your first burst of fervor? If it had been kept up, to what a high degree of virtue you would have already attained!

Affections and Resolutions.

Point II: Happiness of a fervent religious

Consideration: There is nothing more true than that the fervent religious is happy. .With fervor we have everything, and without it nothing. With fervor there is purity and peace of conscience, there is perfect happiness; labor is no longer a burden, and the yoke of religious life becomes light and sweet, the greatest sacrifices become delightful, and we heap up merits in a brief space of time. We become a consolation to our superiors and edification to our brethren; we draw down benedictions from heaven on our community, and on our good works and undertakings. Lastly, with fervor we make constant progress in virtue, obtain final perseverance, and a weight of glory in heaven.

Application: If you have not always been very fervent, you have at least been so at times; and did you not then understand the reality of all these blessings of fervor? Were you not happy then? Did you not feel the truth of the Psalmist's words, *that it is sweet to serve the Lord*? Rekindle, then, your fervor, if it has grown cold; see by what means you once obtained it, and be assured that you

can preserve it by the same means.
Affections and Resolutions.

Point III: Misery of the lukewarm religious

Consideration: "If thou beginnest to grow lukewarm, thou wilt begin to be uneasy. A negligent and lukewarm religious man has trouble upon trouble, and on every side suffers anguish, because he has no comfort within, and is hindered from seeking any without." Thus does the author of the *Imitation* describe a lukewarm religious. He is indeed miserable, for he is the slave of his passions; he is daily staining his soul with sin; he seeks peace, and cannot find it; he carries the yoke of religion without its consolations; he labors hard, and reaps little for eternity. Finally, he runs the risk of losing his vocation, and with it the friendship of God and final perseverance.

Application: Let these thoughts inspire you with a great fear, or rather a lively horror of lukewarmness, and especially because our vicious nature leans towards it. If you have fallen into it, come out of it, with a holy indignation against yourself – even today, when God speaks to your heart – and vigorously begin again to practice the means of preserving fervor. Make some very definite resolutions for this end, and place them at the feet of Jesus, and beg of Him in your fervent Colloquy that He will bless them and render them fruitful.
Colloquy.

July 14: Sermon on the Mount: Persecutions

1st prelude: Imagine you hear Jesus saying these words: "Love your enemies; do good to them that hate you; and pray for them that persecute you."
2nd prelude: Beg the grace of a generous conformity to the doctrine, the precepts, and the example of Jesus Christ in respect to persecutions.

Point I: Doctrine of Jesus Christ on persecutions

Consideration: Both the doctrine and life of Jesus Christ were a condemnation of the sins and hypocrisy of the Pharisees. It was enough to draw down upon Him their hatred, calumnies, and deadly persecution. We have made an especial profession of being the disciples and apostles of Jesus; is it, then, any wonder that we are an object of hatred to the wicked? The Lord has foretold us what we have to expect from them. "The servant is not greater than his master. If they have persecuted Me, they will also persecute you: they will deliver you up in councils, and they will scourge you in their synagogues. The brother also shall deliver up the brother to death, and the father the son; and you shall be hated by all men for *My name's sake*."

Application: We have all witnessed the blind fury of irreligious hatred, and we may perhaps be the victims of it. But, far from being cast down or made sorrowful by such thoughts, our hearts should be set on fire and filled with joy by recalling those other words of our Lord to our minds: "Blessed are ye when they shall revile you and persecute you, and speak all that is evil against you untruly, for My sake. Be glad and rejoice, for your reward is very great in heaven. For so they persecuted the prophets that were before you."

And besides, is not the glory of being thus made like to the Son of God on earth before we join Him in heaven a sufficient cause for holy joy and pride?

Affections and Resolutions.

Point II: Precepts of Jesus Christ in regard to persecutions

Consideration: Let us now meditate on the precepts that our Lord commands us to follow in respect to those who persecute us, or rather the Church of Jesus Christ in our persons. "Love your enemies; do good to them that hate you; and pray for them that persecute and calumniate you; that you may be the children of your Father who is in heaven, who maketh His sun to rise upon the good and the bad." What wonderful gentleness is contained in these words! Are they impossible to obey? No, says Saint Jerome; for we see them fulfilled in Saint Stephen, the first martyr, and those who followed him. All of them, when dying, prayed for their murderers. We find them obeyed again by the first Christians, of whom the Apostle says boldly, "We are reviled, and we bless: we are blasphemed, and we entreat."

Application: The Church, which is the interpreter of Jesus Christ, teaches us in what way we should pray for our enemies, by the words which she has placed in the Litany of the Saints: "That Thou wouldst vouchsafe to humble the enemies of holy Church: we beseech Thee hear us." We thus ask that by temporal misfortunes they may be rendered powerless to do harm, and that, like Saul thrown from his horse and deprived of his sight, they may feel the hand of God, recognize their errors, and humbly implore pardon, that they may be converted, and make a good death. It is by humiliation only that these poor creatures will be brought back to God; and if we could obtain such a result by our prayers, we should have done an immense good.

Affections and Resolutions.

Point III: Conduct of Jesus Christ in persecutions

Consideration: The Lord was not contented, says Saint Augustine, with giving us His precepts, and promising great rewards to those who kept them, He chose to give us also His example. When He was dying, He prayed also for His enemies: "Father, forgive them, for they know not what they do."

Application: If we meditate on the charity and the heroic gentleness of a God who had been calumniated, hated, put to death by His creatures, those whom He had loaded with blessings, all the difficulties and the seeming impossibilities of pardoning offences, of returning good for evil, will disappear.

Colloquy with Jesus dying on the cross.

July 15: Sermon on the Mount: We should fly from Vainglory

1st prelude: Imagine you hear Jesus Christ saying, "Take heed you do not your justice before men, to be seen by them."

2nd prelude: Beg for grace to understand the difference of acting to please men and God – *God only*.

Point I: Acting to please men

Consideration: The Lord, having warned us against the violence of persecutions, now puts us on our guard against the dangers and snares of vainglory. "Take heed that you do not your justice before men, to be seen by them, otherwise you shall not have a reward of your Father who is in heaven." Then it is plain from the words of the infallible Truth that it is in the intention that the merit of our actions consists. If we perform them to please God, they are meritorious; if they are done from vainglory, they have no merit, or are worthy of punishment.

Application: Pride, or an inordinate desire for vainglory, is, as it were, identified with us since original sin. From this springs continual and secret seeking of self, or of the esteem of men in everything we do in public; and this is simply vainglory. It is a subtle temptation, and may be compared to a worm gnawing away at fruit. The greatest saints, notwithstanding the constant vigilance with which they watched over their souls, were fearful of being surprised into it, remembering our Lord's warning, "Take heed; be on your guard." What fear, then, ought you to have of losing the merit of your good works, you who watch so little over yourselves, your thoughts, and your actions! Take this matter into serious consideration; it is worth the trouble.

Affections and Resolutions.

Point II: Acting so as to please God

Consideration: "If thy eye be single, thy whole body shall be lightsome." These words are easily understood: the eye of our body, of our material acts, is, according to Saint Jerome, the understanding which never acts without an intention. If this eye be simple and sinless, it will always enable us to see God, our last end; and our acts will tend simply and directly to Him; we shall do them with the intention of pleasing Him, as the only Author of all goodness and beauty. "To the only God be honor and glory."

Application: Great, indeed, is the Christian and the religious who has God in view in all his actions. He is constantly raising himself to the heights of heaven; he identifies himself, so to speak, with the Divinity, having but one will with it, and happy is he; for God, who sees the secrets of all hearts, will reward even the smallest action, however indifferent in its nature. It is our Lord Himself who says, "Thy Father, who seeth in secret, will repay thee." Are we trying to attain this happiness? We cannot gain it without great purity of conscience and a continual vigilance over self. How do we stand?

Affections and Resolutions.

Point III: Acting so as to please God only

Consideration: If it be a great and happy thing to act habitually for God, how much more great and happy is it to be doing what is seen only by God, and to reach such a point as to lose sight entirely of self, and to be safe from any temptation to vainglory; and, without regard to the promised reward, to be entirely occupied with the thought of God's glory! This is the ideal of absolute perfection; we ought to aspire after it, although we cannot fully attain it.

Application: Do not be cast down because of this inferiority. It will all end in heaven; and while waiting for that, let us do our best often to renew a pure intention; and if while fulfilling your duties you are praised, and the devil of pride tempts you to vainglories, say with Saint Bernard, "I did not begin for thee, and I will not stop for thee" – *Non propter te coepi, nec propter to desinam.* Colloquy.

July 16: Sermon on the Mount: The Lord's Prayer, or Paternoster

1st prelude: Imagine you see Jesus surrounded by His Apostles and a great multitude of people.
2nd prelude: Ask to understand the Lord's Prayer rightly.

Point I: Introduction of the prayer

Consideration: Jesus, after having condemned the hypocrisy of the Pharisees for pretending to make long payers in public, deigned to give us that wonderful prayer, called the Lord's Prayer, or the *Paternoster*. "When ye pray, ye shall not be as the hypocrites, and speak not much as the heathens; thus therefore shall you pray: Our Father, who art in heaven, hallowed by Thy name. Thy kingdom come. Thy will be done on earth, as it is in heaven. Give us this day our supersubstantial bread. And forgive us our debts, as we also forgive our debtors. And lead us not into temptation. But deliver us from evil. Amen.

Application: We are all convinced that the Paternoster is the most excellent of all prayers; most pleasing to God and profitable to ourselves. Yet do we always recite it with the reverence and devotion this conviction should produce? That we may do so, let us meditate on each word. "Our Father, who art in heaven." Our Lord teaches us in this that we should recollect ourselves before we pray, and think to whom we are going to speak, and raise our thoughts to God in heaven. Then, in teaching us to call God our *Father*, He shows that we should pray with filial confidence; and to cement a close union between us all, and remind us to pray for one another, we are to say *our* Father, and not *my* Father. Affections and Resolutions.

Point II: First petition of the Paternoster

Consideration: "Hallowed be Thy name." By the name of God we mean all His attributes, and we ask that they may be known, served and glorified by all men (*Cat. De Mal.*, sec. 27). The first petition of the Paternoster reminds us of the end of our creation, and our first duty – that of sanctifying or glorifying God in ourselves, and as much as we can in others. But as we are incapable of it by our own strength, we earnestly as for grace for ourselves and for all men; saying these words, "Hallowed be Thy name." And thus, by seeking before all other things the glory of our Heavenly Father, we are bringing about our own salvation.

Application: What sort of efforts do we make, and with what success, that our Heavenly Father may be sanctified and glorified, first in ourselves, by purity of conscience, according to Saint Paul's words, "Sanctify the Lord in your hearts, having a good conscience"; then by our brethren, by our regularity, our modesty, our conversations, our zeal, in such a way as to force them, in a manner, to glorify God, the only Author of all that is good and edifying in us, "that they may see your good works, and glorify your Father, who is in heaven"?

Affections and Resolutions.

Point III: Second petition

Consideration: "Thy kingdom come." We are not asking by these words that God may reign over creation, for that He has done from the beginning, but we ask that He may reign over the hearts of men, so that they may all submit of their own free will to His holy laws. We beg also that our Heavenly Father will hasten the day when, all reunited together round His throne, we shall reign eternally with Him in heaven.

Application: We ought to unite action with prayer, and try before all things to live as worthy children of our Heavenly Father, that He may reign over our minds and hearts; that all our thoughts, words and actions may be ruled according to His holy will; and we should endeavor to let God reign over others by all the direct or indirect means in our power. And we have so many. Let us see in what way we can improve upon the past.

Colloquy with our Father who is in heaven.

July 17: Sermon on the Mount: The Lord's Prayer continued

1st prelude: Imagine you see Jesus surrounded by His Apostles and a great multitude of people.
2nd prelude: Ask to understand the Lord's Prayer rightly.

Point I: Third petition of the Paternoster

Consideration: "Thy will be done on earth, as it is in heaven." Our Lord means us to ask for what is more perfect and more glorious to His Heavenly Father than the simple fulfillment of His will or of His commandments – i.e., that His holy will may be done in us as perfectly as it is by the angels and saints in heaven; that at least we should feel an ardent desire of approaching this perfection; and that we should incessantly beg for the grace of which we stand in need.

Application: By our religious profession we are bound, more than the generality of the faithful, to tend towards perfection, and it is much easier for us than they to approach more nearly to it; for, first the good pleasure of God as to the details of life is clearly manifested to us by our rule, and in case of doubt by our superiors, the interpreters of the will of God; secondly, the assurance that we are doing what is most agreeable to God, the good example of our brethren, and the grace of our state make the execution of it easier, sweeter, and doubly meritorious. Happy and glorious is our lot! It ought to convince us that it bears a close resemblance with that of the blessed in Paradise.

Affections and Resolutions.

Point II: Fourth petition

Consideration: Our Lord, after having taught us how we ought first to seek the glory of our Heavenly Father, teaches us what we should ask for ourselves: "Give us this day our daily bread." "Our bread," all that is necessary to sustain our corporal life, and also the food for our spiritual life: "daily," to remind us that, whether rich or poor, we stand in continual need of help from our Heavenly Father: "this day," to teach us that we should renew our prayer daily, lean upon God's providence, and not disquiet ourselves about the future.

Application: Recall to your mind, one by one, all the years of your life, especially those you have passed in religion, and see with what liberality, or rather prodigality, your Father who is in heaven has provided for all your wants. What gratitude have you shown for this? If a superfluity has been given to you, have you not abused it, or only made it the means of satisfying your irregular appetites?

Affections and Resolutions.

Point III: Fifth petition

Consideration: "Forgive us our debts, as we also forgive our debtors." We now humbly beg our Father in heaven to forgive us our sins, and the punishment due to them. Our Lord promises that His Father will grant our request, but on one condition that on our side we will pardon those who have offended us. "If you will forgive men their offences," He said, "your Heavenly Father will forgive you also your offences; but if you will not forgive men, neither will your Father forgive you your offences"; and therefore He added these words to the fifth petition, "as we also forgive our debtors."

Application: Every day say the words, "Forgive us our trespasses"; but, alas, they bear little fruit, because they are said with very little or no compunction. Neither recollected nor interior, we do not see the faults which we commit daily, and we do not weigh them with the "weights of the sanctuary," as the saints did, who confessed every day with tears and groans. Let us weep as they did at our Father's feet, and He will remit them and forget them if we will stifle that feeling of anger which rises even involuntarily in our hearts against those who have offended us. Do you do this?

Colloquy with our Father who is in heaven.

July 18: Sermon on the Mount: The Lord's Prayer continued

1st prelude: Imagine you see Jesus surrounded by His Apostles and a great multitude of people.

2nd prelude: Ask to understand the Lord's Prayer rightly.

Point I: Sixth petition

Consideration: And do not allow us to yield to temptation: such is the sense or interpretation of the words, "And lead us not into temptation"; it is evident that the word "lead" does not mean "draw" or "impel." God could not draw or impel us into the snares laid to tempt us to sin. The impulse to sin, or temptation, as it is called, comes from the devil, the world, and our corrupt nature. We bear about the germ of it within us; how can we, then, be ever free from temptation? Consequently, when we say "Lead us not into temptation," we are not asking to be exempted from temptation, but begging and entreating our Father to make allowance for our weakness, to turn away from us hurtful temptations, to show us the snares of the devil, to remind us in time of need of the eternal truths, finally, to give us superabundant graces, not only that we may not yield to temptation, but that they may be turned to our spiritual advancement; as it is written, "God is faithful, who will not suffer you to be tempted above that which you are able, abut will make also with temptation issue, that you may be able to bear it."

Application: This is what we ask of God; but what does He ask from us, so that our prayers may infallibly be granted? He asks that we distrust ourselves, that we fly from the common causes of temptation, the occasions of sin; that we do not delay to pray in temptation; and if it is in an obstinate one, that we make it known to our spiritual father, resolved to follow his advice faithfully, that we may avoid all delusion.

Affections and Resolutions.

Point II: Seventh petition

Consideration: "But deliver us from evil." By this petition, as by the preceding ones, we ask for many things in a few words; to be preserved from all evil or temporal misfortune, sickness, war, famine, reverses of fortune, persecutions, calumnies, defamation, etc.; we ask to be preserved from falling into mortal sin – an evil infinitely greater than all imaginable temporal misfortunes, an evil in God's sight, the greatest evil that can befall man; we ask to be preserved or raised out of the habit of mortal sin; but above all things, to be preserved from dying in mortal sin, that evil without hope and without remedy – from eternal damnation.

Application: We should ask to be preserved from some of these evils *conditionally* only, so far as is good for our greatest interest – eternal salvation. Some temporal evils, borne with patience and resignation, purify and sanctify us; they are a supernatural blessing. But how often it happens that we make them an occasion of impatience or discouragement, or murmuring against Providence! In saying "deliver us from evil," we ask that such a

misfortune may never happen to us, and that we may not lose any of the hidden treasures of adversity and suffering. What a wonderful prayer the Paternoster is! It is indeed a universal prayer, containing all that is best to ask for the glory of God and our own happiness. Such thoughts as these ought to make us say it with an ever-fresh satisfaction and devotion.
Affections and Resolutions.

Point III: Conclusion of the Paternoster

Consideration: The seven petitions of the Paternoster are followed by the word "Amen" – so be it – a brief but expressive desire by which we virtually repeat all and each petition.

Application: As the word Amen contains the whole substance of the Lord's Prayer, let us learn the habit of saying it with attention and *feeling*, adding to it sometimes these words: "Yes, my soul, let it be thus, let it be thus."
Colloquy.

July 19: Sermon on the Mount: Laying up Treasures

1st prelude: Behold Jesus sitting in the midst of His Apostles.
2nd prelude: Beg for grace faithfully to fulfill the three necessary conditions of laying up great spiritual treasures in a short time – the *state of grace, a pure intention, sanctification of crosses.*

Point I: The state of grace

Consideration: "Lay not up to yourselves treasures on earth, where thieves break through and steal," and which the great robber Death steals away in an instant, leaving nothing behind except regret, too often despair. Let us leave the blinded worldling to find out the solution of the grand problem, "How to realize a great fortune in a short time." But we, following our Lord's counsel, "Lay up to yourselves treasures in heaven, where thieves do not break through and steal," will try to solve one infinitely more interesting – how we can in a short time lay up imperishable treasures of glory and happiness in heaven. The solution is not difficult, and consists of three things – "a state of grace, a pure intention, sanctification of crosses."

Application: If, then, during the brief time of life, we wish to lay up much treasure in heaven (and who does not wish it?), we must be always in a state of grace, for faith teaches us that all good works without charity – *i.e.*, done by a man in mortal sin – gain no merit for heaven: while every good action of the *just*, with the help of grace, will receive an eternal reward. And what a great number of good actions are done in a day, a week, a month! If the religious state possessed no other advantage but that of preserving us in sanctifying grace, how grateful we ought to be to God for having called us to it!

Affections and Resolutions.

Point II: A pure intention

Consideration: Amongst the numerous actions which fill up one day, there are many which in their nature are neither good nor evil before God, but simply indifferent; such as eating, drinking, sleeping, studying, manual labor, receiving or making visits, taking recreation, etc.; but we can render them meritorious by a pure intention. Saint Paul assures us of this when he says, writing to the Corinthians, "Whether ye eat or drink, or whatsoever else you do, do all to the glory of God"; which is equivalent to saying, "Do what is pleasing to God and meritorious to yourself."

Application: It would be folly indeed not to turn this second means of increasing our spiritual riches to profit, especially as it is so easy. What is easier than to offer to God in our morning prayers *all* our actions, protesting that we wish to perform them as well as possible, with the single motive of pleasing Him, and doing His most holy will? What is easier, again, than to renew this intention often in the course of the day? Our actions will be more meritorious, and we shall have less reason to feast lest vainglory should take somewhat from the purity of our first intention, or entirely corrupt it. With what care and what vigilance do you strive after a pure intention? Do you form one fervently and with great intensity of will in the morning? Do you renew it during the day?

Affections and Resolutions.

Point III: Sanctification of crosses

Consideration: The great means of laying up treasures in heaven in a short time is, say the Doctors of the Church, to labour without ceasing for the glory of God and the good of souls; but especially to suffer much, and to bear it with patience and entire resignation to the will of God in all the crosses which it pleases Him to send us.

Application: Let us dig into this rich mine of supernatural

merit: we have not far to look. Misery, suffering and crosses are the heritage of humanity, and no one is exempt from them. But what good does that do us? Let us rather sanctify them, make them meritorious, and of value for eternity, by accepting them as from the hand of God, and bearing them for love of the sufferings of Jesus Christ. Have we done this?
Colloquy.

July 20: Sermon on the Mount: Various Precepts

1st prelude: Behold Jesus preaching to the crowd, who listen attentively to Him.
2nd prelude: Beg for grace to follow His teaching in all things.

Point I: Not to judge others

Consideration: "Judge not, and you shall not be judged; condemn not, and you shall not be condemned; for with what judgment you judge, you shall be judged: and why seest thou the mote that is in thy brother's eye, and seest not the beam that is in thy own eye?" Powerful are the words which our Lord uses to induce us to abstain from judging our neighbours. These judgements are almost always presumptuous, and often very sinful; because we can only judge from appearances, which are always deceitful; because we often go so far as to judge and condemn their *intentions*, which God alone can penetrate, and alone has the right to judge; finally, because these judgments are dictated almost always by jealously or wounded self-love, which blinds us to such a degree that, as our Lord says in figurative language, we do not remark in ourselves faults and failings a thousand times worse than those which we see in others.

Application: In practice, when we are tempted to despise, to judge, or condemn our brethren, let us think of those divine words on which we have meditated, or of those other words which also fell from our Savior's lips: "As long as you did it to one of these My least brethren, you did it to Me." Let us think that what seems blameable or even sinful to us may be perhaps a meritorious act of virtue in the eyes of God, who alone can justly understand our actions and intentions; or rather let us say to ourselves, "Why occupy myself with others? It is not for their acts, but for my own, that I shall have to answer to the Judge of all men. If I had always acted in this way, what a loss of time, what troubles, and what sins I should have avoided!"

Affections and Resolutions.

Point II: The narrow path

Consideration: "Enter ye in at the narrow gate, for wide is the gate and broad is the way that leadeth to destruction, and many there are that go in thereat. How narrow is the gate and strait the way that leadeth to life, and few there be that find it." We naturally ask, "What is the connection between these terrific words of our Lord and the doctrines He was preaching?" but it is soon explained. The Lord knew that we should try in course of time to misinterpret the sense of these doctrines, and to make them give way to the false maxims of the world, the habits and customs of the multitude, and He therefore warned us against these false interpretations.

Application: By embracing the yoke of religion we happily have entered the narrow path that leads to life. But, alas, even there also we find means of enlarging the way, so that two paths may be seen; one is that of the fervent, who are faithful to the maxims and holy practices of the novitiate; and the other, that of the lukewarm, the degenerate religious, who are guided more by the maxims of the world than the teaching of Jesus Christ. In which of these two classes are you to be found?

Affections and Resolutions.

Point III: Not to listen to false prophets

Consideration: "Beware of false prophets, who come to you in the clothing of sheep, but inwardly they are ravening wolves. By their fruits you shall know them." This second warning of our Lord has the same purpose as the first – to make us vigilant; not only against heretics and unbelievers in disguise, but also against the examples and the snares of those of our brethren who may unfortunately have strayed from the right path.

Application: As tares are found among the wheat even on well-cultivated soil, so even is it possible to meet dissipated religious in the holiest communities; and they are the more dangerous if they have talent and seniority. *"By their fruits ye shall know them"*; by their want of discipline, their manner, their spirit of unkindness, of murmuring, criticizing, etc. Pity them, and pray for their conversion; but fly from familiarity with them, and draw closer to

those who are distinguished by their fervor and regularity. Have you understood this and acted upon it?
Colloquy.

July 21: The Leper's Prayer and his Cure

1st prelude: Imagine you see the leper before our Lord, and saying to Him: "Lord, if Thou wilt, Thou canst make me clean."
2nd prelude: Beg for the same feelings which the leper had when he made this prayer.

Point I: Prayer of the leper

Consideration: It pleased our Divine Lord to confirm His wonderful and austere teaching by miracles. The first was the case of the leper: as soon as the poor man saw our Lord afar off he was filled with hope; and fearless of a rebuff, as everyone else was, he came to Him, says the Evangelist, "beseeching Him, and kneeling down said to Him, Lord, if Thou wilt, Thou canst make me clean."

Application: Let us try to profit by our reflection on the qualities of this leper's prayer: first, it was made with profound respect and deep humility; he fell down on his knees before Jesus and adored Him as the Ambassador and Son of God; then he had an ardent faith in the omnipotence of Jesus; he firmly believed that our Lord could cure the leprosy *if He so willed*; he had an entire confidence in the goodness of Jesus, whose praises he had heard, and he had a perfect resignation: "Lord, if Thou wilt," if it is pleasing to Thee, Thou canst cure me. If we made all our prayers with the same feelings, they would be always efficacious.
Affections and Resolutions.

Point II: Cure of the leper

Consideration: In this second point let us bend our whole attention to the Person of our divine model and Saviour, Jesus Christ. How did He receive the leper? How did He answer his prayer? Though He was pressed upon by the crowd, He received him with great sweetness, without showing any impatience or disgust at the sight or smell of the leprosy. He listened gently to his prayer, and wrought a miracle. "Jesus, having compassion on him," says Saint Mark, "stretched forth His hand, and touching him, saith to him, I will; be thou made clean. And when He had spoken, immediately the leprosy departed from him."

Application: This wonderful miracle greatly increased the faith of the multitude in the teaching of Jesus Christ; and it ought to be no less useful to us, especially when we compare our conduct with that of our Lord. Examine yourself; ask yourself, "When someone comes to beg a service from me at a busy moment, especially if his appearance and manner are disagreeable, how do I receive him and listen to him? Is it impatiently, or crossly, or even harshly; putting him off to another time? If it be thus, I am far from resembling my divine model, Jesus, whom I have resolved to imitate as closely as possible." See in what respect your conduct is in contrast with our Lord's, and try to correct it.

Affections and Resolutions.

Point III: Gratitude of the leper

Consideration: We can easily imagine what was the joy and gratitude of the leper so suddenly cured. But our Lord did not suffer him to express it before the witnesses of the miracle: "See thou tell no man; but go, show thyself to the high priest, and offer for thy cleansing the gift that Moses commanded for a testimony to them." But the leper was so overcome with joy that he forgot our Lord's injunction, and *began to publish* and blaze abroad the word.

Application: See how our Lord avoided rather than sought the praise and applause of men, so that God only might receive the glory. Do we not do the exact contrary? Let us learn also, like the leper, to show our gratitude to Jesus Christ; and to spread abroad as much as we can the knowledge of the love of Jesus Christ. Let us examine ourselves.

Colloquy with Jesus, the Divine Physician of our souls.

July 22: Mary Magdalen at the Feet of Jesus in the House of Simon the Pharisee

1st prelude: Imagine you see Magdalene in the midst of the guests washing the feet of Jesus with her tears.

2nd prelude: Beg that you be animated with the same feelings as she had at that moment.

Point I: Entrance of Magdalene into the banquet-hall

Consideration: "And one of the Pharisees desired Him to eat with him. And He went into the house of the Pharisee, and sat down to meat; and behold, a woman (according to the most general opinion, this woman was Mary Magdalen, the sister of Lazarus) that was in the city, a sinner, when she knew that He sat at meat in the Pharisee's house, brought an alabaster box of ointment." She not only entered the house, but went into the banquet-hall, and cast herself at the feet of Jesus. How much it must have cost her to brave human respect in this way! Weight all the circumstances of it. But she was entirely possessed by the love of Jesus, who had already delivered her from seven devils; and, prevented by grace, she was impatient to give Him a proof of her sincere repentance, and to make a public reparation for the scandal she had given. An occasion offered itself, and she eagerly seized it, trampling under foot all human considerations.

Application: Let us learn from this to follow the impulse of grace promptly and generously; to seize upon all the occasions which Providence gives us of doing good, and especially of repairing the harm caused by our bad example; and for this end to brave, if need be, human respect, the ridicule or criticisms of the world. Have you acted thus?

Affections and Resolutions.

Point II: Magdalene gives proofs of her repentance and love

Consideration: As soon as Magdalene saw our Lord, she went straight to Him, and "standing behind at His feet, she began to wash His feet with tears, and wiped them with the hairs of her head, and kissed His feet, and anointed them with the ointment." Mary Magdalene thus shows us what *perfect* contrition is. She is filled with the deepest sorrow, and inflamed with ardent love. She has no other regret than that of having offended God, and no other desire than that of pleasing Him.

Application: When we are at the feet of our confessor, who, in the Sacrament of Penance, holds the place of Jesus Christ to us, let us try to fill our hearts with feelings of perfect contrition. We shall certainly do it if we bring before our minds its immense advantages – a more entire or even total remission of our sins, and the strength to resist temptations, and overcome all obstacles to our sanctification.

Affections and Resolutions.

Point III: Reception that our Lord gave to Magdalen

Consideration: "The Pharisee who had invited Him, seeing it, spoke within himself, saying, This man, if He were a prophet, would know surely who or what manner of woman this is that toucheth Him, that she is a sinner." Jesus instantly took up her defence, and said, "Simon, dost thou see this woman? I entered into thy house, thou gavest Me no water for My feet; but she with tears hath washed My feet. My head with oil thou didst not anoint; but she with ointment hath anointed My feet. Wherefore I say to thee, many sins are forgiven her because she hath loved much. And He said to her, Thy sins are forgiven; go in peace."

Application: Do you wish to know the way of satisfying God's infinite justice for those numerous faults into which, from human infirmity, you fall daily? The Lord tells you what it is: "Love much, and many sins will be forgiven you." Frequently make acts of love, even if it be only these few words: "My God, I love Thee; pardon me for having offended Thee." And often, say ascetical writers, this act will be one of perfect contrition, though you have not had the intention of making one.

Colloquy.

July 23: The Centurion's Servant of Capharnaum

1st prelude: Imagine you see our Divine Lord looking graciously upon the Centurion.

2nd prelude: Beg for the knowledge and love of Jesus Christ.

Point I: Charity and confidence of the centurion

Consideration: The miraculous cure of the leper wrought at the very gates of Capharnaum was as a ray of light to the Roman centurion who commanded the little garrison of that town. Though but a pagan, he acknowledged Jesus the Master of creation; and hearing that He was near the town, he hoped to obtain a favour from Him, in the cure of a servant who was dear to him, and who suffered from palsy; and he sent Jewish elders to Jesus. They pleaded his cause, saying, "He is worthy that Thou shouldst do this for him; for he loveth our nation, and he hath built us a synagogue."

Application: How beautiful is the charity of this Gentile in respect, not of relation or friend, but of a servant! It was an active, generous charity. After having spent much for him on physicians, he hastened to seek help from Jesus, exposing himself to the blame and ridicule of the other pagans. It was a disinterested, universal charity: at his own cost he had built a synagogue for a subjugated people, whose frequent revolts had made them odious to their conquerors. If such was the charity of a man who understood neither its motives nor its supernatural merit, what ought to be ours in respect to our brethren in Jesus Christ! What shame it will be for us if our charity is less active, less generous, less disinterested than his! Is it not so sometimes? Let us reflect, and examine ourselves, entering into details.

Affections and Resolutions.

Point II: Humility and lively faith of the centurion

Consideration: "And when He had entered into Capharnaum, there came to Him a centurion, beseeching Him, and saying, Lord, my servant lieth at home sick of the palsy, and is grievously tormented. And Jesus saith to him, I will come and heal him. And the centurion, making answer, said, Lord, I am not worthy that Thou shouldst enter under my roof; but only say the word, and my servant shall be healed. For I also am a man subject to authority, having under me soldiers; and I say to this, Go, and he goeth; and to another, Come, and he cometh; and to my servant, Do this, and he doeth it." His meaning was, "Far easier is it, then, for Thee, who art Master of all creation, to speak to the malady, and it will obey Thee. My servant will be cured."

Application: We all feel the greatest admiration for this centurion, who had been prevented and enlightened by grace. What great humility, what ardent faith, expressed with the frankness and simplicity of a true soldier, was his! And what confidence he had in our Lord's goodness! He told his story, made his petition, and had so firm a conviction of our Lord's power and mercy, that he could not doubt the result. Why have we not always this faith and confidence in our prayers? We say it is because we are so unworthy; but the centurion had a deeper conviction of this than any one of us. It is, in reality, because we lack a sufficient knowledge of the power and love of our Divine Lord.

Affections and Resolutions.

Point III: Reward given to the centurion

Consideration: The centurion's prayer, so beautiful in its simplicity, delighted the heart of Jesus. "He marveled," says the Evangelist, "and said to them that followed Him, Amen I say to you, I have not found so great faith in Israel. And Jesus said to the

centurion, Go and as thou hast believed, so be it done to thee. And his servant was healed in that same hour." This, then, was the reward of the centurion: the immediate and complete cure of his servant, extraordinary praise bestowed on him by the Incarnate Word, and an *everlasting* celebrity through the whole world; for the words which his faith, humility and confidence brought to his lips are placed by the Church in the mouths of both priests and faithful at the moment of communion.
Application and Colloquy. Let us bless and exalt God's liberality towards us. We are the living proof of it. Let us make a return for it by a continual and entire self-immolation.

July 24: On Faith

1st prelude: Imagine you hear Jesus Christ saying to the centurion, "As thou hast believed, so be it done to thee."
2nd prelude: Beg for increase of faith.

Point I: Nature and necessity of faith

Consideration: Faith is the first in the order of virtues; for by it, enlightened from on high, we know God, His infinite attributes, His will, His good pleasure, and His intentions for us in this world and the next. It is evident, as says the Apostle, what "without faith it is impossible to please God"; it is impossible to perform a meritorious and supernatural act of virtue. That we may be able to do so as soon as possible, faith was given to us by baptism on our entrance into life; but as the Apostle tells us, "not of yourselves, for it is the gift of God."

Application: Faith being the foundation of all virtue, this latter will be so much more perfect as our faith is greater and more ardent. Let us do all we can to increase it. We cannot give it to ourselves, but we can increase it, like any other grace; first by prayer, after the example of the Apostles, when they cried out, "Increase our faith"; again, by a continual exercise of it, doing everything in a spirit of faith, so that we may live by faith; as it is written, "The just shall live by faith." Especially should we try to grow familiar with the thought of God's presence. If we were penetrated with it, we should never sin; we should pray well, be humble and modest in prosperity, strong and courageous in trials and temptations; we should do even the smallest thing with the greatest care, with a pure intention and ardent love; in one word, we should excel in virtue and live like saints.

Affections and Resolutions.

Point II: Excellence and advantages of faith

Consideration: Faith raises us above material things, above what we perceive by our senses and understanding; it raises us unto the invisible, unto God, and the heights of His infinite perfections; it opens to us the splendor, glory and happiness of our future country, Paradise. By faith our thoughts and aspirations become great and noble; we disdain all that is not eternal, we have no other ambition than that of laying up treasures in heaven. Faith raises us above ourselves, our weakness, our inconstancy; we become strong, invincible, even terrible to the devils, like to the first Christians, to those millions of martyrs who, says Saint Paul, triumphed by faith over threats and persuasions, over the horrors of prison and exile, even over cruel suffering and death. Read that wonderful picture of faith (Hebrews xi). By faith even our most ordinary actions become noble, meritorious, often heroic before God.

Application: These thoughts will doubtless rekindle in your heart an ardent desire of excelling in faith, that lively faith which proves itself by works and by a holy life. By these merits, *i.e.*, by the conformity of our actions with our faith, we can judge of its worth and degree. "Try your own selves," says the Apostle, "if you be in the faith"; if there be not a contradiction between what you believe and what you do. You believe, for instance, that your immortal soul is worth far more care than your body; yet do you not act as though it were otherwise? You believe that God sees you, observes you, reads the depths of your heart; but how often does it happen that when alone you act as if there were not witness of your falsehoods, your grave negligences and omissions, of your vain and useless thoughts? You believe that without the spirit of prayer, which supposes both recollection and mortifications, you will be a religious only in name and in habit; yet you prepare your meditation carelessly, you make few efforts to become recollected and mortified. Judge for yourself, after this examen, and see what you have to do from this day forward.

Colloquy.

July 25: Message of Saint John Baptist to Jesus

1st prelude: Behold Saint John Baptist in prison.
2nd prelude: Beg for resignation and constancy like the saints in adversity.

Point I: Captivity and zeal of Saint John Baptist

Consideration: "Now when John had heard in prison the works of Christ, sending two of his disciples he said to Him "Art Thou He that art to come, or look we for another?" Why did the holy precursor send his message? He knew well that our Lord was the Messiah. He did not want to be released from prison, for he knew that "blessed are they that suffer persecution for justice' sake." But he wished his disciples to see Jesus, to know Him, to attach themselves to Him, and follow Him.

Application: We are here taught most practical lessons. John the Baptist had lived a holy life, and he was thrown into prison, apparently abandoned. The Lord did nothing for him, but he never complained; his patience was not exhausted, his faith was unshaken. And I, who have done so little – I give way to impatience, to complains and mistrust, when I do not succeed in my undertakings, or when I am left to myself in trouble. Then, again, the holy precursor was suffering the agony of a harsh captivity; he was severely tried, both physically and morally; but none of this could quench the ardour of his zeal. He still fulfilled the mission which had been given to him. How far am I from possessing such strength of mind, such heroic constancy! A little indisposition, a slight suffering, is sufficient to cast me down, and to make me neglect the whole or part of my duty to God and my neighbor, and to act as if I had no one else to occupy myself about in this world. Is this not true?

Affections and Resolutions.

Point II: Answer of Jesus to the messengers of Saint John

Consideration: When the disciples asked, "Art Thou He that art to come?" (the Messiah promised by the Prophets) – our Lord answered them by actions, working various miracles before their eyes which had been foretold by the prophet Isaias; proving to them thus, both by miracles and the accomplishment of prophecy, that He was really the Messiah. Then when He sent them away, He said, "Go and relate to John what you have heard and seen."

Application: After the example of our Divine Master we should show more by our actions than by our words that we are truly the children of that God who is purity, sanctity, and goodness itself; let us prove to the world that we are the children and heirs of our Holy Founder by reproducing His virtues in us, by showing that we are animated by His spirit. Of what use is it to bear a noble name if our conduct is not in accordance with it? Besides, will not our words be far more persuasive if our life is in conformity with them? Are you convinced of this?

Affections and Resolutions.

Point III: Our Lord's praise of Saint John the Baptist

Consideration: One of the greatest glories of Saint John the Baptist is that he was publicly praised by the Son of God, who only can justly appreciate virtue, because He alone can see the depths of the heart. "And when they went their way," says the Evangelist, "He began to speak to the multitude concerning John. What went you out into the desert to see? A reed shaken with the wind? But what went you out to see? A man clothed in soft garments? But what went you out to see? A prophet? Yea, I say to you, and more than a prophet."

Application: The praise of men is worth nothing. It is vain, because they see only the exterior. But let us try to be worthy of approbation from Him who sees the heart, and who will judge us. The means of obtaining it is to make the two virtues which He especially praised in His precursor our own: *i.e.*, perseverance in a holy life, and an entire mortification of our disorderly inclinations. But, alas, is it not precisely in these things we are wanting? Like the "reed shaken by the wind," we are perpetually inconstant to our resolutions, bringing nothing to a good end, gratifying our senses and our ease. Let us acknowledge this, and humble and correct ourselves.

Colloquy.

July 26: Various Effects of our Lord's Miracles

1st prelude: Imagine you see Jesus surrounded by the crowd; praised by some, criticized by others.

2nd prelude: Beg for grace to draw great fruit from this meditation.

Point I: The miracles of Jesus enlighten and touch the humble

Consideration: The miracles wrought before the eyes of Saint John's messengers were almost immediately followed by a double miracle – the deliverance and cure of a possessed man. "Then was offered to Him one possessed with a devil, blind and dumb; and He healed him, so that he spoke and saw. And all the multitudes were amazed, and said Is not this the Son of David?" (the Messiah, who is to come of that race).

Application: Recognize in this possessed man the misery of the Christian in a state of mortal sin. 1. He is really in the possession of the devil, and will remain in it for all eternity if he dies in his sin. 2. He is blind to the horror of his state, to the enormity of his sins, and the fatal effects they will have upon him in time and in eternity. 3. He is also dumb – dumb as to prayer, dumb as to asking counsel, often dumb as to making a sincere confession. If you have lived – and that, perhaps, for a long time – in this state, and have happily escaped from it, humbly acknowledge that you owe it to a miracle of grace and mercy from Jesus Christ. How many others have persevered in it, and have been surprised by death!

Affections and Resolutions.

Point II: They blind and harden the proud

Consideration: The people who were free from prejudice and malice formed a wise judgment concerning our Lord and His actions; but the Scribes and Pharisees, governed by pride and jealousy, shut their eyes to the light, and hardened themselves in their hatred of Jesus. However, they could not deny the fact of a double miracle having taken place; so they attributed it to the devil. "He hath Beelzebub; and by the prince of the devils He casteth out devils," they said, speaking against even common sense. The Lord confuted them by saying, "If Satan cast our Satan, he is divided against himself: how then shall his kingdom stand?"

Application: We have heard the language of those whom passion has blinded, and we see that it is absurd, and fully displays the motives of those who use it. Have you not often remarked the same, and have you not been the occasion of others making the same about you? On the other hand, consider the calm and dignified language of our Divine Lord. He simply refuted in a tone of authority the horrible accusation by which they hoped to destroy His influence; and He did this only to preserve the people from

being deceived. May His conduct be our model! If it be necessary to justify ourselves, let us do it calmly, not from self-love or vanity, but from zeal for religion. Have we acted thus?
Affections and Resolutions.

Point III: Praise given to some, condemnation to others

Consideration: "I confess to Thee, O Father, Lord of heaven and earth, because Thou hast revealed these things to little ones." Thus does the Son of God praise the simple faith and humble docility of the people; and His words are full of consolation and encouragement. But terrible is the language in which He describes the pride and hypocrisy of the Pharisees and Scribes who taught the people error: "O generation of vipers, how can you speak good things, whereas you are evil?" How terrific, also, are the threats and reproaches that He pronounces at the same time upon the impenitent cities: "Woe to thee, Corozain; woe to thee, Bethsaida: for if in Tyre and Sidon had been wrought the miracles that have been wrought in you, they had long ago done penance in sackcloth and ashes. And thou, Capharnaum, shalt thou be exalted up to heaven? Thou shalt go down even unto hell. For if in Sodom had been wrought the miracles that have been wrought in thee, perhaps it had remained unto this day; but I say to you, that it shall be more tolerable for the land of Sodom in the day of judgment than for thee."

Application: We who live in the midst of a great abundance of grace and means of sanctification must take care not to draw down on ourselves such severe reproaches, such terrific threats; we must abhor all that savours of the pride and hypocrisy with which the Pharisees were reproached, and strive with all our hearts to preserve the simplicity of the dove and the humble docility of childhood, at whatever age or whatever degree of knowledge we may have arrived.
Colloquy.

July 27: Raising of the Widow's Son at Naim

1st prelude: Imagine you see a funeral procession, and Jesus saying to the corpse, "I say to thee, arise."
2nd prelude: Beg the grace of drawing great fruit from this meditation.

Point I: Jesus meets a funeral procession

Consideration: The miracles wrought upon the leper and the centurion's servant, which had excited such wonder, were followed by one still more striking – the resurrection of a dead man. Saint Luke tells us that "He went into a city called Naim, and there went with Him His disciples and a great multitude. And when He came nigh the gates of that city, behold a dead man was carried out, the only son of his mother, and she was a widow; and a great multitude of the city was with her."

Application: What a wonderful picture is here brought before our eyes! How strongly it shows us the folly of those who place their happiness and their hopes in the things of this world! A mother clad in widow's weeds, robbed of all other joys, has still one consolation left to her – an only son. With what happiness does she see him advancing in years, and how often does she dwell hopefully upon his future! Vain is her calculation, fleeting her joy! Death in an instant puts an end to it all, and she is left in solitude and despair. She is an image of the world, the history of those who place their happiness in it.

Affections and Resolutions.

Point II: Jesus, touched with compassion, raises the dead

Consideration: The crowd which went before Jesus stopped silently at the entrance of the town before the funeral procession, which was coming out at the same moment. Every eye was fixed on the desolate mother, who was weeping and crying out with anguish; "whom when the Lord had seen, being moved with mercy towards her, He said to her, Weep not. And He came near and touched the bier. And they that carried it stood still." Then, speaking in that tone of authority which belonged to Him as the Master of life and death, He said, "Young man, I say to thee, Arise." And he that was dead sat up, and began to speak; and He gave him to his mother.

Application: When you see the sweetness and tenderness of the Heart of Jesus for a stranger who had asked nothing from Him, ought you not to blush at your want of confidence in Him? How often you are heard to say, "I try in vain to be as fervent again as I once was; or I strive in vain to bring back this young man, or this sick person, or this hardened sinner, to the right path: it will require nothing less than a miracle." That may be; but why hesitate

to ask for this miracle of grace? Why doubt that you will obtain it? Is it not doing an injury to the Heart of Jesus to believe that He will do less for the life of a soul than that of the body? It is supposed by many of the Fathers that in our Lord's mind the bodily resurrection which He wrought at the gates of Naim was a figure of the spiritual resurrections which the Apostles and their successors were to accomplish in every quarter of the world. And then it was *because of his mother* that Jesus raised the dead man. Be careful, when you desire to obtain any great favor, to implore the intercession of your Mother, of Mary, and you will feel redoubled confidence.
Affections and Resolutions.

Point III: Jesus blessed by the crowd

Consideration: When the multitude who surrounded Him saw the miracle He had wrought, "there came a fear on them all"; and they glorified God, saying, "A great prophet is risen up among us, and God has visited His people."

Application: God is continually working miracles of power and goodness, both in the order of nature and grace. We must not merely look on them, but, imitating these good people, show our gratitude by praising and blessing God, and by trying, when occasion offers, to inspire others with the same feelings of admiration and gratitude. How have you acted in this respect?
Colloquy with our Blessed Lady.

July 28: Return of the Devil; or falling back into Sin

1st prelude: Imagine you see a house invaded for the second time by an enemy.
2nd prelude: Beg for grace to know and to avoid the snares of the devil.

Point I: The devil driven out

Consideration: Magdalene, when she had once been delivered from the seven devils who possessed her, never gave them admittance again. All do not imitate her. Our Lord warns us against the terrible misfortune, and unveils to us the machinations of the devil: "When an unclean spirit is gone out of a man, he walketh through dry places seeking rest, and findeth none." The insult of his expulsion will not let him rest. He wearies himself to find out the means of regaining what he has lost, and is determined to overcome every obstacle. "Then he saith, I will return into my house from whence I came out."

Application: Do we take as much trouble to keep ourselves in grace and fervor as the devil does to rob us of them? Alas, scarcely have we gone back to God by a good confession, or regained fervor by a good retreat, than we lose our compunction, become dissipated, delude ourselves by a false security, and have no fear of the enemy, who is watching us, and lying in wait for the moment when he can take us by surprise. How often have we fallen back into sin! How many means of sanctification have we lost which might have been prevented if we had been on our guard, watching and praying! What does experience say to you in this respect?
Affections and Resolutions.

Point II: The devil returning

Consideration: The devil does not confine himself to plans and resolutions: he takes the most violent means, bringing against us, if necessary, an infernal legion, and coming, he findeth it, says our Lord, empty, swept and garnished (by grace). Then he goeth and taketh seven other spirits more wicked than himself. This means many others more crafty, more wily than himself, who attack us on all sides, in all ways, by joy and sorrow, by pleasure and pain, by prosperity and adversity, by love and by hate, by presumption and by despondency or despair.

Application: The devil carefully watches our state and the dispositions of our hearts whilst we either neglect to examine ourselves, or do it very superficially. The devil does not rely on his own strength, but seeks for help; whilst we, confiding too much in ourselves, do not, even in the most violent temptations, run for aid to God and to the saints. Our pride prevents us form manifesting ourselves to the spiritual directors, and seeking aid and counsel from them; and pride separates us from God, and deprives us of the grace we need to sustain us. How terrible is this! It is thus that we also come to the assistance of our greatest enemy.
Affections and Resolutions.

Point III: The devil triumphant

Consideration: When by presumption, or negligence, or weakness, we have opened our hearts to the devil, what takes place? He enters in and dwells there, says our Lord, and the last state of that man is made worse than the first. Why is this? Because, by repeated sin, the horror of it diminishes, the withdrawal of so much grace weakens the soul, and light and faith are darkened, bad habits are formed, and become, as Saint Augustine said, speaking from experience, a second nature – *Fit habitus peccandi, et habitus fit altera natura*. It is the greatest misery that can befall us.

Application: Let us try to understand this misery. Let us have a lively fear of a habit even of venial sin, and especially of a state of lukewarmness. It is so difficult to get out of it, more so for a religious than for a secular, who is less familiar with holy thoughts, and less guilty of ingratitude toward God. When such a thing takes place, says Saint Bernard, "I look upon a change as more wonderful than the raising of the dead to life." Let us see how we stand, what we have to fear, what remains for us to do. Colloquy.

July 29: Our Lord's Teaching on Family Ties

1st prelude: Imagine you see Jesus instructing the people, and receiving an invitation to come to His Mother and His brethren. **2nd prelude**: Beg for detachment from all undue natural affection for your relations.

Point I: Relationship of Jesus Christ, and with Jesus Christ

Consideration: An apparently accidental incident interrupted our Lord's discourse. People came to tell Him that His Mother and other near relatives were come from Nazareth, and stood without seeking to speak to Him. "And one said to Him, Behold Thy Mother and Thy brethren stand without, seeking Thee. But He answering him that told Him, said, Who is My Mother, and who are My brethren? And stretching forth His hand towards His disciples, He said, Behold My Mother and My brethren," or those who stand to Me in the place of mother and brethren.

Application: What does our Divine Lord teach us by this? That when the glory of God, the salvation of souls, or our own sanctification is in question, we ought to forget all that attaches us to earth, and that, when necessary, we should sacrifice the affection we have for our relations to the obedience and fidelity we owe to God. In other words, we ought to love our relations and friends only in God, for God and as God. This is the meaning of that rule which bids the religious to try to turn the affection which they naturally and lawfully have for their parents, brothers and sisters into a spiritual love. Have you conformed to these rules of conduct?

Affections and Resolutions.

Point II: How we can become brethren of Jesus Christ

Consideration: "For whosoever shall do the will of My Father that is in heaven, he is My brother, and sister, and mother." He that does the will of God can become the brother of Jesus Christ in this sense – that by his conformity in all things with the will of God, which is also that of Jesus, he possesses a perfect *fraternity* of thoughts and feelings with Him; in this sense, again, that by faithfully fulfilling the divine will, he possesses that charity which makes us adopted children of God, and thus *brothers* of Jesus Christ. He Himself gave that name to His disciples when, after His resurrection, He said to the holy women, Go, tell My brethren that they go into Galilee."

Application: How important, then, it is for us to make great efforts to excel in the practice of a perfect conformity of our will with that of God! Besides many other advantages which we all know, it brings us the title of *brothers* of Jesus Christ; it identifies us, so to speak, with Him, and makes us partakers of all those immense blessings which He won by His Passion and His death. What value do we set on this practice? What progress have we made in it?

Affections and Resolutions.

Point III: How we can become the mother of Jesus Christ

Consideration: "For whosoever shall do the will of My Father that is in heaven, he is My brother and sister and mother." Is My mother? There is something, then, greater still than becoming the brother of Jesus Christ – something more marvelous, more inexplicable. Pope Saint Greogry thus explains it: "He becomes the mother of Christ who, by his preaching, causes Him to be born in the hearts of men by making Him known and loved by those who were strangers to Him." This is truly a spiritual maternity, but is it less noble and less meritorious than maternity according to the flesh?

Application: We can all attain this divine maternity, although we be neither preachers nor confessors, by trying by every means in our power to help on any work for the propagation of the faith; by offering to God our prayers, our communions, our penances, and our sufferings for the conversion of infidels, heretics and schismatics; by trying to cause Jesus Christ to be born and to live in the souls of others whenever an occasion presents itself. Have you done this? How can you improve on what you have done? Colloquy.

July 30: Of misplaced Affection towards our Relations

1st prelude: Listen to Jesus Christ saying: "He that loveth father or mother more than Me is not worthy of Me."
2nd prelude: Beg the grace of freedom from all misplaced affection.
There are three things especially which tend to produce and develop in the heart of a religious a misplaced affection towards relations; three things therefore against which we should be on our guard, *i.e., unnecessary visits, misplaced compassion and misplaced zeal.*

Point I: Unnecessary visits

Consideration: The religious who tries to create and multiply motives and excuses for visiting his relations exposes himself to great dangers, and even to losing his vocation, or at least the spirit of his vocation. Saint Basil tells us this, and explains it thus: These misplaced visits cannot fail – 1st, to turn away the attention of the religious from what he should do for God, his own perfection and zeal for souls; 2nd, to fill his imagination with memories and dangerous ideas at the sight of certain persons or places which witnessed his falls in past life; 3rd, to deprive him of peace of soul by keeping him always in anxiety about his relations, their affairs, their undertakings, their successes, their reverses, their domestic afflictions, etc.; 4th, to cause him to lose, little by little, the spirit of his holy vocation.

Application: If experience has not taught you the truth of these observations, return thanks to God, and strengthen the determination, which every good religious ought to have, of avoiding all visits to relations which are not required for very solid reasons.

Affections and Resolutions.

Point II: Misplaced zeal

Consideration: Masters of the spiritual life call *misplaced* that zeal which religious imagine they have about their relations even when they desire to reclaim them from sin. They say that this mission does not devolve on the religious. There is reason to fear, unless it be imposed by obedience, that it may do much harm; and they cite a number of instances where attention to relations by religious has caused them to imbibe the spirit and love of the world. How much stronger reason is there for looking on the eagerness that a religious has about the temporal affairs of his family as misplaced and dangerous, whether it be schemes for their fortune or elevation, or whether it be to deliver them from some pecuniary or commercial embarrassment!

Application: We should always remember that we are dead to the world, and live only to God; that we should be entirely devoted to the great business of our sanctification; and that the less we occupy our mind with our relations and friends, the more readily God will hear the prayers we offer up for their temporal and spiritual happiness. Have you always acted according to these truly wise counsels?

Affections and Resolutions.

Point III: Misplaced compassion

Consideration: That feeling of compassion which causes us to share in the sufferings of our relations is not an imperfection; but if it disturbs our peace and prevents our fulfillment of duty, and if it goes so far as to make us waver in our vocation and abandon it that we may help our family, it is worse than misplaced, it is sinful. The compassion for relations has been, says Saint Jerome, to many religious an occasion of apostasy and damnation. *Quanti monachorum dum patris matrisque miserentur, suas animas perdiderunt (Req. Monach.).*

Application: If we are ever tried by these great temptations, let us recollect that we are publicly engaged to the service of God not by *conditional* but by *absolute* vows, and that He, for whose love we have left our relations, knows how to turn the trials He is pleased to send us to our good. However, these temptations find little entrance into the hearts of religious, unless they be lukewarm, and little attached to their vocation. Colloquy.

July 31: Feast of Saint Ignatius of Loyola, founder of the Company of Jesus

1st prelude: Imagine you see the saint in heavenly glory.
2nd prelude: Beg of him to obtain for us fidelity to grace.
Saint Ignatius was born in 1491; first Superior-general of the order, 1541; bull of approbation issued September 21, 1540; died July 31, 1556; beatified 1609; canonized 1622.

Point I: Wonderful operations of grace in Saint Ignatius

Consideration: *Gratia Dei, sum id quod sum* – "By the grace of God, I am what I am." These words of the Apostle can most suitably be placed in the mouth of Saint Ignatius. There are, indeed, few saints in whom the operations of grace were more manifest and more wonderful. We see how gradually it brought him to the end destined for him. In the divine decrees Ignatius was to found a religious order intended to arrest the progress of heresy in the sixteenth century, and to repair the losses it would cause the Church. Yet, up to the age of thirty years he pursued the phantom of military glory, till at last, wounded and exhausted, he laid himself down on a bed of suffering. Then did grace begin its work, first by showing him the nothingness of this world, and inspiring him with the desire of repairing his past faults by severe penance. While he thus devoted himself for ten whole months in the grotto of Manresa, he was prepared by divers trials and frequent ecstasies for the interior life and the direction of souls. He became a consummate master of the spiritual life, as we discover by his wonderful book of the *Spiritual Exercises* which he then wrote. But he was further destined to become an apostle, and the father of a vast number of apostolic men; and yet Ignatius was an uneducated man! Grace gave him the desire and means of acquiring knowledge by secretly leading his steps to the University of Paris. For there, prepared for him and ready for his hands, were the young student who were to form the nucleus of the new order he was to found. The unction of grace drawn from the spiritual exercises made them united in one desire of consecrating themselves for ever to God by the vows of religion, of offering themselves to the Vicar of Jesus Christ to be sent to preach anywhere, and particularly to devote themselves to the education of youth. They carried out their intention; and Pope Paul III, after reading the summary of the rules of the Institute, presented to him under the title of the *Company of Jesus*, cried out, *Digitus Dei est hic* – "The finger of God is here" (1540). Ignatius, guided by grace, governed the infant society so wisely for sixteen years, that it received the commendation of the Council of Trent, and extended rapidly to the ends of the earth. He himself was fifty-three years later reckoned among the saints (1609).

Application: Recall to your mind your past years, and especially the beginning and the progress of your vocation, and you will be firmly convinced that an especial grace has also prevented and sustained you throughout.

Affections and Resolutions.

Point II: Saint Ignatius's wonderful correspondence with grace

Consideration: As soon as the light of grace penetrated into the soul of Ignatius, he set himself to repair the past, and to attain what his vocation required from him. He secretly left the castle of Loyola, hung up his sword before the altar of our Lady in the sanctuary of Montserrat, clothed himself as a poor man, and begged his bread as such; he made a general confession with tears and sobs, and retired to Manresa, where he inflicted sufferings in his body the very history of which makes us shudder. Having thus become a new man in Jesus Christ, and being consumed with divine love, he gave himself up to zeal for souls; but that he might attain more success with others, he pursued the study of letters at Alcala, and afterwards at Paris applied himself to the higher sciences. With invincible perseverance he overcame the difficulties which he had to encounter in this long course of study, and especially in the formation and establishment of the new order, the plan of which he had learnt by grace. While he composed the Constitutions, he withdrew himself from others, was almost always on his knees, fasting or praying, that all of them might be in accordance with the will of God, and of a nature to bring about the *greater glory of God.* We should remark that these last words, which became the motto of the saint, were repeated in the Constitutions more than three hundred and sixty times. For Ignatius, absolutely dead to self-love and worldly glory, lived for God only. It was the fruit of his unwavering fidelity to grace.

Application: After the example of Saint Ignatius, let us cooperate generously and perseveringly with grace. It will be our

counsel in doubts, our consolation in troubles, our support in the spiritual combat. It will bring us that crown of glory promised to those who, taking it for their guide, seek in everything the *greater glory of God.*
Colloquy.

August 1: Parable of the Sower

1st prelude: Behold Jesus sitting in a boat and speaking to the multitude assembled on the shore of the lake.
2nd prelude: Beg the grace of attaining the end that our Lord proposes to us in this parable.

Point I: Seed falling by the wayside

Consideration: We have now come to that time in our Lord's ministry (towards the middle of the second year) when it pleased Him to present great truths to the people under the familiar but attractive form of parables. One of the most remarkable was the sower. "The sower," said He, "went out to sow his seed. And as he sowed, some fell by the wayside; and it was trodden down, and the fowls of the air devoured it. And other some fell upon a rock, and as soon as it had sprung up, it withered away, because it had no moisture."

Application: Let us tarry here, that we may study the practical lessons of the first part of the parable. Our Lord Himself explains them to us. The seed is the word of God, and they by the wayside are they that hear; then the devil cometh and taketh the word out of their heart, lest believing they should be saved. Two things are here pointed out to us as preventing us from deriving the fruit which our meditation on the Word of God ought to produce; the first is dissipation of mind, which the devil makes use of to banish good thoughts from our hearts; the second, hardness of heart, which prevents them from penetrating into our souls, and taking root there. A careful examination will convince you of this.
Affections and Resolutions.

Point II: Seed sown among thorns.

Consideration: "And other some," continues our Lord, "bel among thorns, and the thorns growing up with it choked it." At the request of the Apostles, the Divine Master deigned to explain this second part of the parable also. "And that which fell among thorns are they who have heard, and going their way, are choked with the cares and riches and pleasures of this life, and yield no fruit."

Application: Let us pity the lot of those Christians who are obliged, by their position, to live and work out their salvation in the midst of the troubles of the world. What perpetual difficulties they meet with in trying to listen to the Word of God, and to rule their conduct by it! And faith also is, as it were, stifled and dead in the greater number of men. We should, then, be fools and our own enemies if, after having with great pain torn ourselves away from the anxieties and dissipation of the world, we let ourselves be drawn into them again, either by too frequent intercourse with people of the world and by useless visits, or by giving too much time and attention to reading the newspapers, or listening to the conversation of the day, or by letting ourselves be surrounded by our relations, who try to interest us in their temporal affairs, their enterprises, their plans for success and fortune, their sorrows and domestic disputes. It is evident that if we yield to the snare of the devil, our fate will be the same as that of seculars – that the germ of progress, even the germ of religious life, will be stifled in us. We ought, then, to be on our guard. Have you always done this?
Affections and Resolutions.

Point III: Seed falling on good ground

Consideration: "And other seed fell on good ground, and being sprung up, yielded fruit a hundred fold" – meaning, according to the explanation of Jesus Christ, "That on the good ground are they who, in a good and very good heart, hearing the word keep it, and bring forth fruit in patience: the one thirty, the other sixty and another a hundred."

Application: We desire to be in this last number. What means should we take to attain it? Our Lord has told us to hear and meditate on the divine word with a heart free from disorderly affections, and above all things desirous of knowing the truth, and decided to embrace it. Is this our habitual state? Let us see in what we can and ought to improve.
Colloquy with our Divine Master.

August 2: Feast of Saint Alphonsus Liguori, Founder of the Order of the Most Holy Redeemer

Saint Alphonsus Liguori was born at Naples 1696; ordained priest 1726;

first Superior of his congregation 1732; bishop 1762; resigned his see 1775; died August 1, 1787; beatified 1816; canonized 1839.

1st prelude: Imagine you see the saint in ecstasy before our Lady's image.
2nd prelude: Beg the grace of walking courageously in the saint's footsteps.

Point I: Saint Alphonsus incites us to labor

We ought to seek in the lives of the saints not only lessons, but encouragement. We shall find many of these in the life of Saint Alphonsus. First of all, we find a powerful encouragement to labor, which, in the hard kind of life we have embraced, is often very necessary for us. From his ordination until his extreme old age, the saint never ceased to preach, to hear confessions, to give retreats and missions. To these labors he added, for thirteen years, the government of a diocese and that of his numerous congregation for forty-two years more. Here was enough, indeed, to fill up a life of any man; but Alphonsus had made a vow *never to lose time*, and, incredible though it seems, he also found time to compose (besides a great number of small treatises) more than fifty-two books, some of which, such as his *Moral Theology* and *Glories of Mary*, are so filled with quotations that it is evident he had read the works of all who had written before him about moral sand our Lady. And laboring thus, the saint, though feeble in health, lived ninety years.

Application: Take care not to imitate those religious who are so occupied about their health that they withdraw from work, never dare to undertake anything great or laborious, and finally become a burden to the community and to themselves. Rather imitate those who, though feeble in health, seek a remedy for their habitual infirmities in labor. Regular work prolongs life, and Saint Alphonsus is a proof of it.

Affections and Resolutions.

Point II: Saint Alphonsus incites us to zeal

Consideration: The long life of the saint was an uninterrupted exercise of zeal. He exercised it in almost every town and village in the kingdom of Naples, and his zeal was always rewarded by extraordinary conversions, often by striking miracles. More than a hundred of these are cited in the process of his canonization:

sometimes he was seen to be raised from the ground while he celebrated or preached; at times, interrupting the sermon, he asked prayers for some great person who was dying in a distant spot; sometimes he pointed out to those who consulted him what they had hidden in the depths of their hearts; often, with the sign of the cross, he cured those dangerously ill; and sometimes, even, he was present at the same time in two places – thus, without leaving Naples, he was present at the death of Pope Clement IX (22 September 1774).

Application: If we wish to obtain great favors from God, we should be zealous. This we can all be in different ways. But after the example of the saint, we should exercise our zeal with a pure intention, having nothing in view but the glory of God and the good of souls. Is it thus that we have always acted?
Affections and Resolutions.

Point III: Saint Alphonsus incites us to devotion to our Lady

Consideration: There are few saints who have had such a tender love for Mary, and who have increased the devotion to her so much by their sermons and writings. Among the latter, the incomparable treatise of the *Glories of Mary*, full both of unction and learning, has been translated into all languages, and has given everywhere a fresh impulse to the devotion to the Queen of Heaven. And she in return was pleased to pour favors on Alphonsus, and even to glorify him before men. One day in particular, when preaching at Amalfi before an immense audience, he invoked Mary, and suddenly he was lifted some feet above the pulpit, and shone radiantly with a celestial light, which streamed upon him from an image of Mary (1756).

Application: let us cherish deep feelings of filial love to Mary in our hearts; let us try to spread devotion to her, and we also shall experience the effects of her power and maternal love.
Colloquy.

August 3: Parable of the Cockle and the Wheat

1st prelude: Behold Jesus Christ giving and explaining this parable.
2nd prelude: Beg the grace of really understanding its meaning, and of profiting by it.

Point I: General application of the parable

Consideration: "The kingdom of heaven [the Church] is likened to a man that sowed good seed in his field. But while men were asleep, his enemy came and oversowed cockle among the wheat, and went his way. And when the blade had sprung up and brought forth fruit, there appeared also the cockle. And the servants said to him, Wilt thou that we go and gather it up? And he said, No; lest perhaps gathering up the cockle, you root up the wheat also together with it. Suffer both to grow until the harvest, and in the time of the harvest I will say to the reapers, Gather up first the cockle, and bind it into bundles to burn; but the wheat gather ye into my barn."

Application: After having attentively considered the parable, as it came from the lips of our Divine Lord, meditate on the explanation of it, which, at the request of the Apostles, He deigned to give. "He that soweth the good seed," said He, "is the Son of Man; and the field is the world, and the good seed are the children of the kingdom, and the cockle are the children of the wicked one, and the enemy that sowed them is the devil. But the harvest is the end of the world, and the reapers are the angels. The Son of Man shall send the angels, and they shall gather out of His kingdom all scandals and them that work iniquity, and shall cast them into the furnace of fire. There shall be weeping and gnashing of teeth. Then shall the just shine as the sun in the kingdom of their Father. He that hath ears to hear, let him hear." These latter words were frequently used by our Lord to excite and fix the attention of His hearers.

Affections and Resolutions.

Point II: Particular application of the parable

Consideration: We may also understand by the field in which the good and bad seed grew together any religious community, however small it may be. The wheat, or good seed, represents those fervent religious who, filled with a spirit of their vocation, are always advancing in virtue until they attain perfection; the cockle, or bad seed, denotes the lukewarm religious too often mixed up with the good seed even in the holiest communities, all those who by their singular and difficult character, are a trouble to others and cause them suffering, or who, by their irregularity and their evil influence, prevent the good from growing in virtue, or even draw the weak into disorder.

Application: Many practical reflections present themselves to the mind. First, if you have to watch or govern others, take care not to shut your eyes to faults or the beginnings of irregularity, under the pretext that they are not great faults. Evil, like the cockle, is always growing, and it becomes difficult to root it up. Secondly, if you are responsible only for yourself, and unhappily see that some of your brethren more or less resemble those whose sad picture has just been traced, do all you can to make them better, but do not be filled with an impetuous and bitter zeal, begging God that He would deliver you from them. As long as it pleases Him to keep them, they can greatly help on your spiritual progress by trying your patience, charity and zeal. And then there is always a hope that they may see their faults, and become models of penance and fervor. Thirdly, look into yourself, and beg of god to give you light; examine carefully your manner of behaving to others, and see if, in some respects, you are not the cockle about which you are so impatient and unmerciful. Alas, those words of our Lord, "Why seest thou the mote that is in thy brother's eye, and seest not the beam that is in thy own eye?" is but too often verified, so terribly does self-love blind us about ourselves. See, after these reflections, what there is to reform in your judgments of others, or your own conduct, and make resolutions accordingly.

Colloquy with the Lord our God.

August 4: Feast of Saint Dominic, Founder of Friars Preachers

Saint Dominic was born 1170; first Superior-general of the order, approved by Honorius III, 1216; first master of the sacred palace, 1217; died 1221; canonized by Gregory XVIII, 1234.

1st prelude: Behold the saint praying before he went to preach the Word of God.

2nd prelude: Beg the grace of following in the saint's footsteps.

Point I: Saint Dominic a model of disinterestedness and abnegation

Consideration: Dominic was born of a rich and illustrious family of Castile, and was gifted with great eloquence. At an early age he was called to the priesthood, and his preaching was very popular among his fellow citizens. But God called him to a greater apostolate – that of converting the obstinate heretics of Languedoc, of evangelizing many countries, and of perpetuating his work by a new religious order. He obeyed the voice of God, and broke all the ties which bound him to earth – possessions, honor, and family. He clothed himself in a poor garment, often went barefoot, lived on alms, and strove to die entirely to himself by a continual abnegation, and to live for God only. Then he gathered companions round him, whom he inspired with the same feelings of disinterestedness, abnegation and zeal.

Application: By following this line of conduct, Dominic became a *man of God – homo Dei*; a man powerful in word and work, and the founder of an order which has rendered great service to religion and given the Church many saints and illustrious theologians. By following the same line of conduct, by detaching ourselves entirely from all earthly things and from ourselves, by perfect abnegation, we shall be able to follow the impulses of grace, and to labor successfully in our Lord's vineyard. Have we done this? After having generously given up all things, have we taken anything back?

Affections and Resolutions.

Point II: Saint Dominic a model of penance and of mortification

Consideration: It is not enough for a preacher of the Gospel to renounce the possession of this world, the esteem of men and of himself; we must also, as Saint Paul says, bear the marks of the Lord Jesus in our body – always bearing about in our body the mortification of Jesus. Saint Dominic understood this, and his mode of life was very austere; notwithstanding the great fatigue of his apostolate, he forbade himself the use of meat entirely, and made it a rule for his order; he fasted almost continually, and during the greater part of Lent he only took bread and water; he slept on a plank, often passed the night in prayer, and inflicted severe penances on his body.

Application: If you cannot go so far on the road of penance and mortification, you can at least mortify continually the disorderly appetites of the flesh; you can practice the penances which a wise director has permitted or counselled you; you can habitually mortify your eyes, your ears, your taste, and all your sense; you can, by an *entire* and *constant* fidelity *to all* the points of the rule and of religious discipline, live under restraint, which is a continual penance. Have you done this? To animate yourself to it,

think of the joy you will have at death at having done it, or of the sorrow if you have neglected it.
Affections and Resolutions.

Point III: Saint Dominic a model of charity and gentleness

Consideration: Though Saint Dominic was severe to himself, he was full of gentleness, goodness, and compassion for others, especially those who were drawn into the heresies of the Albigenses. They were cruel and fanatical schismatics, who used fire and sword against their opponents. Against them, all efforts had been tried in vain, even the arms of the Crusaders. It was reserved for Saint Dominic to win the glory of converting them by his gentleness and charity, by the unction of his words, and by his miracles, among which was the raising to life of three dead persons. But, nevertheless, the saint drew his power chiefly from prayer, fasting, humility, confidence in God, and especially from his tender devotion to the Queen of Heaven. It was she who taught him that easy and successful way of honoring her Divine Son by the recital of the Rosary, which, owing to his zeal, became a universal practice.
Colloquy.

August 5: Parables of the Mustard-seed, the Leaven, and the Hidden Treasure

1st prelude: Imagine yourself to be among the people hearing Jesus.
2nd prelude: Beg the grace of understanding the meaning of His words, and of drawing fruit from them.

Point I: Parable of the mustard-seed

Consideration: Let us ponder over three other parables which our Divine Master has deigned to give for our instruction and encouragement. The first is the grain of mustard-seed. "The kingdom of heaven is like to a grain of mustard-seed, which a man took and sowed in his field; which is the least indeed of all seeds, but when it is grown up it is greater than all herbs, and becometh a tree, so that the birds of the air come and dwell in the branches thereof." Our Lord foretold the marvelous increase of the Church. How little was she during the mortal life of Jesus Christ; how little on the day of Pentecost! It was an imperceptible seed; but, made fruitful by the dew of grace, heated by the words of the Apostles, by the blood of martyrs, and the sweat of missionaries, it has become a majestic tree, which over shadows the whole earth. In its shade the kings of the earth and the princes of knowledge who were prefigured by the birds of the air, come to seek that peace of heart and happiness which the world cannot give them.

Application: Is not this mustard-seed a figure also of the religious order to which you belong, and in which your days pass away peacefully and full of merit for eternity? Remember how feeble it was in the beginning, and how it has extended and taken root, thanks to the holy lives and labors of those who laid its foundations. It is for you, now united in the same intention as your brethren, to strengthen and adorn the work of your predecessors. Each one can and ought to do his part, and that by an exact observance of the rule and constitutions, by prayer and good example. Have you thought of this?

Affections and Resolutions.

Point II: Parable of the leaven

Consideration: "The kingdom of heaven is like to leaven, which a woman took and hid in three measures of meal until the whole was leavened." This parable can be applied to the precious Blood of Jesus Christ, which is given to us in Holy Communion as a sacred leaven. It enters within us, raises us above our weaknesses, gives supernatural strength to the three powers of our soul, and transforms us in a wonderful manner into Jesus Christ, according to the words, "He that drinketh My Blood abideth in Me, and I in him."

Application: Take great care in preparing yourselves well to receive within your breast this heavenly leaven. What wonders it will work in you! It will give you a supernatural strength; it will make you invincible; it will make you men after the heart of God – spiritual and heavenly.

Affections and Resolutions.

Point III: Parable of the hidden treasure

Consideration: "The kingdom of heaven is like unto a treasure hidden in a field, which a man having found, hid it, and for joy thereof goeth and selleth all that he hath, and buyeth that field." The religious can easily perceive the meaning of this parable; he knows at once that the hidden treasure of which Jesus Christ speaks is Christian perfection, concealed from the eyes of the world in the religious state, and that he is the happy mortal who has taken possession of this wonderful treasure.

Application: Recall the joy that filled your soul when you were given the definite possession of the treasure which you had found, of pronouncing the vows of religion. This remembrance will often be very useful to you, especially if it happens that you are tempted against your vocation, or experience a certain natural disgust for the labors or the office which is assigned you.

Colloquy.

August 6: Parables of the Pearl of Great Price, the Net and the Householder

(If anyone prefers to make a meditation on the mystery of the day, *The Transfiguration*, it will be found as given for September 2nd.)

1st prelude: Imagine yourself to be among the people hearing Jesus.

2nd prelude: Beg the grace of understanding the meaning of His words, and of drawing fruit from them.

Point I: Parable of the pearl of great price

Consideration: "The kingdom of heaven," said our Lord, "is like to a merchant seeking good pearls, who, when he had found one of pearl of great price, went his way, and sold all that he had and bought it." By *pearls* our Divine Lord meant those virtues with which the soul should be adorned for the coming of her Spouse. All are precious, more precious than the purest gold and silver. But there is one that excels all others, and it is charity, the queen of virtues. To her belongs the kingdom of heaven; and our glory will be proportioned to the degree of our charity.

Application: We have not to seek for this pearl above all price, for it was given to us in holy Baptism. But we can lose it; and the devil – who was the first to lose it, and with it heaven – has sworn to snatch it from us. Rage and envy are continually suggesting to him new methods of taking us by surprise. We ought, then, to be very prudent, and distrustful of ourselves. Are we so? We can also embellish this pearl, we can increase in charity. We have no lack of means for doing so. We know them, but how do we make use of them?

Affections and Resolutions.

Point II: Parable of the net cast into the sea

Consideration: "The kingdom of heaven is like to a net cast into the sea, and gathering together of all kinds of fishes, which, when it was filled, they drew out, and sitting by the shore, they chose out the good into vessels, but the bad they cast forth. So shall it be at the end of the world. The angels shall go out, and shall separate the wicked from among the just, and shall cast them into the furnace of fire." This net means, of course, the Church, which, being spread over the whole world, receives and contains within her bosom the just and sinners, the elect and the condemned.

Application: You may see also under the figure of the *net*, the order or institute to which you belong. Many subjects enter it, and form a large body; but are all good who belong to it? Are they what they ought to be by virtue of their vows, and the strict obligation they have contracted? Alas, among them can be found the wicked and hypocrites. But the day of manifestation and of separation will come for them as for all impenitent sinners; how terrible, then, will be their shame, and their eternal despair!

Affections and Resolutions.

Point III: Parable of the householder

Consideration: Our Lord asked His disciples, "Have ye understood all these things? They say to Him, Yes." Then, desiring to make them understand by another parable the use they ought to make of the treasures of light with which He was enriching them, He added, "Therefore every scribe instructed in the kingdom of heaven is like to a man that is a householder, who bringeth forth out of his treasure new things and old," and he gives them to his children according to their needs.

Application: This is a command to those who have to instruct, it matters not what class of persons not to content themselves with repeating precisely the same things, but to study constantly either to acquire fresh knowledge, or to be able to set forth the truths unchangeable in their nature under new, more attractives, and striking forms, or to find new methods of exciting and keeping up emulation among young people if we are called upon to direct them. How do you act? With what perseverance and success?

Colloquy.

August 7: Jesus admired, but ill-treated, in His Country

1st prelude: Behold Jesus speaking to His fellow citizens in the synagogue of Nazareth.
2nd prelude: Beg for grace to draw great fruit from this meditation.

Point I: Jesus admired at Nazareth

Consideration: After having given the parables we have been meditating on, Jesus, says the Evangelist, "came to Nazareth, where He was brought up. And when the sabbath was come, He began to teach in the synagogue; and many hearing Him were in admiration at His doctrine, saying, How came this man by all these things? And what wisdom is this that is given to Him, and such mighty works as are wrought by His hands?"

Application: Why did our Lord, after an absence of two years, spend some days at Nazareth? Did He wish to enjoy rest in the midst of acquaintances and friends, or to gain their applause? No; it was to give them a mark of His affection, to do them service, and to sanctify them. We learn from this that we are not forbidden to love our country, our countrymen, or our friends, or even to visit them, in the exercise of our ministry; but that it should be always done in a way worthy of a religious, so as to edify them, to glorify God, to do good to souls; never for motives of sensuality or vanity. What has been your way of thinking and acting in this matter? Affections and Resolutions.

Point II: Jesus despised at Nazareth

Consideration: The Nazarenes began by receiving our Lord well; but their feelings soon changed to jealousy. They thought that His great renown threw them into the shade. Envy led them to despise Him. Then they took scandal, and ended in disbelief. "Is not this the carpenter, the son of Mary, the son of Joseph, the brother of James, and Joseph, and Jude, and Simon? Whence, therefore, hath He all these things? And they were scandalized in regard of Him." As if He had usurped the title of teacher in Israel, or because His family were lowly they needed not to believe in Him.

Application: Here we have an example of the fatal effects of envy. The envious cannot bear to see others above them in learning, in merit, in success, or credit with others, especially if they are inferior to them in birth or younger in age. They are ingenious in finding out their faults, either real or imaginary; and very often they make out that the good they do and the praise they receive is a crime. We see this hideous passion of envy very plainly in the Nazarenes. We blame them for it; but let us search the depths of our own hearts, question our own conduct without hiding anything from ourselves, and we shall probably find enough to make us blush for ourselves, enough to make us dread for ourselves the consequences of envy.

Affections and Resolutions.

Point III: Jesus ill-treated at Nazareth

Consideration: The Nazarenes, thinking Jesus to be like other men, expected that His answer to their reproach to His humble birth would have been to work many miracles among them; but they were unworthy of such a favor, and our Lord told them so in these words: "Doubtless you will say to me this similitude, Physician, heal thyself; as great things as we have heard done in Capharnaum, do also here in thy own country. And He said, Amen, I say to you, that no prophet is accepted in his own country." And, says Saint Luke, "all they in the synagogue, hearing these things, were filled with anger. And they rose up and thrust Him out of the city; and they brought Him to the brow of the hill whereon their city was built, that they might cast Him down headlong."

Application: We see to what terrible lengths uncontrolled passions can lead us. Let us look into ourselves and see if there be any dangerous passion which we are hiding form ourselves; and, profiting by the proverb quoted by our Lord, "Physician, heal thyself," let us strive earnestly to fight against it. God will help us, and we shall soon subdue it.

Colloquy.

August 8: Mission of the twelve Apostles

1st prelude: Behold Jesus surrounded by His twelve Apostles at the moment when He sends them to preach in different parts of Galilee.

2nd prelude: Beg the grace of really understanding the conduct of our Lord in this action.

Point I: Mission of the Apostles

Consideration: Our Lord left Nazareth by a miracle, chained down the arms which were raised against Him, and went to teach in the surrounding country. And seeing the multitudes, "He had compassion on them," says the Evangelist, "because they were distressed, and lying like sheep that had no shepherd. Then He saith to His disciples, The harvest indeed is great but the laborers are few. Pray ye therefore the Lord of the harvest, that He send forth laborers into His harvest." Having thus inflamed their zeal, He put them to the trial, sending them forth two and two in diverse directions to preach the *kingdom of God* to those who could not come to hear it for themselves.

Application: Let us take notice of our Lord's conduct towards His disciples; it has formed the rule of all founders of religious orders. First He prepared them for the apostolic life by forming them to solid virtues, and inflaming them with zeal; then He teaches them how to practice it by His words and example. It is like a first novitiate; He made them follow a second one by giving them an easy mission; and He took care they should go two together, thus establishing that wise rule of a companion, so that each may be to the other a sort of angel guardian, a counsel in doubt, and a support in trouble. Do you value as you ought this plan of action, so well adapted to our nature and our weakness? Affections and Resolutions.

Point II: Powers and instructions given to the Apostles

Consideration: Before the Apostles set forth, Jesus, says Saint Luke, "gave them power over all devils, and of curing diseases and infirmities." Then He gave them His instructions: "Take nothing for your journey, neither staff nor scrip, nor bread nor money; neither have two coats; for he workman is worthy of his meat. Freely ye have received, freely give. And in whatsoever town or city you enter, inquire who in it is worthy, and there abide till you go thence. And whosoever shall not receive you, nor hear your words, going forth out of that house or city, shake the dust from your feet for a testimony to them."

Application: We learn from this what the spirit is which He wishes His missionaries to be filled with – the spirit of confidence in Him, who always proportions His commands to the means for executing them; the spirit of entire disinterestedness; the spirit of perfect trust in Providence, who will never let really disinterested laborers want any necessary; the spirit of mortification and indifference, which is contented with the hospitality provided by Providence, and does not desire to gratify any sensuality or vanity; finally, the spirit of gentleness towards the ungrateful and obstinate. Such is the spirit which should animate us. Are we possessed by it? What efforts do we make to perfect it in us? Affections and Resolutions.

Point III: Success and return of the Apostles

Consideration: "And going out, they went about through the towns preaching the gospel, and healing everywhere. And they cast out many devils, and anointed with oil many that were sick, and healed them. And the Apostles, coming together unto Jesus, related to Him all things that they had done and taught; and He said to them, Come apart into a desert place, and rest a little."

Application: Here, again, are beautiful instructions for the religious who have to spend a longer or shorter time out of the community, whether in the exercise of their sacred ministry, or upon business, or to nurse the sick, or for any other reason. On their return, they should faithfully observe two things: first, they should give their superior an *exact* account of all that they have done, and of all that has happened to them; then they should follow our Lord's counsel, recollect themselves and renew their fervor by retirement and prayer. How have you done both these things? Colloquy with Jesus Christ.

August 9: Jesus strengthens the Apostles against Persecutions

1st prelude: Behold Jesus in the midst of the twelve Apostles who have returned from their mission.
2nd prelude: Beg for the heart of a true Apostle of Jesus Christ. The Apostles are forewarned and strengthened against the persecutions which await them.

Point I: By our Lord's predictions

Consideration: During the weeks that the Apostles spent on their mission they had met neither with contradictions or ill-treatment. They might have thought it would be so always, and this would have been a fatal error. Therefore their Divine Master undeceived them by predicting that the great mission which should hereafter be given to them would be a very different one, and that their position in the midst of pagan nations would be like that of sheep without defense against wolves. "Behold, I send you as sheep in the midst of wolves." What an image! What an idea it must have given the Apostles of the terrible battles they would have to undergo!

Application: The forewarnings of these trials greatly strengthened the faith and courage of the Apostles and first Christians in the future; nothing surprised or overcame them. And we who are disciples and apostles of Jesus Christ should remember that crosses of all kinds are to be our portion in this world, and that when they fall on us we should be neither astonished nor cast down. We ought to be more surprised that we are not called to bear harder trials, to fight greater battles, more worthy of a soldier of Jesus Christ. Have you thought and reasoned thus?

Affections and Resolutions.

Point II: By the martyrdom of Saint John Baptist

Consideration: The martyrdom of Saint John Baptist, which took place during the Apostles' mission, served to confirm the idea that our Lord had given them of the fate which awaited them. The life of the holy precursor had been a continual apostolate, distinguished by the purest and most disinterested zeal that could be imagined. The Apostles had witnessed this; they had heard him praised by our Lord, and now they knew that John had fallen a victim to his zeal; that Herod had sacrificed him to the vengeance of a shameless woman; that after he had been kept a year and a half in chains he had been beheaded, while the Divine Master made no opposition. It was sufficient to make them understand what He had said to them before: "Blessed are those who suffer persecution, because theirs is the kingdom of heaven."

Application: While we remember the glorious martyrdom of Saint John the Baptist, we should renew the resolution of braving the fear of men in the zealous accomplishment of our duties. Let us give ourselves up again without reserve into the hands of God, and He will draw good out of the evil they may do us. The cruel suffering inflicted on Saint John won for him the martyr's crown and the glory of being the precursor of the Messiah in limbo, as he had been on earth.

Affections and Resolutions.

Point III: By the example of Jesus Christ Himself

Consideration: Let us now consider the encouragement that Jesus gave His disciples. He assures them "that every hair of their heads is numbered, that men can kill the body only, and that he that loseth his life for God shall find it again glorified in heaven. But more than all else was the encouragement of His own example: "If they have persecuted Me, they will also persecute you." "The disciple is not above the master, nor the servant above his lord." What greater encouragement could our Lord give to His Apostles, and to ourselves especially, when this likeness between the servant and his lord is to extend to the next world, as He assures us in another place: "And I dispose unto you, as My Father hath disposed to Me, a kingdom"! If we have these consoling thoughts always before our minds, far from flying from crosses, says the author of the *Imitation*, we shall desire them.
Colloquy with Jesus.

August 10: On the Spirit which should animate us in the Exercise of our Zeal

1st prelude: Imagine you hear the Apostle saying, "God has made us fit ministers of the New Testament, not in the letter, but in the spirit."
2nd prelude: Beg the grace of acquiring a high degree of the spirit which should animate our zeal.

Point I: The spirit of poverty and humility

Consideration: In the preceding meditation we found wonderful encouragements for the exercise of zeal, let it cost us what it may. Let us try now to understand well which is the spirit that should animate our zeal and render it fruitful. It is no other than the spirit of our vocation. The more we excel in it, the more successful and pleasing to God will our zeal be. The first thing necessary for a religious is the spirit of poverty, of an entire detachment from the world and from himself. This should be also the spirit of an apostolic man. "Freely ye have received," says Jesus Christ, "freely give." Men desire that in laboring for them we should act only from supernatural motives, and have nothing but the good of their souls in view. If they believe only that we are guided or influenced by vainglory, this will withdraw their confidence and separate them from us; how much more if we justify their suspicion!

Application: When you are nursing the sick, have you a temporal advantage chiefly in view? Have worldly calculations any weight with you in exercising your sacred ministry? Is it not entirely or partly vainglory rather than the glory of God which stimulates you in study, in teaching, in preaching? Be persuaded that it is thus if it pains you when others succeed better than yourself, or when you are employed in matters the world thinks little of, or when you are passed by unnoticed, etc. This matter is worthy of a serious examination, and the more so because self-love is apt to take us by surprise in it, and should therefore be feared.

Affections and Resolutions.

Point II: The spirit of obedience and indifference

Consideration: As religious we ought not only to be detached from the world and its vanities, but also from our own will; we should try to excel in the spirit of obedience. This is the spirit which should distinguish an apostolic man. Our mission comes to us from God through our superior; it is He who has to assign to us the portion of the vineyard which He wishes us to cultivate; it is He who says, "*Ite in vineam meam.*" You will go thither; you will do this; and you will do it in such a manner. The religious who rebels against this order of things, and does what he pleases, deprives himself of an especial help from Providence, and of all consolation in adversity; he runs the risk of laboring without success and without much merit.

Application: Will not all these grievous consequences follow you if you deceive your superiors, or if you morally force them in their arrangements for works of zeal? Can you then say confidently, "I am doing the work that God has given to me under obedience, and I am doing it in the way that He wishes I should do it?" Oh, how many there will be some day who will repent of having been victims of these sad delusions! Act in such a way that you may not be among the number.

Affections and Resolutions.

Point III: The spirit of mortification and sacrifice

Consideration: As religious we ought to excel also in the spirit of mortification and sacrifice; and the exercise of zeal requires it. Great patience, courage and generosity are necessary in the case of sick people, teaching classes, general surveillance, and all that education demands, and also in assiduity by day and night in the confessional, preaching, and direction of souls.

Application: Happy is the religious who from his novitiate devotes himself to the acquisition of the spirit of mortification; his zeal will be ardent, ingenious, persevering, and even heroic if need be. How many souls he will save! Miserable, on the other hand, is he who has not learnt to mortify himself and sacrifice himself; his zeal will be weak and languishing, and there is great fear that many souls will perish eternally from his fault. Which of these religious do you resemble?

Colloquy.

August 11: Continuation of the subject: On the Spirit which should animate us in the Exercise of our Zeal

1st prelude: Imagine you hear the Apostle saying, "God has made us fit ministers of the New Testament, not in the letter, but in the spirit."

2nd prelude: Beg the grace of acquiring a high degree of the spirit which should animate our zeal.

Point I: The spirit of purity and sanctity

Consideration: The end of this meditation, like the preceding one, is to convince us that the more we excel in the spirit of our holy vocation, we shall excel in zeal, because it is that spirit which attaches to it success. This thought ought to stimulate us to attain it in perfection. The state of grace, purity of conscience, sanctity, is what our vocation demands from us; and by the spirit of purity we shall please God. "Be clean." "You shall be holy, because I am holy." And also, by avoiding sin, by being always united to God by sanctifying grace or charity, we shall draw God's blessing down on our works of zeal, and may hope to see them fully succeed, and produce abundant and lasting fruit. Our Lord assures us of it: "He that abideth in Me and I in him, the same beareth much fruit." On the other hand, the Apostle cries out, "If I have not charity, I am become as sounding brass." I may raise my voice, I may entertain my audience; but I shall not convert anyone.

Application: If then you wish that your zeal should be blessed by God, you ought not only to keep yourself in the state of grace, you ought also to strive after great purity of conscience and sanctity. What efforts are you making to attain this end? What horror have you of the slightest faults? What means do you take to avoid them? With what earnestness do you purify yourself in the Sacrament of Penance?

Affections and Resolutions.

Point II: The spirit of charity and gentleness

Consideration: A tender and compassionate charity, together with great meekness, the fruit of humility, is certainly the spirit of our Divine Master and model. "Love one another, as I have loved you." And again, "Learn of Me; for I am meek and humble of heart." Such is the spirit which should distinguish those who profess to follow closely in the footsteps of Jesus, and especially those who profess to follow Him in the path of zeal. He desires that our charity should be absolutely free from all rancor or revenge: "Pray for them that persecute you; do good to them that hate you and calumniate you." He desires that our meekness should be without disguise, like that of sheep and doves: "I send you as sheep among wolves." "Be simple as doves." By following these precepts of our Lord and His wonderful example, the Apostles and their successors converted the world and changed wolves into lambs.

Application: By charity and gentleness we shall succeed in the efforts we make for the conversion and sanctification of souls. The ardour of our zeal must be tempered by charity, patience, and gentleness. Rudeness and harshness of speech exasperate people and close their hearts against us; charity and gentleness open their hearts and give us the mastery over them. Has not experience taught you this?

Affections and Resolutions.

Point III: The spirit of piety and prayer

Consideration: Without a tender and solid piety, without the habit and spirit of prayer, we shall never be religious, save in name; we shall be incapable of that virtue which both God and man demand from us. Still more shall we be incapable of producing fruit in souls. The success of our zeal must come from God: without grace our efforts will be useless. "Neither he that planteth is anything, nor he that watereth; but God that giveth the increase."

Application: You complain that your zealous efforts only meet

with indifference and insensibility; but is not the fault your own? Souls are gained, say the saints, at the price of blood, because the blood of God has flowed for them – *Sanguine emendae sunt animae.* What extraordinary means do you use? How many mortifications and penances, how many prayers and novenas, do you offer for this intention? Perhaps you are contented with purely human means, and therefore what success can you expect? Be a man of God – *homo Dei* – a man of prayer and mortification, and all will yield to your zeal.
Colloquy.

August 12: Feast of Saint Clare, Foundress of the Order of Poor Clares

Born 1193; died 1253; canonized 1255.

1st prelude: Behold the saint in glory, surrounded by a vast number of children whom she has led to heaven.
2nd prelude: Beg of her to obtain for you the spirit of your holy vocation.

Point I: Saint Clare's spirit of generosity

Consideration: God called Clare to spread and perpetuate among women the spirit and austere rule of Saint Francis, her fellow citizen. Her parents, who were of the highest rank in Assisi, wished to keep her in the world; but the saint, at the age of eighteen, fled from her father's house, had her long hair cut off, and was clothed in the habit of penance by Saint Francis in the convent of Portiuncula. God rewarded this great generosity. He sent Clare a great number of companions, who formed the nucleus of the new order of which she was elected first Abbess (1212). After the example of their foundress, they all practiced austerities till then unknown among women: they went barefoot, slept on boards, kept perpetual abstinence, fasted a great part of the year, abstaining then even from milk, eggs and fish; they wore a rough hair shirt, and rose in the night to chant the Divine Office together. The saint found means of practicing still greater severities. (It is an astonishing thing that after seven centuries have gone by, we see the daughters of Saint Clare living in a number of towns and persevering even in our days in all these austerities in spite of the weak health and the prejudices that now exist.)

Application: Of what is not generosity capable? It knows neither obstacles nor impossibilities. How mortified we should be, and what great progress we should make in virtue, if we were animated by it as Saint Clare was!
Affections and Resolutions.

Part II: Saint Clare's spirit of poverty

Consideration: Saint Clare's esteem for poverty was astonishing. She chose for herself the worst and meanest things in the house; she laid down in her Constitutions that the life was to be a common one; that no sister – not even the superioress – was to possess anything of her own; and that the community were to have no endowments, but always subsist by their labor and the alms of the faithful. She firmly resisted Popes Gregory IX and Innocent IV, who wished her houses to have fixed revenues like those of other religious. (Later on, some of these houses accepted endowments with the permission of Pope Urban IV. They were henceforth called Urbanists, or *Rich Clares*. They have never prospered as the *Poor Clares* have done.) When people said her poverty was exaggerated, she replied that Jesus Christ had understood and practiced it in this manner, and that, if observed in this way, it would preserve her convents from relaxation, a worldly spirit, divisions and views of personal interest.

Application: Take into serious consideration the motives that the saint gave for her great esteem of evangelical poverty, and you will esteem and love it as she did; and far from finding its observances too severe, you will continue to preserve it by your example, and to transmit it intact to those who come after you. How far have you contributed to this up to the present time?
Affections and Resolutions.

Point III: Saint Clare's spirit of piety

Consideration: Saint Clare found consolation and strength in religious duties, in frequent communion, and in mental and vocal prayer, to which she gave a great part of the night. By her prayers she miraculously preserved her convent from the invasion of the Saracens and the town of Assisi from great misery. She was so humble and grateful that she looked on herself as a debtor to her fellow citizens, from whom she and her community received their daily subsistence. She made it a rule to pray much for them.

Application: We should also pray much for our benefactors,

and try to make people of the world understand how much they owe to those holy beings who, hidden in their cloisters, raise their suppliant hands to heaven for them, and turn aside the punishments they have deserved by their sins.
Colloquy.

August 13: Miracle of the Multiplication of the Loaves

1st prelude: Behold the Apostles distributing the miraculous bread to the multitude.
2nd prelude: Beg for redoubled love and devotion to Jesus Christ.

Point I: Occasion of the miracle

Consideration: The desert place where Jesus had led His Apostles on their return from their mission was soon besieged by an immense crowd of people. "Jesus had compassion on them, and from a rising ground, where He stood with the twelve, He spoke of the *kingdom of God*." The time went on, the day declined, and still the crowd remained motionless, hanging on the words of Jesus. The Apostles said to Him, "This is a desert place, and the hour is now past; send away the multitudes, that going into the towns they may buy themselves victuals. But Jesus said to them, They have no need to go; give you them to eat." It was evident that, in spite of their want of faith, He was about to work a miracle.

Application: After the example of these good Israelites, let us seek, according to the Lord's precept, "the kingdom of heaven and His justice" before all other things. Have we not to reproach ourselves with being more occupied with our bodily wants, our health and our comforts, than with the means of glorifying God, and of increasing in virtue and sanctity? Alas, many religious have to reproach themselves with it; and the knowledge of it causes their want of confidence in God when human means fail them. Have you not experienced this?
Affections and Resolutions.

Point II: Greatness of the miracle

Consideration: "Jesus saith to Philip, to try him, Whence shall we buy bread, that these may eat? Philip answered Him, Two hundred pennyworth of bread is not sufficient for them, that every one may take a little. Now there were about five thousand men, besides women and children. Andrew, brother of Simon Peter, saith to Him, there is a boy here that hath five barley loves and two fishes; but what are these among so many? And He said to His disciples, Make them sit down by fifties in a company. And taking the five loaves and two fishes He broke and distributed to His disciples to set before the multitude. And they did all eat and were filled. And there were taken up of the fragments that remained twelve baskets."

Application: Five thousand persons fed and satisfied with five loaves and two fishes; what a wonderful miracle! "Would that I could have witnessed it!" you say involuntarily. But, says Saint Augustine (Tract 24, *in Joan.*), you witness a similar one when you see that from some seeds sown in the ground every year God feeds millions of men.

Affections and Resolutions.

Point III: Effects of the miracle

Consideration: They were instantaneous, for all the people cried out, "This is of a truth that Prophet that is to come into the world!" Strengthened in their faith, their love and devotion for our Lord increased; they wanted to "take Him by force and make Him a king"; but "Jesus fled again into the mountain Himself alone."

Application: When we visit Jesus Christ on our altar, and especially when we receive Him in Holy Communion, of which the multiplication of the loaves was a type, let us imitate these pious Israelites and reawaken in our hearts the feelings of love, faith, devotion and gratitude that Jesus loves so much to see in us.

Colloquy.

August 14: Eve of Our Lady's Assumption

1st prelude: Behold the Apostles surrounding the deathbed of our Lady.

2nd prelude: Pray for the grace of a happy and holy death.

It was the will of God that the humiliation of death should precede the glory of Mary's assumption, so that she might be made in all things like her Divine Son. Let us occupy our thoughts today, then, with her death. It was real, though exempted from all suffering.

Point I: It was free from regrets

Consideration: Saint Alphonsus tells us that it is generally three things which make death painful to us; the first is, attachment to earthly possessions. "O death," says Ecclesiasticus, "how bitter is the remembrance of thee to a man that hath peace in his possessions!" He has laid up these possessions with much labor for many years, and he is to be separated from them with bitter and useless regret. There was nothing of this with Mary. From the age of three years she made the sacrifice of parents, of friends, and of all the world could offer her, and all her affections were fixed on God. She had nothing to regret on earth. Her only desire was to leave it, that she might fly to heaven and be there eternally united to the only object of her love – Jesus.

Application: By the vow of poverty, and by renouncing all the affections of flesh and blood, you have broken the ties which bind you to earth; you can leave it without sorrow or regret. If you are faithful to your vocation till the end, your death will be but an easy passage from earth to your home.

Affections and Resolutions.

Point II: It was free from remorse

Consideration: One of the most ordinary sufferings of death is the remorse which the heart of the dying person feels at the thought of his sins, and of God's justice. But remorse could find no place in the heart of our Lady, the purest of creatures. In all her long life there had not been a shadow of sin, but an uninterrupted series of heroic acts of virtue, which seemed to say to her, "We are your works; we will not leave you alone; we will go with you to the throne of God to add lustre to your triumph."

Application: Endeavor to efface the last traces of your past sins by penance; redouble your vigilance over yourself, that you many not commit them again; and then, far from experiencing remorse at the hour of death, you will be full of confidence and joy in the blessed expectation of an eternal reward.

Affections and Resolutions.

Point III: It was free from fear

Consideration: "Often," says Saint Bernardine of Siena, "when thinking of those words of the Holy Ghost, 'Man knoweth not whether he be worthy of love or hatred,' I have trembled from head to foot, and been in a kind of agony." The uncertainty about eternal salvation is the third and the greatest thing which fills the dying with fear and anguish, and not without cause. But what reason for fear could the Mother of God have, who saw the throne of glory prepared for her in heaven by the side of her Divine Son? She longed, therefore, for the moment which should break the bonds that bound her to earth.

Application: You have had no revelation about your salvation, and often doubts and fears harass and trouble your soul; but, on the other hand, what sure grounds of confidence you possess! First, the words of Jesus Christ: "Every one that hath left house, or lands, or brethren, for My name's sake, shall possess everlasting life." Then there is the saying of the Fathers: "A servant of Mary shall never perish." Expand your heart, then, with entire confidence; your Mother will give you an hundredfold. She will assist you in your last moment, as she did visibly Saint Stanislaus Kostka, who died saying that he saw our Lady coming to him. Today, then, the eve of the most solemn of her feasts, prepare yourself by holy affections and ardent desires to celebrate this feast worthily, so that you may obtain a large share in the favors which she delights to pour on her devoted children on the anniversary of her Coronation. Colloquy.

August 15: Feast of Our Lady's Assumption

1st prelude: Behold Mary carried by angels to the highest heaven.
2nd prelude: Beg the grace of worthily celebrating the great feast of today.

Point I: Resurrection of Mary

Consideration: Our Lady's death was a privileged one, and so was her resurrection. Saint John Damascene relates it from tradition, and the revelations of Saint Bridget confirm it. The Apostles were miraculously brought to Jerusalem at the time of our Lady's death, and they buried her body in Gethsemani, in a new sepulchre. Saint Thomas arrived afterwards, and at his entreaty the Apostles opened the grace, and found nothing there but the winding-sheet and lilies, from whence they concluded that Jesus, desiring not to tarry in glorifying His Mother, had raised her up, and brought her by angel hands to be associated in body and soul with Him in heavenly glory and felicity. The Church has adopted this belief, and made it an article of faith.

Application: Let us rejoice in the glorious resurrection of our dearest Mother. Let us rejoice in union with the angels, with the

Church, and with all her devout children. Let us rejoice, also, for ourselves at the thought of our own joyful resurrection. It is true it will not immediately follow our death; but it is not less certain, and if we choose, it will not be less glorious.

Affections and Resolutions.

Point II: Assumption of Mary

Consideration: *Assumpta est Maria in caelum* – "Mary is assumed into heaven." Let us hear and meditate on what Saint Anselm and Saint Bernard say of this great mystery. They tell us of the legions of angels who came down from heaven and bowed low before the Virgin Mother, then reverently raised her into the heavenly regions. They tell us that millions of the blessed in Paradise went out to meet her, and cried out, astonished at her divine beauty, *Quae est ista que ascendit de deserto, deliciis affluens?* – "Who is this that cometh up from the desert flowing with delights?" They tell us that Mary triumphantly entered heaven, was received and conducted by her Divine Son to the throne of the Eternal Father, in the midst of the acclamations of angels and saints: "Hosanna, glory and honor to the daughter of David! Blessed is she that cometh to us like a queen, in the name of the Lord!"

Application: The honors and joys of a mother are also those of her children. Let us, then, be filled with holy joy on this anniversary of the assumption of our beloved Mother, and of her glorious entrance into heaven; let us remember that she was raised so high because she was the humblest of creatures, and that she enjoys all this felicity because she was the *queen of martyrs*.

Affections and Resolutions.

Point III: Coronation of Mary

Consideration: The coronation of Mary, as queen of heaven and earth, is the completion of the glorious mystery of this day. Try to gain an idea of it. Imagine you see the Virgin Mother at the feet of the Eternal Father, who places the crown on her head, the scepter in her hand, and proclaims her queen of angels and of men, dispenser of His grace, mother of mercy. Fancy you hear the joyful cries of the inhabitants of heaven, Hosanna, glory and honor to our queen! Hail, holy queen, mother of mercy! Reign over us, thou and thy Divine Son!

Application: Let us united ourselves in heart and mind with the

inhabitants of the Church triumphant; let us repeat with holy enthusiasm these same expressions of joy and jubilation, the same declarations of love and devotion. Then, reflecting that she is nearest to Jesus in glory because she followed Him the most closely on the day of His Passion, let us offer ourselves to bear our cross generously with Jesus, to carry it even to the heights of Calvary, and to die with Jesus on the cross.
Colloquy.

August 16: The Night that followed the Miracle of the Loaves

1st prelude: Behold the Apostles struggling against the tempest on the sea of Galilee.
2nd prelude: Beg for confidence in God, and perseverance under all the trials of life.

Point I: The great fatigue of the Apostles

Consideration: The day which was closed by the miracle of multiplying the loaves was a very fatiguing one for Our Lord and His Apostles; from early morning till late at night they had not a minute's rest. And not even was night to bring it them. No sooner had the Apostles fed the five thousand guests and gathered the fragments of the repast than our Lord "immediately obliged His disciples," says the Evangelist, "to go up into the ship that they might go before Him over the water to Bethsaida." He did this that they should not be influenced by the people who wanted to proclaim Him king of Israel. He Himself "fled again into the mountain to pray"; and there, after that tiring day, He passed the night in vigil.

Application: The kind of life to which it has pleased God to call us requires much labor and constant fatigue. In truth, the rule tempers this very wisely; but how often it happens that, in consequence of unforeseen circumstances, we must watch and labor at night after working hard all day! How does the lukewarm religious act then? He complains and murmurs, or at least tries to make up for it by idle condolences or human consolations. The humble and fervent religious, on the contrary, thinks he is only doing his duty; that what he does is very little in comparison to what the saints have done, and what worldly people do for interest or for vanity. He delights in leaving one labor for another, and

when necessary, his very exhaustion is the means of his finding fresh strength. Which of these two do you resemble?
Affections and Resolutions.

Point II: The painful night spent by the Apostles struggling against the storm

Consideration: Though the Apostles had put to sea by the express orders of Jesus, they met with contrary winds. In vain did they try to coast along the shore till they reached the port of Bethsaida; they were always driven back. They continued then to struggle till after midnight, "when the sea arose by reason of a great wind that blew, and the ship was tossed by the waves." What did our Lord do? He saw their fatigue and suffering. He saw them "laboring in rowing," and He watched over their safety. But He delayed coming visibly to their succor and causing the storm to cease. Why did He act thus? Saint John Chrysostom tells us it was "to train them to increase their faith, humility and confidence, and that they might have a keener sense of the blessing of divine help."

Application: Thus does God act towards us, and for the same ends. At times He allows that in fulfilling certain duties of our office, or in the execution of enterprises undertaken under obedience and with the best intentions, we should meet with contradictions and difficulties, or that we should not have immediate success. Often, also, He allows us to be troubled for a long time by mental sufferings or violent temptations in spite of the means we employ and the prayers we offer up to be delivered. What ought we, then, to do? To take care not to give way to distrust or discouragement, as if God had forsaken us, to be convinced that He sees our sufferings and our labors; that He is near us and sustains us by His grace, and that He *does not ask from us success but fidelity*; and finally, that after having tried us, He will give us at the fitting time the peace and joy of His sensible presence. See whether in these matters you can amend your way of thinking or acting. Make your resolutions.
Colloquy.

August 17: Continuation of The Night that followed the Miracle of the Loaves

1st prelude: Behold Saint Peter walking on the water to meet

Jesus.
2nd prelude: Beg the grace of increasing in the knowledge and love of Jesus Christ.

Point I: Jesus, walking on the water, goes towards the boat of the Apostles

Consideration: When the hour fixed by the divine decree had come, which was to bring help to the Apostles, "about the fourth watch of the night," just at day-break, Jesus, says the Gospel, "came to them, walking upon the sea." They saw Him afar off, not clearly, the darkness of the night not being quite gone; they were troubled, saying, "It is an apparition."

Application: The Apostles were under a great delusion in supposing that the person of Jesus Christ was an apparition; but are not delusions, if not as great, at least more blameable, because they spring from our passions? Do we not sometimes take Jesus Christ, *i.e.*, the lights, the inspirations, the thoughts, or the salutary fear that comes to us from on high, for phantoms and fancies? One the other hand, do we not take the fancies of our imagination, the inordinate desires of our hearts, the longings of our pride, for inspirations? And taking Jesus Christ for a phantom, or a phantom for Jesus Christ, is equally insulting and blameable.
Affections and Resolutions.

Point II: Jesus comforts His terrified Apostles

Consideration: The human figure that the Apostles saw from afar, like an apparition walking in the water, drew nearer, and seemed coming towards them. They were terrified at the sight, and cried out; and immediately He spoke to them, and said, "Be of good heart, it is I; fear ye not."

Application: The Apostles were on the sea by the express command of Jesus; they had therefore a right to count on His help; and it did not fail them. Let us learn from this that in the works of zeal or charity laid on us by obedience, and in which we are often exposed to many temptations and dangers, we may always count on an especial assistance from God. This is very encouraging.
Affections and Resolutions.

Point III: Jesus permits Saint Peter to come to Him, walking on the water

Consideration: As soon as Saint Peter heard the voice of his dearest Master, he said, as if beside himself, "Lord, if it be Thou, bid me come to Thee upon the water; and He said, Come. And Peter going down from the boat, walked upon the water to come to Jesus. But seeing the wind strong, he was afraid; and when he began to sink, he cried out, saying, Lord save me! And immediately Jesus, stretching forth His hand, took hold of him, and said to him, "O thou of little faith, why didst thou doubt? And when they were come up into the boat, the wind ceased," and presently the ship was at the land to which they were going. And, adds Saint Matthew, "they that were in the boat came and adored Him, saying, Indeed Thou art the Son of God."

Affections: This passage of Holy Scripture is full of practical instruction for us. We see the ardent love of Saint Peter, impatient to be with his Divine Master again; we see his lively faith rewarded by a wonderful miracle; and then we see the astonishing inconstancy of that same faith, ready to defy all perils in one moment, and at the next failing because of a gust of wind. On the other hand, we see the wonderful goodness of Jesus Christ: He puts forth His hand to His disciple and raises him up, while He says to him words which humble and encourage him at the same time: "O thou of little faith, why didst thou doubt?" What faith have we, or what love?

Colloquy.

August 18: Faith of the Genesarenes: Miraculous Cures

1st prelude: Behold Jesus in the midst of sick people, who are trying to touch the hem of His garment.

2nd prelude: Beg the grace of real admiration for their faith.

Point I: Prompt and lively faith of the Genesarenes

Consideration: The boat which carried Jesus and His Apostles came ashore in the morning at the country of Genesar, or Genesareth. Already the fame of the miracle of the multiplication of the loaves wrought the day before had been spread around during the night by witnesses of it coming from the other side of the lake or sea of Galilee. As soon, therefore, as the Genesarenes, who were simple, truthful men, heard that Jesus had arrived, they ran to Him from all parts with a lively faith, and recognized Him as the great Prophet, the Ambassador of God, their Messiah. Every heart inclined towards Him; Jesus was as in the midst of His children.

Application: If our faith was more ardent, our hearts, too, would incline also, and even fly towards Jesus the moment we enter the holy place where He dwells; when at the voice of the priest He comes down upon the altar; when, to pour His blessings on us, He comes out of His Tabernacle, shows Himself to us, unveils to us His Heart burning with love, and says to us, "Come to Me, all you that labor and are burdened, and I will refresh you."

Affections and Resolutions.

Point II: The faith of the Genesarenes was an active and charitable one

Consideration: "Faith worketh by charity," says the Apostle. It manifested itself by charity among those of the good Genesarenes who first had the happiness of recognizing the Saviour. They were anxious that others should share their happiness, and, running through that whole country, they began to carry about in beds those who were sick.

Application: This charity for the sick was very praiseworthy, and touched the compassionate Heart of our Divine Lord. Ah, would that we had the same zeal for our brethren's salvation! Would that we profited by all the occasions which so often present themselves, of making them think of their own souls, showing them their spiritual maladies, and persuading them to come to Him who can cure them! This would by charity indeed to them, and very meritorious for us; in future let it be thus.

Affections and Resolutions.

Point III: The faith of the Genesarenes was full of confidence and respect

Consideration: The faith of the Genesarenes was rewarded by a number of miraculous cures. Saint Mark tells us whithersoever He entered "on His way to Capharnaum, into towns, or into villages or cities, they laid the sick in the streets, and besought Him that they might touch the hem of His garment; and as many as touched Him were made whole."

Application: Let us remark the extreme goodness, condescension, and patience of the Savior, our divine model. He suffers Himself to be approached, touched, and pressed upon by a crowd of sick people, blind, lame, and suffering from every kind of disease, who contended which should touch Him first and obtain

relief; and He never complained; He showed neither emotion nor impatience. Try to form yourself on this admirable model. Remark, also, that the condition to which our Lord had this time attached a cure was the touching of His garment. Interpreters tell us that He did this to make us understand what signal graces and favors are attached to the immediate contact with His Body in Holy Communion, of which He was going to speak that very same day in the synagogue of Capharnaum.
Colloquy.

August 19: The Lord's Discourse about the future Institution of the Eucharist

1st prelude: Behold Jesus teaching in the synagogue of Capharnaum.
2nd prelude: Beg from Him a docile mind and devoted heart.
Point I: Reproach that Jesus addressed to the men of Capharnaum

Consideration: Jesus, after having spent the whole day in travelling through the country of Genesar curing the sick, came towards evening on the sabbath to Capharnaum, and without taking any rest went to the synagogue. He found a numerous assembly there; the greater part of those who, on the day before, had been fed and satisfied with the miraculous bread. Their eagerness to see Jesus again, however praiseworthy in itself, had not merit, and was even worthy of blame because they were only actuated by a purely material and sensual motive, as we learn from our Lord's reproof: "Amen, amen I say to you; you seek Me, not because you have seen miracles, but because you did eat of the loaves and were filled."

Application: Have you not often lost the merit of your good works from interested motives? Your *eager* willingness to go to a distance to fulfil some office of your sacred ministry, or to change your residence or office for instance, was not the motive principally that the journey had attractions for you? Or was it not from vainglory or hope of some earthly blessing? That you may judge correctly about it, examine whether you have the same eagerness about those things which flatter your pride or sensuality as for those for which you have a repugnance.
Affections and Resolutions.

Point II: Revelation which our Lord made

Consideration: Jesus, wishing gradually to prepare men's minds to believe the wonderful miracle of the Eucharist, took advantage of this earthly disposition of the people of Capharnaum to tell them of it. He said to them, "Labor not for the meat which perisheth, but for that which endureth to everlasting life, which the Son of Man will give you. I am the living bread which cometh down from heaven. The bread that I will give is My flesh for the life of the world. The Jews therefore strove among themselves, saying, How can this man give us His flesh to eat?" And Jesus, far from denying the sense of the real presence, answered, "Amen, amen I say to you, except you eat the flesh of the Son of Man, and drink His Blood, you shall not have life in you; for My flesh is meat indeed, and My blood is drink indeed. He that eateth My flesh and drinketh My blood, abideth in Me and I in him. Your fathers did eat manna and are dead. He that eateth this bread shall live for ever."

Application: When we consider these wonderful words flowing from the lips, or rather the heart of our loving Saviour, we are drawn to thank Him with our whole hearts; 1st, for having given us all that He could give us, in bestowing himself to be the food of our souls; 2nd, for having taught this extraordinary mystery ins o clear and precise a manner that it is impossible to doubt it; 3rd, for having allowed us to be born in the bosom of the Catholic Church, where we have so often had the happiness of receiving this mysterious food.

Affections and Resolutions.

Point III: The men of Capharnaum are scandalized, and many desert Him. The Apostles are faithful.

Consideration: "Many, therefore, of His disciples," says Saint John, "hearing it, and unable to understand the mystery, said, This saying is hard, and who can hear it? And after this many of His disciples went back and walked no more with Him. Then Jesus said to the twelve, Wilt thou also go away? And Simon Peter answered Him, Lord, to whom shall we go? Thou hast the words of eternal life; and we have believed and have known that Thou art the Christ, the Son of God."

Application: Let us, with Saint Peter, declare our inviolable attachment to the person of our Divine Master. But knowing how

naturally inconstant we are, let us beg and implore Him to help us, to defend us against our own weakness, and against the snare of our enemies.
Colloquy.

August 20: Feast of Saint Bernard, second Founder of the Cistercian Order

1st prelude: Behold the saint in glory.
2nd prelude: Beg that he will obtain for us an ardent desire of perfection.
Born near Dijon 1091; died 1153, at Clairvaux, in the diocese of Langres; canonized 1165. He founded 160 monasteries.

Point I: Life of Saint Bernard in the world

Consideration: Bernard had the happiness of being born of parents who were pious as well as noble. His mother early taught him the love of chastity and a tender devotion to our Lady. Her pains were well rewarded. Bernard, endowed with natural eloquence, together with rare mental powers, made astonishing progress in study. His chastity was heroic; and to punish himself for an imprudent glance, he threw himself into the water during a frost; and as time went on he celebrated the praises of Our Lady with a success that none have ever surpassed. When he was twenty-three, he felt himself called to embrace the rigorous reform of the Cistercians, recently established by Saint Robert of Molesmes. He followed this vocation with such fervor that he not only overcame the opposition of his brothers, but induced them, as well as twenty-five other gentlemen, to follow him. Then all, together making thirty in number, entered Citeaux the same day, and the following year (1114) made their profession into the hands of the Abbot, Saint Stephen.

Application: Look into yourselves, remember the happy circumstances of your parentage, your education, and especially your vocation, and you will see that God has not been less prodigal of His favors to you than towards Saint Bernard.
Affections and Resolutions.

Point II: The saint's life in the solitude of the cloister

Consideration: The marvel of Saint Bernard's cloister life was, that his first fervor never relaxed, and therefore in a few years he became the model of eminent virtue. The mortification of his senses became almost natural to him. After passing a year at Citeaux, he did not know, as some circumstance proved, what kind of ceiling there was to the dormitory, nor how many windows there were in the choir of the church. He was equally mortified in other things; his usual food was brown bread dipped in warm water, and only under obedience was he induced to take sometimes, for the sake of his health, herb-pottage, seasoned with a little oil and honey. Dead to the world and to himself, he had no will or preference of his own, unless it was to undertake the lowest and most unpleasant offices in the community. Prayer was his greatest delight, and the time for it always seemed to him too short. One might say that his prayer was uninterrupted, for he never lost the presence of God even in his intercourse with people of the world; and therefore he possessed an unction which won the hearts of all who came near him. To stimulate his fervor, the saint often said to himself, "Bernard, Bernard, why art thou come hither?"

Application: "Would that I had been," say you, "in my turn, constant in following my first fervor! To what degree of perfection should I not now have attained?" Do not be contented with this barren regret, the past is no longer yours, but redouble your fervor in order to regain what you have lost.

Affections and Resolutions.

Point III: Life of the saint in the midst of the turmoil of business

Consideration: The peace and happiness that Bernard tasted in the solitude of the cloister were unspeakable; often he was heard to cry out, "Oh, happy solitude! Oh, only abode of happiness!" But God allowed this solitude to be often broken. The wisdom of which this saint, when Abbot of Clairvaux, gave so many brilliant proofs, drew the attention of the whole Church on him; kings and princes entreated him to arbitrate in their disputes; the Sovereign Pontiffs obliged him to undertake long and arduous journeys to pacify nations, to direct councils, to put an end to schisms or to preach crusades. In the midst of all these honors, in this turmoil of business, the saint lost none of his humility or of his union with God. Wherever he went he carried his solitude with him, says his biographer. Let us try to do the same.

Colloquy.

August 21: Third Easter and Third Year of the Ministry of Jesus Christ: Hypocrisy and Envy of the Pharisees

1st prelude: Behold Jesus discoursing with the Scribes and Pharisees.
2nd prelude: Beg for a lively horror of hypocrisy, and a great love of solid virtue.

Point I: Jesus dispenses Himself from observing a point of law

Consideration: Jesus, having spent the sabbath at Capharnaum, "walked in Galilee, for He would not walk in Judea, because the Jews sought to kill Him." Our Lord was not going, then, this year to keep the Pasch at Jerusalem. The law, indeed, ordered it; but He had the right of dispensing with His own law, and the plot against His life was a reason for such dispensation.

Application: We ought to learn from this not to judge our superiors when we see them do or omit something contrary to the rule, or some point of discipline. Have they not the right to dispense themselves for good reasons as well as to dispense others? We do not generally know their reasons, they are not obliged to tell us them, and often they cannot. Our Lord also teaches us, by His example, to protect ourselves by flight and other natural means from the persecution of the wicked, from the evil they desire to do us, from their hatred of God. To act otherwise, when there is nothing to prevent us, would be presuming on grace. God gives the grace of martyrdom to whom and when he pleases. It would also be helping an evil by facilitating its execution. Affections and Resolutions.

Point II: Jesus blames the Pharisees for putting vain observances above the law

Consideration: The Jews of Jerusalem, thwarted in their murderous designs, tried at least to lower Jesus in the minds of the people. This is why, as Saint Mark tells us, "Scribes and Pharisees came to Him from Jerusalem"; they came to spy upon Him, to find Him out in some fault; when they had seen some of His disciples eat bread with common, that is, with unwashed hands, they found fault, and asked Him, "Why do not Thy disciples walk according to the tradition of the ancients?" Their words betrayed their hypocrisy and envy; for they knew that the words of Isaias, "Wash yourselves, be clean," were to be taken in a spiritual sense. Our

Lord made them feel it, by saying, "Hypocrites, having the commandment of God, you hold the tradition of men, the washing of pots and cups, and many other things." Then He spoke to the people whom these hypocrites tried to deceive, saying: "Hear ye Me, and understand: not that which goeth into the mouth defileth a man, but what cometh out of the mouth, this defileth a man."

Application: The two great vices of the Scribes and Pharisees were hypocrisy and envy, and we detest them both; but are we entirely free from them? Let us seriously examine our thoughts and our words. What are they in relation to those of our companions, whose merit and success eclipse ours?

Affections and Resolutions.

Point III: Jesus proves that the transgressions of the law come from the heart

Consideration: "And when He was come into the house from the multitude, Peter said to Him, Expound to us this parable. But He said, Are you also yet without understanding? There is nothing from without a man that entering into him can defile him. But the things which proceed from out of the mouth, come forth from the heart, and those things defile a man. For from the heart come forth evil thoughts, murders, adulteries, fornications, thefts, false testimonies, blasphemies. These are the things that defile a man. But to eat with unwashed hands doth not defile a man."

Application: These words clearly prove, 1st, that what God especially asks from us is purity of heart; 2nd, that temptations, thoughts, images, impressions, which come to us from without cannot defile our hearts if we deny them entrance; 3rd, that we ought carefully to watch over the affections of our hearts. How do we act? Is there not something kept back? Is there not in some corner of our heart a little idol, an inordinate affection, whose existence we deceive ourselves about?

Colloquy.

August 22: The Woman of Canaan

1st prelude: Behold the Canaanite at the feet of Jesus.

2nd prelude: Beg for faith and perseverance like hers.

Point I: Wonderful faith and prayer of the woman of Canaan

Consideration: Jesus, proceeding still further from Jerusalem, went northwards towards the extreme limits of Galilee, and from thence into Phenicia, a country partly inhabited by the descendants of the ancient Canaanites. He had not the intention of then evangelizing that strange and idolatrous country. "He entered," says Saint Mark, "into a house in the coasts of Tyre and Sidon, and He would that no man should know it, and He could not be hid"; for a woman who was a gentile (and whom we must suppose was prevented by grace), "as soon as she had heard of Him [and before He had gone into the house], crying out, said to Him, Have mercy on me, O Lord, Thou Son of David; by daughter is grievously troubled by a devil."

Application: Admire the qualities of this woman's prayer, that you may make them your own. 1st, She runs to Jesus without hesitation or delay; 2nd, she draws near Him, animated with a lively faith in His omnipotence as God, and in His compassion as man – *Lord, Son of David*; 3rd, she is full of the idea that she is but a humble suppliant, and feels that she is helpless – "Have mercy on me"; 4th, she has perfect abnegation and resignation, she tells of her daughter's misery, and leaves her entirely to the goodness of Jesus. Is it thus that you draw to God, that you pray?
Affections and Resolutions.

Point II: The persevering faith and prayer of the Canaanite

Consideration: It would seem that our Lord chose, for our instruction, to try the faith and perseverance of this woman severely, and she has been celebrated for it in the whole world. 1st, "He answered her not a word," says the Gospel, as if He did not deign to listen to her; 2nd, when the Apostles pleaded for her, saying, "Send her away, for she crieth after us" (and she will make You known). He answered, "I was not sent but to the sheep that were lost of the house of Israel." It was equivalent to a refusal; but the woman was not rebuffed; she "came into the house, fell down at His feet, and adored Him, saying, Lord, help me: and she besought Him that He would cast forth the devil out of her daughter."

Application: One of the principal reasons why our prayers are not heard is our want of perseverance. We wish to obtain from God some great favor for ourselves or for a friend: we begin a novena for this intention: the first two or three days we faithfully say the prayers we promised: but is it the same on the sixth or seventh? Is it not difficult to keep up our fervor? Does it not happen that after having begged some favor two or three times without obtaining it, we leave off asking, as if we were fearful of importuning our good God? But does not the example of the Canaanite prove that a holy importunity is pleasing to God? What ought we to think of this? Affections and Resolutions.

Point III: The faith and prayer of the Canaanite are victorious

Consideration: The faith and perseverance of the Canaanite had already triumphed over severe trials. Our Lord chose, however, to make her submit to one more before He granted her prayer. He said, "Suffer first the children to be filled: for it is not good to take the bread of the children and cast it to the dogs." But these harsh words did not dismay the suppliant. She answered and said to Him, "Yea, Lord, for the whelps also eat under the table of the crumbs of the children." Our Lord seemed as if He were conquered, and said to her, "O woman, great is thy faith; be it done to thee as thou wilt; and her daughter was cured from that hour."

Application: This daughter, the object of so much care, is, according to Saint Jerome (in Saint Matthew xv), an excellent type of our soul; and the anxiety of the mother the type of that assiduous care we ought to take for that soul, that we may preserve it not only from the possession of the devil, but also from the influence which this wily and malicious spirit tries to exercise upon it. Perhaps you suffer him to do so without knowing it, because you are not sufficiently recollected, nor *vigilant in prayer*. Colloquy.

August 23: The Value of our Souls

1st prelude: Imagine you hear Jesus Christ saying: "What shall a man give in exchange for is soul?"
2nd prelude: Beg the grace of really understanding what is the value of our souls.

Point I: A soul is worth more than the whole world

Consideration: "Nothing is of equal value to a soul, not even the whole world," says Saint John Chrystostom – "*Nihil amimae aequiparari potest, ne universus quidem mundus*." One soul is worth infinitely more than all that this vast universe in its grandeur and beauty can offer our senses, because all of it is material and will be destroyed, while our soul is a spiritual being, immortal and intelligent, and destined for a supernatural life.

Application: From this indisputable truth the doctors of the Church drew and equally indisputable conclusion, *i.e.*, the loss of the whole world is preferable to that of one soul; and yet how many souls are perishing every day and every minute! "I have seen them in a vision," said Saint Teresa, "falling into hell like the leaves fall from the trees in autumn." From that time she redoubled her prayers, her tears and her penances for the conversion of those who were walking in the path of perdition. And I – what pains do I take in saving souls?

Affections and Resolutions.

Point II: Our souls are of greater value than the blood of a God

Consideration: By the rebellion or the sin of the first man our souls fell under the power of the devil, and he was also condemned to eternal death. The God made man, Jesus Christ, only could redeem him, for so He willed it. But what was to be the price of that redemption? "O man," cries Saint Augustine, "will you learn the true value of your soul? See what the Son of God has done for the ransom of your soul, and you will know what it is worth" – *Vide quanto emit, et videbis quid emit (in Ps. xliii)*. And what has been given for it? By what has it been redeemed? "Not with corruptible things, as gold and silver," says Saint Peter; "but with the precious blood of Christ" – *Non corruptibilibus auro vel argento redempti estis, sed pretioso sanguine Christi*. Our Lord, then, who alone can judge things at their true value, did not think it too much to give the last drop of His blood for our souls.

Application: And I – what have I done for my soul? Do I esteem and love it next to God? Do I not think more of my reputation or of my body than my soul? The least imputation troubles and pains me, and yet I do not care for the numberless stains by which venial sin defaces my soul. "I am eager to enrich my mind with knowledge, and I am slow and remiss in adorning my soul with virtues and merits. Under a little suffering, or in a slight bodily indisposition, I send for the doctor or infirmarian, and I have courage, if need be, to submit to painful remedies; but when my soul is wasting away with a disease which may be fatal, I neglect to send for the spiritual physician, or to employ the remedies his experience and zeal suggest to me."

Affections and Resolutions.

Point III: Our souls are, in a certain sense, of greater value than God Himself

Consideration: Why have many saints allowed themselves to use such an expression? 1. Because a soul is a breath of the Divinity; He "breathed into his face the breath of life, and man became a living soul." 2. Because God made it to His own likeness; and it is the living image to God on the earth. 3. Because God-made-man has sacrificed Himself for it: "He offered Himself for me," says the Apostle. 4. Because God will give Himself to the soul as its reward – *Ego sum merces tua magna nimis.*
Colloquy.

August 24: Jesus returns to Galilee, where He cures one born deaf and dumb

1st prelude: Behold the deaf and dumb in a suppliant attitude before Jesus.
2nd prelude: Beg Jesus to preserve us from, or if need be to cure us of, spiritual deafness and dumbness.

Point I: Jesus leaves Phoenicia, and returns to Galilee

Consideration: Saint Mark, after having told us the history of the Canaanite, immediately adds, "And again going out of the coasts of Tyre, He came by Sidon to the sea of Galilee, through the midst of the coasts of Decapolis." No other miracle or conversion is recorded in Phoenicia. We must conclude, then, that our Lord had no other view in going there than to reward this heathen to lead her into the way of salvation, and convert her to the faith of the true God by the miracle wrought upon her daughter; in one word, to save a soul.

Application: Our Divine Lord teaches us by this that we look on the salvation of a single soul as the worthy fruit of a laborious mission. This is a very consoling thought for a Brother of Charity, for instance, who has but one sick person to nurse, for a teacher who has only one pupil to educate, for a missionary who appears to convert but very few sinners. Our Lord teaches us to exercise our zeal and charity equally in a wide or narrow circle; the merit of both consists in obedience. You believe this divine teaching; do you make it the rule of your conduct? By obedience you are sometimes sent to a great and honorable mission, sometimes to a small, insignificant one; for the first you prepare carefully and eagerly, for the other with indifference and uneasiness. Why this contrast? From zeal for God's glory? Not at all; but from your vanity. Examine your conscience, and it will answer you.

Affections and Resolutions

Point II: The Lord cures the deaf mute

Consideration: Jesus had scarcely entered Galilee when "they bring to Him," says the Gospel, "one deaf and dumb, and they besought Him that He would lay His hands upon him. And taking him from the multitude apart, He put His fingers into his ears, and spitting, He touched His tongue; and looking up to heaven, He groaned, and said to him, EPHPHETA, which is, "Be thou opened." And immediately his ears were opened, and the string of his tongue was loosed, and he spoke right."

Application: The Gospel history appeals both to our eyes and hearts; it is a picture. Let us look at it in detail, and the application will present itself. Begin with the PERSONS. 1. The multitude – they run towards Jesus from all sides, and cannot leave Him; and I am so tardy in going to visit Him in the Blessed Sacrament, and always so ready to leave Him. 2. The PERSON OF JESUS CHRIST – His every feature, His whole bearing, breathes gravity, sanctity, unspeakable sweetness; oh, what a contrast to my levity, my worldly manners, my rudeness! 3. The deaf mute – he could only express his feelings by looks of love and confidence; Jesus understood them, and was touched. A look of love and compassion cast on my crucifix can draw down many graces on me, and I neglect to do it! Let us next contemplate the ACTIONS – they are full of mystery and of lessons. Jesus take the deaf mute apart to teach us to avoid ostentation; He touched his ears with His fingers and his tongue with saliva, He raised His eyes and breathed a sigh towards heaven, to let us understand that the cure of spiritual deafness and dumbness is difficult, that it is above our strength; but that we can obtain it by earnest prayers and many entreaties from God. How have I profited by these lessons of my Savior's?

Affections and Resolutions

Point III: Jesus is admired and praised

Consideration: Having witnessed the miracle wrought upon the deaf mute, and on many others who were cured the same day of different infirmities, "they wondered and said, BENE OMNIA FECIT" – He hath done all things well.

Application: How happy should we be if these words could in all truth be graven on our tombs, BENE OMNIA FECIT – "He hath done all things well." Well before God, by doing all things in their proper order with great fervour and purity of intention; well before men, by acting under obedience and giving edification. Let us not neglect any means that we may obtain such a testimony. Colloquy.

August 25: Second Multiplication of the Loaves

1st prelude: Imagine you see a plain where are seated four thousand men divided into bands, who are miraculously fed with seven loaves.
2nd prelude: Beg for deep feelings of faith, confidence and love.

Point I: The miracle

Consideration: The second multiplication of the loaves took place in the same way as the first. Saint Mark tells us of it thus: "In those days again when there was a great multitude, and they had nothing to eat; calling His disciples together, He saith to them, I have compassion on the multitude, for behold they have now been with Me three days, and have nothing to eat; and if I shall send them away fasting to their homes, they will faint in the way, for some of them come from afar off. And His disciples answered Him, From whence can any one fill them here with bread in the wilderness? And He asked them, How many loaves have ye? Who said, Seven. And taking the seven loaves, giving thanks, He broke and gave to the disciples for to set before them; and they set them before the people. And they had a few little fishes, and He blessed them, and commanded them to be set before them. And they did eat and were filled, and they took up that which was left of the fragments seven baskets; and they that did eat were four thousand men, besides women and children."

Application: How full of encouragement and consolation are the words, "I have compassion on the multitude"! It was so like the Heart of Jesus – always watchful, always alive to our wants, to our sufferings of soul and body. What strength there is in that thought! "They have now been with Me three days." Our good Master, then, keeps and exact account of the time, the days and the minutes that we give to His service; and "some of them come from afar off." Not only does He reckon the time of our service, but He weighs its merit, that He may one day reward it. What an encouragement! "If I shall send them away fasting to their homes, they will faint in the way." His solicitude for us extends even to our future. That future which is hidden from us, and which terrifies us so often, He sees IN REGARD TO EACH OF US; He sees what will be for our happiness; and He sees the means of driving away what will do us harm, and of gaining what is advantageous and necessary for us; when necessary, He will work a miracle to procure it for us. We see the proof of this in the above.

Affections and Resolutions.

Point II: Mystical meaning of the miracle

Consideration: Interpreters point out many mysterious differences between the first and second multiplication of the loaves. First, they figure the different way in which Our Lord acts towards the synagogue and the Church, between the faithful of the Old Law and the New. In the first miracle, the old law was figured by the number of five, signifying the five books of the Pentateuch in which this law was contained; at the second, the new law was figured by the number of four, to signify the four gospels in which it is contained. At the first, it was said that the people sought Jesus because of the miracle; at he second, no mention is made of their motive, because Christians who live according to the Spirit should detach themselves from earth and devote themselves to spiritual things. At the first, only barley bread was given, the food of slaves; at the second, wheaten bread, the food of children. At the first, there remained twelve baskets, which figured the twelve patriarchs of the old law; at the second, seven, which represent the seven gifts of the Holy Ghost, and the seven Sacraments instituted for our nourishment in our journey towards eternity.

Application: Let us admire the economy of the divine wisdom in both the old and new law; let us thank God that we were born children of the new law, and thus favored beyond the Jews. We possess the truth, they had but the shadow; we possess the Incarnate Word, they had but the promise of Him; finally, we are fed with His Body and His precious Blood, they had only the manna, which was but the type of it. But if we enjoy greater

advantages than they, God also requires from us a still greater sanctity. Are we trying to attain it?
Colloquy.

August 26: Jesus in the Country of Magedan, where He is Tempted by the Pharisees Together with the Saducees

1st prelude: Behold Jesus discoursing with the Pharisees and Sadducees.
2nd prelude: Beg the spirit of truth and simplicity.

Point I: Jesus dwells in the country of Magedan

Consideration: Immediately after the miracle of the multiplication of loaves, Our Lord went up into a ship with His disciples. He passed the eastern shore of the sea of Galilee and came to the land of Magedan, a country which had not yet been evangelized. Interpreters remark on this occasion, that as we follow the footsteps of Our Divine Lord, we easily see that His design was to make Himself known to all the house of Israel, so that there should not be a province in Judea which had not been enlightened by His teaching, and witnessed His miracles. It was a figure of what His Apostles were to do in the whole world.

Application: Compare your conduct with that of your divine model. When you have succeeded in some public matter, you like to remain at the scene of the occurrence to attract observation; when you have not succeeded, you are eager to escape notice, and to get away. Jesus does the opposite. He was always eager to hide Himself from the sight and applause of those who were astonished at a wonderful miracle. Acknowledge that your conduct is little in conformity with that of your Divine Master.
Affections and Resolutions.

Point II: Jesus reproves the Pharisees, and leaves them

Consideration: The Gospel tells us nothing of the preaching and miracles of Jesus in Magedan, but it relates the hypocritical alliance between the Pharisees and Sadducees, who were vehemently opposed to each other, but, like all sects, could agree in hostility towards our Lord. "And there came to Him the Pharisees and Sadducees tempting, and they asked Him to show them a sign from heaven." They desired to lower Him in the opinion of the people, by taxing Him with impotence if He did not work the wonder, or sacrilege if He did perform it. “But Jesus knowing their malice, sighing deeply in spirit, saith, A wicked and adulterous generation seeketh after a sign, and a sign shall not be given it but the sign of Jonas the prophet. And He left them and went away.”

Application: Let this teach us to do for the good cause what the impious do for an evil one. They had mutually sacrificed themselves and their own opinions, that they might attack Jesus Christ and His Church. Let us detest all egotism, jealousy and obstinate attachment to our own judgment. Let us be united in heart and mind in our prayers and efforts, losing sight of ourselves, and seeking only the triumph of the good cause, of truth over error. How have you acted?

Affections and Resolutions.

Point III: Jesus reproves the Apostles for their lack of faith and intelligence

Consideration: Our Lord having fulfilled His mission in Magedan, went up into the ship to return to Galilee. During the voyage, desiring to guard His Apostles against error, He said to them, “Take heed, and beware of the leaven of the Pharisees and Sadducees.” They interpreted these words in a material sense, and reflected that they had forgotten to bring enough bread, and thought He referred to that. And Jesus knowing it, said, “Why do you think within yourselves, O ye of little faith, for that you have no bread? Do you not remember the seven loaves among four thousand men, and how many baskets yet took up? Why do you not understand that it was not concerning bread that I said to you, Beware of the leaven of the Pharisees and Sadducees? Then they understood that He said they should beware of the doctrine of the Pharisees and Sadducees.”

Application: Are we not to blame as much as the Apostles for our want of confidence, and our little comprehension of spiritual things, when we have received so many proofs of the divine protection, and have been for so long a time in the school of perfection?

Colloquy.

August 27: Cure of the Blind Man of Bethsaida

1st prelude: Behold Jesus laying His hands on the eyes of the blind man.
2nd prelude: Beg for great light and unction from the Holy Ghost.

Point I: Jesus listens to the prayers made to Him on behalf of the blind man

Consideration: "And they come to Bethsaida, and they bring to Him a blind man, and they besought Him that He would touch him. And taking the blind man by the hand, He led him out of the town, and spitting upon his eyes, laying His hands on him, He asked if he saw anything. And looking up, he said, I see men as it were trees walking."

Application: He led the blind man out of the town, and spat upon his eyes; and emblem, says Venerable Bede, of the unction of the Holy Ghost. What does our Lord teach us in this? That to obtain perfect knowledge, and taste or unction for the things of God, we ought from time to time, in retreat, to isolate ourselves completely form the world and all the occupations of exterior life. The rule makes a RETREAT once a year a sacred obligation. Happy should we be if, like contemplatives, we could pass our whole life in it. But we can really do still better by joining the sweetness of contemplation to the merit of action, by keeping ourselves in the spirit of retreat by recollection and the interior life. Its it not from this want of recollection that, like the blind man, you see the things of the supernatural order so dimly? that you so often judge rashly, that you see things in a wrong light?
Affections and Resolutions

Point II: Jesus gives sight to the blind man only by degrees

Consideration: "After that, again He laid His hands upon his eyes, and he began to see, and was restored so that he saw all things clearly." This miraculous cure is remarkable as being the only one our Lord performed by degrees. Some believe that the dispositions of the blind man were at first very imperfect, and gradually became perfect. Other interpreters think that our Lord wished to prefigure the slow and gradual progress of grace in the soul.

Application: Let us learn form this that God generally acts in our hearts according to the dispositions He finds in them. If they

are good, He does great things; if they are imperfect, He does less; and therefore it is that many people have such little light in their ordinary devotions, particularly in their reception of the Sacraments, because their lack of diligence and fervor arrests the flow of grace from God, and prevents Him from carrying out the full designs of His mercy. Does not experience show us this? Let us learn also not to be discouraged or to lose patience when, after a certain time of prayer and endeavor, we still see our pious desires unrealized, and we have not obtained the entire cure of some spiritual infirmity, or gained a higher degree of virtue. God has His own times. By degrees, He leads us to His ends. Perseverance will infallibly lead us to them. What is your perseverance?
Affections and Resolutions.

Point III: Jesus bids the blind man go to his home, and not to remain in Bethsaida

Consideration: "And He sent him into his house, saying, God into thy house, and if thou enter into the town, tell nobody." Our Lord bade him go home and recollect himself, reflect on the grace he had received, and give thanks to God. He forbade him to satisfy the curiosity of the inhabitants of Bethsaida, to punish them for deriving so little fruit form the number of miracles wrought in the midst of them, as we learn from our Lord's words on another occasion, VOE TIBI, BETHSAIDA – "Woe unto thee, Bethsaida."

Application: We should always have before our mind the benefits God has given us; we should have an ardent gratitude for them, and a great dread of not profiting by them. Have we anything to reproach ourselves with on these points?
Colloquy.

August 28: Feast of Saint Augustine, Bishop of Hippo, and Founder of the Orders which bear his Name*

*Born 354; baptized 387; made bishop 395; died 430

1st prelude: Imagine you see the saint holding in his hand a burning heart.
2nd prelude: Beg that he will obtain for you compunction of heart.

Point I: His estrangement from God

Consideration: Augustine was richly endowed with natural

gifts. He had rare eloquence, and profound and subtle genius, but they were all worse than useless to him. The sense of his superior talents and the praises he received filled him with pride, estranged him from God, from humble submission to the Church, and cast him into the heresy of the Manichees. Having lost the fear of God, he became the slave of his passions, and led a sinful life until he was thirty years old. His great genius did indeed make him feel the shame of being thus enchained by vice. He blushed for himself, he desired to be free, but he had not the strength to do it. It needed a miracle of grace to bring him back to God, and to himself.

Application: Remember your youth. Had it not some resemblance to that of Augustine? Were there not moments of passion when you deliberately abandoned God and give yourself up to the delusions of this proud world? Was there not a considerable time passed in estrangement from God, in slavery to some shameful passion? If your conscience tells you it was so, thank our Lord for having, by a miracle of grace, rescued you from the abyss and brought you back to Him. If by an especial privilege He preserved you from the contagion of vice, thank Him for it still more.

Affections and Resolutions

Point II: His return to God

Consideration: It cost Augustine a long and severe struggle before he broke his chains and triumphed over his habits of sin. He says in his CONFESSIONS that these habits had become a sort of second nature; that it seemed impossible for him to become chaste, to live in sobriety and purity; but that this fancied impossibility was really only a want of an energetic will and a neglect of prayer. “I was like,” he says, “to a man who wishes to rise at a certain hour, and when the time comes, yields to the pleasure of giving way, and falls asleep again.” But grace at last triumphed over this inveterate sinner. He became the model of true penitents; the most glorious champion of the faith; the scourge of heretics; the light and one of the most illustrious fathers of the Church.

Application: It may happen that a religious loses his first fervor and contracts bad habits: the habit of giving way to idleness; transgressing many of his rules without scruple; of omitting for idle reasons his spiritual exercises, or going through them very negligently; of praying without respect or devotion; of permitting familiarities and dangerous curiosities; of criticisms or uncalled-for murmurs without remorse, etc. Though these habits are not as revolting as those Augustine had contracted, they are not less difficult to root up. "I have rarely seen it done," says St. Bernard. We must not, however, despair. All things are possible to grace; but it must have a generous and continual co-operation. If, then, you say it is impossible, you deny the truth; you expose your own cowardice. What ought you to think about this?

Affections and Resolutions

Point III: His love for God

Consideration: Augustine is generally represented holding a burning heart in his hand, as a symbol of his ardent love, a love which was principally manifested by his indefatigable zeal. From the day of his baptism, which he received at the age of thirty-two from the hands of St. Ambrose, he never ceased for the forty-three remaining years of his life to preach and write. He brought many sinners back to God, and many heretics and schismatics, so numerous in his days, to the unity of the faith. The influence of his zeal is still felt; it has survived him, after fifteen centuries have passed, in his innumerable ascetical and dogmatical writings, in the religious orders which he founded, especially in those women, so admirable for their charity and zeal, who, under the name of Augustines, serve the hospitals in so many towns.

Colloquy.

August 29: Confession and Primacy of Saint Peter

1st prelude: Behold Jesus saying, "Thou art Peter, and on this rock I will build My Church."

2nd prelude: Ask for a tender love for the Church of Jesus Christ.

Point I: The divinity of Jesus Christ is revealed to Saint Peter

Consideration: "And Jesus and His disciples went out into the town of Cesarea Philippi, and in the way He asked His disciples, saying to them, Whom do men say that I am? But they said, Some John the Baptist, and others Elias, and others Jeremias, and others one of the former prophets risen again. And Jesus saith to them, But whom do ye say that I am? Simon Peter answered and said, Thou art Christ, the Son of the Living God. And Jesus answering said to him, Blessed art thou, Simon Bar Jona, because flesh and blood have not revealed it to thee, but My Father who is in heaven."

Application: How much instruction there is in all this! 1st, before He chose the chief of the Apostles, Jesus prayed as He had prayed before He chose the twelve; we ought to begin all our actions with prayer. 2nd, He asked what had been said of Him, not from vanity, but that His Apostles might acknowledge His divinity, that Peter especially might proclaim it solemnly. Do we wish to know what is thought and said of us only with the desire of becoming better?

Affections and Resolutions

Point II: The primacy of the Church is given to Saint Peter

Consideration: The solemn profession of the divinity of Jesus Christ made by Saint Peter, enlightened from him with predilection, said, "And I say to thee that thou art Peter, and upon this rock I will build My Church, and the gates of hell shall not prevail against it." These words clearly show us that the Church will endure as long as the world; that she will be violently persecuted, but that at last she will triumph over all persecution.

Application: Combats and victories; this is, then, what Jesus predicted for His Church and her visible Head., Nineteen centuries have borne witness to the truth of the prophesy. We must not, then, be cast down or even surprised at the universal conspiracy hatched in our days against the Church and her Chief, with more unity and cleverness than ever; she will come out victoriously from this great trial as she has so often done before; but until that moment comes, what sorrows she has to endure, what a loss of souls to suffer! It is our task above all others – we who are her privileged children, the advanced guard of her Church – to console her, to make it up to her, to come to her aid by redoubling our fervor, our prayers, and satisfactory works. How do we act? Do we not content ourselves as so many others do with sighing in secret over the troubles of our Mother, or in uttering barren invectives against her persecutors?

Affections and Resolutions.

Point III: The keys of the kingdom of heaven are promised to Saint Peter

Consideration: Our Lord did not think it enough to give Saint Peter the primacy of order and jurisdiction in the Church militant; He willed that his power should extend to the Church triumphant;

for as soon as He had said, "Thou art Peter, and on this rock I will build My Church," He added, "and I will give to thee the keys of the kingdom of heaven: and whatsoever thou shalt bind upon earth, it shall be bound also in heaven; and whatsoever thou salt loose upon earth, it shall be loosed also in heaven."

Application: The astonishing power which Jesus Christ thus gave to Saint Peter, and by him to the Sovereign Pontiffs, not only raised them above the kings of the earth, but also above the other Apostles. For He said to all, "Receive ye the Holy Ghost; whosesoever sins ye remit, they shall be remitted," etc. But to Peter alone did He say, "I will give thee the keys of the kingdom of heaven," a symbol of supreme power. Let us rejoice for the Prince of the Apostles; let us rejoice still more for ourselves; for these keys were not given for himself, but for us – to open to us the doors of heaven.

Colloquy.

August 30: Jesus Foretells His Passion, and Teaches Self-Denial

1st prelude: Behold Jesus going before us carrying His cross.
2nd prelude: Beg for the spirit of abnegation, and love of the cross.

Point I: Jesus makes known to the Apostles His Passion and death

Consideration: The Apostles, though they believed in the divinity of their Master, still dreamed of His future royalty on earth, and this thought gratified their vanity. Jesus chose to undeceive them at once. "He began to teach them that He must go to Jerusalem, and suffer many things form the ancients and scribes and chief priests, and be put to death, and the third day rise again." Upon which Peter, actuated by a mistaken zeal for His Mater's glory, cried out, "Lord, be it far from Thee; this shall not be to Thee." He was thus opposing the designs of the Son of God become the Son of Man to redeem mankind by the mystery of the cross. "Therefore, turning towards Peter, He threatened him, saying, Go behind me, Satan;* thou art a scandal unto Me, because thou savorest not the things that are of God, but the things that are of men." (*This word in Hebrew signifies ADVERSARY, and is given to Lucifer, because he is the great enemy of God and men.)

Application: May not this last reproach be addressed somewhat to you? Do you not show more taste for the study of sciences, for secular reading, but all that can increase your reputation and your bodily welfare, than for the study of sanctity, for spiritual reading, for the practice of humility, mortification, and piety? Examine yourself, and have the courage to answer yourself in all sincerity. Affections and Resolutions.

Point II: Jesus enjoins on us absolute self-denial

Consideration: Man redeemed from eternal ruin by the death and resurrection of the Redeemer cannot attain to eternal life and glory save by following in the footsteps of Him who has made an entire abnegation of Himself. Our Lord wished to make this fully understood, not only by His Apostles, but by all. "And calling the multitude together, with His disciples, He said to them, If any man will follow Me [in the way that leads to eternal life], let him deny himself."

Application: The self-denial which our Lord rigorously exacts from us extends to everything which is an obstacle to eternal salvation. Life even is not excepted. For, said Jesus Christ, "whosoever shall save his life [at the expense of what he owes to God] shall lose it; and whosoever shall lose his life for My sake and the Gospel, shall save it." It is as if He said, The true life of man is not his precarious existence in this world, but his future life eternally happy or unhappy; and he who would save or prolong his present life at the expense of what he owes to God, will lose that life of eternal happiness; while, on the contrary, he who prefers to lose it rather than be false to God, will be sure of a happy eternity. He will have saved all, while the other will have lost all without gaining anything in return. For, our Lord adds, "what shall it profit a man, if he gain the whole world and suffer the loss of his soul; or what shall a man give in exchange for his soul?"

Affections and Resolutions.

Point III: Our Lord lays on us an obligation of carrying the cross after Him

Consideration: Jesus, after having said these memorable words, "If any man will come after Me, let him deny himself," added, "and take up his cross daily, and follow Me."

Application: This last condition, though it may be very contrary to our inclination, is far less difficult to execute than the first; for

let us remark well, it is not HIS cross that Jesus obliges us to carry, but our OWN, much lighter than His; besides, it is not He who lays it on us, the conditions of life make it inevitable that we should have one. But if we bear it after Him for supernatural motives, to satisfy with Him divine justice, to resemble Him more closely, and have a greater share in His glory in heaven, it will appear light to us; little by little we shall come to love it; it will be a happiness to us.
Colloquy.

August 31: On the Three Degrees of Self-denial or Humility

1st prelude: Behold our Blessed Lady standing under the cross of Jesus.
2nd prelude: Beg for a love of suffering and contempt endured for Jesus.

Point I: First degree of self-denial or humility

Consideration: "That forsaking of ourselves and of creatures on which Jesus Christ insists so strongly has many degrees, and especially three. The first consists in the habitual disposition of losing all things – possessions, reputation, health, life itself – and to suffer all things rather than commit a mortal sin. This first degree is necessary for all Christians; without it, an act of love would be a lie in their mouths, and they will be out of the way of salvation.

Application: Let us thank God for having called us to this state of life, where all are supposed to be, and to continue, in this first degree. But do not let us be under any delusion; we cannot keep ourselves in it save by the assistance of grace, and in certain circumstances of a special grace. Besides, in changing our dress we have not changed our nature. We are always men feeble and inconstant. Let us, then, be humble, always distrustful of self, and prompt in having recourse to prayer in temptations. However, the religious who, on principle, is contented with the first degree, will be little worthy of the name he bears, and by no means sure of salvation.
Affections and Resolutions.

Point II: Second degree of self-denial or humility

Consideration: This second degree consists in the habitual

disposition of losing all and suffering all rather than commit a deliberate venial sin. Every true religious ought to strive to attain it, to be able to witness to himself that he has attained the second degree; for if not, 1st, it is with difficulty he will keep in the first, or rather he will not do it; experience teaches us too often the truth of those words of the Holy Spirit: QUI SPERNIT MODICA PAULATIM DECIDET – "He that contemneth small things shall fall little by little." 2nd, He cannot imagine he is fulfilling the obligation he has contracted before God of tending to perfection, for nothing is more opposed to perfection than venial sin. 3rd, He can never enjoy true peace of heart, because he is resisting God's designs for him: QUIS RESTITIT DEO, ET PACEM HABUIT? – "Who hath resisted him, and hath had peace?" 4th, He will never be fit to do great things for the salvation of souls.

Application: It is in our power to attain the second degree, and to remain in it. The proof of it is given to us in the acts of beatification and in the lives of many servants of God. It is said in the lives of the Venerable Luis du Pont and Bellarmine that they made a vow of never voluntarily committing a venial sin, and they were faithful to their vow until death. What they did with the help of grace we can also do; but have we seriously resolved on it? What means have we employed? With what perseverance? Affections and Resolutions.

Point III: Third degree of self-denial or humility

Consideration: This third degree consists in the disposition of rather being poor with Jesus Christ in his poverty than in abundance; of being rather forgotten and despised with Jesus Christ, who was humiliated and insulted, than to live in honor; to be rather on the cross with Jesus crucified than to enjoy the consolations and delights of this life, IN ORDER THAT WE MAY HAVE A GREATER RESEMBLANCE TO JESUS, our divine model, and be better able to prove our love.

Application: This habitual disposition, or third degree of humility, is not impossible to human weakness sustained by grace. Witness the Apostles and an infinity of martyrs who rejoiced in being stripped of all, scoffed at, spit upon, condemned to death for the name of Jesus; witness also so many persons educated in luxury and delights whom we see vowing themselves for love of Jesus to poverty, and the austerities of the cloister. These examples

tend to encourage and stimulate us; and besides, what blessings belong to this third degree! It is the perfect imitation of Jesus Christ; it gives peace and joy of heart in the midst of tribulations, an abundance of divine blessings, the assurance of salvation, the pledge of greater glory in heaven. How are you relatively to this third degree? What has been the end of those resolutions made in so many retreats, that you would neglect nothing that would enable you to attain it?
Colloquy.

September 1: Feast of the Holy Guardian Angels

1st prelude: Behold young Tobias traveling in company with the angel Raphael.
2nd prelude: Beg for a true and solid devotion to your guardian angel.

Point I: What is the dignity of our angel guardians?

Consideration: Among the most precious gifts of God's mercy to men should be reckoned that communion or spiritual intercourse which He has established between us and the holy angels, the order which He has given to these blessed spirits to take care of each of us; for, says the Psalmist, "He hath given his angels charge over thee, to keep thee in all thy ways." But what are these guardian angels? They are pure spirits, created after the image of God, endowed with beauty, power, agility, and intelligence, which are beyond all human conception. They are in regard of God and heaven, where He manifests His glory, what the princes and first dignitaries of a kingdom are in regard of a king and his court. This angel, then, who is day and night by my side, is a prince of the celestial court, whose dignity infinitely surpasses that of the greatest monarchs of the earth.

Application: I believe this truth, but I scarcely ever think about it. When I am alone, I think and act as if no creature were near me witnessing my sufferings and my actions. If I had a more lively faith, what consolation and what a charm I should find in conversing with this holy and wonderful friend, in telling him all my troubles and anxieties; in asking for counsel, strength, and courage in my doubts, sufferings and temptations! We read in the lives of many saints that their ardent faith and tender devotion towards their angel guardian obtained for them the grace of seeing him and conversing familiarly with him. We find this especially in the lives of Saint Camillus, Saint Frances of Rome, and Saint Rose of Lima.

Affections and Resolutions

Point II: What services do our angel guardians render us?

Consideration: "He hath given His angels charge over thee, to keep thee in all thy ways." In obedience to this command, our angel guardian, 1st, watches with tender care over the preservation of our body, our health, and our life, which are exposed to so many dangers, 2nd, he takes still greater care of our immortal soul and of our spiritual interests; he teaches us, brings good thoughts to our minds, shows us the snares laid for us, secretly reproves us for our faults, and draws us by gentle inspirations to perform our duties. 3rd, he does for us what Raphael did for young Tobias – he guides us through the dangers of this life. 4th, he assists us especially at the hour of death.

Application: Let us admire and imitate, as much as we can, three things – 1st the PERFECT INDIFFERENCE of these angels about all that they are desired to do; 2nd, their RECOLLECTION AND PURITY in the midst of the noise and corruption of the world; 3rd, their IMMOVABLE PEACE, notwithstanding their ill success in their good offices.

Affections and Resolutions

Point II: What are our obligations towards our angel guardians?

Consideration: Saint Bernard says there are three in particular – respect for his presence, devotion or gratitude for his charity, confidence in his vigilance. No one can deny these obligations; but the greater number of men, even at the present day, never think of them. This is an additional reason why we should fulfill them carefully.

Application: How can we fulfill them? We can and ought to testify, 1st, our RESPECT, by acting in his sight, especially when we are alone, as if we were in the company of some great person. The following thought will help us in doing so: "One day my angel will bear witness for or against me of what I am doing at this moment." 2nd, our DEVOTION or gratitude, by being very docile to his inspirations, and thanking him EVERY NIGHT for what he has done for us. 3rd, our CONFIDENCE, by consulting him and

invoking him in all our doubts and wants, with the conviction it will never be done in vain.
Colloquy.

September 2: Transfiguration of Our Lord

1st prelude: Behold Jesus in glory on Mount Tabor.
2nd prelude: Beg the grace of drawing fruit from meditating on this great mystery.

Point I: Mystery of the Transfiguration

Consideration: "Jesus taketh unto Him Peter and James, and John his brother, and bringeth them up into a high mountain apart. And He was transfigured before them. And His face did shine as the sun, and His garments became white as snow. And behold there appeared to them Moses and Elias, talking with Him. And Peter answering said to Jesus, Lord, it is good for us to be here; if Thou wilt, let us make here three tabernacles, one for Thee, and one for Moses, and one for Elias. And as he was yet speaking, behold a bright cloud overshadowed them. And lo, a voice out of the cloud saying, This is My beloved Son, in whom I am well pleased; hear ye Him. And the disciples hearing, fell upon their face, and were very much afraid. And Jesus came and touched them, and said to them, Arise, and fear not; and they, lifting up their eyes, saw no one, but only Jesus."

Application: Every detail of this great event is given to us; we might imagine we had seen it, for it is a picture rather than a history. Let us attentively contemplate this picture, considering one by one the PERSONS, their WORDS, and their ACTIONS. Beautiful thoughts and most practical lessons are contained in this contemplation. Do not let us fear to devote too much time to them. If they occupied the whole of our meditation, it would be every useful to us.
Affections and Resolutions.

Point II: Motives for the Transfiguration

Consideration: Eight days had passed away since Jesus foretold His Passion and death to His Apostles; since He had openly declared that they also must be ready to forsake all things, even life itself, for His sake and the Gospel. Their master's words had saddened the disciples, and awakened doubts that might weaken their faith; and to cure this our Lord chose to give them at once a striking proof of His divinity, and a foretaste of the happiness prepared for them in heaven. Such was the principal reason for the Transfiguration.

Application: This is how God is accustomed to act towards us; if He allows sad memories and alarming prospects to throw us into desolation, doubt or dejection, He takes care to put an end to it by sending a ray of celestial glory before our eyes, which immediately sends away our darkness and our anguish, expands our hearts, and fills them with the sweetest confidence and joy.

Affections and Resolutions.

Point III: Saint Peter's rapture

Consideration: When Peter, transported out of himself at the sight of the glorified humanity of Jesus, cried out, "Lord, it is good for us to be here: let us make three tabernacles," Saint Mark tells us, "he knew not what he said" – NON ENIM SCIEBAT QUID DICERET – because he did not understand the end our Lord had in view in manifesting His glory. Later on, he understood it, as he explains to us in his Second Epistle, chapter 1.

Application: Let us enter today into the wishes of our loving Savior; let us gather thoughts of courage and generosity from His glorious Transfiguration; let us say, "If a momentary glimpse of the glorified humanity of Jesus Christ can transport an Apostle with joy and happiness, what will it be to contemplate Him eternally in heaven!" And in striving after this happiness, which is promised to us, we will cry out with Saint Paul, "The sufferings of this time are not worthy to be compared with the glory to come, that shall be revealed in us."

Colloquy.

September 3: The Lunatic Child Possessed by a Devil

1st prelude: Behold the father of the lunatic kneeling at the feet of Jesus.

2nd prelude: Ask for lively sentiments of faith, zeal, and compassion for the unfortunate.

Point I: A lunatic child whom the Apostles could not cure is brought to Jesus

Consideration: Then Jesus came down from Mount Tabor, the

day after the Transfiguration, "and coming to his disciples, He saw a great multitude about them, and the scribes disputing with them." The subject of the dispute was the failure of an exorcism which the Apostles had attempted in the absence of their Master, as the Gospel tells us: "And He asked them, What do you question about among you? And one of the multitude answering said, I have brought my son to Thee, having a dumb spirit, who, wheresoever he taketh him, dasheth him; and he foameth , and gnasheth with the teeth, and pineth away; and I spoke to thy disciples to cast him out, and they could not."

Application: See here the cruelty and tyranny of the devil. God had allowed him to possess this child and to ill-treat him from time to time. Then the devil tormented him AS OFTEN as he could, AS MUCH as he could, and, had he been able, would have done so yet MORE. For, as Saint Mark says, "oftentimes hath he cast him into the fire, and into waters to destroy him." What horror, then, should we have of him! And yet Christians give themselves up to him body and soul by committing mortal sin! Yet religious, too, follow his treacherous suggestions by yielding to the thoughts and desires of vainglory, ambition, envy, and sensuality! Have you been among the number?

Affections and Resolutions.

Point II: Jesus reproaches the Apostles, the Scribes and the people

Consideration: After having heard what had happened, the most gentle Jesus, seeing the multitude scandalized by the failure of which the Scribes accused the Apostles, pronounced these words of bitter indignation, "O incredulous generation, how long shall I be with you? how long shall I suffer you?"

Application: Notice how differently our Savior acted here from what He afterwards did in His Passion. THEN no complaint escaped Him. NOW He complains bitterly. Ah, it is our little faith and our resistance to grace which make the sufferings He then endured with so much love to be of no avail. And you, too, have you never given him cause to complain? Perhaps in many respects.

Affections and Resolutions.

Point III: Why the Apostles failed to cure the lunatic

Consideration: The reason is clearly shown in our Lord's answer to the Apostles when they asked, "Why could we not cast him out?" Jesus said to them, "Because of your unbelief. For, amen I say to you, if you have faith as a grain of mustard-seed, you shall say to this mountain, Remove from hence hither, and it shall remove; and nothing shall be impossible to you. But this kind is not cast out but by prayer and fasting."

Application: Three things are here plainly taught us – 1st, that we, who are called to work for the conversion of sinners, to deliver them from the tyranny of the devil, ought to have faith in a higher degree than the great body of the faithful; 2ndly, that the greater our faith is, the more able shall we be to do great things for the glory of God and the salvation of our neighbor; 3rdly, that in certain cases our faith, to be availing, must be accompanied by acts of corporal penance, which our Lord includes under the single word FASTING. Have we been always thoroughly convinced of these truths? Does our conduct show that we have? What remains for us to do?

Colloquy with our Divine Savior.

September 4: The Cure of the Child Possessed by a Devil

1st prelude: Behold Jesus commanding the devil to go out of the child.

2nd prelude: Ask for a lively horror of everything which can admit the devil into your heart.

Point I: Jesus commands the child to be brought to Him

Consideration: "The nature of God is goodness," says Saint Leo – NATURA DEI BONITAS. Jesus here gives a proof of it, for He bids the fathers, to whom He had just before addressed a well-merited rebuke, to bring his son. "And as he was coming to Him, the devil threw him down and tore him."

Application: Two things are here shown us: first, that God's anger and indignation, which in the next world are eternal, but in this are temporary, often, like heralds, precede His mercy. As the prophet Habacuc says, "When Thou art angry, Thou wilt remember mercy" – CUM IRATUS FUERIS, DOMINE, MISERICORDIAE RECORDABERIS. So, too, the holy Job: "Although He should kill me, I will trust in Him" – ETIAMSI OCCIDERIT ME, IN IPSO SPERABO. Our hope and our confidence should remain unshaken, even when God chastises us or seems to forsake us. Secondly, we see that it is especially when

we make a firm resolution to free ourselves from sin or tepidity that the devil redoubles his efforts to overthrow us, to make us desperate or disheartened. Beware lest you fall into this snare.
Affections and Resolutions.

Point II: Jesus commands the devil to go out of the child

Consideration: Jesus, seeing the child rolling on the ground and foaming before Him, "asked his father, How long time is it since this hath happened unto him? And he said, From his infancy. But if thou canst do anything, help us, having compassion upon us. And Jesus saith to him, If thou canst believe, all things are possible to him that believeth." The father saw at once that the doubt which he entertained of the power of Jesus stood in the way of the favor which he asked, and he cried out with tears, "I do believe, Lord; help Thou my unbelief" – CREDO, DOMINE, ADJUVA INCREDULITATEM MEAM – that is to say, "I do believe as far as I can; of thy mercy supply what is lacking to my faith; help me to believe as I ought."

Application: Imitate this suppliant father. Begin by doing what you can, and ask God to do the rest; then await the answer and the final result. It is a blessed truth which St. Augustine so beautifully expresses in those words which the Council of Trent has literally adopted: DEUS IMPOSSIBILIA NO JUBET; SED JUBENDO MONET FACERE QUOD POSSIS, ET PETERE QUOD NON POSSIS, ET ADJUVAT UT POSSIS – "God does not demand of us impossible things; but by His demands He means us to do our utmost, to ask for what we cannot do, and He helps us to do it." Have we done this? Have we not contented ourselves with simply asking, and making no effort? or, presuming on our strength, have we not neglected to pray?

Affections and Resolutions.

Point III: Jesus gives back the child perfectly cured to the father.

Consideration: The father's faith, now made perfect, is rewarded. "Jesus," says Saint Mark, "threatened the unclean spirit, saying to him, Deaf and dumb spirit, I command thee, go out of him and enter not any more into him." The devil obeyed, but in the manner of a devil: "And crying out, and greatly tearing him, he went out of him; and he became as dead, so that many said, He is dead. But Jesus, taking him by the hand, lifted him up; and he arose. And Jesus restored him to his father. And all were astonished at the mighty power of God."

Application: We have presented to us here a picture of the violent disturbance into which the devil throws a soul that he is compelled to leave. It is a kind of agony, but an agony through which a soul passes from death to life, from habitual tepidity to fervor, to the full vigor of the spiritual life. Perhaps you know something of it by experience. However that may be, learn from this example how to direct and encourage the souls committed to your care.

Colloquy with the Divine Savior.

September 5: The Journey from Mount Tabor to Capharnaum, the Passion Repeatedly Foretold

1st prelude: Picture to yourself Jesus, on His way, conversing alone with His Apostles.

2nd prelude: Ask for grace to understand, reverence, and love spiritual things.

Point I: Jesus foretells His Passion a second time.

Consideration: It was the month of August, in the third year of the preaching of Jesus. Hitherto His ministry had scarcely extended beyond the bounds of Galilee. Now Judea was to be the scene of His labors. But before going there, He wished to pay one last visit to Capharnaum, where He had lived so much. On the way from Mount Tabor to this city He permitted no one to accompany Him except His Apostles, that He might talk to them of the great mystery, of the insults and the cruel death which He was about the suffer in the capital of Judea. "He said to them, The Son of Man shall be betrayed into the hands of men, and they shall kill Him; and after that He is killed, He shall rise again the third day."

Application: In the first place, mark WHEN IT WAS that our Lord reminded Himself and others of His Passion. It was when all smiled upon Him; when the fame of His miracles had won for Him a general popularity. When success attends us, when men praise us, let us not yield to thoughts or words of vanity, but rather let us strive to be humble. Let us remember that we are unprofitable servants, doomed to wither, to die; uncertain too, whether we merit love or wrath. Have you done this? In the second place, mark WHY it was that Jesus so often foretold His approaching

Passion. It was to make them understand that He would suffer of His own free will, and out of love for man, and to prevent them from being scandalized when the time came. Do good, so that what you do may prove to be good under any circumstances.
Affections and Resolutions.

Point II: Jesus is not understood by His Apostles.

Consideration: "But they understood not this word," says Saint Luke, "and it was hid from them, so that they perceived it not." In truth, they understood the expressions, "to be delivered up," and "to be put to death," which were plain enough; but they could not understand their meaning, because their love for Jesus and their own ambitious views made them reject the literal sense of the words. "And they were afraid to ask Him concerning this word"; afraid, doubtless, of learning more than they wished to know. "And they were troubled exceedingly."

Application: Can you see in this no point of resemblance between yourself and the Apostles, who were still so imperfect? How many things, for instance are told you again and again by your superiors, by your director – things which you do not understand because you do not wish to understand them, because they cross your inclination, because they urge you to painful efforts. For example, this excessive liberty in which you indulge your eyes or your tongue is a fatal occasion of sin. Until you totally renounce these undue familiarities, you will have neither peace nor purity of conscience. Has not your want of diligence and care made you responsible for the sins of others? Have not your judgments, your complaints, your irregularities given grave scandal to your brethren?
Affections and Resolutions.

Point III: Jesus foretells His resurrection as well as His death.

Consideration: "The Son of Man shall be betrayed into the hands of men, and they shall kill Him; and after that He is killed, He shall rise again the third day." It is important to notice here that Jesus Christ never separates the prediction of His glorious resurrection from that of His Passion.

Application: He does this for our encouragement, that the thought of our resurrection and the joys of heaven which are promised us may support us in the spiritual combat, in every imaginable sacrifice and suffering. Quicken your faith; summon up your courage. Colloquy.

September 6: The Didrachma

1st prelude: Behold Saint Peter drawing up the fish in which he will find the money required to pay the tax.
2nd prelude: Ask for Saint Peter's simplicity, humility and faith.

Point I: Jesus was exempt from paying the tribute

Consideration: The Gospel only mentions one act of our Lord in this His last visit to Capharnaum: "And when they were come to Capharnaum, they that received the didrachmas came to Peter, and said to him, Doth not your Master pay the didrachmas? He said, Yes. And when he was come into the house, Jesus prevented him, saying, What is thy opinion, Simon? The kings of the earth, of whom do they receive tribute or custom? of their own children or of strangers? And he said, Of strangers. Jesus said to him, Then the children are free." "Still more," he would say, "is the only begotten Son of the King of Heaven free." Undoubtedly this title exempted the Savior from all tribute to earthly kings. His exemption rested on good grounds.

Application: Do the dispensations which we claim from the rule, from work, from penance, always rest upon grounds equally good? Of a truth, there is no lack of excuses. Our age, our health, our business or else our seniority, our merit, our great services. But are not self-deception, self-love, idleness, tepidity, too often at the root of it all? The more we naturally crave for dispensations, the more rigidly should we scrutinize our motives.
Affections and Resolutions.

Point II: Jesus pays the tribute.

Consideration: Though Jesus need not have paid the tribute, yet He did pay it, to avoid giving scandal to the people, who as yet were ignorant of His right of exemption as the Son of God. But He paid it, so to speak, as God, by a striking and singular miracle. He said, then, to Peter, "Go to the sea, and cast in a hook, and that fish which shall first come up, take; and when thou hast opened its mouth, thou shalt find a stater; take that, and give it to them for Me and thee." By this command He severely tested the Apostle's obedience. It stood the trial, and gained the reward.

Application: Learn from this – 1st, Never to put a stumbling-

block in your brother's way, even though in so doing you commit no sin yourself. 2nd, Not to ask yourself, when an opportunity of doing good is presented to you, "Am I obliged to do this?" This would be a bad return for the generosity which God daily shows to you. 3rd, Not to criticize, but to adore, in all humility, the wonderful ways in which God sometimes pleases to work out His good pleasure. 4th, Blind obedience.
Affections and Resolutions.

Point III: Jesus pays for Saint Peter as well as for Himself

Consideration: "Take that, and give it to them for Me and for thee." The tribute was demanded of Jesus only as Head of the College of Apostles. Notwithstanding, He wished for Peter to pay it too. Why did He make this distinction, which in some degree raised the Apostle to the level of his Master? Commentators tell us that it signified to Peter the confirmation of the primacy which had already been given him. This fresh proof of love which our Lord gave to Saint Peter was the reward of his faith and obedience.

Application: Strive to deserve the love of our Divine Master and Savior. Congratulate Saint Peter on the exalted rank to which he was raised. Do we rejoice at this? It was for our welfare that this was done. It is to the supremacy of Saint Peter and of his successors that we owe the unbroken unity of the faith, and the undecaying vigor of the Church, our mother, to whom we owe all that is good, whether natural or supernatural. Do we think enough of all this?
Colloquy.

September 7: The Apostles Dispute as to Which of Them Shall Be the Greatest

1st prelude: Consider our Lord saying, "If any man desire to be first, he shall be the last of all, and the minister of all."
2nd prelude: Ask for grace to become little in your own eyes.

Point I: The ambition of the Apostles

Consideration: The marks of honor and distinction which the Savior had given to Saint Peter aroused the jealousy of the other Apostles. They fell into dispute when their Master had left them for a moment to speak with Peter. But Jesus, who, as Saint Luke tells us, "saw their thoughts," wished to correct them, and asked them, "What did you treat of in the way? But they held their peace; for in the way they had disputed among themselves which of them should be the greatest." AT ILLI TACEBANT: SIQUIDDEM IN VIA DISPUTAVERANT, QUIS EORUM MAJOR ESSET.

Application: You are horrified at the conduct of the Apostles. "What!" you say; "their Master had just been telling them of the cruel death He was about to suffer; but did it make no impression on them? Were they so selfish as to have no thought for Him, but only for their own miserable ambition?" Your indignation is natural; but perhaps you would judge them more leniently if you thought of the weakness of human nature, and especially of your own. Have you not often given way to thoughts of ambition and vainglory after meditating on the humiliations of our Blessed Lord? or knelt humbly in the confessional, and then immediately afterward lost your temper because someone made a harmless joke at your expense? Perhaps even in the confessional itself you took offence at the penance enjoined upon you.

Affections and Resolutions.

Point II: The Apostles taught to be humble

Consideration: Ambition, like every other passion, is ingenious at concealing the end at which it is aiming. We see a proof of this in the case of the Apostles. They came to Jesus and asked a general question, without appearing to refer to themselves: "Who, thinkest thou, is greater in the kingdom of heaven?" Jesus, who knew their motive for asking Him, not wishing to rebuke them too severely, said, "If any man desire to be first, he shall be the last of all, and the minister of all."

Application: We all wish to be great in the sight of God – great in heaven. Jesus Christ here shows us how to become so: by making ourselves little, the least of all, in our own eyes. Would you know if, by God's grace, you have attained to this? Can you bear to be overlooked, to be passed by as something beneath notice, and yet not lose your peace and joy of heart? Are you glad when the lowest office, the meanest work, is allotted to you – when, in fact, you are made, as Jesus says, "the minister of all"?

Affections and Resolutions.

Point III: The Apostles are bid to become as little children

Consideration: The Apostles, engrossed as they were in thoughts of earthly greatness, could understand but little of the abnegation and humility which Jesus taught them. To set it before them more clearly and plainly, He "called unto Him a little child, and set him in the midst of them, and said, Amen, I say to you, unless you be converted, and become as little children, you shall not enter into the kingdom of heaven. Whosoever therefore, shall humble himself as this little child, he is the greater in the kingdom of heaven."

Application: To please God, we must have a share of His special grace and love, by which we obtain this childhood of the spirit, and become in virtue what children are in nature – pure, simple, humble, gentle, obedient. This is not easy. We shall not become so without generous and persevering efforts. Are we making such efforts? What success have we had hitherto? Colloquy with Jesus, who became for us a little child, wrapped in swaddling-clothes and cradled in a manger.

September 8: Feast of the Nativity of Our Blessed Lady

1st prelude: Unite yourself in spirit to the angels who surround the cradle of Mary.
2nd prelude: Ask for grace to grow in knowledge, love and devotion to Our Lady.

Point I: The Nativity of Mary, the subject of our joy

Consideration: One of the brightest days in the history of the world is the birthday of her who should change the face of the earth, who should change the curse into a blessing. She it was who was promised to our first parents when they repented of their sin, as the only hope of salvation for themselves and their posterity; she it was who should bring into the world the Savior so long desired. This great, this glorious day we now commemorate; today we celebrate the birth of the Virgin-Mother Mary. The Church invites us to celebrate it with a great joy, a great solemnity. CUM JUCUNDITATE NATIVITATEM BEATAE MARIAE SOLEMNITER CELEBREMUS. Because her birth has been a cause of joy and blessing to the whole universe – to the angels in heaven, whose queen she was to be – to the holy souls, whose liberator she would become – to the whole race of Adam, whose restorer and mother she would prove. NATIVITAS TUA, DEI GENETRIX, GAUDIUM ANNUNCIAVIT UNIVERSO

MUNDO.

Application: How can we best comply with the invitation of the Church to rejoice as Mary would have us to do? 1. By saluting her as the Dawn of the Son of Justice – as our Queen, our Deliverer, our Mother, wishing ever to be in the number of her devoted subjects, her most loving children. 2. By congratulating her on the extraordinary favors, both natural and supernatural, which God lavished on her from the moment of her birth – favors far higher than any which the greatest saints will ever receive. 3. By promising to do our utmost to spread devotion to her, and to imitate the purity and holiness of her life.

Affections and Resolutions.

Point II: The birth of Mary, the ground of our hope

Consideration: The subjects of a good queen always celebrate with joy the anniversary of her birth. They expect to see this day marked by some special favors, by some unusual bounty; and they are rarely disappointed. But the resources of earthly potentates are limited; so too must be their gifts and favors; they cannot satisfy everyone. Not so with Mary. Jesus has appointed her to be the dispense of the INFINITE merits of His death and Passion. Mary can draw upon this treasure without fear of exhausting it; she can give, then, without stint, if she please; and we know that she does so please, for she is our most tender loving Mother. What may we not hope from her today?

Application: Go to her today with entire confidence. Ask for much – much for yourself, much for others, for your friends, for the order or congregation to which you belong, for all entrusted to your care, for the whole Church, for the two thousand million inhabitants of the world – that all may be united in the same faith, may become one family, one Church – that there may be in reality but one fold and one shepherd. Why do the feasts of our dearest Mother so often pass unmarked by any signal favor? Because we ask for so little; because we pray with so little heart. Let it not be so with you today.

Colloquy.

September 9: Jesus Warns His Disciples Against Scandals

1st prelude: Consider Jesus saying, "Woe to the world because of

scandals."
2nd prelude: Ask for a great fear of giving scandal, and grace to avoid it.

Point I: Scandal in the world

Consideration: The sweet innocence of the little child whom Jesus had set in the midst of the Apostles as their pattern and exemplar caused Him to denounce those who scandalize others, and especially those who scandalize children. Listen to His words: "He that shall scandalize one of these little ones that believe in Me, it were better for him that a millstone should be hanged about his neck, and that he should be drowned in the depths of the sea. Woe to the world because of scandals. It must needs be" – He knew the corruption of the world – "that scandals come; but nevertheless woe to that man by whom the scandal cometh."

Application: You would share our Lord's indignation against scandal, and those who give it, and you would feel that horror of it which He wishes you to feel, if you reflected on the malice and dreadful consequences of this sin. "Sinful about measure" – SUPER MODUM PECCANS PECCATORUM. The fathers, too, speak in terms equally severe of those who give scandal; they call them emissaries and missioners of the devil – devils incarnate, because they lead others into sin as much or even more than the devil does himself – assassins of the soul, a thousand-fold more guilty than murderers of the body – antichrists, undoing the work of Christ – a living plague, spreading everywhere infection and death. In all the years that you have lived in the world have you never given scandal or been scandalized yourself?
Affections and Resolutions.

Point II: Scandal in the cloister

Consideration: When our Lord said so sorrowfully, "Woe to the world because of scandals," did He not think also of religious communities? Is scandal impossible, is it unknown there? Alas, no; for the simple reason that members of such communities are naturally prone to become lax, and so set a bad example. And this of itself is sufficient to commit the sin of scandal. You may not have a direct intention of leading others into sin, but if (as Saint Thomas says), either by word, act, or omission you become an occasion of sin to another, you are guilty of scandal. A superior, for instance, commits it if through negligence or weakness he fails to correct abuses which have crept in, for he is the cause of the laxity and disorders which follow, and become permanent and irremediable. A religious commits it, who, having more or less influence, openly and habitually infringes certain points of the rule of discipline, since others will soon follow him and become as lax as he is; he commits it, who, by his captious criticisms and discontented murmurings, weakens in his brethren the principles of authority and religious obedience; he commits it, who, by his way of ridiculing his superiors, or the practices of humility, mortification, penance, and devotion customary in his convent, causes the want of seriousness in everything, and the total loss of all proper respect.

Application: See if you have not been, in some way, guilty of scandal. If you have, ask pardon for it; do your utmost to repair the mischief you have done. On the other hand, never let a bad example influence you or turn you aside. Follow rather Saint John Berchmans, who drew good out of evil by redoubling his efforts to avoid the sins which he saw in others.

Colloquy.

September 10: Our Lord's Directions for Correction and Pardon

1st prelude: Picture to yourself Jesus surrounded by His Apostles.
2nd prelude: Ask for the spirit of discernment and charity.

Point I: Rules for correction

Consideration: Our Lord talked to His Apostles the whole way from Capharnaum to Jerusalem. He feared lest His denunciation of scandal givers would lead the Apostles to hate them. To remedy this, He showed how His law was emphatically a law of love; that we ought to pity and pray for those who are a cause of offence to us rather than to hate them; that we should do all in our power to bring them to a better mind, especially by a brotherly rebuke. He thought this of so much importance that He gave them detailed directions concerning it: "If thy brother shall offend against thee, go, and rebuke him between thee and him alone. If he shall hear thee, thou shalt gain thy brother. And if he will not hear thee, take with thee one or two more: that in the mouth of two or three witnesses every word may stand. And if he will not hear them, tell the Church; and if he will not hear the Church, let him be to thee as the heathen and the publican."

Application: Our Lord would seem here to point out the way in which the shepherds of the flock should deal with those who trouble it, especially with innovators and dogmatizers. They should first reprove them in private for their errors or scandals; if this fails, then should reprove them before witnesses, and even denounce them; if still they continue obstinate, they should be condemned or excommunicated by a solemn sentence. Laud and magnify the wisdom of this rule which for nineteen centuries has preserved unbroken the faith and unity of the Church. Consider it now in reference to religious, who are especially subject to brotherly reproof. If you see a brother going astray, or committing any fault which could scandalize or mislead the others, tell him his fault privately; if he will not listen to you, do it before a third person; if you see that your remonstrances are WHOLLY INEFFECTUAL, lay the case before the superior. This is the method traced out for you by Jesus Christ. Have you adopted it? Have you not, on the contrary, failed in your duty either through indifference, or by contenting yourself with despising your brother, making no effort to correct him? or by publishing secret faults to those who have no authority in the matter, or by exaggerating them through anger? And when you have been personally offended, have you not been unwilling or refused to make the first advance? Or, if you are in a position of authority over the rest of the community, over pupils or servants, have you not reproved them IN PUBLIC without real necessity, without tact; or IN PRIVATE with heat and sharpness? These are points for self-examination before God.

Affections and Resolutions

Point II: Rules for forgiveness

Consideration: How often should we forgive? How should we forgive? The Apostles seemed to think that our Lord had not been sufficiently clear upon these points. Peter, speaking in the name of the rest, asked, "Lord, how often shall my brother offend against me, and I forgive him? Until seven times? Jesus saith to him, I say not to thee, until seven times; but until seventy times seven." That is to say, always; and always from the bottom of your heart – EX CORDIBUS VESTRIS.

Application: If we carry out our Lord's directions we shall only be doing to our brother what He Himself does to us through the instrumentality of HIs minister in the confessional. We present ourselves there so often, and so often to accuse ourselves of the same faults; and yet He has always forgiven us, and is always ready to do so again, if He sees that we are humble and contrite, and that unreservedly.

In the Colloquy which we are about to make with Him, let us bless and magnify His inexhaustible goodness, patience, and generosity; blushing at our own unwillingness to forgive the little wrongs that we have received – we who have wronged Him so terribly; thinking with shame of the pardons we have granted, and then wholly or in part withdrawn, by bringing up again and resenting old offences. Promise to do better. Ask for grace to help you. Colloquy with our divine and loving Lord.

September 11: Parable of the Unmerciful Servant

1st prelude: Picture to yourself Jesus uttering this parable.
2nd prelude: Ask for grace to gain great benefits from this meditation.

Point I: The mercy and generosity of the king

Consideration: What our Lord had said of the necessity of forgiving, and the gross injustice of those who refuse to do so, was plain enough. But He wished to bring it home to them still further by a parable: "Therefore is the kingdom of heaven likened to a king who would take an account of his servants. And when he had begun to take the account, one was brought to him that owed him ten thousand talents. And as he had not wherewith to pay it, his lord commanded that he should be sold, and his wife and children, and all that he had, and payment to be made. But the servant falling down, besought him, saying, Have patience with me, and I will repay thee all. And the lord of that servant, being moved with pity, let him go, and forgave him the debt."

Application: 1. This king, who so unexpectedly took account with his servants, represents to us the King of kings, who will take account with you at the moment, always so uncertain, of your death. Are you ready to give it? 2. In this immense debt of ten thousand talents, you see to what a sum, in God's estimation, the sins, the faults of every day, amount. Do you think of this? Instead of trying to reduce your debt by the many ways in your power,are you not continually increasing it? On the other hand, in the readiness of the king to forgive the enormous debt of his faithless servant, you see how easy it is to move your Judge, and discharge your debts now in this world. How foolish to keep them for the next, for purgatory!

Affections and Resolutions.

Point II: The hardheartedness and covetousness of the servant

Consideration: "But when that servant was gone out" from the presence of his mater, who had shown himself so tender and generous, "he found one of his fellow servants that owed him an hundred pence; and laying hold of him, he throttled him, saying, Pay what thou owest. And his fellow servant, falling down, besought him, saying, Have patience with me, and I will pay thee all. And he would not; but went and cast him into prison until he paid the debt."

Application: Our Lord evidently wishes to show us how unjust and ungrateful we should be if, after the pardon of our many and great offences, we show any unwillingness to forgive those who have injured us. Yet have we nothing to reproach ourselves with in this? Are we not one of those who always nourish some ill-will against those who have injured, ridiculed, or humbled us, who avoid their presence , or are cool and distant towards them? Do we not expect others to overlook, or put up with, everything from us, while we make no allowance for their feelings?

Affections and Resolutions.

Point III: Application of the parable

Consideration: "The king," informed of his servant's conduct, "called him, and said to him, Thou wicked servant, I forgave Thee all the debt, because Thou besoughtest me; shouldst not thou then have had compassion also on thy fellow servant, even as I had compassion on thee? And his lord, being angry, delivered him to the torturers until he paid all the debt. So also shall my Heavenly Father do to you, if you forgiven not every one his brother from your hearts."

Application: Let these last words sink deeply into your heart. They will silence, when the time of trial comes, the voice of anger, indignation, and revenge. Colloquy.

September 12: Incidents on our Lord's Journey through Galilee

1st prelude: Picture to yourself our Lord as He walked with the disciples.
2nd prelude: Ask for grace to be imbued with the mind and spirit of Jesus.

Point I: Jesus is pressed to hasten towards Jerusalem

Consideration: The Gospel records several remarkable occurrences on the journey which our Lord made by short stages from Capharnaum to Jerusalem. First of all several of His relatives (nephews of Saint Joseph) joined Him on the way, and begged Him to make more speed, so as to reach Jerusalem the first day of the Feast of Tabernacles, which was the 15th of the seventh month, I.E., September. They hoped He would work some great miracles, which would reflect some credit upon them (MANIFESTA TE IPSUM MUNDO – "Manifest Thyself to the world") in the capital – "that Thy disciples also may see Thy works which Thou doest." Jesus answered, "Go you up to this festival today; but I go not up to this festival day." He delayed His arrival until the third day of the feast, because of a plot against His life which was to have been put in execution on the first.

Application: "Manifest thyself to the world"; make yourself a name; strive to be honored, praised, admired. So whispers the innate pride of our hearts. How often have we acted upon the suggestion! How many merits we have lost by doing so! Do you doubt it? Lay your hand upon your heart, and tell me if you do not prefer the society of the rich to that of the poor: if you would not rather fill an important post than a lower one; if you would not rather preach to the noble and the learned than to the uneducated and the poor; if your main object in life is not rather to please man than God?

Affections and Resolutions.

Point II: A Samaritan village refuses to receive Jesus

Consideration: At one place on our Lord's journey through Samaria the inhabitants refuse to receive Him on account of the ancient enmity between themselves and the Jews. "And when His disciples James and John had seen this, they said, Lord, wilt Thou that we command fire to come down from heaven and consume them? And turning, He rebuked them, saying, You know not of what spirit you are. The Son of Man came not to destroy souls, but to save."

Application: In these words our Savior warns us against a spirit of bitterness or cruelty under the name of zeal. We are all prone to this; but we are mistaken if we think it can be pleasing to God. We deceive ourselves when we ask God to punish the wicked or persecutors without delay. Such is not the spirit of Jesus Christ, who came not to destroy, but to save; who bids us pray for our persecutors; who Himself prayed for them on the cross; who (as Saint Peter tells us) "dealeth patiently, not willing that any should perish, but that all should return to repentance."

Affections and Resolutions.

Point III: Another town welcomed the Savior

Consideration: When our Lord was repulsed from the city whose hospitality He had deigned to ask, He made not complaint, but "went into another town."

Application: Happy citizens! What favors will your divine guest not show you! O Jesus, deign to take possession of my heart, to come in and dwell there; make it all your own, your very own. May that blessed promise be fulfilled in Me – "I any one love Me, he will keep My word, and My Father will love him, and We will come to him, and make Our abode with him."

Colloquy.

September 13: Other Events on our Lord's Journey: Healing of the Ten Lepers

1st prelude: Hear Jesus saying to the lepers, "Go, show yourselves to the priests."

2nd prelude: Ask for grace to keep your soul free from the leprosy of sin.

Point I: The prayer of the lepers

Consideration: "As Jesus entered into a certain town there met Him ten men that were lepers, who stood afar off, and lifted up their voice, saying, Jesus, Master, have mercy on us." What is the character of this prayer? It is HUMBLE and RESPECTFUL: conscious of their loathsome appearance, these lepers would not come near Him. It is CONFIDENT: they believed He could cure them where they stood, without any natural remedy. It is FERVENT: their whole heart was in their cry for help. It is TOUCHING: they appeal to Him both as their Savior and their Master. It is CHARITABLE: they ask, not each for himself alone, but for one another, uniting their interests.

Application: Do your prayers possess these characteristics? They will always be heard if they do. Does it seem difficult to pray like this? Have you less need to pray than these poor lepers had? Has not the leprosy of sin made your soul more miserable, more hideous in the sight of God!

Affections and Resolutions.

Point II: The obedience of the lepers

Consideration: "Whom when He saw, He said, Go, show yourselves to the priests." This command supposed that the leprosy would disappear before they presented themselves to the priests. But they had no assurance, no promise that this would be the case. They might naturally have demurred, or at least have asked for some explanation. But they did neither; they obeyed blindly; and they had not been long on the road before their obedience was rewarded: "And it came to pass as they went they were made clean."

Application: Here is a beautiful example of obedience, and a striking proof of the merit and efficacy of BLIND OBEDIENCE. Blind, because it shuts our eyes to the character of our lawful superior – to the reasons of his commands, to the difficulties of executing them – that we may see God alone, in whose name he acts. How precious in the sight of God is this obedience, which the world calls folly! Precious, because in it man sacrifices to God his noblest faculties, the light of his understanding. God has always rewarded it magnificently; often even by miracles. We have a proof of it here. Have you always esteemed as you ought BLIND obedience? Have you practiced it?

Affections and Resolutions.

Point III: Ingratitude of the lepers

Consideration: Of the ten lepers who were cured only one proved grateful. "And one of them, when he saw that he was made clean, went back, with a loud voice glorifying God. And he fell on his face before His feet, giving thanks: and this was a Samaritan." The rest made no other return for the benefit they had received than neglect and ingratitude. "And Jesus answering said, Were not ten made clean? and where are the nine? There is no one found to return and give glory to God but this stranger. And He said to him, Arise, go they way, for they faith hath made thee whole."

Application: We see here how our Lord regards ingratitude and thankfulness, and how careful we should be to make continual acts of thanksgiving to God. GRATIAS AGENTES SEMPER. Do we not often fail to do this? Some danger threatens us – a pestilence, perhaps; we pray to be preserved from it; it passes, and we give no thanks for our deliverance. When we recover from a sickness, we thank God; but when He gives us a much greater favor – uninterrupted health – do we thank Him then? Every day we say grace after meals; how often do we say it from the heart? Colloquy.

September 14: On Confession

1st prelude: Hear Jesus saying, "Go, show yourselves to the priests."
2nd prelude: Ask for grace to make always good confessions.

Point I: Preparation for confession

Consideration: The Fathers tell us that leprosy is a type of sin, which pollutes the soul in the sight of God. By the command which our Lord gave to the lepers to show themselves to the priests, He would have us understand that we also must have recourse to the priest in the Sacrament of Penance. Let us consider now the great blessings contained in this Sacrament, and what we ought to do to approach it worthily. First of all, PREPARATION. It should be serious and careful, but not scrupulous. There are some pious people to whom confession is torture. They weary themselves beyond measure in making their examination of conscience and act of contrition. They never think they have done enough under either head. This is a defect. But there is another defect which religious have much more reason to guard against; and that is, treating confession as a matter of routine, thinking that as everything is included in the ordinary formula of accusation, and examination of conscience is unnecessary. So, to, with regard to their act of contrition: they never think of asking God for grace to make it well. What sort of confession would be likely to follow such a preparation as this?

Application: 1. Have a particular day and particular hour for confession, and keep to it, otherwise you will constantly put it off. 2. On the morning of the day hear Mass with the intention to obtain the grace of perfect contrition. At the Consecration renew your intention, and excite in your heart a sorrow for your sins. You can make your examination of conscience during the first part of Mass. If you do this, all that you will require afterwards is a few moments of preparation immediately before your enter the confessional.

Affections and Resolutions.

Point II: On self-accusation

Consideration: We all know that this should be humble and sincere, or entire. In some cases it may be more difficult for religious to be sincere than for those who can choose their own confessor; but they must remember that no fall, however, grave it may be, could ever surprise a confessor; and this will help them to overcome their false shame, which is the cause of so many sacrileges. We know, too, that the object of frequent confession is to become more and more perfect. To accomplish this, it is much better to confine the accusation of ourselves to certain principal faults than to mention and infinity of defects and natural infirmities, for which it is hard to have true contrition; otherwise our confession will be vague and unprofitable.

Application: Method to adopt: 1. If you have a grave sin upon your conscience, confess that FIRST; for if you begin with lesser faults, your courage may fail you. 2. Confine your EXPLICIT accusation to two or three principal faults, intending to cure yourself of ONE IN PARTICULAR. In this way you will get rid of them all in succession. 3. When in addition, you mention some sin of your past life, try to feel as great compunction for it as if you confessed it then for the first time. This is the easiest way to ensure contrition.

Affections and Resolutions.

Point III: Thanksgiving

Consideration: In order to obtain the best results from frequent confession, it is important – 1st, to make an act of faith in the efficacy of the Sacrament; 2nd, to renew your intention; 3rd, to ask for grace to be faithful to it.

Application: To do this, say, "I believe, my Jesus, that Your Blood, through this Sacrament, has flowed over my soul; that You have purified it and adorned it with fresh gifts. I thank You, and I renew my resolution not to commit again this sin especially. I will impose upon myself a penance if I fall into it again. Bless, O my Jesus, all my efforts."
Colloquy with our Lord, who instituted the Sacrament of Penance.

September 15: Jesus Arrives in Jerusalem after an Absence of Eighteen Months

1st prelude: Behold Him preaching to an immense crowd in the temple.
2nd prelude: Ask for grace to imitate His zeal and patience..

Point I: Diversity of opinions respecting our Lord at Jerusalem

Consideration: Our Lord so arranged His journey that He arrived at Jerusalem on the evening of the third day of the Feast of Tabernacles. He entered with His Apostles quietly and unobserved, and did not show Himself in the temple until the following day, which was the sabbath. He thus frustrated the plot against His life. Nevertheless everyone had been talking of Him, especially since He miraculously cured the ten lepers. "The Jews therefore sought Him on the festival-day, and said, Where is He? And there was much murmuring among the multitude concerning Him. For some said, "He is a good man; and others said, No, but He seduceth the people."

Application: Be not surprised that people should think so very differently about our Lord. It always has been, and always will be, the case with public benefactors. Some praise their zeal; others, even well-meaning people, blame it, or attribute bad motives to it. Do not, then, think it strange if the same thing happens to you – if your superiors or your brethren form different estimates of your fitness for the office of preacher, catechist, professor or director. If you are humble, you will wonder rather that anyone should have a good opinion of you; and so far from being offended or discouraged by criticisms passed upon yourself or your conduct, you will strive rather to profit by them. Have you done so?
Affections and Resolutions.

Point II: Admiration of Jesus

Consideration: The day after His arrival, the fourth day of the feast, "Jesus went up into the temple, and taught. And the Jews wondered, saying, How doth this man know letters, having never learned? Jesus answered them, and said, My doctrine is not Mine, but His that sent Me. He that speaketh of himself seeketh his own glory; but he that seeketh the glory of Him that sent him, he is true, and there is no injustice in him."

Application: The doctrine which we preach in public or teach in private is not our own, but Christ's, who sends us. We should, then, be most careful not to misrepresent it through inaccuracy, or want of preparation, or human respect. See if you have anything to reproach yourself with, either against TRUTH, by falsifying, or against JUSTICE, by seeking your own glory.

Affections and Resolutions.

Point III: The chief men amongst the Jews show their hatred of Jesus

Consideration: The doctors and princes of the nation, afraid of being thrown into the shade, had long tried to ruin Jesus in the popular estimation, and even to raise a tumult in which they might get Him killed without incurring the odium of a murder. The people knew nothing of their intrigues, but Jesus did, and charged them with them openly: "Why seek you to kill Me?" But they pretended to be indignant, and answered, "Thou has a devil: who seeketh to kill Thee?" DAEMONIUM HABES: QUIS TE QUAERIT INTERFICERE?

Affections: Alas, even in these days pride and wickedness conspire to excite the people by lies and calumnies against Christ, His Church, His vicar, His priests – above all, against religious. Be not surprised or disturbed at this; follow your Divine Master, whose only answer to insult and calumny was a still more earnest endeavor to instruct and save the people. Have you done this?

Colloquy.

September 16: Jesus Preaches Again in the Temple

1st prelude: Behold Him preaching to an immense crowd in the temple.

2nd prelude: Ask for grace to imitate His zeal and patience.

Point I: Jesus invites all those who thirst after righteousness

Consideration: Jesus appeared a second time in the temple on the last and most solemn day of the feast; for then the Jews went to drink of the fountain of Siloe, and sprinkled the altar with its water to obtain a fruitful harvest. Our Lord took advantage of the concourse of people to give an instruction, which He began by an allusion to the ceremony of the day: "Jesus stood and cried, saying, If any man thirst, let him come to Me and drink"; that is to say, If anyone thirst for truth and holiness, which give supernatural life and vigor to the soul, let him come to Me; let him believe and hope in Me, the Source of life, and he shall be satisfied; and from his heart, as from a never-failing fountain, the waters of life-giving grace shall spring and flow forth abundantly. "He that believeth in Me, as the Scripture saith, out of his belly shall flow rivers of living water."

Application: Ask most earnestly for this water of the supernatural life, these streams of sanctifying grace, which fill us with the Spirit of God, and enable us to do an apostle's work; to spread around us the sweet savor of Jesus Christ, and a wealth of good works.

Affections and Resolutions.

Point II: Jesus disarms the messengers sent to arrest Him

Consideration: The chief priests and princes had stationed a band of men in the temple with orders to arrest our Lord and bring Him before them if He attempted to preach again. But they were so softened and impressed by the Savior's words that "no man laid hands upon Him. The ministers therefore came to the chief priests and the Pharisees, and they said the them, Why have you not brought Him? The ministers answered, Never did man speak like this Man."

Application: Though our Lord knew perfectly well that men were waiting to seize Him and throw Him into prison, He obeyed the call of love and duty, and entered the temple. Let us imitate His courage and constancy. As religious, as apostles, let neither imprisonment nor death, much less regard for our health or fear of ridicule, turn us from the path of duty. Again, it is said that "no man laid hands upon Him, because His hour was not yet come." His hour – the day when He WISHED to be sacrificed by His enemies. We learn from this that evil will never prevail against us except AT THE TIME and IN THE WAY that God permits. Still,

we ought to be prudent, and make use of wise precautions; for Jesus went not up to Jerusalem until the third day of the feast, and did not show Himself publicly except in the temple.
Affections and Resolutions.

Point III: Nicodemus in the council takes the part of Jesus

Consideration: The chief priests and Scribes, vexed at the failure of their plot, held a meeting in the evening to arrange some plan for securing the person of the Savior. One, however, was found to take His part. This was Nicodemus, the same who came to Jesus by night. He said, "Doth our law judge any man, unless it first hear him, and know what he doth?" To this appeal to the first principles of justice, the answer was, "Art thou also a Galilean? Search the Scriptures, and see that out of Galilee a prophet riseth not. And every man returned to his own house."

Application: We are indignant with these men thus blinded by their passions; but do we not follow their example when we suspect or condemn our brethren without knowing or inquiring into the motives of their conduct?
Colloquy.

September 17: The Woman Taken in Adultery

1st prelude: Picture to yourself our Lord, surrounded by the multitude in the temple, and saying to the adulteress, "Go, and now sin no more."
2nd prelude: Ask for grace to know the mind of Christ, and to be conformed to it.

Point I: Jesus is chosen to judge the case of the adulteress

Consideration: "And early in the morning Jesus came again into the temple: and all the people came to Him, and sitting down, He taught them. And the Scribes and Pharisees bring unto Him a woman taken in adultery, and they set her in the midst, and said to Him, Master, this woman was even now taken in adultery. Now Moses in the law commanded us to stone such a one. But what sayest Thou?" They asked Him as if they intended to abide by His decision. By inviting Him to pass sentence upon the woman, these hypocrites appeared to pay Him great honor, but in reality they only wished to entangle Him, that they might have something whereof to accuse Him.

Application: Consider this most difficult position in which our Lord was placed through the cunning of these wicked men. If He refused the office of judge, He would have seemed to deny His title as the "Sent of God," as emphatically "the Master in Israel"; if He accepted it, He would either be denounced as a violator of the law if He forgave her, or if He condemned her, He would be taxed with cruelty and self-contradiction, because He had said He was come to save, not to destroy. See how Jesus foiled the cunning of His enemies, and even turned it to their own confusion, and you will feel the truth of the words, "There is no wisdom, there is no prudence, there is no counsel against the Lord." You will admire, reverence, and love our Lord more than ever.

Affections and Resolutions.

Point II: Jesus disappoints her accusers

Consideration: Jesus, who knew the intense malice of those who asked Him to try the case of the adulteress, answered nothing, but "bowing Himself down, wrote with His finger on the ground. When, therefore, they continued asking Him, He lifted up Himself, and said to them, He that is without sin among you, let him first cast a stone at her. And again stooping down, He wrote on the ground." Some think that He wrote the secret sins of the accusers. However that may be, "they went out one by one, beginning with the eldest, and Jesus alone remained, and the woman standing in the midst."

Application: Try to have constantly before your mind these words of our Lord, "He that is without sin" – without defect, wrongheadedness, or singularity in his conduct – "let him first cast a stone" at his brethren. We shall then be more dissatisfied with ourselves than with others; we shall then be what humility and true charity require of us, "severe upon ourselves, indulgent to others."

Affections and Resolutions.

Point III: Jesus pardons the adultress

Consideration: When all her accusers were gone, and she was left alone with our Lord, He said to her, "Woman, where are they that accused thee – hath no man condemned thee? Who said, No man, Lord. And Jesus said, Neither will I condemn thee; go, and now sin no more." Doubly saved – body and soul together! What a blessed moment this must have been to her! What reverence, what gratitude, what love must her heart have felt for Jesus her Savior!

Application: Think of all that this same God and Savior has done for you. From how many dangers has He rescued you? how many sins has He forgiven you? You too will glow with love and gratitude. Close this meditation with he outpouring of your heart, and let your actions through the day bear witness to it.
Colloquy with Jesus our Savior and our Pattern.

September 18: Jesus the Light of the World

1st prelude: Picture to yourself Jesus saying, "I am the light of the world."
2nd prelude: Ask for a great gift of divine light.

Point I: Jesus is the Light of the world

Consideration: "I am the Light of the world." With these solemn words our Lord began His third sermon in the temple. To understand what the world owes to the Divine Light incarnate in the person of Jesus Christ, we must consider the state of society before the Incarnation. The most senseless idolatry was substituted for the worship of the only true God; divine honors were given to gods of wood and stone; human sacrifices were offered with the most dreadful cruelty; more than half the world were reduced to a state of slavery, and treated like brute beasts; children were abandoned; and the most shameful excesses, the worst vices, were raised to the rank of virtues.

Application: To whom do we owe our deliverance from all the errors and abominations of Paganism? To Jesus Christ, and to the light of the true faith which, by means of His Apostles, He spread throughout the world. It is to Him alone that we owe all the good, both natural and supernatural, that we enjoy, to Him who enlightens every man that does not willfully close his eyes; to Him who has taught us the nobleness of our origin, the grandeur of our destiny, the duties we owe to God, to our neighbors, and ourselves – duties which, faithfully fulfilled, would undoubtedly make the human race happy, both in this world and the next. What gratitude, then, do we not owe to our Lord? Have you thought enough about this? Do you try to make others feel it?
Affections and Resolutions.

Point II: He that follows Jesus walks not in darkness

Consideration: QUI SEQUITUR ME NON AMBULAT IN

TENEBRIS – "He that followeth Me walketh not in darkness" – in the paths, that is, of vice and error – but in the daylight of truth and virtue. When pagan savages have been brought to Christ, and have learnt and followed the doctrines of His Gospel, this of itself had been sufficient to transform them into models of virtue, gentleness, of heroism; when, on the contrary, any abandon these doctrines, like the followers of Mahomet, they relapse into barbarism; when they alter it by heresy, they fall into a chaos of doubt and human opinions; when they are separated from it by schism, they become the sport of the secular power.

Application: How sweet and consoling it is for us to meditate upon these great truths, for us whom the Lord "Hath called out of darkness," in the persons of our ancestors, "into His marvelous light"; for us who, born of Catholic parents, have been taught from our childhood the knowledge and love of God! Let us take care to show ourselves worthy of this great favor.

Affections and Resolutions.

Point III: He who follows Jesus has the light of life

Consideration: "He that followeth Me walketh not in darkness, but shall have the light of life"; that is to say, the light of the spiritual life which leads to life eternal, to the Beatific Vision. He who lives habitually in a state of grace, except from mortal sin, is sin the first grade of the spiritual life; he who lives exempt from deliberate venial sin, is in the second; he who, entirely detached from the world, aims habitually at the perfect imitation of Christ, is in the third.

Application: You think highly of those who reach this third degree, because they have in this life great spiritual illumination, the source of sweetness unspeakable, and in the next a greater share in the joys of the Beatific Vision. Do not despair of attaining this. Jesus calls you to it; He gives you the means to reach it. Use them with humility, confidence, perseverance, and success will attend your efforts.

Colloquy.

September 19: The Sermon Continued: Contradiction and Violence of the Pharisees

1st prelude: Picture to yourself the Scribes and Pharisees watching Jesus preaching.

2nd prelude: Ask for a great dread of the spirit of contradiction.

Point I: The spirit of contradiction shown by the Pharisees

Consideration: "I am the Light of the world." Our Lord had hardly uttered these solemn words when the Pharisees interrupted Him, saying, "Thou givest testimony of Thyself; Thy testimony is not true. Jesus answered and said to them, Although I give testimony of Myself, My testimony is true, because I am not alone, but I and the Father that sent Me. And in your law it is written , that the testimony of two men is true. They said therefore to Him, Where is Thy Father? Jesus answered, If you did know Me, perhaps you would know My Father also." Then turning to those who believed in Him, He said, "If you continue in My Word, you shall be My disciples indeed; and you shall know the truth, and the truth shall make you free." The Pharisees cried, "How sayest Thou, You shall be free? We are the seed of Abraham, and we have never been slaves to any man. Jesus answered them, Amen, amen I say unto you, that whosoever committeth sin is the servant of sin."

Application: These frequent and impertinent interruptions prove that the Pharisees merely adopted this line of conduct because they felt that our Lord was infinitely their superior in knowledge, holiness, and authority. Their pride was hurt – thence came envy and the spirit of contradiction. Alas, does not this same spirit show itself somewhat in you? and against whom? Is it not against those who in many respects are your superiors, and before whom you should be humble and silent?

Affections and Resolutions.

Point II: Calmness and gentleness of Jesus

Consideration: "Jesus saith to them, If you be the children of Abraham, do the works of Abraham. But now you seek to kill Me, because My words displease you. Neither Abraham nor God is your father, but the devil, whose will you do. Since the day of his first lie, he has not ceased to hate the truth, and you listen to him. But if I say the truth, you believe Me not. Which of you shall convince Me of sin? He that is of God heareth the words of God. The Jews therefore answered and said to Him, Do we not say well that Thou art a Samaritan, and hast a devil? Jesus answered, I have not a devil, but I honor My Father. Amen, amen I say unto you, if any man keep My word, he shall not see death for ever. The Jews therefore said, Now we know that Thou hast a devil. Abraham is dead, and the prophets; and Thou sayest, If any man keep My word, he shall not taste death for ever. Whom dost Thou make Thyself?"

Application: Mark the imperturbable calmness and gentleness of our Divine Master, and try to imitate Him. If it is difficult to do so in many things, yet do not despair. With perseverance and prayer all things are possible.

Affections and Resolutions.

Point III: Dreadful consequences of the spirit of contradiction

Consideration: To the question of the Pharisees, "Whom dost Thou make Thyself?" Jesus replied at once, by declaring that He was the Eternal Son of God. "If I glory Myself, My glory is nothing; it is My Father that glorifieth Me. Abraham your father rejoiced that he might see my day; he saw it, and was glad. The Jews therefore said to him, Thou art not yet fifty years old, and hast Thou seen Abraham? Jesus said to them, Amen, amen I say to you, before Abraham was made, I am." In these short words the Jews understood our Lord to proclaim Himself to be, what in fact He was, the equal of God. They looked upon Him as a sacrilegious blasphemer, and "took up stones to cast at Him; but Jesus hid Himself, and went out of the temple."

Application: To understand this spirit of contradiction, which is the child of pride, and all the horror it deserves, see to what it led those even who were the depositaries of science and law in Israel, to what spiritual blindness and obstinacy, for they neither saw nor wished to see in Jesus the evident tokens that Hew as the Messiah; to what hardness of impiety, to what final impenitence. As our Lord said to them, "You shall die in your sin."

Colloquy.

September 20: Wonderful Cure of the Man Born Blind

1st prelude: Picture to yourself Jesus applying the clay, moistened with spittle, to the eyes of the man born blind.

2nd prelude: Ask for the blind man's faith and ready obedience.

Point I: Cause of the blindness

Consideration: Before leaving Jerusalem, our Lord wished to give His enemies, unworthy thought they were, a still further proof of His divinity – a proof striking, irresistible, of which everyone should hear, and which should afterwards be brought before the synagogue. Saint John tells us, "Jesus, passing by, saw a man who was blind from his birth; and His disciples asked Him, Rabbi, who hath sinned, this man or his parents, that he should be born blind? Jesus answered, Neither hath this man sinned, nor his parents; but that the works of God should be made manifest in him." Of course, our Lord in His answer, and the Apostles in their question, speak only with reference to the blindness. They had doubtless committed sin; "for there is no just man upon earth that doeth good and sinneth not." But the blindness was not sent as a punishment for any sin.

Application: We have here a plain proof that suffering in this world is not ALWAYS the consequence of actual sin. Consequently, afflictions may not be sent as chastisements, but as trials, which God permits to fall upon the just, and even upon the greatest saints, for His own glory, and to increase their merits. So it was in the case of Job, of Tobias, of many other saints, both in the Old and the New Testament; therefore, we should never lose our confidence or get discouraged when the hand of God is upon us; we should rather rejoice as Saint James distinctly tells us. Again, in speaking of the misfortunes of the wicked, we should not always put them down as plain tokens of God's displeasure. Occasions may arise in which the same might be remarked on us. What has been your practice?

Affections and Resolutions.

Point II: Miraculous cure of the bind man

Consideration: "When Jesus had said these things, He spat on the ground, and made clay of the spittle, and spread the clay upon his eyes, and said to him, Go, wash in the pool of Siloe, which is interpreted Sent. He went, therefore, and washed; and he came seeing."

Application: One hardly knows which to admire most, the trial to which the blind man's faith and obedience were subjected, or the readiness with which he did what he was told, without making any objection, as he might naturally have done. Both are wonderful, and full of instruction for us. Let this story confirm our faith, let it teach us to leave ourselves entirely in the hands of God, and to render Him a BLIND obedience. We see here at once the

merit and the recompense – what do we want more to encourage us?
Affections and Resolutions.

Point III: Surprise and doubt of the neighbors

Consideration: The blind man, a beggar by profession, was known to everyone. It was natural that his cure should make a great noise. "The neighbors, therefore, and they who had seen him before that he was a beggar, said, Is not this he that sat and begged? Some said, This is he. But others said, No; but he is like him. But he said, I am he. They said therefore to him, How were thine eyes opened? He answered, That man that is called Jesus made clay, and anointed my eyes and said to me, God to the pool of Siloe, and wash. And I went, I washed and I see."

Application: We see in this candid avowal that the blind man attributed his cure directly to Jesus, because he owed it merely to the means our Savior used. Following this example, let us believe, and openly profess our belief, that it is to God alone that we owe all corporal and spiritual good, as well as all the good we do. This is the way to secure ourselves from vainglory, and to obtain fresh favors from God. Have we done so?
Colloquy.

September 21: The Same Subject Continued

1st prelude: Picture to yourself the blind man standing before the council.
2nd prelude: Ask for his uprightness and generosity.

Point I: The blind man confounds the Pharisees in council

Consideration: The great miracles which our Lord wrought upon the blind man exasperated the Pharisees beyond measure. They determined to damage His reputation, either by questioning the truth of the miracle, or by charging Him with breaking the law by doing it on the sabbath. They had the blind man and his parents brought before the council. The latter declared that he was their son, and that he was born blind. The man on his part declared again that it was Jesus who had spread the clay upon his eyes, and told him to wash, which he did and was cured. Not being able to deny the fact, they tried to rob Him of the seal of His divinity. "This man is not of God," they said, "who keepeth not the sabbath." He must, then, be an agent of the devil, and they tried in every way to make the man think so, but to no purpose. "From the beginning of the world," he said, "it hath not been heard that any man hath opened the eyes of one born blind; unless this Man were of God, He could not do anything." Ashamed and angry at seeing themselves thus refuted by an ignorant beggar, and having no better arguments at hand, "they answered and said to him, Thou wast wholly born in sins, and dost thou teach us? And they cast him out."

Application: It is for our instruction and consolation that the Holy Ghost caused these details to be given. Let us profit by them. Henceforward let us understand better and hate more the base passion of envy. Of what good is it? What did it do for the Pharisees except to cover them with shame and brand them with dishonor? On the other hand, if you are the object of it, fear not; as long as you have truth and virtue on your side, it will do you more good than harm. So it was that everything which our Lord's enemies did against Him through envy ended by adding a proof of the truth of this great miracle, and consequently of His divinity. "To them that love God all things work together for good." What can be more consoling?

Affections and Resolutions.

Point II: The blind man acknowledges and adores his divine Benefactor

Consideration: The uprightness and generosity of the man in glorifying Jesus before the council were magnificently rewarded. "Jesus heard that they had cast him out, and when He had found him, He said to him, Dost thou believe in the Son of God? He answered and said, Who is He, Lord, that I may believe in Him? And Jesus said to him, Thou hast both seen Him, and it is He that talketh with thee. And he said, I believe, Lord; and falling down, he adored Him." Thus was sight given to his soul as well as to his body. Tradition tells us that he attached himself to our Lord's person; that he was one of the seventy-two disciples; that afterwards he was the companion in exile of Lazarus; that he was miraculously landed with him on the coast of Gaul, there labored as an apostle with great success, and died a most holy death at Aix in Provence.

Application: Thank our Lord with all your heart for having

opened your eyes, and revealed Himself to you in a special way; for having made you understand His counsels; for having drawn you to them by the grace of predilection. Ask that you may increase in the knowledge of His divine perfections; that you may love Him more, and try to show your love by making others know and love Him as much as you can.
Colloquy with our loving Savior.

September 22: Mission of the Seventy-two Disciples

1st prelude: Picture to yourself Jesus giving them their instructions.
2nd prelude: Ask for the docility and zeal which they showed.

Point I: Appointment and mission of the seventy-two

Consideration: Jesus, after warning His disciples against the wiles of the Pharisees, left Jerusalem towards the end of the month. He wished to visit and preach in the other towns and villages of Judea. A great work, and but little time to do it in; for the end was approaching – but six months distant. The better to accomplish His purpose, and at the same time to train evangelists who could work at a distance, "He appointed also other seventy-two; and He sent them two and two before His face into every city and place whither He Himself was to come."

Application: You envy the lot of these favored disciples. What happiness, you say, to be the chosen of Christ; to be trained in His school, and upon His model, for one or perhaps for two years, then to have been called and sent upon this mission so full of honor and of merit; to prepare His way before Him, and to win for Him the hearts of men! Doubtless this is a lot worth envying; but has it not fallen upon you also? Have you not enjoyed, are you not still enjoying, as religious, elect followers of Christ, the very same advantages? Your life is devoted to works of charity and zeal; is not this identical with the aim of the seventy-two?
Affections and Resolutions.

Point II: The instructions given to the seventy-two

Consideration: Our Lord gave these new missionaries nearly the same instructions as He had given to the Apostles when He sent them a few months before to preach in Galilee: "Behold I send you as lambs among wolves; carry neither purse, nor scrip, nor shoes, and salute no man by the way. Into whatsoever house you enter, first say, Peace be to this house!… But into whatsoever city you enter, and they receive you, eat such things as are set before you… But if they receive you not, going forth into the streets thereof, say, Even the very dust of your city that cleaveth to us we wipe off against you… I say to you, it shall be more tolerable at that day for Sodom than for that city. Yet know this, that the kingdom of God is at hand," for those who will repent.

Application: Let these divine lessons, these rules of conduct, sink deep into your heart, and, should occasion arise, follow them closely. They may be summed up in these few words: gentleness, disinterestedness, constancy, conciliation, simplicity, recollectedness – all these joined to evangelical firmness, but tempered by mercy and tender calls to repentance. Examine yourself under these heads.

Affections and Resolutions.

Point III: Woes pronounced against the cities which rejected the word of God

Consideration: This third point brings before us something sad, something fearful. The woes which our Lord pronounced against the hardened cities: "Woe to thee, Corazain! Woe to thee, Bethsaida! For if in Tyre and Sidon had been wrought the might works that have been wrought in you, they would have done penance long ago, sitting in sackcloth and ashes. But it shall be more tolerable for Tyre and Sidon at the judgement than for you; and thou, Capharnaum, which art exalted unto heaven, Thou shalt be thrust down to hell."

Application: These woes should inspire us with a wholesome fear. We have been not less favored with the gifts of grace than the inhabitants of Capharnaum. Have we corresponded with them as we should?

Colloquy.

September 23: The Return and Joy of the Seventy-Two

1st prelude: Picture to yourself our Lord surrounded by the joyful disciples.

2nd prelude: Ask for that joy which our Lord would acknowledge.

Point I: Jesus tempers the joy of His disciples

Consideration: The mission of the seventy-two had been a great success, because they had faithfully observed our Lord's directions. Obedience gave them the victory over men and devils, as it is written: VIR OBEDIENS LOQUETUR VICTORIAS – "An obedient man shall speak of victory." "And the seventy-two returned with joy, saying, Lord, the devils also are subject to us in Thy name." This was a legitimate joy; yet we gather from our Lord's reply that it was not altogether free from a vain complacency. He said, "I saw Satan like lightning falling from heaven." As much as to say, Take care, beware of vainglory; it leads to pride, and pride can make you fall, as it made Lucifer and his angels fall from heaven.

Application: Learn from these two things: 1. To follow the rule of obedience; this will ensure us success in all we do. 2. To be on your guard against the insidious attacks, the subtle approach of vainglory, which follows so naturally in the train of success, and which will rob us of all our merit.

Application and Resolutions.

Point II: Jesus corrects the joy of His disciples

Consideration: The joy of the disciples arose from the success they had obtained. Our Lord wished to show them that this motive was not a sound one, inasmuch as success does not depend upon ourselves, does not justify us, and will not always give us a claim to recompense. He pointed out to them, and through them to us, a more substantial motive: "Rejoice not in this, that spirits are subject unto you; but rejoice in this, that your names are written in heaven", or, as he says elsewhere, in the Book of Life.

Application: We may wish for success in our good works, we should even try to obtain it; we may also rejoice if we succeed, and be sorry if we fail; but through it all, our intention must be pure – we must have a single eye to God's glory and our neighbor's good. How comes it that too often failure troubles and disheartens us? Clearly because we think more of our own glory than we do of God. We know that God does not require us to succeed in everything; and if the failure is not the fruit of our own negligence, it will not lessen the reward of our labor. Is it not a spirit of self-seeking which makes us so eager to undertake things which will do us credit, so unwilling to engage in those which cannot bring us into notice? Lift yourself above all this wretched self-love. Raise your thoughts to heaven. Let your happiness and joy consist in pleasing God, in having your name written on the Heart of Jesus, in the Book of Life.

Affections and Resolutions

Point III: Jesus Shares His disciples' joy

Consideration: Our Lord tenderly loved His disciples. He sympathized with them, and rejoiced with them the more, for He knew that the cause of their joy was the gifts bestowed on them by His Heavenly Father. "He rejoiced in the Holy Ghost, and said, I confess to Thee, O Father, Lord of heaven and earth, because Thou hast hidden these things from the wise and prudent and hast revealed them to little ones. Yea, Father, for so it hath seemed good in Thy sight."

Application: When your brother succeeds, rejoice with him. If he surpasses you in ability or in virtue, let no secret jealousy enter your heart, but rather give thanks to God for having enriched him with such gifts. You have a share in them, for we are all members of the same Church. Is this the way in which you have regarded the distribution of God's gifts?

Colloquy.

September 24: The Charity and Loving Calls of Jesus

1st prelude: Listen to Jesus saying, "Come to Me;… take up My yoke upon you, and learn of Me."

2nd prelude: Ask for grace to correspond faithfully to His loving calls.

Point I: Jesus invites us to come to Him

Consideration: Though our Lord devoted Himself especially to His chosen disciples, yet He did not neglect the people. His compassionate love extended to every child of the house of Israel. Later on, it extended to the whole world, through the ministry of His Apostles and disciples. It was to imbue them with this spirit of compassionate universal love that in their presence He uttered these touching words, "Come to Me, all you that labor and are burdened, and I will refresh you." He excepts no one; but prefers those whom the world despises – the poor, the ignorant, the unfortunate.

Application: Here is your pattern. Under obedience you instruct, you nurse, you console the young, the ignorant, the sick, the poor, the imbecile. Attach yourself by preference to the most destitute, the most suffering, the most repulsive. This preference will increase your resemblance to your Divine Master. Never allow yourself to be disgusted or disheartened. Jesus. who acts in and for you, is all powerful. He will sustain you by His grace. He will bring you through all your difficulties, all the trials which your nature shrinks from. "But thanks be to God, who hath given us the victory through our Lord Jesus Christ."

Affections and Resolutions.

Point II: Jesus invites us to take up His yoke, which is sweet and light

Consideration: Jesus, after inviting all those who seek relief from the sufferings inseparable from our human nature, makes a touching appeal to those who, deceived by the fair promises of the devil, have submitted to his yoke, but find that they have but added remorse to their former pains. "Take up My yoke upon you, and learn of Me; because I am meek, and humble of heart, and you shall find rest to your souls. For My yoke is sweet, and My burden light."

Application: We are of the small number who have accepted our Lord's invitation most unreservedly, by leaving all to submit to His law, and to follow His counsels. But, alas, there may have been years of service to the world, of slavery to your passions, before you turned to Him. Yet if it is so, you can better appreciate the difference between the yoke of the devil and that of Christ, you can better understand the solid happiness of your present state, you will give yourself to it with greater fervor! The longer your experience is of the truth of these words, "My yoke is sweet," the greater will be your fervor. "You shall find rest to your soul," an interior rest which the world does not know, and which it cannot give – a rest accompanied often by those spiritual joys which are a foretaste of the bliss of heaven.

Affections and Resolutions.

Point III: Jesus invites us to practice humility

Consideration: "Learn of Me, because I am meek and humble of heart, and you shall find rest to your souls." It is clear from these words that in order to taste this delicious peace which our

Lord promises to those who serve Him faithfully, we must not only be fervent, but also gentle and humble, patiently bearing all injuries, and rendering good for evil.

Application: The way to get and keep these good dispositions, which are so contrary to our natural inclinations, is to have always before you our Lord's example and his glorious promises. This will make everything easy and delightful to us.

Colloquy with our divine and loving Savior.

September 25: Jesus Silences a Scribe who is in Bad Faith

1st prelude: Picture to yourself the Scribe standing before Jesus, and a crowd round them.

2nd prelude: Ask for grace to love God and your neighbors with an upright and generous heart.

Point I: What must we do to be saved?

Consideration: Jesus having entered one sabbath day into the synagogue to teach, as He was wont to do, "a certain lawyer stood up, tempting Him, and saying, Master, what must I do to possess eternal life?" He did not put this question seriously; he only hoped to get some answer from our Lord which might afterwards be turned against Him. Our Lord would therefore have been perfectly justified in treating him with silent contempt, yet, for the sake of those who stood round, He deigned to reply.

Application: If you happen to meet with unprincipled person who ask questions in a captious spirit, or pretend to have doubts about the faith, do not enter into any discussion with them, as if you believed in their sincerity (for they would only laugh at you), unless the honor of our religion required it, or you saw that it would give you an opportunity of explaining things to others who were present. But, in this case, do nothing rashly. Our Lord did not say to all indiscriminately, "I will give you a mouth and wisdom, which all your adversaries shall not be able to resist and gainsay." If you are not a priest or theologian, well-acquainted with the subject, avoid controversy. It may do great harm to religion, as well as to those who hear you, and impiety will triumph.

Affections and Resolutions.

Point II: How we should love God

Consideration: Our Lord, wishing to show the lawyer that it

was not for the sake of instruction that he asked the question, replied, "What is written in the law? How readest thou? He answering said, Thou shalt love the Lord thy God with thy whole heart, and with thy whole soul, and with all thy strength, and with all thy mind, and thy neighbor as thyself. And He said to him, Thou has answered right; this do and thou shalt live."

Application: Give your whole mind to study the practical meaning of each of the terms in this great commandment, so that you may keep it more perfectly.

"WITH THY WHOLE HEART." This is to love nothing so much as God, nothing except in and for God, to be habitually disposed to do anything or suffer anything to please God, to desire only what leads to God, to hate all that turns us from Him.

"WITH THY WHOLE SOUL." This is to be ready to give your life for God, to lose everything rather than lose the grace of God, to banish from your mind every thought which could displease God, or hinder an intimate union with Him.

"WITH ALL THY STRENGTH." This is to spare neither pain nor trouble to advance the glory of God; it is to consecrate to Him our time, our talents, our body, our health, our repose and every energy of our soul.

"WITH ALL THY MIND." This is to be ever striving to come to a better knowledge of the infinite perfections and the will of God, and only to engage in secular studies so far as they make us more fit to work for God. Judge from this how much you love God.

Affections and Resolutions.

Point III: How we should love our neighbor

Consideration: The lawyer, mortified by the exposure of his insincerity, wished to set himself right with the others round him; he therefore asked another question, "And who is my neighbor?" But our Lord, answering him by the parable of the Good Samaritan, laid bare all the pride, malice and selfishness which lurked in his heart, and in those of his colleagues, nominally doctors, but really corrupters of the law.

Application: By trying to justify ourselves like this proud lawyer, we make our position worse both before God and before men.

Colloquy with our Divine Savior.

September 26: Parable of the Good Samaritan: Its Literal Meaning

1st prelude: Picture to yourself a man robbed and wounded, succored by a charitable stranger.
2nd prelude: Ask for a compassionate and generous charity.

Point I: Selfishness of the priests and doctors of the synagogue

Consideration: Our Lord's object in the parable (or, as some Fathers say, the history) of the good Samaritan was publicly to stigmatize the selfish teaching of the doctors of the synagogue, who only recognized as their neighbors those of their own nation who were just, a title which they arrogated to themselves. To the question, "And who is my neighbor?" our Lord replied: "A certain man went down from Jerusalem to Jericho, and fell among robbers, who also stripped him, and having wounded him, went away, leaving him half dead; and it chanced that a certain priest went down the same way, and seeing him, passed by; in like manner also a Levite, when he was near the place and saw him, passed by."

Application: We have here a picture drawn by our Lord Himself of the want of charity amongst the priests and Levites. How consoling it is to turn from this to the boundless charity of our priests, whether secular or religious! There is no disease either of soul or body which they do not seek out and strive to cure. They have filled the world with institutions for the relief of misery in every form: for the child still in its cradle, for the forsaken, the aged, the blind, the deaf and dumb, the insane, the sick of all ages and all ranks, the plague-stricken, the incurable. And everywhere the laity nobly second their efforts; even women, not content with giving their money, give themselves, and seek in far-distant lands for sufferings to alleviate, for souls to win. O Jesus, it is to You, to Your divine teaching, to Your example, that we owe these wonderful effects of charity, which, until Your coming, the world had never seen!

Affections and Resolutions.

Point II: The generous charity of the good Samaritan

Consideration: With the miserable selfishness of the priest and Levite, our Lord contrasts the noble generosity of a Samaritan, whom the Jews would not condescend to recognize as a neighbor.

"But a certain Samaritan, being on his journey, came near him, and seeing him, was moved with compassion. And going up to him, bound up his wounds, pouring in oil and wine; and setting him upon his own beast, brought him to an inn, and took care of him. And the next day he took out two pence, and gave to the host, and said, Take care of him; and whatsoever thou shalt spend over and above, I, at my return, will repay thee."

Application: Our Lord evidently wished us to understand by this, 1st, that we should look upon all, without exception, as our neighbors, even though they may be of a different nation or religion, as were the Jews and Samaritans; 2nd, that the only charity which is worth having is that which shows itself by its deeds; 3rd, that the simple, when their hearts are right, understand their duty better than learned men who are proud; it is a Samaritan who sets an example to a Jew, a layman to a priest. Take care not to be surprised in generosity by pious laymen.

Affections and Resolutions.

Point III: Humiliating confession of the lawyer

Consideration: After our Lord had spoken this parable, He asked the lawyer, "which of these three, in thy opinion, was neighbor to him that fell among the robbers? But he said, "he that showed mercy to him." Thus it was that our Lord, for the second time, condemned him out of his own mouth, and having left him without excuse, He bid him, "Go and do thou in like manner."

Application: FAC SIMILITER. In these last words our Lord tells us that our charity, like that of the Samaritan, should be active and generous, that we should exercise it at the expense of our personal comfort, of our tastes, our health, even of our life, if the salvation of our neighbor requires it. How far does your charity go?

Colloquy.

September 27: Spiritual Interpretation of the Parable

1st prelude: Picture to yourself a man robbed and wounded, succored by a charitable stranger.

2nd prelude: Ask for a compassionate and generous charity.

Point I: The traveler robbed and wounded a type of the sinner

Consideration: The mystical meaning which many Fathers

attach to this parable, and which our Lord may have had in view, is not hard to discover. It is the whole race of man, fallen and bruised by the sin of Adam, raised up again, and finally cured by the Word made flesh, the Redeemer of the world. In a more restricted sense, it is the sinner and his Savior. Consider, first, how all that happened to the unfortunate traveler who fell among the thieves has its counterpart in the soul which falls through mortal sin into the devil's power. It is robbed of all – of its innocence, its bridal robe, of sanctifying grace, of its supernatural beauty which made it like the angels, of its rights of divine adoption, of all its merits. It is covered besides with hideous wounds which sin has made in it; in short, having only fait without charity, it is half dead.

Application: Wretched I should rightly call myself, if in my life I have committed but one mortal sin; wretched, when I think of the state to which I brought myself, and in which I lived for weeks and months; doubly wretched, in that I blinded myself to my misery, and even delighted in it. Where should I be now, if death had surprised me then? But how came this misfortune upon me? Because I WENT DOWN FROM JERUSALEM TO JERICHO; that is to say, because in thought and in affection I went far away from God, from heaven, from my last end, to seek earthly goods and worldly pleasures. Alas, religious though I am, I can still wander away. How I should tremble, then, for my perseverance, tremble lest I should fall, as other religious have done, into the snares which the devils sets for them.

Affections and Resolutions.

Point II: The good Samaritan a type of Christ

Consideration: In the good Samaritan behold the figure of Jesus, our Divine Savior. The resemblance is too strong to be mistaken. The Jew left half dead was, in the eyes of the Samaritan, a stranger, a natural enemy, and moreover a wretch reduced to a horrible and loathsome condition. Yet the moment he saw him, he was touched with compassion, dismounts, and succors him. We also, by sin, have become strangers, enemies, loathsome in the eyes of the Son of God. Yet, at the sight of our misery, He is touched with compassion, comes down from heaven, becomes our neighbor through the Incarnation, rescues us. Now, think of all that the good Samaritan did to console and cure the traveler, and you will see a faint image of what Christ has done for you. He poured over the wounds of your soul the wine of compunction and the oil of sanctifying grace, and He has closed them with the balm of His Precious Blood. Then He laid you, not upon a beast of burden, but upon His own shoulders, like the Good Shepherd, and carried you, a religious, not into an inn, but to a house of His own; charged another with your welfare; Himself directed that all your wants, both bodily and spiritual, should be supplied until He should return to bring you into the palace of His glory.

Application: If you could not help feeling love and admiration for the good Samaritan in the parable, how much more should you feel for the True Samaritan, who every day has shown Himself so good, so generous towards you! But how can you show your love and gratitude? By fervor in serving Him, by obedience to your superiors, who represent Him, by eagerness to assist the poor, the sick, the wretched, in whom He lives, suffers, hungers, as He said Himself, "I was hungry, and you gave Me to eat; sick, and you visited Me. As long as you did it to one of these My least brethren, you did it to Me." In this way show your gratitude.
Colloquy.

September 28: Motives and Conditions of Brotherly Love

1st prelude: Picture to yourself Saint Peter saying, "Before all things have a constant mutual charity among yourselves."
2nd prelude: Ask for a great desire to excel in brotherly love.

Point I: The precept of Christ the first motive of charity

Consideration: Our meditation on the good Samaritan reminds us of the great duty of brotherly love, in which the charm of a religious life should consist. What motives are set before us for cultivating this virtue? 1. Our Lord make it His great commandment. "This is My commandment, that you love one another, as I have loved you." 2. He wishes charity to be the distinctive mark of His true disciples. "By this shall all men know that you are my disciples, if you have love one for another." 3. Having all left our earthly fathers, and having now but one common Father who is in heaven, we are brothers indeed, seated at the same table, walking the same road by the observance of the same rule. 4. In consequence of our frequent communions, the same blood flows through our veins – the Blood of Christ.

Application: If you consider attentively these motives, your love for charity will increase. So, too, will your desire faithfully to observe the conditions under which alone it can exist in community life, and to understand the secret of mutual support, which requires two things. 1. That you should not only bear patiently with the faults of ALL your brothers, but even excuse them, and shut your eyes to them. 2. That you should readily forgive and forget injuries done to you, attributing them to thoughtlessness rather than making a personal matter of them; that no one should ever hear you say, "I keep out of the way of such a brother, or else I should lose my temper – I can't get on with him" or "I try to be on good terms with all, but if any of them offend me, I take care to let him know it, for his own sake." This is not mutual support; this is not the language of charity, but of the world.
Affections and Resolutions.

Point II: Our Lord's example the second motive

Consideration: The whole life of Jesus was one act of love. Far from being a burden to anyone, He passed His life in doing good to all, without complaining of the ingratitude He received in return. He took upon Himself all our sorrows to console them, all our sins to expiate them. After a life of sacrifice, He died the martyr of love, finding excuses even for His executioners: "Father, forgive them, for they know not what they do."

Application: Let us be ready, as our Savior was, to sacrifice our comfort, and , if need be, our health, or even our life, for our brothers. Let us at least be faithful to what, in the second place, the law of mutual support requires – to watch ourselves, to abstain from everything which could hurt or vex another, to become all things to all men. You know that such and such things give offence – alter them. Your jokes are not always taken in good part – leave off making them. On certain days bodily suffering makes you cross – set an especial watch over yourself then, lest others get the benefit of it. How have you observed these necessary rules? In what have you failed most?
Affections and Resolutions.

Point III: Our Lord's threats and promises the third motive

Consideration: It appears from our Lord's words that the sentence which He will pronounce at the last day will depend mainly upon our charity. "Come, ye blessed of my Father;… I was hungry, and you gave Me to eat." And on the other hand, "Depart from Me, you cursed;... I was hungry, and you gave Me not to eat."

Application: How immensely it is for our interest (to put it on the lowest grounds) to excel in charity, and to fight strenuously against our self-love, which is the chief cause of our want of love. Colloquy with our Lord, Sovereign of the Martyrs of Charity.

September 29: Brotherly Love and its Qualities

1st prelude: Listen to our Lord saying, "Love one another, as I have loved you."
2nd prelude: Beg for the spirit of holy charity.

Point I: Our charity should be supernatural and universal

Consideration: Our Lord wishes us to love one another as He has loved us – UT DILIGATIS INVICEM SICUT DILEXI VOS. He has loved us with a love supernatural, universal, active, compassionate, generous and heroic. Such should be the character of our love, Above all, it should be supernatural, based upon faith, which enables us to discern and love in our brother a living image of God, a member of the mystical body of Christ – yes, even Christ Himself, who says that He looks upon that as done to Himself which we do to another. If our charity is supernatural, it will be also universal; for ALL our brothers are children of God, and brothers of Christ.

Application: Do not fall into the mistake of so many Christians, who flatter themselves that they have charity when they have but the shadow of it. Such people are cold and indifferent, except to those whose position or influence makes them desirable acquaintances, or to whom they may have taken a fancy. In this there is not even a shadow of real charity – nothing but selfishness. Beware of such a delusion, and strive to make more progress in true charity, in that which is supernatural, which will make you embrace in Christ all your brothers equally; unless, indeed, it leads you rather to prefer those whom you naturally dislike.
Affections and Resolutions.

Point II: Charity is active and compassionate

Consideration: The charity of Christ was not a mere sentiment, it showed itself in action. His public life, which we have nearly finished, was an unbroken series of acts of charity, of a charity engaging and tender.

Application: Is your charity like this? Is it active? Does it make you anxious to help and comfort your brothers in every possible way? Is it attentive to the needs and sufferings of your brothers, or is it rendered grudgingly, at the instance of humble petitions? When you see a brother in difficulty from overwork or fatigue, are you content with merely expressing your regret; or if sent to help him, do you go with a bad grace? Ah, if you had a more lively faith, you would have a more perfect charity – you would anticipate your brother's wants, remembering that it is to your Lord you do it in the person of your brother.

Affections and Resolutions.

Point III: It must be generous and heroic

Consideration: The love which Jesus bore us regarded not only our bodily needs, but still more the wants of the soul; in all its manifestations it was self-sacrificing, it was heroic. "Greater love than this no man hath, that a man lay down his life for his friends."

Application: Here is the pattern and the measure for your charity. It must be generous, ready (when called upon) to make heroic sacrifices for the temporal and, above all, for the spiritual good of your brothers. In the meantime, we should at least support, encourage and, by our good example, edify them. We should frequently commend them to God, and pray that the community may increase in numbers and in fervor. Have you thus understood and practiced charity?

Colloquy.

September 30: Jesus in the House of Martha and Mary

1st prelude: Picture to yourself Saint Mary Magdalene in contemplation at the feet of Jesus.

2nd prelude: Ask for grace to unite contemplation with activity.

Point I: Jesus visits Martha and Mary

Consideration: Now that He had left Capharnaum, our Lord had no settled home, so He generally relied for food and lodging on the hospitality of others. So, as Saint Luke tells us, "it came to pass as they went that He entered into a certain town; and a certain woman named Martha received Him into her house. And she had a sister called Mary, who, sitting also at the Lord's feet, heard His word. But Martha was busy about much serving."

Application: While we consider these two sisters, so widely differing in character, and yet so closely united to each other, let us think if it is not possible and even necessary to unite the ACTIVE with the CONTEMPLATIVE life – a blessed union, and one most fruitful in merits! In what does it consist? Is it MERELY to add to our works of charity the Office said in choir? If this were all, the union would be neither difficult nor rare – almost every religious would accomplish it. No, it is something more than this – it consists in being HABITUALLY united to God by intention and affection in all exterior work, even amid the distraction and bustle of the world.

Affections and Resolutions.

Point II: Martha complains of Mary: Jesus replies

Consideration: While the evening meal was being prepared Mary sat at our Lord's feet in sweet repose, feeding her soul with the Divine Word. Martha, on the contrary, was engrossed in household matters. MARTHA SATAGEBAT CIRCA FREQUENS MINISTERIUM. Seeing that her sister had no intention of helping her, she thought she might fairly complain: "Lord, hast Thou no care that my sister hath left me alone to serve? Speak to her, therefore, that she help me. And the Lord answering said to her, Martha, Martha, thou art careful, and art troubled about many things. But one thing is necessary. Mary hath chosen the best part, which shall not be taken away from her."

Application: Let us dwell a little on these words, every one of which is full of meaning. 1st, "Thou art careful, and art troubled about many things." How many religious, in other respects fervent and zealous, merit this reproach, because they allow themselves to be engrossed in matters foreign to their office, or do their duty in an excitable, self-seeking spirit, impatient of failure! Might our Lord's words be applied to you? Examine yourself and see.

2nd, "But one thing is necessary." Many things are RELATIVELY necessary, one only ABSOLUTELY – it is to work out your salvation, because no one else can do it for you, and your state in eternity depends upon it. You should think more of this than of anything else. Is it your first thought in the morning, your last at night?

3rd, "Mary has chosen the best part, which shall not be taken away from her." Why did our Lord prefer the part which Mary chose – contemplation? Because it will remain when action is over; because it will be an eternal source of joy to us in heaven as it was of happiness on earth; because contemplation, by revealing to us God's infinite perfections, inflames us with that love from which heroism springs. It was Mary, not Martha, who stood beneath the cross on Calvary.
Colloquy.

October 1: Parable of the Covetous Rich Man: The Danger of Wealth

1st prelude: Listen to these words of Jesus, "Take heed, and beware of all covetousness."
2nd prelude: Ask for grace to value highly your vow of poverty, and to be entirely faithful to it.

Point I: Riches do not make people happy

Consideration: "And one of the multitude said to Him, Master, speak to my brother that he divide the inheritance with me. But He said to him Man, who hath appointed Me judge or divider over you? And He said to them, Take heed and beware of all covetousness; for a man's life doth not consist in the abundance of things which he possesseth."

Application: By declining to enter into the personal question between the two brothers, our Lord teaches us: 1. Not to interfere in our neighbor's temporal affairs, but to concern ourselves solely with his spiritual matters. Is this your practice? 2. To turn all such disputes to good account, by showing the nothingness of riches, their inability to make life either long or happy and the certainty of losing them when death approaches. Happy are we if we can impress these truths upon the minds of men who are ignorant or careless of them. What a service we shall render them, especially if we can turn their thoughts to heavenly treasures! What effort have you made to do this?
Affections and Resolutions.

Point II: Riches a cause of unhappiness

Consideration: In illustration of the truths we have just considered, our Lord spoke this parable: "The land of a certain rich man brought forth plenty of fruits; and he thought within himself, saying, What shall I do, because I have no room where to bestow my fruits? And he said, This will I do: I will pull down my barns, and will build greater; and into them will I gather all things that are grown to me, and my goods. And I will say to my soul, Soul thou hast much goods laid up for many years; take thy rest, eat, drink, make good cheer. But God said to him, Thou fool, this night do they require thy soul of thee; and whose shall those things be which thou hast provided? So is he that layeth up treasure for himself, and is not rich towards God."

Application: What a picture this is of the fate, not only of the rich who are covetous, but of the rich in general! They are really miserable. Their life is passed in calculations, schemes, anxieties by day and night. "What shall I do? Shall I close with this, decide upon that?" Then follows uneasiness; if plans miscarry, bitter regret, sleepless nights, perhaps despair. The rich know no rest, seldom enjoyment. The more their wealth increases, the more do their cares; and when they are preparing to rest and enjoy it, death comes, and all is lost.

Affections and Resolutions.

Point III: Riches often a cause of eternal woe

Consideration: We should think less of riches if we reflect on the numbers who have been eternally ruined, not by them, but by the disorders they occasion. They turn away our hearts and thoughts from God and heaven; they choke our piety, make us neglect religious duties, and insensibly lead us into avarice, injustice, luxury, hardness of heart, and final impenitence. "How hardly shall they that have riches enter into the kingdom of God!" "They that will become rich fall into… the snare of the devil."

Application: Your vow of poverty shelters you from these perils; but while you rejoice at this, remember that it is not the vow, but that which the vow supposes, which will preserve you. It is fidelity to the rule of poverty as your order understands it. Examine yourself minutely upon this point.

Colloquy.

October 2: On Sudden Death

1st prelude: Listen to Jesus saying, "At what hour you think not,

the Son of Man will come."
2nd prelude: Ask for the grace of a sweet and holy death.

Point I: Sudden and unprovided death

Consideration: The story of the rich man, and especially his sad end, had made a great impression. Our Lord took the opportunity to warn them against a surprise by death. "Be you also ready; for at what hour you think not, the Son of Man will come." In fact, nothing is more common than sudden deaths. But are they such a great evil? Certainly not. Sudden death is often a grace, and saints have asked it of God as a favor, that they may escape those assaults which are common to a long and painful agony. It is not, then, sudden death alone which we should fear, but sudden AND UNPROVIDED death – a sudden death in a state of mortal sin. Thus the Church does not bid us say, A SUBITANEA MORTE LIBERA NOS, DOMINE; but A SUBITANEA ET IMPROVISA MORTE, ETC.

Application: What should you do to make this prayer effectual? Never knowingly to remain in mortal sin. To do so would be temerity. Have you been guilty in this respect?
Affections and Resolutions.

Point II: Sudden, but not unprovided, death

Consideration: What is sudden death for the Christian, for the faithful, fervent religious? An instantaneous passage from this world to the next. What would a sudden restoration of sight be to a blind man? And yet how feeble an illustration is this of the transports of delight and joy which a holy soul must feel at its first sight of God; that God for whom it has sacrificed all so generously, in whose service it has passed so many years, borne so many humiliations, privations, sufferings; that God whom it has always feared to offend, to whom it has constantly referred every affection, every action; whom day and night it has adored, sighing for the moment when it should see him face to face! That moment has come. The Heavenly Bridegroom's voice is heard: VENI, SPONSA, VENI; CORONABERIS. INTRA IN GAUDIUM DOMINI TUI.

Application: And shall we dread this moment? Shall we think of sudden death as a calamity, when instantaneously, painlessly, it gives us such unspeakable happiness. Excite in your heart a desire to see and possess your God.

Affections and Resolutions.

Point III: Death which is not sudden

Consideration: To judge by the ordinary course of events, your death will be preceded by an illness more or less protracted. You must, then, learn to be resigned to it, and especially to the loneliness you will then have to bear. You must learn to suffer, and that, too, more than others in the world, for you are not in a hospital, but in a community, where everyone has his own work to do, and where it is impossible for the infirmarian to furnish you with those little luxuries which are lavished on the sick in hospitals.

Application: Happy is he who, while he is still in health, accustoms himself to be left alone, and when in solitude to hold communion with God, with his guardian angel, and the saints, to bear patiently privation and neglect. If you do not learn this, your lot at the last will not be a happy one, nor will your conduct be edifying. Consider this matter, for it is most important.

Colloquy.

October 3: Jesus Cures a Woman who had a Spirit of Infirmity Eighteen Years

1st prelude: Picture to yourself our Lord stretching out His hand over this woman.

2nd prelude: Ask for grace to derive great good from this meditation.

Point I: Wretched condition of the infirm woman

Consideration: Jesus having left Bethany, where we shall often find Him again, continued His ministry, working many miracles, and constantly doing some act of mercy. "And He was teaching in their synagogue on their sabbath. And behold there was a woman who had a spirit of infirmity eighteen years; and she was bowed together, neither could she look upwards at all." How humiliating, how pitiable a state!

Application: The condition to which the Evil Spirit had reduced this poor woman fills us with compassion; yet in it we see but a faint shadow of the miserable state to which the spirit of avarice and impurity reduces so many Christians. It keeps them thus bound, by their thoughts and affections, to the world, to material and sensual pleasures, and so renders them incapable of raising their heart to heaven, to God, or to eternity! We see too in this a faint but sad image of the religious whom the devil of tepidity has changed from spiritual to worldly. In his intentions, his aspirations, there is now nothing exalted, nothing heavenly; he has become incapable of remaining in contemplation of God for long together; an invisible hand bows him down – down to earth, to the flesh. Is this your portrait? Oh, how sad if it be!

Affections and Resolutions.

Point II: The woman cured

Consideration: "Whom when Jesus saw, He called her unto Him, and said to her, Woman, thou art delivered from thy infirmity. And He laid His hands upon her, and immediately she was made straight, and glorified God."

Application: Mark the PLACE and the TIME at which this miracle was wrought. It was in the synagogue, in the place set apart for common prayer, and at the hour when the congregation assembled, that the woman was cured. If she had not been regular in her attendance, she might have missed our Lord, in which case she would have remained a cripple to the end of her days. How important, then, to be punctual at the spiritual exercises of the community! We know not to which of these exercises God may have attached special favors, special graces. Miss one, and you may lose an immense blessing. Do we not sometimes allow trifling matters to keep us away? It was after eighteen years of suffering that the woman's prayers were heard at last. What perseverance! Is yours like this?

Affections and Resolutions

Point III: The ruler of the synagogue: his indignation

Consideration: While "all the people rejoiced for all the things that were gloriously done by Him," the Pharisees were greatly annoyed. The glory of Jesus put them in the shade. To sully that they would have stopped at nothing which envy could suggest, provided only they could make it appear that they were actuated by a great zeal for the law. In this spirit, "the ruler of the synagogue (being angry that Jesus had healed on the sabbath) answering said to the multitude, Six days there are wherein you ought to work; in them therefore come and be healed, and not on the sabbath day." But the hypocrite could not escape the humiliation he so richly deserved. "The Lord answering him said, Ye hypocrites! doth not every one of you on the sabbath day loose his ox or his ass from the manger, and lead them to water? And ought not this daughter of Abraham, whom Satan hath bound, lo, these eighteen years, be loosed from this bond on the sabbath day? And when He had said these things, all His adversaries were ashamed."

Application: Hypocrisy will certainly be exposed some day. Beware of it.

Colloquy with Jesus, our true Physician.

October 4: Feast of Saint Francis of Assisi, Founder of the Order of Friars Minor

1st prelude: Picture to yourself the saint in heaven, surrounded by his spiritual children.

2nd prelude: Ask for the true spirit of religious poverty and humility.

Point I: The poverty of Saint Francis rewarded

Consideration: One might almost say of Saint Francis that he carried the practice of evangelical poverty to excess. When he was about twenty-five years old his father made him renounce in the presence of the Bishop of Assisi his whole patrimony, because he had been profuse in almsgiving, and had offered to rebuild the Church of Saint Damian, which was in a ruinous state. Francis signed the deed without a word: his clothes even he laid at his father's feet, and took his leave, saying that thenceforward he would have no other means of support than God and His Providence. From that time he lived on alms, clothed in a shepherd's cloak, and sheltered by the ruins of Saint Damian. But one day, hearing these words read in the Mass, "Do not possess gold, nor silver, nor money in your purses;… nor two coats, NOR SHOES, nor a staff," he thought he had still too much, and, throwing away his shoes and his staff, he substituted a rope for his leathern girdle, and preached repentance. God deigned to reward so generous a sacrifice by conferring upon the saint extraordinary favors. His voice was irresistible, and disciples were drawn to him in crowds. He formed them into a religious body, and Pope Innocent III approved the rule. Three years later they had sixty convents, built and supported by the contributions of the people, without a penny of their own. So was the poverty of Saint Francis made rich.

Application: Let us, like Saint Francis, look upon poverty as the wall of religion, the root of perfection. Let us love it as a mother. Let it be our glory, not our shame. Let us carefully fulfill its every precept. Have you done so?

Affections and Resolutions.

Point II: The humility of Saint Francis rewarded

Consideration: Think of his marvelous humility. When he was nothing more than the merchant's son at Assisi, unknown to the world, he was great in his own esteem, greedy of notice, prompt to avenge an insult. As Superior-General of twelve thousand religious, admired and praised by all, he was humble, he was nothing in his own eyes, thinking himself unworthy to be raised to the priesthood, wishing only to be forgotten, scoffed at for the sake of God. What brought about this wonderful change? The light which God gave him, and which showed him that all which is good and beautiful in the world or in ourselves comes from and belongs to God. SOLI DEO HONOR ET GLORIA. To us contempt; for we have nothing of our own but original sin, inclination to evil, and inability to perform a single supernatural act.

Application: We know this well enough; it has all been explained and gone through before us. How is it then, that it has not the same effect upon us that it had on Saint Francis? How is it that we are not humble like him? Because we meditate upon these truths superficially, and soon lose sight of them. If we had them always before our eyes, we should become humble too; we, too, would make rapid progress in all virtue, of which humility is the root; we, too, would obtain special graces and special favors, for God ever gives Himself to the humble. Unite yourself, then, on this his feast to his great family, which seven centuries of persecution have not been able to crush, but still remains in all its vigor with a home in every land. Beseech the saint to get you, not his ecstasies, not his stigmata, not his gift of miracles, but his love of poverty, his humility.

Colloquy.

October 5: Deaths of the Tepid and of the Fervent Religious

1st prelude: Picture to yourself Balaam exclaiming, "Let my soul die the death of the just!"
2nd prelude: Ask for the light and strength to know yourself, to amend, and so to secure a holy death.

Point I: Death of the tepid religious

Consideration: "Sickness changes no one, but shows what he is," says the author of the IMITATION; because in sickness it is more difficult to disguise your character. See how true this is in the case of a tepid religious. What is he like in his last illness? As he always was before – exacting, unmortified, complaining, impatient, engrossed in his bodily sufferings, thinking but little of his soul, of eternity. Alas, he shuts his eyes to his danger, notwithstanding every warning. Speak to him of the happiness which death should be to a religious, of the merit he might gain by making a generous sacrifice of his life. Offer to pray with him aloud, or to read him some chapters of the IMITATION – he doesn't care, he hardly listens. But tell him the news of the day, or of some wonderful medicine just discovered, there is no lack of interest then. It is but too plain that he meditates but little upon God or the saints, and shows no eagerness to make frequent Communions, though it could be so easily managed.

Application: The infirmarian and others who see him are grieved to see him in such dispositions. They say among themselves, "I should not like to be as he is in my last illness; what merit he is losing!" Perhaps you say so too, and you would be right. But if you would not be like him then, you must not be like him in health. If you want to know what dispositions you will die in, see what you are living in; if they are like those of the sick man before you, depend upon it you will be no better than he is when your last illness comes. If reformation is needed, oh, begin it now – now, while you are well and strong!

Affections and Resolutions.

Point II: Death of the fervent religious

Consideration: In this case also the remark is true that sickness changes no one, but shows what he is; only we see it under a different aspect. How different it all is now! The more his brethren see of him, the more they esteem him. The virtues which his humility concealed are brought out now, and they see him as he is – a solid religious, dead to the world and to himself, occupied above all with his spiritual concerns. When his illness assumes a serious aspect, he humble asks his superior to tell him what the doctor really thinks of his state; and if the opinion is unfavorable, he immediately makes an offering of his life to God. He is the first to speak of the Sacraments. All through his illness, his conduct is uniformly edifying; patient, resigned, grateful for every service, apparently occupied with one thought, how to make the best use of the time that remains to him. He maintains a constant union of his soul with God by pious affection, and his greatest happiness is to receive Him as often as possible in Holy Communion. If he makes any complaint, it is that he can no longer recite his prayers from his Manual, or read the Holy Scriptures, or the IMITATION, or the Rule, especially those parts which concern the sick; but he makes up for it by asking his brothers to read them aloud, and to speak to him of Jesus and Mary, of the happiness of the religious state, and of the joys of Paradise with which our Savior promises to reward it. During such reading and conversation his soul appears to have a foretaste of the bliss of heaven.

Application: This picture pleases you. You would like it to be reproduced one day in yourself. Live as a fervent religious should live, and you will have your wish. As your life is, so will your death be. Lest you should be overtaken by weakness at the last, and unable to speak, write down NOW the affections you would like suggested to you, and the passages you would like read when you are on your deathbed. If you have not done so already, do it at once.

Colloquy.

October 6: Feast of Saint Bruno, Founder of the Carthusian Order

1st prelude: Picture to yourself the saint exclaiming, “O BEATA SOLITUDO!“

2nd prelude: Ask for the love of silence and retirement.

Point I: God’s Providence in the establishment of the Carthusians

Consideration: Saint Bruno, born at Cologne in the year 1035, of noble and wealthy parents, was destined to transplant into

Europe, under the form of a religious order, the life of the ancient solitaries or contemplatives of the Thebaid. God insensibly led him to the execution of His designs by giving him a great love of solitude, penance, and contemplation. Of his intimate friends there were six who ended by sharing this desire for a solitary life. In the year 1084, Bruno, having resigned his canonry and the chair of theology which he held at Rheims, presented himself with his friends before Hugh, Bishop of Grenoble. The latter, who had been told by God in a vision what to do, led them into the Chartreuse, a rocky desert, covered the greater part of the year with snow and thick fog. There, far removed from every human being (they were four leagues from Grenoble), they built an oratory and little cells a short distance apart, and entered upon a life of penance, prayer, and contemplation, with the greatest possible fervor. Such was the origin of the Carthusian order, which has since obtained a world-wide renown, and which, after nine centuries, still exists where it was first founded.

Application: Recall to mind the history of your own order, and the different circumstances which led you into it. The recollection will increase your trust in God and your love for the religious state. Affections and Resolutions.

Point II: God's Providence in the extension of the order

Consideration: Bruno and his companions would possibly have remained unknown to the world had it not been for a circumstance which God in His Providence brought about for the furtherance of His designs. Pope Urban II, who at Rheims had been a disciple of Saint Bruno, summoned him to Rome to ask his advice on a certain matter. The six original members of the community followed him, and all were received by the Sovereign Pontiff in the kindest manner; their way of life was approved, and a large piece of ground allotted to them within the walls. They there founded a second Chartreuse, which afterwards became the mother of many others. The most famous house in Italy was that "della Torre" in the wilds of Calabria, to which Saint Bruno retired, and where, on October 6, 1101, he breathed his last.

Application: You say that you find it so hard to be recollected, even during prayer. Perhaps, instead of seeking solitude and retirement, like Saint Bruno, you do exactly the reverse. Affections and Resolutions.

Point III: God's Providence in the protection of the order

Consideration: It has been remarked that of all the ancient orders the Carthusian is the only one that has not been reformed, because it never needed it. This phenomenon is a sign of a special Providence of the order. It is further explained by their mode of life differing from that of every other order, in that their separation from the world is COMPLETE, each living in his own separate cell. Added to this, they observe a perpetual fast, silence, and abstinence, even in the case of the sick. The hair-shirt is always worn, and half of every day and night they spend in the choir. Men who live like this are not likely to become lax. Try to imitate them, at least in their love of silence and seclusion.

Colloquy.

October 7: Feast of the Holy Rosary

1st prelude: Picture to yourself the Blessed Virgin Mary teaching Saint Dominic the devotion of the Rosary.

2nd prelude: Ask for grace to appreciate its excellence and advantages.

Point I: The origin of the Rosary

Consideration: For the origin of the Rosary we must go back to the year 1208. It was a time of great trouble, especially in the south of France, where the Albigensian heresy spread death and desolation around. After many vain attempts to extinguish it, Saint Dominic, founder of the order of Friars Preachers, was sent to the infected country. The saint put all his trust in our Lady's protection, and invoked her day and night. His prayers were heard. She appeared to him, and taught him the devotion commonly called the Rosary, promising great and lasting results from the preaching of it. More than a hundred thousand heretics abjured their errors, and the conversion of an immense number of notorious sinners testified to the power of this method of prayer, and caused it to be adopted by the whole of Christendom. The Sovereign Pontiffs erected it into a confraternity, enriched it with many indulgences, and appointed the first Sunday in October with a special office for its commemoration.

Application: The feast is well fitted, 1st, to strengthen our faith in a divine Providence watching over the Church, and supporting it in proportion to the dangers which threaten it; 2ndly, to make us feel the truth of Saint Bernard's remark, "God wishes that we should have everything through Mary"; 3rdly, to increase our confidence in our Lady, and our devotion to the Rosary. Strive to reap these benefits to-day.

Affections and Resolutions.

Point II: The excellence of the Rosary

Consideration: To appreciate the excellence of the Rosary, we must think of its origin, and of the prayers and mysteries which compose it. It comes to us directly from the hand of the Mother of God. It is composed of fifteen decades of the Ave Maria, like the one hundred and fifty psalms of the Canonical Office. Each decade is prefaced by a Pater and a consideration of a mystery in our Lord's life. The whole fifteen remind us of our duty to our Divine Redeemer; of everything necessary, I will not say for salvation, but for the highest perfection.

Application: Are you thoroughly convinced of the beauty and excellence of this devotion, a third part of which you recite daily? The way in which you do recite it will answer my question. Do you not often say it at time and place little suited for prayer? Thus to recite it is to say it (as a holy ascetic once remarked) rather for purgatory than for heaven. Do you not usually forget to meditate on the mysteries? To do this is to lose one great advantage of the Rosary. See in what you have been wanting, and set to work at once to amend it.

Affections and Resolution.

Point III: Method of saying the Rosary

Consideration: It is a general complaint that it is most difficult to say the Rosary with devotion, or rather without continual distractions. One cause of this is the constant repetition, even though the two prayers which compose it are the best in the world. Another cause is, that as it is said without book, there is nothing to fix the eye and arrest the attention. The way to overcome this difficulty is to bring the subject of each mystery before you as vividly as you can, and keep your mind's eye fixed upon it during the whole decade. In this way, even should your attention wander from the words or their meaning, it will at least rest upon the adorable Person of the Lord, which is all that is necessary; for the popular definition of prayer is a raising of the heart to God.

Application: Try this method, and you will find the advantage of thus easily uniting mental and vocal prayer, and of filling your mind with holy thoughts, and your heart with sweet affections. Colloquy.

October 8: Jesus Dines in a Pharisee's House

1st prelude: Picture to yourself our Lord surrounded by the other guests, all of whom are awed by His dignity and majesty.
2nd prelude: Ask for grace to unite in your own person both the interior and the exterior qualities.

Point I: Our Lord rebukes the Pharisee for caring only for the exterior part

Consideration: "A certain Pharisee prayed Him that He would dine with him. And He, going in, sat down to eat. And the Pharisee began to say, thinking within himself, why He was not washed before dinner. And the Lord said to him, How you Pharisees make clean the outside of the cup and of the platter! but your inside is full of rapine and iniquity." Under this figure, in which a man is compared to a vessel, our Lord tells us that we should on no account neglect the exterior, which all can see; but that the interior, the purity of the soul, claims our first regard, for it is this which makes a man's merit in the sight of God.

Application: If, then, we wish to be free from all reproach, our endeavors should be directed chiefly to the formation of our INTERIOR MAN, but not to the exclusion of the EXTERIOR. A religious who neglected the requirements of modesty and niceness in his appearance, or who thought that he need pay no regard to the usages of society, would draw upon himself and his community a general feeling of contempt, to the great injury of religion and of souls.
Affections and Resolutions.

Point II: The religious mindful of the interior part

Consideration: There are three things which go to form the INTERIOR RELIGIOUS upon whom God looks with pleasure: 1. Purity of soul – freedom from stains of sin, not only of mortal sin, but, as far as it is possible, of venial also. The greater the purity, the more readily will God reveal and give Himself to us. 2. Union with God by a spirit of prayer, by habitually making ejaculations, so as to be what the Apostle calls "men of God"; living by God and in God, seeing God in all things, and all things in God. 3. Purity of intention, by which we seek only to please God, and which therefore makes our actions in some sort resemble His.

Application: How do you stand with reference to purity of conscience, union with God, purity of intention? Do you use the means which are necessary to obtain perfection in these three things?

Affections and Resolutions.

Point III: The religious mindful of the exterior part

Consideration: People who only see the outside judge of the interior by the exterior. The religious, therefore, who is engaged in works of zeal and charity, is bound so to comport himself as to gain the respect and confidence of men, that he may win them to God. He must maintain a certain dignity: he must be modest, courteous, and free from affectation: his conversation sensible and edifying; he must be disinterested and zealous, but withal prudent and gentle. However great his knowledge, he must not lose his simplicity; he should be cheerful and light-hearted, and yet persevere the gravity of a religious; equable and gentle in adversity or under persecution, humble when prosperous or successful.

Application: Ask God to show you in which of these qualities you have hitherto been wanting, and to give you grace and courage to acquire it. It is not easy; it requires a constant watchfulness, and yet it is of the first importance. It would be a good plan to make it frequently the subject of your examination of conscience.

Colloquy.

October 9: Parable of the Barren Fig-tree

1st prelude: Picture to yourself our Lord addressing the eager multitude.

2nd prelude: Ask for grace to bring forth the fruits of righteousness.

Point I: Barrenness of the fig-tree, or of the soul of a religious

Consideration: Some Jews having told our Lord of the terrible punishment which Pilate had inflicted on certain Galileans, He took the opportunity of showing them by a parable that they and their whole nation would not be less severely punished if they did not profit by the graces which He had lavished upon them during the three years of His ministry. "A certain man had a fig-tree planted in his vineyard, and he came seeking fruit on it, and found none. And he said to the dresser of the vineyard, Behold, for these three years I come seeking fruit on this fig-tree, and I find none. Cut it down, therefore; why cumbereth it the ground? But he answering said to him Lord, let it alone this year also, until I dig about it, and dung it. And if happily it bear fruit: but if not, then after that thou shalt cut it down."

Application: In this parable, as the Fathers remark, our Lord had not the Jews only in His mind, but those also who in future ages should become the especial objects of God's grace. You then, above all, O religious soul, should lay it to heart; for have you not been transplanted from the cold waste of the world into the garden of religion, there tended with the utmost care, watered with a greater abundance of heavenly dew in a day than many others have in weeks and months? Where, then, is your fruit? What progress have you made since your last retreat, the last monthly recollection? Alas, perhaps none! – nothing but barrenness and graces wasted. Ask God to enlighten you.

Affections and Resolutions.

Point III: Reprobation of the fig-tree, or of the soul

Consideration: Think of the mischief you have done through this barrenness, this tepidity. Not only have you robbed God of the honor due to Him, your Savior, of the fruit of his Passion, your neighbor of the good you might have done him, the community of the blessings which your fervor would have drawn down, your superiors of the joy you might have given them, and yourself of a wealth of merits; not only have you neglected to do the good you might have done, but your conduct has been actively and positively hurtful. Look at the matter in detail, and you will see it has been so. Then think of the dangers to which this barrenness has exposed your soul. "Every tree that bringeth not forth good fruit shall be cut down and cast into the fire. The unprofitable servant cast ye out into the exterior darkness: there shall be weeping and gnashing of teeth."

Application: Among these barren trees, these unprofitable servants, who have incurred the wrath of God, there are perhaps some whom you have known, members of the same community, who have been surprised by an unhappy death and cast into the flames of hell. Oh, surely this thought must inspire you with a holy fear, and induce you to examine yourself in earnest, and make generous resolutions.

Affections and Resolutions.

Point III: The reprieve accorded to the fig-tree, or to the soul

Consideration: The tender-hearted, zealous gardener, who obtained a year's reprieve for the fig-tree, represents our Blessed Lord, who as man intercedes for you with His Father – ADVOCATUM HABEMUS APUD PATREM, JESUM CHRISTUM JUSTUM – who obtains for you a further trial, further graces.

Application: Let this thought increase your confidence and your courage. Say with the Apostle, "I can do all things in Him who strengtheneth me." I will profit, then, by the time and help He gives me. I will seek a director, and say to Him, "Show me how to rid myself once for all of this spiritual stupor, and to bring forth fruits of righteousness in abundance. Cost what it may, I am determined to begin at once." DIXI, NUNC COEPI.

Colloquy.

October 10: The Pharisees Try in Vain to Terrify Our Lord

1st prelude: Imagine you see some of the Pharisees saying to Jesus, "Depart and get Thee hence, for Herod hath a mind to kill Thee."

2nd prelude: Beg the grace of courage and of confidence in the service of God.

Point I: Efforts of the Pharisees to intimidate Jesus

Consideration: Jesus was still keeping away from Jerusalem, evangelizing the countries bordering upon Galilee with great success. This was enough to stir up the envy of the Pharisees, who therefore resolved to hinder His mission, and even to make Him abandon it under some false pretext. They first assumed a hypocritical air, and said to Him, "Master, we hear that Herod, who murdered John the Baptist, hath a mind to kill Thee. Save Thy life, then; depart, and get Thee hence." EXI, ET VADE HINC, QUIA HERODES VULT TO OCCIDERE.

Application: It is in this way that the devil, jealous of the good done by those who devote themselves to works of charity and zeal, tries to hinder their success, and even to drive them away from the place where they are doing good. Sometimes he stirs up false brethren against them, who try to drive them away under the pretext of avoiding disagreements in the community; sometimes he endeavors, and even succeeds, in blackening them in the opinion of their superiors, by intrigue or calumny. You may be the victim of these snares; great servants of God have been so, as we see in the lives of Saint John of the Cross and Saint Francis Regis. But they were not disturbed. They had left their cause in the hands of God, and God sustained them in their trials, and glorified them.
Affections and Resolutions.

Point II: Our Lord's perseverance and firmness

Consideration: Instead of feeling fear and terror, as the Pharisees wished, Jesus answered them calmly and confidently: "Go and tell that fox, Behold I cast out devils and do cures today, tomorrow and the third day," I.E., as long as My mission in these parts requires Me. The Pharisees ought to have been impressed by this courageous answer. He said, as it were, "I do what I have willed, what is necessary for My mission. I fear no one; and I will die only at the time and in the manner that I have appointed."

Application: The just man and the religious who conscientiously fulfill their duty ought to answer with the same courage: "I do what God wills, what obedience has laid on me. I fear Him only; and I will die at the time and in the manner He has resolved that I should die. Happy should I be if I might die a martyr to my duty and to obedience." Is this courage and constancy to be found in you? Judge for yourself; are you not often influenced and upset by fears which are generally imaginary, and induced to ask for a change of dwelling or office because you think your health will suffer, or because you apprehend many difficulties, contradictions, and annoyances? Has not the simple fear that you may not succeed before men in the employment which has been given to you made you resort to false pretenses that you might escape from it?
Affections and Resolutions.

Point III: Our Lord's tenderness for the misery of Jerusalem

Consideration: "It cannot be that a prophet perish out of

Jerusalem." Our Lord gave the Pharisees to understand by these words that He knew the snares they had laid for Him in Jerusalem, and that there indeed He would die, but only because He so willed it. Then thinking of the terrible fate reserved for the inhabitants of Jerusalem, He cried out in grief, "Jerusalem, Jerusalem, that killest the prophets, and stonest them that are sent to thee, how often would I have gathered they children as the bird does her brood under her wings, and thou wouldst not!"

Application: How wonderfully is the tenderness of the Divine Heart manifested to us in these words! Let us try to form our own hearts on the model of this tender and zealous Heart. Let us try also to forget our own troubles, that we may only think how we can relieve the sorrows and needs of our brethren, of all those confided to our care.

Colloquy.

October 11: Parable of the Lost Sheep

1st prelude: Behold Jesus the Divine Shepherd carrying the lost sheep on His shoulders.

2nd prelude: Beg that your heart may expand with confidence and love.

Point I: How the Shepherd seeks the lost sheep

Consideration: This touching parable is the completion of that of the Good Shepherd. Our Lord gave it in the form of interrogation to the Pharisees, who "murmured, saying, This man receiveth sinners, and eateth with them. What man of you, said He, that hath an hundred sheep, and if he shall lose one of them, doth he not leave the ninety-nine in the desert and go after that which is lost until he find it?" Remark the promptitude with which the shepherd seeks his lost sheep: as soon as he sees it is gone he hastens to seek it, without taking time for food. Then consider the perseverance and the solicitude with which he seeks it – nothing discourages him, neither distance, nor accidents, nor fatigue. He never rests until he has recovered his dear sheep.

Application: Has not God really acted thus when you were so miserable as to be lost, to be separated from Him by sin? Were you not immediately recalled by the voice of conscience, by the fear and trouble which He excited in your soul, until finally His grace triumphed over your resistance, and the efforts and deceits of the devil?

Affections and Resolutions.

Point II: How the shepherd treats the sheep he has found

Consideration: When the shepherd at last sees his sheep, he gently calls it to him; and when it has come to him, far from blaming and punishing it, he caresses it and smiles on it to show he is not angry. Nor is this all; moved with compassion, seeing the sheep panting and exhausted, what does this good shepherd do? "He lays it on his shoulders rejoicing," says Jesus Christ, and carries it back to the fold.

Application: Under this image of winning tenderness the Savior of our souls pictures Himself; and this image is a reality. Every penitent sinner affords a proof of it: from the moment he renounces sin, and makes the resolution of returning to God, the reproaches of his conscience cease, and remorse is silent; he feels himself prevented and strengthened by a grace which is so abundant that he is more borne along than treading his way. Nothing now costs him anything; what formerly seemed impossible to him has become easy. And the joy which a priest feels at having saved a soul is communicated to his repentant heart; he tastes a peace and a happiness that he has not known for a long time. What does your own experience tell you?

Affections and Resolutions.

Point III: How the shepherd testifies his joy as having found the lost sheep

Consideration: "And coming home, he calls together his friends and his neighbors, saying to them, Rejoice with me, because I have found my sheep that was lost." And then our Lord Himself deigned to make this consoling application of the words: "I say to you that even so there shall be joy in heaven upon one sinner that doth penance, more than upon ninety-nine just who need not penance."

Application: These divine and wonderful words teach us to appreciate the infinite goodness and mercy of God towards the penitent sinner; and they teach us also the injury it is to God, and the harm we do to ourselves, when, remembering our past sins, we give way to trouble, fear, and discouragement, as if the pardon we have received could be doubtful. Is not this, perhaps, what you have done? If it be so, acknowledge your fault; and if in future you

are tempted to fall into it again, think of what Jesus Christ says, that your conversion has been a subject of joy in heaven among saints and angels. This thought will confirm your confidence, will expand your heart, will help you greatly to make fresh progress in perfection.
Colloquy.

October 12: The Qualities of a Disciple of Jesus: Three Conditions Required

1st prelude: Behold Jesus in the midst of a great multitude.
2nd prelude: Beg the grace of knowing and practicing all that our Divine Lord requires from those who wish to follow Him.

Point I: Estrangement from our relations

Consideration: Among the crowd who followed Jesus, and who listened to Him with very different dispositions from those of the hypocritical Pharisees, many manifested their desire to be numbered among His disciples. But what must have been their surprise when they heard the conditions that the Divine Master had laid down before they could be admitted! The first was: "If any man come to Me, and hate not his father, and mother, and wife, and children, and brethren, and sisters, he cannot be My disciple." That is to say, if he have not the strength to relinquish their friendship rather than that of God; if he have not the courage and determination to resist the, and even give them up, if they oppose the certain will of God in regard to a state of life.

Application: Jesus Christ, then, rigorously demands from us who glory in being His disciples, that in all circumstances we give Him the first place in our esteem as the Sovereign Good, and the first place in our love; that we be entirely detached from the world, and that, at least, we keep our hearts free from all affection to those persons or things who disturb our peace with Him. Has it been thus with you? What are your actual dispositions?
Affections and Resolutions.

Point II: Hatred of ourselves

Consideration: "If any man hate not his own life also, he cannot be My disciple." According to Saint Jerome, our Lord meant that we should be ready to sacrifice our life rather than lose the faith and grace of God- that we should hate and cast away from us all that could flatter our self-love and our senses, all that is capable of soiling our soul in the eyes of God. “To hate one’s self thus in time,” says Saint Augustine, “is to love one’s self in eternity.”

Application: The fulfilment of this second condition, so rigorously exacted by our Divine Master, supposes evidently two things: 1st, great vigilance over all our senses and the most secret movements of our hearts; 2nd, a continual violence against he ambitious aspirations of our minds and the disorderly inclinations of our hearts. These words of our Lord evidently suppose this: “The kingdom of heaven suffereth violence, and the violent bear it away.” Is it not because we fail in this violence and this vigilance over ourselves that we are still so little dead to the world, and its lusts, such weak disciples of Jesus Christ?

Affections and Resolutions.

Point III: Love of the cross of Jesus

Consideration: “And whosoever doth not carry his cross and come after Me, cannot be My disciple.” This third condition is very easily understood; to carry the cross after Jesus is to bear patiently for love of Him all that wearies us, all that goes against our ideas, tastes, and habits; all that is in contradiction to our temper, inclinations, and customs; all that can cause us suffering of mind or body. To carry the cross after Jesus is, says the Apostle, to “bear about in our bodies the mortification of Jesus.” It is to mortify ourselves continually in all things, so that, dead to the world and ourselves, we may live only to God.

Application: Examine carefully how you stand as regards this spirit of mortification and this self-immolation. If you are animated by this spirit, your happiness is certain; if you are a stranger to it, you have everything to fear. Does not the Apostle say this expressly? – “They that are Christ’s have crucified their flesh with the vices and concupiscences… If any man hath not the spirit of Christ, he is none of His.”

Colloquy.

October 13: On the Virtue of Mortification

1st prelude: Behold the Apostle saying, “Mortify your members.”
2nd prelude: Beg for the knowledge, esteem, and practical love of mortification.

Point I: Nature of mortification

Consideration: We bear about in us a strong inclination for all which pleases our senses, and from it springs an infinity of sins and miseries. The resistance to this inclination is what we call mortification. Mortification, then, is an act of the will, by which we repress and kill the vicious desires which spring from concupiscence. If anyone does this from a supernatural motive, and has acquired the habit of doing it, he possesses the virtue of mortification. There is, then, a great difference between an act and the virtue of mortification. This virtue, like all others, has different degrees. It becomes more perfect as we acquire greater facility and perseverance in reducing it to practice.

Application: From your entrance into religion you were taught the knowledge and exercise of mortification, because it is the foundation of the religious life, according to those well-known words of our Lord: "If any man will come after Me, let him deny himself, and take up his cross daily and follow Me." What value do you put upon this virtue? What progress have you made in it? Are you not among that number who began to practice it ardently, but gradually neglected it because it cost them a good deal, and have become strangers to the spirit of mortification?

Affections and Resolutions

Point II: Necessity of mortification

Consideration: All that is without us, as well as that which is within, shows us the absolute necessity of mortification. Without us, we have the precept and example of Jesus Christ, the doctrine and example of the Apostles, and, as we saw in the preceding meditation, we have also the example of all the saints. Where can we find one who has not excelled in the practice of mortification? Within us, we have the experience that if we do not at least continually and energetically fight against the irregular desires of our hearts, we fall into every kind of disorder and excess; as the Apostle reminds us, "If by the spirit you mortify the deeds of the flesh, you shall live."

Application: Without mortification, then, there is no perseverance, no salvation for us. Without mortification it is still more evident there can be no progress in virtue. If you answer truly, must you not acknowledge that to your want of mortification it is owing that you are so inconstant in your resolutions, so far

from attaining the spirit of prayer, so often unfaithful to many points of the rule and certain obligations of your office, that you give so little edification, are so wanting in charity, zeal, patience and resignation! Examine yourself before God.
Affections and Resolutions.

Point III: Excellence and advantages of mortification

Consideration: To be mortified is to die to one's self and the world, to live only to God; it is to conquer, it is to repress, the man of sin in our hearts – that old man who dwells within us – and to let Jesus reign over us as our sovereign Master; it is to overcome all obstacles to perfection; to destroy all that is displeasing to God in us; to love God, as the Apostle Saint John expresses it, "in deed"; and finally it is to follow Jesus, bearing His cross; it is to die upon the cross with Him, as says Saint Paul, "With Christ I am nailed to the cross."

Application: Does it need further argument to induce us to embrace with fervor the holy austerities of mortification? And cannot all of us, though weak in health, mortify ourselves in a number of ways? We know them; at one time we took delight in them; but now? Let us go back to our first fervor. What joy we shall have at death, and what overflowing happiness in eternity! Colloquy.

October 14: The Obligation We are Under of Mortifying Ourselves on Account of Sensuality

1st prelude: Imagine you hear the Apostle saying, "I see another law in my members fighting against the law of my mind."
2nd prelude: Beg the grace of becoming more and more convinced of the necessity of mortification.

Point I: Sensuality impels us towards sin

Consideration: The extreme need we have of mortification arises from that evil leaven which original sin has left in our hearts, and which is nothing else than sensuality; or, as we may define it, an innate and violent inclination for all that pleases the senses or brings enjoyment to the body, and consequently an innate aversion for all that contradicts us. "The imagination and thought of man's heart are prone to evil from his youth."

From this vicious inclination, which will last until death,

springs every kind of disorderly affection which turns us away from God, our last end. He who does not vigorously resist it by a CONTINUAL mortification will certainly be its miserable victim in time and eternity.

Application: Alas, we feel but too keenly this vicious inclination within us; it is constantly impelling us towards disorder. 1. DISORDER IN SIGHT: we feel inclined to look at everything, to read everything, to observe everything; in the house, the conduct of our superiors and brethren; out of it, the objects which strike or please the eye; and from thence springs a multitude of rash judgments, temptations, and sins. 2. DISORDER IN HEARING: we are curious to know all the news of the day, all that is said and done in the house, all that goes on out of the house, and rather the evil than the good: from this spring useless and prolonged visits and conversations, loss of precious time, infractions of the rule of silence, and, what is worse, criticisms, murmuring, detraction, indiscretion, and finally dissipation of mind, void of the heart, an impossibility of recollection, prayer and meditation. 3. DISORDER IN THE TASTE, SLEEP, CARE OF THE BODY: is it not true that we feel tempted to exceed the bounds of temperance, the time given for sleep, the care which we might reasonably take of our body? Such are, then, the effects of sensuality, the disorder which it will certainly engender in all those who do not fight against it by mortification.

Affections and Resolutions.

Point II: Sensuality turns us away from what is good

Consideration: According to the definition given, sensuality is not only that innate and violent inclination for all that pleases the senses, but also an aversion for all that wearies or restrains us. From this proceed transgression of the rule, and the scandal which results from it, so much negligence in fulfilling the duties of our state and our office, so much neglect of spiritual duties, and so much imperfection in all our actions, and finally lukewarmness.

Application: It does not require any great mental effort to prove these truths; we find it within us. Let us appeal to our conscience and ask why we do not observe such and such a point of rule or religious discipline while we observe such another. If we speak the truth, we shall answer, because we do not dislike the one, but the other goes against our taste, character and habits. Why have we

given up and lost sight of the resolutions of our last retreat? They were founded on good motives, and well conceived to assist our spiritual progress. It is true; but they curtailed our liberty of action, they cost us too much. Why are we so often negligent in preparing and making our meditation properly, in rising promptly, in following the exercises of the community? Because we could not do violence to ourselves. These are humiliating avowals, but they should not discourage us. Let us rather take occasion from them to reanimate our ardor and to renew in ourselves the spirit of mortification and of self-abnegation. The harder the combat the more glorious the victory.
Colloquy.

October 15: Feast of Saint Teresa, Foundress of the Reform of Carmel

1st prelude: Imagine you hear the saint saying, "To suffer or to die."
2nd prelude: Beg that she would obtain for you a great love for Jesus.

Point I: Saint Teresa's struggles

Consideration: In the life of this wonderful saint, written by herself, there is a statement on which we ought to fix our attention. She says that the first twenty years of her religious life in the Carmelite Convent at Avila were passed in a continual struggle against the impulse of grace, which pressed her to give up her too frequent and intimate conversations with seculars. "God," says she, "called me on the one hand, and the world drew me away on the other. My soul was always troubled. I passed twenty years in this struggle. My falls were numerous, and I rose again but slowly."

Application: We find in this useful instruction and great encouragement; we see – 1. That one single affection, even thought not a very disorderly one, is an obstacle to peace of soul, spiritual progress, and intimate union with God. 2. That the saints were not of a different nature from us, nor always exempt from weakness or faults. 3. That some of them remained for a notable time in a state of inferiority and spiritual weakness before they sprang forward and attained high perfection. 4. How wrong we are, then, if we despair of ourselves or of grace!

Affections and Resolutions

Point II: Victory of Saint Teresa

Consideration: "One day," says the saint, "when by order of my confessor I earnestly asked God that He would make His will known to me, I had an ecstasy, and I distinctly heard these words: I will that for the future you converse only with the angels." It was the light of grace to Teresa. She gave up for ever her old friends, and longed only for crosses and labors to bear for the love of Jesus. From this moment she made immense progress in perfection, and God poured his choicest gifts upon her. She became the wonder of her times; and the veneration which surrounded her name and writings subsists to this day. On the other hand, the saint obtained what she was always asking for in loving words: "To suffer for Thee, my God, or to die." She had continual bodily suffering, and was for a long time an object of persecution from without. She was treated as extravagant, as a visionary, and a hypocrite, even as one possessed, and a heretic. Her sufferings were equaled only by her deep humility and unshaken patience.

Application: After the example of Saint Teresa, let us try to make sacrifices; let us willingly accept the crosses that it pleases God to send us, and we shall only certainly obtain a large share in the gifts of his liberality.

Affections and Resolutions.

Point III: Reform of Carmel made by Saint Teresa

Consideration: The ancient and illustrious order of Carmel, after its translation into the West (1229), and owing to the troubles of the times, had lost much of its primitive spirit. God inspired Saint Teresa to revive it; and one of the greatest marvels of her life is that she succeeded in causing a very austere reform to be accepted, not only by women, but by men, who recognize her also as their mother. She had to overcome obstacles on all sides. She had to endure many troubles, labors, and mortifications during the last twenty years of her life, which were consecrated to this difficult work. However, her large heart and her confidence in God, together with a wonderful skill in the management of business, carried her through it all. She had the consolation, before she went to heaven, of seeing firmly established seventeen convents of women and fifteen of men, which she had founded herself. After her death, the number greatly increased, and at this day we see the order of Carmel flourishing, producing men and women distinguished by their virtues, their talents and their success in the sacred ministry.

Application: Let us bless God for what He effected in Saint Teresa, and by her in others. Let us congratulate her, and desire that we also may do some great thing for God, or at least sanctify ourselves.

Colloquy.

October 16: Spiritual Advice of Saint Teresa

1st prelude: Behold Saint Teresa writing her spiritual advice.
2nd prelude: Beg the grace of making this advice the rule of your conduct.

Point I: Advice by which to regulate our words

Consideration: Among the numerous writings of Saint Teresa, which are no less admirable and edifying than her life, we find the advice or the rules concerning perfection which she left as a pledge of her love to the children of Carmel. Let us profit by them, and meditate today on some of them.

ADVICE ON USE OF THE TONGUE. Speak little, especially when you are with many people. Never praise yourself, your knowledge, your good actions, or your birth, unless you have reason to hope that it may be of use, and then do it humbly, remembering that these are all the gifts of God. Never excuse yourself, unless there is some strong reason for doing so. Avoid all disputes, and especially in things of little consequence. Speak to everybody with quiet cheerfulness. Never exaggerate things, nor assert anything without being very sure of it. Never speak without thinking what you are going to say, that nothing which can offend may escape you. When any one speaks on spiritual subjects, listen to him with humility. In your discourse, and in the conversations in which you have to take part, always mingle some words which treat of spiritual life, for by this you will avoid idle words and detraction.

Application: After having weighed the wisdom of this advice, put in in practice: see how far you act upon it; then in what you can and will act upon it still further.

Affections and Resolutions.

Point II: Advice by which to regulate our actions

Consideration: Accommodate yourself to the dispositions of the people you have to deal with, and do all you can to gain everybody. Avoid singularity as far as possible, for it is a great evil in the community. Do everything as if you really saw God before you, for it is a sure means of making great progress in virtue. Never let the devotion you have in your heart appear, unless there is some great necessity for it. "My secret is my own," said Saint Bernard and Saint Francis. Avoid curiosity in things which do not concern you; avoid hearing about them. Be gentle to others, severe towards yourself. If you are a superior, never reprove anyone while you are angry, but wait until you are calm. Let your joy be always humble, gentle, modest and edifying. Make known all your temptations, imperfections, and repugnances to your superior and your confessor, that they may give you counsel. Never eat and drink except at the appointed times. Never leave off humbling and mortifying yourself in all things until death; and have a particular devotion to Saint Joseph.

Application: These rules of conduct are not at all above my strength, and I feel what advantages I should derive from following them – peace for my own soul, and edification for my neighbor. Affections and Resolutions.

Point III: Advice for regulating our thoughts and desires

Consideration: Think during the day on what you have meditated in the morning. Often make acts of love for God. Do not think of the imperfections of others, but only of their virtues; as far as regards yourself, think only of your faults. Think that you have but one soul, that you will die but once, that you have but one life, which is short; that there is but one glory, which is eternal; and you will easily detach yourself from things of earth. Seek God in all things, and you will find Him. Let your desire be to see God, your fear be to lose Him, your sorrow not yet to possess Him, your joy all that can lead you to Him; and you will live in great peace.

Application: Make the resolution, after a careful examination, to reform all that is contrary in you to these rules of wisdom. Colloquy.

October 17: Parable of the Groat Lost and Found

1st prelude: Behold our Divine Lord speaking this parable.
2nd prelude: Beg the grace of fully understanding its sense and application.

Point I: The groat is the type of sanctifying grace

Consideration: The parable of the lost groat has the same end as that of the lost sheep, but the application of the types are different. "What woman," said our Lord, still addressing the Pharisees, "having ten groats, if she lose one groat, doth not light a candle and sweep the house, and seek diligently until she find it?" Interpreters tell us that this woman is the type of the Christian who has lost sanctifying grace; but how far short is the type from the reality! The groat is but a piece of money of small value, and sanctifying grace is of infinite price; it is the price of the Blood of our Blessed Lord. The first can only procure us some few earthly advantages; the second can give us the right to a heavenly inheritance; and yet this woman thinks it a great misfortune to have lost her groat, and will take no rest until she has found it.

Application: Terrible is the blindness and misery of many Christians who have lost sanctifying grace by mortal sin; lost it for weeks, for months, for years perhaps, and who do nothing to recover it. They are indeed miserable; for in losing it they have lost God's friendship, lost the right they had acquired in holy baptism to the kingdom of heaven, and the abyss of hell is yawning beneath their feet. If death surprises them in this state, their damnation is certain. Let us compassionate their blindness, and make it practical by seizing every occasion of enlightening them, inspiring them with salutary fear, or at least praying for them.

Affections and Resolutions.

Point II: The groat is a type of the grace of devotion

Consideration: In the woman in this parable we can see, in the second place, the religious who has lost the grace of devotion, or that piety and unction which made him so happy in his vocation, which made the practice of virtue so easy to him, which united him to God even in the midst of a turmoil of business, which made him find a charm not only in his spiritual duties, but even in humiliations, mortifications, and privations of all kinds.

Application: There is no loss we ought to feel so sensibly as the

loss of this grace of devotion, because it is the source of all our blessings. And yet in what way do we try to recover it when we have lost it? Are we not contented with groaning over or complaining of our aridity, of saying with Job, "Who will grant me that I might be as in the days of my youth [I.E., my first fervor], when the Almighty was with me?" Let us do better than this; let us resume our habits of regularity, recollection, and mortification, and especially of our fidelity in performing our spiritual duties; and we shall recover the lost groat, the grace of devotion.
Affections and Resolutions.

Point III: Finding the groat a type of the joy of the angels

Consideration: Consider the joy that this woman felt when she found the groat; she wanted to express her happiness, and so she called "together her friends and her neighbors, saying, Rejoice with me, because I have found the groat which I had lost."

Application: What is the truth which is hidden in this figurative language? No one would ever have discovered it if our Lord had not told it to us, because it is so astonishing. "For so," he concluded, "there shall be joy before the angels of God upon one sinner doing penance." We may add, And also when a lukewarm religious becomes fervent again. Oh, what an encouragement! You, then, who by your long negligence have saddened these blessed spirits, hasten to console them, and to give them joy by a prompt and perfect conversion. Great will be the blessings that will fall on yourself. Can you hesitate?
Colloquy.

October 18: Parable of the Supper

1st prelude: Behold Jesus speaking this parable.
2nd prelude: Beg for grace to overcome, and to help others to overcome, the three obstacles to salvation pointed out by our Lord in this parable.

Point I: Pride is the first obstacle to salvation

Consideration: "A certain man made a great supper, and invited many. And they began all at once to make excuse. The first said to him, I have bought a farm, and I must needs go out and see it. And another said, I have bought five yoke of oxen, and I go to try them. And another said, I have married a wife, and therefore I cannot come. And the master of the house being angry said to his servant, Bring in hither the poor and the blind, that my house may be filled. But I say unto you, that none of those men that were invited shall taste of my supper." Let us consider in this parable the type of the calling to the Faith of Jew and Gentile, the three great obstacles which, according to our Lord, prevent men from partaking of the celestial banquet, eternal salvation.

Application: "I have bought a farm; hold me excused." The schemes for advancement, pride and outward show, by which we wish to rise in the estimation of men, are the first obstacle to salvation. How, in truth, could God give heaven, give Himself, as a reward to those who have done nothing for Him, who have sought in all things their own glory at the expense of that which is due to Him? SOLI DEO HONOR ET GLORIA. Miserable are they indeed! After having PERHAPS obtained a passing glory, they will be cast out with the refuse of the human race into the depths of hell, "an abomination to the Lord" and the saints. ABOMINATIO DOMINO EST OMNIS ARROGANS. Let us thank God for having shown us our true interests; and let us try to undeceive the blinded victims of pride when an occasion offers, and show them on one hand how low a thing it is thus to bow before the opinion of men, and on the other, what true greatness there is in depending only on the Master of the universe, the sole arbiter of our destinies. Affections and Resolutions.

Point II: The second obstacle to salvation is avarice

Consideration: "I have bought five yoke of oxen, and I go to try them; I pray thee hold me excused." Our Lord points out the second obstacle to salvation, cupidity, avarice, or an immoderate desire for riches. How can the avaricious man think of heaven? His days and nights are passed in making calculations, in finding out ways of increasing his possessions, as if he were to live for ever in this world. His god is his money. But this god can neither save him from death nor hell.

Application: What a blessed inspiration have we received in overcoming for ever this obstacle to salvation by the vow of poverty, that happy poverty which provides for all our wants, brings us such peace of heart, and is the pledge of imperishable riches in heaven! How can we show our gratitude towards God? By exercising our zeal, by trying to show men who are avaricious the vanity and deceit of the pursuit and possession of the fleeting things of earth, and in striving to lead their desires and their activity towards the unchangeable and unspeakable possessions of heaven.

Affections and Resolutions.

Point III: The third obstacle to salvation is sensuality

Consideration: "I have married a wife, and therefore I cannot come." In showing this third obstacle to salvation, Jesus Christ does not condemn marriage, as the heretics try to prove; but He teaches us that the attraction of sensual pleasures leads very rapidly to the excess of impurity, and this vice so defiles the soul that the thought of heaven and the INVITATION even to labor for it become odious. He warns us ALL to be on our guard, that we may not be infected by this vice, and that we may labor to cure and save those unhappy beings who are defiled with it.

Application: Let us obey the teaching of our loving Lord, and let us watch and pray that we may never be overcome by sensuality; and let us earnestly beg that He would deign to bless all that we undertake for the conversion of the miserable victims of the spirit of impurity.

Colloquy.

October 19: Parable of the Unjust Steward, and the Practical Lessons which Our Lord Taught by it

1st prelude: Behold the crowd pressing round Jesus and listening to Him.

2nd prelude: Beg the grace of being docile, and faithful to the counsels of Jesus.

Point I: Embarrassment of the unjust steward

Consideration: "A certain rich man," said our Lord, "had a steward, and the same was accused unto him that he had wasted his goods. And he called him, and said to him, How is it that I hear this of thee? Give an account of thy stewardship, for now thou canst be steward no longer." The steward, who could not possibly show his accounts, was in great perplexity. How was he to subsist for the future? "What shall I do?" he said within himself. "To dig I am not able; to beg I am ashamed."

Application: I am this steward; God is that rich Master to

whom all things belong. He has confided a small but precious portion of them to my care: my body and its senses; my soul and its wonderful faculties; my time, my life, my liberty; many gifts of grace, and an infinity of creatures, are placed in my possession. One day, when I am least thinking of it, He will demand a rigorous account of my administration of these possessions; and woe to me if it has not been in conformity with His will and commandments – if I have taken the fruit of these possessions for myself, instead of giving them to Him only. Are my accounts in order? If at this moment He were to call me, and say, "Give an account of thy stewardship," should I be less perplexed than the unjust steward?
Affections and Resolutions.

Point II: Ingenuity of the unjust steward

Consideration: What did the disgraced steward do to get out of this difficulty? He said, "I know what I will do, that when I shall be removed from the stewardship they may receive me into their houses. Therefore, calling together every one of his lord's debtors, he said to the first, How much dost thou owe my lord? And he said, A hundred barrels of oil. And he said to him, Take thy bill, and sit down quickly and write fifty." He did the same with all the other debtors. And the lord commended the unjust steward, forasmuch as he had done wisely; for," added our Lord, "the children of this world are wiser in their generation than the children of light."

Application: The Son of God, in giving us this parable, did not mean to approve the fraud of this steward, but to make us ashamed of the little care we give to our spiritual interests, by showing us that the children of this world are all more industrious and farsighted in the management of their temporal affairs than the children of light – the men devoted to spirituality, OURSELVES – are in the important affair of our sanctification, our eternal happiness. After a careful examination, ought we not to acknowledge this?

Affections and Resolutions.

Point III: Meaning of this parable

Consideration: Our Divine Lord concluded with these words: "And I say to you, Make unto you friends of the mammon of iniquity, that when you shall fail, they may receive you into everlasting dwellings."

Application: We are poor; and how then can we, according to this precept of Jesus Christ, give alms to the poor, that they may intercede for us? We can do it by inducing the rich to give largely, and also by giving spiritual alms, which will, more effectually than temporal ones, enable them to reach heaven, and become our intercessors there. Besides which, faith shows us in the souls in purgatory poor people far more worthy of compassion than the needy we have before our eyes, because they cannot help themselves. Do we not neglect to give them alms, to come to their assistance?
Colloquy.

October 20: Continuation of the Preceding Meditation

1st prelude: Behold the crowd pressing round Jesus and listening to Him.
2nd prelude: Beg the grace of being docile, and faithful to the counsels of Jesus.

Point I: Fidelity in little things

Consideration: Jesus Christ taught several practical lessons from the parable of the unjust steward, which, taken in a wide sense, and relatively to us, contain also maxims in spiritual life. We will meditate on two of them. “He that is faithful in that which is least is faithful also in that which is greater.” These few words teach us how much we should have at heart fidelity in little things as the constant rule of our conduct. There are many motives to induce us to this. 1. MOTIVES AS REGARDS GOD. Our first and highest duty is to love God, and give him proofs of our love and fidelity; doing His holy will in the smallest things is giving Him these proofs, and giving them to Him constantly, almost perpetually; for little things make up the days and minutes.
2. MOTIVES AS REGARDS OTHERS. We all wish to gain many souls, to save the most hardened sinners; but that is impossible unless we have extraordinary graces; and that we may obtain them, we should be generous towards God, faithful in the smallest things, and our success will be certain. 3. MOTIVES AS REGARDS OURSELVES. Our Divine Lord tells us that “he that is faithful in that which is least, is faithful also in that which is greater”; I.E. in great trials, in strong temptations. And the following words are still

more consoling; "Courage, good and faithful servant; because thou hast been faithful in a little, thou shalt have power over ten cities."

Application: Let us weigh carefully the truth of these different motives, and make an act of faith on each of them; then go into detail about your life, and ask yourself whether your conduct is in conformity to these truths – how far you are habitually faithful in little things.

Affections and Resolutions.

Point II: Unfaithfulness in little things

Consideration: "He that is unjust in that which is little is unjust also in that which is greater." This sentence, coming from the lips of the infallible Truth, ought to convince us that habitual infidelity to those points of rule which we count of little importance is very hurtful to us, and may bring fatal consequences to ourselves and many others. 1. We lose an immense treasure of merit for ourselves and for many others. 2. By it our soul incurs many stains which we do not see, but which disfigure it in the eyes of God. 3. It is a great obstacle to the operations of grace, to God's liberality towards us. 4. It brings in relaxation; the bad example of one entices many others, and perhaps ends in universal irregularity. This is the real explanation of what history tells us of the decay or even total ruin of certain communities which had for a long time edified the Church.

Application: We should think most seriously upon this matter, and examine ourselves carefully; and, however it may be with others, take to yourself those words of Jesus Christ: "He who is unjust in that which is little is unjust also in that which is greater"; and if you have any negligence to reproach yourself with, correct yourself from this day forward.

Colloquy.

October 21: Feast of Saint Ursula

1st prelude: Behold the saint in heavenly glory in the midst of a great company of virgins, who bless her as their mother.

2nd prelude: Beg for the spirit of faith, zeal, and generosity that Saint Ursula had.

Point I: Saint Ursula has the glory of virginity and martyrdom

Consideration: Saint Ursula was born about the year 360, in the island of Britain, where Christianity was then flourishing. Her father was Dimnoc, king of Cornwall, and she was well educated. God prevented her with His grace. She made rapid progress in virtue and dedicated her virginity to God. However, her father promised her in marriage to Conan, a Breton prince, who by force of arms had obtained possession of one of the fairest provinces of Gaul, now called Brittany.

Ursula had to embark against her wish, in company with a great many young maidens destined to marry the nobles and warriors among whom Conan had divided his new states. But God had accepted the vow of the saint, and He willed that she should be faithful to it until death. The fleet which carried the virgin train was cast out by a storm on the northern coast, near the mouth of the Rhine, and they fell into the hands of the Huns, an idolatrous and cruel people. Gaunus, their chief, attracted by the beauty of Ursula, endeavored to make her apostatize, that he might marry her. The saint boldly declared that she was the spouse of Jesus Christ, and that she and her companions would die a thousand times rather than be unfaithful to the vows of their baptism. Then the love of the barbarian changed to hatred, and he ordered his soldiers to put them all to death. It was thus that Ursula's head was adorned with the double crown of virginity and martyrdom.

Application: Let us admire and adore the conduct of God towards His elect. He leads them by marvellous ways to their last end. He knows how to turn to His purpose both the fury of the elements and of the wicked. You see it in this instance, and believe it. Why, then, do you let yourself be so easily cast down and discouraged?

Affections and Resolutions.

Point II: Glory of Saint Ursula's apostolate

Consideration: Saint Ursula had that happiness rarely given to women, of gaining the crown of an apostolate as well as those of virginity and martyrdom. She instructed the maidens who were gathered around her, and strengthened them in the faith and love of Jesus Christ, and of chastity. Her zeal bore abundant fruit, for when the hour of trial came all remained faithful unto death. Saint Ursula thus won the glory of having preserved them from ruin, made them children of God, and martyrs, who are venerated and invoked by the whole world. And the glory of Saint Ursula's apostolate did not end with her life; it pleased God to perpetuate it in those numerous communities of virgins who, under the name of Ursulines, devote themselves zealously and successfully to the education of youth, preserving thousands of young persons from the snares of the world and making them children of God. The spirit of Saint Ursula, so faithfully adopted by her followers, is thus communicated to their successors.

Application: Let us try to preserve and perpetuate in ourselves the spirit of the founder, the patron or patroness of the order to which it has pleased God to call us, and we shall live a holy life; and if we are devoted to education, our zeal will be blessed. Let us ask ourselves, then, sometimes, if we have not degenerated from this spirit. And that we may avoid such an evil, let us often read the life of our founder, let us take the constitutions and rules he has given us for the subject of our meditation, and gaze upon a picture which recalls to us his features or his memory; and to these easy methods let us join prayer. Make the resolution of doing this. Colloquy.

October 22: The Apostolate of Education

1st prelude: Imagine you see Saint Ursula instructing and exhorting the vast multitude of young people who have been confided to her care.
2nd prelude: Beg for the necessary talent and zeal to enable you to instruct and exhort profitably.

Point I: Excellence of the work of education

Consideration: In the preceding meditation we had some thoughts on the education of youth, and the nuns of Saint Ursula were the first religious women who devoted themselves to it. At the present day the number of educational orders far exceeds the contemplative. It is the want of the age; and if you are employed in this good work, rejoice, for it is the most excellent of all zealous labors. Education forms men, molds generations, decides the fate of individuals in time and eternity, the fate of families and of kingdoms. Good education gives worthy priests to the sanctuary; legislators and just magistrates to the state; it supplies good children to families, and forms those who are fitted to be the heads of households; it gives protectors to religion, and saints to heaven.

And while the instruction of children and the education of youth is the most striking of all works, it is also the most solid, the most fruitful, the most worthy of the esteem of God and men.

Application: Keep these thoughts always before your mind, and you will not be so easily overcome by ENNUI or despondency, nor seduced by the temptation of giving up education or direction of young people under the pretext of using your talents better in other ways.

Affections and Resolutions.

Point II: Means of succeeding in the work of education

Consideration: The difficulties of giving a Christian education to youth are almost equal to its excellence. To ensure its success we must have more than a good will; we must use the necessary means; we must obtain help from God by an ardent charity, a profound humility, and a great purity of conscience and intention; we must be men of prayer, that grace may sustain our courage and enable us to conquer obstinate, indolent and very passionate natures; we must be closely united to our superiors by obedience, and to our companions by charity, so that there may be perfect unity in our ways of judging and acting; we must be exemplary, so that our life should preach and persuade more than our words, and should contribute to give us authority; we must devote ourselves entirely to the special branch that is given us, no matter what attraction we may feel for other labors or other studies; in one word, we must be men of abnegation, devotion and sacrifice.

Application: See in what way you fail under these different heads.

Affections and Resolutions.

Point III: Precautions to take in the work of education

Consideration: The work of education, especially for those who enter on it while young, is not without its dangers. Many have fallen victims to these; therefore, that you may not share their fate, be on your guard: 1. Against the attraction you feel for some pupils in particular; there is but one step between that and misplaced affections and familiarities. 2. Against dissipation, from whence flow lukewarmness and the loss of the religious spirit. 3. Against the disgust which various contradictions will cause, and which, if you do not take care, will lead to disgust with your vocation. What you ought most especially to avoid in this important work is

partiality, fickleness of temper and conduct, extreme severity and excessive indulgence, anger, harsh language, humiliating remarks, especially in public; unpunctuality in the hours for assembling; want of preparation for what you have to say or teach; routine, or a want of ingenuity in exciting emulation.
Application: Often make an examination on the details contained in this third point.
Colloquy.

October 23: Parable of the Prodigal Son

1st prelude: Behold the prodigal son tearing himself away from the arms of his desolate father.
2nd prelude: Beg the grace of becoming more and more attached to God and your vocation.

Point I: Departure of the prodigal son

Consideration: "A certain man," said our Lord, "had two sons. And the younger of them said to his father, Father, give me the portion of the substance that falleth to me. And he divided unto them his substance. And not many days after, the younger son, gathering all together, went abroad into a far country." The elder son stayed with his father. Who was this father, and who were the two sons to whom our Lord refers? The father is God, and the two sons, says Saint Jerome (EP. AD DAM., 146), represent the two classes into which men are divided – those who remain faithful to God and only desire to live happily under His law, and those who are unfaithful and who want to enjoy unlimited liberty. The prodigal represents the second class; and his misfortunes ought, as our Lord thought, to instruct us and inspire us with a great fear of abusing our liberty.

Application: Have you always belonged to this first class? Has there not been a period in your life when, abusing your liberty, you were living in habitual sin, far from God and heaven, in continual risk of passing into an eternity of misery? God has preserved you from this misfortune; and He has done more – He has opened your eyes, and called you to a state of life where you have many means of repairing your losses and ingratitude. How do you profit by these means?
Affections and Resolutions.

Point II: Delusion of the prodigal

Consideration: The young man, finding himself in possession of a large fortune, entirely independent, and in a country where he was not known, thought himself at the height of happiness. Now he would enjoy himself; no more restraint; every desire of his heart could be satisfied. Such were his delusions. But what happened? "And," says the parable, "he there wasted his substance, living riotously. And after he had spent all, there came a mighty famine in that country, and he began to be in want. And he went and cleaved to one of the citizens of that country. And he sent him into his farm to feed swine. And he would fain have filled his belly with the husks the swine did eat, and no man gave unto him."

Application: The Son of God thus places before our eyes the heartrending picture of a man who thinks he has found happiness by forsaking the divine law to lead a sensual life; and we may also say it is the picture of a religious forsaking his first fervor, freeing himself, and trying to find in creatures, in the satisfaction he gives to his senses, a remedy for the disgust he feels. But what happens? After having in a short time wasted an immense treasure of grace and merit, he feels in his heart a terrible void, which nothing can satisfy, and his mind is filled with sensual and impure thoughts, of which the swine in the parable are a faithful image. He has no peace or rest by night or day. Such is the fate of him who seeks his happiness far from God. Have you not unfortunately experienced something of this kind?

Affections and Resolutions.

Point III: The degradation of the prodigal

Consideration: Besides the hunger and nakedness which the prodigal had to endure, there was the memory of his former position to crown his misery, the thought of his degradation, which was greater than that of those who had formerly been his servants. "How many hired servants in my father's house," he said, "abound with bread, and I here perish with hunger? Keeper of swine, an outcast from human society!"

Application: "Behold," cries our Saint Peter Chrysologus, "the fate reserved for a man who no longer wishes to have God for his Father." SIC INVENIT QUI SE NEGAT PATRI. How degraded he is! Like "the beasts of the field," says the Psalmist; ASSIMILATUS EST JUMENTIS INSIPIENTIBUS.

You have not gone down so low, or you have been quickly raised up from this abasement; but since by your religious profession you are raised above the rest of men, are you always faithful to your high vocation? Do you not sometimes feel humbled in seeing that the faithful in the world find abundant and delicious nourishment in prayer and communion, while you, perhaps, find in them nothing which pleases and strengthens you? Oh, let it not be said of you that you are dying with hunger in the midst of abundance? Colloquy.

October 24: The Prodigal Son, Contemplation

1st prelude: Behold the prodigal sitting on a dunghill surrounded by swine.
2nd prelude: Beg for a great fear of anything that will separate you from God.

Point I: The prodigal son in his father's house

Consideration: Represent to yourselves, in a valley pleasantly shaded with foliage, a spacious house, where peace and affluence abound. There the prodigal son lived in company with a kind and loving brother, under the authority of the best of fathers. What a happy position Providence had given him! Exempt from care, abundantly provided with all that was necessary for the maintenance of life and cultivation of the mind, sharing in the general esteem which his father had won, he only knew the miseries of this world from the lips of others.

Application: Is this not a faithful image of the happiness of the religious life? Do not we also live under the shadow of the sanctuary, far from the cares of the world, with brethren full of charity, under the paternal direction of superiors, who carefully provide for all our wants of body and soul? "Oh, my brothers!" a holy religious used frequently to cry, "let us know how to appreciate our vocation; and we shall lead a joyful and holy life; we shall be always loving and esteeming it more; and this love and esteem for our vocation will assure our perseverance, and will cause us to make great progress." He spoke the truth. If the prodigal had known how to appreciate his happiness, he would never have dreamt of leaving his father's roof.

Affections and Resolutions

Point II: The prodigal far away from his father's house

Contemplation: Let us now contemplate the prodigal in a very different position. He has dissipated his fortune; his evil companions have abandoned him; he finds himself alone, lost, as it were, in a strange country, which is devoured by famine. Vice and hunger have changed him completely. Pale, thin, haggard, and clothed in rags, look at him in this wretched state, amidst a crowd of beggars, holding out his hand for charity, but generally receiving nothing but rebuffs and contempt. What misery!

Application: If unhappily you have become lukewarm, you will see the pitiable state of your soul in the person of this young prodigal. Consider, point by point, all that renders him worthy of pity, and you will find the image of the miseries of your soul. This sight will touch you; you will have pity on yourself, and you will feel the necessary courage and energy to rise out of lukewarmness. Affections and Resolutions.

Point III: The prodigal son depending on his master

Contemplation: Who is this master that the prodigal had? A sordid, avaricious man, without compassion for him who came begging for a morsel of bread. He refused him a lodging; he made him pass days and nights among the swine; he even refused him a share in the food that was given him to feed these vile animals with. What a change, what a heartrending picture! This young man, once so honored in his country, waited on so carefully by a numerous household, sitting day by day at a sumptuous table, is now seated on a dunghill, without help from anyone, despised by everybody, dying with hunger in the midst of swine.

Application: In what lively colors does our Lord paint the abasement and miseries of those who reject His mile and honorable yoke to take service with that unpitying tyrant, the world! And is not this the folly of the greater number of men? Perhaps it was once yours; but light has dawned in your heart, you have seen your error, you have come back to the Lord your God. Attach yourself more and more to Him. Make Him forget your past unfaithfulness by your redoubled fervor in His holy service. Colloquy.

October 25: The Prodigal Son, Continued

1st prelude: Behold the prodigal son bathed in tears in his father's arms.
2nd prelude: Beg that your heart may be expanded by confidence and love.

Point I: Return of the prodigal son

Consideration: Passion blinds us, but adversity teaches us, and makes us look into ourselves. We see the proof of this in the prodigal. IN SE REVERSUS – "Returning to himself," says our Lord, he understood how sinful and miserable he had been to abandon his father. He began to feel remorse, and it was the moment of grace for him; he corresponded with it; he considered what means he should take to rise out of his misery, to save his failing life. He could only see one – that of returning to his father and imploring his pardon. He instantly took the resolution and put it into execution. SURGAM ET IBO AD PATREM – "I will arise, and will go to my father, and say to him, Father, I have sinned against heaven and before thee; I am not now worthy to be called thy son; make me as one of thy hired servants" – he acted on his resolution – "and, rising up, he came to his father."

Application: What does the Divine Author of this parable mean us to learn from this? 1. That the contradictions, humiliations, and troubles of conscience which we have sometimes to endure are the means which God uses to make us look into ourselves, and to help us to rise out of the miserable state of languor in which our soul lies. 2. That in these moments, far from giving way to distrust and discouragement, and thus making our condition worse, we ought rather to consider the means of escaping, and take practical resolutions. 3. That we may be sure to obtain from God strength and perseverance to execute them, we should go to Him not as our Judge, but as our Father. To call Him by the name of FATHER disarms divine justice, and it brings back confidence into our hearts.

Affections and Resolutions.

Point II: The reception of the prodigal son

Consideration: How was the prodigal received by his father? The Lord tells us: CUM ADHUC LONGE ESSET, VIDIT ILLUM PATER IPSIUS – "When he was yet a great way off, his father saw him." At first he did not know him, he was so disfigured by misery; but as soon as he recognized him, says our Lord, he was moved with compassion and ran to him. Then the child fell on his knees, and with a voice broken with sobs made his confession, PATER, PECCAVI – "Father, I have sinned." But the father would not let him finish: he saw that he was penitent, and that was enough; he raised him, "fell upon his neck, and kissed him."

Application: This good and tender father our Lord meant for no other than the Lord our God, our true Father, whose service we have chosen for ever. Oh, how wrong we are, then, when we torment ourselves to no purpose, and do God an injury by giving way so often to servile fear; when we close up our hearts, or doubt about our pardon, or that our past sins are forgotten, as if we were the slaves of a harsh and vindictive master!

Affections and Resolutions.

Point III: Festival given to the prodigal son

Consideration: See, in this third point, how our Lord finishes the picture He has given us of His Heavenly Father in the father in this parable. After having given his penitent son a full pardon and forgotten the past, he chose to reinstate him in all his rights as a son. He called his servants, and said to them, "Bring forth quickly the first robe, and put it on him; and put a ring on his hand, and shoes on his feet; and bring hither the fatted calf, and kill it, and let us eat and make merry; because this my son was dead and is come to life again, was lost and is found."

Application: Every trait of goodness is reproduced to the letter in the conversion of this sinner. God was not contented with forgiving him all; He gave him back all that he had lost – the ROBE of baptismal innocence; the RING, or the pledge of His friendship; the SHOES, that he might walk firmly in the way, or grace to persevere; and the right of sitting down at the eucharistic banquet, where he could be filled with blessings and unspeakable delights. Let us redouble our love and generosity for a God who is so good, so liberal.

Colloquy.

October 26: On the Infinite Goodness of God, Manifested in Preventing Grace

1st prelude: Behold the goodness of God in the father of the prodigal.
2nd prelude: Beg the grace of growing in gratitude and love for God.

Point I: Incomplete idea of God's preventing goodness

Consideration: Let the parable of the prodigal help us to form an idea of God's goodness revealed to us by preventing grace. The father of the prodigal gives us only an idea of it; it is as a faint ray of sunshine compared to the sun at noonday. The extreme goodness of this father in the parable, which touches us and often moves us to tears, only shows us a part of God's mercy, and that the least part; it is the mercy which RECOVERS, but not the mercy which PREVENTS; it is God pardoning the penitent sinner, it is not God SEEKING the ungrateful and obstinate sinner.

Application: Nothing captivates our heart so much as kindness, nothing predisposes us so much in favor of anyone as receiving proofs of kindness from him. Why, then, is it that our hearts give themselves to God with so much difficulty, that we love Him so little? It is because we do not know Him enough, because the memory of His goodness to us is not often enough before our minds. We can easily imagine what feelings of love the prodigal child must have had for his father, who received him so tenderly and gave him so generous a pardon; but has not our Heavenly Father a thousand times more right to our love, when He has first loved us, and has sought us and brought us back when we were rushing to our ruin?

Affections and Resolutions.

Point II: A more complete idea of God's preventing goodness

Consideration: If the type of God's PREVENTING goodness had been complete in the parable of the prodigal, and if God had been entirely represented in it, the father would have followed his son in his mad career; he would have gone to seek him in that distant country whither sin had led him; he would have come to him in the midst of his wanderings or his miseries, not to reproach him, but to beg him to return, to offer him his home and his possessions, to beg him, to press him, to implore him to accept them; for such is the action of that grace that we call PREVENTING. Jesus Christ did not go so far as this in the parable, because to suppose such goodness in an earthly father would have been unlike the reality, for this goodness belongs only to our Heavenly Father, in whom all is infinite.

Application: How many great sinners who have returned to God can bear witness of this truth! Perhaps you yourself have been conquered by the preventing grace and infinite goodness of God, or you have followed, as a director of souls, its marvelous operations in others; and you have exclaimed in the depths of your heart, "The Lord is good!"

Affections and Resolutions.

Point III: It is impossible to give a complete idea of God's goodness

Consideration: Now, however extraordinary the excess of the divine goodness we have just considered may seem, it falls short of the reality. No figure and no comparison can give a complete idea of it, for the simple reason that God's goodness is INFINITE, and our intelligence is essentially FINITE.

Application: We ought, then, to admire and adore the depths of this attribute of this attribute of God's love as an impenetrable mystery which can only be believed by faith. In our conversations and instructions, sermons and exhortations, let us try to make God better known. We do not do it enough; and we may be certain we only do it superficially and coldly.

Colloquy.

October 27: Parable of the Rich Man and Lazarus

1st prelude: Behold the rich man in hell crying out, "I am tormented in this flame."

2nd prelude: Beg the grace of making this meditation very fruitful.

Point I: The parable

Consideration: Our Lord shows us in this parable one of those rich worldlings whose happiness consists in the enjoyments of life, and who have no pity for the suffering. "There was a certain rich man," he said, "who was clothed in purple and fine linen, and feasted sumptuously every day." And then He shows us a poor man in suffering, but pious and resigned. "And there was a certain beggar named Lazarus, who lay at his gate full of sores, desiring to be fed with the crumbs that fell from the rich man's table, and no one did give him; moreover the dogs came and licked his sores. And it came to pass that the beggar died, and was carried by the angels into Abraham's bosom. And the rich man also died, and was buried in hell."

Application: This striking contrast between different classes – great wealth and extreme poverty – we see in our own days; and it will always exist. But what was rarely seen among the Jews we see on all sides among us – many rich people poor in spirit, very generous towards the needy; and many poor people very pious, and wonderfully patient and resigned; from which we may certainly conclude that the final end of both these classes will be a happy one.

Affections and Resolutions.

Point II: Intention of the parable

Consideration: It is evident by the context that Jesus Christ gave this parable that He might destroy that prejudice that exited among the Jews – that prosperity in this world was the proof of virtue and its reward, and adversity or poverty the punishment of sin; from which they drew the conclusion, 1st, that he who was born or became miserable was a sinner and unworthy of pity, as we see from the history of the man born blind (Saint John, chapter ix); 2nd, that man's greatest happiness consisted in possessing the good things of this world. Modern prejudices do not go as far as this; but is the thirst for riches and enjoyments less? Does it not turn many Christians away from the path of salvation, and lead them to hell?

Application: Upon us falls the mission of enlightening and undeceiving the victims of those blind prejudices which lead them to eternal ruin. That our mission may be successful let us try in our intercourse with them to fill their minds with those eternal truths on which we meditate so often; and to say we have no opportunity of doing so is to accuse ourselves of want of zeal. Do we deserve such a reproach?

Affections and Resolutions.

Point III: The fruit of this parable

Consideration: What fruit ought we in particular to derive from meditation on this parable? A sovereign contempt for all that ends with time, and is worth nothing in itself for eternity; such as the pleasures of life, the favor of men, the renown gained by talent, superiority, remarkable deeds, success in the management of affairs; and, on the other hand, a great esteem for virtue, humiliations, and sufferings endured to please God and to atone for our sins.

Application: If, then, from want of talent, or health, or success in studies or business, you are put in an inferior place, out of the way, looked down upon in a manner, while perhaps you have to endure great corporal sufferings, take care not to give way to depression, despondency, or murmuring; think rather that God in His mercy deals thus with you that you may have occasions of practicing patience, humility and resignation, and of laying up an immense treasure of merits for eternity. Give thanks, then, to God, and esteem yourself. See what there is to correct in your judgment and in your conduct.

Colloquy.

October 28: The Rich Man in Hell

1st prelude: Imagine you hear Jesus Christ say, "And he was buried in hell."

2nd prelude: Beg of God that you may never lose a salutary fear of hell.

Point I: The thought of hell

Consideration: Yesterday's meditation on the fate of the rich man in eternity directs our thoughts to hell. Let us dwell on this thought. We ought sometimes to meditate on it, so that it may be engraven on our minds, and keep us in a salutary fear of God. For we also, though we may be religious, though we may be priests, might have moments of darkness, of delirious passion, when ONLY the fear of eternal torments can keep us to our duty. This, doubtless, is why our Lord so often spoke of hell in instructing the people, and even to the Apostles in particular.

Application: We can also make this meditation on hell a help to our spiritual progress. Saint Francis Borgia found it aided him in attaining great virtues. Placing himself in spirit on the borders of the abyss, and fixing his eyes on the awful number of angels and men whom sin had cast in there, he said to himself, "There is thy place, Francis; there is the torment thou hast deserved." From this the saint gained that wonderful humility, that profound contempt of himself, whose record in his life seems past belief. From this he gained that mistrust of his own light, that love of obedience and direction in the smallest things, that he might not, as he said, "fall into the snares of the devil"; from this proceeded his unshaken patience in the hardest trials of his life, and his mortification and penances carried almost to excess; from this proceeded that continual increase of fervor and charity; the flames of hell kindled in him the fire of divine love; from this he gained a zeal by which he was consumed, and which made him undertake great things for the salvation of others. Let us imitate the saint. The contemplation of hell, MADE IN THIS WAY, will cause us to make progress in every kind of virtue.

Affections and Resolutions.

Point II: The torment of hell

Consideration: As it is absolutely impossible for us to form an exact idea of the future life, and particularly of hell and of all the torment the damned souls have to endure, we should meditate carefully on the words of the sentence which Jesus Christ will pronounce at the great Judgment-day on the lost: "Depart from Me, you cursed, into everlasting fire." Depart from Me! Hell is, then, the loss of God, the eternal separation from Him, the only and infinite happiness of the life to come. The damned can never have even a consoling thought. CURSED! – cursed by God, of a God who will have no further mercy on them. Cursed in their souls, in the memory and understanding; remorse and despair at having lost heaven for vain, vile, criminal and shameful things. Cursed in their bodies, in every bodily sense at once – in their sight, hearing, smell, and taste. Into everlasting fire! To die slowly consumed by fire is a cruel death, but to live in fire without ever dying! what a life, what an eternity!

Application: Beg of God that these terrible truths may be engraven in your mind; it will preserve your compunction, distrust and contempt of self; it will make you victorious over your passions, humble in prosperity, generous, and courageous in all that is painful to nature in your vocation and office; it will be the pledge of your final perseverance, of your eternal salvation.

Colloquy.

October 29: Affability, Gentleness and Zeal of Jesus

1st prelude: Behold our Lord laying His hands on little children.
2nd prelude: Beg the grace of showing forth in yourself the virtues of Jesus Christ.

Point I: Gentleness of Jesus

Consideration: A fact that the Evangelists tell us, as if incidentally, shows us how affable and gentle our Divine Lord was, and that He was always the same – always gracious and easy of access. While He was engaged in a grave discussion with the Scribes and Pharisees on the laws of marriage and the prerogatives of virginity, "little children were presented to Him, that He should impose hands upon them and pray." It was evidently an ill-chosen time on the part of the mothers. "And the disciples rebuked them." But Jesus said to them, "Suffer the little children, and forbid them not to come to Me."

Application: Affability, or that habit of receiving and listening with composure and gentleness to those who come to us at all times, is a very precious and necessary quality, not only for superiors in regard to their subjects, but for religious who are devoted to works of zeal and charity. Do you fail in this respect? Is not your manner often cold, sometimes disagreeable and repulsive? Perhaps you are gentle and affable to strangers, but harsh or dry towards your brethren and your inferiors.

Affections and Resolutions.

Point II: Tenderness of Jesus

Consideration: Our Divine Master not only allowed these mothers to approach Him and present their little children, but He chose to manifest His interest and fatherly tenderness towards these little ones. "And embracing them, and laying His hands upon them, He blessed them."

Application: How great was the tenderness shown by our dear Lord! He saw in each of these children the living image of his Heavenly Father – a soul of infinite price created for heaven, but coveted by the devil. You may also feel tenderness for the children you have to guard and educate, but is it founded on supernatural motives? Is it animated by faith? Is it free from all admixture of over-natural, earthly, or sensual affection? Watch over yourself on this point; distrust yourself. Those who were more confirmed in virtue than you, have been led, little by little, into errors which were terrible for themselves and terrible for the body to which they belonged.

Affections and Resolutions.

Point III: Zeal of Jesus

Consideration: There is another circumstance of this presentation of little children to our Divine Lord to be remarked. He took occasion from it to exercise His zeal for the surrounding multitude; for immediately after saying, "Suffer little children to come to Me," He added, "for such is the kingdom of God. Amen, I say to you, whosoever shall not receive the kingdom of God as a little child shall not enter into it." By these words our Lord warned His hearers against the example of the proud and obstinate Pharisees, and exhorted them to listen to His divine teaching, and follow it with the simplicity and docility of a child.

Application: After the example of Jesus, do you seek and seize upon occasions of prosecuting the salvation of others and of your brethren? Is this zeal shown in your conversation and correspondence? What good can often be done by a few words said to the purpose! And you have neglected to do this good; God will demand an account from you of it. Try, then, to repair the past.

Colloquy.

October 30: Parable of the Pharisee and Publican

1st prelude: Behold the Pharisees listening spitefully to the words of Jesus.

2nd prelude: Beg the grace of listening to his words with joy, and profiting by them.

Point I: The Pharisee's prayer

Consideration: Under the type of the parable which forms the subject of this meditation, Jesus, while He confounded the Pharisees, gave us most profitable instruction; let us try to draw fruit from it. "Two men," said He, "went up into the temple to pray; the one a Pharisee, and the other a publican. The Pharisee, standing, prayed thus with himself: O God, I give thee thanks that I am not as the rest of men – extortioners, unjust, adulterous, as also is this publican. I fast twice in the week; I give tithes of all that I possess."

Application: In this pretense of a prayer made by the Pharisee our Lord shows us certain marks and effects of pride which escape the eye of man, but which are very guilty in the eyes of God; such as esteem of ourselves at the expense of others whom we depreciate; a secret satisfaction in our good actions – even our penances, our acts of humility, and the special favors bestowed on us by God's liberality. Is there nothing of this in you? Examine and see, for this is a subtle matter. It was a subject of continual alarm, even for great saints. Do you think you should fear self-love less than they did?

Affections and Resolutions.

Point II: The publican's prayer

Consideration: That the odious pride hidden in the Pharisee's prayer might be still more thoroughly exposed, our Lord contrasts with it that of the publican, one of those men whose profession caused them to be generally looked upon as sinners. "And the publican, standing afar off, would not so much as lift up his eyes towards heaven, but struck his breast, saying, O God, be merciful to me a sinner!"

Application: Our Lord gives us, in this publican, a model of prayer. The most essential quality for prayer is humility; and there was humility in his choice of a positions, humility in h is whole demeanor – with his face ben towards the ground, he struck his breast as though he were a criminal before a judge; there was humility in his words – he acknowledged that he was guilty, and had no other title to pardon than the divine clemency. It is humility, then, a profound conviction of our misery, which makes our prayers pleasing to God, and efficacious. Is it not, perhaps, because you have not this conviction in the depth of your heart, or that it is not sufficiently rooted there, that your prayers are so feeble and produce so little effect?

Affections and Resolutions.

Point III: The judgment passed by our Lord on the prayers of the Pharisee and publican

Consideration: It is probable that the Jews who saw these two men enter the temple to pray thought that one had made a wonderful prayer, pleasing to God, because they had a high idea of his sanctity; while the other had only made it as a matter of form, and gained no merit. But the judgments of God, who sees the heart, are different from those of men. What did our Lord say? "I say to you, this man [the publican] went down to his house justified rather than the other; because every one that exalteth himself shall be humbled, and he that humbleth himself shall be exalted."

Application: Let us take care, then, not to judge by appearances, for they are often deceptive. Let us also be far from leaning on the judgments of men, or seeking consolation from them, or think we are safe only because our brethren or our superiors have a good opinion of us. Let us remember it is God who will judge us; and go straight to Him, asking Him often in the simplicity of our hearts that He will show us what is displeasing in us to Him, and what He desires from us; so that we may destroy the one and acquire the other. What joy we shall have at death, if we have acted in this way!

Colloquy.

October 31: Vigil of All Saints

1st prelude: Behold the saints in glory.

2nd prelude: Beg the grace of obtaining due dispositions with which to celebrate the great feast of tomorrow.

Point I: The combats of the saints

Consideration: The saints were not born saints, but they became such. Children of Adam, as well as we are, they had to struggle against the inclinations of their own hearts, and against the attractions of vice. Many of the, besides, had to choose between their conscience and the most terrible threats of impious and powerful men. They resisted, they fought, determined to die rather than to commit iniquity. POTIUS MORI QUAM FOEDARI – Rather die than live dishonored. Such as their war-cry. Truth sustained them and made them invincible.

Application: What encouragement there is in these thoughts! The saints were not better off than I am. Many had more violent passions to overcome than I have, and greater obstacles to surmount. I have as many means of sanctification as they had, or rather, as a religious, I have stronger and better means than many of them had. Why is it, then, that I do not resemble them more? Because I have been weak or cowardly in the combat; because my will lacks energy, for sanctity requires a strong will, and we must do violence to self. "The kingdom of heaven suffereth violence, and the violent bear it away."

Affections and Resolutions.

Point II: The victories of the saints

Consideration: The saints were ardent in their combat, and persevering in their efforts; they persevered to the end, fulfilling the condition to which Jesus Christ has attached the victory: "He that shall persevere to the end, he shall be saved." They triumphed over everything – the ridicule, seduction, and threats of the world; the malice and rage of the devil; all the torments invented by the hatred of tyrants; and, what is still more difficult, over the weakness and inclination of their own hearts.

Application: What we generally are wanting in is not a good will, not good resolutions, but fidelity in carrying them out – PERSEVERANCE. To what high perfection you would not have attained if you had faithfully carried out the plan of life laid down for you during your novitiate, or even the resolutions made in your annual retreats! But, alas, our resolutions, far from holding good for one year, cannot do so for one day. Does it not often happen that you have lost sight by noon-day of the purpose that you formed in the meditation of the same day?

Affections and Resolutions.

Point III: The happiness and glory of the saints

Consideration: Today we must chiefly meditate on the reward of the saints. Let us remember how they fought, how they persevered, and how Almighty God at length permitted them to taste and see the bliss promised to those who endure to the end. The rewards of God partake of His nature; and our most lofty imaginations are but the shadow of the glories and the joys prepared for us above. "Eye hath not seen, nor ear heard, neither hath it entered into the heart of man, what things God hath prepared for them that love Him."

Application: These thoughts will serve to enflame and strengthen us. We shall be ready to exclaim with Saint Paul "that the sufferings of this time are not worthy to be compared with the glory to come that shall be revealed to us." Far from allowing ourselves to be overcome by difficulties, we shall, as did Saint Francis Xavier and Saint Teresa, sigh after humiliations, trials and sufferings. Let this be the fruit of our meditation and our preparation for All Saints, offering our fasting and abstinence for the same intention.

Colloquy.

November 1: Feast of All Saints

1st prelude: The glory and happiness of the saints in heaven.

2nd prelude: Ask for grace to conceive their bliss.

This festival speaks of heaven. Let us go there in spirit; let us try to form some idea of it.

Point I: Heaven excludes all evil

Consideration: Supposing a stranger called together the inhabitants of a certain parish, and told them that after having made a tour of the world, and crossing unknown seas, he had at length discovered an island free from all extremes of heat and cold, enjoying a uniform temperature, a soil so fertile that it needs no cultivation, where evil passions are unknown, and where there is neither pain, sickness, old age, nor death; would not his hearers think that his discovery was neither more nor less than a beautiful dream or a poetical imagination?

Application: But this beautiful dream, this poetical imagination, really exists in heaven, as our faith tells us. "Death shall be no more, nor mourning, nor crying, nor sorrow," are the words of Saint John in the Apocalypse. Oh, if heaven were no more than this, it would not be surprising that men should be willing to make the greatest sacrifices in order to attain it, nor that those who heard and believed the stranger's tale should sell all they had, and embark at once to that fortunate island, to escape infirmity and death!

Affections and Resolutions.

Point II: Heaven contains all good

Consideration: In heaven we shall possess God, an infinite Being, comprehending in Himself all possible perfections; thus our happiness will be likewise perfect – perfect as regards all the faculties of the soul, memory, and understanding; our thoughts sweetened and purified beyond our conception; our knowledge superior to that of the most learned here below; our will satisfied by the instantaneous accomplishment of every desire; perfect also as to the senses of our bodies; glorified like that of our Lord after His resurrection. All that can charm the eye, delight the ear, the taste, or smell, will be ours without measure or fear of excess, for concupiscence will no longer exist.

Application: Thus our happiness will be perfect in heaven, so we say and believe, we, envying the saints who are in possession of it, yet, strange to say, clinging the while to this miserable world, our place of exile! How little we think of the joys above! Oh, if like Saint Paul we had been caught up into the third heaven, and tasted its delights, were it only for a moment, what a change would it make in us! We should care for nothing on earth; we should languish and sigh after heaven alone.

Affections and Resolutions.

Point III: Heaven ensures us the eternal possession of all good

Consideration: Our appreciation of the unspeakable bliss promised us in heaven must be infinitely heightened by the thought that we shall enjoy it for ever without fear of loss or change. But will not this endless enjoyment produce weariness or satiety? Away with such an idea! God being infinite, and His beauty and excellence infinite, the blessed will always be able to discover in Him fresh perfections and fresh sources of joy, which will be inexhaustible, for the finite can never exhaust the infinite.

Application: If we allow such thoughts to sink deeply into our minds, we shall long, as the saints did, for heaven. We shall exclaim with the Psalmist: "Who will give me wings like a dove, and I will fly and be at rest?" With Saint Paul, "I desire to depart and to be with Christ"; and with Saint Ignatius, "How vile appear the things of earth when I contemplate those of heaven!"

Colloquy.

November 2: Feast of the Holy Souls: Why and How We Should Help the Holy Souls

1st prelude: Place purgatory before your eyes.

2nd prelude: Ask for true devotion to the holy souls.

Reasons for helping these holy souls:

Point I: As regards Almighty God

Consideration: These souls are exceedingly pleasing to God, being united to Him by a higher degree of sanctifying grace than those of the greatest living saints whose salvation is yet uncertain, whilst theirs is assured. The Beatific Vision is theirs already; and God would permit them to enjoy it at once, absolving them from all debts contracted by sin, were it not for His eternal decree, by virtue of with the time of their expiation can be shortened by prayer alone. He Himself asks our prayers in the name of the love He bears to these exiled souls. Can we refuse Him?

Application: Thus it is clear that Almighty God has in a certain sense placed the fate of the holy souls in our hands, and that if we show ourselves unmindful of them we neglect God Himself. Surely none of us would run the risk of incurring such a reproach. Let us on this solemn day renew our fervor on behalf of these suffering souls. We have many means of helping them – so many partial and plenary indulgences to be gained so easily. Do you make use of them? Do not hesitate, for in doing so you lose nothing and gain greatly.

Affections and Resolutions.

Point II: Reasons drawn from the state of the holy souls themselves

Consideration: 1. Because they suffer so grievously. Saint Thomas tells us the least pain in purgatory surpasses all that the martyrs endured. And not only do they suffer grievously, but for so long a time – during centuries, as we may see from the Church permitting perpetual commemorations on their behalf. 2. Because they can do nothing for themselves. 3. Because they so beseechingly entreat our help. 4. Because they ask it in the name of charity, in the name of our Lord, who in some sort suffers in them, saying, “I was in prison, and you did not visit Me.” 5. Because many of them appeal to your justice, to your gratitude; they are your relations, your friends, your benefactors.

Application: The truths laid down by the doctors of the Church in respect to the holy souls teach us not to limit our charity on their behalf. Some of the faithful have engaged themselves by vow to make over all their good works to the souls in purgatory. Benedict XIII approved of this heroic act, and, what is more, encouraged it by three special favors. 1. Wherever a priest who has made it celebrates, the altar is privileged. 2. All the faithful can gain a

plenary indulgence every time they communicate, and on every Monday they hear Mass. 3. All these indulgences can be applied to the souls in purgatory.
Affections and Resolutions.

Point III: Reasons as regards ourselves

Consideration: Charity towards ourselves as well as towards our neighbor should induce us to help the holy souls. Both in life and death we receivc immense advantage from so doing. 1. In thinking of the rigorous justice of God, we acquire a deeper hatred of sin and a stronger motive for expiating our past offences. 2. We make friends and advocates for ourselves with God. 3. We shorten our own time in purgatory; for our Lord Himself says, "Blessed are the merciful, for they shall obtain mercy."

Application: Begin by offering up your Communion and the indulgence attached for the holy souls; then consider what you will add for the future to what you have hitherto done on their behalf.
Colloquy.

November 3: On Death

1st prelude: Imagine a religious on his deathbed.
2nd prelude: Ask that you may obtain from the thought of death a strong desire of leading a holy life.

Point I: The mystery of death

Consideration: From the souls in purgatory we are brought today to the thought of death, so nearly are the two subjects connected. We all know that we shall die only once; that on this death of ours our eternal salvation depends; that thus it is the most momentous business of our whole existence, and should therefore be our chief concern during life. But the mystery is, that it is not so; that, on the contrary, we think of nothing so seldom as of death; and if the thought comes into our minds, we chase it away as unpleasant and untimely.

Application: Is not this really the case as concerns yourself? Can you say that at least once a week you seriously ask yourself the question, "Were I to die now, what should I fear or hope? How should I wish to have lived?" Perhaps you answer in the negative; perhaps even when the death of one of your brethren brings your own end before you, you instinctively turn away from the unwelcome idea, saying, "I am still young; or perhaps I am older than he who is gone, but I am strong and healthy; I need not think about dying yet."

What folly! What can be its cause? for to every effect belongs a cause. But is not the true cause in reality this: that if we seriously and frequently thought of death, we should feel obliged in conscience to live in a more holy and mortified manner, which we are not disposed to do? Let us be sure that while we banish the thought of death, we only enjoy a false peace, which can serve no good end.

Affections and Resolutions.

Point II: Preparation for death

Consideration: Today for me, tomorrow for thee. Imagine that this tomorrow has come for you; that you are stretched motionless on your deathbed, your life ebbing away from you, and your soul on the point of appearing before its Judge. Then ask yourself two questions: first, have I nothing which troubles my conscience at this awful hour, which makes me fear the sight of God? Oh, if you answer yes, do as you would wish to have done then: lay your doubt before your confessor in all simplicity, and follow his advice confidently. Second question: ask yourself an account of your past life. Will you not be forced to exclaim, as so many others have done, "Would to God I had been a more fervent and more mortified religious! How many my omissions, how great my negligence, sin and folly! O Lord, give me back health, allow me time for penance, and I will live differently, and atone for what is past!"

Colloquy.

November 4: Parable of the Laborers in the Vineyard in its Literal Sense

1st prelude: Behold our Divine Lord.

2nd prelude: Ask for grace to obey His will.

Point I: The call of the laborers

Consideration: Our Lord says in this parable "that the kingdom of heaven is like to a householder, who went out early in the morning to hire laborers into his vineyard; and having agreed with them for a penny a day, he sent them into his vineyard. And going out about the third hour, he saw others standing in the market place idle; and he said to them, Go you also into my vineyard, and I will give you what shall be just; and they went their way. And again he went out about the sixth and the ninth hour, and did in like manner; but about the eleventh hour he found others standing, and said to them, Why stand you here all day idle?… He saith to them, Go you also into my vineyard."

Application: In the literal sense of this parable, the master of the house is Almighty God, the Father of the whole human family; the vine the human family, bearing within itself the promised Messiah; the laborers the patriarchs, prophets, judges and teachers sent by God, during successive ages of the world, to keep alive in the hearts of men the advent of that expected Messiah; whilst the penny agreed upon as their hire is redemption – the heaven opened by that Messiah, and promised by Him to all who have diligently labored.

Affections and Resolutions.

Point II: The payment of the laborers

Consideration: "When evening was come, the lord of the vineyard saith to his steward, Call the laborers, and pay them their hire, beginning from the last even to the first." This inversion in the order of payment is interpreted as a prophesy of the fact, according to the words of our Lord, that the last shall be first, and the first last; that though the Jews were called first into the kingdom of God, they shall nevertheless be the last to enter it as a nation, because they will resist to the end of time the light of grace, a small number alone excepted. Thus our Lord adds, "many are called [that is, all the Jews], but few are chosen" out of their number amongst the elect.

Application: This is the true sense of the well-known verse, "Many are called, but few chosen," which, falsely applied to Christians, has too often discouraged pious souls. If you have been amongst them, see your error, and take care, if it is your duty to instruct others, that you give this, the true meaning.

Affections and Resolutions.

Point III: Murmurs of the laborers

Consideration: "When, therefore, they were come, … they received every man a penny; but when the first also came, they thought that they should receive more; … and they murmured against the master of the house, saying, These last have worked but one hour, and thou hast made them equal to us, that have borne the burden of the day and the heats. But he answering said to one of them, Friend, I do thee no wrong; didst thou not agree with me for a penny? ... Is it not lawful for me to do what I will? Is thy eye evil because I am good?"

Application: Our Lord predicts the murmurs of the converted Jews, which we read of in the Acts of the Apostles, when they saw the Gentiles received into the Church on the same footing as themselves. Let us learn to avoid all pretension, and to have a horror of every species of jealousy.

Colloquy.

November 5: Parable of the Laborers in the Vineyard: Its Moral Acceptation

1st prelude: Behold our Divine Lord.
2nd prelude: Ask for grace to obey His will.

Point I: The call of the laborers

Consideration: This vine – the care of the Master of the household, Almighty God – is our soul, created in His own image, made fruitful by the Blood of His Son. He gives it over to us; He exhorts us from the morning of life to its close to cultivate it with all diligence, that it may yield the fruits of holiness in abundance, stimulating our zeal by the hope of a reward eternal as to its duration, infinite as to its objects. What powerful motives to incite us to this labor in our youth, in manhood, in old age!

Application: How have you labored during your youth in the world? in religion? in the novitiate? in your studies? in the various employments confided to your charge? If your early years are not all spent, redouble your diligence in making a good use of them. If you are at the sixth or ninth hour, more advanced in life, fully occupied at home or abroad, beware lest dissipation or tepidity make you forget the interests of your soul. On the contrary, strive to become more and more fervent.

Affections and Resolutions.

Point II: Payment of the laborers

Consideration: Remark that the laborers are not paid "til evening was come." God does not reward the labors of life until its close – at the hour of death, or rather in eternity, which we reach through death. Life ought not to see long; it is, after all, but a day which is quickly passed. "One day in the sight of the Lord is as a thousand years," in the world of the Apostle Saint Peter, "and a thousand years as one day." Observe, besides, that the steward is commanded to call ALL the laborers and that all receive the same wages, which signifies that all the elect will be admitted alike into heaven, and will equally share its bliss according to their several capacities, though at the same time their capacities may be infinitely varied. We may also learn, from seeing that those who had worked but one hour received the same wages as those who had borne the labor and heat of the day, that it is fervor, and not the number of years we have spent in religion, which is of value in the sight of God.

Application: Renew your fervor at this consoling thought, and do not be discouraged if you have only given yourself entirely to God late in life.

Affections and Resolutions.

Point III: Murmurs of the laborers

Consideration: Who are those who murmur? They who were called the first, and who labored the whole time. Wherefore do they murmur? Because the others received the same as themselves, and even seemed to be preferred to them, being the first summoned for payment.

Application: Here is a lesson for those who have grown old in religion, and who stand in danger of falling into certain defects, such as vanity, an eagerness for distinction and privileges, suspicion, jealousy, ill-humor, and, what is worst of all, spiritual lukewarmness induced by decay of bodily strength. Let us guard against these defects by watchfulness and prayer, saying with David, "Unto old age and gray hairs, O God, forsake me not."

Colloquy.

November 6: On Zeal for Souls

1st prelude: Imagine our Lord saying, "God you also into My vineyard."

2nd prelude: Ask for grace to understand the grandeur and merit of zeal.

Point I: Nothing is greater in the sight of God than zeal

Consideration: In the exercise of zeal we spread and build up the kingdom of God by gaining Him new subjects; we thus cooperate with God the Father in the work of creation, by teaching men to know, love and serve Him; with God the Son in the work of redemption, by making fruitful that Blood He poured out for the salvation of man; with God the Holy Ghost in His office of Sanctifier, by strengthening the elect in love of virtue, and hatred of sin. In the words of Saint Denis the Areopagite, of all divine things, the most divine is to cooperate with God in the salvation of souls.

Application: Let us rejoice if we are called to this exercise in zeal, in which all is great and nothing small, if we consider the end in view. The distinctions which we may be sometimes tempted to draw between teaching children or grown persons, rich and poor; between preaching in a cathedral or in a country village; between attending the deathbed of a beggar or of a noble, are nothing more nor less than vanity. Have we never made any of these distinctions, so unworthy of the faith we profess, and so often injurious in their consequences?

Affections and Resolutions.

Point II: Nothing more agreeable to the sight of God than zeal for souls

Consideration: This is self-evident, since the zeal in question has not only the glory of God for its end, but the salvation of souls, a single soul being of more value in His eyes than anything else in the world. If we call to mind all that our Lord did and suffered for the salvation of man, His labors, His tears, His humiliations, and His death, we shall required no other argument to convince us of the esteem which He attaches to zeal for souls.

Application: This the Apostles understood, and were thus inspired to undertake such distant journeys and arduous labors, to brave perils of every kind, and finally death amidst frightful tortures. What proofs do you give of sharing their ardor? Do you neglect no occasion of exercising this zeal? How do you cultivate the vine committed to your care? Are you not of the number of those who form great designs for the future, neglecting the present?

Affections and Resolutions.

Point III: Nothing more meritorious in the sight of God than zeal for souls

Consideration: Since nothing is more agreeable to God, it follows that nothing is more meritorious, and consequently that nothing will be more magnificently rewarded. These are the words of the Holy Ghost: "They that instruct many to justice shall shine as stars for all eternity"; or, as Saint James has it, "He who causeth a sinner to be converted from the error of his ways shall save his soul from death, and shall cover a multitude of sins."

Application: What encouraging reflections for the different members of a religious community, for those who spend their life in the labors of Martha, for those who are preparing for their ministry, or who, having engaged in it, are compelled to remain inactive through sickness or old age! For all, as members of one body, cooperate towards the same end; either in providing for the wants of their brethren, or by offering to God their studies, their sufferings and their prayers, for those laboring for the salvation of souls.

Colloquy.

November 7: The Rich Young Man Called to Evangelical Perfection

1st prelude: Imagine the young man kneeling at the feet of our Lord.

2nd prelude: Ask the grace of increasing in the perfection of our vocation.

Point I: The question the young man asks our Lord

Consideration: On one occasion, when our Lord was preaching in the country round about Jordan, a certain young man appeared before Him, and addressed Him in these words: "Good Master, what good shall I do, that I may have life everlasting?"

Application: This young man gives us an example of fervor, respect, humility and zeal; but what we should principally remark is, that he does not ask our Lord what sins he should avoid in order to gain heaven, but what good he should do. Unfortunately we, for the most part, follow an opposite course; our faults and the means of overcoming them form the almost exclusive subject of our examinations and resolutions. In future let our first thought on rising be the good we may do that day, reviewing the actions which will occupy us, and seeing how we may most perfectly perform them, asking God's blessing upon them, and taking the necessary resolutions.

Then at night, when we make our examination, let us thank God (filled with joy) for the good He has enabled us to do, resolved to do still better in time to come. Thus we shall serve God with love and confidence, and shall infallibly make greater progress than in perpetually dwelling upon our sins and imperfections.

Affections and Resolutions.

Point II: The answer our Lord gives the young man

Consideration: Our Lord answers the young man by saying, "If thou wilt enter into life, keep the commandments." And the young man replies, "All these have I kept from my youth; what is yet wanting to me?" Jesus says again to him, "If thou wilt be perfect, go sell what thou hast and give to the poor, and thou shalt have treasure in heaven; and come follow Me."

Application: What splendid inducements were here held out by our Lord to the young man whom, looking on, He loved, as Saint Mark tells us! In place of perishable, He offered him eternal wealth; instead of limited earthly possessions, the boundless kingdom of heaven, and the enjoyment of glory and happiness therein proportioned to the greatness of his sacrifice. What blessedness for the young man, had he understood and followed the counsels of his Divine Lord!

Affections and Resolutions.

Point III: Sadness of the young man

Consideration: But the young man, instead of being filled with joy and gladness at these words of our Lord, was, as the Gospel says, "struck sad at the saying, and went away sorrowful; for he had great possessions."

Application: Here we are tempted to inquire the end of this young man; was he saved or lost? Saint Augustine thinks that he was not saved, not because he did not follow the counsel given, but because his want of resolution led him to fall an easy prey to the temptations of wealth, which he would have avoided in following his vocation. Our Lord's words on the departure of the young man give great weight to this opinion: "How hardly shall they who have riches enter into the kingdom of God!"

Let us thank God for the grace which has overcome the obstacles to our holy vocation.
Colloquy with Our Divine Lord.

November 8: Sickness and Death of Lazarus

1st prelude: Imagine our Lord having just received the message from the sisters of Lazarus.
2nd prelude: Ask for great confidence in God, joined to perfect resignation.

Point I: The message from the sisters of Lazarus

Consideration: The resurrection of Lazarus is doubtless one of the most striking of those miracles by which our Lord deigned to prove His divinity, being performed in the neighborhood of Jerusalem in favor of a wealthy and well-known personage, who had lain for four days in the grave, and in the presence of a number of distinguished citizens. Let us first consider the message sent to our Lord as soon as Martha and Mary were aware of the serious character of their brother's illness. It ran thus: "Lord, he whom Thou lovest is sick."

Application: From this we may learn, 1st, that in all our afflictions we should PROMPTLY have recourse to God, and not wait til we have exhausted all human means of aid; 2ndly, that we need not set forth many motives in our petitions for God's assistance. This is what Saint Augustine says in speaking of the message of Martha and Mary, which he calls a model of prayer.
Affections and Resolutions.

Point II: The reply of Jesus

Consideration: "This sickness is not unto death, but for the glory of God, that the Son of God may be glorified by it." Such was the sole answer of our gracious Lord to the message of Martha and Mary. Later on He said to His disciples, "Lazarus our friend sleepeth." From these mysterious words those who heard them naturally gathered that our Lord thought the state of the sick man in no way alarming. But what could the sisters have thought as they watched beside their dying brother, after having implored our Lord's aid with such confidence? It was, indeed, enough to overcome their faith and resignation; but they never murmured; even the very words of Mary used when she first saw our Lord showed that her faith in Him was still unshaken: "Lord, if Thou hadst been here, my brother had not died."

Application: Where are your faith and resignation when, after having prayed long and earnestly, you find what you have asked still denied? Do you not yield to thoughts injurious to God, or at least to impatience, to murmuring and discouragement, saying to yourself what others say aloud, "What is the use of prayer?" Affections and Resolutions.

Point III: The delay in our Lord's departure

Consideration: Saint John tells us that Jesus loved Martha and her sister Mary and Lazarus. But in spite of this, and though He intended giving proof of His affection by working so great a miracle on their behalf, it was our Lord's will to try them in the furnace of affliction. Thus He permitted Lazarus to die, and seemed regardless of the grief of the sisters; remaining three days in the place where He was, and then taking two days in crossing the Jordan and reaching Bethany, which therefore He did not reach until four days after the death of Lazarus.

Application: Thus our Lord deals with His chosen ones. If you meet with many and bitter trials, conclude therefore that He loves you, and is preparing for you superabundant happiness and glory, and take courage from the thought.

Colloquy.

November 9: First Incident on the Journey to Bethany: Third Prediction of the Passion

1st prelude: Imagine our Lord on His way thither, surrounded by His Apostles.

2nd prelude: Ask that you may always bear in mind the remembrance of His Passion, and derive great fruit from doing so.

Point I: Our Lord predicts His Passion for the third time

Consideration: On the journey to Bethany our Lord spoke for the third time, and in a more detailed manner, of His Passion to be accomplished in the course of a few weeks, saying, "Behold, we go up to Jerusalem; and the Son of Man shall be betrayed to the chief priests and to the scribes and to the ancients, and they shall condemn Him to death, and shall deliver Him to the Gentiles; and they shall mock Him, and spit upon Him, and scourge Him, and kill Him; and the third day He shall rise again."

Application: Do not these frequent references of our Lord's to His approaching Passion show that it was ever in His mind and dear to His Heart? For as He Himself said, "out of abundance of the heart the mouth speaketh." If, therefore, we desire to please His Sacred Heart and obtain signal favors from it, let us always try to remember what He suffered fro us; let us speak of it to others, and make it the subject of our visit to the Blessed Sacrament.

Affections and Resolutions.

Point II: Our Lord's prediction not understood by the Apostles

Consideration: Though our Lord spoke of His approaching Passion and death with the utmost plainness, the Apostles, as Saint Luke says, "understood none of these things." They even went so far as to discredit the predictions of their Master, Saint Peter exclaiming, in the words related by Saint Matthew, "Lord, be it far from Thee; this shall not be unto Thee"; so blinded were they still by their prejudices respecting the temporal glory of the promised Messiah.

Application: Let us learn to be more indulgent, or at least to show more moderation towards those who differ from us, and not to accuse them too readily of incredulity or impiety, either on account of their errors in matters of faith or their aversion to certain religious institutions and practices. How many amongst them are, like the Apostles, the victims of ignorance or of prejudice! Are we ourselves wholly free from prejudice? Do not we sometimes say, "I could not do without this, I could never do that, live in that place," etc.? All such ideas are the fruit of prejudice; that is, of an opinion formed before experience; which subsequent events, to our great surprise, often wholly remove.

Affections and Resolutions.

Point III: Reasons for our Lord's prediction

Consideration: Our Lord, though He well knew His Apostles would not understand Him when He spoke of His Passion, did so for three reasons: 1. That they might not be scandalized when they saw Him, their Master, treated exactly according to His predictions, and learn that His sufferings were caused much more by His love than by the malice of His enemies. 2. To awake in their hearts towards Him the feelings of love and generosity so richly His due. 3. To make them see that the kingdoms and thrones

He had promised them could only be purchased by suffering and humiliation.
Colloquy with our Lord on the cross.

November 10: Second Incident on the Journey to Bethany: The Inconsiderate Request of the Sons of Zebedee

1st prelude: Imagine the Apostles James and John, accompanied by their mother, making their request to our Lord.
2nd prelude: Ask for humility as the fruit of the meditation.

Point I: The inconsiderate request of the two Apostles

Consideration: "Then" – that is to say, directly after our Lord's prediction of His Passion – "came to Him the mother of the sons of Zebedee, with her sons, adoring and asking something of Him; and they said, Grant that we may sit one on Thy right hand, and the other on Thy left, in Thy glory." Such a demand, made at such a time, fully confirms what has just been said concerning the ignorance and prejudice of the Apostles.

Application: But still more astounding than their ignorance is the astonishing lengths to which their ambition carries them. Not content with our Lord's promise that they should one day sit on twelve seats judging the twelve tribes of Israel, they aspired to sit, the one on His right hand, the other on his left. What could lead two poor sinners to form such lofty pretensions? Alas, we may find the cause within ourselves! Ambition springs from pride, and pride is deeply rooted in every human heart, whatever its state or condition, and is the source of all the dissensions, disputes, and apostasies which have invaded even the sanctuary of religion. Be on your guard, therefore, and fear falling victim to its insidious advances.
Affections and Resolutions.

Point II: Our Lord's reply to the Apostles

Consideration: Our Lord's reply to this ill-timed demand was sufficiently humiliating: "You know not what you ask. Can you drink the chalice that I shall drink?" – referring to the sufferings and humiliations of which He was so soon to drain the very dregs. He continues: "My chalice, indeed, you shall drink; but to sit on My right or left hand is not Mine to give, but to them for whom it is prepared by my Father."

Application: The practical conclusion we should derive from these words of our Lord appears to be this: that all our requests should be made under the condition of their being for our good; for often we, too, know not what we ask; even things which seem to us to tend to the glory of God and the welfare of our own or our neighbors' souls would, on the contrary, prove injurious to us. Affections and Resolutions.

Point III: The indignation of the other Apostles: the admirable lesson given by our Lord

Consideration: "And the ten hearing it," Saint Matthew continues, "were moved with indignation against the two brethren. But Jesus called them to Him and said, You know that the princes of the Gentiles lord it over them, and they that are the greater exercise power upon them. It shall not be so among you; but whoever will be the greater among you let him be your minister, and he that will be first among you shall be your servant. Even as the Son of Man is not come to be ministered unto, but to minister, and to give His life for the redemption of many."

Application: Let us endeavor to apply these words of our Lord to ourselves, so as to derive great practical fruit from them, examining ourselves as to our past conduct, and resolving for the future to make it more conformable to religious perfections. Colloquy.

November 11: Third Incident on the Journey to Bethany: The Cure of the Blind Man at Jericho

1st prelude: Imagine our Lord approaching Jericho, surrounded by the multitude.

2nd prelude: Ask for grace to pray well

Point I: The blind man crying aloud as our Lord passes by

Consideration: "Now it came to pass, when He drew nigh to Jericho, that a certain blind man sat by the wayside begging; and when he heard the multitude passing by, he asked what this meant; and they told him that Jesus of Nazareth was passing by; and he cried out, saying, Jesus, Son of David, have mercy on me! And they that went before rebuked him that he should hold his peace; but he cried out much more, Son of David, have mercy on me!"

Application: Let us consider the qualities of the prayer of this blind man. 1. It was well-timed; he learned that our Lord was passing; moved by grace, he seized the opportunity, he cried out at once, and he was heard, and healed by a miracle. Had he at all delayed, would he ever have received his sight? 2. It was fervent: uttered from the depths of a heart conscious of its misery. Why are our prayers so cold? Because we do not feel our misery. 3. It was pressing and persevering: he cried out, and ceased not to cry, thought our Lord did not appear to heed him, and those by his side rebuked him. Is it not our want of perseverance that renders our prayers so often of no effect?

Affections and Resolutions.

Point II: Our Lord commands the blind man to be brought to Him

Consideration: Though our Lord seemed at first not to heed the cries of the blind man, wishing to test his faith and confidence, His Heart was full of compassion for his state. "He commanded him," as the Gospel says, "to be brought to Him, and when he was come near, He asked him, saying, What wilt thou that I do to thee? But he said, Lord, that I may see."

Application: If God does not immediately grant our petitions, it is for our good. He requires us to express them, not because they are unknown to Him, but for our own advantage; in so doing, we recognize that all benefits flow from Him alone, and show our filial confidence in our Heavenly Father.

Affections and Resolutions.

Point III: Our Lord heals the blind man

Consideration: How wonderfully were the faith and perseverance of the blind man rewarded! "And Jesus said to him, Receive thy sight; thy faith hath made thee whole. And immediately he saw and followed Him, glorifying God. And all the people, when they saw it, gave praise to God."

Application: Remark our Lord's goodness on this occasion. Not only does He give sight to the bodily eyes of the blind man, but He opens the eyes of his soul. In his Benefactor the blind man recognizes the promised Messiah; he follows Him, he blesses Him, and the surrounding multitude are infected by his enthusiasm.

Let us, after his example, praise, adore and glorify our Divine Lord, from whom we have received even greater favors than the blind man of Jericho. Let us try to know and love Him more and more, and to make others know and love Him also.

Colloquy with our Lord, our Master and Physician.

November 12: Fourth Incident on the Journey to Bethany: The Wonderful Conversion of Zacheus

1st prelude: Imagine our Lord in the house of Zacheus.
2nd prelude: Ask our Lord to sanctify you as He sanctified Zacheus.

Point I: Zacheus seeks to see our Lord

Consideration: The miraculous cure of the blind man being noised abroad throughout the then flourishing and important city of Jericho, our Lord was triumphantly received on His entrance in this very place where, fifteen ages before, Joshua had been victorious, but where He came not to execute justice but mercy, and to call sinners to repentance. Amongst these sinners was, as Saint Luke tells us, a man named Zacheus, who was chief of the publicans, and rich. This man sought to see Jesus where he was, but he could not for the crowd, because he was of low stature, and running before he climbed up into a sycamore tree, that he might see Him, for He was to pass that way.

Application: The desire of Zacheus to behold the Author of so great a miracle was, doubtless, very natural; but it was not so much founded upon curiosity as upon grace, according to the opinion of commentators. It was his eagerness and generosity that obtained him such signal favors. Oh, if our dispositions resembled his, what graces and favors would be ours likewise!

Affections and Resolutions.

Point II: Zacheus honored by a visit from our Lord

Consideration: The Evangelist continues: "When Jesus was come to that place, looking up He saw him, and said to him, Zacheus, make haste and come down, for this day I must abide in thy house." What must have been the surprise and delight of Zacheus at these gracious words! No wonder, as Saint Luke says, that he made haste and came down, and received Jesus with joy.

Application: When our Lord deigns to visit you in Holy Communion, let no ill-timed fears prevent your opening your heart to Him with joy and confidence, but welcome Him after the example of Zacheus.

Affections and Resolutions.

Point III: Zacheus converted and sanctified by our Lord's visit

Consideration: As our Lord entered into the house of Zacheus, grace entered with Him, and made this man, regarded as a sinner, a just man and a saint. (Saint Clement relates that Zacheus afterwards became a follower of Saint Peter, and was ordained by him Bishop of Cesarea.) His works gave proof of the change. "Behold, Lord," he said, "the half of my goods I give to the poor; and if I have wronged any man anything, I restore him fourfold. Jesus said to him, This day is salvation come to this house; ... for the Son of man is come to seek and to save that which was lost."

Application: Let us imitate Zacheus in his generosity, by putting our good resolutions into practice immediately, and making what amends we can for any injury or scandal we may have caused; thus shall we secure our Lord's favor, and be sure of one day hearing from His lips words of blessing and salvation. Colloquy with our Divine Lord.

November 13: The Resurrection of Lazarus: Our Lord Arrives at Bethany

1st prelude: Imagine Lazarus coming forth from the tomb.
2nd prelude: Ask for lively faith in the great mystery of the Resurrection.

Point I: Our Lord's interview with Martha and Mary

Consideration: "Jesus therefore came," relates Saint John, "and found that he [Lazarus] had been four days already in the grave... Martha therefore, as soon as she heard Jesus was come, went to meet Him, but Mary sat at home. Martha therefore said to Jesus, Lord, if Thou hadst been here, my brother had not died. Jesus saith to her, Thy brother shall rise again. Martha said to Him, I know that he shall rise again in the resurrection at the last day. Jesus saith to her, I am the resurrection and the life; he that believeth in Me, although he be dead, shall live; and every one that liveth and believeth in Me shall not die for ever. Believest thou this? She saith to Him, Yea, Lord, I believe that Thou art Christ, the Son of the living God, who art come into this world."

Application: Imagine our Lord asking you the same question, "Believest thou this?" and strengthen your faith in the great and consoling mystery of the Resurrection. If you penetrate it deeply, you will in future be capable of greater sacrifices; you will not so much fear injuring your health.

Affections and Resolutions.

Point II: Our Lord at the grave of Lazarus

Consideration: When Mary heard from her sister that our Lord was come, she rose up, and, followed by the Jews that were with her in the house, went to meet Him; and, as the Gospel continues, "when she was come where Jesus was, she fell down at His feet, and saith to Him, Lord, if Thou hadst been here, by brother had not died. Jesus therefore, when He saw her weeping, and the Jews that were come with her weeping, groaned in spirit and troubled Himself, and said, Where have you laid him? They say to Him, Lord, come and see. And Jesus wept. The Jews therefore said, Behold how He loved him. But some of them said, Could not He that opened the eyes of the blind have caused that this man should not die? Jesus therefore, again groaning in Himself, cometh to the sepulchre. Now it was a cave, and a stone was laid over it."

Application: Let us observe: 1. That Mary, as soon as she heard that Jesus was come, left all those that were trying to console her, to throw herself at the feet of Jesus; let us, too, learn from her to find our best consolation at HIs feet before the Blessed Sacrament. 2. That we are not forbidden to be moved by the sorrow of our friends and relations, since our Lord Himself wept at beholding the sorrow of Martha and Mary. 3. That, not satisfied with bestowing His compassion on their sorrow, our Lord removed its cause by restoring to them the object of their love. Let us do as He did as far as lies in our power; true it is we cannot restore life to the dying, nor riches to those who have lost them, but we may bring back those to the fold who were dead in sins, and restore them to the riches of God's grace.

Affections and Resolutions.

Point III: Resurrection of Lazarus

Consideration: "Jesus saith, Take away the stone… They took therefore the stone away; and Jesus, lifting His eyes to heaven, said, Father, I give Thee thanks that Thou hast heard Me. And I knew that Thou hearest Me always; but because of the people who stand about have I said it, that they may believe that Thou hast sent Me. When He had said these things He cried with a loud voice, Lazarus, come forth. And presently he that had been dead came forth."

Application: Let us admire the power and goodness of our Divine Lord, who worked this stupendous miracle not so much for Lazarus as for the Jews and for ourselves, that we might believe in Him, love Him, and serve Him with all the powers of our soul. Colloquy with our Lord.

November 14: The Chief Priests and the Rulers Conspire Against Christ

1st prelude: Imagine the council-room with the chief priests and rulers assembled.
2nd prelude: Ask an increase of love towards our Lord.

Point I: The jealousy our Lord's enemies conceived against Him

Consideration: We learn from Saint John that "many of the Jews who had come with Martha and Mary, and had beheld the resurrection of Lazarus, believed"; but he goes on to say, "some of them went to the Pharisees and told them the things that Jesus had done. The chief priests therefore and the Pharisees gathered a council and said, What do we? for this Man doth many miracles. If we let Him alone, all will believe in Him."

Application: Here are clear proofs of the jealousy and hatred the chief priests and Pharisees bore our Lord, both because He made the people believe in Him and because He rebuked their own pride and hypocrisy. It was passion that blinded them, and that at last led them to put to death Him who had come to save them. In the same manner how many priests, and even religious, distinguished by their learning and talents, have been similarly deceived! Let their example make us fear for ourselves. Affections and Resolutions.

Point II: Pretexts for the hostility the chief priests and Pharisees bore our Lord

Consideration: Passion is ever ashamed to declare itself openly, and seeks to veil itself under specious pretexts. Thus the chief priests and the Pharisees reasoned, saying, "If we let Him alone, so will all believe in Him; and the Romans will come and take away our place and nation."

Application: Do not we often see in these our days men as distinguished amongst their fellows as these Scribes and Pharisees,

who league themselves together against our Lord and His Church? They would not for the world acknowledge that their passions make them persecutors of all that is holy; they pretend that they are influenced only by the good of humanity, and unfortunately succeed in inducing many to join them.
Affections and Resolutions.

Point III: The enemies of our Lord openly declare their resolve to put Him to death

Consideration: At length the hostility of the priests and Pharisees bursts forth undisguised. "One of them, named Caiphas, being the high priest that year, said to them, You know nothing, neither do you consider that it is expedient for you that one man should die for the people, and that the whole nation perish not. And this he spoke not of himself, but being the high priest of that year, he prophesied that Jesus should died for the nation, and not only for the nation, but to gather together in one the children of God that were dispersed. From that day therefore they devised to put Him to death. Wherefore Jesus walked no more openly among the Jews, but he went into a country near the desert, unto a city that is called Ephrem."

Application: The prophetic words of Caiphas show us that in the supernatural order the power of the priest is derived from his office, and not from his personal character. This is our security in the reception of the Sacraments. The flight of our Lord teaches us, besides, that to hide from persecution is not cowardice, and that a contrary conduct would oftentimes be rashness.
Colloquy with our Divine Lord.

November 15: Our Lord's Abiding at Ephrem: On our Annual Retreat

1st prelude: Imagine our Lord and His Apostles retiring into the desert.
2nd prelude: Ask the grace of a due appreciation of an annual retreat, and that you may benefit by it.

Point I: Importance of the retreat

Consideration: Jesus, we are told, "went into a country near the desert, unto a city that is called Ephrem, and there He abode with His disciples." We find that He remained there six days. This retirement of our Lord's, a fortnight before His Passion, forcibly reminds us of the annual retreat prescribed us by our rule. That we may profit as we ought by so great a means of grace, let us bear in mind the ends proposed: 1. To sound the depths of our hearts, to learn to know ourselves, and to see how we stand as regards our vocation and the observance of our vows. 2. To repair what is past by a good confession or a review of the year, accompanied by perfect contrition. 3. To lay down a rule of life for the future, and to renew our fervor, diminished as it is by the advance of time. It is true that our spiritual exercises ought to sustain and increase our fervor in the service of God; but these valuable instruments of perfection are apt to lose their efficacy by use, and the chief end of the retreat is to impart a fresh vigor to our daily practices of piety, and to lead us to fulfill them better for the future.

Application: These considerations will serve to show the importance of this retreat, and the danger incurred by those who make it carelessly. Has your conscience nothing to reproach you with on this subject?

Affections and Resolutions.

Point II: Means of making the retreat well

Consideration: To do so: 1. Think how reasonable it is that you who have labored for the salvation of others during a whole year should at least take a week to busy yourself exclusively about your own soul. 2. Remember that God has from all eternity attached special graces to this retreat: your perseverance, your eternal salvation, may depend upon it; perhaps even it may be His design that it should serve as your preparation for death. 3. Excite within yourself an earnest desire of making it well, with a lively confidence that God will enable you to gather abundant fruit from it. 4. Pray much: the more wretched you feel yourself, the greater should be your confidence, joining mortification to prayer, and having a special devotion to our Blessed Lady.

Application: Think what a rigorous account God will ask you of this retreat. Think how many lost souls, had they received such a grace, it would have made saints. Think of your own salvation; think of the salvation of your neighbors, for theirs may depend upon the use you make of this retreat.

Affections and Resolutions.

Point III: Means of preserving the fruits of the retreat

Consideration: 1. To write down clearly, before coming out of retreat, what change you should make in any part of your conduct as regards men, as regards God, and what habits you should adopt for the future as regards God, as regards men. 2. To make these points successively the matter of your particular examination. 3. To make them the matter of your meditation every Sunday or Monday. 4. To examine yourself more thoroughly upon them on the day of your monthly retreat, and to give an account of them to your Director. Have you employed these means constantly since your last retreat?

Application: See in what respects you have failed. Make a resolution not to do so for the future, but to be faithful to them until your next retreat.

Colloquy with our Lord.

November 16: On the Duty of Praying Always

1st prelude: Imagine our Lord saying to you, "Pray always."

2nd prelude: Ask for the grace of doing so.

Point I: How we can pray always

Consideration: A time of danger and temptation was now at hand for the Apostles; more than ever they required to strengthen themselves by prayer. Therefore their Divine Master told them to pray ALWAYS, because in all situations of life grace is needed, either to enable men to struggle successfully against temptation, or to enable them to fulfill their obligations as Christians or religious. "Ask, and it shall be given you," is the condition imposed by our Lord Himself; hence the maxim, "All by prayer, nothing without prayer."

Application: But in practice how are we to pray always? It can be done in various ways; one is by familiarizing ourselves with some ejaculatory prayer, which by frequent use springs from the heart to the lips without the slightest effort. The venerable Louis de Ponte was so accustomed to repeat, "PROPTER TE, For Thy sake, my God," that his communications with heaven may be said to have been almost uninterrupted; he, indeed, prayed always. How happy should we be if we were thus ever united to God by prayer! and what strength it would give us in time of temptation! But it is in our power to obtain it, as others have done, but only by constant

and generous effort.
Affections and Resolutions.

Point II: Against discouragement in prayer

Consideration: The Gospel continues: "We ought always to pray, and not to faint." The same lesson is contained in the parable which follows – that of the unjust judge, who is for a long time appealed to in vain by a poor oppressed widow. But at length the judge is compelled to do her justice, "because," as he says, "she is troublesome to me, I will avenge her."

Application: It was very necessary that our Lord, after having exhorted us to pray always, should urge upon us to continue in prayer, and not to give way, as we are often inclined to do, to discouragement and weariness. How many persons who at first prayed with fervour and confidence, finding their petitions unanswered, have lost heart and abandoned prayer! Had the widow of the parable thus acted, she would have obtained nothing. We are often discouraged, besides, by the remembrance of our unworthiness, our faults, and our falls. We should console ourselves by reflecting that nothing is more pleasing to God than the prayer of a humble and contrite heart; that the greater our miseries, the more abundant His mercies; that the promise of our Lord, "Ask, and it shall be given unto you," proves that it is our prayer and not our merits that draws down on us the favor of heaven; and that ofttimes, if we do not receive what we have asked, we obtain other and more precious graces.
Colloquy with our Lord.

November 17: The Supper at Bethany

1st prelude: Imagine Saint Mary Magdalene anointing our Lord's feet.
2nd prelude: Ask for grace to love our Lord as she did.

Point I: The conduct of Saint Mary Magdalene

Consideration: Mary had anointed the feet of our Lord on a previous occasion, and also in the house of Simon of Bethany, probably the same Saint Mark speaks of as Simon the leper. At this second supper, eight days before the passion, Lazarus being present, "Mary," in the words of Saint John, "therefore took a pound of ointment of right spikenard, of great price, and anointed the feet of Jesus, and wiped His feet with her hair; and the house was filled with the odor of the ointment." This holy woman took every opportunity of showing the love and gratitude she bore our Lord. She had formerly taken pleasure in adorning her hair, and in rich perfumes; now she makes a sacrifice of both in His service.

Application: Let us also, following the example of this great penitent, lose no opportunity of showing love and generosity towards our Lord. Let us offer to Him in particular what it costs us most to relinquish, our judgment and our liberty, yielding them up willingly under the yoke of obedience. Let us be, as Saint Paul expresses it, "the good odor of Christ," diffusing it around us by giving an example of perfect regularity, anointing the feet of our Lord by cherishing in a peculiar manner the poor suffering members of His mystical body.

Affections and Resolutions.

Point II: Conduct of Judas

Consideration: Judas, far from being edified at the holy prodigality of Saint Mary Magdalene, vented his vexation in complaints hidden under the mask of charity. "Why," said he, "was not this ointment sold for three hundred pence, and given to the poor? Now he said this," adds Saint John, "not because he cared for the poor, but because he was a thief, and, having the purse, carried the things that were put therein."

Application: We are justly indignant at the behavior of Judas, who, though one of the twelve, has become a thief, a hypocrite, and the censor of his Divine Master; whilst we admire the unruffled sweetness of our Lord, who, though He knew the hearts of all men, and that of Judas in particular, abstained from a word of reproach, as if, by sparing his reputation before men, He still hoped to win the traitor back. He merely blamed him indirectly whilst praising Mary Magdalene. "Let her alone," He said, "that she may keep it against the day of My burial; she hath wrought a good work upon Me. Amen I say to you, wheresoever this gospel shall be preached in the whole world, that also which she hath done shall be told for a memorial of her."

Affections and Resolutions.

Point III: Conduct of the inhabitants of Jerusalem

Consideration: These may be comprised in four classes: 1. Those who, having been converted by the resurrection of Lazarus, had recognized Jesus as the Messiah, and flocked to Bethany to pay Him homage. 2. Those who had been drawn thither by curiosity. 3. The largest number, the wholly indifferent, who remained at home, disdaining to make inquiry concerning the reported miracle. 4. The bitter enemies of our Lord, the chief priests, who, as Saint John says, "thought to kill Lazarus also, because many of the Jews by reason of him went away and believed in Jesus."

Application: We may learn from this that the triumphs of the Church are ever followed by the same effects – the conversion of the well-disposed, and the consolation of the faithful; an increase of hatred in the declared enemies of Christ, and the indifference of the greatest number, who are entirely absorbed in pleasure and in mere material interests. Let us derive as fruit from it an increase of zeal for the glory of our Lord and for the conversion of sinners. Colloquy.

November 18: Our Lord's Entry into Jerusalem

1st prelude: Imagine our Lord seated on the foal of an ass, approaching the town in triumph, surrounded by an admiring crowd.

2nd prelude: Ask that the love of Jesus may triumph over your heart, and over the hearts of all mankind.

Point I: Preparations for our Lord's entry

Consideration: "And on the next day [after the feast at the house of Simon], He went before, going up to Jerusalem… And when He was come nigh to Bethphage and Bethania, unto the mount of Olivet, He sent two of His disciples, saying, Go into the town which is over against you, at your entering into which you shall find the colt of an ass tied, on which no man ever hath sitten; loose him, and bring him hither; and if any man shall ask you why do you loose him, you shall say thus unto him, Because the Lord hath need of his service." Here we know not what to admire most – the foreknowledge of our Lord, which nothing escapes, and the free domain He possesses over the goods of His creatures, the prompt obedience of His disciples in executing an order which must have seemed to them rash and dangerous; or the eagerness with which the inhabitants of Bethany complied with the request of the messengers of Jesus.

Application: Let us learn: 1. To abandon ourselves to the providence of God, who watches over each one of us, knowing all that happens to us, and turning it in His love to our profit. 2. To offer Him unreservedly health, talents, learning, etc. 3. Not to hesitate when obedience imposes on us duties apparently difficult. If we act in a spirit of faith like the disciples, all difficulties will speedily disappear.

Affections and Resolutions.

Point II: Glories of our Lord's triumph

Consideration: What sweetness and majesty united in our Lord, what enthusiasm in the people on the occasion of His entry! "They took," says the Gospel, "branches of palm in their hands, and spread their garments in the way, and cried, saying, Hosanna to the Son of David; blessed is He that cometh in the name of the Lord; hosanna in the highest!"

Application: If you should happen to be praised for your zeal or charity, to become the object of reverence, perhaps even to be regarded as a saint, repress all emotion of vanity, refer all your success to God alone, and remember that only five days after the triumphal entry of our Lord into Jerusalem, the very same streets re-echoed with the cry of "Crucify Him, crucify Him!"

Affections and Resolutions.

Point III: The envy of the Pharisees

Consideration: Though the Scribes and Pharisees could not but see the accomplishment of the prophesy of Zachary in the triumphal entry of our Lord, pride and jealousy prevented their admitting it. They said among themselves, "Do you see that we prevail nothing? Behold, the whole world is gone after Him." Some even went so far as to say to our Lord, "Master, rebuke They disciples"; to whom He said, "I say unto you, If these should hold their peace, the stones will cry out." How wonderfully were these words of our Lord fulfilled on the day of His Passion! For when the terrified disciples stood silent on Calvary, the rending of the rocks bore testimony to the divinity of their Master.

Application: If you feel vexed at the success of any of your colleagues, do not give way to the jealousy of the Pharisees. Thank God that good is done, whoever may be the instrument.

Colloquy with our Lord.

November 19: Jesus Weeps over Jerusalem

1st prelude: Behold our Lord weeping over Jerusalem.
2nd prelude: Ask that you may never cause Him such grief as He experienced at the sight of that faithless city.

Point I: The infidelity of Jerusalem: the first motive of our Lord's tears

Consideration: The acclamations of the crowd increased as the procession approached the town; but our Lord, in the words of Saint Luke, seeing the city, wept over it – not at the thought of the cruel death awaiting Him there (that He had long desired and expected: a year before He had said, "I have a baptism wherewith I am to be baptized; how am I straitened until it be accomplished!"), but at the thought of the blindness of the inhabitants of that devoted city, who would for the most part persist in rejecting Him, and who were to be so fearfully chastised in consequence. It was the thought of their eternal reprobation that drew from His lips those touching words, "If thou also hadst known, and that in this thy day, the things that are to thy peace, but now they are hidden from thy eyes."

Application: Let us learn from these tears of our Divine Lord: 1. To be less taken up with our own petty miseries, and more concerned at the sight of so many blind and hardened sinners, and to use prayers, tears, penances, and mortifications for their conversion. 2. To keep alive within ourselves a spirit of compunction, which, alas, perhaps we only know by name. 3. To fear above all things, as the saints did, not to co-operate sufficiently with the grace of God.
Affections and Resolutions.

Point II: The destruction of Jerusalem: the second motive of our Lord's tears

Consideration: Our Lord loved Jerusalem tenderly. His Heavenly Father had made it the home of His chosen people, and the abiding-place of His Temple, and called it the Holy City, the City of God. How the thought of its total destruction must have grieved His Sacred Heart when He uttered the fearful prophecy, "For the days shall come upon thee, and thy enemies shall cast a trench about thee, and compass thee round, and straiten thee on every side, and beat thee flat to the ground, and thy children who are in thee; and they shall not leave a stone upon a stone, because thou hast not known the time of thy visitation!" Our Lord still hoped by this terrible warning to convert the unbelieving Jews; and the prophecy was not fulfilled for thirty-eight years, when the Romans, the instruments of God's vengeance, laid siege to Jerusalem, and, after reducing it by famine, laid it waste exactly as our Lord had described.

Application: The destruction of Jerusalem is a figure of the desolation caused by mortal sin in the faithless soul, which loses all its beauty in the sight of God, and becomes a hideous ruin, deprived of all the rights bestowed in holy baptism, of sanctifying grace, peace and happiness, of all acquired merits, and finally, the reward of heaven. O mercy of God, if this desolation be not ours! Let this thought increase our zeal and fervor.

Colloquy with our compassionate Lord.

November 20: Principal Events of Palm Sunday

1st prelude: Behold our Lord teaching in the Temple.
2nd prelude: Ask for the grace to follow His example.

Point I: Our Lord sought by the Gentiles

Consideration: The great event of this day is the triumphal entry of our Lord into the holy city. The Gospel continues: "He entered Jerusalem, and into the Temple," where, according to Saint John, there were certain Gentiles, "who came up to adore on the festival day; these therefore came to Philip, who was of Bethsaida of Galilee, and desired him, saying, Sir, we would see Jesus. Philip cometh and telleth Andrew. Again, Andrew and Philip told Jesus."

Application: Let us, after the example of our Lord, hasten into His sanctuary to thank Him for any success we may have obtained; and, if obedience sends us into any town or village, let us first of all, if possible visit the church to adore our Lord, and ask His blessing on our labors. Does not our indifference and lukewarmness in this respect contrast unfavorably with the behavior of the Gentiles mentioned above?

Affections and Resolutions.

Point II: Our Lord foretells His approaching death

Consideration: Our Lord, having granted the request of the

Gentiles, foretells in their presence and in that of the multitude His approaching death, speaking of it under the guise of a parable, which would shortly be made clear to them. "The hour is come," He said, "that the Son of Man should be glorified. Amen, amen I say to you, unless the grain of wheat falling into the ground die, it bringeth not forth much fruit." Thus our Lord speaks of His death and of its fruit, the conversion of the Gentiles.

Application: What a lesson for ourselves! Our Lord gave His life for the salvation of souls, and we will not suffer; we would choose another road to heaven for ourselves and others than the royal road of the cross. What extraordinary blindness!

Affections and Resolutions.

Point III: Jesus is troubled

Consideration: "Now is My soul troubled," continues our Lord. Wherefore was He thus troubled? It was at the thought of the cruel and shameful death which awaited Him. But He goes on, "Father, save Me from the hour"; and then adds, "Father, glorify Thy name." A voice therefore came from heaven: "I have both glorified it and will glorify it again."

Application: We learn from this that the trouble we feel at some prospective humiliation or affliction is not an imperfection, still less a fault, since our Lord Himself experienced it. But do we do as He did – sanctifying it by prayer and submission to the holy will of God?

Colloquy.

November 21: Our Blessed Lady's Presentation in the Temple

1st prelude: Imagine our Blessed Lady, almost an infant, offering herself in the Temple.

2nd prelude: Ask for the grace to imitate her generosity.

Point I: Mary gives herself to God without delay

Consideration: The Church this day celebrates the presentation of our Blessed Lady in the Temple, whither she was brought by her parents at the age of three years, and confided to the care of the pious women employed in the service of the Temple, and whom, according to custom, she was to assist and remain with until she should be of marriageable age. But the holy child entertained views widely different. Enlightened by grace from above, she had already chosen to belong to God alone, and had bound herself to Him by a vow of virginity – the first of all the daughters of Judah!

Application: You esteem our Blessed Lady happy in having such pious parents, and in understanding at so tender an age the privilege of thus consecrating herself to God. But had you not also a holy mother, who offered you to the Lord in your infancy, and thus inspired you in later years with the idea of ratifying that offering of your own free will? But if not, at least you gave yourself entirely to God on the day of your First Communion. Have you always been faithful? Have you not, little by little, lost sight of your promises? Perhaps bad example has led you into sin, or you may have long lived in certain habitual sins. What an injury to God! What an injury to yourself!

Affections and Resolutions.

Point II: Mary gives herself to God without reserve

Consideration: Our Blessed Lady's sacrifice on the day of her presentation was perfect and entire. She gave up everything for the love of God – the society of her parents, the goods of the world – all, even the most innocent pleasure of sense, and, by her vow of virginity, the hope cherished by so many of the women of Judah of becoming the mother of the promised Messiah. Her liberty only remained; and that too she gave up, Saint Anselm tells us, by a promise of obedience to the high priest Zachary. Thus her sacrifice was entire, and, what is more, perfect from the love and fervor with which she made it.

Application: We also have offered ourselves wholly and entirely to God and His love by our religious vows. We ought each day to renew this offering of ourselves, because the obligations it involves recur each day; but do not we do so without much reflection, perhaps making certain reserves as to the use of our tongues, our eyes, or our other senses, or as to the affections of our hearts, which we divide between God and the creature?

Affections and Resolutions.

Point III: Mary gives herself irrevocably to God

Consideration: Mary never sought to take anything back from the offering she had made; but day by day she made it more complete, more agreeable to God, thereby imprinting upon it the seal of perfection. The Almighty in return poured out fresh graces upon her, and Mary faithfully corresponded with each and all. This may serve to make us understand how truly the Archangel Gabriel saluted her as "full of grace," "blessed among women," on the day of the Annunciation. But who can form an idea of the treasures of grace, acquired during the long course of years which followed the Incarnation, with which our Lady entered the courts of the heavenly Jerusalem?

Application: How far we are from imitating the constancy of our Blessed Mother! How faithless are we to our best-grounded resolutions! We seem to make promises to God only for the purpose of breaking them. Let us blush for our weakness, and take advantage of this festival to give ourselves entirely and irrevocably to God.

Colloquy.

November 22: The Events of Monday in Holy Week: Our Lord Curses the Barren Fig Tree

1st prelude: Imagine our Lord cursing the barren fig tree.
2nd prelude: Ask that you may bring forth abundant fruits of salvation.

Point I: Our Lord's hunger

Consideration: On the evening of Palm Sunday our Lord returned to Bethany, but returned to Jerusalem on the following day. On His way thither, Saint Matthew relates that He was hungry. It seems probable that our Lord had fasted all the day before, and must therefore have been greatly suffering from want of food.

Application: Our Lord, we know, frequently fasted, and the Holy Spirit no doubt specially mentions His hunger in this place for the encouragement of those who imitate His example and suffer likewise. But it is rather the spiritual than the bodily hunger of our Lord that we should here consider. How can we relieve it? By the fruit of our good works and virtues we may set before Him daily an abundant feast. But do you do so? Do not your days bring forth little but vain and barren projects? Humble yourself, and redouble your fervor.

Affections and Resolutions.

Point II: Our Lord finds no fruit on the fig-tree

Consideration: In the words of Saint Mark, "And when He had

seen afar off a fig-tree having leaves, He came, if perhaps He might find anything on it: and when He was come to it He found nothing but leaves, for it was not the time for figs." This barren tree offers a striking image of the Jewish nation, whose religion now only consisted in outward forms and in a blind adherence to the letter of the law, without imbibing its spirit or practicing the virtues it prescribed.

Application: The fig-tree also is an image of those weak and lukewarm Christians who neglect the practice of good works, and content themselves with mere prayers and outward practices, and also of the religious who has lost the spirit of his state, who performs all his exercises and actions mechanically, without the heart or mind taking part in them. Let us examine ourselves, and fear lest we fall into this state, as we may so easily do through negligence and dissipation.

Affections and Resolutions.

Point III: Our Lord curses the barren fig-tree

Consideration: "And He saith to it [the fig-tree], May no fruit grow on thee henceforth for ever! And immediately the fig-tree withered away; and the disciples seeing it wondered, saying, How is it presently withered away!"

Application: How much greater will be the astonishment of the sinner, surprised by death in the midst of his vain projects of future conversion, when he hears the fearful words, "Depart from Me, ye cursed, into everlasting fire," and finds his regrets useless, and the time for bringing forth works of penance gone for ever! Let this thought inspire us with zeal for the conversion of sinners, and also for our own conversion and sanctification.

Colloquy.

November 23: Principal Events of Tuesday in Holy Week; The Widow's Mite, the Scribes and Pharisees

1st prelude: Imagine our Lord praising the poor widow, and confounding the Scribes and Sadducees.

2nd prelude: Ask that you too may merit the praises of Jesus.

Point I: Our Lord praises the poor widow

Consideration: Our Lord, having returned to Jerusalem, spent a great part of the day in the Temple teaching, chiefly in parables;

and there, in the words of Saint Mark, "He beheld how the people cast money into the treasury, and many that were rich cast in much. And there came a certain poor widow, and she cast in two mites, which make a farthing. And calling His disciples together, He said to them, Amen I say to you, this poor widow hath cast in more than all they who have cast into the treasury; for all they did cast in of their abundance, but she of her want cast in all she had, even her whole living."

Application: If old age or ill-health prevents your being employed in great labors for the service of God, or if, being young and strong, you are employed in things apparently trifling, learn from these words of our Lord that He judges our actions according to the spirit, generosity, and intention with which they are performed.

Affections and Resolutions.

Point II: Our Lord answers the Scribes concerning the tribute-money

Consideration: The Scribes and Pharisees, in order to ensnare our Lord, hoping to render Him either odious to the people, or criminal in the eyes of the Roman government, came to Him with a cunningly-devised question: "Tell us, therefore, what dost Thou think: is it lawful to give tribute to Caesar or not? But Jesus, knowing their wickedness, said, Why do ye tempt me, hypocrites? Show me the coin of the tribute. And they offered Him a penny; and He saith to them, Whose image and inscription is this? They say to Him, Caesar's. Then He saith to them, Render therefore to Caesar the things that are Caesar's, and to God the things that are God's. And hearing this, they wondered, and leaving Him, went their way."

Application: We do wrong to yield to fear and discouragement when we see the enemies of religion craftily endeavoring to ensnare. Such a weakness is injurious to God and hurtful to ourselves.

Affections and Resolutions.

Point III: Our Lord answers the Sadducees concerning the Resurrection

Consideration: After our Lord had thus confounded the Scribes, the Sadducees came to Him on a similar errand. "Master," they said, speaking of a woman who had successively married seven brothers, "at the resurrection, therefore, whose wife of the seven shall she be, for they all had her? Our Lord answered, In the resurrection they shall neither marry nor be married, but shall be as the angels of God in heaven."

Application: They shall be as the angels of God in heaven. What consoling words! Like those angels who are pure spirits? Yes, because our body shall rise, as the Apostle says, a spiritual body, possessed of angelic qualities – agile, lucid, subtle, and incorruptible – but still capable of enjoying sensible pleasures, the nature of which we are not now capable of conceiving. If we could picture this happy state with lively faith, we should continually sigh after its possession.

Colloquy.

November 24: Continuation of the Events of Tuesday in Holy Week: Parable of the Husbandmen and the Vineyard

1st prelude: Imagine our Lord in the Temple.
2nd prelude: Ask that you may gather abundant fruit from this meditation.

Point I: The care bestowed upon the vineyard

Consideration: "There was a man, a householder, who planted a vineyard, and made a hedge round about it, and dug in it a wine-press, and built a tower, and let it out to husbandmen, and went into a far country." It must have been almost impossible for the Jewish priests and rulers not to have understood the meaning of this parable, so clearly does it refer to Almighty God and His chosen people, whom He blessed above all others, and who made so ungrateful a return. In the same parable we see a striking exposition of the advantages and obligations of the religious state.

Application: In the first place, we see described the advantages of the religious state. Almighty God, the Father of the whole human family, is also the Founder and Father of the religious state, and of each particular Order. "I planted thee a chosen vineyard," He says by His prophet. The hedge enclosing this chosen vineyard is the triple rampart of vows, rules and the watchfulness of superiors; the wine-press, pouring out its costly juice, is an image of the religious state, from which, more than any other, flows and inexhaustible stream of grace and merit; the tower in the midst represents the tabernacle, from whence our Lord watches with a special care over those admitted to his vineyard, which He has let out to us that we may labor in it and cultivate it, whilst He appears to be at a great distance from us because hidden from our eyes, though near in reality, observing if we are faithful and diligent, and preparing us a reward proportioned to our deserts.

Affections and Resolutions.

Point II: Ingratitude and sin of the husbandman

Consideration: "When the time of the fruits was nigh, he sent his servants to the husbandman, that they might receive the fruits thereof; and the husbandmen, laying hands on his servants, beat one, and killed another, and stoned another. Again he sent other servants, and they did to them in like manner; and, last of all, he sent to them his son, saying, They will reverence my son… And taking him, they cast him out of the vineyard and killed him."

Application: Here our Lord refers not only to the obstinate and ungrateful Jews, but to those unhappy religious who – despite the warnings of their superiors, the representatives of God, and the inspirations of their angel guardians – leave the vine committed to their care uncultivated, and consequently produce no fruit.

Affections and Resolutions.

Point III: Punishment of the husbandmen

Consideration: "When, therefore, the lord of the vineyard shall come, what will he do to these husbandmen?" This is the question with which our Lord concludes the parable. And the Jews standing by reply, unconsciously pronouncing their own condemnation: "He will bring those evil men to an evil end; and will let out his vineyard to other husbandmen, that shall render him the fruits in due season." And our Lord confirms it in these terrible words: "Therefore I say unto you, that the kingdom of God shall be taken from you, and shall be given to a nation bringing forth the fruits thereof."

Application: Many religious, after long years of profession, have incurred the like penalty; would you avoid it? Be wholly unreserved with your spiritual director; not only as to your sins, but as to your temptations, your fears and doubts, and follow his advice exactly.

Colloquy.

November 25: Completion of the Events of Tuesday in Holy Week: Our Lord Foretells the Last Judgment

1st prelude: Imagine our Lord coming in the clouds of heaven with great power and majesty.
2nd prelude: Ask that you may be always prepared to appear before the judgment-seat of God.

Point I: Signs preceding the Last Judgment

Consideration: Our Lord passes on from predicting the destruction of Jerusalem to describe the signs which shall herald the Last Judgment: "And there shall be signs in the sun and in the mood and in the stars, and upon the earth distress of nations by reason of the confusion of the roaring of the sea and of the waves. Men withering away for fear and expectation of what shall come upon the whole world, for the powers of heaven shall be moved."

Application: During His mortal life our Lord is known only as the tender Lover of mankind, the good Shepherd come to seek and save; but at this last judgment, in which He will appear to justify the dealings of Providence before the eyes of the universe, and to put to confusion the enemies of God and His Church, He comes clothed with power and majesty to appal those who have abused His long-suffering and mercy. Let us bear in mind this last judgment, and the terrible sentence to be pronounced against impenitent sinners, when tempted to evil.
Affections and Resolutions.

Point II: The order of the Last Judgment

Consideration: "Then shall appear the sign of the Son of Man in heaven;... and they shall see Him coming in the clouds of heaven with great power and majesty; and He shall send His angels with a trumpet and a great voice; and they shall gather together His elect from the four winds, from the farthest parts of the heavens to the utmost bounds of them... And all nations shall be gathered before Him; and He shall separate them one from another, as the shepherd separateth the sheep from the goats; and He shall set the sheep on his right hand, but the goats on his left. Then shall He say to those that shall be on His right hand, Come, ye blessed of My Father, possess you the kingdom prepared for you from the foundation of the world; and to them also that shall be on His left hand, Depart from Me, ye cursed, into everlasting fire, which was prepared for the devil and his angels."

Application: Let us try to imagine the joy that will fill the hearts of the blessed at the sight of the sign of the Son of Man in heaven; they who have so generously carried their own cross here will gaze with delight upon the cross of Jesus. Consider this confusion of those faithless or hypocritical religious, whom our Lord will be forced to place on His left hand, their companions the vilest reprobates. How terrible will be this separation between the members of the same community! Where would you stand, were you to die this moment?

Affections and Resolutions.

Point III: On preparation for the Last Judgment

Consideration: When will this last judgment be? Our Lord says, "Of that day or hour no man knoweth, neither the angels in heaven." But we all know that death is near at hand to each one of us, and that judgement follows death as certainly as death life. "Take ye heed, watch and pray, for ye know not when the Lord of the house cometh; and what I say to you I say to all, Watch." These are the words of Christ Himself.

Application: Would you hope for and not fear the Last Judgment? Prepare yourself, then, by a holy life. "Be ye also ready," says our Lord; live ever prepared. Do you do so?

Colloquy.

November 26: Principal Events of Wednesday in Holy Week: Our Lord Rebukes the Pharisees

1st prelude: Imagine our Lord denouncing the Pharisees.

2nd prelude: Ask that you may never deserve such reproaches.

Point I: They are reproved because they regard only the outward marks of piety

Consideration: On this, the evening preceding Holy Thursday, when the princes and doctors of the nation, gathered together in council under Caiphas, had determined to put our Lord to death, and Judas agreed to betray Him into their hands for thirty pieces of silver, our Lord, as usual, taught in the Temple, and took the opportunity of denouncing the Pharisees, who misled the people by an outward semblance of virtue and religion. "Woe to you, Scribes and Pharisees, hypocrites, because you tithe mint and anise and cummin, and leave the weightier things of the law; you make clean the outside of the cup and the dish, but within you are full of rapine and uncleanness; blind guides, who strain out a gnat and swallow a camel; you are like to whited sepulchres, which outwardly appear to men beautiful, but within are full of dead men's bones and of all filthiness."

Application: Did our Lord address these bitter reproaches to the Pharisees alone? Did He not have in His mind those Christians, those religious, who are prone to scruples and accuse themselves of trifles, whilst they make no account of grave omissions in the discharge of their duties? Truly these, when they examine their conscience, strain out a gnat and swallow a camel. Are there not others who only care for appearances, who wish to be regular and virtuous in the eyes of men, whilst in the sight of heaven they are unclean and mere whited sepulchres? Do you belong to either of these two classes?

Affections and Resolutions.

Point II: Our Lord rebukes the Pharisees because they are severe towards others and indulgent towards themselves

Consideration: We find in general that hypocrites are loud in their censure of others, whilst they allow themselves great liberties. The Pharisees belonged to this class; and therefore our Lord again denounced them, saying, "Woe to you, Scribes and Pharisees, hypocrites, because you shut the kingdom of heaven against men!" and again telling the people that "they bind heavy and insupportable burdens, and lay them on men's shoulders, but with a finger of their own they will not move them."

Application: No doubt you condemn the conduct of these hypocritical Pharisees, as did our Lord; but are you not disposed to exact much from others, your subordinates, which you do not think is required from yourself? Do you practice what you preach and advise others to do?

Affections and Resolutions.

Point III: Our Lord rebukes the pride and avarice of the Pharisees

Consideration: Our Lord has another subject of condemnation for the Pharisees – their pride and self-interest. He says all their works they do to be seen of men; for they make their phylacteries broad, and enlarge their fringes, and they love the first places at feasts, and the first chairs in the synagogues; whilst they devour the houses of widows, praying long prayers; "for this you shall receive the greater judgment."

Application: The world often complains that the ministers of religion are proud and self-interested. Let us never give it any grounds for addressing such reproaches to ourselves; let us carefully examine our intentions, words and behavior before God, and see if our conscience is clear as regards these points. Colloquy with our Divine Lord.

November 27: Events of Holy Thursday: The Paschal Supper

1st prelude: Imagine our Lord surrounded by His Apostles in the supper-chamber at Jerusalem.
2nd prelude: Ask that you may draw abundant fruit from this meditation.

Point I: Preparations for the Paschal Supper

Consideration: Our Lord left Jerusalem on Wednesday evening, and slept at Bethania, returning to the city towards sunset the next day, the first day of the Azymes, or feast of unleavened bread. Then, as Saint Mark relates, the Apostles came to Him, saying, "Wither wilt Thou that we go and prepare for Thee to eat the Pasch? And He sendeth two of His disciples, and saith to them, Go ye into the city, and there shall meet you a man carrying a pitcher of water; follow him, and whithersoever he shall go in, say to the master of the house, The Master saith, Where is my refectory, where I may eat the Pasch with My disciples? And he will show you a large dining-room furnished, and there prepare ye for us. And His disciples went their way, and came into the city, and they found as He had told them, and they prepared the Pasch." (These preparations consisted in procuring a paschal lamb with was slain in the Temple and then roasted, unleavened bread (azymes), wine and lettuce or other vegetables.)

Application: This supper-chamber, renowned through the whole world since our Lord honored it with His presence, is an image of our heart, which our Lord deigns to make His dwelling-place in Holy Communion. To receive Him, it must be, first, large and spacious in desires and generosity. Never let us resemble those who are satisfied with giving our Lord only what they cannot refuse him under pain of mortal sin. Secondly, it must also be well

furnished – adorned with virtues, with true humility, lively confidence, and ardent love.
Affections and Resolutions.

Point II: Hour of the Paschal Supper

Consideration: "And when the hour was come, He sat down, and the twelve Apostles with Him; and He said to them, With desire I have desired to eat this Pasch with you before I suffer."

Application: Remark our Lord's exactness in fulfilling all the precepts of the law; His calmness at the near approach of His Passion, which must have been forcibly brought before Him at the sight of the Paschal lamb, the type of the Lamb slain from the beginning of the world – that Passion to be that day consummated on the cross. ("That day"; that is, according to the Jewish mode of reckoning, from sunset to sunset. Thus the Paschal Supper, the instituting of the Eucharist, the agony in the Garden, and our Lord's death and burial, all took place in one day from Thursday to Friday evening.)
Affections and Resolutions.

Point III: Our Lord predicts the treachery of Judas

Consideration: Judas, as we know, had on the day before promised to deliver his Lord into the hands of His enemies for thirty pieces of silver. As it would have been inconsistent with our Lord's glory to have appeared ignorant of this base betrayal, He predicted it during the Paschal Supper in this words: "Amen I say to you, one of you that eateth with Me shall betray Me." We hear that the Apostles began to be sorrowful, and to say to Him one by one, "Is it I?" But Judas does not seem to have manifested any emotion, despite our Lord's awful denunciation of His treacherous follower: "It were better for him if that man had never been born."

Application and Colloquy: Let us, at this sad spectacle of weakness and treachery in the person even of an Apostle, humiliate ourselves profoundly before God, and beseech Him to preserve us in His holy fear by aid of His all-powerful grace.

November 28: The Events of Holy Thursday, Continued: Our Lord Washes His Apostle's Feet

1st prelude: Imagine our Lord at the feet of His Apostles.
2nd prelude: Ask that you may learn what our Lord intended to

teach us by this action of His.

Point I: Our Lord at His Apostles' feet

Consideration: The figures of the old law were about to give place to the realities of the new – the Paschal Supper to that Eucharistic Feast in which the Lamb of God gives Himself for the food of His creatures. But before proceeding to the institution of this ineffable mystery, it was our Lord's will to perform an action of almost incomprehensible humility – to wash the feet of His Apostles, not excepting Judas, intending by it to give us some idea of the purity of soul with which we ought to approach Holy Communion. Saint John says "that when supper [the Pasch of the old law] was done, knowing that the Father had given Him all things into His hands, and that He came from God and goeth to God, He riseth from supper, and layeth aside His garments, and, having taken a towel, girdeth Himself; after that He putteth water into a basin, and began to wash His disciples' feet, and to wipe them with the towel wherewith He was girded." The Apostle, it would seem, only insists upon the divinity of our Lord the better to express the depth of His humiliation in the performance of this action, usually the office of slaves at nobles' tables.

Application: It may have been your duty to perform offices towards your brethren, the poor, or the sick, which the world calls humiliating and disagreeable, and your pride and delicacy have made you dislike and neglect them: perhaps you have even tried to avoid them; if so, what regret you ought to feel when you call to mind the eternal Son of God washing the feet of poor sinners, those even of His betrayer Judas!

Affections and Resolutions.

Point II: Our Lord at the feet of Saint Peter

Consideration: Saint John continues: "He cometh therefore to Simon Peter. And Peter saith to Him, Lord, dost Thou wash my feet? Jesus answered and said to him, What I do thou knowest not now, but thou shalt know hereafter. Peter saith to Him, Thou shalt never wash my feet. Jesus answered him, If I wash thee not, thou shalt have no part with Me. Simon Peter saith to Him, Lord, not only my feet, but also my hands and my head. Jesus saith to him, He that is washed needeth not but to wash his feet, but is clean wholly; and you are clean, but not all."

Application: We may here admire Saint Peter's humility and

respect for his Divine Master; but let us take care that we never go against the manifestation of God's will. It is a good thing to fly honors, benefices, and superiorships. The saints have done so; but to persist in refusing to accept them, in spite of the express orders of our superiors, would be false humility and sheer perversity. We may also so characterize the conduct of certain persons who, acting contrary to the commands of their confessors, remain away from Holy Communion on the pretext of being unworthy, because they are not allowed to make general or useless confessions.
Affections and Resolutions.

Point III: Our Lord instructs His Apostles

Consideration: Then being sat down again He said to them, Know you what I have done to you? You call Me Master and Lord, and you say well, for so I am. If, then, I being your Lord and Master, have washed your feet, you ought also to wash one another's feet; for I have given you an example, that as I have done to you, so you do also."

Application: Our Lord here gives us His example as the rule of our words, thoughts and actions – in short, of our whole conduct, not by way of counsel but express precept; but does it not rather seem that instead of its being thus commanded us, it should be considered as our honor and glory to tread in the footsteps of our Master, God made man? Why are not His humility, His zeal, His charity and self-sacrifice our daily model? He Himself says, "If you know these things, you shall be blessed if you do them."
Colloquy with our Divine Lord.

November 29: Continuation of the Events of Holy Thursday: The Eucharistic Supper

1st prelude: Imagine our Lord in the midst of His Apostles.
2nd prelude: Ask to increase in the knowledge and love of our Divine Lord.

Point I: The wonders of the Holy Eucharist

Consideration: After our Lord had finished that act of profound abasement so significative of the preparation required for the eucharistic feast, He sat down to the table with the Apostles, to institute that new sacrifice of infinite merit in which He Himself was to be both priest and victim, and giving Himself to His creatures, as He was about to die for their sakes, not for that night only, but to the end of time, knowing, as Saint John says, that His hour was come, that He should pass out of this world to the Father; having loved His own who were in the world He loved them to the end. O wonderful excess of divine love!

Application: Let us consider amongst the wonders of the eucharistic feast, firstly, the infinite wisdom of our Lord manifested therein, dying for mankind, yet perpetually remaining with them; secondly, His infinite power by changing bread into His body, living and united to His divinity as it is in heaven, so that the accidents of the substance are wholly destroyed, and that He is present in each and every fragment of the Sacred Host, and this by a few words uttered, not by Himself only in that upper chamber, but by the humblest of His priests at any time and in any spot of the world; lastly, His infinite goodness. The height of human love can go no further than to give its life for the beloved object; but our Lord did yet more – after dying for man He remains ever with him to console him, to guide him, to offer Himself for his daily and to be his daily food. All this He does in the Sacrament of the Holy Eucharist, foreseeing the ingratitude of mankind towards Him therein, and the horrible profanations to which He would be exposed.

Affections and Resolutions.

Point II: Historical exposition of the Holy Eucharist

Consideration: Call to mind the simple words in which the institution of the Holy Eucharist is given inn the Gospel narrative: "And whilst they were at supper Jesus took bread, and blessed and broke and gave to His disciples, and said, Take ye and eat; this is My Body. And taking the chalice, He gave thanks, and gave to them, saying, Drink ye all of this."

Application: Think each time that you have the happiness of being present at Holy Mass of the wonders of the Last Supper; fancy you hear our Lord saying, "Do this for a commemoration of Me"; and behold Him, in the person of the priest, changing bread and wine into His adorable Body and Blood.

Colloquy with our Divine Lord.

November 30: Continuation of the Events of Thursday Evening: Our Lord's Discourse after Instituting the Holy Eucharist

1st prelude: Draw near in spirit to the Apostles, that you may bear and taste the sweetness of our Lord's words.
2nd prelude: Ask that they may bring forth in you the fruits of holiness.

Point I: Our Lord's tender love for His Apostles

Consideration: A father who sees the moment of his death or departure from his children at hand feels the strength and tenderness of his love for them redouble. Thus, when our Lord knew that His hour was come, His words and actions revealed a still deeper love for His followers than He had before manifested; for the first time He calls them His little children: "Little children, yet a little while I am with you"; and seeing them troubled at His words, He continues, "And if I shall go and prepare a place for you, I will come again, and will take you to Myself, that where I am you also may be; I will not leave you orphans; I will come unto you;… and I will ask the Father, and He shall give you another Paraclete, that He may abide with you for ever… In the world you shall have distress; but have confidence, I have overcome the world." And again, "Amen, Amen, I say to you, if you ask the Father anything in My name, He will give it you."

Application: What feelings of joy and confidence should fill our hearts at these blessed words, addressed as much to each one of us as to the Apostles! He has promised, besides, to everyone that has left house, or brethren or sisters, or father or mother, or wife or children, or lands, for His name's sake, an hundredfold, and to possess life everlasting. Let the thought console you in sadness, and bring you peace and confidence.

Affections and Resolutions.

Point II: Our Lord commands His Apostles to love one another

Consideration: As a tender father on his deathbed exhorts his weeping children to live in love and unity, our Lord commands His Apostles to love one another as He had loved them. He calls it His commandment, meaning thereby to lay a peculiar stress upon it obligation; adding, "By this shall all men know that you are My disciples, if you have love one for another."

Application: Do you wish to make your Lord the model of your conduct? to draw near His Sacred Heart? Resolve to excel in fraternal charity.
Colloquy.

December 1: Continuation and End of the Events of Holy Thursday: The Prayer of Our Lord

1st prelude: Imagine our Lord raising His eyes to heaven, surrounded by His Apostles.
2nd prelude: Ask that you may comprehend the prayer of our Lord, and profit by it.

Point I: Our Lord prays for Himself

Consideration: Our Lord had begun His public life by prayer; He ends it in like manner. "He lifted up His eyes to heaven," Saint John tells us, "and said, Father, the hour is come; glorify Thy Son, that Thy Son may glorify Thee." He asks to be loved, known, and served by all men, but only for the glory of His Father; He prays also for His elect, "that they may know Thee, the only true God, and Jesus Christ whom Thou hast sent." He asks it as the price of His merits: "I have glorified Thee on earth; I have finished the work which Thou gavest Me to do."

Application: We may here learn from our Lord: 1. Not only to begin all our good works by prayer, but to end them in like manner, by asking God's blessing on them. 2. To be zealous for our own souls, glorifying God by a holy life, that we may attain salvation. Many, whilst they are watchful for the souls of others, neglect their own. 3. To perform all our actions with great care and diligence, so that at the end of our lives we may be able to say as our Lord did, "I have finished the work which Thou gavest me to do."
Affections and Resolutions.

Point II: Our Lord prays for His Apostles

Consideration: Remark that our Lord first asks that His Apostles may be united in heart and mind: "Holy Father," He prays, "keep them in Thy name whom Thou hast given Me, that they may be one, as We also are." Next, that they may preserve their innocence in the midst of the temptations of the world: "I pray not that Thou shouldst take them out of the world, but that

Thou shouldst keep them from evil." Lastly, their sanctification: "Sanctify them in truth," that is, in the practice of the truths I have taught them.

Application: What sacrifices do you make to maintain: 1. With those about you that union of heart and mind so strongly insisted on by our Lord? 2. That purity of conscience? 3. That holiness of life that consists in the practice of virtues not only exterior but interior?

Affections and Resolutions.

Point III: Our Lord prays for all the faithful

Consideration: Our Lord continues: "And not only for them [His Apostles] do I pray, but for them also who through their word shall believe in Me; that they may all be one, as Thou, Father, in Me and I in Thee, that they also may be one in Us." He asks for them, besides, that they may be partakers of His glory: "Father, I will that where I am they also whom Thou hast given Me may be with Me, that they may see My glory which Thou hast given Me."

Application: Blessed prayer of our Lord, that after nineteen hundred years still produces such wonderful effects!

Colloquy.

December 2: Eve of the Feast of Saint Francis Xavier: Motives of Confidence in this Great Saint

Born 7th April 1506; first vows at Montmartre, 15th August 1534; priest and solemnly professed, 1537; sailed for the Indies, April 1541; entered Japan, August 1549; died 2nd December, 1552.

1st prelude: Imagine Saint Francis Xavier interceding for us in heaven.

2nd prelude: Ask that you may understand the three great motives which should induce us to ask his intercession with confidence.

Point I: The credit this saint possesses with Almighty God

Consideration: We may form some idea of the credit Saint Francis Xavier enjoys with God by calling to mind the favors and miracles obtained by his invocation in various parts of the world. Besides the twenty-four persons whom he raised from the dead, and the eighty-eight other miracles mentioned in the process of canonization, it has been judicially proved that since his death his intercession has restored to life twenty-seven others in the Indies.

The Bishop of Malacca has deposed to eight hundred miracles in his diocese alone; and in many localities of Europe where this saint is particularly honored – for instance, in Palermo, in Calabria and Oberburg in Lower Styria – extraordinary favors have been obtained by devoutly invoking him.

Application: Do not such considerations inspire you with unbounded confidence in this great saint – you in particular who, as a religious vowed to the active service of God, to a certain degree resemble Saint Francis Xavier? Choose the favors you desire he should obtain for you, and what means you should make use of to efficaciously implore his intercession.

Affections and Resolutions.

Point II: The charity of Saint Francis Xavier

Consideration: Saint Francis Xavier's charity for his neighbor may be called his ruling passion. More than once he might be seen, though Legate Apostolic, beginning from door to door in Goa for both Portuguese and Indians in distress. His charity was generous and heroic; nothing – neither danger nor death – could stay it; it was universal; none were excluded from it. If the saint showed any preference, it was for those who blamed or opposed him.

Application: The charity of Xavier being not less great now than during his life on earth, his credit with God is increased rather than diminished. How, then, can we fear to invoke him and not be heard? Why should he have less charity for you than for others? Hitherto it may be that want of confidence has prevented your obtaining what you asked; this want of confidence often proceeds from an error against which we need warning: we believe ourselves unworthy to be heard. We are too apt to think that the efficacy of prayer depends wholly on the merit of the man who offers it.

Affections and Resolutions.

Point III: Saint Francis Xavier's insatiable zeal for souls

Consideration: Saint Francis Xavier was specially distinguished by zeal for souls, shown in his eagerness for their conversion to the faith, and which no difficulty nor danger could diminish. Once when his friends entreated him not to expose himself to certain death by a voyage to a distant and solitary island, he replied, "Would not traders go thither were gold to be found there; and can I hesitate when there are souls to be saved instead?"

Application: We, like Saint Francis Xavier, have left everything to devote ourselves as he did for the salvation of our neighbor, and thus may believe that he will regard us with peculiar favor, and be one of our warmest intercessors with heaven, drawing down blessings both on ourselves and on our undertakings.
Colloquy.

December 3: Feast of Saint Francis Xavier

1st prelude: Imagine the saint looking down upon us from heaven.
2nd prelude: Ask that you may understand the wonders which grace worked in Saint Francis Xavier.

Point I: The admirable works of the saint

Consideration: We may say with Bourdaloue that in Saint Francis Xavier were renewed all the prodigies worked by the Apostles; endowed as they were with miracles and the gift of tongues, he equaled and even surpassed many of them in the number of conversions he effected, and the distances he traversed, computed at three times the circumference of the globe, baptizing with his own hand more than twelve hundred thousand heathen, visiting over two hundred kingdoms, overturning innumerable idols, planting churches in every place, and even penetrating Japan, where the sound of the Gospel had until then never reached.

Application: On hearing of such wonders we are sometimes tempted to complain of our limited sphere of action, and to think that if it were enlarged we could better imitate so great a saint and do more in the service of God, whilst we neglect our own obligations and the observances of our state. Fatal illusion! Thus certain young Jesuits, students at Coimbra, were greatly desirous of following Saint Francis Xavier to India; he replied, "Brothers, I highly approve of your zeal; but be not deceived, no one can excel in great matters who has not first excelled in lesser ones." Meditate and profit by this answer.
Affections and Resolutions.

Point II: Admirable humility of Saint Francis Xavier

Consideration: The humility of Saint Francis Xavier was not less wonderful than his miracles. Whilst his name was resounding throughout the whole world, he disappeared from his own eyes, hidden as it were in God, esteeming himself an unworthy servant;

when congratulated on his success, he replied, "If God works any good through me, it is due to the prayers and merits of my brethren in Europe." From this humility sprang his profound respect for his superior, Saint Ignatius, to whom he never wrote but on his knees, entreating him in nearly every letter to send someone who would watch over, direct, and stimulate him.

Application: Humility should surely be easy to us who do so little for God, yet we are still full of ourselves and sensitive to a degree; why are we so different from Saint Francis Xavier? Because we do not know ourselves as he did. "Know yourself," says Saint Augustine, "and you will be humble."

Affections and Resolutions.

Point III: Admirable piety of Saint Francis Xavier

Consideration: Another wonderful feature in the character of this great saint was that he united in the highest degree the perfections of the contemplative life with those of the active. Even during his sleep he held communication with God; his favorite ejaculation was, "O most Holy Trinity!" and whenever he kissed the crucifix he bathed it with his tears. God was pleased to work a miracle in honor of the saint's devotion at five thousand miles' distance from the scene of his labors, in the castle of his family; where, during the ten years of his missionary life in India, the crucifix was found on each successive Friday covered with sweat.

Application: We complain of a distaste for prayer, of the coldness of our Communions, attributing both to the multiplicity of our occupations. Saint Francis Xavier is a proof of our own error. If we applied ourselves as he did to prayer with fidelity and perseverance, we should lose all that we complain of, and receive piety as well as the other gifts of God.

Colloquy.

December 4: On Generosity

1st prelude: Contemplate our Lord carrying the generosity of His love for us so far as to sacrifice Himself on the altar of the cross.

2nd prelude: Ask for a spirit of generosity in the service of God.

Point I: The nature of generosity

Consideration: The generosity in the service of God which we have so recently been admiring in Saint Francis Xavier may be defined as a moral or an acquired virtue, which leads a man to surmount courageously all the difficulties of his state, office, spiritual exercises, etc.

Application: If we really comprehend what generosity is, we shall appreciate and desire it. How is it to be acquired and increased? By considering the greatness of the God we serve, His goodness, His love for us, the many claims He possesses to our gratitude and entire devotion. If such thoughts were always before our minds as they were before that of Saint Francis Xavier, we should be generous as he was, and ready to do and dare all for the glory of God and the salvation of souls.

Affections and Resolutions.

Point II: Necessity of generosity

Consideration: If you reflect upon the definition of generosity above given, you will easily perceive its necessity. To the ungenerous, the fulfilment of duty becomes a painful burden, imperfectly performed, or thrown upon others, leaving them old and invalided before their time. They go back instead of advancing in virtue; their charity, mortification, and zeal languish; their spiritual exercises suffer, and are gone through with tepidity and indevotion. Without generosity, what becomes of regular observance and religious discipline? For instance, we find pretexts for not rising promptly, and this first imperfection leaves its mark on the whole day; we become accustomed to habitual infractions of the rule, and at last are regular only in name.

Application: If experience has unfortunately taught you that these are indeed the sad consequences of want of generosity in the service of God, humiliate yourself before Him, asking Him to renew in you the spirit of this necessary virtue.

Affections and Resolutions.

Point III: The advantages of generosity

Consideration: The greatness of the advantages of generosity is admirably summed up in these few words from the SPIRITUAL EXERCISES: “In proportion as a soul is generous in the service of god, she experiences the effects of her liberality, and becomes day by day a more fit recipient of heavenly gifts and graces.” This explains to us the rapid progress made by the saints in the practice of the most exalted virtues.

Application: You desire to resemble the saints in this respect;

you can do so according to the measure of grace given you. Two things are needed, as Saint Thomas a Kempis tells us: “forcibly to draw one’s self from what nature is viciously inclined to, and fervently to follow up the good one is most in need of” (IMITATION, Book I, chap. xxv).
Colloquy.

December 5: Preparation for the Feast of the Immaculate Conception

1st prelude: Imagine a field covered with thorns and briers; in the midst, a lily of dazzling whiteness.
2nd prelude: Ask that we obtain a due appreciation of the motives which should induce us to prepare carefully for this feast, motives as regards God, our Lady and ourselves.

Point I: Motives regarding God

Consideration: What was the intention of the Most High in thus preserving our Blessed Lady from the stain of original sin inherited by every other descendant of Adam? He willed to glorify her above all the saints of both the Old and the New Law, because He had chosen her as the Mother of the eternal Word according to the flesh. and what is our intention in celebrating this festival, and in thus preparing for it beforehand? Our intention is that of God Himself; we unite ourselves to Him in the work of glorifying our Blessed Lady.

Application: We can best prepare ourselves for this feast: 1. By often saying to ourselves that the whole Catholic world, joined to the heavenly host, is making ready to celebrate this stupendous privilege of our dearest Mother. 2. By exciting in us an ardent desire to yield to none in celebrating it worthily.
Affections and Resolutions

Point II: Motives regarding our Blessed Lady

Consideration: The privilege of her Immaculate Conception is that dearest to the heart of our Blessed Lady, and to possess it she would willingly have sacrificed all the others bestowed upon her, the divine maternity not excepted. How pleasing to her, therefore, must be our devout preparation for this festival!

Application: How can we best please our Blessed Lady in this preparation? By carefully avoiding all that is displeasing to her, or

that can tarnish the purity of our soul in her eyes.
Affections and Resolutions

Point III: Motives regarding ourselves

Consideration: God wills, the doctors of the Church teach us, that all graces come to us through our Blessed Lady's hands. She intercedes for all the faithful, but, like an earthly mother, has a peculiar predilection for those of her children who try to please her SPECIALLY. By devoutly celebrating this festival, instituted in honor of her dearest privilege, we are sure of not only becoming agreeable to her, but of sharing her special favors; and by thus defending the interests of our Blessed Mother, we most effectually provide for our own.

Application: A third means of preparation for this great festival is to redouble our fervor, and to excite within ourselves those virtues which are particularly dear to our Blessed Lady, such as humility, charity and piety.
Colloquy.

December 6: Second Day of Preparation: On Avoiding Venial Sin

1st prelude: Imagine a field covered with thorns and briers; in the midst, a lily of dazzling whiteness.
2nd prelude: Ask that you may have an ever-increasing horror of venial sin.

Point I: Venial sin disfigures us in the eyes of our Blessed Lady

Consideration: With the view of pleasing our Blessed Lady, and of obtaining her special favors, let us endeavor to acquire great purity of conscience, and principally by avoiding venial sin, because it is specially odious to her. Every venial sin, it is certain, disfigures us in her eyes, tarnishing as it does the beauty of a soul purchased by the blood of her Divine Son.

Application: What a powerful inducement for avoiding venial sin, above all habitual venial sin! How can we hope to obtain signal favors from that purest of mothers if soiled by its approaches? Perhaps it is your venial sins which have hitherto prevented her granting your request.
Affections and Resolutions

Point II: Venial sin is in some sort cruelty towards our Blessed

Lady

Consideration: This may at first appear an exaggeration, but it is not so in reality. Venial sin it was as well as mortal that caused the sufferings of our Lord; venial sin even now can wound His Sacred Heart, and through the Son grieves the Mother.

Application: What, then, have I done as often as I have deliberately committed a venial sin? I have said, if not in words, in act, "O Mary my Mother, I love thee with all my heart; I love Jesus thy Divine Son; I would not for the world wound Him mortally, but I care little for wounding Him slightly." Can we hope to obtain anything from her immaculate Heart whilst we thus treat Him who is her very life?

Affections and Resolutions

Point III: Venial sin separates us from our Blessed Lady

Consideration: The child who tenderly loves his mother suffers in her absence and pines for the moment of beholding her. Thus Saint Stanislaus and several other saints tenderly devoted to our Blessed Lady sighed after death, that they might enjoy the sight of their beloved Mother, and be eternally united to her in heaven.

Application: But what have you done in so heedlessly committing venial sin, adding fresh debts to your already heavy account? You have added to your purgatory, to the time which is to keep you away from your Mother perhaps by years. How is it that this thought has not restrained you?

Colloquy.

December 7: Third Day of Preparation: On the Practice of Virtue

1st prelude: Imagine a field covered with thorns and briers; in the midst, a lily of dazzling whiteness.

2nd prelude: Ask by the Immaculate Conception of our Blessed Lady the grace of growing in virtue.

Point I: Mary a model of humility

Consideration: Let us try on this the eve of this great feast to obtain our dearest Mother's favors by exciting ourselves to the practice of humility, obedience, and patience, three virtues by which she was especially distinguished. It was her humility that raised her to those surpassing heights of grace and glory. All her life she loved to be hidden, forgotten and considered as nothing. Already the Mother of God, she makes herself the servant of her cousin Elisabeth. During her thirty years' residence at Nazareth she passes for an ordinary woman. During our Lord's public life she hides herself when He is honored and followed, and appears only when He is despised and deserted. she is not present when He enters Jerusalem in triumph, but she is to be found at the foot of the cross on which He dies loaded with insults.

Application: Has not my conduct been precisely the reverse of all this? Have I not been vain of the little good there is in me, avoided humiliations, and sought the esteem and applause of men? What should I do in future?

Affections and Resolutions

Point II: Our Blessed Lady a model of obedience

Consideration: The manner in which our Lady practiced obedience shows how highly she esteemed this virtue, and how greatly she desires to see it practiced by her children. Her obedience was supernatural, and thus was blind, universal, and heroic. She obeyed a heathen emperor by her journey to Bethlehem, the Mosaic law by conforming to the rite of purification, from which in reality she was exempt, and, though superior in merit and dignity to Saint Joseph, she obeyed him in everything as her lawful spouse.

Application: If you would be a true child of Mary you must be obedient not only in easy things but in all; your obedience must be based on love and faith, seeing God in the person of your superiors, and receiving their orders as the expression of His will. Have you done so?

Affections and Resolutions

Point III: Mary a model of patience

Consideration: Another virtue which specially distinguished our Lady was her patience, her entire and perfect resignation to the divine will in every event of her life. No creature had ever so many or so painful sufferings, no mother was ever so wounded through her affections, but never did murmur or complaint hover on her lips; she was modest in prosperity, not cast down in adversity, even rejoicing in tribulation, because it made her more like to her Divine Son, and gave her an opportunity of showing Him her love.

Application: We are frequently called upon to practice patience and resignation. How are we affected by adversity? Are we not tempted to discouragement, and when prosperous, are we not disposed to vanity and boasting? Let us ask our Blessed Lady to make us docile hearers of these words of our Lord's, "Learn of Me, because I am meek and lowly of heart, and you shall find rest to your soul."

Colloquy.

December 8: Feast of the Immaculate Conception

1st prelude: Imagine the Holy father Pius the Ninth, surrounded by all the members of the Sacred College, and a multitude of bishops from the four quarters of the world, proclaiming the dogma of the Immaculate Conception.

2nd prelude: Ask that your love for our Blessed Mother may ever increase in strength and perfection.

Point I: Feast of the Immaculate Conception

Consideration: On this day, so dear to Mary's children, we celebrate in the first place the moment in which Almighty God showed her through the distance of ages to our first parents as the Virgin Mother of the Divine Redeemer, the woman destined to crush the head of the serpent. And as by eternal decree she was miraculously exempt from all stain of original sin, and endowed with the richest treasures of grace and sanctity, it is meet that we should honor her glorious prerogatives by this special Feast of the Immaculate Conception.

Application: What is our first obligation on this great day? We should join in spirit with the blessed in heaven, and rejoice with our dear Mother, not only for her own sake, but for ours, her children, who are partakers of her glory and happiness.

Affections and Resolutions

Point II: The anniversary of the promulgation of the Immaculate Conception

Consideration: Secondly, we are called upon to celebrate that ever memorable day, the 8th of December, 1854, which raised the Immaculate Conception of our Blessed Lady from a pious belief to the dignity of a dogma of the Infallible Church, causing universal joy amongst the entire body of the faithful, and recalling to mind the enthusiasm awakened by so many centuries before when the

Council of Ephesus proclaimed Mary the Mother of God.

Application: The rulers of the Church and the faithful in general had the same object in view in so ardently desiring the dogmatic definition of our Lady's Immaculate Conception; they knew that it would to a certainty bring down abundant graces from the Queen of Heaven; and we, this day and during the following week, should implore her powerful protection on behalf of the whole Church, that she may confound the machinations of the enemies of religion, behold her Son's desire accomplished, and the whole world "one fold and one shepherd."

Affections and Resolutions

Point III: The Immaculate Conception as the precursor of the Incarnation

Consideration: The Immaculate Conception may be fitly called the precursor of the Incarnation; long ago the Prophet Isaias had foretold the sign that should proclaim the blessed moment of Redemption to be at hand, that a Virgin Mother should arise, and, still greater wonder, be the Mother of a God made man.

Application: In seventeen days we shall celebrate the festival of the Nativity, of the birth of God made man. There seems to be a special intention in these two feasts coming so near together; as if the one were to serve as preparation for the other. Let us prepare for it to the utmost of our power.

Colloquy.

December 9: Series of Meditations on the Divine Attributes, the Existence of God

1st prelude: Imagine that you hear the Almighty saying through Moses, "I am who am."

2nd prelude: Ask Almighty God to give you a lively sense of His presence and His majesty.

Point I: My reason reminds me of God

Consideration: All that is within me cries out unceasingly, "Remember thy Creator"; my reason, also, however little I consult it, says, "I exist, therefore God exists." Nothing cannot proceed from nothing; if there had ever been a moment in which nothing existed, nothing would ever have existed. An eternal, uncreated and infinite Being there then must have been from all time; reason proclaims it, faith affirms it. I believe in God the Father Almighty, Creator of heaven and earth.

Application: I think so often of myself, of all around me, and yet so little of God, from whom I derive my being, my very thoughts. I need something exterior to myself to remind me of Him, when all that is within me ought to bring Him to my mind and make me praise, love and adore Him. Must I not be habitually dissipated to live thus as it were a stranger to myself?

Affections and Resolutions

Point II: The universe reminds me of God

Consideration: It is impossible not to call to mind the Creator of heaven and earth when we call to mind the stupendous works of His hands. If a clock reminds us of a clockmaker, a palace of its architect, how much more must the sight of this vast globe, and the still vaster planetary system, of which it is but an infinitesimal part, cause us to bow in adoration before its mighty Author, and exclaim with the royal prophet, "The heavens show forth the glory of God, and the firmament declareth the work of His hand. O Lord our God, how admirable is Thy name in the whole earth!"

Application: Why does not the sight of the wonders of creation bring God continually before us, and fill us with the profoundest adoration? It is because we have become so accustomed to them from infancy, and we require therefore to make special meditation upon God and His works in order that the subject may produce its due effects upon us.

Affections and Resolutions.

Point III: The testimony of the whole world reminds me of God

Consideration: Every age and people have paid their homage to God and to His attributes. Cicero, the prince of Roman orators, says: "There is no nation to be found so savage as to be ignorant of the existence of God." And again, "Where is the man so deprived of reason, who, when he gazes upwards, is not convinced that there is a God who governs the world?" The chief of the first American tribe visited by the Spaniards, when groaning under the tyranny of his conquerors, reproved them in these words: "White men, you are stronger than ourselves, but one day the Great Spirit who reigns above will punish you as you deserve."

Application: Oh, in what sublime concert all creatures from every age unite in bearing testimony to Almighty God! All nature

proclaims Him and calls upon us to bless and glorify Him. "He made us, and not we ourselves." "O praise the Lord, all ye nations: praise Him, all ye peoples."
Colloquy.

December 10: On the Divine Attributes, Continued

1st prelude: Imagine that you hear the Almighty saying through Moses, "I am who am."
2nd prelude: Ask for an increase in the knowledge and love of God.

Point I: God, an infinite Being, our sovereign good

Consideration: As God is in His essence infinite and eternal, His perfections are necessarily countless and immeasurable. From Him all existing or possible creatures derive their being – innumerable worlds, nations, kingdoms and empires, the ranks of the heavenly host, the infinite variety of animals, plants and minerals, each precious stone, each delicious scent or sweet sound. Whoever possesses God possesses and enjoys all these things; but as they are nothing in comparison to God the sovereign good, he enjoys incomparably more in the possession of God alone than he would in possessing them all without God, their author and their source.

Application: Do not such reflections show you more clearly than ever your enviable lot in giving up all for God, to ensure His eternal possession here and hereafter? And do not they make you feel the force of God's promise to His faithful: "I am thy protector, and thy reward exceeding great."? And of the favorite ejaculation of so many saints: "My God and my all!"
Affections and Resolutions.

Point II: God an incomprehensible Being

Consideration: The creature being finite, the Creator infinite, and the finite not being capable of comprehending the infinite, it follows that God cannot be comprehended by any created intelligence, not even by the very angels themselves. The knowledge of the wisest of men, of the highest of saints, is unequal to the task. He is, as the Psalmist says, "an ocean without shore or bottom." Those blessed souls admitted to the Beatific Vision in all its fullness, who contemplate Him through all eternity, ever find fresh beauties and perfections which eternity itself cannot exhaust.

Application: As long as we live let it be our endeavor to increase in the knowledge of God; for the more we know Him the more we shall love Him; and in proportion to our love here will be our glory hereafter, and consequently our eternal bliss in heaven. Affections and Resolutions.

Point III: God an eternal, unchangeable Being

Consideration: God has existed from all eternity; He could neither spring into being from Himself, nor at the command of another. His eternity is infinite, incomprehensible. Saint Augustine speaks well when he says, "Eternity is God." This eternal God exists purely and simply, without division of past and future. He is likewise unchangeable both in will and action. When we read in the Scriptures that He repented Himself, or that He was moved, it is a mere mode of expression adapted to our feeble intelligence.

Application: "From all eternity God has loved me, bringing me out of nothing into eternity – into a forever blessed eternity, if I so will. With what love and gratitude should I not be filled at the thought? Should it not make me constant and unchangeable in my service of God?" This should be our practical conclusion. Colloquy.

December 11: On the Divine Attributes, Again

1st prelude: Imagine a single ray which gives light to the whole world.

2nd prelude: Ask God to enlighten and to inflame you with His love.

Point I: Simplicity of God

Consideration: The infinite perfection of God does not admit the idea of form or composition, from which the angels, the simplest of created beings, are not excluded. He is a spirit, infinitely pure and simple, despite His immensity and His various attributes. These perfections or attributes are divided and distinguished, because otherwise we could neither conceive nor express them; but in reality the power, justice, wisdom and mercy of God are one – the infinite, unchangeable, and eternal Being whose relations with creation are only those of cause to effect, of the Creator to the creature. These things are infinitely above our feeble comprehension, but they are nevertheless the teachings of faith.

Application: Our Lord teaches us to aspire to the infinite perfections of God the Father: "Be ye therefore perfect, as also your Heavenly Father is perfect." We can best do so by the practice of simplicity. True simplicity consists in abhorring and avoiding all duplicity and affectation in word or action, particularly in our relations with superiors. To them we should freely open our whole hearts, and stand before them such as we believe ourselves to be before God, disclosing motives and intentions with entire frankness and sincerity. Do we act thus?
Affections and Resolutions.

Point II: Immensity and omnipresence of God

Consideration: Although God in His essence is absolutely simple, He is also immense and illimitable. "Heaven and the heavens of heaven cannot contain Thee." He is therefore everywhere present; He is with us in prayer, in temptation, in sorrow, in each and every action. His goodness preserves, His wisdom guides, and His power directs us. It matters little where obedience places us, for we can go nowhere where He is not. "In Him we live and move and are," says Saint Paul, just as a fish exists, lives and dies in the water that surrounds and sustains it. "As often as I breathe I converse with God," said a holy Father of the Desert.

Application: These truths should lead us: 1. To behave with the same propriety at every time and in every place, remembering that we are never alone, unseen or unheard. 2. To be content with pleasing God alone, and not to seek the esteem and approbation of men, even of our superiors. 3. To find a pure intention and frequent ejaculatory prayers much easier in practice. 4. To be persevering and courageous in difficulty and in suffering. Even if we seem abandoned by man, God our all will be our witness and our reward. Thus shall we become truly interior servants of God, and holy religious.
Colloquy.

December 12: On the Divine Attributes, Continued, the Omnipotence, Sanctity and Happiness of God

1st prelude: Imagine you hear our Lord saying, "The things that are impossible with men are possible with God."
2nd prelude: Ask for the knowledge and love of God.

Point I: Omnipotence of God

Consideration: Whenever we call to mind the creation of the world, we are at once struck with the omnipotence of God; to create, that is, to make anything out of nothing, presupposes infinite power. God is, therefore, omnipotent. "God the Father Almighty, Creator of heaven and earth," by a word, or rather by an act of His will, formed out of nothing this vast and wonderful universe. "By the word of the Lord the heavens were established, and all the power of them by the spirit of His mouth." And a single act of His will could as instantly recall the whole into nothing, or as instantly create millions of new worlds.

Application: A few years ago I did not exist. It was the power and goodness of God that drew me out of nothing. "He made us, and not we ourselves," says the Psalmist. I therefore belong entirely to Him, and should make use of all my bodily and mental faculties only according to His holy will manifested to me by His commandments, by my rule, and by my superiors. "Be thou faithful unto death," so runs His promise, "and I will give thee the crown of life."

Affections and Resolutions.

Point II: Sanctity of God

Consideration: The sanctity of God being inherent to His infinite essence, is likewise necessarily infinite. "Holy, holy, holy, Lord God Almighty!" sing the blessed in heaven before His throne. In virtue of this His attribute God loves above all things the good that we do, whilst He hates the evil in like proportion. "Thou hast loved justice and hated iniquity." This attribute besides renders God incapable of erring in what He has revealed to us, or of being unfaithful to His promises.

Application: "You shall be holy, for I am holy." Holiness is not enjoined, it is commanded us. How, then, can I obtain this sanctity which God requires of me? 1. By carefully preserving my soul from every stain, and by purifying it as perfectly as possible from those which it contracts despite my vigilance. 2. By adorning my soul with virtues in order to please God, creating anew His image within me "in justice and holiness of truth."

Affections and Resolutions.

Point III: Happiness of God

Consideration: God, as well as being infinitely holy, powerful, wise and just, is necessarily infinitely happy, or to speak more accurately, He is to Himself and in Himself supreme and infinite bliss, the source from which angels and saints draw throughout all eternity joys which are never exhausted and are ever new.

Application: Let us rejoice that we are called to share in the blessedness of the saints, even in that of God Himself; above all, let us rejoice in the thought that this blessedness is increased according to our merit. "In My Father's house there are many mansions," says our Lord; and again, "Lay up to yourselves treasures in heaven."

Colloquy with our Divine Lord.

December 13: On the Divine Attributes, Continued, the Knowledge, Beauty and Sweetness of God

1st prelude: Think you hear these words of Saint Michael the Archangel, "Who is like unto God!"

2nd prelude: Ask for an increase of the knowledge and love of God.

Point I: The knowledge and understanding of God

Consideration: Both our natural understanding and our acquired knowledge are limited in their extent, and subject to error; but it is not so with God. God, being an infinite and eternal Being, has neither past, future, limits nor change. He sees at once and without effort all that actually is, all that is possible, all that has been or will be, our thoughts, dispositions, and intentions, whether for good or for evil, the most secret aspirations of our hearts. "All things are naked and open to His eyes."

Application: These thoughts are full of consolation for the religious who strives to live in the fear of God, and who can truly say with Saint Peter, "Lord, Thou knowest all things, Thou knowest that I love Thee"; but they are as full of terror for the religious who is satisfied with being one only exteriorly, and who seeks the applause and esteem of men, whilst in the eyes of God he is a worldly-minded hypocrite, a whited sepulchre, full within of dead men's bones and all filthiness, like the Scribes and Pharisees rebuked by our Lord.

Affections and Resolutions.

Point II: The beauty of God

Consideration: Call to mind the numberless beauties of this vast universe. Above us extends the firmament, studded with a million resplendent stars at night; in the day made brilliant by the glorious sun, that rises and sets with equal splendor. Around us we behold fields, woods, valleys, and hills adorned with an infinite variety of trees, plants, flowers and fruit, inhabited by every species of animal, many of surpassing beauty of form and color. And the beauties of our mind and soul, and those of the angels, if we could see them, would be found infinitely superior to all created things; yet all are but the feeblest reflection of the infinite beauty of God. Ah! could we but behold it for a moment only, nothing here would ever charm us more; we should see that nothing was worth loving but God alone.

Application: If the sight of any earthly beauty ever tempts you, turn away your eyes quickly, and raise them towards God, the Infinite Beauty, saying with the Psalmist, "Show us Thy face, and we shall be saved." If the temptation continue, implore, as He did, the help of the Most High: "O Lord, come to my assistance; Lord, make haste to help me."

Affections and Resolutions.

Point III: The sweetness of God

Consideration: Mildness or sweetness is one of the most beautiful qualities of man, therefore it proceeds from God, the source of all beauty, and as He is infinite, He possesses it in infinite perfection. "O taste and see that the Lord is sweet," are the words of King David. If he imposes commands upon us, He strengthens us to fulfil them by His powerful grace, He encourages us by the hope of a magnificent reward; and if we fail, He is ever ready to pardon. "He is bountiful to forgive."

Application: Do you deserve it to be said of you, as has been said of so many saints, "Severe to himself, indulgent to others"? Where are your mildness and sweetness? See how far you have failed, and how you should correct yourself. Colloquy.

December 14: On the Divine Attributes, Continued, the Providence, Justice and Mercy of God

1st prelude: Imagine you hear David saying, "The Lord ruleth me, and I shall want nothing."
2nd prelude: Ask for an increase of the knowledge and love of God.

Point I: The providence of God

Consideration: When we call God the Father Almighty, Creator of heaven and earth, we acknowledge His providence, shown in His care for all His creatures, but for man most particularly, made in His own image, and for a supernatural end. No earthly father could, without sin, be indifferent as to his children's welfare; how much more, then, must our merciful Heavenly Father interest Himself in our happiness! He cares for each one of the two thousand million who people this globe as if he were alone upon earth, because, by reason of His immensity, He is everywhere equally present. Holy Scripture thus touchingly speaks of the paternal tenderness of God, confirmed by the belief of every nation: "Behold, I have graven thee in My hands; thy walls are always before My eyes. Can a woman forget her infant, so as not to have pity on the son of her womb? And if she should forget, yet will not I forget thee."

Application: The admirable and amiable action of Divine Providence you must have frequently remarked upon in observing the general course of events, and that of you own life in particular. ADMIRABLE, because it can draw good from evil, as in the case of Joseph becoming the deliverer of his brothers who sold him; and uses the machinations of the wicked to advance the cause of God and His Church, as is proved by the experience of nineteen hundred years. AMIABLE, because it has led you, despite dangers and obstacles, to the blessed end of your vocation. Affections and Resolutions.

Point II: The justice and mercy of God

Consideration: These two divine attributes are far from being contradictory; one is the necessary consequence of the sanctity of God, which obliges Him to punish sin and reward virtue; the other is the consequence of His goodness, which we instinctively acknowledge when we call Him the good God. This goodness is spoken of as patience or longanimity awaiting the penitent, as mercy in the pardon of the sinner. "He is compassionate and merciful, long-suffering and plenteous in mercy." As God is infinite, so are His justice and mercy, rewarding the just with everlasting glory, and the wicked with everlasting punishment. "But He delayeth not His promises," writes Saint Peter, "as some imagine, but dealeth patiently for your sake, not willing that any should perish, but that all should return to penance." Witness the pardon graciously extended to the good thief, and to so many other illustrious penitents.

Application: Are you not yourself a living proof of the long-suffering and mercy of God, whom you have so often provoked, even perhaps after having often received His loving forgiveness? And He has returned you good for evil. Have you not cause to blush at your severity towards your brethren, or towards sinners who do not amend as quickly as you desire? Ask pardon, and promise for the future to endeavor to imitate the long-suffering and patience of God.

Colloquy.

December 15: The Divine Attributes, Continuation and End, Greatness and Immensity of God

1st prelude: Recall the words of the Psalmist, "Great is the Lord, and greatly to be praised; and of His greatness there is no end."

2nd prelude: Ask for an increase in the knowledge and love of God.

Point I: The greatness of God in His works

Consideration: Greatness commands respect, and respect is a part of the homage we owe to God. As it comprehends in itself the rest of the divine attributes, the Holy Scriptures are filled with the idea of the infinite greatness of God. "Of His greatness there is no end," writes King David. To form some idea of His greatness, let us remember that this world of ours is only one of a vast system of planets, and yet is 27,000 miles in circumference, and would take two years and a half to be completely traversed at the rate of thirty miles a day. The sun, being nearly three million miles in circumference, could not be traversed at the same rate of speed in less than 274 years; yet this sun, so immeasurably greater than our universe, is supposed to be infinitely inferior to certain of the fixed stars. And all this greatness, as compared to that of God, is as a grain of sand to a mountain!

Application: Let us bear such thoughts in mind at prayer, in our visits to the Blessed Sacrament, and at Communion also; when tempted to offend God, or to excite sorrow for having offended Him, they will prove very useful.

Affections and Resolutions.

Point II: The greatness and immensity of God

Consideration: To form some idea of the greatness and immensity of God, we may again call the sun to mind, and reflect that it is distant from us at least 95,000,000 miles. Imagine, if you can, so vast a space; but there are planets twenty times further removed from us than the sun; even their distance is nothing in comparison to that of the fixed stars. The light of some of these fixed stars, astronomers are of opinion, has not yet reached us, though it has been travelling towards us at the rate of 12,000,000 miles a minute since the creation of the world. And each of these stars is the centre of a planetary system vastly greater than our own. But what are the millions of worlds, that surpass calculation or even conception, compared to God? The wise man answers, "As the least grain of the balance, and as a drop of the morning dew that falleth upon the earth."

Application: It is this great God who deigned to become man – who became an infant for our sake in the stable of Bethlehem. Oh, incomprehensible mystery of self-abasement! We are on the point of commencing the novena that precedes the feast of Christmas; let us endeavor to do so worthily, and to derive from it due fruit.

Colloquy with the Lord our God.

December 16: Novena for the Preparation of Christmas, Reasons for Making it Well

1st prelude: Ponder the words of Isaias the Prophet, "Prepare ye the way of the Lord; make straight in the wilderness the paths of our God."

2nd prelude: Ask that you may have a due appreciation of the reasons for making this novena with suitable dispositions.

Point I: Characteristics of this festival: our first reason

Consideration: The feast of Christmas is at once the first and last of the ecclesiastical festivals; it is the last in the order of time, coming as it does at the close of the year; but it is the first in the order of our Lord's life, and as such we may not doubt it was celebrated each returning year by Him and by His Blessed Mother.

Application: Are not these sufficient reasons for endeavoring to celebrate this novena, not only with joy and eagerness, but with particular devotion? Should we not endeavor, besides, to make reparation for the lukewarmness with which we have too probably celebrated the previous festivals of the year?

Affections and Resolutions.

Point II: The example of the Church: our second reason

Consideration: Remark in how many ways our Holy Mother the Church distinguishes the festival of Christmas: 1. She precedes it by the four weeks' preparation of Advent. 2. She permits Holy Mass to be celebrated at midnight. 3. She permits every priest to say three Masses in honor of the threefold birth of our Lord – His being born of His Father from all eternity, His temporal birth at Bethlehem, and His spiritual birth in the hearts of the Faithful. 4. She dispenses from abstinence whenever Christmas Day falls on a Friday.

Application: We, the devout children of a holy Mother, should see from these things how earnestly the Church exhorts us to prepare ourselves for this great festival. She not merely counsels us, she as it were obliges us to do so; but it is surely an obligation full of sweetness to celebrate as fervently as possible the birth of Him who is at once our Redeemer and our Father.

Affections and Resolutions.

Point III: Graces attached to the Festival of Christmas: our third reason

Consideration: Our Lord, who is ever ready to dispense graces and favors to all that ask them, is, we may believe, specially disposed to grant our requests on this joyful day upon which for the love of us He entered this vale of tears, the consoler of our exile, and our exceeding great reward.

Application: We may therefore confidently hope to obtain at this holy season all the graces that we most require, either in effectually overcoming our habitual defects, or in advancing to that degree of perfection to which God has called us, but on the sole

condition that we prepare ourselves to receive them. Let us see what special favor we desire from the Holy Child, and decide upon the particular practices of this novena.
Colloquy.

December 17: Dispositions Requisite for the Success of this Novena

1st prelude: Imagine you hear these words of Moses, "Do what is pleasing in the sight of the Lord thy God."
2nd prelude: Ask earnestly for the light and strength you need in making this novena.

Point I: Ardent desire

Consideration: No one is disposed to bestow gifts and favors upon those who do not value them. The gifts of divine grace are above all price. Whoever does not ardently desire them shows that he cannot fittingly appreciate the, and will therefore have but a trifling share in the blessings of this holy season. This fervent desire is what our Lord requires of you in the first place.

Application: To further stimulate this ardent desire, reflect on your poverty and misery, on your weakness in virtue, and the little preparation you have yet made for a holy death. Such thoughts will cause you to sigh for the coming of your Lord, as the sick man does for the visit of his physician.
Affections and Resolutions.

Point II: Great confidence

Consideration: To ardent desire we must join great confidence. When we invoke God with entire confidence, we glorify Him by proclaiming his power, His goodness, and His munificence: and to do so is, for that reason, very pleasing to Him. We see in the Gospel that our Lord made this confidence one of the principal conditions for obtaining His favors. When two blind men came to Him to be healed, He asked them first, "Do you believe that I can do this unto you?" And when they replied in the affirmative, He continued, "According to your faith be it done unto you"; and at once restored their sight.

Application: Want of confidence is a defect to be found in most of our prayers. We feel too often a lurking presentiment that our petitions will not be granted – a presentiment founded on the imperfect idea we entertain of the goodness of God, contrasted with our own unworthiness, saying, "What can so miserable a creature as myself expect from Almighty God?" We are mistaken: it is precisely because we are so weak and miserable, so incapable by ourselves of either strength or virtue, that we have so imperative a claim on the goodness of God. Our Lord has said, "They that are in health need not a physician, but they that are ill." Affections and Resolutions.

Point III: Great generosity

Consideration: Our Lord desires to bestow His gifts upon us, but He requires us to co-operate with Him, and to co-operate generously. His liberality will be in proportion to ours, and consequently the graces and favors of this holy season to our generosity toward Him during the novena.

Application: Should not such thoughts stimulate us to make special efforts during these few remaining days? Let us see what in us is displeasing in the sight of God, and what He particularly asks from us, that we may destroy the one and acquire the other. Colloquy.

December 18: Obstacles to the Success of the Novena

1st prelude: Imagine you hear the voice of the prophet Isaias saying, "Prepare ye the way of the Lord, make straight His paths."
2nd prelude: Ask for grace to surmount the three principal obstacles to the success of the novena.

Point I: First obstacle: Indifference

Consideration: A benefactor is naturally indisposed to grant fresh favors to those who, after receiving kindness at his hands, treat him with carelessness or indifference. For instance: a father has six sons, he prepares a great feast for them: five seem to care little or nothing about it; the youngest, on the contrary, spares neither pains nor toil to make all pass off as brilliantly as possible: the father has done his part; with which of his sons is he best pleased? No doubt with the youngest; can you blame him?

Application: The practical lesson is easily seen; equally clear is the answer to the question, Why do so many Christians, so many religious even, receive no extraordinary favors at this Christmas festival? Draw a suitable conclusion.

Affections and Resolutions.

Point II: Second obstacle: Dissipation of mind

Consideration: The second obstacle, from which the first generally springs, is dissipation. In the midst of the bustle of the world, the thousand bits of news of the day, the anxiety and pressure of household cares, commerce, employment, business, the mind of man can hardly take in or dwell on thoughts regarding faith, or do what the interests of his own soul require, or prepare rightly for the great solemnities of religion, and especially the feast of Christmas. The greater number of men are in this miserable state; and, alas, it is to be feared that many will only leave the turmoil of temporal business to enter upon a miserable eternity.

Application: Let us thank God that we have left the turmoil of the world; but let us remember that dissipation can also penetrate into the interior of religious houses and prevent religious from preparing themselves to keep the great feasts of the year as they ought. This will certainly be the fate of him who goes into the world more than he need, who devotes himself with too much natural impetuosity to his employment, even if it be the sacred ministry, and who does not love silence, retreat, and recollection. See how far you recognize yourself in this picture, and what you have still to do that Jesus Christ may be born in your heart on the glorious feast of Christmas.

Affections and Resolutions.

Point III: Third obstacle: Want of perseverance

Consideration: The third obstacle to the success of our novena is our inconstancy, the levity of our minds, that excessive fickleness of our will which makes us begin good works and never finish them, continually change our good resolutions, or give them up almost as soon as we have formed them. Does not experience tell us, regarding novenas in particular, that as soon as the first day is over we relax our observance of the practices agreed upon, omit them occasionally, and even forget them altogether?

Application: Let the experience of the past give us a lesson; let it be in this novena of preparation for the loveliest of feasts as an ever-warning voice reminding us of our inconstancy, keeping us continually on our guard against ourselves, stimulating and persevering our fervor until the closing day.

Colloquy.

December 19: On the Mystery of Christmas

1st prelude: Behold Saint John the Evangelist writing, "The Word was made flesh, and dwelt among us."
2nd prelude: Beg the grace of understanding the wonderful mystery of God becoming a mortal and feeble man.

Point I: Who is this Word made flesh?

Consideration: Who is this Word, become visible to our eyes in mortal flesh? The Word Eternal, the second Person of the Holy Trinity, consubstantial with the Father; it is God, Creator of heaven and earth, become a mortal man and still remaining God, uniting, without mixture of alteration, the human and divine nature in one divine Person. What a mystery of wisdom, power and love! But especially, what a mystery of abasement! The omnipotent God become a little child for us!

Application: If your faith in this mystery of abasement was more lively, instead of cherishing feelings of vanity and murmuring when you are humiliated, you would be ashamed of even an involuntary feeling of vanity, and you would love and seek for humiliations. Such were at least the feelings and dispositions with which the memory of the cradle of Bethlehem, and those words of the Apostle, "Emptied Himself, taking the form of a slave," inspired the saints.

Affections and Resolutions.

Point II: Why did the Word become flesh?

Consideration: We know why the Word became a passible and mortal man, but we do not think enough of it; it was to raise us up from degradation, and save us from that eternal perdition which we had incurred from the rebellion of our first parents. No creature, neither man nor angel, could ever do it; because divine justice demanded a satisfaction equal to the offence, and proportioned to the infinite Majesty of God; a satisfaction of which a creature, who is essentially limited is incapable. The Incarnate Word alone could do both, in suffering for us as man and as God, and making those sufferings of infinite value.

Application: It is entirely by the mystery of the Incarnation that we have regained our former dignity of children of God, and our rights to a heavenly inheritance, and that we have the consoling prospect of passing from this sorrowful life to the joys of a blessed eternity. What deep gratitude we owe to our Savior God, who wrought this mystery of reconciliation, as Saint Paul says, "when we were enemies"!

Affections and Resolutions.

Point III: Why was the Word made flesh so greatly humiliated?

Consideration: It would have been sufficient for the Son of God, in order to redeem us and repair what we had lost, to have united Himself to a body exempt from suffering , like that of Adam before he sinned, and to breathe forth one sigh for guilty man; but He chose to endure all the humiliations and all the infirmities of our humanity, and to born like other men. And why? Because He wished to draw all hearts to Him, and bind them to Him for ever by this manifestation of an EXCESS OF LOVE; as Saint John the Evangelist expresses it, "PROPTER NIMIAM CHARITATEM SUAM DILEXIT NOS."

Application: And the greater number of men give no other return to all their Redeemer's love for them than indifference, forgetfulness, and ingratitude! And we, who by many titles belong to this God of love, how do we love Him? Is it not with reserve, with parsimony; only doing what He has the strict right to demand from us? And if we do anything beyond that, is it not coldly and with many imperfections? That we may repair the past and give a proof of our good will, let us today add something to what we had resolved to do during the novena.

Colloquy.

December 20: Election, Prerogatives and Dispositions of the Mother of the Word Incarnate

1st prelude: Behold the Archangel Gabriel saying to Mary, "Thou shalt conceive and shalt bring forth a Son, and thou shalt call His name Jesus."

2nd prelude: Beg the grace of increasing in the knowledge, esteem and love of our Blessed Lady.

Point I: Election of the Blessed Virgin

Consideration: No man has the power of choosing his mother, for it is evident that he who does not exist can do nothing. But there was one man who could do it, the Man God, Jesus our

Savior. Essentially eternal according to His divine nature, He could and did from all eternity choose her who was to be the Mother of His human nature, for He had determined to come into the world as other men did. His choice fell on the daughter of Joachim and Anne, the issue of the royal blood of David, and, by alliance, of the priestly line of Aaron; and by this choice of divine predilection Mary became the most excellent and happiest of creatures.

Application: Let us rejoice in the thought of the election made by the Incarnate Word of the Blessed Virgin; let us rejoice still more because, by the gift of the same Word, Mary has become our own Mother; but never let us forget that, as children of that holy and perfect Mother, we should strive after sanctity and perfection, even if we were not obliged to do so by our vows. For this end let us redouble our efforts during this novena.

Affections and Resolutions.

Point II: Prerogatives of the Blessed Virgin

Consideration: "God does not leave His works incomplete," says the theologian Saint Thomas; "he always proportions His graces and prerogatives to the dignity to which He pleases to call His creature, so that it may worthily fulfill its obligation." It please Him to call the Virgin Mary to the greatest dignity to which human creature can be raised, therefore He gave her extraordinary and exceptional graces and prerogatives: 1. He preserved her from original sin. 2. He confirmed her in grace, so that the beauty of her soul was never tarnished by the least actual sin. 3. He gave her the joys of maternity together with the glory of virginity. 4. He endowed her with the plenitude of the gifts and graces of the Holy Ghost from the first moment of her existence. 5. From this moment also, according to the opinion of many of the Fathers, He gave her the use of reason, so that she was not a minute without loving her God and increasing her merits.

Application: When God has called you by the choice of his gratuitous predilection to the religious state, raised you, perhaps, to the priesthood, and thus given you a greater dignity than other men, He has not left His work incomplete – He has proportioned the help of His grace to it; He has given you special and super-abundant graces. How have you corresponded with them?

Affections and Resolutions.

Point III: Dispositions of the Blessed Virgin

Consideration: The life of our Lady, from her birth to the moment of the Incarnation, was a continual preparation for that great even. She prepared for it by great watchfulness over all her senses and the movements of her heart, although she had not to fear, like we have, a surprise from disorderly passions. She prepared herself by retirement from the world, solitude, silence, and recollection; living from three years old in the Temple, there she prepared herself by continual prayer and meditation, together with ardent desires, to see the Savior of the world.

Application: It is by attaining similar dispositions and by employing these same means that we ought to prepare for the great feast of Christmas. Have you done it? See in what you have failed, and try to make up for it by fervor during the days that still remain of this novena, and your desires will be fulfilled; Jesus will come to you with an abundance of His benedictions.
Colloquy.

December 21: On the Circumstances of the Time in which Our Savior Appeared

1st prelude: Behold the Apostle saying, "When the fullness of the time was come, God sent His Son."
2nd prelude: Beg the grace of waiting patiently for the time of God's visits and consolations.

Point I

Consideration: When did the Savior of the world appear upon the earth? Four thousand years after He was promised to our first parents, after forty centuries of preparation, waiting, sighs, and desires for Him from the just men of the Old Testament. And why did He delay His coming for so long a time? The Fathers answer, "If the satisfaction and restoration had closely followed the offence, man would never have learnt the full extent of the moral degradation caused by sin, nor the impossibility of raising himself out of it, and consequently the greatness of the benefit of redemption." In the meantime the world was not left without means of salvation. It had the promise and certainty of a Redeemer, and men could be saved by the expectation and merits of the future Redeemer; and history shows us
this EXPECTATION generally existed among all nations.

Application: It is God's will that we should have a deep conviction of our misery and helplessness before He visits us and bestows His gifts, that we may appreciate them better, be more grateful, and derive greater profit from them.
Affections and Resolutions.

Point II

Consideration: When did the Savior of the world appear on earth? When all the prophesies and types announcing the qualities of the Messiah were ENTIRELY accomplished by these divers figures and prophesies, which became century after century more precise and detailed, God willed to prepare the world by degrees to believe the most wonderful of all mysteries – the divinity of the Gospel, and the institution of the Church of Christ.

Application: Thus also does God deign to condescend to our weakness. He helps us to believe, by multiplying when necessary motives for our faith, just as He helps us to practice virtue and to obey Him in difficult matters by multiplying the succors of His grace. Have you not experienced this in critical circumstances, particularly as regards your vocation?
Affections and Resolutions.

Point III

Consideration: When did the Savior of the world appear on earth? The fortieth year of the reign of the Emperor Augustus, when nearly all the people of the known world submitted to the Roman empire and were ruled by the same laws, and the whole world was at peace. This immense extent of the Roman empire, the fourth of the monarchies foretold by Daniel, together with universal peace after seven centuries of war, was visibly arranged by Providence to facilitate the propagation of the Gospel, which was to form out of all nations one family in Jesus Christ.

Application: If we follow with the eyes of faith the events which the course of ages displays on the world's stage, we shall see in our own days the working of Divine Providence, which so wonderfully causes everything to carry out His eternal designs and the salvation of His elect. Let us take care not to reason about public events as the men of this world generally do; they look on them as a game or the result of chance, of prudence or imprudence on the part of statesmen. But we, better enlightened, should reason as men of faith; let us see and bless the hand of God in everything

which happens, and behold Him directing the course of events towards ends often far from our thoughts. In this way we shall please God, edify others, and do good to ourselves. We shall grow in faith, hope and love of God.
Colloquy.

December 22: Benefits which We Owe to the Word Incarnate

1st prelude: Behold the Infant Jesus weeping for us in the manger of Bethlehem.
2nd prelude: Beg the grace of appreciating the principal benefits which we owe to His immense love.

Point I: Benefit of existence

Consideration: Saint John begins his Gospel with these sublime words: "In the beginning was the Word, and the Word was with God, and the Word was God. All things were made by Him, and without Him was made nothing that was made. And the Word was made flesh, and dwelt among us." It is, then, by this Eternal Word, who in time united Himself to our mortal nature, that this universe has been created out of nothing; and as nothing which it contains was made without Him, we also have been made by Him, and to Him we owe the blessing of existence in time and eternity, the one being inseparable from the other.

Application: During this time, when we are preparing ourselves to celebrate worthily the anniversary of the human birth of the Eternal Word, it is natural we should think of our won birth, and of Him to whom we owe it. And with what a burst of love and gratitude we ought to think of it, who have received the plenitude of the gifts of life, being born by a special providence AFTER the Incarnation of the Son of God! Do we think of this often enough, with enough affection and gratitude?
Affections and Resolutions.

Point II: Benefit of redemption

Consideration: Another blessing that we owe to the Incarnate Word is that of redemption – that act of unspeakable love by which He willed to take on Himself the sentence of death pronounced against our first parents, to expiate in His own person the sin imputed to us all, and to wash away in His Blood the stains of our own iniquities. "Christ hath redeemed us from the curse of the law," says Saint Paul; "who hath washed us from our sins in His own Blood," adds Saint John. This second benefit is greater than the first of creation in t his sense, that, as Saint Augustine says, "It would have availed us nothing to have been born, if we had not been redeemed: QUID NASCI PROFUIT, NISI REDIMI PROFUISSET?" In this sense also, that the benefit of redemption is a greater proof of the love of the Divine Word. Creation cost Him only a word; redemption cost Him the shedding of His Blood.

Application: It was in the stable of Bethlehem that the "Word made flesh" began the work of our redemption, offering His first tears to divine justice,, and offering Himself as a victim of expiation. What should this wonderful mystery of love produce in those who meditate on it? "They also who live," says the Apostle, thus redeemed from death, "may not now live to themselves but unto Him who died for them and rose again." Consider, then, how ungrateful and guilty you are in thinking of yourself before all things; in seeking after your comfort and honor rather than the good pleasure of your Savior; and is not this what you have very often done?

Affections and Resolutions.

Point III: Benefit of the divine adoption

Consideration: It was not enough for the love of the Incarnate Word to rescue us from slavery, and reconcile us with His heavenly Father; He also willed that we should become His adopted children and heirs. This benefit of the divine adoption, which surpasses all that we can imagine, He accomplished by uniting in His person the human and divine natures. "When the fullness of time was come," says the Apostle, "God sent His Son… that we might receive the adoption of sons;… and if sons, heirs also: heirs, indeed, of God, and joint-heirs with Christ."

Application: How noble would be our thoughts, how holy would be our lives, if the memory of these things were always before our minds! Let us strive to make it so.

Colloquy.

December 23: On those qualities of the Infant Jesus Proposed for our Imitation

1st prelude: Listen to Jesus Christ saying, "Unless you be

converted and become as little children, you shall not enter into the kingdom of heaven."
2nd prelude: Beg the grace of understanding how we can become by grace what little children are by nature.

Point I: The natural purity of infancy

Consideration: When we think of the mystery of Christmas – of the Word "made flesh" become "a little child for us" – we should look on this child as like other infants, endowed with the same NATURALLY good qualities; but as the Infant Jesus had the full use of His reason, we should consider these qualities in Him as SUPERNATURALLY good, raised to the dignity and merit of virtues, and we should try to retrace them in ourselves. The first of these qualities is purity, freedom from the least stain of actual sin, of which infancy is incapable. In the Infant Jesus this purity was a virtue, not only because He was sanctity itself, but because He detested sin above all things. He offered His tears for the expiation of the world, and to obtain the necessary grace to preserve us from sin.

Application: If we desire to please the Infant Jesus, and to obtain a large share of His favor, let us try to become by virtue what He was by essence, and what little children are by nature, exempt from sin; let us strengthen ourselves, especially during this novena, in the determination of losing everything and suffering everything rather than commit a deliberate venial sin. Let us keep in this disposition from love, rather than fear or any other less perfect motive.

Affections and Resolutions.

Point II: The natural humility of infancy

Consideration: Humility, or rather freedom from all thoughts of vanity, is another characteristic of infancy. But this humility has no merit, because the child is incapable of appreciating the dignity of man, and of feeling the humiliations he has to endure. It was not thus with the Infant Jesus. He perfectly knew and appreciated the dignity of His Person, the respect and sovereign homage which were due to Him. On the other hand, He felt vividly the extreme humiliations He had to endure, the loneliness in which He was left, the disdain and contempt of the world. But He did not complain, took no vengeance, accepted all and bore it all of His own choice, out of zeal for the glory of His Heavenly Father, so terribly outraged by our pride and rebellion.

Application: It is by accepting from supernatural motives the humiliations of all kinds that we shall become like little children, and pleasing to the Incarnate Word, the Infant Jesus. Let us strengthen our generous resolution of striving to attain the third degree of humility.

Affections and Resolutions.

Point III: Natural obedience of infancy

Consideration: Little children are naturally obedient: incapable of making a reasonable opposition, they give themselves up. They do not examine, or criticize, or murmur, but their obedience is not meritorious. Not so with the Incarnate Word, become a little child for us. He had a perfect use of reason; He was infinite wisdom; He saw and felt all the imperfections in the orders given to Him; but He did not show it even by the least gesture. He submitted to all, and in all, with a perfect conformity of judgment and will.

Application: Happy are the religious who have striven, and by virtue have become as obedient as children are by nature. Let us try to be among this happy number.

Colloquy.

December 24: Christmas Eve, What our Thoughts, Feelings and Occupations Today Ought to Be

1st prelude: Imagine you hear the chant of those words of today's office, "Today you shall know that the Lord will come, and tomorrow you shall see His glory."

2nd prelude: Beg of God that all our thoughts, feelings and actions may prepare us for the great feast of tomorrow.

Point I: What our thoughts today should be

Consideration: Man is essentially a thinking being. Our mind is always acting, and we are always thinking of something. But often we take no account of our thoughts, they are not actually good or bad, but vague. Let us try to prevent this today, and fix them on the great event whose joyous anniversary we are about to keep.

Application: Let us think today, specially during the Mass, of the confession we are going to make, and try to obtain perfect contrition; let us think frequently during our work of the things that were done on this day – of the journey made by Mary and

Joseph from Nazareth to Bethlehem; let us accompany them in spirit during their three days' travel; let us share in some sense their fatigue and difficulties; from time to time let us look at our Lady, and admire the calm serenity with which she endures all the various accidents, and even the affronts, which she receives at Bethlehem, where they refuse her hospitality. Jesus, whom she bore within her, made up for all. These thoughts will keep us in recollection, and in those holy dispositions which the Church desire to communicate to us today.

Affections and Resolutions.

Point II: What our feelings ought to be

Consideration: The heart experiences all kinds of impressions. We cannot always control them as we wish, but we can by efforts of our will induce certain feelings or affections.

Application: Let us make use of this dominion of our will, and entertain during this day the feelings which are fitting, as Christmas night draws near; feelings of admiration at the thought of a God made man – a little infant – for us; feelings of desire to have Him spiritually born in our hearts; feelings of fear lest we should not give Him worthy hospitality; feelings, on the other hand, of confidence in His infinite goodness, hoping to share largely in His gifts.

Affections and Resolutions.

Point III: What our occupations ought to be

Consideration: Our occupations are nearly all arranged beforehand, and fill up the day. Our kind of life is laborious, and we have but few free moments. In this sense all our days are alike. It is to be wished, however, that this day might be an exception, that we might live as contemplatives, entirely devoted to meditation on those great events we are about to celebrate. Unfortunately, it is just the contrary; the eves of great feasts are days of great labor. We shall all be busier than usual today in one way or another.

Application: Let us make this apparent obstacle into a means of preparation for the feast; let us accept the increase of work and fatigue with a good heart, in the spirit of penance and expiation. Such is the spirit of the Church in making this day a fast. While we are laboring, let us entertain tender and pious affections for our Lady, who had to bear such hard trials today, especially when she was refused accommodation at Bethlehem, and was obliged to bring her Divine Son into the world in a stable open to the air, in the middle of the night. Thus, while we all go about our numerous occupations, we shall unite contemplation to action, and we shall prepare an acceptable hospitality for the Infant Jesus in our hearts. Colloquy.

December 25: Christmas Day

1st prelude: Behold the manger of Bethlehem.
2nd prelude: Beg the grace of sharing the feelings which Mary, Joseph and the shepherds experienced at the sight of the Infant Jesus.

Point I: Contemplation of the Infant Jesus, so sweet and loving

Consideration: CHRISTUS NATUS EST NOBIS: VENITE, ADOREMUS – "Jesus is born for us; come, let us adore Him!" Such is the invitation which the Church on this night gives to all the faithful. Respond quickly to it, O my soul! Go in spirit to Bethlehem, and contemplate the features of our Savior. What a sight of unspeakable love meets our eyes! God, Creator of the world, became a little infant, stripped of all the splendor of His divinity, that He might take away all fear from us and draw all hearts to Him. What love thus to annihilate Himself for us; and how He loves us! See how He stretches out His little hands towards you, saying in His heart those words which He afterwards repeated, "Come to Me, all you that labor and are burdened, and I will refresh you." "I came not to judge the world, but to save the world."

Application: Who can contemplate this Divine Child, whose love has made Him come down from heaven into the stable that He may raise us to heaven, and not love Him in return? Who can hear the language of His loving and compassionate heart, and not be filled with feelings of the sweetest and most entire confidence, whatever may have been his past unfaithfulness?
Affections and Resolutions.

Point II: Contemplation of the Infant Jesus, so poor and suffering

Consideration: PROPTER VOS EGENUS FACTUS EST, CUM ESSE DIVES. Jesus, says the Apostle, "being rich," with all the treasures of the world, "became poor for your sakes" – poor unto extreme indigence, suffering cruelly from the want of many necessities of life. Contemplate, O my soul, the place of His birth, and all that is around it. What do you see? An abandoned stable, open to the wind; a manger, and in it a little straw. Such is the cradle of the new-born Child, Jesus our Savior. What poverty and what suffering! Thus, then, from His entrance into the world He fulfilled the prophecy of Isaias – VIRUM DOLORUM – "a man of sorrows."

Application: Jesus endured the effects of extreme poverty without complaining. He embraced them by choice, and from love; and why? To teach us to despise the possessions and delights of life, which are the greatest obstacles to salvation, and also that he might induce us to follow His example by embracing poverty and mortification, which will surely lead us to the possession and unspeakable delights of heaven.

Affections and Resolutions.

Point III: Contemplation of the Infant Jesus, so humble and gentle

Consideration: DISCITE A ME, QUIA MITIS SUM ET HUMILIS CORDE – "Learn of Me" – from this state of voluntary abasement and loneliness to which I am reduced without a sign of impatience – "for I am meek and humble of heart." What a mystery! What a depth of abasement! The Omnipotent, the Infinite Wisdom is nothing more in the eyes and estimation of men than a little infant – a type of weakness and ignorance – despised by the world, laid on a little hay in a cave between two animals, as if He were unworthy of having a place among the children of men.

Application: Behold, O my soul, to what an excess of humiliation a God made man has reduced Himself, to teach thee to humble thyself, and bear patiently wounding remarks and contempt, no matter from whence it comes. What gratitude oughtest thou to show Him!

Colloquy.

December 26: Feast of Saint Stephen, First Martyr

1st prelude: Behold the saint, ready to die, lifting his eyes towards heaven and praying for those who stone him.

2nd prelude: Beg the grace of sharing the lively faith, the strength of soul, and the heroic charity of the holy martyr.

Point I: Lively faith of Saint Stephen

Consideration: Stephen shared the prejudices of his nation concerning the temporal greatness of the Messiah. But the preaching of Jesus dispelled these ideas, and from henceforth he attached himself to our Lord, and became His faithful disciple. It is believed that he was of the number of the seventy-two. Later on he was elected and ordained a deacon, having received the gift of eminent faith with the fulness of the Holy Ghost. VIRUM PLENUM FIDE ET SPIRITU SANCTO. He preached with fervor, and worked wonderful miracles, which were followed by numerous conversions.

Application: We have had the grace of getting rid of the false ideas of the world about grandeur and the happiness of having great possessions; we have had the grace of following the precepts of Jesus Christ and preferring voluntary poverty in the religious state. This is one of the most precious gifts of faith; but has this faith been fruitful in works of zeal and sanctity, as was that of Saint Stephen?

Affections and Resolutions.

Point II: Courage of Saint Stephen

Consideration: The success of the holy deacon's preaching soon raised a persecution against him. The doctors and princes of the nation dragged him before the SANHEDRIM, or highest court of the Jews, and false witnesses accused him as a blasphemer. Stephen knew instantly that he must either conceal the truth or risk his life in its defense. He did not hesitate, and courageously proved before his judges the divinity of Jesus Christ, and reproached them for having put the Messiah to death and obstinately resisted the Holy Spirit; and then, enlightened by a heavenly vision, he cried out, "Behold, I see the heavens opened, and the Son of Man standing on the right hand of God!" At these words his enemies could bear it no longer; they ran on him, and dragged him out of the city to stone him. The saint did not resist, but endured death joyfully in testimony of his faith, receiving thus the first martyr's palm towards the end of the year in which Jesus Christ died.

Application: Martyrdom, probably, will never be our lot; but let us take comfort, for the Doctors of the Church maintain and prove that the total immolation a man makes of himself by the religious profession is indeed a true martyrdom, "less terrible in its

sufferings," says Saint Bernard, "but more painful because of its duration – HORRORE QUIDEM MITIUS, SED DIUTURNITATE." (SERM. 3, Cant.) This is true, but it applies to a fervent and mortified religious. We can be such, but are we?
Affections and Resolutions.

Point III: Saint Stephen's heroic charity

Consideration: Exhausted from loss of blood, and on the point of death, the saint forgot himself. After the example of his Divine Master, he begged pardon for his murderers. "He cried out with a loud voice, saying, Lord, lay not this sin to their charge; and when he had said this, he fell asleep in the Lord."

Application: Thus did the first martyr fulfill the precept Jesus Christ has given to us all: "Pray for them that persecute you; do good to them that hate you." How do you fulfill this on occasions of far less importance, where the victory over self is infinitely easier?
Colloquy.

December 27: Jesus Announced to the Shepherds and Glorified by the Angels

1st prelude: Behold the shepherds listening to the words and son of the angels.
2nd prelude: Beg the grace of experiencing the feelings which the angels imparted to the heard of the shepherds.

Point I: Announcement of the Messiah

Consideration: For the world's salvation Jesus was born at Bethlehem, and He wished that men should know it, but not the rich, proud, and sensual men of the world, only poor shepherds, simple, laborious, and unworldly. "And there were in that same country shepherds watching and keeping the night watches over their flocks; and behold an angel of the Lord stood by them, and the brightness of God shone round about them, and they feared with a great fear. And the angel said to them, Fear not, for behold I bring you good tidings of great joy, that shall be to all the people; for this day is born to you a Savior, who is Christ the Lord, in the city of David."

Application: Our vocation makes us like these happy shepherds; like them, we live out of the world, a simple, chaste,

poor and very laborious life. We may, then, hope that Jesus will make Himself known to us also, that He will deign to let the brightness of His light shine round about us, and give us tidings of great joy. That we may more surely obtain these favors, let us watch over our senses and the movements of our hearts.
Affections and Resolutions.

Point II: Distinctive signs of the Messiah

Consideration: "This day is born to you a Savior," said the angel; "and this shall be a sign unto you – you shall find the Infant wrapped in swaddling clothes, and laid in a manger." The infancy of Jesus a sign of humility; the swaddling clothes a sign of poverty; the manger, or the roughness of the cradle, a sign of mortification. Such is the threefold sign which the angel gave to the shepherds and to us all, as a proof that Jesus was really the promised Savior of the world, and, in fact, as our Savior He had to expiate our sins, which all proceed from three sources – pride, avarice and sensuality. He had also to show and encourage us, by His example more than by His words, how to adopt the only means which will succeed in keeping us from sin. He was doing both when He came into the world with the tokens of humility, poverty and mortification.

Application: We have often read or listened to the Gospel we have meditated on today without understanding its meaning, without seeing the wonderful conformity of the signs given by the angel with the qualities of the promised Savior. Let us conclude from this that in meditation we should make a great point of the considerations, and study them deeply. From the light which comes into our minds should spring the affections of our hearts.
Affections and Resolutions.

Point III: Glorification of the Messiah

Consideration: One angels, supposed to be the Archangel Gabriel, was sent to announce the birth of Jesus; but when it pleased God to glorify His Son He sent legions of angels. "And suddenly there was with the angel a multitude of the heavenly army, praising God, and saying, Glory to God in the highest, and on earth peace to men of good will."

Application: By His deep humiliation Jesus merited this burst of praise. He had repaired the glory of God, and brought peace and joy to men of good will. These holy and encouraging thoughts out

not to be lost upon us, but should strengthen a good will in us, that energetic will ready to die to self, to seek in all things nothing but the greater glory of God; and we shall find peace of soul, and be glorified in our turn.
Colloquy.

December 28: The Shepherds Go to Bethlehem

1st prelude: Behold the shepherds hastening to Bethlehem.
2nd prelude: Beg for the feelings which filled the shepherds' hearts when they saw the Infant Jesus.

Point I: The shepherds exhort each other to go to Bethlehem

Consideration: After the angels departed from them into heaven, the shepherds said one to another, "Let us go over to Bethlehem, and let us see this word that is to come to pass, which the Lord hath showed to us." It would seem from this passage that after the celestial vision disappeared, the shepherds began to doubt. The event of which they had been told was so extraordinary – the Messiah born in such abjection; so unlike the idea of that temporal greatness which they had formed about Him. Many of them hesitated about going to the spot pointed out. And then they had their flocks to keep, and to walk nearly two miles in the midst of the night. But the more fervent prevailed over the others, and at last they all set out without delay.

Application: Happy is the religious community where there is a unity of desires and efforts to attain perfection; when each member animates and encourages the others in doing well; when there is no other ambition than that of excelling in respect, humility and charity. Does it not depend on you to make the community in which you live like this?
Affections and Resolutions.

Point II: The shepherds go to Bethlehem with eagerness

Consideration: When the shepherds had determined on going, they set out at once, walking quickly in spite of the darkness and the fatigue of their vigil. The Gospel tells us they "came with haste." Why did they have such promptitude of will and action? 1. The angel's words had given them a lively faith. 2. They ardently desired to see and adore the Messiah and Savior. 3. They hoped to receive blessings and favors.

Application: Every day when you awake your good angel invites you to come to the cradle of your loving Savior, to come and visit Him in the Sacrament of His love, and to consecrate the first-fruits of the day to Him. Oh, what graces and blessings belong to this first visit to the Blessed Sacrament! Convinced of this truth from the beginning of your novitiate, you made the resolution of never missing it by your own fault. Are you faithful to this resolve? Do you break it sometimes, perhaps frequently, and why? Because you do not rise with promptitude and eagerness, because you reason and dispute with sleep and sensuality; and thus time passes away, the propitious moment is lost.

Affections and Resolutions.

Point III: The shepherds find and adore their Savior

Consideration: The shepherds, having reached the placed pointed out by the angel, "found Mary and Joseph, and the Infant lying in the manger." With their bodily eyes they only saw an ordinary infant; but with the eyes of faith they saw under that veil of feebleness the infinite majesty and goodness of God their Savior. What joy they felt before the Divine Child, and what special graces they carried away with them!

Application: We have the same God on our altars, veiled under still greater feebleness. Let us visit Him, then, often, animated with the same faith and feelings as the shepherds had. Here we can truly say that all depends on faith. Let us try to revive and strengthen it in us as we go towards the sanctuary, by representing Jesus to ourselves in a visible form; for instance, in the first visit we pay in the morning, as a loving child calling us to Him, and holding out His little hands full of heavenly gifts.

Colloquy.

December 29: Return of the Shepherds and their Zeal

1st prelude: Behold the shepherds speaking with transport of the Messiah to those whom they meet on the road.

2nd prelude: Beg the grace always to leave the presence of Jesus with the same feelings as the shepherds did.

Point I: The shepherds spread the Good News everywhere

Consideration: The shepherds, having adored their Savior and laid their simple offerings at His feet, "returned glorifying and praising God for all the things they had heard and seen, as it was told unto them." Such was the effect of that divine love which the shepherds had acquired at the manger. Jesus was in their hearts and on their lips. They wanted to make Him known and loved by all the world; they spoke of Him with transport to all those whom they met, entreating them also to go and adore their Messiah. Love had made them into apostles.

Application: If Jesus is in our hearts, He will also be often on our lips. He has told us, "out of the abundance of the heart the mouth speaketh." Animated by His love, and with zeal for His glory, we will try to make Him loved and served as much as we can by all the world. We shall be watchful and ingenious in seizing on every occasion of attaining this great end: and these occasions will not fail us. You will know by these signs if Jesus is in your heart. Examine yourself.

Affections and Resolutions.

Point II: Men are indifferent to their story

Consideration: "And all that heard wondered." And certainly what the shepherds told was enough to astonish the Jews of Bethlehem – the Messiah born in a stable, the appearance, words, and songs of angels! We should have thought that they would have run to the stable to adore their Savior, and disputed who should have the honor of lodging Him, of having Him with them. But they did nothing; they wondered and reasoned, and then became indifferent, and forgot Him.

Application: What will it serve us, if, after having meditated with feelings of admiration on the wonderful mysteries of the Incarnation and birth of the Eternal Word, we do not practice the virtues of which Jesus gave us the example?

Affections and Resolutions.

Point III: Mary keeps the memory of these things in her heart

Consideration: "But Mary kept all these words, pondering them in her heart." The conduct of our Lady is a singular contrast with that of the Jews. She kept all these things; she impressed deeply in her mind all that was said and done concerning her Divine Son. he meditated on them all day, and laid up a treasure of precious teaching to be communicated later on to the disciples and Apostles. It is believed that it was from her that Saint Luke learnt the details he wrote in his Gospel about the Incarnation, adoration of the shepherds, the visitation and purification.

Application: Our dear Mother teaches us how we ought to profit by our meditations, recalling to our mind from time to time during the day the good thoughts we have had, and trying to revive in our hearts the affections which proceeded from them. See in this matter how you have failed, and what you ought to correct.
Colloquy.

December 30: On the Fervor which the Love of Jesus demands from Us

1st prelude: Behold the Apostle saying to us, "Be ye thankful, in spirit fervent, serving the Lord."
2nd prelude: Beg earnestly for a spirit of fervor in God's service.

Point I: Motives for fervor as regards God

Consideration: The meditations we have been making on the Incarnation and Nativity of the Eternal Word have reminded us of the unspeakable love which God has for men - for each of us. Love demands love. And the Apostle says that it ought to manifest itself especially by our fervour in the service of God. Let us end this long series of meditations by some thoughts which will maintain and increase our fervour. The first is, the benefit of creation, which supposes God to have decreed an ETERNAL love for us; and we have only a little time in which to love Him meritoriously.

Application: This thought was continually in the minds of the saints; it preserved their fervour and stimulated them to acts of virtue more and more perfect. "What!" said they; "God has lovingly been occupied with me for all eternity; I have only a little time in which I can make him a return for it; and by my lukewarmness in His holy service shall I lose part of this brief time, shall I share my heart between Him and creatures? No, it shall never be! Courage, my soul; redouble thy fervour and generosity as thou drawest near to the end."
Affections and Resolutions.

Point II: Motives of fervor as regards ourselves

Consideration: If the love and service of God require fervour, a true love of ourselves does so also. Why have we left the world and entered religion, at the price perhaps of heroic sacrifices? Was it that we might lead an ordinary course of life, such as we could have done by remaining in the world? No, certainly not. It was to do penance for past sins, to have our purgatory in this life, to live and die as saints, to attain a high degree of glory in heaven. And all this is impossible without great fervour in God's service. All religious who have the attainment of the great end for which they entered religion at heart should especially dread degenerating little by little from their first fervour, and falling into lukewarmness.

Application: "Have I preserved in my first fervour, or is it decayed?" It is natural to ask this important question at the end of a year; it is not difficult to answer it. You have but to review the time of your novitiate, to compare your way of acting then with what you now do in various points, such as rising, visits to the Blessed Sacrament, corporal penances, the additions of mediation, particular examen, etc. Make this comparison; by your own judge.
Affections and Resolutions.

Point III: Motives of fervour as regards others

Consideration: A religious, no matter to what order he belongs, ought to devote himself to others, and try to help them. He should come between an offended God and guilty men, that he may keep back the punishments which they have deserved. He must, then, be closely united to God by ardent love, and be dear to the Heart of God, and then he will have influence with Him, and a great power of intercession. And this, again, supposes more than an ordinary generosity and fervour.

Application: You desire ardently to do great good among souls and to save many. The great means of succeeding is to sanctify yourself with the hope of doing service to others. "For them do I sanctify Myself," and Jesus, speaking to His Apostles of His Father, "that they also may be sanctified." Be fervent, then, in God's service, and you will be an apostle.
Colloquy.

December 31: On the last day of the year

1st prelude: Imagine you see a merchant making up his accounts for the past year.
2nd prelude: Beg the grace of really knowing your past life, that you may regulate the future.

Point I: What has this year been to you?

Consideration: On God's side this year has been for you an uninterrupted series of benefits in the order of nature and grace. He has preserved your life and health in the midst of so many dangers, from which thousands of others have suffered. He has provided, like a father, for all your needs, you have been in want of nothing; and with fatherly solicitude He has watched over the interests of your soul, turned away temptations from you, under which you would have given way, and sustained you in difficult circumstances by extraordinary graces. Review every day of the year, and you will not find one in which some signal favor was not bestowed.

Application: But what has this year been on your side? Has it been what God had the right to expect from you in return for so many benefits? Has it been a year of fervour in His holy service, of progress in His love? Has it not been marked, on the contrary, by many rapines in the holocaust? by much unfaithfulness, cowardice, ingratitude?

Affections and Resolutions.

Point II: What remains to you of this year? Nothing; for it has passed.

Consideration: What remains on the last day of the year of the number of things that succeed each other so rapidly? There is nothing; all is passed; the suffering that it cost us to do right, and the enjoyment that we had in doing wrong. All the efforts and the sacrifices which the fervent religious made in going through his spiritual exercises, in sanctifying all his actions, in resisting his disorderly inclinations, in bringing his senses under the yoke of discipline and rule, that he might live in the exercise of a continual mortification - all is passed away. On the other hand, the lukewarm religious has nothing left of the satisfaction which he sought for in an easy and relaxed life, against his conscience, hurtful to his eternal interest, and disedifying to others. For both of these all is passed; and if the memory of it is with them today, it is a happy and encouraging remembrance for one, bitter and depressing for the other.

Application: Profit by these salutary reflections. Recollect yourself, beg God to enlighten you, and see which of these two religious you resemble. If it is the first, let your heart expand with joy; but if it be the second, the memory of this year should excite bitter regret in your soul for having thought so little of the severe account that God will demand from you, and the merit you have lost.

Affections and Resolutions.

Point III: What remains to you of this year? All of it; nothing is passed

Consideration: If on the last day of the year we may truly say that all is passed away, we may also as truly say in another sense that nothing is passed; because in reality the fruit of our works remains, waiting for reward or punishment, and not a single thought, word or action is excepted; God has weighed them all in the balance of His infinite justice; all will be abundantly rewarded or severely punished.

Application: If this truth had always been before our minds, how eagerly we should have seized on every occasion of doing some good, how carefully we should have avoided the smallest faults, and how precious this year would have been before God! Let us try to secure this happiness during the year which is about to begin.

Colloquy.

www.ingramcontent.com/pod-product-compliance
Ingram Content Group UK Ltd.
Pitfield, Milton Keynes, MK11 3LW, UK
UKHW041953190726
13854UKWH00005B/1942